T0137857

Communications in Computer and Information Science 2077

Rationale

The CCIS series is devoted to the publication of proceedings of computer science conferences. Its aim is to efficiently disseminate original research results in informatics in printed and electronic form. While the focus is on publication of peer-reviewed full papers presenting mature work, inclusion of reviewed short papers reporting on work in progress is welcome, too. Besides globally relevant meetings with internationally representative program committees guaranteeing a strict peer-reviewing and paper selection process, conferences run by societies or of high regional or national relevance are also considered for publication.

Topics

The topical scope of CCIS spans the entire spectrum of informatics ranging from foundational topics in the theory of computing to information and communications science and technology and a broad variety of interdisciplinary application fields.

Information for Volume Editors and Authors

Publication in CCIS is free of charge. No royalties are paid, however, we offer registered conference participants temporary free access to the online version of the conference proceedings on SpringerLink (http://link.springer.com) by means of an http referrer from the conference website and/or a number of complimentary printed copies, as specified in the official acceptance email of the event.

CCIS proceedings can be published in time for distribution at conferences or as post-proceedings, and delivered in the form of printed books and/or electronically as USBs and/or e-content licenses for accessing proceedings at SpringerLink. Furthermore, CCIS proceedings are included in the CCIS electronic book series hosted in the SpringerLink digital library at http://link.springer.com/bookseries/7899. Conferences publishing in CCIS are allowed to use Online Conference Service (OCS) for managing the whole proceedings lifecycle (from submission and reviewing to preparing for publication) free of charge.

Publication process

The language of publication is exclusively English. Authors publishing in CCIS have to sign the Springer CCIS copyright transfer form, however, they are free to use their material published in CCIS for substantially changed, more elaborate subsequent publications elsewhere. For the preparation of the camera-ready papers/files, authors have to strictly adhere to the Springer CCIS Authors' Instructions and are strongly encouraged to use the CCIS LaTeX style files or templates.

Abstracting/Indexing

CCIS is abstracted/indexed in DBLP, Google Scholar, EI-Compendex, Mathematical Reviews, SCImago, Scopus. CCIS volumes are also submitted for the inclusion in ISI Proceedings.

How to start

To start the evaluation of your proposal for inclusion in the CCIS series, please send an e-mail to ccis@springer.com.

Joaquim Filipe · Juha Röning
Editors

Robotics, Computer Vision and Intelligent Systems

4th International Conference, ROBOVIS 2024
Rome, Italy, February 25–27, 2024
Proceedings

 Springer

Editors
Joaquim Filipe
Polytechnic Institute of Setubal
Setúbal, Portugal

Juha Röning
Biomimetics and Intelligent Systems
University of Oulu
Oulu, Finland

ISSN 1865-0929   ISSN 1865-0937 (electronic)
Communications in Computer and Information Science
ISBN 978-3-031-59056-6   ISBN 978-3-031-59057-3 (eBook)
https://doi.org/10.1007/978-3-031-59057-3

This Springer imprint is published by the registered company Springer Nature Switzerland AG
The registered company address is: Gewerbestrasse 11, 6330 Cham, Switzerland

Paper in this product is recyclable.

Preface

This book contains the proceedings of the 4th International Conference on Robotics, Computer Vision and Intelligent Systems (ROBOVIS 2024). This conference was organized and sponsored by the Institute for Systems and Technologies of Information, Control and Communication (INSTICC) and held in cooperation with the ACM Special Interest Group on Artificial Intelligence (ACM SIGAI) and endorsed by the International Association for Pattern Recognition (IAPR).

This year ROBOVIS was held in Rome, Italy as a hybrid event, from 25 to 27 February.

The purpose of ROBOVIS, the International Conference on Robotics, Computer Vision and Intelligent Systems, is to bring together researchers, engineers and practitioners who are interested in sharing their research and experience in the thematic areas of this conference. Robotics is a field that is closely connected to Computer Vision and Intelligent Systems. Research and development of robots requires technologies originating from the other two areas; research work in Computer Vision has often been driven by needs in Robotics; Intelligent Systems models and software have often been developed aiming at applications in the areas of physical agents, i.e. robots, or in areas related to scene understanding, video and image processing, and many other aspects of computer vision. There is a need for a venue where these three research communities, often isolated, meet and discuss innovation possibilities driven by the intersection of these highly synergetic fields.

The high quality of the ROBOVIS 2024 program was enhanced by three keynote lectures, delivered by experts in their fields, namely: Arianna Menciassi (Scuola Superiore Sant'Anna of Pisa, Italy), Vittorio Murino (Istituto Italiano di Tecnologia, Italy) and Jean Ponce (Ecole normale supérieure-PSL, France and New York University, USA - Distinguished IAPR Speaker).

ROBOVIS 2024 received 33 paper submissions from 17 countries, of which eight submissions were accepted as full papers. The high quality of the papers received imposed difficult choices in the review process. To evaluate each submission, a double-blind paper review with three reviews per submission was performed by the Program Committee, whose members were highly qualified independent researchers in the ROBOVIS topic areas.

All presented papers will be submitted for indexation by DBLP, Google Scholar, EI (Elsevier Engineering Village Index), The Institution of Engineering and Technology (IET), Japanese Science and Technology Agency (JST), Norwegian Register for Scientific Journals and Series, Mathematical Reviews, SCImago, Scopus, zbMATH and Web of Science/Conference Proceedings Citation Index.

As recognition for the best contributions, several awards based on the combined marks from the review process, as assessed by the Program Committee, and the quality of the presentation, as assessed by session chairs at the conference venue, were conferred at the closing session of the conference.

Building an interesting and successful program for the conference required the dedicated effort of many people. Firstly, we greatly thank the authors, whose research and development efforts are recorded here. Secondly, we thank the members of the program committee and additional reviewers for their diligence and expert reviewing. Finally, we acknowledge the professional support of the ROBOVIS 2024 team for all organizational processes.

We hope that all colleagues who participated in the conference and/or read its proceedings find this a fruitful and inspiring conference. We hope to contribute to the development of the Robotics, Computer Vision and Intelligent Systems community and look forward to having additional research results presented at the next edition of ROBOVIS, details of which are available at https://robovis.scitevents.org/.

February 2024

Joaquim Filipe
Juha Röning

Organization

Conference Chair

Joaquim Filipe   Polytechnic Institute of Setubal/INSTICC,
Portugal

Program Chair

Juha Röning   University of Oulu, Finland

Program Committee

Victor Alchanatis	Agricultural Research Organization, Israel
Yannick Aoustin	LS2N, France
Shafriza Nisha Basah	University of Malaysia Perlis, Malaysia
Mohammed Benbrahim	Université Sidi Mohamed Ben Abdallah, Morocco
Jonas Beskow	KTH Royal Institute of Technology, Sweden
Mahdi Bodaghi	Nottingham Trent University, UK
Stefano Borgo	ISTC CNR National Research Council, Italy
Sofiane Boucenna	ENSEA Graduate School, France
Ivan Buzurovic	Harvard University, USA
François Charpillet	Loria - Inria Lorraine, France
William Cockshott	Glasgow University, UK
Micael Couceiro	Ingeniarius, Lda. & University of Lisbon, Portugal
James Crowley	Univ. Grenoble Alpes, France
Arturo De La Escalera	Universidad Carlos III de Madrid, Spain
František Duchon	Slovak University of Technology in Bratislava, Slovak Republic
Nils Einecke	Honda Research Institute Europe GmbH, Germany
Ahmed El-Sayed	University of Bridgeport, USA
Arturo Espinosa-Romero	Autonomous University of Yucatan, Mexico
Daniele Fontanelli	Università degli Studi di Trento, Italy
Luigi Freda	Independent Researcher, Italy
Udo Frese	University of Bremen, Germany
Yakup Genc	Gebze Technical University, Turkey

Luis Gerardo De La Fraga	Cinvestav, Mexico
Arturo Gil Aparicio	Miguel Hernandez University, Spain
Hilario Gómez-Moreno	Universidad de Alcalá, Spain
Hideki Hashimoto	Chuo University, Japan
Michael Jenkin	York University, Canada
Wlodzimierz Kasprzak	Warsaw University of Technology, Poland
Azfar Khalid	Nottingham Trent University, UK
Hubert Konik	Université Jean Monnet, Laboratoire Hubert Curien, France
Alexandros Kouris	Samsung AI Center Cambridge and Imperial College London, UK
Claudio Loconsole	Universitas Mercatorum, Italy
Alexandre Meyer	Claude Bernard University Lyon 1, France
Enrique Moltó	IVIA, Spain
Vicente Morell Giménez	University of Alicante, Spain
Huu-Cuong Nguyen	Can Tho University, Vietnam
Martin Otis	Université du Québec à Chicoutimi, Canada
Igor S. Pandžic	University of Zagreb, Croatia
Soon-Yong Park	Kyungpook National University, South Korea
Jorge Peña Queralta	University of Turku, Finland
Andreas Pichler	PROFACTOR GmbH, Austria
Salvatore Pirozzi	Università degli Studi della Campania Luigi Vanvitelli, Italy
David Portugal	University of Coimbra, Portugal
Mark Post	University of York, UK
Anthony Remazeilles	TECNALIA, Spain
Raúl Sánchez-Yáñez	Universidad de Guanajuato, Mexico
Pedro Santana	ISCTE - University Institute of Lisbon, Portugal
Saeed Shiry Ghidary	Staffordshire University, UK
Amin Shoukry	Egypt-Japan University of Science and Technology, Egypt
Aiguo Song	Southeast University, China
Marc Stamminger	Friedrich-Alexander-Universität Erlangen-Nürnberg, Germany
Paolo Stegagno	University of Rhode Island, USA
Frieder Stolzenburg	Harz University of Applied Sciences, Germany
Ryszard Tadeusiewicz	AGH University of Science and Technology, Poland
Ruwan Tennakoon	RMIT University, Australia
Flavio Tonidandel	Centro Universitario FEI, Brazil
Roberto Vezzani	Unimore, Italy
Miguel Villarreal-Cervantes	Instituto Politécnico Nacional, Mexico

Mattias Wahde	Chalmers University of Technology, Sweden
James Whidborne	Cranfield University, UK
Shih-Hung Wu	Chaoyang University of Technology, Taiwan, Republic of China
Yuming Zhang	Univ. of Kentucky, USA
Jianmin Zheng	Nanyang Technological University, Singapore
Cezary Zielinski	Warsaw University of Technology, Poland
Djemel Ziou	Universite de Sherbrooke, Canada
Ali Zolfagharian	Deakin University, Australia

Additional Reviewers

Giovanni Flores-Caballero	UNAQ, Mexico
Michele Mirto	Università della Campania, Italy
Alam Gabriel Rojas-López	Instituto Politécnico Nacional, Mexico

Invited Speakers

Vittorio Murino	Istituto Italiano di Tecnologia, Italy
Arianna Menciassi	Scuola Superiore Sant'Anna of Pisa, Italy
Jean Ponce	Ecole normale supérieure-PSL, France and New York University, USA

Invited Speakers

Learning with Privileged Information and Distillation for Multimodal Video Classification

Vittorio Murino

Department of Computer Science, University of Verona, Verona, Italy

Abstract. Diverse input data modalities can provide complementary cues for several tasks, usually leading to more robust algorithms and better performance. However, while a (training) dataset could be accurately designed to include a variety of sensory inputs, it is often the case that not all modalities are available in real life (testing) scenarios, where a model has to be deployed. This raises the challenge of how to learn robust representations leveraging multimodal data in the training stage, while considering limitations at test time, such as noisy or missing modalities. In this talk, I will present a new approach for multimodal video action recognition, developed within the unified frameworks of distillation and privileged information, named generalized distillation. Particularly, we consider the case of learning representations from depth and RGB videos, while relying on RGB data only at test time. We propose a new approach to train an hallucination network that learns to distill depth features through multiplicative connections of spatio-temporal representations, leveraging soft labels and hard labels, as well as distance between feature maps. Subsequently, we improve the hallucination model to distill depth information via adversarial learning, resulting in a clean approach without several losses to balance or hyperparameters to tune. We report state-of-the-art results on video action classification on multimodal datasets such as NTU RGB D, UWA3DII, and Northwestern-UCLA.

Brief Biography

Vittorio Murino is full professor at the University of Verona, Italy, and has also a double appointment with University of Genova. He took the Laurea degree in Electronic Engineering in 1989 and the Ph.D. in Electronic Engineering and Computer Science in 1993 at the University of Genova, Italy. From 2009 to 2019, he worked at the Istituto Italiano di Tecnologia in Genova, Italy, as founder and director of the PAVIS (Pattern Analysis and Computer Vision) department, with which he is still collaborating now as a visiting scientist. From 2019 to 2021, he worked as Senior Video Intelligence Expert at the Ireland Research Centre of Huawei Technologies (Ireland) Co., Ltd. in Dublin. His main research interests include computer vision and machine learning, nowadays focusing on deep learning approaches, domain adaptation and generalization, and multimodal learning for (human) behavior analysis and related applications, such as video surveillance and biomedical imaging. Prof. Murino is co-author of more than 400 papers published in refereed journals and international conferences, member of the technical committees of important conferences (CVPR, ICCV, ECCV, ICPR, ICIP, etc.), and guest co-editor of special issues in relevant scientific journals. He is also member of the editorial board of Computer Vision and Image Understanding and Machine Vision & Applications journals. Finally, prof. Murino is IEEE Fellow, IAPR Fellow, and ELLIS Fellow.

There's Plenty of Room at the Bottom: Opportunites and Challenges for Microrobotics

Arianna Menciassi

Scuola Superiore Sant'Anna of Pisa, Italy

Abstract. Robotics is becoming more and more pervasive, and people are already familiar with robots moving around them. On the other hand, there is another class of robots operating in areas where traditional robots and human operators cannot work. They are called microrobots and can find multiple applications for healthcare, remote inspections and environmental remediation. Microrobots require a change of paradigm in design, manufacturing and control They are difficult to be seen and difficult to be tracked and navigated. They have limitations in terms of autonomous powering and they can be even dangerous if they are lost in delicate environments, such as the vessels of the human body. This talk will present the opportunities and challenges offered by microrobotics and will focus on issues related to navigation, safe control, tracking and vision of microrobots, based on the research experience of the speaker.

Brief Biography

Arianna Menciassi was born in Pisa, Italy, in 1971. She graduated in Physics at the Pisa University (1995), she obtained the PhD (1999) at Scuola Superiore Sant'Anna (SSSA, Pisa, Italy) and she was visiting professor in different universities in France since 2014 (Pierre and Marie Curie, in Paris, Besancon University, in Besancon). She is Full Professor of Biomedical Robotics at SSSA and team leader of the "Surgical Robotics & Allied Technologies" Area at The BioRobotics Institute. She is the Coordinator of the PhD in Biorobotics since 2018, and she was appointed in 2019 as Vice-Rector of the Scuola Sant'Anna. Her main research interests involve surgical robotics, microrobotics for biomedical applications, biomechatronic artificial organs, smart and soft solutions for biomedical devices. She pays a special attention to the combination between traditional robotics, targeted therapy and wireless solution for therapy (e.g. ultrasound- and magnetic-based). She served in the Editorial Board of the IEEE-ASME Trans. on Mechatronics and she has been Topic Editor of the International Journal of Advanced Robotic Systems (2013-2020). In 2018 she has been appointed as Editor of APL Bioengineering and of the IEEE Transactions on Medical Robotics and Bionics. She is Associate Editor for Soft Robotics and she serves as Associate Editor of the IEEE Trans. on Robotics from Jan. 2021. She is Co-Chair of the IEEE Technical Committee on Surgical Robotics.

She is serving in the Steering Committee of iSMIT. She received the Well-tech Award (Milan, Italy) for her researches on endoscopic capsules, and she was awarded by the Tuscany Region with the Gonfalone D'Argento, as one of the best 10 young talents of the region. Recently, she has been awarded with the KUKA Innovation Award, for her activities on robotic assisted focused ultrasound.

Physical Models and Machine Learning for Photography and Astronomy

Jean Ponce

Ecole normale supérieure-PSL and New York University, France

Abstract. We live in an era of data-driven approaches to image analysis, where modeling is sometimes considered obsolete. I will propose in this talk giving back to accurate physical models of image formation their rightful place next to machine learning in the overall processing and interpretation pipeline, and discuss two applications: super-resolution and high-dynamic range imaging from raw photographic bursts, and exoplanet detection and characterization in direct imaging at high contrast. This is joint work with Theo Bodrito, Yann Dubois de Mont-Marin, Thomas Eboli, Olivier Flasseur, Anne-Marie Lagrange, Maud Langlois, Bruno Lecouat and Julien Mairal.

Brief Biography

Jean Ponce is a Professor at Ecole Normale Supérieure - PSL, where he served as Director of the Computer Science Department from 2011 to 2017 and a Global Distinguished Professor at the Courant Institute of Mathematical Sciences and the Center for Data Science at New York University. He is also the co-founder and CEO of Enhance Lab, a startup that commercializes software for joint demosaicing, denoising, super-resolution and HDR imaging from raw photo bursts. Before joining ENS and NYU, Jean Ponce held positions at Inria, MIT, Stanford, and the University of Illinois at Urbana-Champaign, where he was a Full Professor until 2005. Jean Ponce is an IEEE and an ELLIS Fellow, a member of the Academia Europaea, and a former Sr. member of the Institut Universitaire de France. He has served as Program and/or General Chair of all three top international Computer Vision Conferences, CVPR (1997 and 2000), ECCV (2008) and ICCV (2023, upcoming). He has also served as Sr. Editor-in-Chief of the International Journal of Computer Vision and Associate Editor for Computer Vision and Image Understanding, Foundation and Trends in Computer Graphics and Vision, the IEEE Transactions on Robotics and Automation, and the SIAM Journal on Imaging Sciences. He currently serves as Scientific Director of the PRAIRIE Interdisciplinary AI Research Institute in Paris. Jean Ponce is the recipient of two US patents, an ERC advanced grant, the 2016 and 2020 IEEE CVPR Longuet-Higgins prizes, and the 2019 ICML test-of-time award. He is the author of "Computer Vision: A Modern Approach", a textbook translated in Chinese, Japanese, and Russian.

Contents

Compute Optimal Waiting Times for Collaborative Route Planning 1
  Jörg Roth

Robot Vision and Deep Learning for Automated Planogram Compliance
in Retail 21
  Adel Merabet, Abhishek V. Latha, Francis A. Kuzhippallil,
  Mohammad Rahimipour, Jason Rhinelander, and Ramesh Venkat

Park Marking Detection and Tracking Based on a Vehicle On-Board
System of Fisheye Cameras 31
  Ruben Naranjo, Joan Sintes, Cristina Pérez-Benito, Pablo Alonso,
  Guillem Delgado, Nerea Aranjuelo, and Aleksandar Jevtić

Analysis of Age Invariant Face Recognition Efficiency Using Face Feature
Vectors 47
  Anders Hast, Yijie Zhou, Congting Lai, and Ivar Blohm

Uncertainty Driven Active Learning for Image Segmentation
in Underwater Inspection 66
  Luiza Ribeiro Marnet, Yury Brodskiy, Stella Grasshof,
  and Andrzej Wąsowski

Enhancing Connected Cooperative ADAS: Deep Learning Perception
in an Embedded System Utilizing Fisheye Cameras 82
  Guillem Delgado, Mikel Garcia, Jon Ander Íñiguez de Gordoa,
  Marcos Nieto, Gorka Velez, Cristina Pérez-Benito, David Pujol,
  Alejandro Miranda, Iu Aguilar, and Aleksandar Jevtić

Weapon Detection Using PTZ Cameras 100
  Juan Daniel Muñoz, Jesus Ruiz-Santaquiteria, Oscar Deniz,
  and Gloria Bueno

Improving Semantic Mapping with Prior Object Dimensions Extracted
from 3D Models 115
  Abdessalem Achour, Hiba Al Assaad, Yohan Dupuis,
  and Madeleine El Zaher

Offline Deep Model Predictive Control (MPC) for Visual Navigation 134
  Taha Bouzid and Youssef Alj

BiGSiD: Bionic Grasping with Edge-AI Slip Detection 152
Youssef Nassar, Mario Radke, Atmaraaj Gopal, Tobias Knöller,
Thomas Weber, ZhaoHua Liu, and Matthias Rätsch

GAT-POSE: Graph Autoencoder-Transformer Fusion for Future Pose
Prediction 164
Armin Danesh Pazho, Gabriel Maldonado, and Hamed Tabkhi

UCorr: Wire Detection and Depth Estimation for Autonomous Drones 179
Benedikt Kolbeinsson and Krystian Mikolajczyk

A Quality-Based Criteria for Efficient View Selection 193
Rémy Alcouffe, Sylvie Chambon, Géraldine Morin, and Simone Gasparini

Multi-UAV Weed Spraying 210
Ali Moltajaei Farid, Malek Mouhoub, Tony Arkles, and Greg Hutch

Human Comfort Factors in People Navigation: Literature Review,
Taxonomy and Framework 225
Matthias Kalenberg, Christian Hofmann, Sina Martin, and Jörg Franke

Region Prediction for Efficient Robot Localization on Large Maps 244
Matteo Scucchia and Davide Maltoni

Utilizing Dataset Affinity Prediction in Object Detection to Assess
Training Data 260
Stefan Becker, Jens Bayer, Ronny Hug, Wolfgang Huebner,
and Michael Arens

Optimizing Mobile Robot Navigation Through Neuro-Symbolic Fusion
of Deep Deterministic Policy Gradient (DDPG) and Fuzzy Logic 278
Muhammad Faqiihuddin Nasary, Azhar Mohd Ibrahim,
Suaib Al Mahmud, Amir Akramin Shafie,
and Muhammad Imran Mardzuki

DAFDeTr: Deformable Attention Fusion Based 3D Detection Transformer 293
Gopi Krishna Erabati and Helder Araujo

MDC-Net: Multimodal Detection and Captioning Network for Steel
Surface Defects 316
Anthony Ashwin Peter Chazhoor, Shanfeng Hu, Bin Gao,
and Wai Lok Woo

Operational Modeling of Temporal Intervals for Intelligent Systems 334
J. I. Olszewska

A Meta-MDP Approach for Information Gathering Heterogeneous
Multi-agent Systems 345
*Alvin Gandois, Abdel-Illah Mouaddib, Simon Le Gloannec,
and Ayman Alfalou*

Interacting with a Visuotactile Countertop 361
*Michael Jenkin, Francois R. Hogan, Kaleem Siddiqi,
Jean-François Tremblay, Bobak Baghi, and Gregory Dudek*

A Color Event-Based Camera Emulator for Robot Vision 375
*Ignacio Bugueno-Cordova, Miguel Campusano,
Robert Guaman-Rivera, and Rodrigo Verschae*

Fast Point Cloud to Mesh Reconstruction for Deformable Object Tracking 391
Elham Amin Mansour, Hehui Zheng, and Robert K. Katzschmann

Estimation of Optimal Gripper Configuration Through an Embedded
Array of Proximity Sensors 410
*Jonathas Henrique Mariano Pereira, Carlos Fernando Joventino,
João Alberto Fabro, and André Schneider de Oliveira*

The Twinning Technique of the SyncLMKD Method 426
*Fabiano Stingelin Cardoso, Ronnier Frates Rohrich,
and André Schneider de Oliveira*

Intuitive Multi-modal Human-Robot Interaction via Posture and Voice 441
*Yuzhi Lai, Mario Radke, Youssef Nassar, Atmaraaj Gopal,
Thomas Weber, ZhaoHua Liu, Yihong Zhang, and Matthias Rätsch*

Virtual Model of a Robotic Arm Digital Twin with MuJoCo 457
*Bernardo Perez Inturias, João Pedro Garbelini Marques de Oliveira,
and Mauricio Becerra Vargas*

Author Index 471

Compute Optimal Waiting Times for Collaborative Route Planning

Jörg Roth[✉]

Faculty of Computer Science, Nuremberg Institute of Technology, Nuremberg, Germany
Joerg.Roth@th-nuernberg.de

Abstract. Collaborative routing tries to discover paths of multiple robots that avoid mutual collisions while optimising a common cost function. A collision can be avoided in two ways: a robot modifies its route to pass another robot, or one robot waits for the other to move first. Recent work assigns priorities to robots or models waiting times as an 'action' similar to driving. However, these methods have certain disadvantages. This paper introduces a new approach that computes theoretically optimal waiting times for given multi-routes. If all collisions can be avoided through waiting, the algorithm computes optimal places and durations to wait. We used this approach as component to introduce a collaborative routing system capable of solving complex routing problems involving mutual blocking.

Keywords: Pathfinding · Collaborative Routing · Collision Avoidance · Multi-Robots

1 Introduction

The routing problem for a single robot in a known environment has been extensively researched, and we have efficient solutions for it. However, planning routes for multiple robots in the same environment is much more challenging. From the perspective of a single robot, all other robots are dynamic objects that need to be bypassed. If we knew all routing tasks in advance, we could compute paths that avoid collisions directly.

Recent work tries to overcome the combinatorial problem that occurs when dealing with multiple robots and thus high-dimensional configuration-spaces. The notion of collision between routes has to consider space *and* time. This means that two routes only cause a problem if the robots enter the spatial collision in an overlapping time interval. To solve spatio-temporal collisions, we have two options: First, one robot (or both) may use another route. Second, one robot waits (or drives slower) and thus enters the position in question later.

Usually, waiting in place or driving slower is modelled as a single action, in the same way as driving with normal speed. This, however, is critical when the planning algorithm assumes fixed time intervals: a waiting cycle usually is not a whole multiple of a base cycle. Moreover, robots may drive at different speeds that result from their driving abilities.

In this paper, we go in another direction. We first answer the following question: If we knew all optimal individual routes beforehand, what are optimal waiting times that avoid spatio-temporal collisions and minimize a common cost function for all robots? This cost function is modelled as black box, i.e., our approach does not make any assumptions. It should not be confused with the cost function that each robot tries to minimize for its individual route. To give an impression, the common cost function may be *the average driving time of all robots*, whereas the individual cost function may be the *shortest path*.

Our goal is to find the optimal answers to the following questions:

- Which robot needs to wait?
- When should a robot wait?
- How long should a robot wait?

in order to optimise the common cost function.

Our approach is not restricted to certain routing graphs. Even though we present our evaluation using a grid graph, we may apply any routing graph. In addition, we do not require all robots to move to the next node at the same time. This means that edges may span different distances or robots may have different speeds.

The detection of spatial collisions is performed by a black box function. Usually, we assume a collision occurs if two robots are closer than a pre-defined distance. In particular, we do not only assume a collision, if two robots reside on the same routing graph node (that is, which many other approaches do).

We do not make any assumption about the type of robot. The word *driving* can be replaced by any movement, e.g., *walking*, *swimming*. We assume a certain individual routing approach that is able to compute optimal routes for an individual robot, i.e., when it does not have to care about other robots.

Once we are able to compute optimal wait times, we demonstrate how to use it as a building block to heuristically solve complex collaborative routing problems. We also consider scenarios in which robots first have to leave a narrow area, wait at free places and then re-enter in different ordering.

2   Related Work

Many collaborative routing approaches are based on A* [17]. Either A* is used to compute individual routes (first ignoring other robots), or A* uses combined vertices, which map all configurations of individual robots to a single composite state. In the latter case, A* tries to plan step-by-step, whereas each step represents simultaneous actions of all robots. Such steps also are 'waiting'.

A common classification to distinguish existing work is to consider *centralized* and *distributed* approaches [18].

Centralized solutions assume an instance that has the overall knowledge about the environment and routings tasks of all robots, whereas distributed solutions only partly know the problems and react to collisions with other robots [19]. One issue of distributed approaches is communication between robots: as they compute parts of the overall solution, they have to inform each other. This, however, may result in unwanted waiting of some robots on the computations of others [12].

We further divide solutions into *global* and *decoupled*, where global do search over the multiple robot steps and decoupled look for single routes and try to combine them to collaborative routes without collisions [11].

A class of approaches assigns *priorities* to robots [10]. The highest priority robot ignores all other robots while planning. The second considers the first one as obstacle etc. [1] incorporates the knowledge about higher priority robots into the cost function to avoid collisions; [2] uses a reservation table for this. [3] starts with individual routes, then integrates bypasses at every collision. To speed up the route planning, certain positions that support bypasses are precomputed. [9] used a randomized scheme for prioritisation of robots.

[6] uses a conflict tree to model mutual collisions, whereas each node represents a set of constraints on the motion of the robots. Its extension [16] speeds up execution of internal A* with the help of heuristics that select most promising nodes to expand.

[7] applies probabilistic search to solve to collaborative routing problem. Probabilistic search has a long tradition in single-robot planning [20], whereas a benefit is to support higher-dimensional configuration spaces without to suffer from long runtimes. Thus, probabilistic approaches may also deal with multiple routes. We may achieve asymptotic correctness, but cannot expect deterministic results. Also genetic planners [15] use random components to optimise results.

[8] shifts the problem from workspace to trajectory planning. This is much harder, as also driving constraints of robots have to be considered. The authors introduce *safe corridors* to address this problem. They use a priority based optimisation of trajectories. [13] uses special polynomials the model trajectories. [14] addresses the problem of pure grids: even though suitable for graph generation, resulting trajectories often are difficult to drive by robots. Thus the authors suggest other patterns to fill the space.

Mechanisms are suggested that reduce the huge number of multi-states during planning. [2] introduced a planning window: the cooperative planning only plans a part of the route of all robots, then plans the next parts starting from the new position. [4] proposed a so-called *operator decomposition*: instead of considering all combinations of robot actions from a certain multi-state, the multiple robots are considered one-by-one. Even though the branching factor after all single-robot actions remains the same, additional techniques may reduce the complexity. [5] identifies independent parts of the problem, i.e., subsets robots that may not influence each others. This significantly reduces the tasks as problems may independently be solved.

Discussion

Computing optimal waiting times does not play an important role in former work. Waiting may be more efficient than bypassing a collision. This, however, is difficult to decide when the optimal waiting state and time are not available. Many existing approaches assume a fixed waiting cycle that is modelled as a robot's single action besides driving to the next place. This, however, does not take into account the whole potential of waiting: First, it is not clear where to optimally wait, as the waiting may occur anywhere, not only shortly before a collision. Second, waiting should not be modelled as a single-step action, as waiting may be shorter or longer, dependent on the situation and collision conditions. In addition, if waiting is modelled in the same way as driving actions, the planning complexity is unnecessarily increased, as unreasonable patterns of waiting and driving have to be considered.

We further want to solve difficult problems in narrow environments, where robots have to drive to a free place to wait until a blocking situation has been resolved. This cannot be solved by prioritisation, as no single robot is able to drive a direct path. Global planners may solve this problem, however with the drawback of a long runtime, if free places are far away from optimal paths.

In the following, we first present an approach to compute optimal waiting times for given routes.

3 Optimal Waiting Times

3.1 Introductory Considerations

We assume that multiple robots simultaneously begin driving from their start position and follow their routes. When a robot finishes its route, it stops and remains at the target. This, in particular, means that finished robot may be an obstacle for other robots. We also support routes that visit any route point (including the target) multiple times. Such routes may occur, if robots have to move outside a crowded area in order to resolve a mutual blockade.

Our approach computes waiting times to avoid collisions in the computed robot routes, while optimising a common cost function. If two robots should enter the same place in the same time, one robot has to wait somewhere beforehand in order to delay its movement. This can be arbitrarily complex. E.g., if a robot wants to enter a long hallway, it may have to wait at the entrance for other robots to come out of the hallway. The problem is difficult because of three effects:

- The waiting position very often is not directly before two robots meet, but somewhere before.
- It is not clear, which robot of both waits for the other. If we have more than two robots, we get a high number of possible combinations.
- The duration to wait is not obvious. If we have non-trivial routing graphs, each transition between nodes may require a different time. Thus, waiting durations usually are not whole multiples of a certain clock time.

The input of our algorithm is a set of pre-computed routes for each robot. They also define the desired speeds between nodes. We do not make any assumptions about the routes, i.e., they even to not have to be optimal for the individual robot. The outputs are routes with additional time intervals of zero speed. A later step may re-define the speeds and, e.g., replace normal driving plus waiting time by slower driving. This, however, does not influence a plan, as we actually compute the times between leaving one node and entering another.

Our approach takes the routing graphs of the robots, created for their individual path planning. We work on these graphs, but detect spatial collisions *geometrically*, mainly using the distance. The detection of collisions, however, may be arbitrarily complex and may also consider the robot's orientation. We shift the detection to a black box function, we later call *coll*.

Spatial collisions on graphs may either occur on the nodes (*vertex conflicts*) or on connections between nodes (*edge conflicts*). In our approach we assume a dense graph, where nodes are geometrically closely distributed among the area. In such a graph, edge conflicts cannot appear without vertex conflicts of connected nodes. Graphs that are based on, e.g., grids fulfil this condition. Other approaches for routing graph generation such as visibility graphs may produce long edges. However, we may easily split long edges into smaller parts, if we artificially introduce new vertexes.

Our approach computes all configurations of waiting times that provide a conflict-free driving. The developer defines a common cost function (we later call *evaluate*) to find the best configuration for a specific application. We, e.g., may minimize the sum of squares of running times. Our approach does not require a specific cost model, but takes the common cost function as black box. Note that common cost functions such as *time of first completion* or *time of last completion* are not reasonable as $n-1$ robots may be delayed without affecting the overall result.

3.2 Model and Definitions

In the following, the letters a, b, ... indicate robots. If we iterate through the robots' routes, we use the letters $i, j, ...$ (later also p, q) as indices for route points. Let r_a denote the route for robot a with route points r_{ai}. We finally use r_{a1} for the first and r_{alast} for the last route point of r_a.

To introduce the notion of time, let $r_{ai}.t$ denote the planned point in time, when a robot approaches route point r_{ai}. Further let $r_{ai}.\Delta t$ denote the optimal driving time (computed by the individual route planner) required for the robot to drive to the next route point *without* waiting.

Finally let $r_{ai}.w$ denote the waiting time duration that is computed by our approach to avoid collisions. We get $r_{ai+1}.t = r_{ai}.t + r_{ai}.\Delta t + r_{ai}.w$. Both $r_{ai}.\Delta t$ and $r_{ai}.w$ are zero for r_{alast}.

We further get a *time collision* (i.e., overlapping time interval) for route points r_{ai} and r_{bj}, if

$$r_{ai}.t < r_{bj+1}.t \text{ and } r_{bj}.t < r_{ai+1}.t \tag{1}$$

This, however, is not applicable for last route points. Then we get a time collision, if

$$r_{alast}.t \leq r_{bj} + 1.t \tag{2}$$

Two last points of different routes always have a time collision.

We detect a *spatial collision* by a function $coll(r_{ai}, r_{bj})$. This can be an arbitrary function that expresses proximity. Best practice is a function that computes the geometric distance between route points and checks, if they are closer than the two robot extents, including a safety buffer. We define all colliding route points to a given point r_{ai} by

$$C(r_{ai}) = \{r_{bj} | coll(r_{ai}, r_{bj})\} \tag{3}$$

We finally assume a *spatio-temporal* collision, if we both have a time and spatial collision for the same route points. We call the set of all *spatio-temporal collisions* $T(r_{ai})$.

According to formula (1) and (2), we count waiting and driving time to the current route point. We may think of an immediate switch to the new point after waiting. Of course, we could apply a more precise approach. E.g., we could interpolate the actual position between route points for any point in time. There are several reasons for our model. First, we may have the chance to later replace waiting times by slow driving, thus the actual speed is not obvious at this stage. Second, we later want to have the chance to replace next route points, thus an interpolation would cause another position. Finally and most important, our approach must be able to detect spatial collisions *before* we define the actual timing. This would not be possible, if the position is time-dependent. In dense route networks, the impact of this simplification is low.

3.3 The Idea

We have a collision-free configuration of waiting-times, if $T(r_{ai}) = \{\}$ for all robots and routing points. Then, each spatial collision of r_{ai} must occur after or before r_{ai}. To resolve collisions, we have a decision of two possibilities, which leads to a total amount of $2^{numberOfSpatialCollisions}$ permutations. This usually is far too large for a complete check, thus we have to look for a means to reduce this huge number. For this, we split any $C(r_{ai})$ in two sets $A(r_{ai})$, $B(r_{ai})$, of which A specifies route points after r_{ai} and B route points that occur before r_{ai}. More precisely, we get $C(r_{ai}) = A(r_{ai}) \dot\cup B(r_{ai})$, where

$$
\begin{aligned}
A(r_{ai}) &= \{r_{bj} \in C(r_{ai}) | r_{bj}.t \geq r_{ai+1}.t)\} \\
B(r_{ai}) &= \{r_{bj} \in C(r_{ai}) | r_{bj+1}.t \leq r_{ai}.t)\}
\end{aligned}
\tag{4}
$$

Some properties of A, B:

$$
r_{bj} \in A(r_{ai}) \text{iff } r_{ai} \in B(r_{bj})
\tag{5}
$$

For all $i' \leq i$ and $j' \geq j$ we get

$$
\begin{aligned}
&\text{from } r_{bj} \in A(r_{ai}) \text{ and } r_{bj'} \in C(r_{ai'}) \text{ follows } r_{bj'} \in A(r_{ai'}) \\
&\text{from } r_{ai} \in B(r_{bj}) \text{ and } r_{ai'} \in C(r_{bj'}) \text{ follows } r_{ai'} \in B(r_{bj'})
\end{aligned}
\tag{6}
$$

This is a result of (4) and an ascending ordering of route times. The last property is not obvious:

$$
\text{if } r_{bj} \in A(r_{ai}) \text{ and } r_{bj-1} \in C(r_{ai}) \text{ follows } r_{bj-1} \in A(r_{ai})
\tag{7}
$$

The proof: if $r_{bj-1} \in B(r_{ai})$ then from (4) would follow $r_{bj}.t \leq r_{ai}.t$, but from $r_{bj} \in A(r_{ai})$ follows $r_{bj}.t \geq r_{ai+1}.t$. Both cannot be possible. The result is counterintuitive, as r_{bj-1} appears before r_{bj} and still must appear later than r_{ai} in order to avoid a collision. Figure 1 illustrates the reason.

Robot b bypasses robot a at points that spatially collide with r_{ai}. If we knew that r_{bj} appears after r_{ai} then r_{bj-1} must also appear after r_{ai} or would timely collide. We later assign the direct predecessor of r_{bj} that is in C also to A. Moreover, we can apply this rule multiple times, as long as we get an uninterrupted sequence of spatially colliding route points. Note there is an analogous property of (7) with B.

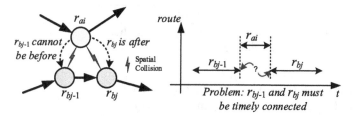

Fig. 1. Reason for ordering of subsequent spatial collisions.

To present our approach, we finally need the transitive hulls of A and B.

$$A^*(r_{ai}) = \begin{cases} A(r_{ai}) & i \text{ is last route point} \\ A(r_{ai}) \cup A^*(r_{ai+1}) & \text{otherwise} \end{cases} \tag{8}$$

A^* specifies the minimum set of route points that must appear after r_{ai}. To also consider (7), we additionally define

$$A^+(r_{ai}, r_{bj}) = A^*(r_{ai}) \cup \{r_{bj'} \cdots r_{bj}\} \tag{9}$$

where j' is the lowest number for which $\{r_{bj'}...r_{bj}\} \subseteq C(r_{ai})$. A^+ specifies minimum set of route points that must appear after r_{ai}, if we assume r_{bj} appears after r_{ai}. B^*, B^+ are defined in an analogue manner.

3.4 The Algorithm

We now can put it together (Algorithm 1). The approach: We know that in the final configuration all spatially colliding route points must be timely ordered *after* (i.e., in set A) or *before* (i.e., in set B). We start with an unknown ordering U. We iteratively put unknown route points either into A or B.

We first need two procedures *moveA*, *moveB* that register a pair of colliding route points in a given order. These procedures also apply the rules of the last section to specify the order of further collisions pairs. We define *moveB* analogously, if we replace $A \leftrightarrow B$ throughout the code.

The final approach works as follows:

- We go through all permutations of *after* or *before* for each pair of spatially colliding route points and call *moveA* or *moveB* respectively. A permutation is completely checked, if U is empty for all colliding pairs or if a *failure* occurred.
- Once we knew the timely ordering of spatially colliding route points, we can specify the minimal waiting times to fulfil the timely ordering.
- Once we know the waiting times, we can assign a cost value and detect the successful permutation with lowest.

Algorithm 1. moveA.

$moveA(r_{ai}, r_{bj})$ // r_{bj} should appear after r_{ai}
if $r_{ai}=r_{alast}$ or $r_{bj}=r_{b1}$: return *failure*;

for each pair (r_{pk}, r_{ql}) with $r_{ql} \in r_{pk}.C$
                  and $r_{pk} \in B^+(r_{bj}, r_{ai})$ // r_{pk} must be before r_{bj}
                  and $r_{ql} \in A^+(r_{ai}, r_{bj})$ {   // r_{ql} must be after r_{ai}
     if $r_{ql} \in r_{pk}.A$ // after relation already registered
         continue;   // $\Rightarrow$ do nothing
     if $r_{ql} \in r_{pk}.B$ or $r_{pk} \in r_{ql}.A$ // contradiction already registered
         return *failure*;   // $\Rightarrow$ inconsistency
     $r_{pk}.A \leftarrow r_{pk}.A \cup \{r_{ql}\}$;   // register r_{ql} after r_{pk}
     $r_{pk}.U \leftarrow r_{pk}.U \setminus \{r_{ql}\}$;   // and not longer unknown
}
return *success*;   // All pairs (and dependent pairs) registered

---

Algorithm 2. computeWaitingTimes

$computeWaitingTimes$(set of routes R)
for each route $r_p \in R$ {
    for each route point r_{pi} in r_p
      $r_{pi}.U \leftarrow C(r_{pi})$; $r_{pi}.A \leftarrow \{\}$; $r_{pi}.B \leftarrow \{\}$; // initialize A, B, U
    for each $r_{bj} \in r_{p1}.C$: $moveA(r_{p1}, r_{bj})$;   // No other route point must before a start
    for each $r_{bj} \in r_{plast}.C$: $moveB(r_{plast}, r_{bj})$; // No other route point must after a target
    if any of these $moveA/moveB$ fail, return *failure*;
}

$R_{opt} \leftarrow none$;   // The current optimum
$open \leftarrow \{R\}$;   // Route set candidates, start with the given route
while $open \neq \{\}$ {
    $R' \leftarrow$ poll any element of $open$;
    if all U in R' are empty {
      $setWaits(R')$;
      if $setWaits$ was successful {
        $evaluate(R')$;
        if evaluation is better than of R_{opt}: $R_{opt} \leftarrow R'$;
      }
    }
    else {
      choose a pair r_{ai}, r_{bj} of R' where $r_{bj} \in r_{ai}.U$;
      make a copy R'_a of R'; call $moveA(r_{ai}, r_{bj})$ on R'_a; if *success*: $open \leftarrow \{R'_a\}$;
      make a copy R'_b of R'; call $moveB(r_{ai}, r_{bj})$ on R'_b; if *success*: $open \leftarrow \{R'_b\}$;
    }
}
return R_{opt};

According to the rules stated in the last section that are integrated into *moveA* and *moveB*, a certain ordering of a single pair additionally specifies the ordering of many other pairs. Usually, we thus only need to test few candidates, as either all other pairs are defined or we get a *failure*. This is why this approach does not have to deal with a combinatorial explosion.

To compute all waiting times, we execute the pseudo code in Algorithm 2.

To complete this approach, we have to define *setWaits*. This function computes the waiting times w for all route points, based on their ordering. If we knew all waiting times of spatial collisions in $r_{ai}.B$ (i.e., all collision of which we know, they have to be before r_{ai}), we are able to define the time of a routing point r_{ai}. The respective other robots must leave the routing points in B, before robot a enters r_{ai}. If the planned time to leave the predecessor r_{ai-1} was too early, to robot a had to wait there, i.e., apply a time $r_{ai-1}.w > 0$.

We now iteratively define the waiting times. For this, we assign a state to each routing point r_{ai}:

- *unprocessed*: $r_{ai}.t$ is unknown,
- *processed*: $r_{ai}.t$ is known, but not $r_{ai}.w$,
- *fully processed*: $r_{ai}.t$ and $r_{ai}.w$ are known.

Initially, we consider all r_{a1} as *processed* and set $r_{a1}.t = 0$.

For $i > 0$, if all in $r_{ai}.B$ are *fully processed*, we consider r_{ai} as *processed* and r_{ai-1} as *fully processed* with

$$r_{ai}.t = \max(r_{ai-1}.t + r_{ai-1}.\Delta t, \max_{r_{bj} \in B(r_{ai})} (r_{bj}.t + r_{bj}.\Delta t + r_{bj}.w))$$
$$r_{ai-1}.w = r_{ai}.t - r_{ai-1}.t - r_{ai-1}.\Delta t \qquad (10)$$

We iterate through all routes and look for route points that fulfil the condition above. We stop, if all route points apart of the last are *fully processed* and the last are *processed*. Note that $r_{ai}.\Delta t$ and $r_{ai}.w$ are zero for last route points.

There is, however, the possibility, we could not find any *unprocessed* route point where all in B are *fully processed*. In this case we stop with a failure. Figure 2 shows such a constellation.

We have a chain r_{ck-1} before r_{bj} before r_{ai} before r_{ck}. This, however, is unsolvable, as there must a time interval between r_{ck-1} and r_{ck} to integrate r_{bj} and r_{ai}, but r_{ck-1} and r_{ck} must be time connected as they are subsequent route points.

This situation is similar to those addressed by formula (7), but we have more than two robots. This means *moveA* and *moveB* could produce illegal permutations without creating a failure. In principle, we could detect such situations beforehand, but this would require to execute a time-consuming loop detection. We thus shift it to *setWaits* to detect such situations. Note that these situations require three conditions. First, more than two robots must drive across the same points. Second, any two involved routes must not fulfil the left-hand side of (7) otherwise *moveA*, *moveB* would avoid the situation. Third, there must be a chain that begins with a route point and ends with the predecessor. As a consequence, such situations occur very rarely.

Some words about the evaluation of routes. To find the optimal set of waiting times, all candidates have to be evaluated. As our approach iterates through all possible orderings

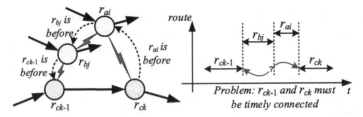

Fig. 2. Situation where *setWaits* fails.

of colliding route points, the evaluation function does not have to fulfil any properties and can be considered as black box. As sequence of route points are given, an evaluation does not have to reflect the actual driving costs (e.g., route lengths or driving time) – it only has to consider the amount of waiting time. It, e.g., could return the average completion time or the square sum of completion times for evaluation.

4   Extending the Approach for Collaborative Routing

4.1   Introduction

The approach presented in the last sections computes optimal waiting times for *known* routes. However, it is not obvious, which routes were optimal, if we had to consider mutual collisions. Good first candidates for optimal routes are *individual optimal routes* – routes that are optimal, if a robot only considers its own routing task and stationary obstacles, but no other robots. In a lucky scenario, individual optimal routes also are optimal for collaborative routing. But:

- An individual optimal route may have waiting times, thus a *suboptimal* individual route would be quicker.
- It could be required to first drive to a waiting place, to allow other robots to bypass places.

In this section, we present an approach that addresses these problems. It is important to note that even our waiting approach computes an optimal solution for given routes, the extension in this section usually does not compute optimal routes. In most cases, our approach discovers at least one solution (if it exists). In rare cases, the approach fails, even though a solution exists. We come back to this point later.

Our goal to present a heuristic approach for collaborative routing mainly is to justify the approach of optimal waiting of the last sections. We want to demonstrate, that once we were able to compute waiting times, we may use this as building block to compute collaborative routes.

The idea of our collaborative routing is to produce candidates of routes, we call *tasks*. We start with a task that contains all *individual* optimal routes. We produce further tasks, if we take existing tasks and modify one route (and thus produce non-optimal individual routes). For all tasks we check, if *computeWaitingTimes* is successful. We stop, until we have a predefined number of successful tasks, of which we return the best one (in terms of the common cost function) as result.

4.2 Critical Collisions

The key elements of our approach are *critical collisions*. Critical collisions are spatial collisions that are impossible to solve with waiting times. Once detected, we do not have to check, if *computeWaitingTimes* fails and instead must modify the set of routes.

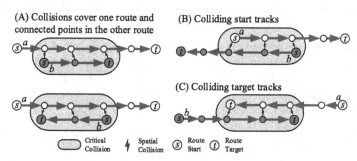

Fig. 3. Critical collisions.

Figure 3 illustrates all constellations of critical collisions. In (A) robot a must wait for b, but if b stays in the target, a is blocked forever. In (B) both robots meet in the collision area, have to wait and are forever blocked. In (C) one robot first enters the collision area and the second can thus not reach its target.

We can define the rules more formally. For a subset of route points $\{r_{i1}...r_{im}\}$ let

$$C^*(\{r_{i1}, \cdots, r_{im}\}) = \bigcup_{r_i \in \{r_{i1}, \cdots r_{im}\}} C(r_i) \tag{11}$$

denote the set of spatial collision in other routes. We then have a critical collision of routes r_a, r_b type (A), if there is an uninterrupted subroute $r_{ai},..., r_{ak}$ of r_a where

$$\{r_{ai}, \cdots, r_{ak}\} \subseteq C^*(\{r_{b1}, \cdots, r_{blast}\}) \text{ and}$$
$$\{r_{b1}, \cdots, r_{blast}\} \subseteq C^*(\{r_{ai}, \cdots, r_{ak}\}) \tag{12}$$

For type (B) we need start subroutes $r_{a1},...$ of r_a and $r_{b1},...$ of r_b where

$$\{r_{a1}, \cdots\} \subseteq C^*(\{r_{b1}, \cdots\}) \text{ and}$$
$$\{r_{b1}, \cdots\} \subseteq C^*(\{r_{a1}, \cdots\}) \tag{13}$$

For type (C) we need target subroutes..., r_{alast} of r_a and..., r_{blast} where

$$\{\ldots, r_{alast}\} \subseteq C^*(\{\ldots, r_{blast}\}) \text{ and}$$
$$\{\ldots, r_{blast}\} \subseteq C^*(\{\ldots, r_{blast}\}) \tag{14}$$

We finally call all involved route points (of both rout3es) *critical members*.

4.3 Resolving Critical Collisions

As we already mentioned, we usually do not achieve the theoretical optimal routes. Only the waiting times for a given set of routes are optimal for these routes.

To resolve a critical collision, we have to modify at least one route point in order to invalidate the conditions (12), (13) or (14). It is sufficient to integrate a single point that does not spatially collide with other critical members. We call such a route point the *intermediate (im)*. Our approach to create new routes works as follows:

- We randomly choose one critical member.
- We identify the closest node (in terms of routing costs) in the routing graph that does not spatially collide with any other routing points. This is our *im*.
- We split the respective route into $s \rightarrow im$ and $im \rightarrow t$. We then call the individual route planning to compute the least-cost routes for both splits.

We can easily identify an *im* using a Dijkstra approach. We iteratively expand a least-cost graph until a candidate with the given properties has been found.

It is obvious, a route through *im* is not optimal anymore, if we consider the individual route. On the other hand *im* cannot be member of any critical collision as only nodes that are members of a C can be critical members. This we decrease the overall amount of critical members.

Figure 4 illustrates the approach. We have two examples of critical collisions. Figure 4 (left) shows a critical collision of type (A). Several solutions solve the problem and depend on the environment. If we, e.g., select the centre point of route b to create the *im*, the respective route can entirely be changed (first solution) or we only make a short bypass through *im*. The latter solution could be required, if there are certain obstacles below route b.

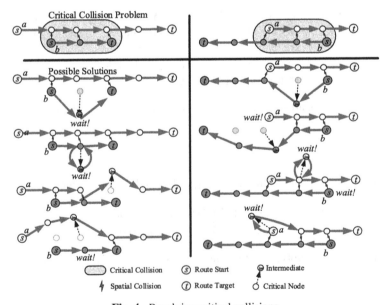

Fig. 4. Resolving critical collisions.

One could argue, a simple solution would be to penalize a single collision member and call the route planning again. This, however, could not solve all problems. Figure 4 bottom right shows such a situation: robot a first has to drive in the wrong direction in order to avoid the critical collision. Such bypasses could be very long: we may think, e.g., of two robots in a narrow maze that want to swap their positions. Both robots first have to drive out the maze, change their ordering and re-enter it. We thus apply a mechanism introduced in [21] to create bypasses. Note that any mechanism that creates alternative routes based on penalizing route points (e.g., [1]) always creates routes that visit each route point only once, which does not solve complex routing problems.

4.4 Putting All Together

We now are able to sketch the collaborative routing approach.

A routing *task* is a set $\{(s_a, im_a, t_a, r_a), (s_b, im_b, t_b, r_b), \ldots\}$ where im may be null. The route either is the individual shortest path from s to t (null im) or the concatenation of individual shortest paths from s to im and from im to t.

The algorithm starts with individual optimal routes. If either we detect a critical collision or the computation of waiting times failed, we create route modifications that may solve the problems. We store new routing tasks in an *open* list. To avoid checking the same routing task multiple times, we additionally manage a *closed* list. We stop, if we cannot produce any new modification or if we produced enough successful tasks. The overall result is the tasks that produced best costs. We get the pseudo code in Algorithm 3.

The approach can be applied in different ways. We, e.g., may stop, if the first task was successful (without considering the costs). The opposite mode may be to run, until the *open* list was empty (thus all produced task modifications were checked). Best-practice is something in between, we called it *best of k*: we iterate the while loop, until we have a predefined number of k successful tasks – the final result then is the best of these k tasks. As alternative: we also could simply run until a pre-defined computation time has been reached.

We finally have to consider the limits of the approach. Again note that it not produces theoretical optimal multi-routes, even if we checked all tasks. It was intended to produce near-optimal routes and at least one solution for most routing problems.

There is, however, a reason, this approach sometimes does not offer a solution for a solvable problem. To resolve critical collisions, we shift a collision member away from *any* collision (critical or non-critical). In very narrow scenarios, however, it could be required to shift a critical collision to *another route*, without producing a new critical collision. In this case, our approach failed. We could, e.g., produce more task modifications to solve this problem. This, however, would cause a combinatorial explosion and made this approach inappropriate.

To sum up: whenever we had enough space to resolve any critical collision, our approach generates at least one solution.

Algorithm 3. collabroute.

modifiyTask(Task *task*, routepoint r_{ai})
compute an intermediate *im* to r_{ai}; // see last section
create new task *t'* with *im* in the respective route;
return *t'*;

collabroute()
open←{initial task with individual optimal routes};
closed←{}; *solutions*←{};
while *open* is not empty {
　　currT←poll any element of *open*;
　　if *currT*∈*closed* continue while loop;
　　closed← *closed*∪{*currT*};
　　if *currT* contains critical collisions {
　　　　for all critical members r_{ai}
　　　　　　open←*open*∪*modifiyTask*(*currT*, r_{ai});
　　}
　　else {
　　　　computeWaitingTimes(routes in *currT*);
　　　　if not *successful* {
　　　　　　for all pairs (r_{ai}, r_{bj}) of spatial collisions {
　　　　　　　　open←*open*∪*modifiyTask*(*currT*, r_{ai});
　　　　　　　　open←*open*∪*modifiyTask*(*currT*, r_{bj});
　　　　　　}
　　　　}
　　　　else { // successful!
　　　　　　solutions←*solutions*∪{*currT*};
　　　　　　if enough *solutions* break while loop;
　　　　}
　　}
}
select the solution in *solutions* with best costs as result;

5　Evaluation

We conducted several experiments to verify and evaluate both the approach to compute waiting times and the collaborative routing. It turned out, it was an advantage to have a full collaborative planning approach (even though heuristically) for evaluation, as we were able to produce a huge number of different calls of *computeWaitingTimes* with realistic routing problems.

For the routing environment we used an 8-connected grid world. It is important to mention that our approach also works on any other routing network, e.g., visibility graph or Voronoi regions. However, the grid world makes it easy to create scenarios that challenge the algorithm. We made the following assumptions:

- We have square cells with width 1.
- Two robots collide, if their distance is less than 2. This means, between two robots there has to be at least a single cell in between.
- A robot may reside in a neighbour cell of a cell occupied by an obstacle.
- A robot has a speed of 1/time unit.

We created 6 scenarios with different problem levels, sizes and number of robots (Table 1, Fig. 7, 8).

Table 1. Test Scenarios.

No	Description	Number of Robots	Occupied Area
#1	Narrow aisle – robots first have to leave and enter in other order	3	26×3
#2	Narrow aisle with two evasion bays	2	26×3
#3	Large area with bottleneck	4	55×15
#4	Crossing of narrow aisles – all robots want to go over the center	5	26×11
#5	Sparsely occupied area – most robots have to pass center	8	36×11
#6	Large maze with narrow aisles	5	35×12

Our first goal was to evaluate *collabroute*. It strongly depends on the strategy that decides to end the loop. We tested *best of k* with different k. We first want to investigate how the average routing costs of result routes depend on k. To make the results comparable between the different scenarios, let q denote the ratio of average routing costs of collaborative routes to individual optimal routes. Obviously, $q \geq 1$ and $q = 1$ only, if the individual optimal routes do not have mutual spatio-temporal collisions. In scenario #1 it is not even possible to get close to 1 because all robots first have to move out of the aisle (Fig. 7). Figure 5 shows q for different k.

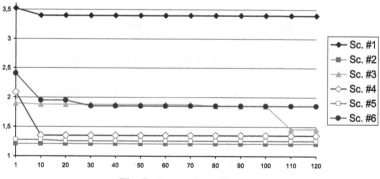

Fig. 5. Ratio q for different k.

For $k = 1$ we stop with the first successful task. For higher k we spend more runtime to potentially get better result. We see, the first result already is suitable for many scenarios. In scenarios #3, #4, and #6 the values of q get significantly lower for higher k.

We additionally want to investigate the influence of k to the runtime. We first use the number of iterations in the while loop of *collabroute* as a measure of runtime (Fig. 6).

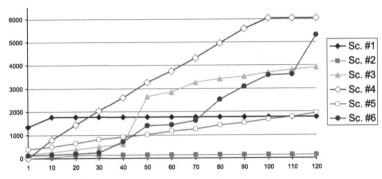

Fig. 6. Number of total iterations for different k.

If the *open* list gets empty, the loop finishes, even though the amount k of successful results has not be reached (scenarios #1 and #2). If the *open* list contains candidates, we approximately get a linear increase. Steps may occur (scenarios #3 and #6) if we have long rows of task candidates in the open list with critical collisions. If we compare Figs. 5 and 6 we see that higher values of k do not pay off, as the runtime significantly increases without considerable better routes. We decided to choose $k = 10$ for further experiment. Table 2 shows more detailed statistics of the computation of collaborative routes with *collabroute*. The runtime measurements were made on an i9-10900K (3.7 GHz).

Table 2. Statistics of *collabroute* for $k = 10$.

| No | Avg. Computation | | Avg. Collaborative Routes | | | Avg. Indiv. Optimal | |
	Iterations	Time [ms]	Run Length	Waiting Time	Driving Time	Driving Time	q
#1	1771	431	30.9	5.4	36.3	10.7	3.40
#2	28	4	19.9	1.3	21.2	17.5	1.21
#3	261	481	34.1	24.8	58.9	31.4	1.88
#4	792	1356	13.8	2.9	16.7	12.3	1.35
#5	488	2745	17.0	2.4	19.4	15.2	1.28
#6	151	1322	39.4	32.7	72.2	37.0	1.95

Different scenarios result in different runtimes. Not surprisingly, the number of robots has the greatest impact on runtime.

We also see how *collabroute* forms the respective solutions. In all scenarios, the routes were modified. The three centre columns indicate the actual output, whereas an additional column shows the driving times (i.e., route lengths) of individual optimal routes. We see the run lengths for the collaborative routes are at least slightly longer than the individual optimal routes. Additionally, waiting times have been integrated to avoid spatio-temporal collisions.

The column *Iterations* indicates the number of iterations in the while loop.

We get a large range of runtimes (column *Time*) for the different scenarios from 4 ms to 2.7 s. The runtimes reflect the complexity of the scenarios. Note that the first results are available very quickly, e.g., 650 ms for scenario #5.

Table 3 shows statistics of *computeWaitingTimes*. We indicate averages of all calls made during a single call of *collabroute*. Here, Iterations shows the number of iterations in the while loop of *computeWaitingTimes*. We also counted the maximum of elements in the *open* list of all iterations to get an indication of required memory. Finally, we counted the number of *moveA* and *moveB*.

Again the number of robots has the largest influence on runtime. In narrow scenarios, the amount of spatial collisions increases quadratically. Moreover, *moveA* and *moveB* iterates over the set C, and *computeWaitingTimes* iterates over the set U (initially C), thus the amount of elements in C highly influences the runtime.

Note, we intentionally created very difficult scenarios in order to challenge the approach.

Figures 7, 8 show two scenarios as sequences of images. Also for complex problems we get reasonable solutions. Even the problem, where robots have to drive outside and area and re-enter in another ordering (Fig. 7) is solved.

Table 3. Statistics of *computeWaitingTimes* for $k = 10$.

No	Iterations	Computation Time [ms]	Max *open* list Elements	Number of *moveA*/moveB
#1	159.80	9.04	3.07	356.88
#2	28.00	0.29	1.91	60.73
#3	443.10	37.50	3.60	912.20
#4	1521.65	62.78	7.55	3068.10
#5	2965.70	225.91	8.20	5840.10
#6	976.58	98.79	4.17	1969.42

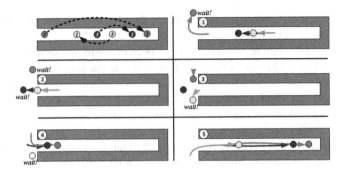

Fig. 7. Result for scenario #1.

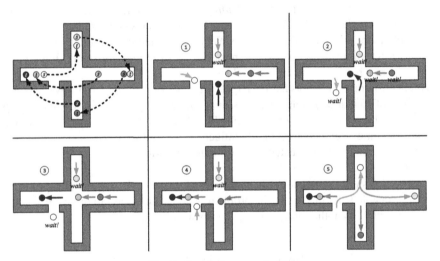

Fig. 8. Result for scenario #4.

6 Conclusions

This paper presented a two-fold approach: an algorithm for theoretically optimal waiting times efficiently is able to decide, if discovered routes can collaboratively be used, and if, where to wait. This makes it possible to evaluate multi-route candidates. A second algorithm produces candidates that avoid critical collisions – collisions that make any solution impossible. A critical collision can be bypassed, if one involved robot integrates a suitable intermediate point into its route. We thus are able to produce new multi-route candidates and stop, if we had enough.

The approach can be applied to all routing networks and is not restricted to grid-based graphs. In addition, we do not require the robots to synchronously move to next nodes: we may have different robots speeds, and even different speeds of one robot in its route. We do not apply a prioritisation approach. We even create routes for difficult scenarios, where robots first have to drive far away from start and target to a free place and re-enter a narrow area in another order.

References

1. Geramifard, A., Chubak, P., Bulitko, V.: Biased cost pathfinding. In: Proceedings of the Second Artificial Intelligence and Interactive Digital Entertainment Conference, 20–23 June 2006, Marina del Rey, California (2006)
2. Silver, D.: Cooperative pathfinding. In: AIIDE'05: Proceedings of the First AAAI Conference on Artificial Intelligence and Interactive Digital Entertainment, June 2005, pp. 117–122 (2005)
3. Wang, C.K.H., Botea, A.: MAPP: a scalable multi-agent path planning algorithm with tractability and completeness guarantees. J. Artif. Intell. Res. **42**(1), 55–90 (2011)
4. Standley, T.: Finding optimal solutions to cooperative pathfinding problems. In: AAAI'10: Proceedings of the Twenty-Fourth AAAI Conference on Artificial Intelligence, July 2010, pp. 173–178 (2010)
5. Standley, T., Korf, R.: Complete algorithms for cooperative pathfinding problems. In: IJCAI'11: Proceedings of the Twenty-Second international joint conference on Artificial Intelligence - Volume One, July 2011, pp. 668–673 (2011)
6. Sharon, G., Stern, R., Felner, A., Sturtevant, N.R.: Conflict-based search for optimal multi-agent pathfinding. Artif. Intell. **219**, 40–66 (2015)
7. Svestka, P., Overmars, M.H.: Coordinated motion planning for multiple car-like robots using probabilistic roadmaps. Robot. Auton. Syst. **23**(3), 125–152 (1998)
8. Li, J., Ran, M., Xie, L.: Efficient trajectory planning for multiple non-holonomic mobile robots via prioritized trajectory optimization. IEEE Robot. Autom. Lett. **6**, 405–412 (2021)
9. Bennewitz, M., Burgard, M., Thrun S.: Optimizing schedules for prioritized path planning of multi-robot systems. In: Proceedings - IEEE International Conference on Robotics and Automation (2001)
10. van den Berg, J., Snoeyink, J., Lin, M., Manocha, D.: Centralized path planning for multiple robots: optimal decoupling into sequential plans. In: Robotics: Science and Systems V, University of Washington, Seattle, USA (2009)
11. Cáp, M., Novák, P., Kleiner, A., Selecký, M.: Prioritized planning algorithms for trajectory coordination of multiple mobile robots. IEEE Trans. Autom. Sci. Eng. **12**(3), 835–849 (2015)
12. Cáp, M., Novák, P., Selecký, M., Faigl, J., Vokřínek, J.: Asynchronous decentralized prioritized planning for coordination in multi-robot system. In: 2013 IEEE/RSJ International Conference on Intelligent Robots and Systems (IROS), 3–7 November 2013, Tokyo, Japan, pp. 3822–3829
13. Park, J., Kim, J., Jang, I., Kim, H.J.: Efficient multi-agent trajectory planning with feasibility guarantee using relative Bernstein polynomial. In: 2020 IEEE International Conference on Robotics and Automation (ICRA), IEEE, pp. 434–440 (2020)
14. Yu, J., Rus, D.: An effective algorithmic framework for near optimal multi-robot path planning. In: Proceedings International Symposium on Robotics Research (2015)
15. Davies, T., Jnifene, A.: Path planning and trajectory control of collaborative mobile robots using hybrid control architecture. J. Syst. Cybern. Inform. (JSCI) **6**(4), 42–48 (2008)
16. Li, J., Ruml, W., Koenig, S.: EECBS: a bounded-suboptimal search for multi-agent path finding. In: Proceedings of the AAAI Conference on Artificial Intelligence (AAAI), pp. 12353–12362 (2021)
17. Hart, P., Nilsson, N., Raphael, B.: A formal basis for the heuristic determination of minimum cost paths. IEEE Trans. Syst. Sci. Cybern. **4**(2), 100–107 (1968)
18. Latombe, J.: Robot Motion Planning. Kluwer Academic Publishers, Boston (1991). ISBN 0-7923-9206-X
19. Azarm, K., Schmidt, G.: A decentralized approach for the conflict-free motion of multiple mobile robots. In: Proceedings of the IEEE/RSJ International Conference on Intelligent Robots and Systems (IROS), Osaka, Japan, pp. 1667–1674 (1996)

20. LaValle, S.M.: Rapidly-exploring random trees: A new tool for path planning, TR 98-11, Computer Science Dept., Iowa State University, 1998, 98–11
21. Roth, R.: Efficient computation of bypass areas. In: Gartner, G., Huang, H. (eds.) Progress in Location-Based Services 2016. Lecture Notes in Geoinformation and Cartography(), pp. 193–210. Springer, Cham (2016). https://doi.org/10.1007/978-3-319-47289-8_10

Robot Vision and Deep Learning for Automated Planogram Compliance in Retail

Adel Merabet[1]([⊠]), Abhishek V. Latha[2], Francis A. Kuzhippallil[2], Mohammad Rahimipour[1], Jason Rhinelander[1], and Ramesh Venkat[3]

[1] Division of Engineering, Saint Mary's University, Halifax, NS B3N 3C3, Canada
adel.merabet@smu.ca
[2] Computing and Data Analytics, Saint Mary's University, Halifax, NS B3N 3C3, Canada
[3] Sobey School of Business, Saint Mary's University, Halifax, NS B3N 3C3, Canada

Abstract. In this paper, automated planogram compliance technique is proposed for retail applications. A mobile robot with camera vision capabilities provides the images of the products on shelves, which are processed to reconstruct an overall image of the shelves to be compared to the planogram. The image reconstruction includes image frames extraction from live video stream, images stitching and concatenation. Object detection, for the products, is achieved using a deep learning tool based on YOLOv5 model. Dataset, for algorithm training and testing, is built to identify the products based on their image identification, number, and location on the shelf. A small scale of shelves with products is built and different cases of products on shelves are tested in a laboratory environment. It was found that YOLOv5 algorithm detects various products on shelves with a precision of 0.98, recall of 0.99, F-measure of 0.98, and clarification loss of 0.006.

Keywords: Robot · Image · Deep learning · Object detection · Planogram · Retail

1 Introduction

Inventory management involves a sequential process of order, storage, usage, and selling of products with the intent of revitalizing the company's profit margin. The expeditious evolution of customer habits, customer satisfaction, and supply chain has made the essentiality of the development of smart, efficient, and fast inventory management system inevitable. The emerging demands have led retail companies to focus on the scope of automating several aspects of inventory management with the reliance on the fusion of robotics and artificial intelligence (AI).

Planogram is the blueprint of the shelves, which provides information about the products present and their respective positions on the shelves. Planogram compliance involves verifying if the current arrangement of the products matches with the planogram. Currently, most retail companies perform manual planogram compliance. The limitation of this approach is the increased risk of human errors, time consumption, and manual labor. The combination of computer vision and deep learning can provide an automated

J. Filipe and J. Röning (Eds.): ROBOVIS 2024, CCIS 2077, pp. 21–30, 2024.
https://doi.org/10.1007/978-3-031-59057-3_2

solution to effectively undertake planogram compliance swiftly, effectively, and cost-efficiently. Various approaches have been used to execute planogram compliance. In [1], support vector machine (SVM) is used to achieve an object detection accuracy of 69% and further able to improve accuracy to 81% with slight modifications in height and width of the images. Other works focused on implementing detection of products on the shelf, estimation of empty space on the shelf and identification of any change between two images taken at different times [2, 3]. Various techniques such as image differencing, principal component analysis, change vector analysis and Kauth-Thomas transformation are used to detect the difference between multiple images. Furthermore, SVM, a derivate of change vector analysis, is used to classify objects through using multiclass discriminative classifier.

Recent advances in object detection include the use of deep learning techniques to ensure planogram compliance [4–7]. These techniques are more robust and accurate if the dataset is large. Convolution neural network (CNN) is used for object detection and identifying products on the shelf. This network is trained on different image datasets and the overall prediction accuracy is high. Variants of CNN such as region-based-CNN (R-CNN) and fast R-CNN techniques have been employed with good accuracy. R-CNN uses region-based extraction, and it is faster and more accurate than other conventional CNN but computationally expensive [8–10]. The recent approach for real-time object detection system is You Only Look Once (YOLO) technique that can tackles two issues in planogram compliance [11]. Firstly, shelf monitoring to determine the changes in the stock and availability of products. Second, to ensure compliance. Different versions of YOLO have been investigated for object detection. The training of the YOLO model requires labeling the images of the products and the racks of the shelves for best detection and classification.

In this work, the automated planogram compliance includes a series of steps that are executed sequentially using the robot vision system for capturing images and computer vision and deep learning technique (YOLOv5) for object detection and classification for planogram compliance [12]. The proposed solution presents a smart, efficient, and cost-effective approach to inventory management that can help retail companies automate the planogram compliance and increase sales and profits. The integration of emerging technologies has the potential to revolutionize the inventory management process and enable retail companies to be competitive in this industry.

2 Images Capturing and Shelves Image Reconstruction

2.1 Robot Vision System and Images Capturing

The reconstruction of the image of shelves with the products, to be compared to the planogram, is achieved using the robot vision system shown in Fig. 1. It includes a mobile platform and a tower of three cameras that visualize the three racks (rows) of the two shelves. In this procedure, the robot moves along the shelves where the cameras continuously capture live video with the frames (images) of the shelves. Each camera visualizes one rack of the shelves.

During the live video capture, the following operations are executed in this order:

(a)   (b)

Fig. 1. Robot vision system. (*a*) Open structure robot to capture images of products on shelves. (b) Robot structure with cover.

Frame Extraction. The camera video produces 30 images per second. However, only one (01) frame per 180 frames is extracted to avoid redundancy in extracted frames and reduce the image stitching time for reconstructing the entire shelf.

Blur Detection. A Laplacian filter, based on a second order derivative filter, is used for edge detection to ensure the extracted images are not blurred. The filter checks for blur based on the variance of the image. If an image contains low variance, below a predefined threshold, then the image is declared blurred, as low-variance images have minuscule edges.

Images Storage. The images captured, and found not blurred, are stored in three image folders namely *images1*, *images2*, and *images3*. Each folder number corresponds to the rack (row) of the shelves. Examples of images, captured by the robot vision system, are illustrated in Fig. 2. The image folders are transferred to another remote host computer via the secure copy protocol (SCP) command for processing the shelves image reconstruction.

2.2 Shelves Image Reconstruction

The overall image of the shelves, to be used in the planogram compliance, is reconstructed using a procedure that includes image stitching and concatenation.

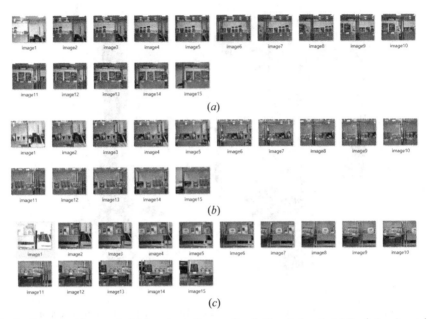

Fig. 2. Storage of images in folders depending on the shelf rack (row). (*a*) Rack (row) number one. (*b*) Rack (row) number two. (*c*) Rack (row) number three.

Image Stitching. This maneuver allows stitching the individual frames of each row to create a panoramic image. It is achieved using the function *cv2.stitcher* from the *OpenCV* library. The image stitching for each row is depicted in Fig. 3.

Concatenation. Once the individual row-wise images are stitched, the overall image of the shelves is generated through performing a vertical concatenation. The function *vconcat* is used to achieve concatenation. The vertical concatenation is performed since each camera is used to capture the entire row of the shelves. Hence each stitched image represents a single row of shelves. The result of the concatenation, that represents the overall shelves image to be compared to the planogram, is illustrated in Fig. 4.

Fig. 3. Row stitched image. (*a*) Rack (row) number one. (*b*) Rack (row) number two. (*c*) Rack (row) number three.

Fig. 4. Concatenated images to reconstruct the entire shelves image.

3 Planogram and Database

The planogram is built using two versions, graphical and textual, as shown in Fig. 5.*a* and *b*, respectively. It includes the placement of each product on the shelves. Information about the products includes number identification (ID), name, quantity, price, image ID, description and class label. This information is recorded and tabulated in database tables and maintained in Microsoft SQL server as illustrated in Fig. 6. Furthermore, locations of the products on the shelves are tabulated in a database as shown in Fig. 7.*a*. Planogram compliance operates on the principle of sequence matching between the products locations in the planogram and their locations extracted from the actual image of the shelves involved in the planogram compliance. The original sequence, built for the products' locations in the planogram, are labeled in classes and coordinates as shown in Fig. 7.*b*.

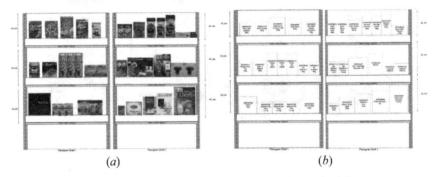

(*a*)   (*b*)

Fig. 5. Planogram. (*a*) Graphical version. (*b*) Textual version.

	Id	Name	Qty	Price	Image	Description	Class_labels
1	6900463430	Ritz Low Sodium	1	17.99	C:\Users\franc\Documents\Francis SMU\Image Proce...	Ritz Low Sodium 200g	0
2	6900463319	Ritz Cheese	1	18.42	C:\Users\franc\Documents\Francis SMU\Image Proce...	Ritz Cheese 180g	1
3	8919463314	Great Value Coconut Lime	1	7.65	C:\Users\franc\Documents\Francis SMU\Image Proce...	Coconut Lime 300g	2
4	7919463387	Bear Paws	3	23.41	C:\Users\franc\Documents\Francis SMU\Image Proce...	Bear Paws 200g	3
5	1509443378	President Choice Cranberry Tea	1	16.33	C:\Users\franc\Documents\Francis SMU\Image Proce...	President Choice Cranberry Herbal Tea 40g	4
6	4249768010	Heinz Alpha Getti	2	61.50	C:\Users\franc\Documents\Francis SMU\Image Proce...	Heinz Alpha Getti 250g	5
7	4249768550	Unico Diced Tomatos	1	2.50	C:\Users\franc\Documents\Francis SMU\Image Proce...	Unico Diced Tomatos 796ml	6
8	4249768760	Nescafe Coffee Hazlenut Flavour	1	12.50	C:\Users\franc\Documents\Francis SMU\Image Proce...	Nescafe Coffee Hazlenut Flavour 100g	7
9	4249768765	Nescafe Coffee Original Flavour	1	12.50	C:\Users\franc\Documents\Francis SMU\Image Proce...	Nescafe Coffee Original Flavour 100g	8

Fig. 6. Example of the database of products on the shelves.

	Item_ID	Shelf_no	Row_no	Column_no
1	6900463430	1	1	1
2	6900463319	1	1	2
3	8919463314	1	1	3
4	7919463387	1	1	4
5	1509443378	1	1	5
6	4249768910	2	1	1
7	4249768910	2	1	2
8	4249768550	2	1	3
9	4249768760	2	1	4

(a)

	A Class_labels	B Shelf_no	C Row_no	D Column_no
1				
2	0	1	1	1
3	1	1	1	2
4	2	1	1	3
5	3	1	1	4
6	4	1	1	5
7	5	2	1	1
8	5	2	1	2
9	6	2	1	3
10	7	2	1	4
11	8	2	1	5
12	9	2	1	6

(b)

Fig. 7. Databases for planogram compliance. (*a*) Products locations. (*b*) Class labels for all products and locations.

4 Object Detection

Object detection of the products on the shelves, as shown in the shelves image shown in Fig. 6, is carried out using the deep learning model YOLOv5, which is a predefined convolutional neural network architecture [12]. YOLOv5, for object detection, is composed of multiple convolutional layers and predicts the object class, bounding box location, and the confidence score for each object in the input image. Furthermore, it uses extensive data augmentation techniques during training to improve the robustness of the network. This includes random cropping, flipping, rotation, and color jittering. The network is trained using both images and instance-level annotations. The following procedure is applied for the YOLOv5 object detection:

Products Dataset. The dataset includes information about each product as specified in the table of Fig. 6. Due to the limited number of products and to enlarge the amount of data for the training, augmentation is being used to increase the number of images per product. Then, the dataset is divided into two sets, one for the training and the other for testing at rates of 80% and 20%, respectively.

Dataset Annotation. This step involves annotating the images and extracting the coordinates information in YOLOv5 format. It is achieved using the tool MakeSense AI [13].

Architecture and Training. The YOLOv5 architecture is defined as illustrated in Fig. 8 and the parameters are assigned as specified in Fig. 9 [12]. Then, the dataset is fed to the network for training.

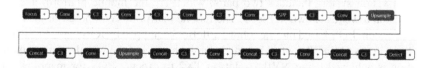

Fig. 8. YOLOv5 architecture [12].

Fig. 9. YOLOv5 architecture and parameters.

Testing. The generated image of all products on shelves, illustrated in Fig. 4, is fed to the trained YOLOv5 to detect the objects. The network output provides information about the object detection that includes the class label of the object, and bounding box coordinates. This information is stored in a text file to generate the sequence of the status of the racks (rows) of the shelves.

5   Planogram Compliance

The products are identified from the reconstructed shelves image, Fig. 4, and the sequence is generated by the YOLOv5; then this generated sequence is compared to the original sequence of the existing planogram shown in Fig. 8. If the generated sequence, from the YOLOv5, is the same as the sequence of the planogram, the products arrangement on the shelves match the planogram, and the products are placed in the correct locations. Otherwise, some products are missed or misplaced due to the discrepancy between the two sequences. The missing products are detected when the two sequences have different lengths. The misplaced products are detected based on the mapping of the two sequences elements. If there is any violation occurring at any index, then the product information is stored, and its actual position is displayed in the shelves' reconstruction image and the real position is displayed in the planogram image to show which action is required to make necessary corrections.

6   Experimental Results

The robot vision system includes two parts, which are the mobile platform and the camera vision tower as shown in Fig. 1. The mobile platform is composed of the robot operating system ROS-based mobile robot TurtleBot3 equipped by Raspberry Pi 3 to run the ROS and uses *OpenCR* control board to run the motors of the wheels. Autonomous navigation is achieved using NVIDIA Jetson TX2 to execute ROS for mapping and movement toward the target. The vision tower includes three cameras (See3CAM_30–3.4 MP autofocus USB camera with liquid lens) and NVIDIA Jetson Nano to capture images from the video streams of the three cameras and wirelessly transfer them to a host computer for image processing. The shelving unit includes two shelves with three racks (rows) on each shelf. A total of 28 grocery products and others are arranged on the two shelves as shown in Fig. 1. The planogram is illustrated in Fig. 5. Information about the 28 products and their locations on the shelves is tabulated as shown in Fig. 6 and 7.

The YOLOv5 model, with the architecture shown in Fig. 5, is trained using an augmented number of the images captured by the robot vision system. The training occurs using different numbers of epochs. The network output, for object detection, is evaluated using performance indicators: precision, recall. F1-score and clarification loss. It can be observed, from the results shown in Table 1, that increasing the number of epochs to 200 provides better outcome based on the performance indicators. The visual result for object detection is illustrated in Fig. 10, where it can be observed that all products are detected with high accuracy. Then, the sequence of the coordinates of the products locations, based on the YOLOv5 output, is compared with the original sequence from the planogram to show a perfect compliance.

Table 1. YOLOv5 Performance.

Case	No. of Epochs	Precision	Recall	F1-Score	Clarification Loss
1	50	0.88	0.50	0.64	0.043
2	150	0.86	0.96	0.91	0.013
3	200	0.98	0.99	0.98	0.006

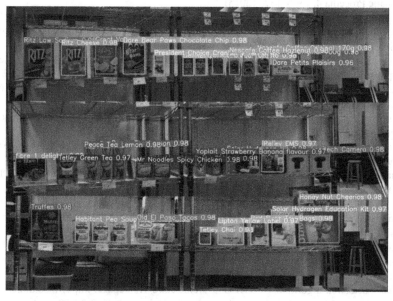

Fig. 10. Object detection using YOLOv5 trained under 200 epochs.

7 Conclusions

Planogram compliance is a major aspect of retail, which has scope for automation to increase the efficiency, speed of compliance checks, and report generation. In this work, a robot vision system is proposed to navigate in a store and collect images of products on shelves. Computer vision tools are used to reconstruct a complete image of the shelves involved in the planogram compliance. Deep learning tool, based on YOLOv5, is used to detect the products and their locations on the shelves to compare with planogram for compliance. The experimentation, conducted on a small scale, has shown that the robot vision system and the deep learning tool provides accurate results for planogram compliance. Future works include the assessment of the proposed solution in a real retail store with multiple shelves.

Acknowledgment. This work is financially supported in part by the David Sobey Centre (DSC) for Innovation in Retailing & Services (DSC) of the Sobey School of Business at Saint Mary's University.

References

1. Gul, V., Kuzu, R.S.: Toward retail product recognition on grocery shelves. In: 6th International Conference on Graphic and Image Processing, vol. 9443, pp. 1–2 (2015)
2. Latha, P., Vaiapury, K.: An automated vision based change detection method for planogram compliance in retail stores. Comput. Vis. Bio Inspired Comput. 399–411 (2018)
3. Minu, S., Shetty, A.: A comparative study of image change detection algorithms in Matlab. Aquatic Procedia **4**, 1366–1373 (2015)
4. Ciregan, D., Meier, U., Scmidhuber, J.: Multicolumn deep neural networks for image classification. In: IEEE Conference on Computer Vision and Pattern Recognition, Providence, RI, USA (2012)
5. Wang, J., Huang, C., Zhao, L., Li, Z.: Lightweight identification of retail products based on improved convolutional neural network. Multimed. Tools Appl. **81**, 31313–31328 (2022)
6. Wei, Y., Tran, S., Xu, S., Byeong Kang, B., Springer, M.: Deep learning for retail product recognition: challenges and techniques. Comput. Intell. Neurosci. **2020**, 1–23 (2020)
7. Wajire, P., Angadi, S., Nagar, L.: Image classification for retail. In: 2020 International Conference on Industry 4.0 Technology, pp. 23–28, Pune, India (2020)
8. Hinton, G.E., Osindero, S., The, Y.-W.: A fast learning algorithm for deep belief nets. Neural Comput. **18**(7), 1527–1554 (2006)
9. Zhao, Z.Q., Zheng, P., Xu, S.T., Wu, X.: Object detection with deep learning: a review. IEEE Trans. Neural Netw. Learn. Syst. **30**(11), 3212–3232 (2019)
10. Saqlain, M., Rubab, S., Khan, M.M., Ali, N., Shahzeb, A.: Hybrid approach for shelf monitoring and planogram compliance (Hyb-SMPC) in retails using deep learning and computer vision. Math. Probl. Eng. **2022**, 1–18 (2022)
11. Redmon, J., Divvala, S., Girshick, R., Farhadi, A.: You only look once: unified, real-time object detection. In: Proceedings of the 2016 IEEE Conference on Computer Vision and Pattern Recognition, Las Vegas, NV, USA (2016)
12. Object detection algorithm — YOLOv5 architecture Homepage. https://medium.com/analytics-vidhya/object-detection-algorithm-yolo-v5-architecture-89e0a35472ef. Accessed 26 May 2023
13. https://www.makesense.ai/. Accessed 26 May 2023

Park Marking Detection and Tracking Based on a Vehicle On-Board System of Fisheye Cameras

Ruben Naranjo[1,3]([✉]), Joan Sintes[2], Cristina Pérez-Benito[2], Pablo Alonso[1], Guillem Delgado[1], Nerea Aranjuelo[1], and Aleksandar Jevtić[2]

[1] Vicomtech Foundation, Basque Research and Technology Alliance (BRTA), Mikeletegi 57, 20009 Donostia-San Sebastián, Spain
rnaranjo@vicomtech.org

[2] FICOSA ADAS, SLU, Polígon Industrial Can Mitjans, 08232 Viladecavalls, Spain
joan.sintes@ficosa.com

[3] University of the Basque Country (UPV/EHU), Donostia-San Sebastián, Spain

Abstract. Automatic parking assistance systems based on vehicle perception are becoming increasingly helpful both for driver's experience and road safety. In this paper, we propose a complete and embedded compatible parking assistance system able to detect, classify, and track parking spaces around the vehicle based on a 360° surround view camera system. Unlike the majority of the state-of-the-art studies, the approach outlined in this work is able to detect most types of parking slots without any prior parking slot information. Additionally, the method does not rely on bird-eye view images, since it works directly on fisheye images increasing coverage area around the vehicle while eliminating computational complexity. The authors propose a system to detect and classify, in real time, the parking slots on the fisheye images based on deep learning models. Moreover, the 2D camera detections are projected in a 3D space in which a Kalman Filter-based tracking is used to provide a unique identifier for each parking slot. Experiments done with a configuration of four cameras around the vehicle show that the presented method obtains qualitative and quantitative satisfactory results in different real live parking scenarios while maintaining real-time performance.

Keywords: Park marking detection · Vehicle perception · Advanced Driver-assistance systems

1 Introduction

The proliferation of vehicles in today's bustling urban landscapes has spurred an escalating demand for intelligent vehicular safety and assistance systems. Advanced Driver Assistance Systems (ADAS) play a pivotal role in enhancing road safety and elevating the overall driving experience. Among these innovations, parking assistance systems have gained significant attention due to their potential to redefine the entire parking experience.

Incorporating parking slot detection not only expedites the parking process and reduces traffic congestion but also assists in accurately positioning vehicles within parking lots. Moreover, it is an enabling technology for autonomous driving, being a key

© The Author(s), under exclusive license to Springer Nature Switzerland AG 2024
J. Filipe and J. Röning (Eds.): ROBOVIS 2024, CCIS 2077, pp. 31–46, 2024.
https://doi.org/10.1007/978-3-031-59057-3_3

component for Autopark systems, which are currently of great importance in the automotive industry.

One of the major difficulties this field has to overcome is the large variability in parking slot types and shapes, shown in Fig. 1, as well as obstructions and occlusions from already parked vehicles and nearby obstacles such as pedestrians, trees and bushes, light poles and signage, etc. Additionally, parking assistance systems must process data in real-time to provide timely feedback to drivers which demands efficient and fast algorithms to achieve it. In order to be effective in real-world scenarios, parking assistance systems also need to be robust to daytime and weather changes.

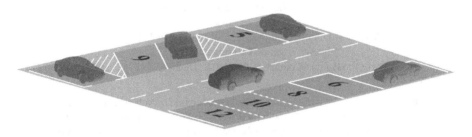

Fig. 1. Parking assistance system to detect, classify and track parking slots with varied marking designs and parking layouts.

In this paper, we present a lightweight parking assistance system, able to detect, classify, and track parking slots around the vehicle in real-time. The proposed method is able to detect parking slots independently of their shape and orientation. Additionally, by working directly on the fisheye images the system covers a bigger area around the vehicle while removing any pre-processing step.

We evaluate the proposed system by using an in-house recorded and annotated dataset. This dataset is captured in different parking environments, including different parking shapes (lateral, parallel, and diagonal), different border types (x-shape, l-shape, t-shape), and different day-light conditions. The metric used to evaluate the entire system including detection, tracking, and localization is an adaptation of the HOTA Metric (Higher Order Tracking Accuracy) [10] for polygon shapes.

In summary, the main contributions are:

– The proposal of a parking assistance system to detect, classify and track parking slots that is robust to varied marking designs, parking layouts, and weather conditions.
– The usage of fisheye images as input without the need of any pre-processing step such as bird-eye view.
– A scalable system, compatible with different camera configurations and the main automotive embedded platforms, while maintaining real-time performance.

This paper consists of five sections. Section 2 describes the related prior work, Sect. 3 introduces the proposed methodology, Sect. 4 presents a range of experiments including quantitative and qualitative results and finally in Sect. 5 conclusions are drawn.

2   Related Work

There has been a variety of research on the detection of parking slots around the vehicle which can be categorized into two groups based on the technology used: non-visual detection methods and visual detection methods. On the one hand, non-visual detection methods primarily utilize ultrasonic sensors [15], short-range radars [13], or lidars [7], which emit microwave signals to gauge the distance between the sensor and its surroundings using "time of flight" (TOF). This microwave-based approach is robust against changes in nearby lighting conditions and boasts straightforward data processing. Consequently, non-visual methods often meet the requirements for measuring parking slot distances and accuracy in many scenarios, but they do come with some drawbacks. Most of these approaches are based on recognizing free spaces between vehicles that have already been properly parked to infer vacant parking slots, and thus, their usability is limited and cannot perform well in open environments. Moreover, ultrasonic radars and short-range radars are characterized by their small coverage, due to the restricted directionality and short operational range, and the lack of resolution causing a limited perception of parking slot characteristics [11]. Laser scanners such as lidars, produce more stable and high-precision results in exchange for a high cost, increasing the overall cost of the vehicle which results in a low scalability option.

On the other hand, visual methods predominantly employ monocular RGB cameras [2,8] or RGB-Depth (RGB-D) cameras for image acquisition, and with the use of computer vision techniques they try to identify parking slots. These methods employ parking slot markers such as line segments and corner points to identify parking slots. Compared to non-visual methods, they are not limited by parked vehicles around and can also detect occupied slots. An early approach to visual detection of parking slots is to rely on low-level visual features for an initial detection [9,16] and extract the parking slot from that. With the advancement of Artificial Intelligence techniques in the image domain, some recent studies have trained Deep Learning models to detect parking slots. Most of these focus on object detection architectures, either two-stage [21], or one-stage detectors [17,19] and achieve a significant improvement over previously discussed methods, identifying the most common parking markers with high precision. Some studies leverage image segmentation techniques [4,20] and graph neural networks [12]. As far as the author's knowledge all of these methods are based on Bird-Eye-View image, obtained through an image stitching pre-processing step. Moreover, at present, there is a lack of publicly available datasets for fisheye images that also include tracking information, which difficult the comparison between our systems and other state-of-the-art studies.

While these approaches offer accurate visual assistance and provide rich image data, the majority of them are limited to detection on single frames without providing any temporal information which limits their usability in real-life scenarios. Additionally, they are built on high-end GPUs, which entail a significant increase in the cost of the vehicle and hinder the scalability of the technology.

3   Methodology

We propose a parking assistance system that allows the vehicle to perceive and recognize its surroundings, being able to localize and identify over time parking slots on the vehicle's surroundings while determining its occupancy by classifying it as free or occupied. This data may act as the fundamentals for Autopark systems that need to track those parking slots before and during the parking maneuver and know which parking places are free to park. The overall system architecture is shown in Fig. 2, which highlights the four main subsystems.

In this section we first describe our surround view setup, then we present the park marking detector. After that, we detail the 3D object estimation and finally the tracking method and multi-camera fusion.

3.1   Surround View System

In this work, we proposed a setup based on a surround-view system composed of four High Dynamic Range (HDR) 1.4Mpx fisheye cameras. These cameras are located on the front, back, left, and right of the vehicle. By strategically placing and orienting this 180-degree field of view cameras around the designated area, this setup offers a 360-degree panoramic view of the vehicle's surroundings, ensuring that no blind spots are left unchecked as shown in Fig. 2. Should be noted that the system does not rely upon the number of cameras, since it is completely scalable to setups with more or less cameras, and therefore different coverage areas. The four fisheye images serve as the starting point for our vehicle perception method.

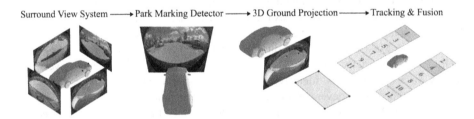

Surround View System ⟶ Park Marking Detector ⟶ 3D Ground Projection ⟶ Tracking & Fusion

Fig. 2. Pipeline of our parking assistance system to detect, classify, and track parking slots for Surround View Systems.

3.2   Park Marking Detection

The aim of this module is to detect marked parking slots on fisheye images. To accomplish that, we had to deal with some requirements regarding functionality, flexibility, and efficiency. Due to lens distortion and perspective, traditional detectors for rectangular bounding boxes and oriented bounding boxes are not suitable for this use case. Therefore a polygon shape must be used to define the detections. Additionally, to detect parking slots in real-life scenarios we have to take into consideration several factors that contribute to their variability such as varied marking designs, parking lot layouts, weather conditions, wear and tear as well as vehicle occlusions. Also, the system must be able to run in real-time while being efficient and portable to embedded platforms.

To attain the constraints mentioned above we use an adapted version of the YoloV5 [5] to extract polygons bounding boxes instead of rectangular bounding boxes. For enhanced detection reliability, we trained and validate it with our in-house recorded and labeled dataset of 194K images that considers two classes, free and occupied, and significant diversity. The main advantage of our method is that the park marking detector is not limited to any parking shape, border type, color, floor type, or low-level visual features since the neural network will learn it implicitly as long as it is considered in the training dataset.

Furthermore, looking for a flexible and efficient solution applicable to various automotive embedded platforms we have made some layer adjustments to be fully compatible with on of the most used platforms in the automotive industry currently, Texas Instruments TDA4VM hardware [3]. A critical aspect of ensuring compatibility of this kind of systems with an embedded platform is the compatibility of the deep learning model, in our case the Park marking detector should be compatible with the target platform, TDA4VM. This compatibility guarantees that the model can later be ported to embedded systems, which will make the method compatible with automotive standards, lighter and without the need for expensive resources such as GPUs to perform in real time. These advantages make it a solution that can move from theory to practice as a market product.

Fig. 3. Inference results of our park marking detection module on fisheye images.

By including large variability in terms of parking definitions, scenarios, and weather conditions, the network achieves robust and accurate detections due to a comprehensive training environment, as seen in Fig. 3. Meanwhile, the network achieves fast inference times. Our park marking detector module takes 7ms to infer detections in four fisheye images at the same time with an Nvidia GeForce RTX 3060 Mobile.

3.3 3D Ground Projection

The aim of this module is to estimate the 3D position of the 2D image points. Estimating the 3D position of the parking slots from 2D image detections is a crucial step in our park marking detector and tracker system. This process enables us to transform all the detected slots from the four cameras into a common coordinate system, facilitating accurate spatial understanding of the surrounding scene. To achieve this, we make use of both extrinsic and intrinsic parameters obtained during camera calibration. Extrinsic parameters account for the camera's position and orientation in the world, allowing us to relate image pixels to real-world coordinates. Intrinsic parameters, on the other hand, pertain to the camera's internal characteristics like focal length and distortion coefficients, which correct lens distortions and enable accurate mapping of image coordinates to the camera's sensor plane. By leveraging these calibrated parameters, we can effectively bridge the gap between 2D image detections and their 3D spatial projection, as shown in Fig. 4.

Since we focus on the area around the vehicle it is fulfilled that almost in all the cases the parking slots in this area will be located at the same plane than the vehicle, therefore we can assume that the parking slots detected are located in the ground plane $Z = 0$. Taking into account this assumption, given a 2D point p in image coordinates the corresponding 3D point p' is computed as follows:

1. Given the ground plane in world coordinates system with norm vector $N = (0, 0, 1)$, we transform the plane to the camera coordinate system by:

$$N' = P^{-1} \cdot N \qquad (1)$$

where N' is the ground plane in camera coordinates system and P corresponds to the projection matrix defined by $P = [R|t]$.

2. Compute the ray in 3D space X_d that pass through the corresponding 2D point on the image plane:

$$X_d = K^{-1} \cdot \begin{bmatrix} x \\ y \\ 1 \end{bmatrix} \qquad (2)$$

where K^{-1} corresponds to the inverse of the camera intrinsic matrix and x, y is the 2D point in the image plane $p = [x, y]$.

3. Given the ray in 3D space X_d undistort it by using the camera distortion coefficients to obtain X_u.

4. Compute the 3D projection p'_c in camera coordinates system of the 2D point defined by:

$$p'_c = X_u \cap N' \qquad (3)$$

where $\cap$ corresponds to the intersection between ray X_u and plane N'.

5. Transform the resulting 3D point p'_c in camera coordinates system to world coordinates system:

$$p' = P \cdot p'_c$$

Note that in our case the world coordinate system used corresponds to the vehicle coordinate system in which the origin is located on the ground, below the midpoint of the rear axle. The x-axis points forward from the vehicle, the y-axis points to the left, as viewed when facing forward and z-axis points up from the ground to maintain the right-handed coordinate system.

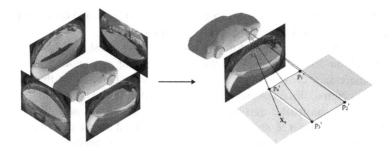

Fig. 4. 3D ground projector representation. 2D image points are projected to 3D space.

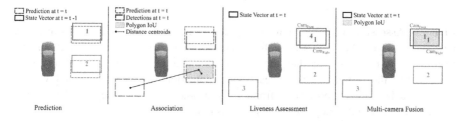

Fig. 5. Tracking and multi-camera fusion module composed of prediction, association, liveness assessment, and fusion steps.

3.4 Tracking and Multi-camera Fusion

Given the 3D positions of the parking slots detected by each of the four cameras, the multi-camera parking slot tracking module proposed in this paper utilizes a Kalman filter [5] approach for its effectiveness in achieving accurate and computationally efficient tracking. This module aims to estimate the 3D position and trajectory of each parking slot around the vehicle and assign it a unique identifier over time, similar to proposed in [1]. The tracking and multi-camera fusion approach is performed in four steps: prediction, association, liveness assessment, and fusion as shown in Fig. 5. Note that the height of the parking slots is not tracked since we assume they are located in the ground plane and their height should stay as $Z = 0$.

Prediction. The prediction step is used to estimate the state vector of a parking slot at the next time based on the previous state vector and a dynamic model of the system. In our model, we utilize a state vector to represent the current state of a parking slot. This vector incorporates the position and velocity components for each parking slot corner coordinate in the 3D space. The Kalman filter algorithm utilizes the state vector to continuously enhance predictions by incorporating new measurements, thereby ensuring robust and precise tracking of parking slots.

Association. The association is probably the most critical part during tracking and multi-camera fusion since it is in charge of determining which detections from the camera sensors correspond to which tracked parking slots. Correctly associating detections to tracked objects ensures robustness to real-world noisy environments and provides consistency over time, enhancing the accuracy of the system.

During association, a likelihood matrix is computed that assigns a likelihood value to each prediction-detection pair. With the aim of reaching maximum accuracy while avoiding unnecessary computations, the likelihood value is based on the CameraID, Object Class, centroid distances and polygon Intersection Over Union (Polygon IoU).

This way, we construct a maximization unbalanced assignment problem to associate detections with tracked objects, having the likelihood matrix described above as our cost matrix. To solve the assignment problem we use a generalization of the Hungarian algorithm [6] since it keeps a low complexity, solving the optimization problem in strongly-polynomial time.

Liveness Assessment. In order to minimize the effect that false positives and false negatives have on the system as well as manage memory resources, we implement a liveness assessment process that handles the initialization and termination of tracked objects. For the initialization process, when detections are not associated with an already tracked object for several frames, these objects become new tracked objects and are included in the output of the system as real parking slots.

The process for tracked object termination is based on a similar concept, instead of removing a parking slot from the list of tracked objects as soon as it is not associated with a detection on a frame, it is kept on the background. Once the tracked object has not been assigned a detection for several frames, we consider the object is lost or out of view and remove it from the list of tracked objects.

Multi-camera Fusion. As a result of the surround view system configuration, some angles of the scene are viewed by two cameras at the same time. In consequence, parking slots located in the overlapping area are tracked by two different cameras simultaneously. Multi-camera fusion, the last step of the pipeline, is performed to create a unified and more comprehensive view of the scene and thus, improve the accuracy and robustness of the system.

Parking slots tracked that are close to each other are analyzed during the period of time that both have been present on the scene so far. In case the mean overlapping area of the slots over this time exceeds a certain value, both tracked objects are considered to be the same parking slot on the scene and thus are assigned with the same identifier, as shown in Fig. 2. By analyzing it over a period of time the system offers robustness to misdetections and occlusions.

Keep in mind that the work has been conducted using a four fisheye cameras setup positioned around the vehicle, that is sufficient to cover the entire vehicle surroundings by fusing adjacent pairs of cameras. However, the system is compatible with other camera setups with two or more cameras.

4 Experiments

The proposed system is an integral component responsible for collecting and processing sensor information from the surroundings of the vehicle. An accurate and timely perception of the environment is crucial for the safe and efficient operation of autopark systems and parking assistance systems. Therefore, extensive experimentation is vital to ensure the reliability and robustness of the system.

In this study, we evaluate the performance of our vision-based parking assistance system. We conduct our experiments on our own recorded and labeled dataset containing real-world images and artificially generated images, explained in Sect. 4.1. In Sect. 4.2 and Sect. 4.3 we prove numerically and visually the performance of our method in different real-world scenes containing large variability in terms of parking lots definitions.

4.1 Dataset

To cope with the shortage of public available datasets for training and validation, specially with labeled data for a fisheye Surround View System (SVS) we have created an in-house dataset based on real and simulated scenarios. This dataset consists of a total of 194K images from two different sources: recorded data and simulated data.

On the one hand, by means of Ficosa's recording car equipped with state-of-the-art surround view system, we captured a wealth of diverse data across various environments and parking lot scenarios. This vehicular data collection ensured a comprehensive and dynamic dataset that encapsulated real-world scenarios containing a large variability in terms of parking lot type, orientation, and corner shapes, as shown in Fig. 6.

Furthermore, WebLabel [18] annotation tool played a pivotal role in the dataset creation process by facilitating the manual labeling and annotation of the collected data. This meticulous annotation process ensured that the dataset was enriched with valuable ground truth information, making it a robust resource for subsequent research and analysis. A total of 30 video sequences of 30 s duration were recorded and labeled across 12 different parking scenarios providing us with a total of 90k real-world annotated images. Of this set of images 49%, 30%, and 21% contain lateral, parallel, and diagonal parking, respectively. Furthermore, 44%, 25%, and 21% of these parking lots contain t-shape, l-shape, and x-shape border types, respectively.

On the other hand, we employed rFpro [14] simulation software to enrich the dataset with various environmental scenarios, including challenging conditions by considering three different daylight levels (daylight, sunset, night), three weather conditions (clear sky, cloudy, rainy), and three markers visibility cases (10%, 30%, 50%). Figure 7 shows some generated samples included in our dataset. This approach allowed us to precisely control and replicate these conditions, overcoming the logistical difficulties of real-world data collection. By doing so, we ensured the availability of a diverse dataset that enhanced the credibility and applicability of our research findings, making it a pivotal aspect of our study.

Finally, to train and test the system the dataset was split into 70% for training and 30% for testing.

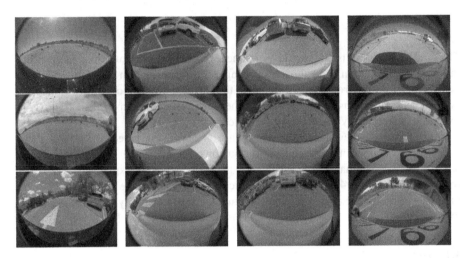

Fig. 6. Recorded sample images of Ficosa's dataset.

4.2   Quantitative Results

Our work has been evaluated under the the Higher Order Tracking Accuracy (HOTA Metric) [10] which has been widely used to evaluate object detection and tracking algorithms in autonomous driving systems. The HOTA metrics provide a comprehensive evaluation of the performance of the detection and tracking algorithms by considering both the spatial and temporal accuracy by means of a combination of detection, association, and localization accuracy.

Table 1 shows the HOTA score as well as the detection accuracy (DetA), association accuracy (AssA), and localization accuracy (LocA). In addition, in Table 1 and Table 2, GTIDs, represent the total number of unique object identities tracked within the sequences, reflecting the count of distinct entities under tracking. On the other hand, GTDets, denote the overall number of objects in the dataset, encompassing all instances, whether they belong to unique identities or not.

Experiments show that the parking assistance system is robust in real live scenarios both detecting and tracking free parking slots and occupied parking slots. However, camera positioning and consequently, the point of view of that camera, may difficult the task of detecting parking slots. It can be reflected in Table 1 in which the front and rear cameras tend to perform worse than the side cameras in terms of detection accuracy, consequently affecting the final HOTA score. It makes sense since both front and back cameras are less tilted than side cameras, causing the vertices of those furthest parking lots to be closer together, and consequently, complicating its correct detection. Despite the camera positioning, results reveal high scores in localization accuracy, a crucial aspect for auto-park systems and parking assistance systems.

In terms of class, occupied class shows lower overall HOTA scores, than free class. The main reason is the partial occlusion of the parking slot caused by the car parked on it. Consequently, one or more vertices are not visible and the method needs to estimate them. This can be observed since detection accuracy decreases for occupied classes on

Fig. 7. Generated samples using rFPro simulation environment with different daylight conditions.

Table 1. HOTA metrics on the test set for real-world data captured by Ficosa.

Real world annotated data								
Class	Camera	HOTA	DetA	AssA	LocA	Dets	GTDets	IDs	GTIDs
Free	Front	57.28	47.91	70.26	86.84	6134	6059	123	114
	Right	65.44	61.08	70.90	86.66	8955	9623	103	81
	Left	57.12	51.36	63.92	88.69	6505	7375	88	55
	Rear	40.77	32.49	52.55	79.76	3830	5245	134	110
	Combined	**55.15**	**48.21**	**64.41**	**85.49**	**25424**	**28302**	**448**	**360**
Occupied	Front	54.44	46.56	64.24	84.64	5791	5016	115	93
	Right	60.03	55.96	65.16	85.04	6887	6548	89	54
	Left	49.33	46.12	53.00	87.74	6499	7551	77	48
	Rear	38.21	27.90	57.40	78.29	2460	3949	98	85
	Combined	**50.50**	**44.14**	**59.95**	**83.93**	**21637**	**23064**	**379**	**280**

Table 2. HOTA metrics on the test set for real-world data captured by Ficosa considering three different parking types.

Real world annotated data								
Class	Type	HOTA	DetA	AssA	LocA	Dets	GTDets	IDs	GTIDs
Free	Parallel	38.99	29.28	53.44	84.84	3340	5236	76	50
	Lateral	58.96	51.29	69.13	88.51	13873	15560	249	220
	Diagonal	48.80	43.07	56.55	80.45	11550	12742	199	140
Occupied	Parallel	46.15	38.27	59.11	81.65	5847	6852	88	65
	Lateral	52.84	45.51	61.99	86.27	13199	14216	237	183
	Diagonal	46.61	41.81	56.61	80.04	8434	8848	142	97

Table 3. Performance evaluation of the system.

Platform	Configuration	Latency↓	fps↑	Precision	Layers Quantized
PC	CPU	160 ms	6.25 fps	32 bits	None
	CUDA	25 ms	40 fps	32 bits	None
	TensorRT	12 ms	83.3 fps	16 bits	None

all the cameras. Even so, despite the higher complexity of managing challenges of the environment and parking visibility, the detection and tracking system maintains reliable performance without a big drop in results.

Table 2 shows the HOTA score for the three different parking types. Notably, there are certain parking types within the dataset, such as parallel parking slots, that lack sufficient representation due to a low quantity of samples, and consequently show lower overall HOTA scores. In contrast, results reflect a significant improvement in performance for those parking types with a larger presence on the dataset, such as lateral parking slots.

Despite the high complexity and variability of parking slot definition and parking areas, which poses a big challenge for the detection and tracking algorithms, the algorithm demonstrates the system's robustness and adaptability. These findings underscore the system's suitability for real-world applications across diverse parking areas, parking definitions, and marking types.

Furthermore, a thorough performance analysis of the method was conducted, and the results are presented in Table 3. The analysis involved computing the performance of a built-in PC featuring an i7-11800H CPU and an NVIDIA 3060 Mobile GPU using a four camera setup with resolution of 1344×968 pixels each. The latency ranges from 12 to 160 milliseconds, per frame with the lowest latency achieved using TensorRT. These results demonstrate the system's adaptability to different hardware configurations as well as the ability to work on real-time applications.

With the intention of developing a method that can be used in real live scenarios and automotive standards compatible, this work is focused on the challenging step of the process, make the parking slot detection step compatible and portable to embedded hardware. As mentioned in Sect. 3.2, the necessary layer adjustments has been done to the network, getting a fully TDA4VM hardware compatible slot detection network that is ready to be subsequently ported to the embedded platform.

4.3 Qualitative Results

We present the qualitative results of our study, offering insights from an in-depth analysis of visual data. These findings reveal the nuances, complexities, and unique perspectives related to our parking assistance system, complementing the quantitative data and providing a comprehensive understanding of the phenomenon.

Figure 8 shows the results of our method applied to scenes in which lateral parkings predominate. Results show high performance across the three facets of detection, association, and localization. The method demonstrates robustness when confronted

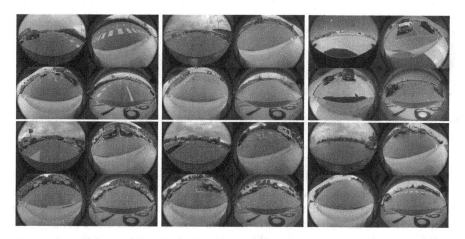

Fig. 8. Results samples on test data with lateral parkings.

with diverse ground types, including asphalt and cobblestones, as well as situations where line visibility is compromised. Furthermore, our approach exhibits resilience when dealing with different corner types, such as l-shape, x-shape, or t-shape configurations. These robust characteristics underscore the versatility and effectiveness of our method in real-world scenarios, making it a valuable asset for autopark systems.

Figure 9 shows the results of our method applied to scenes in which parallel and diagonal parkings predominate. Results showcase its effectiveness in most scenarios. However, in certain cases, challenges arise in localization and detection, primarily attributed to the limited availability of data, specially for parallel parkings. Despite occasional difficulties, our method consistently excels in detecting and associating park markings, emphasizing its overall efficacy in real-world applications.

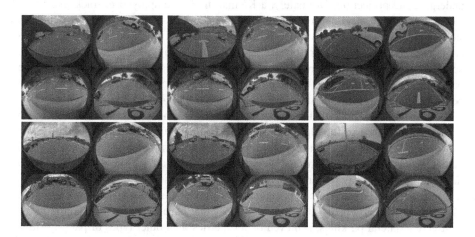

Fig. 9. Results samples on test data with parallel and diagonal parkings.

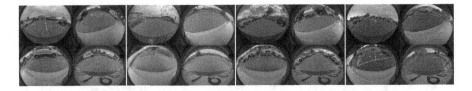

Fig. 10. Results samples on challenging conditions, e.g. colored parkings, low line visibilities, and high-density scenarios.

Figure 10 shows results of our method on challenging conditions such as low line visibility, colored parking slots as well as high density of occupied parking slots. The method excels in robustly detecting parking slots of different colors and different line visibility. This versatility is particularly valuable in environments where parking slots are differentiated by a diverse range of hues. However, the method's performance may be influenced in scenarios with high parking slot occupancy, primarily impacting detection, localization, and subsequently, association between cameras. Finally, we can correlate quantitative results explained in Sect. 4.2 by noticing some difficulties in the detection and localization in those cases where park marking lines are very close to each other, e.g. on diagonal parking slots, specially for front and rear cameras due to its orientation and visual perspective.

5   Conclusions

In this paper, we present a vision-based novel system to detect, classify and track parking slots for a Surround View System equipped with, but not limited to, four fisheye cameras that offer complete 360° coverage around the vehicle.

The proposed pipeline consists of three phases. Firstly, a deep learning model is applied to identify and classify parking spots. Following this, the identified data points undergo a 3D projection. Ultimately, a Kalman filter is employed to track these projected points in the final phase. Our approach has been designed to apply the detection step in each camera independently offering a huge versatility for other types of camera configurations and avoiding pre-processing such as stitching, which adds computational complexity and significantly reduces useful image information. In addition, it has also been designed to be portable to an automotive embedded platform, specifically, it has been implemented following the requirements of the TDA4 platform.

The results show not only the ability to work in real-time with the 4 cameras but also a good performance of the algorithm in terms of the HOTA metric. Although results show good performance overall, we observe better results on the side cameras due to having more tilt than the front and side cameras, which affects the distance between the vertices of far-away parking slots. In addition, we observe a better detection accuracy on free parking slots since occupied parking slots tend to have occlusions from the parked vehicles. Finally, those parking types that have better representation on the dataset, e.g. lateral parkings, achieved better metrics than other types of parking slots. Experiments on computing performance reveal that the proposed system can work with a configuration of four cameras in real-time.

Moving forward, our work will focus on balancing and extending the recorded dataset, specially for parallel parking slots, in order to improve the parking slot detection and classification model, as well as, removing the flat-world constraint to broaden the operational domain of the system. We will continue porting the model to Texas Instruments TDA4VM hardware which will allow us to compare embedded model with PC model. Finally, we see potential for experimenting with data fusion to leverage vehicle GPS data and improve the tracking capabilities of the system.

Acknowledgments. This work has received funding from the Ministerio de Ciencia, Innovación y Universidades of the Spanish Government, programme "Misiones CDTI", under project "Movilidad2030" (EXP 00129266/MIG 20201040).

References

1. Delgado, G., et al.: Virtual validation of a multi-object tracker with intercamera tracking for automotive fisheye based surround view systems. In: 2022 IEEE 14th Image, Video, and Multidimensional Signal Processing Workshop (IVMSP), pp. 1–5 (2022). https://doi.org/10.1109/IVMSP54334.2022.9816285
2. Huang, C., Yang, S., Luo, Y., Wang, Y., Liu, Z.: Visual detection and image processing of parking space based on deep learning. Sensors **22**(17), 6672 (2022)
3. Instruments, T.: TDA4VM Jacinto processors for ADAS and Autonomous Vehicles silicon revisions 1.0 and 1.1 (2021). https://www.ti.com/lit/ds/symlink/tda4vm.pdf
4. Jian, D.H., Lin, C.H.: Vision-based parking slot detection based on end-to-end semantic segmentation training. In: 2020 IEEE International Conference on Consumer Electronics (ICCE), pp. 1–4. IEEE (2020)
5. Kalman, R.E.: A new approach to linear filtering and prediction problems (1960)
6. Kuhn, H.W.: The Hungarian method for the assignment problem. Naval Res. Logist. Quart. **2**(1–2), 83–97 (1955)
7. Lee, B., Wei, Y., Guo, I.Y.: Automatic parking of self-driving car based on lidar. Int. Arch. Photogrammetry, Remote Sens. Spat. Inf. Sci. **42**, 241–246 (2017)
8. Lee, Y., Park, M.: Around-view-monitoring-based automatic parking system using parking line detection. Appl. Sci. **11**(24), 11905 (2021)
9. Li, Q., Lin, C., Zhao, Y.: Geometric features-based parking slot detection. Sensors **18**(9), 2821 (2018)
10. Luiten, J., et al.: HOTA: a higher order metric for evaluating multi-object tracking. Int. J. Comput. Vision **129**, 548–578 (2021)
11. Ma, Y., Liu, Y., Zhang, L., Cao, Y., Guo, S., Li, H.: Research review on parking space detection method. Symmetry **13**(1), 128 (2021)
12. Min, C., Xu, J., Xiao, L., Zhao, D., Nie, Y., Dai, B.: Attentional graph neural network for parking-slot detection. IEEE Robot. Autom. Lett. **6**(2), 3445–3450 (2021)
13. Prophet, R., Hoffmann, M., Vossiek, M., Li, G., Sturm, C.: Parking space detection from a radar based target list. In: 2017 IEEE MTT-S International Conference on Microwaves for Intelligent Mobility (ICMIM), pp. 91–94. IEEE (2017)
14. rFpro: https://rfpro.com/applications-autonomous-vehicle-development/adas-autonomous-vehicles/rfpro-synthetic-training-validation-data/. Accessed Oct 9 2023
15. Shao, Y., Chen, P., Cao, T.: A grid projection method based on ultrasonic sensor for parking space detection. In: IGARSS 2018–2018 IEEE International Geoscience and Remote Sensing Symposium, pp. 3378–3381 (2018)

16. Suhr, J.K., Jung, H.G.: A universal vacant parking slot recognition system using sensors mounted on off-the-shelf vehicles. Sensors **18**(4), 1213 (2018)

17. Suhr, J.K., Jung, H.G.: End-to-end trainable one-stage parking slot detection integrating global and local information. IEEE Trans. Intell. Transp. Syst. **23**(5), 4570–4582 (2021)

18. Urbieta, I., et al.: WebLabel: OpenLABEL-compliant multi-sensor labelling. Multimedia Tools Appl., 1–20 (2023)

19. Xie, Z., Wei, X.: Automatic parking space detection system based on improved YOLO algorithm. In: 2021 2nd International Conference on Computer Science and Management Technology (ICCSMT), pp. 279–285. IEEE (2021)

20. Zhou, S., Yin, D., Lu, Y.: PASSIM: parking slot recognition using attentional semantic segmentation and instance matching. In: 2022 IEEE 5th International Conference on Big Data and Artificial Intelligence (BDAI), pp. 169–175. IEEE (2022)

21. Zinelli, A., Musto, L., Pizzati, F.: A deep-learning approach for parking slot detection on surround-view images. In: 2019 IEEE Intelligent Vehicles Symposium (IV), pp. 683–688. IEEE (2019)

Analysis of Age Invariant Face Recognition Efficiency Using Face Feature Vectors

Anders Hast$^{(\boxtimes)}$, Yijie Zhou, Congting Lai, and Ivar Blohm

Uppsala University, Uppsala, Sweden
anders.hast@it.uu.se
https://andershast.com

Abstract. One of the main problems for face recognition when comparing photos of various ages is the impact of age progression on facial features. The face undergoes many changes as a person grows older, including geometrical changes and changes in facial hair, etc. Even though biometric markers such as computed face feature vectors should preferably be invariant to such factors, face recognition generally becomes less reliable as the age span grows larger. Therefore, this study was conducted with the aim of exploring the efficiency of such feature vectors in recognising individuals despite variations in age, and how to measure face recognition performance and behaviour in the data. It is shown that they are indeed discriminative enough to achieve age-invariant face recognition without synthesising age images through generative processes or training on specialised age related features.

Keywords: Age-invariant face recognition · Biometric markers · Discriminative methods

1 Introduction

The overall aim of this paper is to analyse how to achieve age-invariant face recognition (AIFR) based on Face Feature Vectors (FFV) only, without synthesising age images through generative processes or training on specialised age related features.

Facial features are a commonly used biometric marker that can be captured using images or videos. Generally, biometric markers are physical or behavioural characteristics that can be used to identify individuals, such as fingerprint patterns, voice prints, iris patterns, or as in our case facial features. Face recognition (FR) techniques are based on the analysis of unique features of the face, which can be represented by FFVs. These vectors can be used to match a face with a known identity in a database of faces, providing a useful tool for identification and verification. For example, FR can ensure that only authorised personnel can operate or interact with a robot. Moreover, FR can enhance the interaction between humans and robots by allowing the robot to recognise and respond to individual users.

However, one of the main challenges of FR is to handle the impact of age progression on facial features. As people grow older, their faces undergo various changes, including geometrical changes, as well as changes in facial hair, and other factors such as the presence of glasses. Even though computed FFVs should be invariant to such

J. Filipe and J. Röning (Eds.): ROBOVIS 2024, CCIS 2077, pp. 47–65, 2024.
https://doi.org/10.1007/978-3-031-59057-3_4

factors, FR becomes less reliable as the age span grows larger. This paper analyses the varying effectiveness of FFVs in recognising individuals as age varies. Moreover, different suitable measurements will be discussed and how to safely clean the data.

2   Previous Work

AIFR methods can be categorised into two types: generative and discriminative methods. Generative methods [4,7,8,17,28,29] transform the recognition problem into general FR by simulating the aging process by synthesising extracted features or face images [25] into the same age group. Discriminative methods, on the other hand, aim to find robust features that are not affected by age. Both methods aim to improve FR by minimising the effect of age variation. In this work the focus is on Discriminative methods that are using the FFVs from any FR pipeline, without producing any specialised age related features.

Sawant and Bhurchandi [30] discuss the challenges faced by practical AIFR systems due to variations and similarities in appearance between persons. They extend the previously mentioned definition, each handling the problem from a different perspective, adding deep learning approaches. The performance of generative approaches depends both on models for ageing and age estimation, while discriminative approaches rely on local features and learning methods. Deep learning methods have improved AIFR performance but require large training data, which is a challenge when using small databases.

Discriminative methods for AIFR have received relatively limited attention compared to other aspects of FR. However, some important papers have been published in this area, which will be briefly explained before the analysis made later in this paper. First let us look at some papers that propose specialised age related features.

Gong et al. [9] proposed to use Hidden Factor Analysis, to separate aging variation from features using a probabilistic model with two latent factors: an age-invariant identity factor and an age factor affected by aging. In order to estimate both the latent factors and model parameters, an Expectation Maximization learning algorithm was employed. Similarly, MTLFace was introduced by Huang et al. [13,14] where they propose to decompose the features related to both age and identity. Zheng et al. [43] developed AE-CNN, a novel CNN based FR network, which also separates age-related variations from person specific features. Furthermore, Wang et al. [38] introduced a similar approach, which they call OE-CNN that enhances AIFR by separating deep face features into two orthogonal age- and identity-related components.

Xu and Ye [40] proposed to use nonlinear factor analysis and a coupled auto-encoder networks (CAN) for efficient AIFR. Yan et al. [41] propose MDF, which is based on face time series, using multi-feature fusion and decomposition with self-attention.

However, the focus in this paper lies on discriminative FFVs, just like Zhifeng et al. [20] who proposed a discriminative model for AIFR, which addresses the face aging problem in a more direct way without relying on a generative ageing model. Their approach take advantage of a patch-based local feature representation approach, together with a multi-feature discriminant analysis (MFDA) method. Ling et al. [21,22] propose what they call a gradient orientation pyramid, for obtaining a robust FFV, which captures hierarchical facial information and performed well for AIFR on challenging passport databases.

Gong et al. [10] proposed a new maximum entropy feature descriptor (MEFD), which extracts discriminatory and expressive information by encoding the microstructure of facial images in terms of maximum entropy. Li et al. [19] proposed an hierarchical learning model for AIFR. The first level extracts features from microstructures that optimise information in local patterns. The second level involves refining these features using a refinement framework to create a discriminative FFVs.

3   Face Recognition Methods

In this work, we used and compared two major pipelines for FR, which are freely available. Nevertheless, other approaches could also have been used to produce FFVs, such as *FaceNet* [31], *SphereFace* [23], *CosFace* [37], and [36,39], just to mention a few.

3.1   InsightFace

InsightFace [15] is a FR pipeline in Python, which is based on PyTorch and MXNet. It provides state of the art algorithms for all main steps in the FR process, such as face detection using *RetinaFace* [6]. Highly discriminative FFVs are extracted for each detected face, based on the Additive Angular Margin Loss (ArcFace) [5]. All provided models, ($buffalo\_l$, $antvelope2$, $buffalo\_m$ and $buffalo\_s$), produce 512 long FFVs. One of the reasons we chose *InsightFace* as the main pipeline in this work, was because it was ranked fourth in the 2020 top 10 trending AI libraries. Hence, it is easy to obtain, download and use for testing and exploring FR. And, as shall be shown it also outperformed the following pipeline.

DeepFace.   The DeepFace [32–34] framework, is also based on python, and it is lightweight and can be used both for FR as well as analysis of other attributes, such emotion, gender, age and race. Its hybrid FR framework provides state of the art models, which can be combined in different ways. However, in this work, the *RetinaFace* backend was used for face detection and two different models ($Facenet512$ and $ArcFace$) were used for creating the FFVs, which both are 512 long. *DeepFace* can produce FFVs of other lengths (e.g. 128 and 4096) but the mentioned ones were chosen as they are of the same lengths as those produced by *InsightFace*. Even though this pipeline is more versatile than *InsightFace*, it has one drawback. Just because it is lightweight and fast, the alignment of faces seem to be its weak link as will be discussed later.

4   Datasets

During the automated FR process for both datasets used, certain images were eliminated if the faces were not detected properly or if they contained more than one face. Furtermore, any duplicate face images, mislabeled identities, or any corrupt FFVs were also removed. These were identified by comparing all FFVs from face images of the

Fig. 1. Examples of faces resulting in corrupt FFVs or being mislabeled.

same identity and determining if more than 50% of the comparisons had a similarity less than 0.1. This means that such a face image was not considered to be the same person as in the other face photos of the same label, i.e. more than 50% of the intra matches are considered false matches. Hence, this face image is either mislabeled or in some sense very hard. For example, very blurry faces, people doing very extreme grimaces, or faces being more or less obscured by hands or people wearing big dark sunglasses would typically yield very low similarity. Generally, as we shall see, the similarity between FFVs of the same person are greater than 0.2, even for extreme age differences. However, in such cases, some moderately problematic images may have a similarity less than 0.1, but not for cases with smaller age spans unless they are indeed to be considered corrupt. Therefore, the requirement of 50% with a similarity less than 0.1 ensures that not all such moderately problematic images will be eliminated, but just the ones that are extremely hard to identify, like in Fig. 1.

However, these hard cases were excluded as the primary objective of utilising these datasets is to ascertain the possibility of achieving AIFR, rather than authenticating the challenging scenarios mentioned earlier. Figure 2 shows the distribution among certain age groups in the two datasets used.

4.1 AgeDB

A subset of the *AgeDB* dataset [27] was obtained from the original $16,516$ images We selected images, requiring that each identity should have at least 30 different face images, and that those should have a variation in age, covering at least three different decades, i.e. $(0-10, 11-20, 21-30, 31-40, 41-50, 51-60, 61-70$ and 70+$)$. Some 9700 face images were extracted (depending on the model used), after the aforementioned cleaning process, yielding about 36 face images for each identity. This procedure will ensure that there are indeed several face images at hand of the same identity covering different ages, i.e. decades. Therefore, it is possible to analyse how well FR works for different ages with varying age spans.

Figure 3a give at hand that the FFVs are suitable for AIFR on the *AgeDB* dataset, since each person cluster very well despite the age span. Here t-SNE [24] was used to create a scatter plot, where each colour represents a person, i.e. identity.

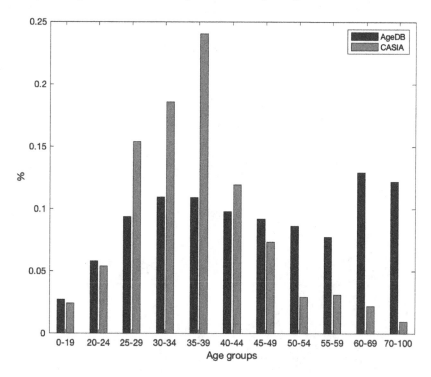

Fig. 2. Bar graph illustrating the relative size of age groups in AgeDB and CASIA datasets.

4.2 CASIA

The *CASIA-WebFace* [42] originally contains about $500k$ images. However, the afore-mentioned selection process produced a much smaller dataset that contains over 65000 face images depending on the model used, resulting in more than 50 face images per identity on average. Even if it is noew more feasible to handle, it is still quite a lot larger than the *AgeDB* dataset.

A similar scatter plot for the *CASIA* dataet is shown in Fig. 3b, and it is obvious that this set is both larger and more varied than the *AgeDB* dataset. As will be show later, the FFVs are indeed suitable for AIFR also on this more challenging dataset.

4.3 LFW

The $13,233$ images in the *Labeled Faces in the Wild* (LFW) dataset [12, 18] contains 5749 different identities. It is rather unbalanced, since 4069 identities have just a single image, while the remaining 1680 identities have two or more images. After FR, cleaning and also removal of single image persons, 6209 face images of 1174 persons remained. This dataset has very little variation in age and is used here for comparison to understand the difference between a dataset with small age variation compared to those with large age variation.

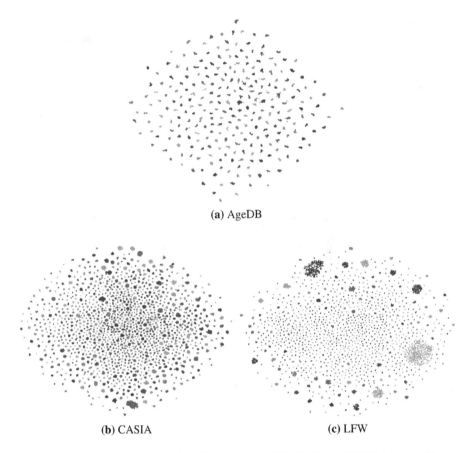

(a) AgeDB

(b) CASIA   **(c)** LFW

Fig. 3. Scatter plots of the result of t-SNE on the AgeDB, CASIA and LFW datasets. Clusters are formed for each label, even if the age varies within each cluster. AgeDB is visually more homogenous than CASIA.

5   Measurements Used in the Experiments

In this section, three different measurements are explained that were used and evaluated in the experiments.

5.1   Similarity Between FFVs

In order to define the performance measurements used, we must first define the *similarity* measurement. Even though several such measurements exist, it was chosen here to use the *cosine similarity*, which is defined as

$$\text{cosine similarity} := \frac{u \cdot w}{\|u\|\|w\|} \tag{1}$$

where u and w are FFVs.

The name itself, comes from the fact that the cosine of the angle between two normalised vectors can be computed using the dot product directly. Even if the value could theoretically vary between -1 and 1, it seldom falls below $-0,3$ for the models in *Insightface*. Furthermore, a value of 1 means that the face images in question actually are the very same image, i.e. they are duplicates, which were already removed in the aforementioned cleanup process. Later it will be discussed that this value usually lies around 0.65 for face images taken under similar circumstance of the same person, such as is the case for the images in the *LFW* dataset. And as we will see, for AIFR this value drops to around 0.5 for the other two datasets. The cosine similarity for comparing two different people usually lies around 0. Furthermore, the threshold or decision boundary, i.e. to tell whether two face photos of the same person are at hand, lies around 0.2 for AIFR, and can be set a bit higher when there is no age variation.

5.2   Mean Average Precision

The performance for retrieval systems is often measured by computing the so called mean Average Precision (mAP) [1]. This is done by computing all the similarities with respect to the query feature vector, compared to all other feature vectors in the system, and then sorting them on the obtained similarities. Let us assume that class label k contains m_k persons (identities), i.e. FFVs, belonging to the same class (or identity). Then the Average Precision (AP) will be 1 if all its m_k closest neighbours do belong to the same class label. However, if any of the close neighbours does not belong to the same class, then the AP will subsequently be lower. The mAP is defined as

$$\text{mAP} = \frac{1}{n} \sum_{i=1}^{n} AP_i \tag{2}$$

where, for each FFV, AP is defined as

$$\text{AP}_i = \frac{\sum_{k=1}^{n} P@k \times r(k)}{m_k} \tag{3}$$

where $P@k$ is the precision for the n items in the sorted list. Here $r(k)$ is a binary relevance function, which indicates whether the k-th item in the retrieved list belongs to the class in question, or not. I.e. in our case it tells whether the item has the same identity as the query image.

5.3   Bhattacharyya Measurements

Both the Bhattacharyya distance and coefficient [2] are being used, not only in statistics, but also i fields such as image processing, pattern recognition, e.g. for support vector machines, neural networks and other machine learning algorithms [35]. They are named after Anil Kumar Bhattacharyya, an Indian statistician who introduced this concept in 1943. These measurements facilitate comparison of image similarity and clustering of data points through analysis of their probability distributions. Both the Bhattacharyya distance and coefficient are restricted within the range of 0 and 1.

Here the Bhattacharyya coefficient, will be used for computing intra- and inter similarities, as explained in the next section [11]. It is a similarity measure between two probability distributions, where 0 indicates no overlap between the distributions, and 1 indicates that the two distributions are identical. It has a simple intuitive explanation since it basically is the dot product of the normalised distributions, and therefore measures how much overlap there is between the two distributions. It is generally defined as

$$BC = \sum_{i=1}^{n} \sqrt{p_i q_i} \tag{4}$$

where p and q are the two distributions, both of length n, of the intra- and inter similarities respectively.

6 Results

In the first experiment, both *InsightFace* and *DeepFace* was used on the smaller *AgeDB* dataset, and the two aforementioned measurements were taken. This was done both on the whole dataset, as well as for different age groups. This allowed for understanding which pipeline and models to use in the subsequent experiments using the larger *CASIA* dataset.

6.1 Similarity Distributions

Figure 4 displays histograms representing the intra similarity distribution (cosine similarity between different FFVs belonging to the same identity - shown in blue bars) and the inter similarity distribution (similarities between FFVs of one identity and FFVs of all other identities- shown in red bars), compare to [11]. The distributions for $buffalo\_l$ and $antelopev2$ are shown in Fig. 4a and 4b respectively. They are indeed quite similar. However, a few differences are noticeable. The peak for the intra similarities are further away from the peak of the inter similarities for $antelopev2$ than for $buffalo\_l$. Misclassifications mostly occur in the overlapping region between the two distributions, which is measured by the Bhattacharyya coefficient. The decision boundary that could be used for a classifier, lies in the middle of this overlap, i.e. where it has its maximum, is a 0.22 for the former and 0.2 for the latter model.

For comparison the histogram for the *LFW* dataset is shown in Fig. 4c. One can note several things. First of all the overlap between the distributions is very small. Secondly, the peak for the intra similarities are even further away from the peak of the inter similarities, and the similarity for the same identities now lie around 0.67 instead of 0.57 for $antelopev2$ and 0.52 for $buffalo\_l$. Finally, the decision boundary is moved up to 0.26.

6.2 Pipeline Performance

In Table 1 the results from the first experiment are shown. It is clear that *InsightFace* generally performs better than *DeepFace* (the two last models in the table). The reason

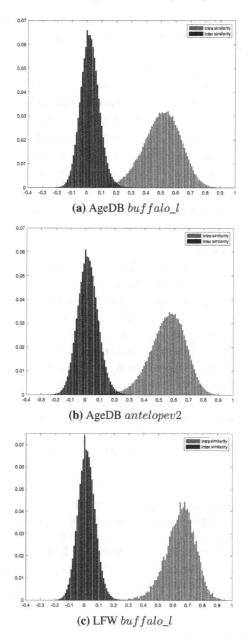

(a) AgeDB *buffalo_l*

(b) AgeDB *antelopev2*

(c) LFW *buffalo_l*

Fig. 4. Bar plot of a histograms of intra similarity (blue bars = same identity) and inter similarity (red bars = different identities) between FFVs. Note how the centre of the peak of the blue bars are located differently. (Color figure online)

for this can be deduced when looking at the sizes of the obtained datasets, which are substantially smaller for the $Facenet512$ and $ArcFace$ models than for the four first models. This implies that $DeepFace$ will produce more corrupt FFVs and it was also

Table 1. Results on the *AgeDB* dataset for Different models. The number of features extracted, mean Average Precision and the Bhattacharyya coefficient are given.

Model	Size	mAP	Coeff.
buffalo_l	9728	0.98038	0.07681
antelopev2	9728	**0.98740**	**0.06565**
buffalo_m	9729	0.97989	0.07770
buffalo_s	9743	0.92075	0.15497
Facenet512	9524	0.55024	0.41574
ArcFace	9507	0.60164	0.40998

Table 2. The mean Average Precision using different models on various age groups in the AgeDB dataset.

Age span	*buffalo_l*	*antelopev2*	*buffalo_m*
0–19	0.94086	**0.95240**	0.94298
20–24	**0.99212**	0.98879	0.99195
25–29	**0.99086**	0.98816	0.99301
30–34	0.99369	**0.99474**	0.99360
35–39	0.99679	**0.99715**	0.99618
40–44	0.99242	**0.99442**	0.99202
45–49	0.99109	**0.99323**	0.99051
50–54	**0.99791**	0.99768	0.99741
55–59	**0.99953**	0.99736	0.99551
60–69	**0.99572**	0.99490	0.99465
70–100	0.99576	**0.99623**	0.99557
Mean	0.9897	**0.9905**	0.9894

visually deduced that it especially has problems with profile faces. This is probably due to its lightweight alignment procedure, which is fast but also less exact.

The results in the table can be compared to the *LFW* dataset, with its distributions depicted in Fig. 4c, which had a mAP of 0.9987 and Bhattacharyya coefficient equal to 0.0079 for the *buffalo_l* model. Keep in mind that this dataset have almost no age variation. Hence, the results for *AgeDB* are still pretty good, even if the Bhattacharyya coefficient is almost 10 times higher, but the mAp is only 1.87% higher.

6.3   Age Group Performance

Next, the same measurements where computed for different age groups using the *AgeDB* dataset as shown in Table 2. The age groups where chosen so that there were not too few images in each group especially in the highest and lowest groups, as depicted in Fig. 2.

Table 3. The mean Average Precision using different models on various age groups in the CASIA dataset.

Age span	$buffalo\_l$	$antelopev2$	$buffalo\_m$
0–19	0.96276	**0.97188**	0.96017
20–24	0.97197	**0.98039**	0.97263
25–29	0.97350	**0.98337**	0.97354
30–34	0.97948	**0.98679**	0.97999
35–39	0.98206	**0.98851**	0.98190
40–44	0.98222	**0.98830**	0.98187
45–49	0.97712	**0.98120**	0.97706
50–54	0.97950	**0.98476**	0.98027
55–59	0.99108	**0.99496**	0.99025
60–69	0.98666	**0.99155**	0.98917
70–100	0.98785	**0.99452**	0.98648
Mean	0.9795	**0.9860**	0.9794

From the Tables 1 and 2 several things are clear. First of all, the mAP is rather high for the *InsightFace*, i.e. close to 1.0, which indicates a very high possibility to perform reliable AIFR, despite the large age span.

All in all, $antelopev2$ yields higher mAP, also when running on the *CASIA* dataset, as shown in Table 3. However, it should be noted that in this case, $antelopev2$ produces only 63558 FFVs, while $buffalo\_l$ produces 63609, $buffalo\_m$ produces 63659 and $buffalo\_m$ will even produce as many as 63786. So, it could be argued that the latter models will capture more faces and are therefore more attractive, even if yielding slightly lower mAP and higher Bhattacharyya coefficients. Nevertheless, using slightly different age groups for readability, the mAP for $buffalo\_l$ is shown as a similarity matrix in Fig. 5a for the *AgeDB* dataset and in Fig. 7a for the *CASIA* dataset. Here the mAP is computed for two age groups only, or only one if it is the very same age group on the diagonal. Obviously, the mAP is generally higher on the diagonal, just as one would expect. In the same way the cosine similarity is higher on the diagonal as shown in Fig. 5b. Figure 6 also shows the mean cosine similarity, as well as the standard deviation for all similarities in each cell in Fig. 5b. Here, the Age group in question is marked with a black empty box. By following the line to the left or right one can determine how the similarity to adjacent groups changes. Figure 7 shows the same Similarity matrices, and the corresponding Shaded bar graph for the *CASIA* dataset is shown in Fig. 7SB.

6.4   Correlation Between Measurements

An experiment was conducted to evaluate the correlation between the mAP and the Bhattacharyya coefficient. First these measures where computed separately for 11 different age groups. Next, grouping was done on persons regardless of age group. In this case 8 groups of people for *AgeDB* and 18 for *CASIA*, in order to capture how the measurements vary with the varying age of the people. Figure 9 shows that there is a clear

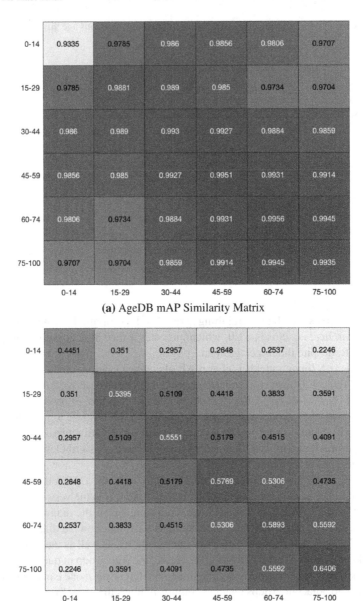

(a) AgeDB mAP Similarity Matrix

(b) AgeDB Cosine Similarity Matrix

Fig. 5. Similarity matrices for both mAP and the cosine similarity. The cosine similarity is higher within a group (intra similarity), than among groups (inter similarity).

correlation between mAP and the Bhattacharyya coefficient. Here both datasets have been used with all four models in *InsightFace*. It makes sense that the values for when

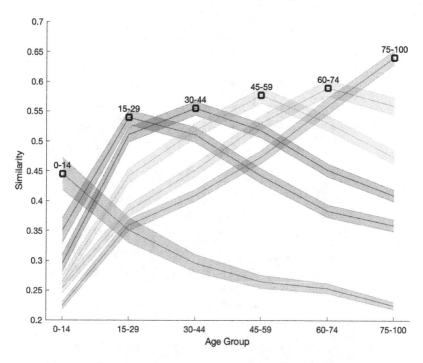

Fig. 6. Shaded bar graph of the same similarities and its standard deviation, between one age group and all other age group. The Age group in question is marked with a black empty box. The cosine similarity is higher within a group (intra similarity), than among groups (inter similarity).

the grouping is done on person are generally higher since it is harder to match FFVs with large age spans.

7   Discussion

The experiments show that *InsightFace* generally works very well compared to *Deep-Face*, which is most probably due to the less accurate alignment procedure of the latter. With that said, it is not necessarily so that the other steps in the pipeline are less accurate, since both pipelines share many common algorithms. Nevertheless, both the mAP is overall quite high and the Bhattacharyya coefficient is generally low, for *InsightFace*, which shows that reliable AIFR can indeed be performed also when there is a rather large age span among the face images. This is especially true for the *buffalo_l* and *antvelope*2 models. Even though the latter is overall giving better values in the measurements, it is also noticeably slower when used in the pipeline. Therefore, we chose to use the former in many experiments, such those reported in Figs. 5 and 7. In other words, these measurements would have been generally higher if the *antvelope*2 model would have been used. Nevertheless, the conclusion is the same, i.e. the FFVs from *InsightFace* are indeed well suited for AIFR and no specialised age related features should be necessary.

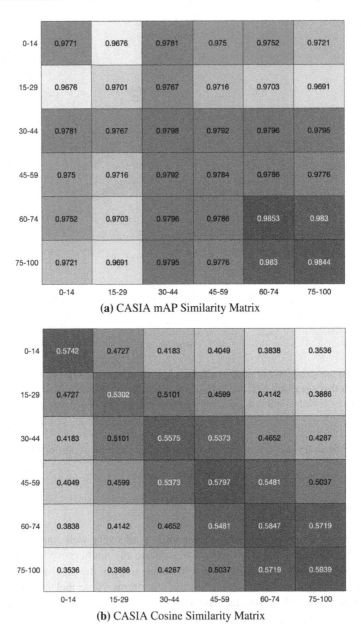

(a) CASIA mAP Similarity Matrix

(b) CASIA Cosine Similarity Matrix

Fig. 7. Similarity matrices for both mAP and the Cosine Similarity. The cosine similarity is higher within a group (intra similarity), than among groups (inter similarity).

The distributions in Fig. 4 are exhibiting Gaussian like curves for intra- and inter similarities, which shows that the number of buckets chosen, were adequate and should not have any detrimental impact on the measurements. This can also be deduced from

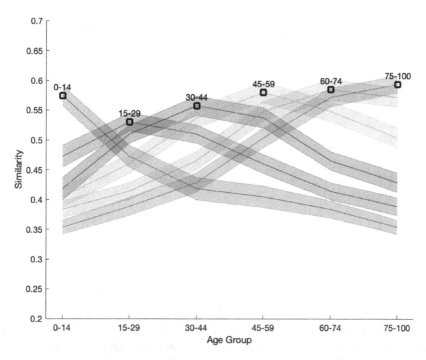

Fig. 8. Shaded bar graph of the same similarities and its standard deviation, between one age group and all other age group. The Age group in question is marked with a black empty box. The cosine similarity is higher within a group (intra similarity), than among groups (inter similarity).

the comparison of the two measurements in the scatter plot in Fig. 9, which do exhibit a clear correlation. However, we chose not to compute the Bhattacharyya coefficient for each age group, since some groups are relatively small as shown in Fig. 2, and therefore the partial distributions would be less exact.

Interestingly, Fig. 6 shows that the older you get and move up the decades, the more similar your face appears to be, within that age group. This is also apparent from looking at Fig. 8, with the exception of the first age group. The reason might be the relatively low number of photographs available in that group, not covering all ages within the group. Moreover, it can be noted that the mAP is highest for the age group 60 − 74 for both datasets and that it is not always following the behaviour of the Cosine similarity. This is because the latter describes the behaviour of the data, while the former describes the performance, and even if they are closely related, they are not always the same.

The threshold for the decision boundary was proven to be smaller for the two datasets with a large age span compared to the one with almost no age variation. This comes as now surprise as the overlap between the distributions, and thereby the Bhattacharyya coefficient, will be smaller. Nonetheless, this investigation gives at hand what values to choose when using the same pipelines and models that were used herein. Even for large age spans the similarity measure is generally over 0.2, which shows that AIFR

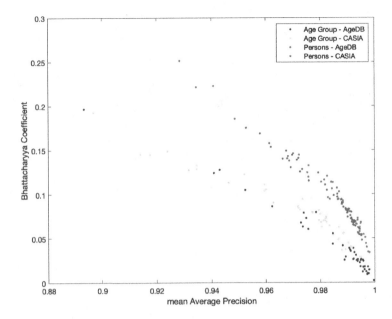

Fig. 9. Scatter plot of the mAP vs. the Bhattacharyya Coefficient. It is apparent that there is a clear correlation between the two measurements. Note that the Coefficient is generally larger when grouping on different persons, than on age groups, since the age will vary more on persons.

can be done with high confidence. This was also confirmed by the high mAP, both within certain age groups and between different age groups.

8 Conclusion

The performed experiments shows clearly that the FFVs obtained from *InsightFace* are suitable for AIFR, especially when using the *buffalo_l* and *antvelope2* models. In other words, they can generally be used as stable biometric markers, and no specialised age related features should be necessary, nor any generative approach for synthesising ageing. *DeepFace* performed a bit worse, which is due to the quick and simple alignment. Therefore, it should be investigated what performance would be the result when using a better alignment approach.

Furthermore, it can be concluded the mAP and Bhattacharyya Coefficient are both good measurements for evaluating the performance for AIFR. These measurements clearly indicate that AIFR can be done despite large age spans, even if there will always be some hard to identify faces.

8.1 Future Work

For future work we propose to use other ways to compute loss than the Additive Angular Margin Loss (ArcFace) approach [5], such as ElasticFace [3], AdaFace [16], and

MagFAce [26]. Furthermore, a more balanced dataset, when it comes to the distribution of face identities among the different age groups, would be useful for future research on the behaviour of different FR methods and pipelines when doing AIFR.

Acknowledgements. This work has been partially supported by the Swedish Research Council (Dnr 2020-04652; Dnr 2022-02056) in the projects *The City's Faces. Visual culture and social structure in Stockholm 1880–1930* and *The International Centre for Evidence-Based Criminal Law (EB-CRIME)*. The computations were performed on resources provided by SNIC through UPPMAX under projects SNIC 2021/22-918 and SNIC 2022/22-1123.

References

1. Beitzel, S.M., Jensen, E.C., Frieder, O.: Map. In: Liu, L., Özsu, M.T. (eds.) Encyclopedia of Database Systems, pp. 1691–1692. Springer, Boston (2009). https://doi.org/10.1007/978-0-387-39940-9_492

2. Bhattacharyya, A.: On a measure of divergence between two statistical populations defined by their probability distribution. Bull. Calcutta Math. Soc. **35**, 99–110 (1943)

3. Boutros, F., Damer, N., Kirchbuchner, F., Kuijper, A.: ElasticFace: elastic margin loss for deep face recognition. In: Proceedings of the IEEE/CVF Conference on Computer Vision and Pattern Recognition (CVPR) Workshops, pp. 1578–1587 (2022)

4. Deb, D., Aggarwal, D., Jain, A.K.: Identifying missing children: face age-progression via deep feature aging. In: 2020 25th International Conference on Pattern Recognition (ICPR), pp. 10540–10547 (2021). https://doi.org/10.1109/ICPR48806.2021.9411913

5. Deng, J., Guo, J., Xue, N., Zafeiriou, S.: ArcFace: additive angular margin loss for deep face recognition. In: Proceedings of the IEEE/CVF Conference on Computer Vision and Pattern Recognition, pp. 4690–4699 (2019)

6. Deng, J., Guo, J., Zhou, Y., Yu, J., Kotsia, I., Zafeiriou, S.: RetinaFace: single-stage dense face localisation in the wild (2019). https://doi.org/10.48550/ARXIV.1905.00641

7. Duong, C., Quach, K., Luu, K., Le, T., Savvides, M.: Temporal non-volume preserving approach to facial age-progression and age-invariant face recognition. In: 2017 IEEE International Conference on Computer Vision (ICCV), pp. 3755–3763. IEEE Computer Society, Los Alamitos, CA, USA (2017). https://doi.org/10.1109/ICCV.2017.403

8. Geng, X., Zhou, Z., Smith-Miles, K.: Automatic age estimation based on facial aging patterns. IEEE Trans. Pattern Anal. Mach. Intell. **29**(12), 2234–2240 (2007). https://doi.org/10.1109/TPAMI.2007.70733

9. Gong, D., Li, Z., Lin, D., Liu, J., Tang, X.: Hidden factor analysis for age invariant face recognition. In: 2013 IEEE International Conference on Computer Vision, pp. 2872–2879 (2013). https://doi.org/10.1109/ICCV.2013.357

10. Gong, D., Li, Z., Tao, D., Liu, J., Li, X.: A maximum entropy feature descriptor for age invariant face recognition. In: 2015 IEEE Conference on Computer Vision and Pattern Recognition (CVPR), pp. 5289–5297 (2015). https://doi.org/10.1109/CVPR.2015.7299166

11. Hast, A.: Age-invariant face recognition using face feature vectors and embedded prototype subspace classifiers. In: Blanc-Talon, J., Delmas, P., Philips, W., Scheunders, P. (eds.) Advanced Concepts for Intelligent Vision Systems, pp. 88–99. Springer Nature Switzerland, Cham (2023). https://doi.org/10.1007/978-3-031-45382-3_8

12. Huang, G.B., Ramesh, M., Berg, T., Learned-Miller, E.: Labeled faces in the wild: A database for studying face recognition in unconstrained environments. Technical Report 07-49, University of Massachusetts, Amherst (2007)

13. Huang, Z., Zhang, J., Shan, H.: When age-invariant face recognition meets face age synthesis: a multi-task learning framework. In: Proceedings of the IEEE/CVF Conference on Computer Vision and Pattern Recognition, pp. 7282–7291 (2021)

14. Huang, Z., Zhang, J., Shan, H.: When age-invariant face recognition meets face age synthesis: a multi-task learning framework and a new benchmark. IEEE Trans. Pattern Anal. Mach. Intell. (2022)

15. InsightFace: Insightface (2023). https://insightface.ai. Accessed 30 Feb 2023

16. Kim, M., Jain, A.K., Liu, X.: AdaFace: quality adaptive margin for face recognition. In: Proceedings of the IEEE/CVF Conference on Computer Vision and Pattern Recognition (2022)

17. Lanitis, A., Taylor, C., Cootes, T.: Toward automatic simulation of aging effects on face images. IEEE Trans. Pattern Anal. Mach. Intell. **24**(4), 442–455 (2002). https://doi.org/10.1109/34.993553

18. Learned-Miller, G.B.H.E.: Labeled faces in the wild: updates and new reporting procedures. Technical Report UM-CS-2014-003, University of Massachusetts, Amherst (2014)

19. Li, Z., Gong, D., Li, X., Tao, D.: Aging face recognition: a hierarchical learning model based on local patterns selection. IEEE Trans. Image Process. **25**(5), 2146–2154 (2016). https://doi.org/10.1109/TIP.2016.2535284

20. Li, Z., Park, U., Jain, A.K.: A discriminative model for age invariant face recognition. IEEE Trans. Inf. Forensics Secur. **6**(3), 1028–1037 (2011). https://doi.org/10.1109/TIFS.2011.2156787

21. Ling, H., Soatto, S., Ramanathan, N., Jacobs, D.W.: A study of face recognition as people age. In: 2007 IEEE 11th International Conference on Computer Vision, pp. 1–8 (2007). https://doi.org/10.1109/ICCV.2007.4409069

22. Ling, H., Soatto, S., Ramanathan, N., Jacobs, D.W.: Face verification across age progression using discriminative methods. IEEE Trans. Inf. Forensics Secur. **5**(1), 82–91 (2010). https://doi.org/10.1109/TIFS.2009.2038751

23. Liu, W., Wen, Y., Yu, Z., Li, M., Raj, B., Song, L.: SphereFace: deep hypersphere embedding for face recognition. In: 2017 IEEE Conference on Computer Vision and Pattern Recognition (CVPR), pp. 6738–6746. IEEE Computer Society, Los Alamitos (2017). https://doi.org/10.1109/CVPR.2017.713

24. Van der Maaten, L., Hinton, G.: Visualizing data using t-SNE. J. Mach. Learn. Res. **9**(11) (2008)

25. Mahalingam, G., Kambhamettu, C.: Age invariant face recognition using graph matching. In: 2010 Fourth IEEE International Conference on Biometrics: Theory, Applications and Systems (BTAS), pp. 1–7 (2010). https://doi.org/10.1109/BTAS.2010.5634496

26. Meng, Q., Zhao, S., Huang, Z., Zhou, F.: MagFace: a universal representation for face recognition and quality assessment. In: CVPR (2021)

27. Moschoglou, S., Papaioannou, A., Sagonas, C., Deng, J., Kotsia, I., Zafeiriou, S.: AgeDB: the first manually collected, in-the-wild age database. In: 2017 IEEE Conference on Computer Vision and Pattern Recognition Workshops (CVPRW), pp. 1997–2005 (2017). https://doi.org/10.1109/CVPRW.2017.250

28. Park, U., Tong, Y., Jain, A.K.: Age-invariant face recognition. IEEE Trans. Pattern Anal. Mach. Intell. **32**(5), 947–954 (2010). https://doi.org/10.1109/TPAMI.2010.14

29. Ramanathan, N., Chellappa, R.: Modeling age progression in young faces. In: 2006 IEEE Computer Society Conference on Computer Vision and Pattern Recognition (CVPR'06), vol. 1, pp. 387–394 (2006). https://doi.org/10.1109/CVPR.2006.187

30. Sawant, M.M., Bhurchandi, K.M.: Age invariant face recognition: a survey on facial aging databases, techniques and effect of aging. Artif. Intell. Rev. **52**, 981–1008 (2019). https://doi.org/10.1007/s10462-018-9661-z

31. Schroff, F., Kalenichenko, D., Philbin, J.: FaceNet: a unified embedding for face recognition and clustering. In: 2015 IEEE Conference on Computer Vision and Pattern Recognition (CVPR), pp. 815–823 (2015). https://doi.org/10.1109/CVPR.2015.7298682

32. Serengil, S.I., Ozpinar, A.: LightFace: a hybrid deep face recognition framework. In: 2020 Innovations in Intelligent Systems and Applications Conference (ASYU), pp. 23–27. IEEE (2020). https://doi.org/10.1109/ASYU50717.2020.9259802

33. Serengil, S.I., Ozpinar, A.: Hyperextended lightface: a facial attribute analysis framework. In: 2021 International Conference on Engineering and Emerging Technologies (ICEET), pp. 1–4. IEEE (2021). https://doi.org/10.1109/ICEET53442.2021.9659697

34. Serengil, S.I., Ozpinar, A.: An evaluation of SQL and NoSQL databases for facial recognition pipelines (2023). https://www.cambridge.org/engage/coe/article-details/63f3e5541d2d184063d4f569, https://doi.org/10.33774/coe-2023-18rcn. preprint

35. Shah, M.H., Dang, X.: Novel feature selection method using Bhattacharyya distance for neural networks based automatic modulation classification. IEEE Signal Process. Lett. **27**, 106–110 (2020). https://doi.org/10.1109/LSP.2019.2957924

36. Shi, Y., Jain, A.: Probabilistic face embeddings. In: 2019 IEEE/CVF International Conference on Computer Vision (ICCV), pp. 6901–6910 (2019). https://doi.org/10.1109/ICCV.2019.00700

37. Wang, H., et al.: CosFace: large margin cosine loss for deep face recognition. In: 2018 IEEE/CVF Conference on Computer Vision and Pattern Recognition, pp. 5265–5274 (2018). https://doi.org/10.1109/CVPR.2018.00552

38. Wang, Y., et al.: Orthogonal deep features decomposition for age-invariant face recognition. In: Ferrari, V., Hebert, M., Sminchisescu, C., Weiss, Y. (eds.) Computer Vision - ECCV 2018, pp. 764–779. Springer International Publishing, Cham (2018). https://doi.org/10.1007/978-3-030-01267-0_45

39. Wen, Y., Zhang, K., Li, Z., Qiao, Y.: A discriminative feature learning approach for deep face recognition. In: Leibe, B., Matas, J., Sebe, N., Welling, M. (eds.) Computer Vision - ECCV 2016, pp. 499–515. Springer International Publishing, Cham (2016). https://doi.org/10.1007/978-3-319-46478-7_31

40. Xu, C., Liu, Q., Ye, M.: Age invariant face recognition and retrieval by coupled auto-encoder networks. Neurocomputing **222**, 62–71 (2017)

41. Yan, C., et al.: Age-invariant face recognition by multi-feature fusion and decomposition with self-attention. ACM Trans. Multimedia Comput. Commun. Appl. **18**(1s) (2022). https://doi.org/10.1145/3472810

42. Yi, D., Lei, Z., Liao, S., Li, S.Z.: Learning face representation from scratch (2014). https://doi.org/10.48550/ARXIV.1411.7923

43. Zheng, T., Deng, W., Hu, J.: Age estimation guided convolutional neural network for age-invariant face recognition. In: 2017 IEEE Conference on Computer Vision and Pattern Recognition Workshops (CVPRW), pp. 503–511 (2017). https://doi.org/10.1109/CVPRW.2017.77

Uncertainty Driven Active Learning for Image Segmentation in Underwater Inspection

Luiza Ribeiro Marnet[1,2]([✉]) [ID], Yury Brodskiy[1] [ID], Stella Grasshof[2] [ID],
and Andrzej Wąsowski[2] [ID]

[1] EIVA a/s, Skanderborg, Denmark
{lrm,ybr}@eiva.com
[2] IT University of Copenhagen, Copenhagen, Denmark
{stgr,wasowski}@itu.dk

Abstract. Active learning aims to select the minimum amount of data to train a model that performs similarly to a model trained with the entire dataset. We study the potential of active learning for image segmentation in underwater infrastructure inspection tasks, where large amounts of data are typically collected. The pipeline inspection images are usually semantically repetitive but with great variations in quality. We use mutual information as the acquisition function, calculated using Monte Carlo dropout. HyperSeg is trained using active learning with an underwater pipeline inspection dataset of over 50,000 images. To allow reproducibility and assess the framework's effectiveness, the CamVid dataset was also utilized. For the pipeline dataset, HyperSeg with active learning achieved 67.5% meanIoU using 12.5% of the data, and 61.4% with the same amount of randomly selected images. This shows that using active learning for segmentation models in underwater inspection tasks can lower the cost significantly.

Keywords: Active learning · Computer vision · Underwater inspection

1 Introduction

Computer vision plays a pivotal role in advancing automation across various applications, such as equipment inspection [2,17,37], autonomous driving [6,7,38], medical diagnoses [10,27,41], underwater debris detection [9,18], and underwater pipeline inspection [15,23]. However, the large amounts of annotated datasets required for training these models presents a major challenge. Annotating such datasets is time-consuming, expensive, or infeasible, especially in domains requiring expert knowledge.

Even though access to large data is important, the quality of the data is critical. Active learning focuses on selecting the smallest sample set that can be used to train a model to achieve the same performance as when training with the entire dataset [5, 30]. This typically involves training the model with few initial samples and selecting additional samples for labeling and retraining the model iteratively [5]. It is known that random selection usually does not perform well.

Partially supported by the European Union's Horizon 2020 research and innovation programme under the Marie Skłodowska-Curie grant agreement No 956200, REMARO.

J. Filipe and J. Röning (Eds.): ROBOVIS 2024, CCIS 2077, pp. 66–81, 2024.
https://doi.org/10.1007/978-3-031-59057-3_5

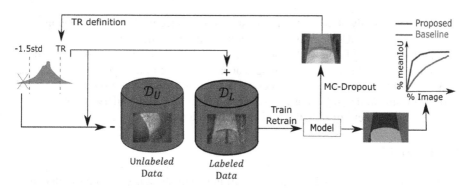

Fig. 1. Our active learning process: After pre-training the model with a small set of randomly chosen images, we start selecting images with uncertainty above a threshold TR (top-left) for training and validation of the model. In each iteration two new thresholds are defined: TR_t for training, and TR_v for validation images. We discard images with an uncertainty below the mean minus 1.5 standard deviations. In this figure, D_U and D_L are the pools of unlabeled and labeled images, respectively. The signs '+' and '−' indicate that the newly selected images are removed from D_U and added to D_L.

Epistemic uncertainty [1] can be used to identify samples that are most informative for training deep learning models. It measures the model's confidence in its predictions based on its level of familiarity with the input data [1,21]. By identifying samples that induce high epistemic uncertainty, the most informative samples can be labeled and added to the training dataset, potentially reducing the labeling effort while improving the model's performance.

In this paper, we investigate the use of epistemic uncertainty for image selection in the field of computer vision applications, cf. Fig. 1, more specifically to enhance the capabilities of autonomous robotic systems. We employ two distinct datasets, one for street view image segmentation, a crucial component in the domain of autonomous vehicle navigation, and the other for segmenting images captured during underwater robotics missions. Segmenting underwater images is a challenging task that can aid in, e.g., underwater autonomous vehicle path tracking, and is especially important for visual inspection of underwater equipment and structures. We demonstrate the performance of the active learning method with epistemic uncertainty when training HyperSeg [25] with real underwater RGB images from various missions and locations. To allow reproducibility, we also apply our approach to the street view dataset CamVid [3,4].

The results for the underwater images are specially important. These images come from a huge pool of images for pipeline inspection, and are semantically similar, but vary in quality due to factors like low and non-uniform illumination, color degradation, low contrast, blurring, and hazing [8,11,32]. Labeling these images requires specialized expertise and constitutes a significant cost for the growing but still small underwater automation industry. Selecting key images representing the different image qualities, reduces the required amount of training data, resulting in lower cost and human effort for labeling, which is valuable for innovating companies in this sector.

To the best of our knowledge, this is the first paper applying active learning for real underwater images. Our contributions include:

- A systematic study of the method against a random selection baseline, showing 6.2% gain in the meanIoU over the baseline in the underwater dataset.
- An active learning framework that uses a threshold for selecting new images instead of the usual fixed percentage of images at each active learning cycle.
- An implementation and reproduction package allowing to reproduce the results on the CamVid dataset using DenseNet and HyperSeg (the underwater imagery is unfortunately security-sensitive and cannot be released).

2   Related Work

In active learning with classical machine learning methods, it is common to select new samples using a metric for capturing uncertainty and another for measuring similarity. The former identifies samples for which the model is unsure about the predicted output, and is used for selecting the most informative samples for the model to learn from. The last aids in selecting representative samples and preventing the selection of redundant samples with similar information.

Thus, the first step in developing an active learning framework is to decide on an uncertainty metric. While the softmax values are often used as a measure that reflects the model's confidence for classification tasks, it has been demonstrated that misclassified samples can have high softmax values [26], for example, when an input out of the distribution of the training dataset is used during inference [13]. Therefore, other methods of capturing uncertainty should be used.

The uncertainty of the predictions, called predictive uncertainty, can be decomposed into epistemic and aleatoric [1]. Epistemic uncertainty reflects the model's lack of knowledge about the input's pattern, while aleatoric uncertainty reflects the data quality itself, e.g. noise caused by the sensor that captures the data. Since the goal of active learning is to select new images that bring knowledge that the model lacks for training, the important uncertainty in this scenario is the epistemic. Methods like Monte Carlo Dropout (MC-Dropout), deep ensembles, and error propagation can be used to access this uncertainty [12].

MC-Dropout is a widely used method for modeling epistemic uncertainty in deep neural networks. During inference dropout layers are used and the same input sample is passed forward multiple times through the model. Since dropout is applied, each pass may produce a different output, and these outputs are used to assess the epistemic uncertainty. If the model is well-trained and the input is similar to what the model has seen during training, the outputs will be similar or identical. On the other hand, if the model does not have enough knowledge about an input, the outputs of each forward pass will be more varied, indicating high uncertainty. Different metrics, such as variation ratio, mutual information, total variance, margin of confidence, and predictive entropy, can be used for that [24].

Ensembles of networks can also be used to predict epistemic uncertainty. In this method, an input sample is passed through the model and the results of each network in the ensemble are used to estimate the uncertainty [33]. Finally, the error propagation method [28] estimates the model uncertainty by propagating the variance of each layer to the output. This variance arises in layers such as dropout and batch normalization and is modified by the other layers of the model.

Deep active learning has been applied to tasks requiring costly labeling, such as medical image analysis. Softmax confidence with a single forward pass was used to evaluate the segmentation uncertainty for pulmonary nodules [36] and membrane [16] images, even if these may not be ideal for deep learning models. Other studies have proposed more reliable approaches. Using different subsets of training samples of biomedical images, a set of segmentation models was trained, and the uncertainty was measured as the variance between their outputs [40]. Different metrics, such as max-entropy and Bayesian active learning by disagreement (BALD), were calculated using MC-Dropout outputs for selecting new images to label for training skin cancer image classifier [14] and to segment medical images [31]. Moreover, a comparison between querying entire medical images and querying image paths concluded that the latter led to better models [22].

More recently, active learning was studied in the autonomous driving context. The Deeplabv3+ architecture with a Mobilenetv2 backbone was trained with uncertainty- and difficulty-driven image selection [39]. A further reduction of labeled pixels was obtained by querying image paths [29,34]. Even though these studies used entropy-based metrics for image selection, the metrics were calculated using a single pass softmax output and did not use MC-dropout.

In this work, we use MC-dropout to guide active learning in real-world problems. We first validate the method with DenseNet and HyperSeg for semantic segmentation [20] on the publicly available street view dataset CamVid [3,4]. We then use active learning with the better-performing model, HyperSeg [25], to obtain a new state-of-the-art model for real-time semantic segmentation in an underwater application. Our underwater dataset contains many images that are hard to segment even for human eyes. The dataset is unbalanced, with some classes appearing in only a few images and occupying a low percentage of pixels. The goal is to analyze the effectiveness of active learning in training the models with only a small percentage of the data and in learning to predict underrepresented classes.

3   Method

We now present an overview of our learning method: the models, the acquisition function, and the entire active learning framework.

Models. We employ two deep learning models for segmentation, DenseNet and Hyper-Seg. DenseNet [19], initially developed for classification, was later extended for segmentation [20]. We choose DenseNet due to its success in accessing epistemic uncertainty using MC-Dropout [21]. We utilize the lighter version, DenseNet-56.

HyperSeg is a state-of-the-art model based on the U-Net architecture [25]. In the decoder, it utilizes dynamic weights, that are generated based on both the input image and the spatial location. Because of its high high mean intersection over union (meanIoU), high frames per second (FPS) rate, and the option to use dropout, we hypothesize that it is an appropriate choice. We use the version HyperSeg-S with efficientNet-B1 as the backbone [35], as it has achieved FPS of 38.0 and meanIoU of 78.4% in the original work. To the best of our knowledge HyperSeg has not been used in similar experiments to this date.

Acquisition Function. We calculate the epistemic uncertainty using MC-Dropout with T forward passes. The metric used was the mutual information, that for a segmentation problem with C classes is calculated for each pixel of the image as:

$$\mathcal{I} = \underbrace{\frac{-1}{\log_2(C)} \sum_{c=1}^{C} p_c^* \log_2(p_c^*)}_{\mathcal{H}} + \frac{1}{T \log_2(C)} \sum_{c=1}^{C} \sum_{t=1}^{T} p_{ct} \log_2(p_{ct}), \qquad (1)$$

where $\mathcal{H}$ is the entropy,
$p_t = (p_{1t}, ..., p_{Ct})$ is the softmax output for a single forward pass t, and $p^* = (p_1^*, ..., p_C^*)$ is the average prediction of the T passes. For each pixel, we predict one value p^*, and a class label c based on the maximum value of p_c^*. We divide the equation by $\log_2(C)$ to normalize the entropy between zero and 1.

Deep Active Learning Framework. In a real-world scenario the images are labeled after being queried. To reflect this, we only use the labels after the images are selected. Our active learning process begins by randomly selecting a constant $P\%$ of the images from both the training and validation sets in the first iteration. The model is then trained with these images. The epistemic uncertainty of each selected image is then calculated as the average uncertainty of each pixel:

$$EU_{\text{img}} = \frac{1}{N} \sum_{i=1}^{N} EU_i, \qquad (2)$$

where EU_i is the epistemic uncertainty for pixel i, Eq. 1, of an image with N pixels. The next step is to calculate the thresholds TR_t and TR_v (Fig. 1) used to decide which images from the unlabeled training and validation datasets, respectively, should be selected for labeling. These thresholds are calculated as:

$$TR = \overline{EU}_{\text{img}} + S\sigma \qquad (3)$$

where $\overline{EU}_{\text{img}}$ and σ are the mean and standard deviation of EU_{img}, for the corresponding training and validation datasets, and S is a positive constant defined by the user. Bigger values of S result in querying fewer images. For the next iteration, the EU_{img} values of the images in the pools of unlabeled (remaining) training and validation data are computed. The images with EU_{img} above the respective thresholds, TR_t and TR_v, are selected for labeling. The model is then retrained with the new and previously selected images.

To accelerate the selection process, images with uncertainty values below 1.5 standard deviations below the mean are excluded from future selection. Since the model's predictions for these samples are relatively certain, using them to retrain the model is unlikely to improve performance. The value of 1.5 was empirically chosen and should be further studied in the future.

Training Details. DenseNet [20] was implemented from scratch and trained following the original paper, which includes pre-training and fine-tuning phases. The model was initialized with HeUniform in the first iteration, and with the weights of the best model from the previous iteration in subsequent iterations. RMSProp optimizer was used with a weight decay of $1e^{-4}$, and horizontal flip was applied to the training and validation datasets. Pre-training was performed using random crops of 224×224. The initial learning rate was $1e^{-3}$ in the first iteration and $1e^{-4}$ in the subsequent ones, with a learning rate decay of $1e^{-4}$. Fine-tuning was performed using 360×480 image resolution, an initial learning rate of $1e^{-4}$, and no learning rate decay. In each iteration, the pre-training process stopped after no improvement in validation meanIoU or validation loss for 150 consecutive epochs, and the fine-tuning process stopped after no improvement for 50 consecutive epochs.

For HyperSeg, we used the source code of the original authors.[1] The model's backbone was initialized with imagenet pre-trained weights in the first iteration and with the weights of the best model from the previous iteration in subsequent iterations. The initial learning rate was 0.001 in the first iteration and 0.00098 in subsequent iterations. The training of each iteration stopped after no improvement in validation meanIoU or validation loss for 10 consecutive epochs. The version chosen, HyperSeg-S, operates on 768×576 resolution.

Both models used a rate of 20% in each dropout layer utilized. DenseNet has a dropout layer after each convolutional layer. Hyperseg can add dropout layers at the end of the encoder and at the end of the hyper patch-wise convolution blocks in the decoder. For HyperSeg, we only used the dropout layer in the encoder. All experiments were developed using PyTorch.

4 Experimental Evaluation

We discuss the optimal number of forward passes T used in MC-dropout, and the impact of applying active learning on the datasets *CamVid* [3,4], and *pipeline*.

Datasets. CamVid [3,4] is a street view dataset for segmentation. It contains video frames captured from the viewpoint of a driving car. The original dataset provides 369 images in the training subset, 100 in the validation subset, and 232 in the testing subset, in a resolution of 720×960. The half-resolution version consists of 367 images for training, 101 for validation, and 233 for testing. Labels for 32 hierarchical classes are provided from which we use 11: 'sky', 'building', 'column-pole', 'road', 'sidewalk', 'tree', 'sign-symbol', 'fence', 'car', 'pedestrian', and 'bicyclist'.

The underwater dataset *pipeline* was provided by our industrial partner's customers and contains images from pipeline surveys. Due to security reasons,[2] the data is not publicly available. The entire dataset comprises 64,920 video frames recorded during surveys of infrastructure. Out of these frames, we reserved 8,896 for testing while the remaining 56,024 images have been randomly split into 70% for training and 30% for validation. The dataset has five classes: 'background', 'pipeline', 'field joint', 'anode', and 'boulder-and-survey vehicle', with respectively 99.9%, 77.1%, 20.3%, 21.0% and

---

[1] https://github.com/YuvalNirkin/hyperseg.
[2] E.g. https://en.wikipedia.org/wiki/2022_Nord_Stream_pipeline_sabotage.

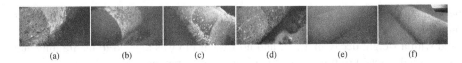

Fig. 2. Example of the pipeline dataset: (a-b) an anode and pipeline, (c) a pipeline and a field joint, (d) a field joint, boulders and pipeline, (e) a pipeline alone, and (f) a pipeline, field joint, and part of a vehicle in the top right (best viewed in color).

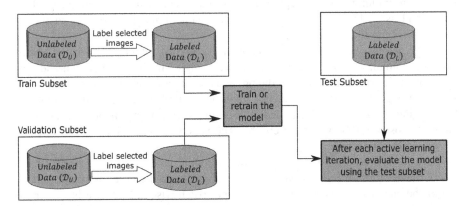

Fig. 3. The two datasets used, CamVid and pipeline, were divided into training, validation, and test subsets. For the active learning experiments, a few images from the training and validation subsets are initially labeled. At each iteration of the experiments, more images are selected, without replacement, from the respective pools of unlabeled images. The selected images are labeled and moved to the pools of labeled data. The entire test subset has labels since the beginning of the experiment.

15.5% of the training and validation images in each class. Figure 2 shows several examples. In the figure, some images have a more brownish background and others are more blueish. Image (e) suffers from higher turbidity than the other images. Marine flora grows on the pipelines in images (a), (c), and (d). Underwater images suffer from low and non-uniform illumination, color degradation, low contrast, blurring, and hazing [8,11,32]. The poor quality is due both to light attenuation and floating particles in marine environments, known as "marine snow" [32]. This causes haziness [11] and reduces visibility to below 20m, sometimes even below 5m. Also, the light is attenuated differently depending on the wavelength. The red light is attenuated faster, while blue is attenuated slower [8] resulting in the blueish hue of images.

We divide the two datasets into three subsets of images: training, validation, and testing. For the experiments with active learning, new images are iteratively selected from the pools of unlabeled training and validation images and added to the respective pools of labeled images, Fig. 3. For the test subset, the labels of all images have been used since the beginning, and this subset of images remains unchanged during all experiments and iterations. The flow diagram in this image shows how the images are moved and applied in each active learning iteration.

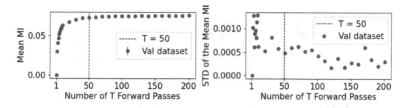

Fig. 4. Study of the number of forward passes T using the CamVid dataset and the model DenseNet. For each number of forward passes T, $\overline{EU}_{img}$ of the validation dataset of CamVid was calculated five times. The graph on the left shows the average of the five results obtained, and the graph on the right shows the standard deviation. Here $\overline{EU}_{img}$ was calculated using mutual information (MI).

The Number of Forward Passes. In many papers the number of forward passes in MC-Dropout is set to $T = 50$, without clear justification. To address this shortcoming, we conducted a study to determine the optimal value of T. Since the epistemic uncertainty per image EU_{img}, Eq. (2), is used for querying new images for being labeled, this study should focus on how the number of passes T affects EU_{img}.

We calculated $\overline{EU}_{img}$ of the dataset for $T = \{1, 2, 3, ..., 10\}$ and $T = \{20, 30, 40, ..., 200\}$. Each value of T was evaluated five times. The study was conducted using DenseNet-56 trained and validated with the complete subsets of CamVid. Figure 4 presents the results for the validation dataset. The graphs illustrate the mean and standard deviation of the results for the five repetitions. The graphs indicate that a stable mean value is achieved after T reaches 50, confirming the choice in published works. Furthermore, the standard deviation is over 100 times smaller than the mean, suggesting that 50 forward passes are enough to obtain a stable result with MC-Dropout. Henceforth in this paper, we define T as 50, in line with other works.

Active Learning for the CamVid Dataset. Figure 5 summarizes the design of experiment that we used. Starting with the experiment using DenseNet, at *step 1*, $P = 10\%$ images are selected for labeling, and the model is trained with the selected images at *step 2*. Two copies of the trained model, A and R, are saved. Model A will be further trained with active learning, and model R with randomly selected images. At *step 3*, the TR_t and TR_v are calculated with Eq. (3), in this experiment with $S = 1.0$, and new images are selected for labeling. After that, model A is retrained at *step 4*.

For evaluation purposes, a second model is trained using randomly selected images. At *step 5*, the same number of images N_{iter} from *step 3* is randomly selected, and model R is retrained at *step 6*. Notice that at each iteration, based on the calculated TR_t and TR_v, a different number of images is selected for training, N_{iter_train}, and validation, N_{iter_val}. Therefore, N_{iter} is different at each iteration. Notice also that the pools of labeled training and validation images, Fig. 3, generated with active learning at *step 3* of Fig. 5 are independent of the pools of images generated with the random selection at *step 5*, which means that the respective unlabeled pools are also independent.

At *Step 7* of Fig. 5, models A and R are evaluated using the test dataset, which remains the same in all iterations. After that, the two models are compared, analyzing

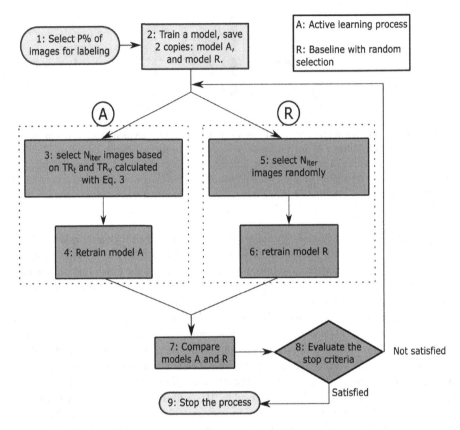

Fig. 5. The experiments begin with the random selection of $P\%$ of training and $P\%$ of validation images for training the model. At *step 3*, N_{iter_train} images are selected for training and N_{iter_val} for validation of model A. Based on the values of N_{iter}, defined at *step 3*, the same amount of images are randomly selected at *step 5*. The pools of labeled training and validation images for model A are composed of the $P\%$ initially selected images plus the images selected based on uncertainty in the iterations performed. The same applies to the pools used for training and validating model R, but in this case, the images are randomly selected. *Step 7* compares the performance of the two models. The whole process stops when the chosen criteria is achieved.

the improvement of active learning against random selection. Finally, *step 8* evaluates the chosen stop criteria, e.g. if all images have been selected, no improvement in mean-IoU on the test set is achieved, or few images have an epistemic uncertainty above the threshold. In this paper, for the CamVid experiments, we stop if very few images with uncertainty above the threshold are left. To observe if the performance of the models would suddenly improve, we keep the experiments running after unlabeled images stopped having uncertainty above the threshold.

Figure 6(a) is a result of *step 7* of Fig. 5, and presents the outcomes of the experiment on the CamVid dataset using DenseNet. The model's meanIoU stabilizes around 59% after iteration 12, using approximately 40% of the training data and slightly over 50% of

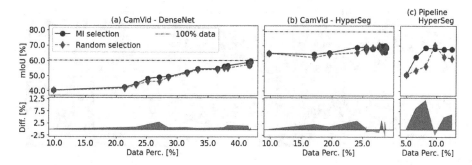

Fig. 6. Results of the active learning experiments. The bottom graphs show the difference in meanIoU between the model trained with active learning vs. trained with random images, where positive values means active learning prevails.

the validation data, which represents around 41% of the data when the weighted mean is calculated for both subsets as shown in Fig. 6(a). After that, only one new image was selected for training and one for validation, indicating that additional images do not contribute significantly to the model's knowledge. Comparatively, training the model with the entire dataset yielded only a slightly higher meanIoU of 60.22% in our implementation. However, the model trained with uncertainty-selected images consistently outperformed the one trained with random images.

Additionally to DenseNet [21], we investigate the performance of HyperSeg, for which we start with $P = 10\%$ images and $S = 1.5$. The model trained with active learning outperformed the model trained with random images until around 25% of the images were queried, Fig. 6(b). After 25% of the images were selected, the performance of the models trained with images queried with uncertainty and randomly were very similar and stabilized around 69.0%. A possible reason for this behavior is that HyperSeg model has excellent generalization capabilities, requiring fewer data to achieve a stable meanIoU close to the performance obtained with the entire dataset. Finally, Fig. 7 and Table 1 show results obtained with the models from the last iterations of the DenseNet and HyperSeg experiments. Table 1 also shows the performance of the models trained with the entire dataset.

In summary, applying active learning to CamVid confirmed the effectiveness of the active learning framework. It further reinforced that when data follows a consistent pattern, adding more samples does not necessarily improve the model's performance. As shown in Fig. 6(a-b), the meanIoU gain for DenseNet from the beginning to the end of the experiment is much more expressive than for HyperSeg. Even though more studies should be performed to analyze this behavior, we hypothesize that it regards the models' structure. HyperSeg apparently has a huge capability of generalization and does not require as much data as DenseNet to achieve the best performance possible.

Figure 8 compares our results with three recent deep active learning methods. Semi supervised semantic segmentation for active learning (S4AL) achieved around 61.4% meanIoU training on 13.8% of the data, which is 97% of the performance obtained with the entire dataset [29]. Similarly, Manifold Embedding-based Active Learning (MEAL) achieved 59.6% meanIoU, which is 81.6% of the overall performance, with just 5% of

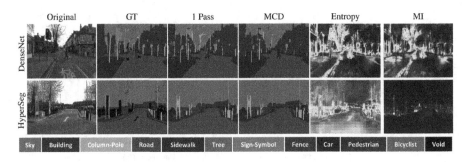

Fig. 7. Test segmentation results for the models trained with CamVid. GT is the ground truth. MCD is the average of the results obtained with MC-dropout. For the entropy and the mutual information (MI) plots, the warmer colors represent higher values. The entropy and MI heatmaps are normalized per experiment (best viewed in color.).

the images [34]. However, these frameworks queried patches of images instead of the whole image.

Difficulty-Aware Active Learning (DEAL) used image-level querying, and achieved 61.64% meanIoU, which is about 95% of the whole dataset performance, using 40.0% of the data [39]. Using DenseNet, we achieved 97.9% of the whole dataset's results with 41.9% of the data. With HyperSeg, we obtained 87.1% performance using only 28.9% of the data. As HyperSeg is a state-of-the-art model tailored for CamVid, the meanIoU is higher than for the other approaches. Notice also that the same framework requires a different percentage of data to obtain results close to the result obtained with 100% of the data when different model architectures are used, as we demonstrated using DenseNet and HyperSeg. Finally, when analyzing the results, it is important to remember that S4AL, DEAL, and MEAL are much more complex frameworks than ours. S4AL uses a teacher-student architecture for allowing semi-supervised training using pseudo labels. MEAL uses uniform manifold approximations and projection (UMAP) to learn a low dimensional embedding representation of the encoder output and uses K-Means++ to find the most representative between the most informative images sampled with entropy. DEAL adds to the CNN structure a probability attention module for learning semantic difficulty maps. Our framework consists of taking an out-of-the-box model without modifications and allowing dropout during the inference phase for using the MC-dropout and calculate the epistemic uncertainty.

Table 1. Results for the CamVid test subset. mIoU refers to meanIoU.

Experim.	% Data	Sky	Build.	Column	Road	Sidew.	Tree	Sign	Fence	Car	Pedes.	Bicyc.	mIoU
DenseNet	100	88.8	74.3	30.8	89.5	77.0	71.3	33.1	32.2	68.1	51.6	45.6	60.2
	41.9	91.9	77.6	28.2	92.0	77.6	74.1	26.5	26.0	70.0	47.5	37.3	59.0
HyperSeg	100	94.5	92.9	50.3	97.4	88.5	86.4	35.3	70.8	94.4	73.8	86.8	79.2
	28.8	85.8	84.5	38.5	94.3	7.2	79.9	47.7	55.5	88.7	46.5	61.0	69.0

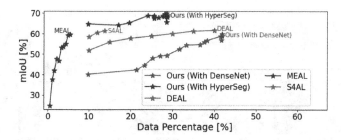

Fig. 8. Comparison of methods on CamVid. The values for DEAL, MEAL, and S4AL were manually extracted from the graphs in the original papers, hence are approximate. For each framework, the markers indicate when new images were labeled, and the models were (re-)trained in the respective original papers (Best viewed online in color.).

The Pipeline Dataset. The active learning process takes longer on this dataset, because it is larger than CamVid. We chose to run this experiment with HyperSeg, as it required less data and fewer iterations in the CamVid experiment, while achieving significantly higher meanIoU than DenseNet.

Figure 6(c) presents the results when starting with $P = 5\%$ of the images and $S = 1.5$. Because the pipeline dataset is huge, analyzing it entirely per iteration is time-consuming. First, the images are shuffled, then EU_{img} is calculated for each image. The image is selected or not based on the thresholds. The iteration stops when a pre-defined number of images is reached or the whole dataset is evaluated. For this experiment, we stop the active learning framework if the meanIoU does not improve significantly anymore. The model trained with uncertainty-based selection outperforms the baseline model trained with randomly selected images. The final meanIoU of the active learning model is 6.17% higher than the baseline. Except for iteration 4, the model trained with active learning was much more stable, presenting better and increasing performance across iterations. Teble 2 presents the meanIoU for the test dataset for the final iteration models with uncertainty-based selection and with the baseline random selection. Note that for the most underrepresented class (boulder and survey vehicle) the model trained with uncertainty-based selection presents the most significant performance gain compared to the model trained with random images. Figure 9 showcases two examples of predictions for test images using the resulting model from the last iteration of this experiment. The entropy plots show higher values for the pipeline and the field joint, the relatively illegible classes, suggesting that using entropy as an acquisition function could yield good results.

Table 2. mIoU for the pipeline test dataset, for the models trained in the final iteration using 12.5% of the data. The percentages over headings indicate the amount of images containing each class in the entire training and validation datasets.

| | 99.9% | 77.1% | 20.3% | 21.0% | 15.5% | |
Selection Criteria	Backg.	Pipe	F. Joint	Anode	B.&S. V.	mIoU
Uncertainty	97.0	84.6	66.3	31.1	58.6	67.5
Random (baseline)	96.2	80.0	61.3	29.0	40.3	61.4

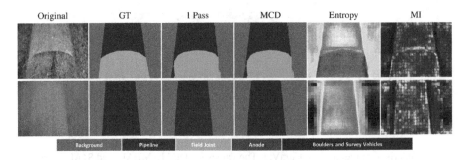

Fig. 9. Example results for pipeline test images. For the entropy and the mutual information plots, the warmer colors represent higher values (best viewed in color).

In Fig. 6 the difference of meanIoU between the models trained with images selected based on uncertainty and the ones trained with randomly selected images is more significant in the pipeline experiment than in the CamVid experiments. The possible reason for that is that the pipeline dataset is much bigger and unbalanced than CamVid, making the selection of images more critical and challenging.

Repeatability. Learning depends on the initial set of images chosen for the first iteration. To test repeatability we reran the CamVid experiment with HyperSeg several times. We use CamVid because it is a smaller dataset than pipeline, allowing to run the experiments faster. While the original setup for CamVid with HyperSeg used $S = 1.5$ for thresholds in Eq. (3), we now used both $S = 1.5$ and $S = 0.5$, the latter selecting more images in each iteration. The top plot in Fig. 10 shows meanIoU results after each iteration for active learning and baseline random-selection models, grouping runs starting with different initial sets of images using four colors. As can be observed in the middle plot, active learning always prevails with $S = 1.5$. The bottom graph shows that for $S = 0.5$ the performance gain was smaller, and in the experiment number 2, in pink, random selection performed better. We hypothesize that as CamVid is a very small dataset and HyperSeg has a strong generalization capacity, when more data is selected the benefit of the uncertainty selection gets much lower. It remains an open question whether retraining the models from scratch at each iteration would prevent them from getting stuck in local minima yielding better performance. Notice that we reported in the previous paragraphs the performance for the experiment 1, in blue. The other experiments presented better meanIoU%. Experiment 4, in yellow, for example, achieved 75.7% meanIoU, 95.6% of the performance with the entire dataset, training on 21.7% of the data.

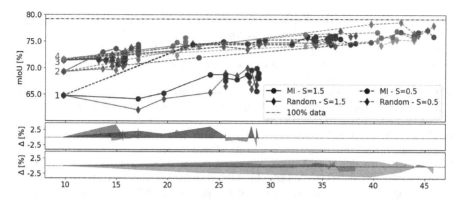

Fig. 10. Study of repeatability of results using the CamVid dataset and the model HyperSeg. Top: Four colors group run for different random initial sets of images. Below: mIoU differences Δ between the active learning and the baseline random selection models for $S = 1.5$ (middle) and $S = 0.5$ (bottom). Positive Δ means active learning prevails. (Best viewed online in color.)

5 Conclusion

We demonstrated the effectiveness of active learning with epistemic uncertainty in an underwater infrastructure inspection task, using HyperSeg, a five-class dataset of more than fifty thousand images, and mutual information as the epistemic uncertainty measure. The HyperSeg structure did not need to be modified, making this method easy to implement. Using active learning for selecting the training images resulted in a model with 6.17% better meanIoU than a baseline model trained with the same number of random images. The model trained with active learning achieved 67.5% meanIoU using only 12.5% of the available data for training and validation. We observed that in the second iteration, the images queried attempted to compensate for the less represented classes in the dataset and the classes with lower performance in the previous iteration. This indicates that the approach helps with unbalanced datasets. Our experiment on the CamVid dataset, a small street view dataset with 11 semantic classes, suggested that the framework used is particularly effective for large datasets but may not provide a significant advantage for small datasets.

References

1. Abdar, M., et al.: A review of uncertainty quantification in deep learning: techniques, applications and challenges. Inf. Fusion **76**, 243–297 (2021)
2. Bouarfa, S., Doğru, A., Arizar, R., Aydoğan, R., Serafico, J.: Towards automated aircraft maintenance inspection. A use case of detecting aircraft dents using mask R-CNN. In: AIAA Scitech 2020 forum, p. 0389 (2020)
3. Brostow, G.J., Fauqueur, J., Cipolla, R.: Semantic object classes in video: a high-definition ground truth database. Pattern Recogn. Lett. **30**(2), 88–97 (2009)
4. Brostow, G.J., Shotton, J., Fauqueur, J., Cipolla, R.: Segmentation and recognition using structure from motion point clouds. In: Forsyth, D., Torr, P., Zisserman, A. (eds.) ECCV 2008. LNCS, vol. 5302, pp. 44–57. Springer, Heidelberg (2008). https://doi.org/10.1007/978-3-540-88682-2_5

5. Budd, S., Robinson, E.C., Kainz, B.: A survey on active learning and human-in-the-loop deep learning for medical image analysis. Med. Image Anal. **71**, 102062 (2021)
6. Chen, X., Kundu, K., Zhang, Z., Ma, H., Fidler, S., Urtasun, R.: Monocular 3D object detection for autonomous driving. In: 2016 IEEE Conference on Computer Vision and Pattern Recognition (CVPR), pp. 2147–2156 (2016). https://doi.org/10.1109/CVPR.2016.236
7. Chen, X., Ma, H., Wan, J., Li, B., Xia, T.: Multi-view 3D object detection network for autonomous driving. In: Proceedings of the IEEE Conference on Computer Vision and Pattern Recognition, pp. 1907–1915 (2017)
8. Chiang, J.Y., Chen, Y.C.: Underwater image enhancement by wavelength compensation and dehazing. IEEE Trans. Image Process. **21**(4), 1756–1769 (2012)
9. Chin, C.S., Bo Hui Neo, A., See, S.: Visual marine debris detection using YOLOV5s for autonomous underwater vehicle. In: 2022 IEEE/ACIS 22nd International Conference on Computer and Information Science (ICIS), pp. 20–24 (2022). https://doi.org/10.1109/ICIS54925.2022.9882484
10. Desai, M., Shah, M.: An anatomization on breast cancer detection and diagnosis employing multi-layer perceptron neural network (MLP) and convolutional neural network (CNN). Clin. eHealth **4**, 1–11 (2021)
11. Duarte, A., Codevilla, F., Gaya, J.D.O., Botelho, S.S.C.: A dataset to evaluate underwater image restoration methods. In: OCEANS 2016 - Shanghai, pp. 1–6. IEEE (2016). https://doi.org/10.1109/OCEANSAP.2016.7485524
12. Feng, D., Harakeh, A., Waslander, S.L., Dietmayer, K.: A review and comparative study on probabilistic object detection in autonomous driving. IEEE Trans. Intell. Transp. Syst. (2021)
13. Gal, Y.: Uncertainty in Deep Learning. Ph.D. thesis, University of Cambridge (2016)
14. Gal, Y., Islam, R., Ghahramani, Z.: Deep Bayesian active learning with image data. In: International Conference on Machine Learning, pp. 1183–1192. PMLR (2017)
15. Gašparović, B., Lerga, J., Mauša, G., Ivašić-Kos, M.: Deep learning approach for objects detection in underwater pipeline images. Appl. Artif. Intell. **36**(1), 2146853 (2022)
16. Gaur, U., Kourakis, M., Newman-Smith, E., Smith, W., Manjunath, B.: Membrane segmentation via active learning with deep networks. In: 2016 IEEE International Conference on Image Processing (ICIP), pp. 1943–1947 (2016). https://doi.org/10.1109/ICIP.2016.7532697
17. Guo, F., Qian, Y., Rizos, D., Suo, Z., Chen, X.: Automatic rail surface defects inspection based on mask R-CNN. Transp. Res. Rec. **2675**(11), 655–668 (2021)
18. Hong, J., Fulton, M., Sattar, J.: TrashCan: a semantically-segmented dataset towards visual detection of marine debris. CoRR abs/2007.08097 (2020). https://arxiv.org/abs/2007.08097
19. Huang, G., Liu, Z., van der Maaten, L., Weinberger, K.Q.: Densely connected convolutional networks. In: Proceedings of the IEEE Conference on Computer Vision and Pattern Recognition (CVPR) (2017)
20. Jégou, S., Drozdzal, M., Vazquez, D., Romero, A., Bengio, Y.: The one hundred layers tiramisu: Fully convolutional denseNets for semantic segmentation. In: Proceedings of the IEEE Conference on Computer Vision and Pattern Recognition Workshops, pp. 11–19 (2017)
21. Kendall, A., Gal, Y.: What uncertainties do we need in Bayesian deep learning for computer vision? In: Guyon, I., rt al. (eds.) Advances in Neural Information Processing Systems, vol. 30. Curran Associates, Inc. (2017). https://proceedings.neurips.cc/paper_files/paper/2017/file/2650d6089a6d640c5e85b2b88265dc2b-Paper.pdf
22. Li, B., Alstrøm, T.S.: On uncertainty estimation in active learning for image segmentation. In: 2020 International Conference on Machine Learning: Workshop on Uncertainty and Robustness in Deep Learning (2020)
23. Medina, E., Petraglia, M.R., Gomes, J.G.R.C., Petraglia, A.: Comparison of CNN and MLP classifiers for algae detection in underwater pipelines. In: 2017 Seventh International Conference on Image Processing Theory, Tools and Applications (IPTA), pp. 1–6 (2017). https://doi.org/10.1109/IPTA.2017.8310098

24. Milanés-Hermosilla, D., et al.: Monte Carlo dropout for uncertainty estimation and motor imagery classification. Sensors **21**(21), 7241 (2021)

25. Nirkin, Y., Wolf, L., Hassner, T.: HyperSeg: patch-wise hypernetwork for real-time semantic segmentation. In: Proceedings of the IEEE/CVF Conference on Computer Vision and Pattern Recognition, pp. 4061–4070 (2021)

26. Oberdiek, P., Rottmann, M., Gottschalk, H.: Classification uncertainty of deep neural networks based on gradient information. In: Pancioni, L., Schwenker, F., Trentin, E. (eds.) ANNPR 2018. LNCS (LNAI), vol. 11081, pp. 113–125. Springer, Cham (2018). https://doi.org/10.1007/978-3-319-99978-4_9

27. Polsinelli, M., Cinque, L., Placidi, G.: A light CNN for detecting COVID-19 from CT scans of the chest. Pattern Recogn. Lett. **140**, 95–100 (2020)

28. Postels, J., Ferroni, F., Coskun, H., Navab, N., Tombari, F.: Sampling-free epistemic uncertainty estimation using approximated variance propagation. In: Proceedings of the IEEE/CVF International Conference on Computer Vision, pp. 2931–2940 (2019)

29. Rangnekar, A., Kanan, C., Hoffman, M.: Semantic segmentation with active semi-supervised learning. In: Proceedings of the IEEE/CVF Winter Conference on Applications of Computer Vision, pp. 5966–5977 (2023)

30. Ren, P.: A survey of deep active learning. ACM Comput. Surv. (CSUR) **54**(9), 1–40 (2021)

31. Saidu, I.C., Csató, L.: Active learning with Bayesian UNet for efficient semantic image segmentation. J. Imaging **7**(2), 37 (2021)

32. Schettini, R., Corchs, S.: Underwater image processing: state of the art of restoration and image enhancement methods. EURASIP J. Adv. Sign. Proc. **2010**(1), 746052 (2010)

33. Shamsi, A., et al.: An uncertainty-aware transfer learning-based framework for COVID-19 diagnosis. IEEE Trans. Neural Netw. Learn. Syst. **32**(4), 1408–1417 (2021). https://doi.org/10.1109/TNNLS.2021.3054306

34. Sreenivasaiah, D., Otterbach, J., Wollmann, T.: MEAL: manifold embedding-based active learning. In: Proceedings of the IEEE/CVF International Conference on Computer Vision, pp. 1029–1037 (2021)

35. Tan, M., Le, Q.: EfficientNet: rethinking model scaling for convolutional neural networks. In: International Conference on Machine Learning, pp. 6105–6114. PMLR (2019)

36. Wang, W., et al.: Nodule-plus R-CNN and deep self-paced active learning for 3D instance segmentation of pulmonary nodules. IEEE Access **7**, 128796–128805 (2019)

37. Wang, Y., Liu, M., Zheng, P., Yang, H., Zou, J.: A smart surface inspection system using faster R-CNN in cloud-edge computing environment. Adv. Eng. Inform. **43**, 101037 (2020)

38. Xiao, X., et al.: BASeg: boundary aware semantic segmentation for autonomous driving. Neural Netw. **157**, 460–470 (2023)

39. Xie, S., Feng, Z., Chen, Y., Sun, S., Ma, C., Song, M.: DEAL: difficulty-aware active learning for semantic segmentation. In: Proceedings of the Asian Conference on Computer Vision (2020)

40. Yang, L., Zhang, Y., Chen, J., Zhang, S., Chen, D.Z.: Suggestive annotation: a deep active learning framework for biomedical image segmentation. In: Descoteaux, M., Maier-Hein, L., Franz, A., Jannin, P., Collins, D.L., Duchesne, S. (eds.) MICCAI 2017. LNCS, vol. 10435, pp. 399–407. Springer, Cham (2017). https://doi.org/10.1007/978-3-319-66179-7_46

41. Zhou, X., Li, Y., Liang, W.: CNN-RNN based intelligent recommendation for online medical pre-diagnosis support. IEEE/ACM Trans. Comput. Biol. Bioinf. **18**(3), 912–921 (2020)

Enhancing Connected Cooperative ADAS: Deep Learning Perception in an Embedded System Utilizing Fisheye Cameras

Guillem Delgado[1(✉)], Mikel Garcia[1,3], Jon Ander Íñiguez de Gordoa[1], Marcos Nieto[1], Gorka Velez[1], Cristina Pérez-Benito[2], David Pujol[2], Alejandro Miranda[2], Iu Aguilar[2], and Aleksandar Jevtić[2]

[1] Vicomtech Foundation, Basque Research and Technology Alliance (BRTA), Mikeletegi 57, 20009 Donostia-San Sebastián, Spain
{gdelgado,mgarcia}@vicomtech.org
[2] FICOSA ADAS, SLU, Polígon Industrial Can Mitjans, 08232 Viladecavalls, Spain
c.perez.benito@ficosa.com
[3] University of the Basque Country (UPV/EHU), Donostia-San Sebastián, Spain

Abstract. This paper explores the potential of Cooperative Advanced Driver Assistance Systems (C-ADAS) that leverage Vehicle-to-Everything (V2X) communication to enhance road safety. The authors propose a deep learning based perception system, on a 360° surround view within the C-ADAS. This system also utilizes an On-Board Unit (OBU) for V2X message sharing to cater to vehicles lacking their own perception sensors. The feasibility of these systems is demonstrated, showcasing their effectiveness in various real-world scenarios, executed in real-time. The contributions include the introduction of a design for a perception system employing fish-eye cameras in the context of C-ADAS, with the potential for embedded integration, the validation of the feasibility of day 2 services in C-ITS, and the expansion of ADAS functions through Local Dynamic Map (LDM) for Collision Warning Application. The findings highlight the promising potential of C-ADAS in improving road safety and pave the way for future advancements in cooperative perception and driving systems.

Keywords: Cooperative advanced driver assistance systems · V2X · Deep learning

1 Introduction

The emergence of Cooperative Intelligent Transport Systems (C-ITS) will revolutionize the way vehicles interact with their near environment. Vehicles are no longer isolated entities; instead, they are increasingly becoming connected devices that communicate with each other and the road infrastructure. While the current vehicles are already equipped with various advanced features, the near future holds the promise of even greater possibilities, with vehicles interacting directly with each other and the road infrastructure through Vehicle-to-everything (V2X) communications. V2X is a fundamental technology of C-ITS that enables vehicles to exchange data with each other and

J. Filipe and J. Röning (Eds.): ROBOVIS 2024, CCIS 2077, pp. 82–99, 2024.
https://doi.org/10.1007/978-3-031-59057-3_6

the surrounding infrastructure. Furthermore, communication between vehicles, infrastructure, and other road users will play a vital role in increasing the safety of future automated vehicles and integrating them into the overall transport system.

Advanced Driver Assistance Systems (ADAS) have also contributed to improving road safety and enhancing the driving experience by reducing risks associated with human factors. According to the study outlined in [17], ADAS play a crucial role in situations where the driver may become distracted, or when there is an overwhelming amount of incoming inputs, such as in highly crowded urban scenarios. This paper explores a new generation of ADAS that share information between vehicles and infrastructure. Our objectives are to provide a comprehensive argument for such systems and to demonstrate its engineering feasibility to deploy embedded systems for Connected Autonomous Vehicles (CAVs) at a large scale.

All the static and dynamic information available through sensors and communication are reported, after a proper process of data fusion, in a structured georeferenced local database named Local Dynamic Map (LDM) which acts as a common layer accessed by all the applications.

To achieve these objectives, we conducted experiments in two distinct scenarios. The first scenario, Urban Road, is situated in a densely populated area with tailored traffic regulations and infrastructure designed for congested traffic conditions, maintaining a speed limit not exceeding 50 km/h. The second scenario is City Traffic (Slow speed), extending our evaluation to another context characterized by slow-speed traffic conditions under 30 km/h. Our proposed perception system, featuring a 360° surround view, is optimized for real-time, 360° visibility around the vehicle. This system is further enhanced through C-ITS, enabling information exchange via V2X messaging. Validation was carried out by implementing a Collision Warning Application atop the LDM, showcasing its practical benefits in urban traffic scenarios where swift information sharing is critical (Fig. 1).

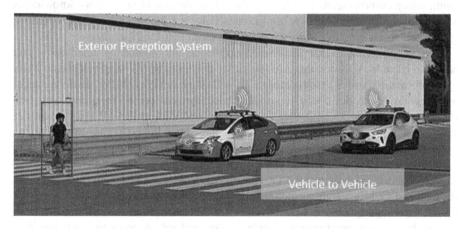

Fig. 1. Collision prevention use case based on the proposed system.

The contribution of this paper can be summarized as the following:

- We introduce our design of a perception system that can provide real-time detection of the vehicle's surroundings for a C-ADAS.
- We provide a comprehensive argument for a C-ADAS from an engineering and scalable feasibility perspective.
- We demonstrate the feasibility of day 2 services [6] in C-ITS, which incorporate advanced cooperative components, allowing vehicles without perception sensors to receive object detections from other vehicles.
- We are expanding the support services available from day 1 to include new applications such as Collision Warning Application and LDM.

The remainder of this paper is organized as follows. Section 2 presents the related works. Section 3 introduces the system architecture of our proposal consisting of cooperative system and in Sects. 4, 5, 6, 7 we detail each module. Section 8 provides experimental results performed with vehicles on urban roads. Section 9 concludes this paper.

2 Related Work

ADAS are considered one of the crucial domains of intelligent transportation systems [20]. In order to further improve road safety, researchers have proposed Cooperative ADAS (C-ADAS), which facilitate cooperation between different systems. The primary differentiation between C-ADAS and conventional ADAS lies in their respective scope of visibility. C-ADAS possesses the capability to anticipate traffic conditions over extended distances, whereas traditional systems are limited to perceiving the environment within a relatively short radius of just a few meters around the vehicle. Several cutting-edge works have made significant contributions to the development of this technology [9]. One frequently observed use case in the literature is cooperative platoon and multiplatoon communication [19]. Nevertheless, to the best of the authors' knowledge, no state-of-the-art approach has been proposed for a scalable embedded cooperative system that solely employs camera-based technology [10, 16, 23, 27, 29].

Automated vehicles that use local information are limited by blind spots and occluded hazards. V2X communications tackle this issue by allowing vehicles to share road information with infrastructure (V2I) and other vehicles (V2V). Different technologies have been developed to support these wireless communications, including Dedicated Short Range Communications (DSRC), C-V2X or ITS-G5 [12]. In the last years, the European Telecommunications Standards Institute (ETSI) has worked on the standarization of the Collective Perception Service (CPS), which allows road users to share information about detected objects by broadcasting Collective Perception Messages (CPMs). ETSI approved the TR 103 562 V2.1.1 [1], as a first attempt to standarize the CPS and CPM generation rules [15]. However, there are no established guidelines for V2X message synchronization or fusion. LDM can serve as a centralised and real-time software component running inside a connected vehicle to merge and store data from different sensors or sources, including V2X. The concept of LDM was firstly introduced in the SAFESPOT European project [4]. One of the key features of the LDM is its ability to integrate data from heterogeneous data sources. Different works such as [26] have worked on the implementation of the LDM based on the SAFESPOT definition. Other works such as [8] extended the LDM concept to a Relational-Local Dynamic Map (R-LDM) by using graph databases. In [14] they also used graph databases focusing in interoperability of the LDM implementation by using a common automotive ontology [28] and using an standard data interface over the OpenLABEL standard. In the PEGA-SUS European project, they extended the 4-layer description to a 6-Layer Model [25], making a clearer distinction between static information layer and adding a digital information layer for V2X and digital map data.

Day 1 / 2 / 3+ are successive C-ITS deployment phases of use cases and technologies. They are different phases of the roadmap built on top of each other. The initial Day 1 phase focuses on cooperative awareness and decentralised notification services involving cooperative vehicles and road infrastructure. With increasing market penetration Day 2 services are enabled improving and complementing the Day 1 services and offering collective perception services. Having these services in the field Day 3+ focuses on real cooperation by sharing intentions and coordination data. Cooperative Day 3 assisted and automated vehicles will share their trajectory and maneuver planning, support negotiation and coordination as well as active VRU advertisement [2]. Collision Warning Application concept can contribute to enhancing road safety and efficiency. In Day 1 C-ITS services, Collision Warning Applications can be beneficial for various purposes, including hazard notifications. By incorporating such algorithms [24], vehicles can estimate the time until a potential collision with these hazards, enabling timely alerts to be sent to nearby vehicles. Day 2 C-ITS services [13], which usually involve more advanced applications, Collision Warning Application can be extended to further enhance safety and traffic flow optimization. For example, Traffic Signal Priority Request by Designated Vehicles aims to prioritize certain vehicles, such as emergency vehicles or public transport, at intersections as [21].

3 System Architecture

In this study, we propose a C-ADAS system that allows data sharing from vehicles equipped with perception systems to surrounding vehicles or infrastructure by using an antenna attached to an OBU attached for communication system. The overall system architecture is shown in Fig. 2, which highlights the four main subsystems, Perception, V2X, LDM, and Applications.

We used two commonly known automotive vehicles to test the proposed architecture, namely a Cupra Formentor and a Toyota Prius. These vehicles were equipped with four vision cameras with fisheye lenses with an overlapping FOV of 189°, a router based on APU2 board with 4G LTE (Long-Term Evolution) and Wifi mini PCI cards, and a differential global positioning systems (DGPS) xNAV550 dual antenna GNSS + IMU. The processing units for these vehicles were an i7-11800H CPU and a NVIDIA 3060 Mobile for Cupra Formentor and a Vecow RCX-15540R-PEG with an i7-9700E 64Gb and 2 NVIDIA 2080Ti for the Toyota Prius. The four cameras are mounted in the vehicle covering the front, back and lateral sides, enabling a comprehensive surround view of the vehicle. The software architecture of this system was established on Robot Operating System (ROS) suite for build-in PCs and Real Time Operating System (RTOS) for TDA4, which is a series of automotive system-on-chip platforms by Texas

Instruments, designed for ADAS and autonomous driving applications. Additionally, both vehicles were equipped with an MK5 OBU from Cohda Wireless, each one connected to a Mobilemark MGW-303 antenna, for V2X communication. The OBUs are connected to the processing units via Ethernet. Despite the availability of multiple sensors on both vehicles, we will utilize the perception of a single vehicle as the sole transmitter while the other is the receiver in the upcoming experiments.

The Perception module plays a critical role in providing real-time information about the surroundings to the transmitter vehicle. This module uses four cameras that capture visual data at a rate of 25 frames per second. The incoming h264 packets, received via the Ethernet protocol using UDP, are processed using Gstreamer and parsed into the desired format for further analysis and processing. The module then publishes the detected objects as 3D cuboids on ROS topic for other modules to access. In addition, geoposition information is also published using the DGPS as ROS topic to provide real-time position of the ego-vehicle. The V2X module enables the wireless exchange of local sensing information between vehicles and infrastructure. In transmission mode, the module continuously reads data from the odometry and perception information publishers in ROS. It then prepares and sends messages in compliance with ETSI CPM message specifications. In reception mode, the module receives data from other vehicles, transforms the perception information from the transmitter to the receiver's coordinates system, and publishes the detections in ROS. The LDM module provides driver-friendly visual traffic information using detections in the ego-car coordinates. The module inputs this information into a database that can be used by agnostic applications to read and develop use cases, such as a Collision Warning application.

4   Perception

This module is in charge of understanding and interpreting the traffic scene surrounding the vehicle, where the vehicle is moving in an urban area at a speed limit of less than 50 km/h. The task of achieving this goal is complex and requires real-time inference processing, starting with a proper perception of the elements that make up the scene, including the characteristics of the infrastructure in which the vehicle is moving.

To address these challenges, a vision-based approach is proposed. Recent advances in deep neural networks have led to the development of multiple systems that have significantly improved the performance of detection algorithms. Among these systems, those that utilize four to six fisheye cameras offer an advantage due to their wide field of view, enabling the coverage of the entire surrounding of a vehicle with a small number of sensors. In contrast, other systems that use LiDAR to enhance the accuracy of perception tend to be computationally and economically expensive [30]. For this reason, our focus is on perception using cameras to provide real-time performance and keep costs low.

The proposed perception system for this project has been validated in previous studies [7], and it consists of an object detector, a 2D Kalman filter, a 2D to 3D projection, and a final 3D Kalman filter that fuses IDs from multiple cameras entirely programmed in C++. This work extends the previous work by improving the system's speed and embedding it onto a board for production, using TDA4VM from Texas Instruments (TI). This facilitates its deployment on resource-constrained devices.

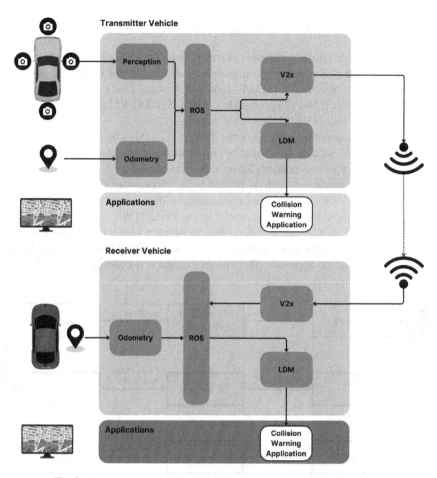

Fig. 2. General overview of the architecture of the proposed C-ADAS.

4.1 Embedded Computing

By leveraging embedded computing in RTOS, we can reduce the latency and bandwidth requirements of intelligent systems, making them more responsive and efficient, while also increasing their scalability by processing data closer to the source. In situations characterized by the coexistence of numerous vulnerable road users and vehicles, it becomes imperative to meticulously observe and track these entities. When employing cameras operating at a frame rate of 25 frames per second, this necessitates the execution of the data processing pipeline within a stringent time frame of less than 40 milliseconds (ms) to ensure the preservation of pertinent information. Furthermore, the strategic placement of processing resources in close proximity to the data source assumes paramount significance. This strategic positioning serves a dual purpose: firstly, it mitigates the introduction of extraneous latency that may result from offloading processing tasks to cloud-based infrastructures, and secondly, it serves as a proactive measure to fortify the system against potential external security breaches and attacks.

The complete perception pipeline is ported to the TDA4VM processor, that allows dedicated hardware to accelerate deep learning tasks using the DSP C7x alongside the Matrix Multiply Accelerator (MMA) Tensor Processing Unit (TPU). The proposed setup is composed by: TDA4VM processor, J721EX-SOMXEVM evaluation board and a surround view of four D3's IMX390 2MP cameras.

Our proposed solution is built upon the TIOVX API [5], which is an implementation of the OpenVX Standard provided by Texas Instruments. Our approach involves developing a library of independent kernels that are optimized for specific hardware components of the processor, such as Digital Signal Processors (DSPs) or the Multipoint Control Unit (MCUs), and then concatenating them using index parameters to form a complete graph that can be executed on the FreeRTOS system. The pipeline is executed in parallel, as the four incoming images of each iteration are replicated until the 3D tracker module, thereby enabling full hardware utilization and lower latency compared to a sequential approach. The flow of execution is illustrated in Fig. 3.

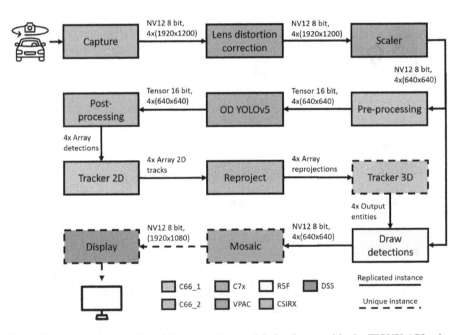

Fig. 3. Comprehensive pipeline of the perception module implemented in the TIOVX API using the TDA4 platform. The diagram illustrates the replicated instances of components for each camera and highlights the target where the processing takes place.

Our implementation of the TIOVX pipeline performs a high degree of flexibility concerning the configuration to be deployed and parameter tuning, thereby facilitating performance optimization for specific use cases. Additionally, it offers the capability to customize the processing pipeline to fulfill specific integration requirements by employing dynamic pipelining of incoming inputs. This customization fulfills the desired latency requirements for each iteration execution.

To achieve maximum hardware utilization, our approach involves creating multiple instances of the graph, each of which is executed in parallel based on the sequential utilization of the target hardware within the concatenated kernels. To enable interconnection between these instances, we have implemented a queuing system that creates intermediate buffers between kernels. This system enables incoming images to be processed in the order of the pipelining.

Our proposed AI model is seamlessly integrated into the TDA4 platform by employing platform-specific techniques to optimize execution latency. This is achieved through a quantization process utilizing mixed precision, where the floating-point inference is transformed into a mixed implementation. Specifically, certain layers are quantized to fixed-point 8-bit inference, while the most critical layers retain a higher precision of floating-point 16-bit.

The selection of which layers to quantize is determined through a benchmarking process, aiming to minimize the gap between the floating-point and fixed-point models. This approach significantly improves the inference latency. The layers that define the backbone and the final layers responsible for producing the desired results are maintained in floating-point precision. By adopting this methodology, we effectively optimize the overall performance and latency of the inference process.

5   V2X Communication

This subsystem manages the CPS among the connected vehicles. An end-to-end pipeline that allows real-time V2X communications is proposed, from the generation of CPM messages in the transmitter vehicle and their transmission via ITS-G5, to the CPM reception and decodification in the receiving vehicle.

In order to execute the wireless communications among the vehicles, each vehicle was equipped with a Cohda Wireless MK5 OBU, which is connected to a Mobilemark MGW-303 antenna that allows DSRC communications. The OBU is as well connected, via Ethernet, to the embedded board or vehicle PC in which the ADAS applications are run.

Figure 4 shows a high level architecture of the V2X transmission module. A client application in the embedded board is subscribed to the perception and vehicle odometry ROS topics. For every perception message received in each frame, this client fills out all the information required for the CPM generation in a JSON format, including the position, classification, object ID and time of measurement for each perceived object. This JSON is then sent to the OBU by UDP socket. UDP was chosen for this point-to-point communication because of its low latency compared to other scalable protocols, e.g., MQTT. Inside the OBU, a V2X stack is executed, which generates and transmits CPMs regularly at 10 Hz. Even though the system is compliant with ETSI TR 103 562 V2.1.1, it defines a set of rules for defining the CPM transmission frequency between 1–10 Hz [11]. In this study, we performed all tests using the highest and most demanding frequency rate. The content of the transmitted CPM is updated by the last JSON received through UDP. As the maximum standard frequency rate of the CPM is 10 Hz and we are processing the images at 25 Hz, the possible loss of packages due to UDP communications is not critical in this pipeline.

The V2X stack running at the onboard OBU on the receiver vehicle receives the transmitted CPMs through ITS-G5 and parses the content of the messages into JSON format. The JSONs are sent, via UDP, to the onboard processing unit of the vehicle, so the information included in the CPM can be published as ROS topics, loaded to LDM and consumed by the ADAS applications.

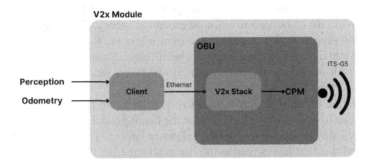

Fig. 4. Architecture of the proposed V2X module.

6   LDM

In this work, each vehicle (Transmitter and Receiver) uses LDM as a centralized database for data management in order to store and retrieve the information generated from the different data sources of the system, mainly focusing on dynamic and static information. For our LDM implementation, InfluxDB has been selected as our time-series database (TSDB) engine, a popular open-source database designed for storing time series data and optimized for fast writes and queries, making it an excellent choice for our real-time data management requirements [18]. A high-level architecture of the components and data inside LDM can be seen in Fig. 5.

The LDM uses information of the geopositioning provided by the DGPS, which receives real-time corrections from an RTK base station, obtaining centimeter level precision positioning. Thanks to this, data received from CPM messages can be transformed from the local coordinate system of the transmitter vehicle into the local coordinate system of the receiver vehicle. The generated CPM messages are decoded, transformed into geopositioned detected objects and inserted inside the LDM of the receiver vehicle. Data from the surroundings of the vehicles are downloaded from Open Street Maps (OSM) providing static road information to the vehicles. Consequently, it becomes feasible to leverage a real-time database to record and monitor the precise spatial coordinates of the egocar as well as the various objects comprising the scene. Thanks to the data inserted in the LDM, a real-time visualization of the data accessible to each vehicle can be visualized by using RVIZ or by interconnecting open-source dashboard and analytics solutions such as Grafana to our TSDB, as can be see in Fig. 6.

LDM Module

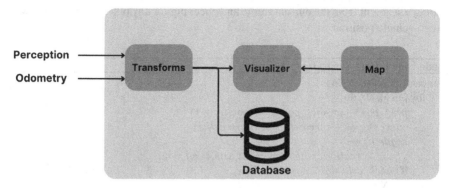

Fig. 5. Architecture of the proposed LDM module.

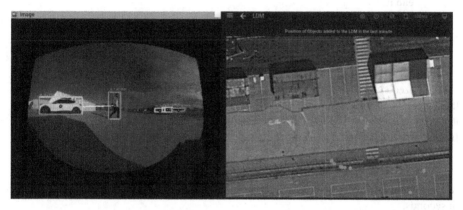

Fig. 6. The left image shows the view of the front camera in ROS. The right image shows the geoposition of the detected objects using Grafana in green and the blue colored dot is the current position of the egocar. (Color figure online)

7   Applications

The incorporation of static and dynamic objects into the database via LDMs enables the development of multiple applications aimed at enhancing the safety and efficiency of the transportation system. This framework facilitates the creation of a diverse range of applications that utilize a common database. This data can be used to detect and prevent potential collisions, even in situations where the driver's visibility is limited, ultimately improving road safety.

Therefore, we implemented a Collision Warning application. The algorithm of this application calculates the time remaining before a potential collision between our car and obstacles based on their relative speed and distance, typically measured in meters and meters per second, using a time-to-collision metric (TTC).

We employed a 3D tracking module [7], which utilizes a Kalman filter to enhance the trajectory of objects in a top-view plane. The system, as described in Algorithm 1, uses this module to predict the position of each tracked object for the next 50 frames, creating a segment from the current frame and checking for any potential collisions with the ego vehicle position.

Pseudo-code 1. Get collision frame number.

```
for each object track do
    for i in [0, 49] do
        pred_pos ← predict_position(track, i + 1)
        current_pos ← predict_position(track, i)
        segment ←
                create_segment(current_pos, pred_pos)
        if check_collision(segment) then
            N = i
            time_to_collision = N * 0.04
        end if
    end for
end for
```

In order to determine whether the object has collided with the ego vehicle, an ego-vehicle-sized cube is constructed in 3D space. The next step involves checking whether the trajectory of all tracked objects intersects with this cube during a given frame. By iterating over the next 50 frames at the current frame, any collisions occurring in the N frame can be determined to a specific time of collision, usually measured in seconds.

$$time\_to\_collision = N * 0.04\,s \qquad (1)$$

where N is the frame where we detect a hit and $0.04s$ is the frame rate of the cameras in seconds.

8   Experiments and Results

Here, we provide experimental results to evaluate our proposed system with two vehicles.

8.1   Experimental Setup

The main objective of our experiments was to test the capability of the transmitter vehicle to transmit its sensing information to the receiver vehicle via wireless communications. With the support of our system, we expected the receiver vehicle to merge remote information while driving.

The experiments were performed in two different scenarios. The first scenario, Urban Road, is located within a locality, which includes traffic rules and infrastructure adapted to the characteristics of a dense traffic environment. The speed limit does not exceed 50 km/h. The second scenario is in City Traffic (Slow speed). These types of roads are in urban areas, are usually one-way and require a speed limit of lower than 30 km/h due to the influx of Vulnerable Road Users (VRUs) and are often very congested environments, see Fig. 7.

Fig. 7. Left column shows examples of City Traffic scenarios, while the column in the right shows examples of Urban Road scenarios.

8.2 Perception Evaluation

In this study, we evaluate the performance of the perception module of a vehicle in two different scenarios: Urban Road and City Traffic. The experiments were conducted using the Higher Order Tracking Accuracy (HOTA) metrics [22], which combines detection accuracy (DetA), association accuracy (AssA), and localization accuracy (LocA). In addition, GT_IDs, or Ground Truth IDs, represent the total number of unique object identities tracked within the sequences, reflecting the count of distinct entities under tracking. On the other hand, GT_Dets, or Ground Truth Detections, denote the overall number of objects in the dataset, encompassing all instances, whether they belong to unique identities or not.

The dataset consists of 39 recorded videos, with a varying duration between 30 s and 1 min and have been labelled taking into consideration that the same object might appear in different cameras and should be labelled with the same identifier. It is important to highlight that certain classes such as Bicycle, Bus or Truck were not captured for specific scenarios during the recording of real videos, as their occurrence or likelihood of being recorded is relatively low.

Our experiments in Table 1 show that the perception module is robust in both environments. However, as a result of utilizing a dataset that closely reflects real-world conditions and scenarios, certain limitations have been observed. Notably, there are certain classes within the dataset that lack sufficient representation due to a low quantity of samples. For instance, the truck class consists of only 24 distinct objects and 2831 detections within a single scenario. Similarly, the bicycle and bus classes exhibit a limited number of samples, with only 6 objects each. Conversely, classes with a larger number of samples demonstrate more reliable and accurate performance results.

For car tracking, it is evident that the HOTA scores are generally higher in the city traffic context compared to urban road scenarios. This suggests that the tracking system performs better in the complex and crowded environment of city traffic, where precise association and localization are crucial. In contrast, trucks exhibit lower HOTA scores overall, with a more significant drop in association accuracy in city traffic, indicating challenges in tracking larger vehicles.

Bicycles show lower overall HOTA scores, with limited data available for city traffic. The results reveals that association accuracy is particularly challenging for bicycles, which may be due to their smaller size and varying trajectories. Person tracking showcases reasonably high HOTA scores, especially in urban road scenarios, indicating that the tracking system effectively handles pedestrian movements.

Motorcycles exhibit varying HOTA scores, with better association accuracy in urban road scenarios. This variation suggests that the tracking performance is context-dependent and might be influenced by the speed and maneuverability of motorcycles.

Bus tracking, on the other hand, shows limited data and lower HOTA scores in urban road scenarios. Further data collection and analysis may be needed to draw more conclusive insights.

Traffic sign and traffic light tracking generally display moderate to high HOTA scores, with better performance in urban road scenarios. These objects are often stationary, which facilitates their tracking.

Despite the higher complexity and variability of the traffic patterns in the city traffic scenario, which poses a greater challenge for the detection and tracking algorithms, the algorithm performs well without a big drop in results. The experiments conducted in both scenarios demonstrate the system's robustness and adaptability to varying urban conditions. Despite the challenges of the environment, the tracking system maintains reliable performance, especially for well-represented object classes. These findings underscore the system's suitability for real-world applications across diverse urban contexts. Specially in the City Traffic scenario, where lower speeds and higher congestion are factors, precise association and localization are particularly crucial, which is reflected in the HOTA scores.

Furthermore, a thorough performance analysis of the perception module was conducted, and the results are presented in Table 2. The analysis involved comparing the performance of a built-in PC featuring an i7-11800H CPU and an NVIDIA 3060 Mobile GPU with that of the embedded TDA4VM system.

In the case of the PC, the latency ranges from 9 to 180 milliseconds, with the lowest latency achieved using TensorRT. These results demonstrate the system's adaptability to different hardware configurations. Furthermore, precision configurations are explored, with variations in the number of bits used for computation.

On the TDA4VM platform, latency values ranging from 26 to 60 milliseconds are observed, depending on the precision configuration. Notably, the "Fixed point" configuration achieves the lowest latency of 26 milliseconds, indicating efficient real-time processing capabilities. This configuration employs 8-bit precision across all layers of the perception module.

An important advantage of utilizing affordable embedded systems, such as the TDA4VM, is their capability to meet the demanding requirements in terms of price, performance and energy consumption for autonomous driving applications. In spite of the PC platforms exhibiting the most favorable latency characteristics when configured

Table 1. Metrics from urban and city traffic scenarios using real videos recorded by FICOSA.

Class	Context	HOTA	DetA	AssA	LocA	GT_IDs	GT_Dets
Car	Urban road	52.87	47.56	59.22	85.85	547	46874
	City traffic	56.61	53.42	60.34	85.30	1361	115924
Truck	Urban road	-	-	-	-	-	-
	City traffic	27.19	27.57	27.23	82.97	24	2831
Bicycle	Urban road	18.37	11.79	28.71	76.82	6	1838
	City traffic	-	-	-	-	-	-
Person	Urban road	41.90	39.56	45.06	77.50	284	16235
	City traffic	37.69	35.12	41.2	66.6	417	21222
Motorcycle	Urban Road	26.64	25.47	30.84	73.75	69	3067
	City traffic	36.63	34.9	38.91	69.4	74	3541
Bus	Urban Road	7.04	4.65	10.66	82.96	6	281
	City traffic	-	-	-	-	-	-
Traffic Sign	Urban road	47.99	38.71	60.32	78.90	211	11658
	City traffic	44.33	34.08	58.63	70.76	314	9215
Traffic Light	Urban road	27.62	22.55	35.79	76.22	35	1580
	City traffic	39.53	37.75	41.92	65.03	11	118

Table 2. Performance evaluation of the perception module.

Platform	Configuration	Latency↓	Precision	Layers quantized
PC	**CPU**	180 ms	32 bits	None
	CUDA	23 ms	32 bits	None
	TensorRT	9 ms	16 bits	None
TDA4VM	**Floating-point**	60 ms	16 bits	None
	Mixed	30 ms	8 & 16 bits	Frst and last layer in 16 bit
	Fixed point	26 ms	8 bits	All the layers

with TensorRT, it becomes evident that there exists a substantial trade-off in terms of cost-effectiveness associated with this advantage. However, by leveraging these embedded systems, it becomes feasible to implement high-end deep learning solutions at a cost-effective level, ensuring compatibility with the actual needs of autonomous driving systems. This module is integrated with the others components, enabling parallel execution with other available hardware resources. This parallelization ensures optimal hardware utilization throughout the entire pipeline.

This capability of embedded systems makes them an ideal choice for the scalability of C-ITS, as they can seamlessly integrate with all necessary software and hardware components to achieve optimal performance. By harnessing the potential of embedded systems, C-ITS can be designed to deliver reliable and efficient operation in a cost-effective manner, thereby enhancing accessibility for consumers.

8.3 Communication Evaluation

The ETSI establishes a maximum end-to-end latency of 100 ms as a service requirement for information sharing for automated driving between User Equipment (UE) supporting V2X application [3]. This end-to-end latency is measured at the application level. In order to evaluate our communication module, we monitored the end-to-end latency of our system, and compared the results with the 100 ms latency requirement.

To monitor the end-to-end latency, we set up two nodes, 5 m away from each other, and measured round-trip time (RTT). The sender attached its CPU clock (at the application level) to the CPM in the *generationDeltaTime* field. Once the message arrived at the receiver, the receiver sent the message back to the sender without any message modification. The sender can compare current local CPU clock with the CPU clock included in the message retransmitted from the receiver. In this evaluation, we use half of RTT as the communication latency. The measurements were conducted for one hour, and with a varying number of up to 40 perceived virtual objects per message, this includes different field information such as position or identifier, we do not include any features from the image. The measurements were performed in an open public area, which means the delay can be affected by uncontrollable environmental interference.

Table 3 shows the average latency obtained in our experiments, as well as the standard deviation, 95th and 99th percentile, maximum latency, and the percentage of CPMs with a latency lower than the 100 ms threshold. These metrics are dissected for different sizes of CPMs, as the number of objects included in the message affected in the latency. Overall, up to 20 perceived objects, the end-to-end latency requirement was always fulfilled. For CPM messages with more than 20 perceived objects, the end-to-end latency was still under 100 ms in over 99% of the messages.

Table 3. Metrics from CPM end-to-end latency tests, in milliseconds, for different sizes of CPMs.

Number of Objects	Mean	σ	95%	99%	Max	% of CPMs under 100 ms
0 - 10	42.57	12.83	63.00	66.00	92.00	100%
11 - 20	51.32	13.87	73.00	82.31	88.00	100%
21 - 30	57.32	14.04	78.00	90.00	105.00	99.91%
31 - 40	61.43	14.70	84.00	97.00	113.00	99.44%

8.4 System Limits

After completing the implementation and integration of our functional system, we conducted field tests to validate the expected functionality of the system. As we previously mentioned, we verified with different metrics that each of the components were functioning properly and integrated with each other as intended. Therefore, real-world scenarios were utilized to validate the expectations of the whole system, see Fig. 8. The primary use case for testing the system was to evaluate its ability to detect a pedestrian crossing the street when the transmitter vehicle could observe them but the receiver could not in real-time. We validated the system's ability to appropriately transmit and receive detection information via the V2X module in real-time, visualizing it in the LDM and we verified that the Collision Warning application could alert the driver before visual confirmation. Our results demonstrated that the system consistently and successfully performed this task, meeting the set expectations and functioning of all system components.

During the field tests, we discovered areas of opportunity for system enhancement. One notable aspect to consider is the precision of the perception module's detection capabilities, especially when it comes to accurately locating objects situated at a considerable distance from the vehicle in three-dimensional space. While the system demonstrated commendable performance across various scenarios, achieving really precise object localization in 3D, in these particular instances, posed a challenge. In C-ADAS, where ensuring effective communication among receiving vehicles and maintaining the precision of the elements inserted in the LDM are areas of consideration, the 2D to 3D projection module presents itself as an aspect worthy of attention for further improvement. However, it is worth highlighting that the proposed system boasts a versatile design, empowering us to explore alternative perception approaches and integrate more advanced detection methods or state-of-the-art algorithms.

Overall, the system validation demonstrated that our functional system is capable of performing its intended tasks consistently. We also identified the system's limitations and are working to improve its performance in those areas.

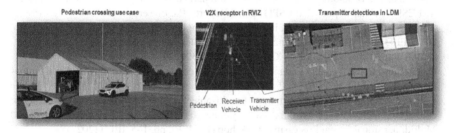

Fig. 8. The left image depicts the pedestrian use case, in which the transmitter vehicle is able to detect the pedestrian while the receiver vehicle cannot. The central image displays the detections received via V2X in RVIZ in the receiver vehicle. The rightmost image depicts all the detections transmitted by the transmitter vehicle and visualized in the LDM.

9   Conclusions

In conclusion, our perception system has demonstrated real-time detection capabilities, effectively showcasing the feasibility and effectiveness of embedded systems in C-ADAS. Our study provides a compelling case for C-ADAS, emphasizing their engineering feasibility, and achieving real-time end-to-end latency for communications in day 2 services of C-ITS. The interconnection between modules enables scalable and streamlined development in a platform specifically designed for OEMs, facilitating a simple and efficient workflow. In addition, there is potential for scalability through increased inter-unit communication. Moving forward, our future work focuses on improving camera-based detection algorithms to enhance the accuracy of the detected object sent via CPM. In order to mitigate redundant detections in LDM, it is necessary to incorporate an association of perceived objects originating from different CPMs. We also plan to perform an in-depth analysis of the C-ADAS system using synthetic data due to the complexity of the validation using real scenario data.

Acknowledgments. This work has received funding from the Ministerio de Ciencia, Innovación y Universidades of the Spanish Government, programme "Misiones CDTI", under project "Movilidad2030" (EXP 00129266/MIG 20201040).

References

1. ETSI TR 103 562 V2.1.1, "Intelligent Transport Systems (ITS); Vehicular Communications; Basic Set of Applications; Analysis of the Collective Perception Service (CPS); Release 2" (2019)
2. Car-to-Car Communication Consortium. http://www.car-2-car.org (2023). Accessed 15 Dec 2023
3. 3GPP: Service requirements for enhanced v2x scenarios. Technical Specification (TS) 22.186, 3rd Generation Partnership Project (3GPP) (2019)
4. Andreone, L., Brignolo, R., Damiani, S., Sommariva, F., Vivo, G., Marco, S.: D8.1.1 - SAFESPOT Final Report. SAFESPOT Final Report - Public version (2010)
5. Chitnis, K., et al.: Novel OpenVX implementation for heterogeneous multi-core systems. In: 2017 IEEE International Conference on Consumer Electronics-Asia (ICCE-Asia), pp. 77–80 (2017). https://doi.org/10.1109/ICCE-ASIA.2017.8309323
6. Consortium, C.C.C., et al.: Guidance for day 2 and beyond roadmap. In: Car2Car Communication Consortium, C2CCC WP, vol. 2072 (2019)
7. Delgado, G., et al.: Virtual validation of a multi-object tracker with intercamera tracking for automotive fisheye based surround view systems. In: 2022 IEEE 14th Image, Video, and Multidimensional Signal Processing Workshop (IVMSP), pp. 1–5. IEEE (2022)
8. Eggert, J., Salazar, D.A., Puphal, T., Flade, B.: Driving situation analysis with relational local dynamic maps (R-LDM). FAST-Zero Symposium (2017)
9. Elleuch, I., Makni, A., Bouaziz, R.: Cooperative overtaking assistance system based on V2V communications and RTDB. Comput. J. 62(10), 1426–1449 (2019)
10. Elleuch, I., Makni, A., Bouaziz, R.: Cooperative advanced driver assistance systems: a survey and recent trends. In: Abraham, A., Piuri, V., Gandhi, N., Siarry, P., Kaklauskas, A., Madureira, A. (eds.) ISDA 2020. AISC, vol. 1351, pp. 160–170. Springer, Cham (2021). https://doi.org/10.1007/978-3-030-71187-0_15
11. ETSI, T.: Intelligent transport systems (ITS); vehicular communications; basic set of applications; part 2: specification of cooperative awareness basic service. Draft ETSI TS 20(2011), 448–451 (2011)
12. ETSI, T.: Intelligent Transport Systems (ITS); Access layer specification for Intelligent Transport Systems operating in the 5 GHz frequency band. EN 302(663), V1 (2013)
13. European Union: Roadmap for Service Implementation Beyond Initial Deployment. Technical report, Cooperative ITS Services Deployment Support (EU EIP-44) (2021)

14. García, M., Urbieta, I., Nieto, M., González de Mendibil, J., Otaegui, O.: ILDM: an interoperable graph-based local dynamic map. Vehicles **4**(1), 42–59 (2022). https://doi.org/10.3390/vehicles4010003

15. Garlichs, K., Günther, H.J., Wolf, L.C.: Generation rules for the collective perception service. In: 2019 IEEE Vehicular Networking Conference (VNC), pp. 1–8. IEEE (2019)

16. González-Saavedra, J.F., Figueroa, M., Céspedes, S., Montejo-Sánchez, S.: Survey of cooperative advanced driver assistance systems: from a holistic and systemic vision. Sensors **22**(8), 3040 (2022)

17. Goodall, N.J.: Potential crash rate benchmarks for automated vehicles. Transp. Res. Rec. **2675**(10), 31–40 (2021).https://doi.org/10.1177/03611981211009878

18. Hao, Y., et al.: TS-benchmark: a benchmark for time series databases. In: 2021 IEEE 37th International Conference on Data Engineering (ICDE), pp. 588–599 (2021). https://doi.org/10.1109/ICDE51399.2021.00057

19. Hussain, R., Zeadally, S.: Autonomous cars: research results, issues, and future challenges. IEEE Commun. Surv. Tutor. **21**(2), 1275–1313 (2018)

20. Koesdwiady, A., Soua, R., Karray, F., Kamel, M.S.: Recent trends in driver safety monitoring systems: state of the art and challenges. IEEE Trans. Veh. Technol. **66**(6), 4550–4563 (2016)

21. Lee, Y.J., Dadvar, S., Hu, J., Park, B.B.: Transit signal priority experiment in a connected vehicle technology environment. J. Transp. Eng. Part A Syst. **143**(8), 05017005 (2017). https://doi.org/10.1061/JTEPBS.0000062

22. Luiten, J., et al.: HOTA: a higher order metric for evaluating multi-object tracking. CoRR abs/2009.07736 (2020)

23. Massow, K., Thiele, F.M., Schrab, K., Bunk, B.S., Tschinibaew, I., Radusch, I.: Scenario definition for prototyping cooperative advanced driver assistance systems. In: 2020 IEEE 23rd International Conference on Intelligent Transportation Systems (ITSC), pp. 1–8. IEEE (2020)

24. Qu, C., Qi, W.Y., Wu, P.: A high precision and efficient time-to-collision algorithm for collision warning based V2X applications. In: 2018 2nd International Conference on Robotics and Automation Sciences (ICRAS), pp. 1–5 (2018)

25. Scholtes, M., et al.: 6-layer model for a structured description and categorization of urban traffic and environment (2021)

26. Shimada, H., Yamaguchi, A., Takada, H., Sato, K.: Implementation and evaluation of local dynamic map in safety driving systems. J. Transp. Technol. **05**(02), 102–112 (2015). https://doi.org/10.4236/jtts.2015.52010

27. Sualeh, M., Kim, G.W.: Visual-lidar based 3D object detection and tracking for embedded systems. IEEE Access **8**, 156285–156298 (2020). https://doi.org/10.1109/ACCESS.2020.3019187

28. Urbieta, I., Nieto, M., García, M., Otaegui, O.: Design and implementation of an ontology for semantic labeling and testing: automotive global ontology (ago). Appl. Sci. **11**(17) (2021). https://doi.org/10.3390/app11177782

29. Wang, K., Li, Z., Sun, Y., Qiao, X., Wang, F.Y.: An embedded system for vision-based driving environment perception. In: 2006 2nd IEEE/ASME International Conference on Mechatronics and Embedded Systems and Applications, pp. 1–5 (2006). https://doi.org/10.1109/MESA.2006.296998

30. Wang, P.: Research on comparison of lidar and camera in autonomous driving. In: Journal of Physics: Conference Series, vol. 2093(1), p. 012032 (2021). https://doi.org/10.1088/1742-6596/2093/1/012032

Weapon Detection Using PTZ Cameras

Juan Daniel Muñoz⬛, Jesus Ruiz-Santaquiteria⬛, Oscar Deniz$^{(\boxtimes)}$⬛,
and Gloria Bueno⬛

VISILAB, E.T.S. Ingeniería Industrial, University of Castilla-La Mancha, Ciudad Real, Spain
{juandaniel.munoz,jesus.ralegre,oscar.deniz,
gloria.bueno}@uclm.es

Abstract. Massive shooting in public places are a stigma in some countries. Computer vision techniques are being actively researched in the last few years to process video from surveillance cameras and immediately detect the presence of an armed individual. The research, however, has focused on images taken from cameras that are (as is the typical case) far from the entrance where the individual first appears. However, most modern video surveillance cameras have some pan-tilt-zoom (PTZ) capabilities, fully controllable by the operator or some control software. In this paper, we make the first (as far as the authors know) exploration on the use of PTZ cameras in this particular problem. Our results unequivocally reveal the transformative impact of integrating PTZ functionality, particularly zoom and tracking capabilities, on the overall performance of these weapon detection models. Experiments were carefully executed in controlled environments, including laboratory and classroom settings, allowing for a comprehensive evaluation. In these settings, the utility of PTZ in improving detection outcomes became evident, especially when confronted with challenging conditions such as dim lighting or multiple individuals in the scene. This research underscores the immense potential of modern PTZ cameras for automatic firearm detection. This advancement holds the promise of augmenting public safety and security.

Keywords: CCTV video surveillance · Weapon detection · PTZ cameras · Object detection

1 Introduction

Public safety and the prevention of criminal acts are fundamental concerns in our society. In this context, weapon detection has become a priority to ensure secure environments in both public and private spaces. Incidents of armed violence, such as mass shootings, armed robberies, and acts of terrorism, have increased in frequency and magnitude worldwide, leading to a growing demand for effective weapon detection technologies.

Early and accurate detection of weapons is essential for timely prevention and response to risk situations. Identifying individuals carrying firearms, knives, or other dangerous objects allows for immediate intervention, thereby minimizing potential harm or loss of human lives. Furthermore, weapon detection contributes to deterring potential perpetrators and fosters a secure environment that promotes peace and people's confidence.

J. Filipe and J. Röning (Eds.): ROBOVIS 2024, CCIS 2077, pp. 100–114, 2024.
https://doi.org/10.1007/978-3-031-59057-3_7

Situations like the tragic shootings that have occurred in the United States (schools, shopping centers, etc.) could have been mitigated with early detection. The surveillance images captured in such cases show that it should be possible to detect the risk: the left image in Fig. 1 was captured from a security camera during the shooting at Columbine High School; the right image was captured during the shooting at Covenant School in Nashville in 2023.

Fig. 1. Left image: security camera footage of the shooting incident at Columbine. Right image: security camera footage of the shooting incident at Covenant. Sources: [7,10].

Computer vision research has considered the problem of automatically detecting an individual with a weapon. All of the published works, however, have considered images as taken from a static surveillance camera which is far from the individual. In such images the individual and the weapon appear with a small size and sometimes it is difficult even for human operators to discern both. While that is a realistic scenario, it misses on the opportunity of modern PTZ cameras. PTZ cameras have become more compact, and their cost has significantly dropped in the last years, making them a highly viable option when deploying CCTV surveillance systems.

In this paper, we make the first (as far as the authors know) exploration on the use of PTZ cameras in this particular problem of automatic weapon detection from a distance. Two CNN based on object (firearm) detection architectures were used: Faster R-CNN [15] and EfficientDet [17]. The objective of the study is to assess if PTZ capabilities allow for more efficient firearm detection.

The rest of the article is structured as follows. Section 2 reviews existing work on handgun detection using surveillance cameras. Section 3 describes the proposed method. The experiments carried out and the results obtained are summarized in Sect. 4. Finally, conclusions and future work are presented in Sect. 5.

2 Related Work

The detection of weapons has been a subject of intense research and development for several decades and has recently experienced significant advancements due to progress in computer vision and machine learning. Below, we provide a brief review of some articles that have addressed this topic.

In [1], an approach based on deep learning techniques is proposed for real-time weapon detection in CCTV videos. Convolutional Neural Networks (CNNs) are employed to extract discriminant features (shape and texture) and classify images as weapons or non-weapons.

In [16], automatic weapon detection in security systems is also proposed using deep learning techniques. This article describes a study based on three Convolutional Neural Networks (CNNs) applied to the automatic detection of weapons in images extracted from surveillance videos. The models take into consideration not only the discriminant features of potential weapons (shape and texture) but also the pose of the individual carrying the weapon. Thus, the model is provided not only with the (image of the) weapon itself but also with information about the body pose of the individual. As can be expected, this contributed to achieving improved results.

Other relevant studies can be discussed, such as [6]. In this research, the objective is to develop a real-time threat level detection system and the classification of targets (i.e. humans, vehicles, weapons) intended for use in border security. To detect and classify the targets, the authors used an object detector based on the classic Viola-Jones method [18].

With respect to PTZ cameras, in [11], an automated video surveillance system is designed. In that research, the proposed system detects anomalous objects with respect to the object type. The raw object detections are supplied by a convolutional neural network. The system does not need any manually labelled data, since a nonparametric probabilistic model of the object types normally found in the scene is learned in an unsupervised way. A kernel density estimator based on the Dirichlet distribution is proposed for this purpose. The probabilistic model yields an estimation of the probability that an object is anomalous. This information is passed on to a camera control module, which follows and focuses on the object (thanks to the PTZ camera movements, which allow accurate tracking) which is most likely to be anomalous in the current field of view.

In [3], PTZs are proposed for their usage in public places, private security, and military operations. The formal 'PTZ Search Problem' (PTZSP) is introduced, in which a stationary PTZ camera must navigate in a three-dimensional space to detect objects of interest. Rewards and penalties are assigned for each correct and incorrect detection, respectively, as well as for the time expended. The PTZSP is related to the Orienteering Problem with Functional Profits (OPFP) [12], but due to the vast search space, it is challenging to address with existing algorithms. The article proposed a series of simulations in large outdoor environments and various algorithms to solve the PTZSP.

In other works, such as [5], an approach based on background subtraction is proposed for the detection of moving objects in image sequences captured with PTZ cameras. This approach introduces a neural network-based method where the background model adapts automatically and self-organizes to changes in the scene background. A series of experiments with real image sequences are conducted, demonstrating the effectiveness of the presented approach.

As mentioned above, there is no evidence of work where PTZ cameras are utilized for the automatic detection of weapons. The recent lines of research where the body pose and even hand pose (see the recent work [2]) are considered as additional cues show that there is potential for the use of PTZ capabilities in this problem.

3   Tracking/Zoom System

Within the context of this research, the focus is directed towards the most pivotal component: the proposed method for tracking potential handguns. This method represents the cornerstone of our work, as it addresses the critical need for enhanced security measures and real-time threat detection. The method starts from a weapon detector that performs a first detection, which should then be confirmed or discarded thanks to the PTZ capabilities.

This system can be divided in the following steps:

1. Starting from an initial static camera position (Pan = 0.5; Tilt = 0.2; Zoom = 0.0), when a first detection occurs, the current Pan-Tilt-Zoom parameters are obtained, and the camera adjusts its Pan-Tilt to align the detection's bounding box with the center of the frame (with a certain tolerance). This is accomplished by comparing the center of the detection's bounding box with the center of the frame (with a resolution of 640 × 480 pixels in this case).
2. Once it is centered, a zooming procedure begins on the bounding box. Zoom is only applied when the bounding box is centered, meaning that even if zoom has already been applied, if there is any misalignment in the frame, the camera readjusts to the bounding box before continuing to zoom.
3. The zoom is applied based on the size of the bounding box relative to the frame. In other words, if the handgun is far away and a significant amount of zoom has been applied, and suddenly it starts getting closer, with excessive zoom, it would become indistinguishable. To ensure that the bounding box still fits within the frame and the handgun remains visible, the zoom is reduced. This is achieved by dynamically modifying the zoom value at any time depending on the current zoom value.
4. Furthermore, in addition to this, when the camera starts detecting and initiates tracking, if there is no further detection within 3 s from the last one, the camera returns to its initial position in search for a new detection.

To convert the horizontal and vertical distances between the centers of the bounding box and the frame into Pan and Tilt distances (both Pan and Tilt typically have values ranging from 0 to 1) the distances are linearly scaled to values between 0 and 1, which are then passed to a function that moves the camera in Pan and Tilt as necessary. The camera's adjustment also depends on the zoom applied at any given moment, as higher zoom requires smaller adjustments. Expression 1 is used to transform values relative to the frame into values ranging from 0 to 1. The expression provided is for Pan, and a similar approach is applied to Tilt. It is important to note that if the target value is outside these ranges, the camera moves to the minimum or maximum values accordingly.

$$npp = pp + [a - b] \cdot (c - zp) \tag{1}$$

where:

$$a = \frac{dx - dminp}{dmaxp - dminp} \cdot (nmax - nmin) + nmin \qquad (2)$$

$$b = \frac{ref - dminp}{dmaxp - dminp} \cdot (nmax - nmin) \qquad (3)$$

The variables in Expressions 1, 2, 3 are defined as:

- **npp**: the target Pan setting.
- **pp**: the current Pan.
- **dx**: the difference in the x-axis between the center of the frame and the center of the bounding box.
- **dminp**: equal to $\frac{-\text{frame width}}{2}$, which represents the maximum negative horizontal distance between the center of the frame and the center of the bounding box.
- **dmaxp**: equal to $\frac{\text{frame width}}{2}$, which represents the maximum positive horizontal distance between the center of the frame and the center of the bounding box.
- **nmax**: the maximum value in the new range, which is 1.
- **nmin**: the minimum value in the new range, which is 0.
- **ref**: the reference value in the original range [dminp, dmaxp], which is 0.
- **c**: a constant obtained based on the current zoom.
- **zp**: the current zoom value.

4 Experiments

This section provides an overview of the experimental setup and methodology employed in this study. Prior to delving into the specifics, a brief summary of the objectives is presented. Our objective is to compare the effect of PTZ in this problem, with respect to the use of a static non-PTZ camera. Thus, in our case we capture the same scene using two PTZ cameras: one static and the other effectively utilizing the PTZ movements. To ensure uniform conditions. Note that two identical PTZ cameras have been employed to use the same type of sensor and ensure identical conditions. The static camera covers a larger field of view, while the PTZ-enabled camera will adjust and zoom in on any detected handguns.

4.1 Experimental Setup

The cameras used are HIKVISION IP PTZ cameras (HiWatch Series, specifically the model HWP-N2204IH-DE3 [8]). They are positioned side by side, securely mounted on a wooden base (covered with black vinyl) on a tripod to ensure that the captured images are nearly identical (see Figs. 2, 3).

In the experiments, both cameras record video and start the recording at the same time. Firstly, they move to a position of 0.5 in pan (midpoint) and 0.2 in tilt, with the zoom set to 0 (a range between 0 and 1 has been chosen for these values, using the ONVIF protocol). Meanwhile, the camera that applies the real-time model adjusts its PTZ values based on detections, while the other camera remains static. Furthermore, if

Fig. 2. Assembly of PTZ cameras. Left image: position for recording experiments. Right image: attachment of the base.

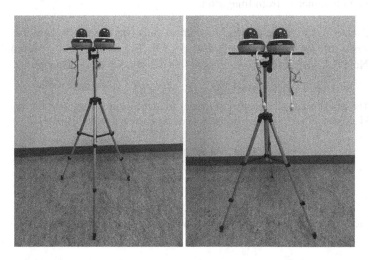

Fig. 3. Assembly of PTZ cameras. Left image: front view. Right image: rear view (Ethernet cable power connection).

the PTZ has already moved from the initial position due to a first handgun detection and then no further detection is obtained 3 s (a user-selected value), it returns to its original position to reevaluate the area.

Of all the possible bounding boxes detected within the same frame, we only take the one with the highest score returned by the model. We retain a single detection per frame, as we evaluate a realistic situation in which, normally, at most, only one gun appears in the scene.

From the generated videos, the bounding box information for each frame is exported to JSON files, which are then compared with their corresponding ground truth annotations (based on Intersection over Union, IoU). By comparing the JSON files (which follow the COCO format in this case), results are obtained.

A wide range of situations has been studied (variations in clothes, lighting conditions, handgun positions, movements, recording angles, etc.) to demonstrate the aforementioned points.

4.2 Model Training

In order to analyze these situations and demonstrate the main objective, it is necessary to train the handgun detection architectures mentioned above (Faster R-CNN and EfficientDet), which are representative of existing work on the subject.

- **Faster R-CNN:** the implementation used for this architecture is available in the Torchvision library [14]. The ResNet101 backbone pretrained on ImageNet [4] was used.
- **EfficientDet:** the implementation used for this architecture is available at [19]. In this case, the "tf efficientnetv2 l" architecture was used as the backbone, also with pretrained parameters from ImageNet.

The dataset used for the training of both models was the pistol dataset created by the University of Granada in a seminal work [13]. The dataset split is summarized in Table 1. Note that there is only one class in this dataset, which is "Handgun".

Table 1. The table displays the number of images from the dataset designated for training, validation, and testing of the detectors. The dataset comprises a total of 3000 images.

Train	Validation	Test	All
2160	240	600	3000

The selected values for the main hyperparameters are included in Table 2.

Table 2. Hyperparameters selected for the training of the detectors. The number of epochs is the number of times the model is trained on the entire dataset; the batch size indicates the number of training examples used in each weight update step during training; the learning rate is a value that determines how much the model's weights should be adjusted in each training step. It controls the rate at which the model learns; the optimizer is an algorithm that adjusts the model's weights during training to minimize the loss function.

	Faster R-CNN	EfficientDet
Number of epochs	50	50
Batch size	4	8
Learning rate	0.001	0.001
Optimizer	SGD	AdamW

4.3 Results

The behavior of the system is studied in various scenarios. The following points outline the cases studied and their corresponding results. This allows for a final comparison between models and situations. In this case, an IoU threshold of 0.2 has been selected to obtain the results. It is an appropriate value in this case because the ground truth bounding boxes are much smaller than those generated by the model. This means that, although both bounding boxes highlight the handgun, with a relatively high IoU threshold, it is not considered a true positive (even though it is) due to the size difference in the bounding boxes (see Fig. 4).

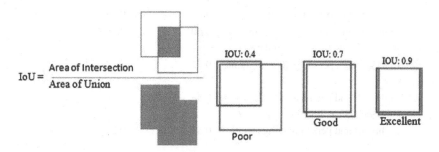

Fig. 4. The image illustrates how Intersection over Union (IoU) is calculated. It is a commonly used evaluation metric in object detection tasks, as it measures the degree of overlap between two bounding boxes. Three cases with different overlaps are shown. As seen in the first case, even though the same object is being identified, the difference in size between the bounding boxes results in a low IoU, potentially leading to a false negative. This is why a small IoU threshold has been chosen. Source: [9].

The metrics used for performance assessment are: *Precision* or ratio of correctly detected objects over all positive predictions of a certain class, *Recall*, or ratio of correctly detected objects over all ground truth objects of a certain class, and *F1-score*, defined as the harmonic mean of precision and recall. In the result tables, only F1-score values (0 to 1 range) are shown.

Different situations were recorded in two locations: a laboratory and a classroom. Also, we studied: variations in clothes, lighting conditions, handgun positions, movements, recording angles, etc. It is important to mention that both cameras, the static PTZ (referred to as the static camera hereafter) and the PTZ camera that applies its characteristics movements (referred to as the PTZ camera hereafter), have been configured in the same way and they apply the model in the same way as well. The only difference between both cameras is that one applies tracking/zoom while the other one remains internally static.

Results with Faster R-CNN. It is important to mention that when applying the model, a confidence threshold of 0.8 was chosen. This means that the model only considers bounding boxes with a score equal to or higher than 0.8, which was selected to mitigate false positives. Additionally, the videos recorded with this model have an average of approximately 150 frames (about 15 s of recording at around 10 FPS).

The results obtained with this detector in the laboratory are shown in Table 3.

Table 3. Results obtained with the Faster R-CNN detector in the laboratory. Various scenarios have been studied, such as how the individual carries the handgun (aggressive aiming or calmly, lowered, without aiming at anyone), variations in lighting conditions at the location, among others. Two columns show the F1-score values obtained for both PTZ and static cameras.

Situation	F1-score PTZ camera	F1-score Static camera
Lights on and person moving away	0.64	0.40
Lights on and person approaching from a distance, then moving away	0.60	0.51
Lights on and person with a handgun down	0.72	0.12
Lights off and person approaching from a distance, then moving away	0.55	0.28
Lights off and person moving away	0.81	0.28

Figure 5 shows an example of the situations analyzed. In this case, a person moves farther away from the camera. Two captures from the PTZ camera's recorded video are shown. In the left image of the figure, there is an initial detection (the bounding box of the detection is a green rectangle) while the camera is in its initial position. In the right frame, it can be seen how the camera has adjusted to the bounding box of the detection and zoomed in, providing a better view of the handgun. This zoom-in helps with subsequent detections.

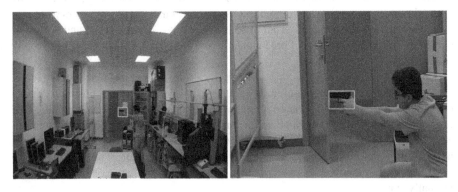

Fig. 5. The scenario involves the lights turned on, and a person moving away from the camera in a laboratory setting. In the left frame, the handgun is detected, and in the right frame the camera adjusts to the bounding box of the detection through Pan-Tilt-Zoom movements. **PTZ** camera. **Faster R-CNN** model.

If we now view the video generated from applying the model to the static camera and extract the same time moments as those shown in Fig. 5, we obtain the frames in Fig. 6. Comparing Figs. 5 and 6, both show detections. However, when looking at the right frames of both figures, the PTZ camera detects the "Handgun", whereas the second one does not. This demonstrates how centering the bounding box and applying zoom contribute to a higher number of detections.

Fig. 6. Scenario with lights on and a person moving away from the camera. Location: laboratory. In the left frame, the handgun is detected, while in the right frame it is not detected because the camera does not apply zoom, and the person moves too far away. **Static** camera. **Faster R-CNN** model.

Moving onto the other location, the classroom, the results obtained are shown in Table 4.

Table 4. Results obtained with the Faster R-CNN detector in the classroom. Various scenarios have been studied, such as the presence of two individuals in the scene, variations in clothes, among others. Two columns show the F1-score values obtained for both PTZ and static cameras.

Situation	F1-score PTZ camera	F1-score Static camera
Lights off and person moving around the scene	0.62	0.52
Lights off and person moving around the scene (2)	0.63	0.41
Lights off and person moving away	0.80	0.43
Lights on and multiple people in the scene	0.76	0.28
Lights on, handgun down, and multiple people	0.86	0.31

One of the studied situations in the classroom is shown in Fig. 7, where there are multiple individuals in the scenery: one with a mobile phone and another with a handgun. Zoom is particularly useful in such cases because it helps to eliminate false positives such as mobile phones (see the top two frames of the figure).

Fig. 7. Scenario with lights on and multiple people in the scene. Location: classroom. In the top left frame (**PTZ** camera), an initial detection is performed on a possible "Handgun". In the top right frame (**PTZ** camera), a significant zoom has been applied to the handgun, reducing false positives. In the bottom frame (**static** camera), a mobile phone is detected as a handgun (false positive). **Faster R-CNN** model.

The model applied to the recording from the static camera performs significantly worse, as evident from the obtained results. Since it does not focus on the handgun, it gives fewer detections and is subject to a higher number of false positives (see the bottom frame of Fig. 7).

Results with EfficientDet. When applying this network, a confidence threshold of 0.55 was chosen. This means that the model only considers bounding boxes with a score equal to or higher than 0.55. This model is not as good as the Faster R-CNN taking into account the obtained metrics. However, our goal is to demonstrate the improvement in the detection rate through the Pan-Tilt-Zoom movements of the camera, even if the model is not performing as good as in the previous case. Videos were recorded in the same locations, but fewer in number since many different cases have already been studied with the Faster R-CNN model. Additionally, the videos recorded with this model have an average of approximately 255 frames (about 15 s of recording at around 17 FPS).

Results obtained in the laboratory are shown in Table 5.

Table 5. Results obtained with the EfficientDet detector in the laboratory. Only a situation has been studied, as all of them have been studied with the other detector. Two columns show the F1-score values obtained for both PTZ and static cameras.

Situation	F1-score PTZ camera	F1-score Static camera
Lights on and person moving away	0.81	0.13

Results with this architecture in the classroom scenario are shown in Table 6.

Table 6. Results obtained with the Efficient detector in the classroom scenario. Various conditions have been studied, such as variations in clothes or in lightning, among others. Two columns show the F1-score values obtained for both PTZ and static cameras.

Situation	F1-score PTZ camera	F1-score Static camera
Lights on and person moving around the scene	0.35	0.10
Lights on and person moving away	0.23	0.13
Lights on and person moving away (2)	0.46	0.27
Lights off and person moving away	0.61	0.03

As shown in Fig. 8, zoom is crucial and the detector works better when PTZ movements are applied.

Fig. 8. Scenario with lights off and a person moving away from the camera. Location: classroom. In the left frame (**PTZ** camera), the handgun is detected after previous detections and zoom application. In the right frame (**static** camera), no detection occurs. **EfficientDet** model.

5   Conclusions and Future Work

Overall, the results show that the use of PTZ capabilities through the implementation of tracking code significantly improves the performance of deep learning models in this problem, as seen in the results tables (much better results when PTZ is employed). E.g., in the case of Faster R-CNN, it is evident that using zoom and tracking is especially important when the handgun is down (see Table 3).

It is worth highlighting that, similar to when the handgun is down, the use of zoom and tracking of the "Handgun" in the situation of multiple people in the scene is crucial. This helps to avoid many false positives (see F1-score values in Table 4).

Comparing models, Faster R-CNN generally provides better results. This is because, as mentioned earlier, EfficientDet does not detect that well in this particular case. A possible solution to this would be lowering the IoU threshold for EfficientDet. However, this could lead to an increment of false negatives, which is undesirable. Also, the architecture could be retrained in order to detect better, but the training of the neural networks is not critical in this study, as the intention is to demonstrate the improvement of the networks when using PTZ capabilities, rather than emphasizing the quality of the models in detection, as seen, e.g., in Table 5. Also, looking at Table 6, when the person moves away from the camera with the lights off, the usage of the tracking/zoom system is clearly significant.

It can be concluded that the objective that motivated the completion of this work has been successfully achieved, demonstrating that the use of PTZ cameras with a tracking/zoom system in the field of video surveillance, and more specifically in handgun detection, provides a significant improvement.

The implemented tracking system presents some limitations, such as locking onto a false positive, preventing it from detecting real handguns. This could be addressed by having the camera return to its initial position after a certain amount of time once tracking has started or, in situations with multiple potential handguns with high confidence, by tracking/zooming to cover all of them. Related to this, it would be interesting to explore scenarios with multiple detections instead of just one, as done in this work (the single detection assumption was made considering a lone shooter, as mentioned earlier). Also, achieving precise tracking/zoom in situations with very rapid movements that could cause the handgun to go out of frame, especially after applying a significant amount of zoom, is essential. Optimizing architectures with the TensorRT library could be considered to increase FPS performance, enabling the camera to react more quickly and make adjustments more frequently. Finally, we could point its ineffectiveness in distant situations initially, as it is necessary for the handgun to be close enough to the camera for an initial detection to occur. Only then can tracking/zoom be initiated, which will be effective in distant situations thereafter.

Future work shall also consider experiments with weapons other than handguns and scenes with multiple handguns.

As demonstrated, there are still many aspects to improve, but this initial exploration has shown that this system indeed offers more advantages than disadvantages.

Acknowledgements. This work is part of project DISARM, Grant PDC2021-121197, funded by MCIN/AEI/ 10.13039/501100011033 and "European Union NextGenerationEU/PRTR". The work has been partially funded by the following projects: SBPLY/21/180501/000025 by the Autonomous Government of Castilla-La Mancha and the European Regional Development Fund (ERDF), and dAIEdge Grant n. 101120726 by the European Commission. Author J. Ruiz-Santaquiteria was supported by Postgraduate Grant from the Spanish Ministry of Science, Innovation, and Universities (grant number PRE2018-083772).

References

1. Bhatti, M.T., Khan, M.G., Aslam, M., Fiaz, M.J.: Weapon detection in real-time CCTV videos using deep learning. IEEE Access **9**, 34366–34382 (2021)
2. Chatterjee, R., Chatterjee, A.: Pose4gun: a pose-based machine learning approach to detect small firearms from visual media. Multimed. Tools Appl. 1–27 (2023)
3. David, P., Harrison, A., Sreenivas, R., Whitman, J.: Context-Aware Visual Search Using a Pan-Tilt-Zoom Camera. Army Research Laboratory, Aberdeen Proving Ground, MD (2023)
4. Deng, J., Dong, W., Socher, R., Li, L.J., Li, K., Fei-Fei, L.: ImageNet: a large-scale hierarchical image database. In: 2009 IEEE Conference on Computer Vision and Pattern Recognition, pp. 248–255. IEEE (2009)
5. Ferone, A., Maddalena, L., Petrosino, A.: Neural moving object detection by pan-tilt-zoom cameras. In: Apolloni, B., Bassis, S., Esposito, A., Morabito, F. (eds.) Neural Nets and Surroundings. SIST, vol. 19, pp. 129–138. Springer, Heidelberg (2013). https://doi.org/10.1007/978-3-642-35467-0_14
6. Goyal, A., et al.: Automatic border surveillance using machine learning in remote video surveillance systems. In: Hitendra Sarma, T., Sankar, V., Shaik, R. (eds.) Emerging Trends in Electrical, Communications, and Information Technologies. LNEE, vol. 569, pp. 751–760. Springer, Singapore (2020). https://doi.org/10.1007/978-981-13-8942-9_64
7. Hernández, E.: Tiroteo en Nashville: cronología de la tragedia en The Covenant School. La Opinión (2023). https://laopinion.com/2023/03/29/tiroteo-en-nashville-cronologia-de-la-tragedia-en-the-covenant-school/
8. HI-WATCH: HWP-N2204IH-DE3 PTZ Camera Specifications (2014). https://www.hi-watch.eu/en-us/product/2014/network-ptz/2-0-mp-4-ir-network-ptz-camera. Accessed 04 Oct 2023
9. Koirala, A., Walsh, K.B., Wang, Z., McCarthy, C.: Deep learning - method overview and review of use for fruit detection and yield estimation. Comput. Electron. Agric. **162**, 219–234 (2019)
10. Lara, A.: 1999: matanza en la escuela de Columbine. Economist & Jurist (2022). https://www.economistjurist.es/articulos-juridicos-destacados/1999-matanza-de-la-escuela-de-columbine
11. López-Rubio, E., Molina-Cabello, M.A., Castro, F.M., Luque-Baena, R.M., Marin-Jimenez, M.J., Guil, N.: Anomalous object detection by active search with PTZ cameras. Expert Syst. Appl. **181**, 115150 (2021)
12. Mukhina, K.D., Visheratin, A.A., Nasonov, D.: Orienteering problem with functional profits for multi-source dynamic path construction. PLoS ONE **14**(4), e0213777 (2019)
13. Olmos, R., Tabik, S., Herrera, F.: Automatic handgun detection alarm in videos using deep learning. Neurocomputing **275**, 66–72 (2018)
14. PyTorch Vision: Faster R-CNN - PyTorch Vision (2015). https://pytorch.org/vision/main/models/faster_rcnn.html. Accessed 05 Oct 2023
15. Ren, S., He, K., Girshick, R., Sun, J.: Faster R-CNN: towards real-time object detection with region proposal networks. In: Advances in Neural Information Processing Systems, vol. 28 (2015)

16. Salido, J., Lomas, V., Ruiz-Santaquiteria, J., Deniz, O.: Automatic handgun detection with deep learning in video surveillance images. Appl. Sci. **11**(13), 6085 (2021)
17. Tan, M., Pang, R., Le, Q.V.: EfficientDet: scalable and efficient object detection. In: Proceedings of the IEEE/CVF Conference on Computer Vision and Pattern Recognition, pp. 10781–10790 (2020)
18. Viola, P.A., Jones, M.J.: Rapid object detection using a boosted cascade of simple features. In: CVPR (1), pp. 511–518. IEEE Computer Society (2001). http://dblp.uni-trier.de/db/conf/cvpr/cvpr2001-1.html#ViolaJ01
19. Wightman, R.: Efficientdet-Pytorch (2022). https://github.com/rwightman/efficientdet-pytorch

Improving Semantic Mapping with Prior Object Dimensions Extracted from 3D Models

Abdessalem Achour[1,3(⊠)] [iD], Hiba Al Assaad[1] [iD], Yohan Dupuis[2] [iD], and Madeleine El Zaher[1] [iD]

[1] LINEACT CESI, Campus of Toulouse, 31670 Labège, France
{aachour,halassaad,melzaher}@cesi.fr
[2] LINEACT CESI, Paris La Dèfense, 92074 Paris, France
ydupuis@cesi.fr
[3] SMI Doctoral School, HESAM University, 75013 Paris, France

Abstract. Semantic mapping in mobile robotics has gained significant attention recently for its important role in equipping robots with a comprehensive understanding of their surroundings. This understanding involves enriching metric maps with semantic data, covering object categories, positions, models, relations, and spatial characteristics. This augmentation enables robots to interact with humans, navigate semantically using high-level instructions, and plan tasks efficiently. This study presents a novel real-time RGBD-based semantic mapping method designed for autonomous mobile robots. It focuses specifically on 2D semantic mapping in environments where prior knowledge of object models is available. Leveraging RGBD camera data, our method generates a primitive object representation using convex polygons, which is then refined by integrating prior knowledge. This integration involves utilizing predefined bounding boxes derived from real 3D object dimensions to cover real object surfaces. The evaluation, conducted in two distinct office environments (a simple and a complex setting) utilizing the MIR mobile robot, demonstrates the effectiveness of our approach. Comparative analysis showcases our method outperforming a similar state-of-the-art approach utilizing only RGBD data for mapping. Our approach accurately estimates occupancy zones of partially visible or occluded objects, resulting in a semantic map closely aligned with the ground truth.

Keywords: Semantic mapping · Data association · Prior knowledge

1 Introduction

Mobile robots are increasingly finding applications across a wide range of settings, including homes, offices, healthcare facilities, and manufacturing environments. To execute their tasks effectively, these robots rely on having an accurate and up-to-date map of their surroundings. Traditional mapping techniques have primarily focused on metric or topological maps, which ensure safe navigation but often lack vital information about the environment, such as object categories and spatial relationships [1]. However, certain tasks demand a more profound cognitive understanding of the environment, such as human-robot collaboration, semantic navigation [2], and object manipulation. Additionally, robots are increasingly transitioning from specialized, single-task machines to

J. Filipe and J. Röning (Eds.): ROBOVIS 2024, CCIS 2077, pp. 115–133, 2024.
https://doi.org/10.1007/978-3-031-59057-3_8

general-purpose systems that operate in diverse environments. To address these challenges, semantic mapping emerges as a promising approach, enriching maps with high-level semantic knowledge, including object categories, shapes, 3D models, and object relationships. This enrichment allows robots to effectively generalize knowledge, learn, and be transparent in their decision-making processes [3].

Our research delves into indoor semantic mapping within the framework of a digital twin—a virtual replica that mirrors real-world entities in real-time. The fast integration of this technology across various applications, such as manufacturing [4], and the numerous studies interested in its adoption in other domains like agriculture [5,6], motivates our focus. Our methodology involves continuously updating a semantic map within the digital twin, providing real-time information on object categories, positions, and occupancy zones. This integrated semantic map serves as a supervision and analysis tool, facilitating swift responses during challenges and significantly enhancing the capabilities of robots. Consequently, robots can adapt their tasks promptly to changing surroundings, have increased flexibility and real-time decision-making capabilities.

Existing literature outlines two approaches to semantic mapping: 2D and 3D. In 2D mapping, the aim is object localization and identification, while 3D mapping delves into the spatial characteristics of objects [7,8]. Choice depends on the intended application. For tasks like semantic navigation [2], a 2D map suffices, enabling navigation using high-level instructions like "Go to the kitchen" or "Transport the box to the garage". Conversely, object manipulation demands 3D models for spatial understanding [9]. Context also matters, in environments where 3D models of objects are available beforehand, prioritizing 2D mapping can be efficient. Real-time applications might favor 2D data for timely decision-making. However, scenarios requiring complex object manipulation, augmented reality applications, and surface mapping in fields like archaeology or geological exploration, necessitate 3D mapping for accuracy.

In the domain of digital twins with accessible 3D models, the need for extensive transmission of additional 3D data might be mitigated. As a result, our research is currently directed towards refining precise 2D mapping, aiming to leverage existing 3D models to streamline data exchange and potentially enhance operational effectiveness. Prior 2D mapping works relied solely on sensor data. For instance, Zhao et al. [10] proposed a solution that incorporates voice instructions to annotate an occupancy grid map with object labels. In contrast, Qi et al. [11] present a different approach, enabling the incorporation of object topological information into an occupancy grid map. This involves utilizing an object detection model and a triangulation algorithm, leveraging odometry and stereo vision data to identify objects within point clouds. Subsequently, they employ minimum bounding rectangles to represent the topological space based on labeled point clouds. Additionally, Zaenker et al. [9] utilize RGBD data to represent the occupancy zones of objects on the occupancy map using polygons. Their approach involves extracting object point clouds and simultaneously labeling them using a detection model. They employ the Quickhull algorithm [12] to approximate the occupation zones from these labeled point clouds. Similarly, Dengler et al. [13] propose an RGBD-based solution. They employ a CNN-based detection model and a segmentation algorithm to identify object point clouds. Then, the occupation zones of objects are determined from the labeled points clouds. Each object's point cloud was projected onto the map plane, and the Quickhull algorithm was used to represent the object's occupation zone through polygons. Furthermore, they introduce a more accurate representation using oriented bounding boxes.

Beyond object recognition, studies have focused on semantic place categorization using sensor data, intending to enable autonomous robots to discern area-specific semantic labels akin to human perception, such as "office" or "kitchen" [14]. Recent methodologies leverage diverse technologies: Hiller et al. [15] utilize 2D laser sensor data, employing image patches from 2D occupancy maps as input for Convolutional Neural Networks (CNNs) to determine precise locations. Kaleci et al. [16] employ a 2D deep learning architecture, annotating occupancy grid maps using laser data, while Posada et al. [17] use CNNs to categorize omnidirectional camera images.

Clearly, the majority of prior works in 2D semantic mapping relied solely on sensor data. In contrast, the focal point of our approach lies in 2D mapping, introducing a major novelty: how to integrate prior knowledge into the semantic mapping process to enhance the quality of the created map ? This approach distinguishes our work from existing methodologies, as it strategically leverages prior knowledge to augment the mapping process. Specifically, in this paper, we propose an RGBD-based semantic mapping solution that utilizes real object models to improve the approximation of the 2D occupation zone of objects. Our solution enables the approximation of complete occupancy zones of objects, even when only partial object representations are available. It achieves this by utilizing predefined bounding boxes derived from the real dimensions of objects extracted from 3D models. The primary advantage of our approach lies in its ability to estimate the occupancy zones of partially visible or occluded objects, leading to a more accurate semantic map that closely aligns with ground truth. We assess the performance of our mapping solution in two distinct office settings and conduct a comparative analysis with an alternative semantic mapping method [13].

Our paper is organized as follows: In Sect. 2, we provide a brief description of the overall semantic mapping process, followed by a detailed description of our method for integrating prior object dimensions extracted from 3D models into the mapping process. In Sect. 3, we present our experimental results, including a discussion of the experimental setup, evaluation metrics, and results analysis. Finally, in Sect. 4, we summarize our findings and discuss potential avenues for improvement.

2   Method Description

In this research, we propose a real-time semantic mapping solution tailored for autonomous mobile robots, leveraging RGBD data. This paper specifically focuses on a novel association approach designed to generate 2D representations of semantic objects using both RGBD data and prior knowledge. The objective of our work is to deploy a semantic map onto a digital twin. This semantic map serves various purposes, primarily enhancing the capabilities of mobile robots and enabling them to perform more complex tasks. What sets our work apart is the utilization of prior knowledge provided by the digital twin, including information about objects existing in the environment and their numerical models. Additionally, our method is designed to be real-time, embeddable, and resource-efficient for deployment on a mobile robot, fulfilling the dual purpose of mapping the environment and updating the digital twin in real-time.

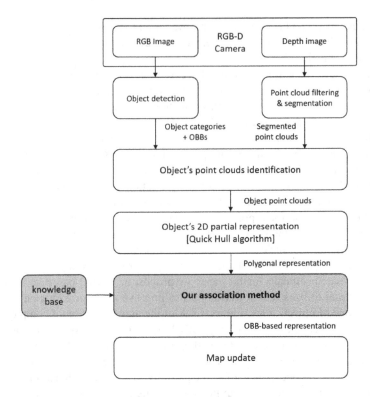

Fig. 1. Enhancing semantic object representation: Integration of our method within the semantic mapping process, based on the framework proposed in [13]. Modules highlighted in blue indicate the incorporation of prior knowledge for improved semantic object representation. (Color figure online)

The overall process is briefly summarized in the following section, followed by a detailed description of our approach.

2.1   The Overall Semantic Mapping Process

There are two major semantic mapping approaches in mobile robotics: mono-robot approaches and collaborative approaches. In mono-robot approaches, a single robot is used for semantic mapping, whereas collaborative approaches involve multiple agents, which can be robots or other entities, working together in various ways to create the semantic map. This paper is interested in mono-robot semantic mapping. Readers interested in collaborative semantic mapping can refer to our review paper [1], where we conducted an in-depth study of both approaches.

Existing literature presents several approaches for semantic mapping. Our method, depicted in Fig. 1, is proposed based on the RGBD-based approach introduced in [13]. This approach assumes the presence of an established occupancy grid map and knowledge of the global pose of the robot. The semantic mapping process involves employing

 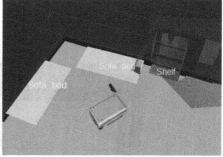

(a) Representation with Convex Polygons   (b) Representation with Rectangular Bounding Boxes

Fig. 2. Semantic object occupancy zone representation.

a detection model to identify objects within the RGB image, combined with a rapid segmentation algorithm for segmenting objects within the depth image. An association step establishes links between each object detection and its corresponding segment in the point cloud, creating object point clouds.

To represent the spatial extent of objects, our method projects object point clouds onto the ground plane and uses the Quickhull algorithm [12] to generate a convex polygonal representation of the object. We choose this algorithm for its computational simplicity and efficiency in approximating convex shapes from point sets. It produces streamlined object representations with minimal computational overhead, making it suitable for real-time mapping applications. Figure 2a illustrates object representations using convex polygons.

It's important to note that the generated polygonal representation captures only the observable portion of the object, as the robot's RGBD sensor detects partial aspects of objects within its operational range and field of view during navigation. To address this limitation, we incorporate prior knowledge of object dimensions from a pre-existing dataset of CAD models to construct a complementary rectangular bounding box representation, as shown in Fig. 2b. This integration of prior information significantly enhances the accuracy and consistency of the resulting map. Moreover, the mapping process is incremental, allowing the assimilation of new information to fill in missing details or update object shapes and positions.

In the following, we assume that the polygon representing the object at each time point has already been constructed using the Quickhull algorithm. We then focus on the association method for the generation of the bounding box representation.

2.2 Prior Knowledge

In our work, prior knowledge consists of a list of objects found in the environment. Each object is described by the dimensions length and width, represented respectively by l and w, of the rectangular bounding box enclosing its 2D projection to the ground. Indeed, bounding boxes are commonly used in many mapping approaches to represent the zone occupied by objects. They allow the representation of a wide variety of objects

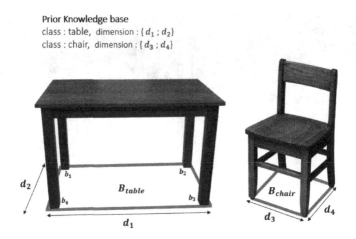

Fig. 3. Example of the prior knowledge base of objects existing in the environment.

in the real world, ranging from simple geometric shapes to complex structures. Even curved objects can often be enclosed within a bounding box that is large enough to contain it without excessive waste of space. Additionally, bounding boxes reduce the complexity of object representation, as they are defined by a few simple parameters such as the center point, orientation, and size.

In our case, the environment being considered is an office environment, so objects such as tables, chairs, desks, etc. may be present. We have adopted a strategy of employing a single model for each object category. This choice is driven by our core objective, which is to validate our mapping technique. While the consideration of multiple models does not currently influence our mapping process directly, it does introduce an additional challenge: the precise association of detections with the appropriate shape in our knowledge base. While this aspect is not our current primary focus, it remains a potential avenue for exploration in our future work.

For instance, when considering the "table" class, there is only one model present in the environment, and consequently, only one set of dimensions $\{l, w\}$ is stored in our prior knowledge base. Using these known dimensions, a predefined bounding box, denoted as $B_o = \{b_1, b_2, b_3, b_4\}$, with vertices defined in a clockwise direction, will be created to represent the occupancy of the object. Figure 3 shows an example of the prior knowledge and predefined bounding boxes for two objects: "table" and "chair".

2.3   2D Geometric Association Method

The objective of our method is to establish a connection between the predefined bounding box B_o and the partial polygon of the object denoted as O_t at time t. This association enables us to estimate the actual occupied area of the object from partial occupancy.

Our approach is designed to determine both the orientation and position of the object by identifying potential connections between the object's bounding box and the edges of its polygon. To accomplish this, we introduce a method involving the generation of

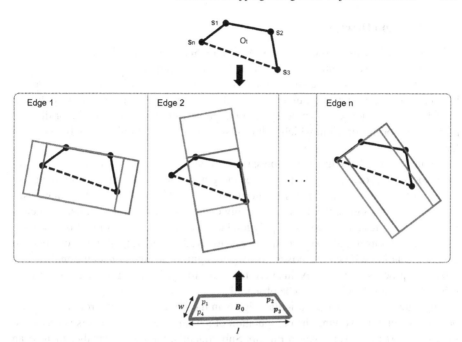

Fig. 4. Generation of candidate bounding boxes: O_t represents the polygon denoting the partial occupancy zone of the semantic object. The green and red boxes are two candidate options for augmenting this polygon. For each selected edge, the box orientation is determined by the edge's orientation, and two potential positions are proposed: the green box is positioned on the left side of the edge, aligned with its right extremum, while the red box is placed on the right side of the edge, aligned with its left extremum. Following the box generation process, the most suitable box will be chosen to represent the object. (Color figure online)

multiple candidate bounding boxes, followed by their association and evaluation, ultimately leading to the selection of the most suitable candidate to represent the object. The method is visually depicted in Fig. 4. In particular, we propose creating two bounding boxes for each edge of the polygon: one shifted to the left (indicated in green) and the other to the right (indicated in red). This approach results in a total of $2n$ potential candidates, each exhibiting distinct positions and orientations, where n represents the number of edges of the polygon. Given that each edge can be associated with either the length or the width of the object, we apply this reasoning initially with bounding box dimensions $\{l, w\}$, and subsequently with dimensions $\{w, l\}$, resulting in a total of $4n$ candidate bounding boxes.

To evaluate the quality of each candidate association, we calculate an association score for each, selecting the bounding box with the highest score to accurately represent the object.

2.4   Algorithm Description

Polygon Simplification and Foreground Edges Selection: The RGBD camera generates a high-density point cloud, leading to densely populated object point clouds. This density often causes over-segmented edges in polygons generated using the Quick-hull algorithm. Consequently, this issue significantly increases the number of potential bounding boxes and extends processing time. Furthermore, this density factor directly affects the scoring function, which will be discussed later, as it relies on polygon edges length.

To tackle this challenge, we propose the introduction of a simplification step before the association process. This step involves merging consecutive edges within the polygon, especially those with angles greater than $178°$. Although these edges may visually appear as a single edge, they are actually composed of multiple smaller segments. Figure 5a provides an example of a polygon before and after undergoing this process.

Moreover, our initial association process involved considering all polygon edges to generate candidate bounding boxes, leading to significant time consumption. To optimize this process, we now exclusively focus on foreground edges in relation to the robot, as they are more likely to be observed.

To determine whether a particular edge is in the foreground of the robot or not, we propose a method involving the computation of a triangle using the edge's vertices and the robot's position, as shown in Fig. 5b. Subsequently, we assess whether there is an intersection between this triangle and the object polygon. If no intersection is detected (the green triangle), the edge is considered to be in the foreground. Conversely, if an intersection is detected (the red triangle), the edge is not considered to be in the foreground. To compute this intersection, we employ the Weiler-Atherton clipping algorithm [18], which effectively clips the polygon using the triangle, generating a new polygon that represents the intersection region.

Establishing Local Reference Frames for Edges: To elucidate the process of generating bounding boxes, our methodology incorporates specific conditions. Firstly, we assume a consistent clockwise arrangement of vertices for the polygon, denoted as $O_t = \{s_i, i = 1, ..., n\}$ at time t. Simultaneously, we ensure that the vertices b_i of the resulting bounding boxes, referred to as $B_o = \{b_1, b_2, b_3, b_4\}$, also maintain a clockwise orientation.

After applying the Quickhull algorithm, the polygon vertices are represented in the global reference frame $R_0(o, \overrightarrow{x}, \overrightarrow{y})$ with coordinates (x_{s_i}, y_{s_i}). This global frame serves as the reference coordinate system for the semantic map and is crucial for the robot's localization and map updates.

Our association method entails the establishment of a local reference frame for each edge of the polygon. This frame serves the purpose of identifying candidate bounding boxes for the edge within its local context and defining the association features required for score computation. Subsequently, the box coordinates are transformed into the global frame to enable map updates. In what follows, we provide a detailed explanation of how the local frame is defined for each edge and the necessary transformations for transitioning between the global frame and the local frame, as well as the reverse transition.

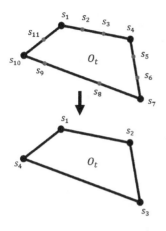

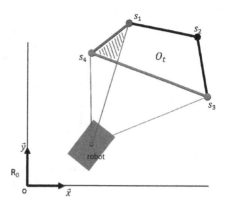

(a) Polygon simplification   (b) Foreground Edges identification

Fig. 5. Illustration of polygon simplification and selection of foreground edges: (a) The simplification step merges consecutive edges in the polygon with angles greater than 178°, resulting in the removal of all red vertices. The total number of edges in the polygon is reduced from 11 to 4. (b) The green edge is considered a foreground edge because there is no intersection between the green triangle and the polygon. In contrast, the red edge is not considered a foreground edge because there is an intersection between the red triangle and the polygon. (Color figure online)

For each edge, denoted as $e_i = \{s_i, s_{i+1}\}$ and represented by the two points s_i and s_{i+1}, we establish a local reference frame $R_i(s_i, \overrightarrow{u}, \overrightarrow{v})$ as shown in Fig. 6a. This local reference frame at point s_i is determined by two essential vectors: $\overrightarrow{u}$, which is a unit vector aligned with the direction of e_i, and $\overrightarrow{v}$, a unit normal vector to e_i pointing inward toward the polygon. Together, the pair of vectors $(\overrightarrow{u}, \overrightarrow{v})$ forms an orthonormal basis for the local reference frame at point s_i.

For $\overrightarrow{u}$, we express it as:

$$\overrightarrow{u} = \begin{bmatrix} \Delta_x & \Delta_y \end{bmatrix}^T \tag{1}$$

Here, Δ_x and Δ_y are determined as:

$$\Delta_x = \frac{x_{s_{i+1}} - x_{s_i}}{\|e_i\|} \qquad \Delta_y = \frac{y_{s_{i+1}} - y_{s_i}}{\|e_i\|}$$

where $\|e_i\|$ represents the norm of the edge. To derive $\overrightarrow{v}$, we apply a rotation of $-\pi/2$ to $\overrightarrow{u}$ using the rotation matrix R_θ :

$$\overrightarrow{v} = R_{\theta=-\pi/2}\,\overrightarrow{u} = \begin{bmatrix} \Delta_y & -\Delta_x \end{bmatrix}^T \tag{2}$$

Now, Eq. 3 is employed to establish the global coordinates (x_b, y_b) in the reference frame R_0 for a given point b based on local coordinates (α, β), as depicted in Fig. 6a:

$$\begin{bmatrix} x_b \\ y_b \end{bmatrix} = \begin{bmatrix} x_{s_i} \\ y_{s_i} \end{bmatrix} + \begin{bmatrix} \Delta_x & \Delta_y \\ \Delta_y & -\Delta_x \end{bmatrix} \begin{bmatrix} \alpha \\ \beta \end{bmatrix} \tag{3}$$

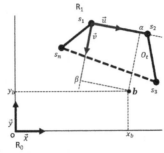

(a) Illustration of the local reference
defined for the first edge

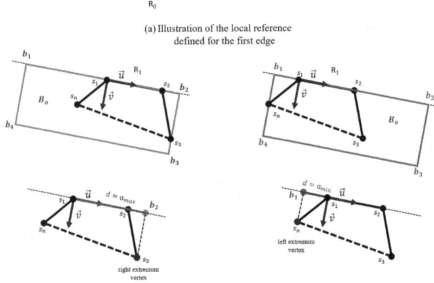

(b) Creation of the shifted left bounding box   (c) Creation of the shifted right bounding box

Fig. 6. Example of creating the predefined bounding boxes for the first edge.

Furthermore, the inverse transformation for Eq. 3 can be obtained as follows:

$$\begin{bmatrix} \alpha \\ \beta \end{bmatrix} = A^{-1}B \quad with \quad A = \begin{bmatrix} \Delta_x & \Delta_y \\ \Delta_y & -\Delta_x \end{bmatrix} \quad and \quad B = \begin{bmatrix} x_b - x_{s_i} \\ y_b - y_{s_i} \end{bmatrix} \qquad (4)$$

Here, the inverse of matrix A, denoted as A^{-1}, is given by :

$$A^{-1} = \frac{1}{det(A)} \begin{bmatrix} -\Delta_x & -\Delta_y \\ -\Delta_y & \Delta_x \end{bmatrix} \qquad (5)$$

With $det(A) = -1$, we can simplify the inverse transformation :

$$\begin{bmatrix} \alpha \\ \beta \end{bmatrix} = \begin{bmatrix} \Delta_x & \Delta_y \\ \Delta_y & -\Delta_x \end{bmatrix} \begin{bmatrix} x_b - x_{s_i} \\ y_b - y_{s_i} \end{bmatrix} \qquad (6)$$

Given Eq. 3 and Eq. 6, we have the ability to either transform the global polygon coordinates into local coordinates for the purpose of generating bounding boxes or utilize the inverse transformation to update the map.

Candidate Bounding Boxes Generation: Now that we have all the essential components in place, we outline the procedure for generating bounding boxes, a fundamental aspect of our solution. The steps for creating shifted bounding boxes within the global reference frame R_0 are as follows:

1. Generation of leftward shifted bounding box:
   - For a leftward shift (Fig. 6b), the Shift Distance (d) along the u-Axis is set to α_{max}, representing the α value of the extremum right vertex. The identification of the right extremum vertex involves calculating local coordinates (α, β) for all polygon vertices using Eq. 6. Subsequently, the vertex with the maximum α value is selected.
   - Further, determining the coordinates of b_2 involves aligning the bounding box edge b_{12} with e_i while ensuring that the edge b_{23} passes from the extremum right vertex with α value equal to α_{max}. Applying Eq. 7 gives the coordinates of b_2.

$$\begin{bmatrix} x_{b_2} \\ y_{b_2} \end{bmatrix} = \begin{bmatrix} x_{s_i} \\ y_{s_i} \end{bmatrix} + \alpha_{max} \, \overrightarrow{u} \tag{7}$$

   - After determining the coordinates of b_2, Eq. 8 is applied to compute coordinates for the remaining bounding box vertices.

$$\begin{bmatrix} x_{b_m} \\ y_{b_m} \end{bmatrix} = \begin{bmatrix} x_{b_2} \\ y_{b_2} \end{bmatrix} + a\overrightarrow{u} + b\overrightarrow{v} \tag{8}$$

   For $m = 1$, $a = -l$ and $b = 0$; for $m = 3$, $a = 0$ and $b = -w$; for $m = 4$, $a = -l$ and $b = -w$.

2. Generation of rightward shifted bounding box:
   - Conversely, for a rightward shift (Fig. 6c), the Shift Distance (d) is set to α_{min}, denoting the α of the extremum left vertex.
   - Further, determining the coordinates of b_1 involves aligning the bounding box edge b_{12} with e_i while ensuring that the edge b_{14} passes from the extremum left vertex with α value equal to α_{min}. Applying Eq. 9 gives the coordinates of b_1.

$$\begin{bmatrix} x_{b_1} \\ y_{b_1} \end{bmatrix} = \begin{bmatrix} x_{s_i} \\ y_{s_i} \end{bmatrix} + \alpha_{min} \, \overrightarrow{u} \tag{9}$$

   - After determining the coordinates of b_1, Eq. 10 is applied to compute coordinates for the remaining bounding box vertices.

$$\begin{bmatrix} x_{b_m} \\ y_{b_m} \end{bmatrix} = \begin{bmatrix} x_{b_1} \\ y_{b_1} \end{bmatrix} + a\overrightarrow{u} + b\overrightarrow{v} \tag{10}$$

   For $m = 2$, $a = l$ and $b = 0$; for $m = 3$, $a = l$ and $b = w$; for $m = 4$, $a = 0$ and $b = -w$.

As previously mentioned, this process is executed twice for each edge. Initially, it is performed using a bounding box with dimensions $\{l, w\}$, where $\|b_{12}\| = l$ and $\|b_{23}\| = w$, resulting in the generation of two candidate bounding boxes for the edge.

Subsequently, the process is repeated with the bounding box having its dimensions flipped to $\{w, l\}$, where $\|b_{12}\| = w$ and $\|b_{23}\| = l$. At this stage, two distinct candidate bounding boxes, differing in terms of both position and orientation, are generated. This approach allows for the consideration of a broader range of potential candidates, ultimately enhancing the final selection.

AssociationScore Computation: In order to select the best bounding box for an object representation, a scoring function is calculated for each generated bounding box to assess the quality of the association. The scoring function, named $S \in [0, 1]$, provides an indication of the deviation between the polygon and the box. The boxes with scores higher than a specified threshold are kept, and the one with the highest score is selected as the final representation of the object. The selection threshold ϵ is determined through testing.

The computation of the S is performed using the following equation:

$$S = 1 - (w_1 \cdot f_1 + w_2 \cdot f_2 + w_3 \cdot f_3) \tag{11}$$

where f_1, f_2 and f_3 are the features that are considered in evaluating the association and w_1, w_2 and w_3 are the corresponding weights, with the constraint $w_1 + w_2 + w_3 = 1$.

Definition of the f_1 equation: The f_1 equation quantifies the quality of the alignment between the created bounding box and its associated polygon. Since bounding boxes are inherently rectangular, they inherently possess angles of 90°. The primary objective of this equation is to minimize its value when the bounding box aligns perfectly with the polygon at a 90° angle.

To achieve this alignment, two conditions must be met. First, as we shift the bounding box to the right, α_{min} should approach zero, signifying that the bounding box aligns with the leftmost edge of the polygon. Second, as we shift the bounding box to the left, $\alpha_{max} - \|e_i\|$ should tend to zero, indicating alignment with the rightmost edge of the polygon. These conditions ensure that the bounding box aligns precisely with the orientation of the polygon, achieving the desired 90° orientation.

The f_1 feature is calculated using the following equation:

$$f_1 = \frac{|\alpha_i| - i \cdot \|e_i\|}{l}$$

In this equation, when performing a right shift, i is set to 0, and α_i corresponds to α_{min}. For a left shift, i is set to 1, and α_i corresponds to α_{max}. The division of the error distance by l serves to normalize the f_1 value within the range of 0 to 1, allowing for meaningful comparisons and assessments of alignment.

Definition of the f_2 equation: The f_2 equation quantifies the offset distance between the length of the bounding box and that of its associated polygon. In our analysis, we define the length of the polygon as the distance between its extreme vertices in the local frame R_i, measured along the direction of the edge used for association, and this length is represented as $|\alpha_{min}| + \alpha_{max}$. The primary objective of f_2 is to minimize the error between the real length (l) and the polygon length ($|\alpha_{min}| + \alpha_{max}$).

The f_2 feature is calculated using the following equation:

$$f_2 = \frac{l - (|\alpha_{min}| + \alpha_{max})}{l}$$

Similar to f_1, the division of the error distance by l serves to normalize the f_2 value within the range of 0 to 1.

Definition of the f_3 equation: The f_3 equation quantifies the offset distance between the width of the bounding box and that of its associated polygon. More precisely, we define the width of the bounding box as the distance from the edge used for association to the lowest vertex in the local frame R_i. This distance is equal to β_{max}, representing the coordinate of the lowest vertex in the local frame R_i. The primary objective of f_3 is to minimize the error between the real width (w) of the object and the width of the polygon (β_{max}).

The f_3 feature is calculated using the following equation:

$$f_3 = \frac{w - \beta_{max}}{w}$$

Similar to f_1 and f_2, normalizing the f_3 value by dividing the error distance by w ensures that it falls within the range of 0 to 1.

The score S is only calculated for boxes that meet two conditions:

$$\begin{cases} |\alpha_i| + (1 - i) \cdot \|e_i\| < l + \psi \\ \beta_{max} < w + \psi \end{cases}$$

where ψ represents a predefined constant to take into account the scaling errors stemming from observation inaccuracies. These two conditions serve to filter out bounding boxes with less relevant characteristics, particularly when the length or width of the bounding box exceeds the actual dimensions of the object it represents. The inclusion of ψ ensures that bounding boxes are not discarded due to scaling errors caused by observation inaccuracies, thus preserving their relevance for analysis.

Regarding the weights, there are many methods to tune them. For the first version of our solution, we propose a method of manually determining them by tuning parameters according to some constraints, testing, and retuning the parameters that give the best results (Sect. 3.2).

3   Experimentation

We evaluated the performance of our semantic mapping approach against Dengler et al. open-source RGBD-based approach [13]. We selected this comparative framework due to its close alignment with our own approach. Dengler et al.'s method, like ours, leverages RGBD data to construct point clouds of objects and employs the Quickhull algorithm to define object occupation zones. However, our approach introduces a novel association solution that enriches object representation through predefined bounding boxes. Therefore, this state-of-the-art method serves as an ideal reference point to accentuate the distinctive contributions of our work.

To ensure a fair comparison, we used the same pre-trained detection model as [13], namely Faster R-CNN [19], trained on the OpenImages dataset [20], encompassing over 600 common object categories found in home and office environments. Our solution's modularity allows for easy substitution of the detection model, as it outputs object categories and detection bounding boxes.

In what follows, we present our experimental setup, highlight the importance of polygon simplification and foreground edge selection solutions to reduce association processing time. Then, we compare the semantic maps obtained by the two approaches.

3.1 Experimental Setup

We conducted experiments to evaluate our approach using a computer equipped with an i7-7700K CPU. Our approach assumes that the robot pose is provided, so we generated a metric map using the ROS gmapping node and used the robot ground truth pose for localization. The experiments were performed in two different environments using the MiR100[1] mobile robot with an Asus Xtion Pro camera that had a resolution of 640×480 pixels. The camera was placed at a height of 1.0 m above the robot and 5 degree pitch angle facing the ground.

We evaluated our solution's performance through tests in simulated environments. Since the association method operates downstream of the mapping process and does not directly depend on low-level sensor data, this type of testing allowed us to assess our solution across various contexts and collect diverse performance metrics. We created three simulated office environments. In this initial solution version, we established a knowledge base comprising four object models: a chair, a table, a shelf, and a sofa bed. Subsequently, we populated all three environments with multiple instances of these four object models. One of these environments served as the test environment, where we exhaustively defined the hyper-parameters as described in Sect. 3.2. We then used these hyper-parameters to obtain validation results in the other two distinct environments (Tables 2 and 3). The first validation environment covers an area of approximately $100\,m^2$ and contains spaced objects along with some partially hidden objects. The second environment shares the same surface area but features a higher object density, with many objects concentrated in the middle and some hidden, making it a more challenging.

3.2 Tuning the Scoring Function Weights

To determine the appropriate weights for our scoring function S, we initiated the process by defining a range of values [0, 1] with a step size of 0.1 for each weight. Subsequently, we conducted an exhaustive grid search to identify the optimal combination of weights. This involved testing numerous combinations, and the one yielding the best results was selected. Given the time-intensive nature of this process, we implemented optimizations inspired by the underlying principles of our method.

One key insight guiding our weight selection was the importance of minimizing the offset angle of association (f_1), as this parameter directly influences the position of the

---

[1] MiR ROS packages: https://www.github.com/dfki-ric/mir_robot/tree/melodic.

Table 1. An illustration of the evolution, on the basis of two sequences, of the total number of edges used for association after polygon simplification and foreground edges selection, as well as the average association time.

Environment	Total number of edges			Average association time per polygon (s)
	Initial polygons [13]	After polygon simplification	After foreground edges selection	
Spaced	12060	4137	**1369**	**0.0037 (0.001)**
Cluttered	25699	6813	**2435**	**0.0039 (0.002)**

bounding box. Consequently, a higher weight was assigned to this parameter. On the other hand, the errors associated with the width (f_3) and the length (f_2) have approximately the same effect on determining the orientation of the bounding box, leading to close weight values for these features.

To streamline the weight selection process, we first fixed w_2 and w_3 to values within the range $[0, 0.5]$, while varying w_1 within the range $[0.5, 1]$. Subsequently, we adjusted the values of w_1 and w_2 to fine-tune the scoring function. Regarding the selection threshold, we systematically tested values within the interval $[0$ to $0.9]$ with a step size of 0.1 and retained the value that produced the best results. The most efficient score function S was obtained for the set of weights $w_1 = 0.5$, $w_2 = 0.3$, and $w_3 = 0.2$. The scaling error constant was set to $\psi = 0.1\,\text{m}$, and the selection threshold was set to $\epsilon = 0.6$.

3.3   Evaluation of Polygon Simplification and Foreground Edges Selection

The number of polygon edges generated by the Quickhull algorithm in Dengler *et al.* is significant. As described in Sect. 2.4, we introduced polygon simplification and foreground edges selection processes to speed up the association processing time. Table 1 illustrates the evolution of the total number of polygon edges after the introduction of these two pre-association steps. The results obtained for a sequence in a cluttered environment and a sequence in a spaced environment show that only 10% of the total number of edges are retained for association, thus the association processing time is reduced by about 10 times compared to using the initial polygons. The last row of Table 1 shows that the association process takes about 4 ms, including the pre-association steps. Since the number of polygon edges varies from object to object, this value is an average of the association time of all polygons processed per sequence.

3.4   Evaluation of the Association Algorithm

We conducted 12 mapping sequences in each validation environment, and for each environment, we defined the waypoints for the robot to follow. The trajectory of the robot varies from one sequence to another, in order to provide a performance that is agnostic to the viewpoints of the different objects in the scene. Figure 7a illustrates the path followed by the robot during the mapping process in the first environment.

We calculated the average metrics for each object class relative to the ground truth map for each sequence in both environments. Subsequently, we averaged the metrics

(a) Ground truth map

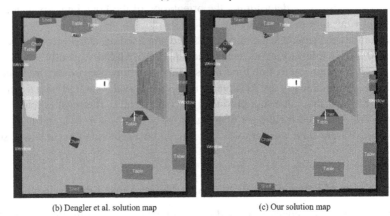

(b) Dengler et al. solution map   (c) Our solution map

Fig. 7. (a) Visualization of the ground truth map, (b) the resulting semantic map from the Dengler *et al.* approach [13], and (c) from our approach.

per object over all sequences in each environment. We utilized the following metrics for our evaluation:

- Intersection over Union (IoU), which measures the overall similarity between two shapes.
- The 2D Center of Mass (CoM) offset, which measures the distance between the center of mass of two shapes and provides information about the magnitude of the object displacement.
- True Positives (TP), which indicate the number of correctly mapped objects for which the IoU relative to ground truth is greater than 0.2.

While the False Positive (FP) metric, which represents falsely mapped instances, is generally used as a complement to TP to evaluate the accuracy of the detection model, we are only interested in evaluating the association method on correctly mapped objects. Therefore, we compute only TP to show the number of objects considered when computing the average IoU and CoM offset metrics.

Table 2. Mapping results for the spaced environment (TP: True Positives, IoU: Intersection over Union, CoM: Center of Mass).

Metrics	TP	IoU		CoM offset (m)	
Class		Our solution	Dengler solution [13]	Our solution	Dengler solution [13]
Chair	48	**0.8216 (0.04)**	0.6559 (0.07)	**0.0455 (0.02)**	0.0782 (0.02)
Table	58	**0.8825 (0.03)**	0.7521 (0.05)	**0.0672 (0.02)**	0.1799 (0.05)
Shelf	12	0.6477 (0.10)	**0.7044 (0.10)**	0.1030 (0.03)	**0.0914 (0.05)**
Sofa bed	24	**0.8241 (0.04)**	0.6709 (0.04)	**0.1078 (0.02)**	0.1770 (0.04)
Total	142	**0.7940 (0.08)**	0.6958 (0.03)	**0.0809 (0.02)**	0.1316 (0.04)

Table 3. Mapping results for the cluttered environment (TP: True Positives, IoU: Intersection over Union, CoM: Center of Mass).

Metrics	TP	IoU		CoM offset (m)	
Class		Our solution	Dengler solution [13]	Our solution	Dengler solution [13]
Chair	48	**0.6435 (0.07)**	0.5510 (0.09)	**0.0731 (0.01)**	0.1046 (0,02)
Table	59	**0.8134 (0.04)**	0.6410 (0.04)	**0.1000 (0.04)**	0.2603 (0.04)
Shelf	37	0.6819 (0.06)	**0.7211 (0.06)**	0.0964 (0.02)	**0.0574 (0.03)**
Sofa bed	34	**0.8669 (0.04)**	0.7708 (0.03)	**0.0778 (0.03)**	0.1001 (0.01)
Total	178	**0.7514 (0.09)**	0.6710 (0.08)	**0.0868 (0.01)**	0.1306 (0.07)

The average results over the 12 sequences for each environment are presented in Table 2 and Table 3. These results were obtained after approximately 54 min of mapping, or about 2 min/sequence for the spaced environment and 2 min and 30 s/sequence for the cluttered environment. A total of 142 objects were mapped in the spaced environment (compared to 52 in [13]) and 178 objects in the cluttered environment (compared to 68 in [13]).

The results depicted in Table 2 shows that our approach incorporating the augmentation step outperforms Dengler *et al.* approach for all objects, except for the shelf, where the results are almost equivalent. Our solution well performs in mapping large objects, such as tables or sofa beds, with large unseen parts, leading to significant improvements in both the average IoU and average CoM offset. We noticed also an enhancement in the shape of foreground objects, like chairs in this environment. Our approach also performs well for the shelf class, but it shows relatively inferior results compared to other objects, similar to Dengler *et al.* solution. This can be explained by the fact that although the orientation of the box was correctly estimated, the offset side was not selected accurately in some cases. Since the object is small, this offset has a substantial influence on the average IoU value.

Similarly, Table 3 shows that our approach performs better for all objects, except the shelf, for the same reason mentioned above. In this setting, there are more partially invisible tables due to the chairs positioned in the foreground, and we can observe that Dengler *et al.* solution performance declines, while our approach still performs well, especially for the table class. Moreover, our approach almost systematically reduces the standard deviation for both environments, and is therefore more stable.

4   Conclusion and Perspectives

In this paper, a 2D semantic mapping approach is presented, designed for mobile robots equipped with RGBD cameras. The method leverages RGBD camera data to initially construct a primitive representation of objects using convex polygons. Subsequently, prior object dimensions obtained from their 3D models are incorporated to enhance this representation. These known dimensions are used to predefine rectangular bounding boxes that accurately cover the real occupied surfaces of the objects. An association method is then introduced to define the best alignment, including correct orientation and position, between these bounding boxes and the polygonal representations of the objects. This approach differs from prior works that solely relied on sensor data for this purpose.

A comparative analysis of our method against the approach presented in [13], conducted in two distinct office settings, demonstrates several notable advantages. Firstly, our solution significantly reduces the complexity of the polygonal representation. Secondly, the use of predefined bounding boxes for object representation significantly enhances the approximation quality for nearly all objects, particularly those that are partially visible or occluded.

Several directions for further improvement of our method can be explored. Firstly, expanding the knowledge base with objects of more complex geometries will allow us to assess how our solution performs in response to such challenges. Additionally, addressing issues arising from limitations in the detection model, such as class confusion or false detections, is a priority for future work. These challenges will be tackled by enriching the knowledge base with additional information about object relationships, including the possibility of object superposition. This supplementary data will be employed to rectify contextual inconsistencies in the map, either in real-time or during post-processing. Lastly, we intend to enhance the method's capability to handle various object models linked to the same label or category.

References

1. Achour, A., Al-Assaad, H., Dupuis, Y., El Zaher, M.: Collaborative mobile robotics for semantic mapping: a survey. Appl. Sci. **12**(20), 10316 (2022)
2. Crespo, J., Castillo, J.C., Mozos, O.M., Barber, R.: Semantic information for robot navigation: a survey. Appl. Sci. **10**(2), 497 (2020)
3. Liu, W., Daruna, A., Patel, M., Ramachandruni, K., Chernova, S.: A survey of semantic reasoning frameworks for robotic systems. Robot. Auton. Syst. **159**, 104294 (2023)
4. Stark, R., Fresemann, C., Lindow, K.: Development and operation of digital twins for technical systems and services. CIRP Ann. **68**(1), 129–132 (2019)
5. Purcell, W., Neubauer, T.: Digital twins in agriculture: a state-of-the-art review. Smart Agric. Technol. **3**, 100094 (2023)
6. Verdouw, C., Tekinerdogan, B., Beulens, A., Wolfert, S.: Digital twins in smart farming. Agric. Syst. **189**, 103046 (2021)

7. Grinvald, M., et al.: Volumetric instance-aware semantic mapping and 3D object discovery. IEEE Robot. Autom. Lett. **4**(3), 3037–3044 (2019)

8. Sünderhauf, N., Pham, T.T., Latif, Y., Milford, M., Reid, I.: Meaningful maps with object-oriented semantic mapping. In: IEEE/RSJ International Conference on Intelligent Robots and Systems (IROS), pp. 5079–5085 (2017)

9. Zaenker, T., Verdoja, F., Kyrki, V.: Hypermap mapping framework and its application to autonomous semantic exploration. In: IEEE International Conference on Multisensor Fusion and Integration for Intelligent Systems (MFI), pp. 133–139 (2020)

10. Zhao, C., Mei, W., Pan, W.: Building a grid-semantic map for the navigation of service robots through human-robot interaction. Digit. Commun. Netw. **1**(4), 253–266 (2015)

11. Qi, X., et al.: Building semantic grid maps for domestic robot navigation. Int. J. Adv. Robot. Syst. **17**(1) (2020)

12. Barber, C.B., Dobkin, D.P., Huhdanpaa, H.: The quickhull algorithm for convex hulls. ACM Trans. Math. Softw. (TOMS) **22**(4), 469–483 (1996)

13. Dengler, N., Zaenker, T., Verdoja, F., Bennewitz, M.: Online object-oriented semantic mapping and map updating with modular representations. CoRR, vol. abs/2011.06895 (2020)

14. Hernandez, A.C., Gomez, C., Barber, R., Mozos, O.M.: Exploiting the confusions of semantic places to improve service robotic tasks in indoor environments. Robot. Auton. Syst. **159**, 104290 (2023)

15. Hiller, M., Qiu, C., Particke, F., Hofmann, C., Thielecke, J.: Learning topometric semantic maps from occupancy grids. In: 2019 IEEE/RSJ International Conference on Intelligent Robots and Systems (IROS), pp. 4190–4197. IEEE (2019)

16. Kaleci, B., Turgut, K., Dutagaci, H.: 2DLaserNet: a deep learning architecture on 2D laser scans for semantic classification of mobile robot locations. Eng. Sci. Technol. Int. J. **28**, 101027 (2022)

17. Posada, L.F., Velasquez-Lopez, A., Hoffmann, F., Bertram, T.: Semantic mapping with omnidirectional vision. In: 2018 IEEE International Conference on Robotics and Automation (ICRA), pp. 1901–1907. IEEE (2018)

18. Weiler, K., Atherton, P.: Hidden surface removal using polygon area sorting. ACM SIGGRAPH Comput. Graph. **11**(2), 214–222 (1977)

19. He, K., Gkioxari, G., Dollár, P., Girshick, R.: Mask R-CNN. In: Proceedings of the IEEE International Conference on Computer Vision, pp. 2961–2969 (2017)

20. Krasin, I., et al.: OpenImages: a public dataset for large-scale multi-label and multi-class image classification, vol. 2, no. 3, p. 18 (2017). Dataset https://github.com/openimages

Offline Deep Model Predictive Control (MPC) for Visual Navigation

Taha Bouzid[1,2(✉)] and Youssef Alj[1]

[1] International Artificial Intelligence Center of Morocco,
AI Movement Mohammed VI Polytechnic University, Rabat, Morocco
bouzid.taha01@gmail.com
[2] ENSAM, Moulay Ismail University, Meknes, Morocco

Abstract. In this paper, we propose a new visual navigation method based on a single RGB perspective camera. Using the Visual Teach & Repeat (VT&R) methodology [8], the robot acquires a visual trajectory consisting of multiple subgoal images in the teaching step. In the repeat step, we propose two network architectures, namely ViewNet and VelocityNet. The combination of the two networks allows the robot to follow the visual trajectory. ViewNet is trained to generate a future image based on the current view and the velocity command. The generated future image is combined with the subgoal image for training VelocityNet. We develop an offline Model Predictive Control (MPC) policy within VelocityNet with the dual goals of (1) reducing the difference between current and subgoal images and (2) ensuring smooth trajectories by mitigating velocity discontinuities. Offline training conserves computational resources, making it a more suitable option for scenarios with limited computational capabilities, such as embedded systems. We validate our experiments in a simulation environment, demonstrating that our model can effectively minimize the metric error between real and played trajectories.

Keywords: Visual navigation · Mobile robots · MPC · Control · Deep learning

1 Introduction

Visual navigation is the task of guiding a robot toward a specific goal using an RGB camera as its primary exteroceptive sensor. In order to achieve this task, existing techniques can be categorized into two main groups: map-based navigation and reactive methods. In the former, the robot relies on a pre-built map representing the environment and tries to reach the goal. In the latter, the robot makes decisions, such as obstacle avoidance, on the fly, without prior knowledge of the environment. In the context of map-based visual navigation, several challenges require careful consideration. First, map-building: The construction of an accurate and informative map is a fundamental step in map-based navigation. These maps can take various forms, including topological graphs [13], metric maps derived for example from SLAM-based techniques [2], or more recent neural implicit representations [21]. Secondly, localization: Precise self-localization within the map is essential for effective navigation. To ensure that the robot knows its position accurately within the environment, localization methods must seamlessly integrate with the chosen map representation. Thirdly, path planning: Efficient global and local path planning strategies are essential for guiding the robot from its current location to the desired goal. These strategies must navigate through the map complexity while optimizing some criteria such as distance, safety, and energy efficiency. Finally, control algorithms: Control algorithms play a crucial role in executing the planned path. These algorithms generate velocities and control signals that are sent to the robot actuators, translating planned actions into physical movement. While control algorithms are critical, they often operate within the context of the chosen navigation approach.

One widely adopted approach for robot control is visual servoing [1], in which the primary objective is to guide the robot toward a desired image using continuous visual feedback. However, visual servoing alone may not inherently address obstacle avoidance, necessitating dedicated routines. Additionally, the non-linear nature of the cost function within the visual servoing framework can limit the convergence domain. In recent years, learning-based methods [9, 12, 20] have gained an increasing interest. Reinforcement Learning (RL) [20], for example, offers a framework where an agent is trained to learn a policy that maps visual observations directly to actions. RL presents substantial challenges, often requiring an extensive number of trial-and-error experiments to converge successfully. While initial training can be conducted in a simulated environment, adapting these learned policies to real-world scenarios remains a complex and ongoing challenge [19]. In contrast, Model Predictive Control (MPC), enables a robot to navigate through its environment by continuously synthesizing future images based on its current state and then planning control actions to achieve desired visual goals. MPC has found applications in diverse problem domains, including trajectory planning [7], humanoid gait generation [17], and wheeled robot control [12].

The main contributions of our work are twofold. First, it introduces VelocityNet as an offline deep MPC navigation system. Second, we adapt the existing network architectures to a single perspective camera. Offline training offers several noteworthy benefits, including enhanced safety, cost-effectiveness, and greater adaptability. It allows training within a simulated environment, which is safer than training the robot in the real world. The approach also has the advantage of being time-efficient. This is because the robot only needs to collect data from its environment rather than undergo training within it, which significantly reduces the time required for the overall process. Offline training does not require access to the real robot, which can save money on hardware and setup costs. We will demonstrate our model's ability to generate precise velocities for a robot to follow a desired trajectory with minimal errors in various scenarios.

This paper is organized as follows: In Sect. 2, we first present work related to visual navigation. Section 3 begins with a description of the simulation environment, followed by an explanation of the architecture and training process of the two proposed network architectures, namely, ViewNet and VelocityNet. In Sect. 4, we define the experimental setup employed in our study. Moving on to Sect. 5, we present the results of our simulations under various motion types. Finally, in Sect. 6, we wrap up the paper with our concluding remarks.

2   Related Work

In this section, we introduce three key techniques for visual navigation: Visual Servoing, Reinforcement Learning (RL), and Model Predictive Control (MPC).

Visual Servoing: Visual servoing (VS) methods have a long history in robotics [1], VS is a closed-loop control technique that uses real-time visual feedback, primarily in the form of extracted image features, to guide the motion or position of a robot or camera. This technique allows a wide variety of tasks designed to locate a system with respect to its environment or to reach a target image, by controlling one or several degrees of freedom. Optimization methods are employed in order to find the optimal control inputs that minimize the error between the desired visual features and the observed ones. VS has been used in the visual path following [3,4]. A visual path is represented by a series of target images and a visual servoing algorithm allows the robot to navigate from its current position to the next key image. VS suffers from a limited convergence area due to a highly non-linear cost function. Furthermore, it is very sensitive to lighting conditions and requires accurate camera calibration. With the development of deep learning architectures, VS can be used to control a robot in a latent space as proposed in [6], where the representations of camera pose and the embeddings of their respective images are tied together. This allows a larger convergence domain and more accurate robot positioning.

Reinforcement Learning (RL) for Visual Navigation: In recent years, the rise of Reinforcement Learning (RL) has revolutionized the field of robotics, particularly in the context of visual navigation. RL has demonstrated its capability to learn control policies directly from visual observations [20], offering the potential to navigate to distant goals while optimizing user-specified reward functions. Researchers have investigated RL-based approaches, training agents to navigate through environments using simulated experiences. Online reinforcement learning for robotic navigation is difficult to implement in real-world settings, as it requires several experiments of trial and error. Offline reinforcement learning methods, which can leverage existing datasets of robotic navigation data, offer a more scalable and generalizable approach. Shah et al. [16] proposed an offline reinforcement learning system for robotic navigation that can optimize user-specified reward functions in the real world, their use of graph search in combination with RL parallels prior work that integrates planning into supervised skill learning methods [15,16] and goal-conditioned reinforcement learning [5]. The transition from simulation to the real world remains a challenging task and requires extensive domain adaptation and robustness to unforeseen real-world conditions. Nevertheless, RL in visual navigation is a promising approach, and the field continues to evolve with innovations in model architectures, training methodologies, and transfer learning techniques. Our work differs from those previous approaches as it focuses on a subset of visual navigation problems known as visual path following. In this approach, there is no need for trajectory planning or graph optimization. Instead, the robot is provided with a trajectory composed of images, referred to as subgoals, which it is expected to follow.

Model Predictive Control (MPC) in Visual Navigation: Model Predictive Control has emerged as a powerful paradigm in visual navigation, allowing robots to predict future images based on their current state and plan control actions accordingly. This approach transcends traditional control strategies, enabling robots to anticipate changes in the environment and adapt their actions proactively. MPC-based methods find applications in various facets of visual navigation, such as trajectory planning [14], obstacle avoidance, and path following [18]. By explicitly accounting for visual feedback and uncertainty, MPC enhances an agent's capability to navigate dynamically in changing environments with agility and precision. Previous approach [12] used an Online Deep Visual MPC-policy learning method that can perform visual navigation while avoiding collisions with unseen objects on the navigation path. However such Online learning methods require a large amount of online experience. The main goal of our approach is to develop an offline Deep Visual MPC-policy learning method and to explore its application to robotic navigation tasks by building a learning-based system for long-horizon planning.

3   Proposed Approach

In this section, we will present the simulated environment and the network architectures used to control the robot, as well as the training process of these networks.

3.1   Simulation Environment

The simulation was conducted in ROS Gazebo. The simulated environment comprises two key models: a house and a robot. Within this environment, the robot is capable of navigating inside the house and collecting the necessary images for training our models.

The House Model: We use the house represented in Fig. 1 for the robot navigation. The robot can move inside this model, capture images, and receive velocity commands to collect a dataset that will be used for training. The house is composed of different rooms, each containing various items of furniture. These items contribute to the photometric richness of the captured images.

We will use a floor that features the shape and colors of a mosaic as shown in Fig. 1. In this manner, the floor will contain various colors and shapes, which will significantly enhance the richness of our model. It's important to note that our models employ CNN layers for feature extraction. Consequently, providing them with a multitude of features can augment their capabilities.

Figure 2 shows the difference between the floor with and without changes, the right image depicts an example of the images that will be used for the training of our model.

The Robot Model: The mobile robot model represented in Fig. 3 that we use in our simulation can move in a 2D space with only two velocities: longitudinal velocity denoted as v_x and angular velocity around the z-axis denoted as ω_z. From now on, for the sake of simplicity, we denote v_x and ω_z as v and ω respectively; We can move our robot by sending twist velocity messages to the corresponding topic dedicated to moving the robot. We attach a forward-looking camera in the front of the robot enabling

Fig. 1. Upper view of the house model.

(a)   (b)

Fig. 2. Images captured from the robot perspective camera, depicting the changes made to the scene by texturing the floor, (a) before texturing, and (b) after texturing.

it to take images from the environment. Hence, we can acquire the dataset images by simulating robot movement within the environment. To extract velocity commands, we can access the twist messages published in the corresponding velocity topic and subsequently link each image to its corresponding velocity command.

Fig. 3. The mobile robot model used in the simulation.

3.2 Future Image Prediction, ViewNet

Figure 4 represents ViewNet architecture inspired from [11]. The network takes as input an image captured from our camera's perspective and a given velocity $\xi_t = (v, \omega)$ and outputs a prediction image. The architecture is based on the Encoder-Decoder (ED) architecture depicted in Fig. 4. The ED takes two inputs: the image input is directly sent to the encoder and the velocity is concatenated with the output of the encoder. The output of the decoder is a two-dimensional flow field image as represented in Fig. 4. The flow field is used to sample the input image and generate the future prediction image. Images synthesized with ViewNet will be used to train VelocityNet within the MPC policy defined in Eqs. (2) and (3).

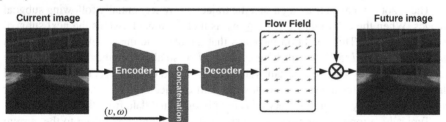

Fig. 4. ViewNet architecture for future image prediction.

3.3 Control Policy with VelocityNet

We present a novel navigation system based only on perspective images from an RGB camera. Our model can generate velocities necessary for a mobile robot to reach subgoal images.

Figure 5 shows the proposed architecture for path following. At time t, VelocityNet takes the robot current image from the camera and the subgoal image as inputs. The visual trajectory is defined by l subgoal images $(I_0, I_1, ..., I_{l-1})$ collected during a previous step, also referred to as the visual teach step.

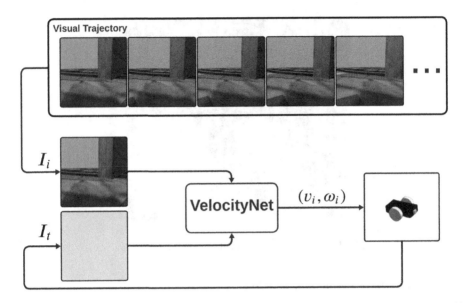

Fig. 5. The proposed path following approach. I_t is the image from the camera attached to the front of the robot at time t, I_i is the subgoal image of index i from the visual trajectory, (v_i, ω_i) are the generated velocities commands to reach the i-th subgoal image.

In the repeat step, the main objective of VelocityNet is to minimize the difference between the current image and the subgoal image at time t. By generating accurate velocities, the robot moves towards the location of the subgoal causing the robot's current camera image to resemble the subgoal image.

The robot can navigate along a specific trajectory by sequentially following subgoal images. When the condition $|I_t - I_i| \leq e_m$ is met the model assigns the next subgoal with index $i + 1$, This condition indicates that the absolute image difference between the current image I_t and the i-th subgoal image I_i is smaller than the threshold e_m. We can experimentally choose a certain value for e_m based on the expected precision and the time required for the robot to follow the entire trajectory. This method allows our robot to follow any given trajectory relying only on visual data from the RGB camera.

Typically, a topological graph is constructed, and the nearest image to the current one is selected from the visual trajectory to initiate the navigation. In our scenario, the robot starts visual navigation from an initial position corresponding to the first image, denoted as I_0, in the visual trajectory. However, the determination of whether the robot should move or not in the presence of a significant disparity between the real-time image and the subgoal image I_0 is governed by Algorithm 1. This algorithm decides whether the robot should navigate to the initial image or proceed to the subsequent subgoal images.

3.4   Training VelocityNet

We employ an offline deep Model Predictive Control (MPC) Policy to train VelocityNet, leveraging existing data collected for training ViewNet. This dataset includes images paired with corresponding velocity commands. As shown in Fig. 6, our training process involves using three consecutive images from the dataset (I_i, I_{i+1}, I_{i+2}) and with their corresponding velocity commands, denoted as (v_{c_i}, ω_{c_i}) and $(v_{c_i+1}, \omega_{c_i+1})$, associated with the initial and second images. The index i can be chosen randomly within the range of subgoal indexes. These velocity commands serve as the control inputs that guide the robot movement from the current image, denoted as I_i, towards the subgoal image I_{i+2} during data collection.

VelocityNet undergoes two forward calculations during training, resulting in two sets of velocities: (v_1^j, ω_1^j) and (v_2^j, ω_2^j), distinguished by the index 'j' ('1' for the upper one and '2' for the other). During the initial forward calculation, we concatenate I_i with I_{i+2} and feed this concatenated data into VelocityNet. The order of concatenation is significant: the first element represents the current image, and the second one depicts the goal image.

In the subsequent forward calculation, we reverse the roles of consecutive images I_i, I_{i+1}, and I_{i+2}, along with their corresponding velocity commands, such that I_{i+2} becomes the current image and I_i becomes the subgoal image. Consequently, the corresponding velocity commands become $-(v_{c_i+1}, \omega_{c_i+1})$ and $-(v_{c_i}, \omega_{c_i})$.

In fact, this second forward calculation was added to the model as a form of data augmentation, aiming to enhance the model's adaptability to various scenarios when dealing with different subgoals. This augmentation helps the model predict accurate velocities.

The generated velocities are used in predicting images via ViewNet, which takes both velocities and images as input, producing prediction images.

The predicted images $(I_{p_1}^j, I_{p_2}^j)$ and the subgoal images (I_i, I_{i+1}, I_{i+2}) are used to compute the image loss as defined in Eqs. (2) and (3). On the other hand, the generated velocities $((v_1^j, \omega_1^j), (v_2^j, \omega_2^j))$ and the velocity commands are employed to calculate the velocity loss as represented in Eqs. (4) and (5).

We define the cost function that corresponds to each calculation as a weighted combination of two components, the image loss J_{img_j} and the velocity loss J_{vel_j}. This function penalizes large velocity changes, which can lead to jerky motion or instability. The defined MPC objective uses a horizon of N time steps. The calculation of the best N upcoming velocity commands involves minimizing the following cost:

$$J_j = w_1 J_{img_j} + w_2 J_{vel_j} \tag{1}$$

where w_1 and w_2 are constant weights and j the index of the forward calculation. The values of w_1 and w_2 can be adjusted to find the right balance between the two objectives. For example, if we want to prioritize smoothness, we can increase the value of w_2. If we want to prioritize accuracy, we can increase the value of w_1. Nonetheless, a larger value of w_2 can make the model memorize the velocity commands linked to each image. However, the intention behind this supplementary factor is not to instruct the model to mimic the precise velocity commands of the robot but to regularize and obtain smooth velocities.

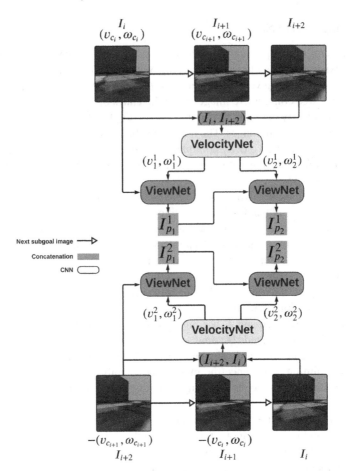

Fig. 6. Offline training process of VelocityNet, the generated velocities and images are used for the loss calculation to update the model.

Image Loss: The image loss can be defined as the mean of absolute pixel difference between the subgoal images (I_i, I_{i+1}, I_{i+2}) and the sequence of predicted images ($I_{p_1}^j$, $I_{p_2}^j$), the image loss for $j = 1$ can be defined as:

$$J_{img_1} = \frac{1}{2n_{pix}} \left(\left| I_{i+1} - I_{p_1}^1 \right| + \left| I_{i+2} - I_{p_2}^1 \right| \right) \tag{2}$$

where $|.|$ denotes the Mean Absolute Error (MAE) function. This function outputs a single value representing the average absolute difference between predicted and subgoal images. Image loss for $j = 2$ can be defined as:

$$J_{img_2} = \frac{1}{2n_{pix}} \left(\left| I_{i+1} - I_{p_1}^2 \right| + \left| I_i - I_{p_2}^2 \right| \right) \tag{3}$$

with $(I_{p_1}^j, I_{p_2}^j)$ are the predicted images generated by the model conditioned on virtual velocities, and n_{pix} represents the number of pixels in the image, $3 \times 128 \times 128$.

Velocity Loss: Training our model based on the image loss alone can help our robot navigate precisely in the environment, but the velocities generated in that case can be fluctuating and non-realistic. As a solution, we propose to add a velocity loss that can help our model generate smooth velocities and minimize the difference between the generated velocities $((v_1^j, w_1^j), (v_2^j, w_2^j))$ and the velocity commands $((v_{c_i}, w_{c_i}), (v_{c_{i+1}}, w_{c_{i+1}}))$, the Velocity loss for $j = 1$ can be defined as:

$$J_{vel_1} = \frac{1}{N} \sum_{n=1}^{N} \left((v_{c_{i-1+n}} - v_n^1)^2 + (w_{c_{i-1+n}} - w_n^1)^2 \right) \tag{4}$$

Velocity loss for $j = 2$ can be defined as:

$$J_{vel_2} = \frac{1}{N} \sum_{n=1}^{N} \left((v_{c_{i+2-n}} + v_n^2)^2 + (w_{c_{i+2-n}} + w_n^2)^2 \right) \tag{5}$$

The loss functions described in Eqs. (4) and (5) employ a normalized summation approach, combining terms with different units. Typically, a weighted sum is employed to prevent one term from overshadowing another due to differences in scale. However, in our formulation, we deliberately opted for equal weighting between the two terms with distinct units. This choice signifies that irrespective of their units, each term contributes equally to the overall loss. The absence of a dominant unit indicates that the chosen formulation successfully mitigates any disproportionate influence of one physical quantity over another.

We define the loss function that will be used in backpropagation as:

$$J = \frac{1}{2} \sum_{j=1}^{N} J_j \tag{6}$$

3.5 Visual Trajectory Following with VelocityNet, Control Algorithm

In Algorithm 1, we describe the control algorithm used to follow the visual trajectory. During real-time operation, the mobile robot will use only the VelocityNet model to navigate between l subgoals. Our model generates two sets of velocities, (v_1, w_1) and (v_2, w_2). The velocity command given to the robot is the first one generated by the model, (v_1, w_1). If the loss condition, $|I_t - I_i| > e_m$ is satisfied, we wait for the robot to execute the twist message for a duration of 0.1 s, and then we send a null-velocity command to initiate a pause while waiting for the VelocityNet model to be calculated. Otherwise, we will switch to the next subgoal and the robot remains stationary, as we've previously published a null velocity command. Thereby we continue this process until we complete the visual trajectory.

Algorithm 1. Visual path following algorithm.

Data: Visual trajectory: A sequence of desired visual states or images (I_i);
Real-time image: The current image or visual state captured by the robot's camera I_t;
Result: Control the robot's motion to follow the visual trajectory

1 initialization;
2 **while** *subgoal index* $< l$ **do**
3   calculate the l1 error between the subgoal and current image;
4   **if** $|I_t - I_i| > e_m$ **then**
5   v, ω = VelocityNet(Real-time image, Subgoal image);
6   publish(v, ω);
7   moving the robot for 0.1 seconds;
8           $v = 0.0$;
9           $\omega = 0.0$;
10   publish(v, ω);
11   **else**
12   subgoal index += 1;

---

4   Experimental Setup

4.1   Network Structure

ViewNet: ViewNet architecture is based on the Encoder-Decoder (ED) architecture. The encoder is constructed by 8 convolutional layers with batch normalization and leaky ReLU function. The encoder produces a 512-dimensional feature vector, which we combine with the two-dimensional velocity vector (v, ω) before inputting it into the decoder. Subsequently, the decoder generates a flow field image with dimensions $2 \times 128 \times 128$ that we use for sampling the input image. The output image from ViewNet is a three-channel (RGB) 128×128 image.

VelocityNet: VelocityNet can generate N steps robot velocities. Concatenated real-time image and subgoal image are input to 8 convolutional layers with batch-normalization and leaky ReLU activation functions, excluding the last layer. In the final layer, the feature is split into two $(N \times 1)$ vectors. The $\tanh(.)$ function is applied to the last layer of VelocityNet to keep the linear velocity within the range of $\pm v_{max}$ and the angular velocity within the range of $\pm \omega_{max}$, where $v_{max} = 0.5\,\mathrm{m/s}$ and $\omega_{max} = 1.0\,\mathrm{rad/s}$.

4.2   Training

We use the simulator previously described to train and evaluate our model based on our MPC approach. VelocityNet and ViewNet are trained on the data collected from the simulation environment by moving the robot in the house model. We collect a total of 7024 images and the corresponding velocity commands. The collected images are of size 800×800, which are then resized to 128×128 before being fed into the network.

The training was performed on a computing infrastructure equipped with NVIDIA T4 GPUs. We train the networks separately, starting with ViewNet. They are both trained using the Adam optimizer with a learning rate of $1e - 4$.

4.3 Parameters

We fix the horizon period to $N = 2$ to limit error accumulation. As shown in Fig. 6, ViewNet takes input images from the dataset or predicted images generated from the previous ViewNet output. Therefore, using ViewNet for a long horizon will cause errors that may accumulate and result in predicted images that differ from the desired ones.

We set the weights w_1 and w_2 in the cost function J_j to 0.8 and 0.3, respectively. We gave the weights those values because the robot is not allowed to memorize the exact velocity commands, but rather to smooth out the velocities generated by the model while prioritizing tracking subgoal images precisely.

The metric error e_m for the subgoal switching condition, $|I_t - I_i| < e_m$, is set empirically to 17. This value represents an optimal choice for achieving precise tracking of subgoals and minimizing the time required to complete the visual trajectory.

Our robot will use only real-time images from the image topic and does not require any additional information from the environment.

5 Results Analysis

Model testing is performed on different scenarios. We collect three different visual trajectories: the first trajectory represents images corresponding to pure translation, the second one corresponds to pure rotation, and the third combines rotation and translation.

We evaluate our model based on these three scenarios and demonstrate that it can perform its required tasks with minimal errors.

5.1 Linear Translation

In this paragraph we describe tests made for pure translation. Throughout the robot movement, we gather the corresponding (x, y) coordinates for each indexed image, representing them as blue points, as illustrated in Fig. 7.

The collected visual trajectory is given to the model, the robot can follow the desired trajectory with minimal photometric error over a series of iterations, as depicted by the red dots.

We can observe a slight deviation in the robot path starting at the location marked by coordinates $(2.25, 2.510)$. These slight variations are permissible as long as the error, expressed as $|I_t - I_i|$, does not exceed the specified limit of e_m. If the main focus is to achieve higher accuracy, the value of e_m can be reduced to minimize these deviations.

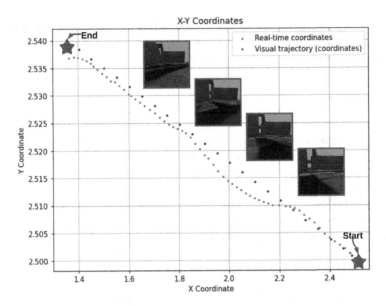

Fig. 7. Evaluation of our predictive model VelocityNet in a linear translation scenario, blue points represent the visual trajectory (x, y) coordinates, while red dots indicate real-time robot coordinates upon receiving generated velocity commands. The figure also displays a sample of four images from the visual trajectory. (Color figure online)

5.2 Pure Rotation

We collected a visual trajectory composed of images during the robot pure rotational movement, as represented in Fig. 8 the robot did successfully reach each subgoal. The figure represents the robot yaw angles collected respectively for each subgoal index.

The collected visual trajectory represents the pure rotation of the robot in both directions. The robot starts rotating clockwise from subgoal 1 to subgoal 171 and then counterclockwise for the rest of the visual trajectory. A similar deviation to what occurred during linear translation was observed within the subgoals range of 79 to 100, slight variations are acceptable as long as the error between the real time image and subgoal image, remains within the specified limit of e_m.

5.3 Combined Translation and Rotation

We gave our model a visual path that incorporates both linear translation and rotation. As shown in Fig. 9, the robot initiates its motion by moving in a linear movement until it reaches the coordinates (2.57, 2.5). Afterward, it starts a rotational movement, and finally, it continues with linear translation until it reaches the end of the trajectory.

Our robot did successfully follow the desired path as shown with red dots in the same figure, however, as we approached the end of the trajectory the robot started to slip away from the desired subgoals.

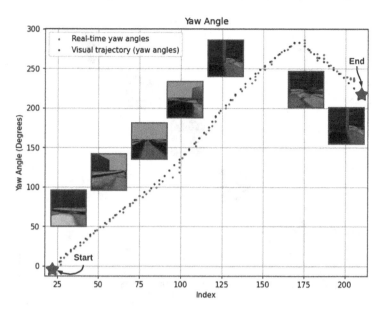

Fig. 8. Evaluation of VelocityNet in Pure Rotation Scenario, blue points represent yaw angles gathered during visual trajectory tracking, while red dots illustrate real-time robot yaw angles in response to the predicted velocity commands, with the index denoting subgoals indices. (Color figure online)

5.4   Statistical Analysis

For each point (x_i, y_i) in the visual trajectory coordinates, we find the nearest point (x_t, y_t) in the real-time coordinates and compute the error between the two points as the following:

$$\text{error}(x_i, y_i) = \sqrt{(x_i - x_t)^2 + (y_i - y_t)^2} \tag{7}$$

We use the same method for the pure rotation scenario; for each angle ψ_i in the visual trajectory yaw angles, we find the nearest angle ψ_t in the Real-time yaw angles, the error can be defined as:

$$\text{error}(\psi_i) = |\psi_i - \psi_t| \tag{8}$$

where i is the index of the subgoal image from the visual trajectory.

In Fig. 10(a) and (b), we can observe the plotted metric errors calculated using Eq. 7 for the selected subgoal indexes. Notably, in the pure translation scenario, these errors exhibit oscillations around the mean value calculated in Table 1. These results demonstrate stability, which is an encouraging sign for a robust model that does not diverge. In the combined rotation and translation scenario, the errors exhibit overall stability, with a slight uptick in error values at the end of the trajectory.

In Fig. 10(c), we can see the yaw angle errors computed using Eq. 8 for the selected subgoal indexes. Similar to the pure translation scenario, the model exhibits indications of stability.

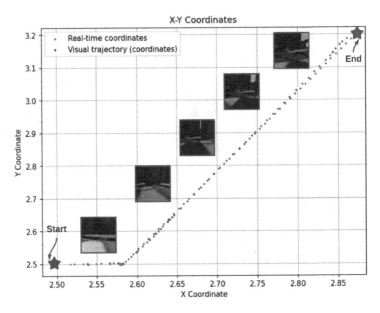

Fig. 9. Evaluation of our predictive model VelocityNet in a (Translation + Rotation) scenario, blue points represent the visual trajectory (x, y) coordinates, while red dots indicate real-time robot coordinates upon receiving generated velocity commands. The figure also displays a sample of images from the visual trajectory. (Color figure online)

Tables 1 and 2 summarize the statistical data of the error results presented above. The mean errors across all scenarios are relatively low.

It's noteworthy that the standard deviation in the scenario involving pure rotation is significantly higher at 1.187 compared to the lower standard deviations of 6.98×10^{-3} in the pure translation motion scenario and 2.203×10^{-3} in the translation+rotation motion scenario. This difference in standard deviations suggests that in the rotation motion scenario, the robot's behavior tends to be less consistent, making its predictions less reliable, and the results more prone to variability.

Table 1. Error statistics for pure translation and translation + rotation scenarios.

	Pure translation	Translation + Rotation
Min (meters)	3.37×10^{-6}	2.13×10^{-4}
Max (meters)	0.025	8.825×10^{-3}
MSE (meters)	0.012	5.04×10^{-3}
Standard deviation (meters)	6.98×10^{-3}	2.203×10^{-3}

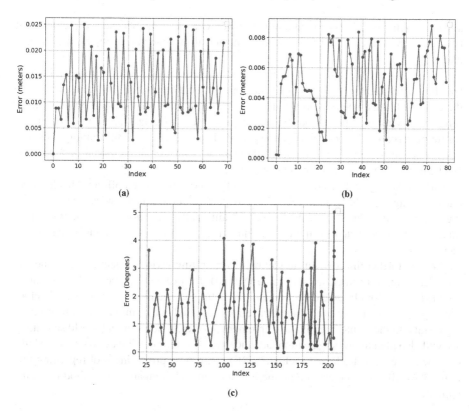

Fig. 10. Quantitative Evaluation of the Three Scenarios: (a) Pure Translation, (b) Translation + Rotation, and (c) Pure Rotational Motion, illustrating Error Plots for the selected subgoals.

Table 2. Error statistics for pure rotation scenario.

	Rotation
Min (degrees)	6.36×10^{-3}
Max (degrees)	5.053
MAE (degrees)	1.578
Standard deviation (degrees)	1.187

6   Conclusion

We proposed a novel way to use MPC policies with deep neural networks, and applied them to visual navigation using an RGB camera. VelocityNet is a neural network that is offline trained with the same goals as an MPC controller. This allows VelocityNet to learn how to generate velocities that minimize the disparity between the current image of the robot and the target images along a visual trajectory. The offline training scheme allows also the use of less computational power. Our experiments showed that a visual navigation system based on VelocityNet can robustly follow visual trajectories in simulation.

Achieving a reasonable balance between how accurately our robot follows its path and the time it takes to complete the trajectory can be a bit challenging. This is because there are instances where the robot may deviate from the path at certain points. Therefore, identifying the appropriate value for e_m is a complex task and could be a topic for future research. VelocityNet is a novel deep-learning approach for training robots to navigate using visual cues. It is more efficient and robust than traditional methods and can be used in a wider range of environments.

One of the key features of VelocityNet is that it can be trained offline. This has several advantages, including the ability to navigate in environments where online training is not feasible due to time constraints. Additionally, VelocityNet can be trained on images that are collected from the environment, which are less time-consuming to collect.

We can further improve our model by incorporating various enhancements, such as the integration of obstacle avoidance. GoNet [10] for instance can be used by monitoring the horizon for obstacle detection and predicting whether the robot-predicted velocities may result in a collision. The metric errors obtained in the simulation show promising results. In the future, we plan to implement our experiments in real-world scenarios. We will also plan to investigate more advanced methods for novel view synthesis. Methods such as Neural Radiance Fields (NeRF) could be a promising tool regarding this issue. We will also increase the prediction horizon and compare our method to online approaches.

References

1. Chaumette, F., Hutchinson, S.: Visual servo control. I. Basic approaches. IEEE Robot. Autom. Mag. **13**(4), 82–90 (2006)
2. Chung, C.M., et al.: Orbeez-SLAM: a real-time monocular visual SLAM with ORB features and NeRF-realized mapping. In: 2023 IEEE International Conference on Robotics and Automation (ICRA), pp. 9400–9406. IEEE (2023)
3. Diosi, A., Remazeilles, A., Segvic, S., Chaumette, F.: Outdoor visual path following experiments. In: 2007 IEEE/RSJ International Conference on Intelligent Robots and Systems, pp. 4265–4270. IEEE (2007)
4. Diosi, A., Segvic, S., Remazeilles, A., Chaumette, F.: Experimental evaluation of autonomous driving based on visual memory and image-based visual servoing. IEEE Trans. Intell. Transp. Syst. **12**(3), 870–883 (2011)
5. Eysenbach, B., Salakhutdinov, R.R., Levine, S.: Search on the replay buffer: bridging planning and reinforcement learning. In: Wallach, H., Larochelle, H., Beygelzimer, A., d' Alché-Buc, F., Fox, E., Garnett, R. (eds.) Advances in Neural Information Processing Systems, vol. 32. Curran Associates, Inc. (2019)
6. Felton, S., Fromont, É., Marchand, E.: Deep metric learning for visual servoing: when pose and image meet in latent space. In: IEEE International Conference on Robotics and Automation (2023)
7. Finn, C., Levine, S.: Deep visual foresight for planning robot motion. In: 2017 IEEE International Conference on Robotics and Automation (ICRA), pp. 2786–2793. IEEE (2017)

8. Furgale, P., Barfoot, T.D.: Visual teach and repeat for long-range rover autonomy. J. Field Robot. **27**(5), 534–560 (2010)

9. Gupta, S., Davidson, J., Levine, S., Sukthankar, R., Malik, J.: Cognitive mapping and planning for visual navigation. In: Proceedings of the IEEE Conference on Computer Vision and Pattern Recognition, pp. 2616–2625 (2017)

10. Hirose, N., Sadeghian, A., Vázquez, M., Goebel, P., Savarese, S.: GONet: a semi-supervised deep learning approach for traversability estimation. In: 2018 IEEE/RSJ International Conference on Intelligent Robots and Systems (IROS), pp. 3044–3051 (2018). https://doi.org/10.1109/IROS.2018.8594031

11. Hirose, N., Sadeghian, A., Xia, F., Martín-Martín, R., Savarese, S.: VUNet: dynamic scene view synthesis for traversability estimation using an RGB camera. IEEE Robot. Autom. Lett. **4**(2), 2062–2069 (2019)

12. Hirose, N., Xia, F., Martín-Martín, R., Sadeghian, A., Savarese, S.: Deep visual MPC-policy learning for navigation. IEEE Robot. Autom. Lett. **4**(4), 3184–3191 (2019)

13. Kwon, O., Kim, N., Choi, Y., Yoo, H., Park, J., Oh, S.: Visual graph memory with unsupervised representation for visual navigation. In: Proceedings of the IEEE/CVF International Conference on Computer Vision, pp. 15890–15899 (2021)

14. MG, H.N., Antony, R.: MPC based path planning for wheeled mobile robots in environments with varying slip. In: Advances in Robotics - 5th International Conference of The Robotics Society, AIR 2021. Association for Computing Machinery, New York (2022). https://doi.org/10.1145/3478586.3478601

15. Savinov, N., Dosovitskiy, A., Koltun, V.: Semi-parametric topological memory for navigation. In: International Conference on Learning Representations (2018). https://openreview.net/forum?id=SygwwGbRW

16. Shah, D., Bhorkar, A., Leen, H., Kostrikov, I., Rhinehart, N., Levine, S.: Offline reinforcement learning for visual navigation. In: 6th Annual Conference on Robot Learning (2022)

17. Tanguy, A., De Simone, D., Comport, A.I., Oriolo, G., Kheddar, A.: Closed-loop MPC with dense visual SLAM-stability through reactive stepping. In: 2019 International Conference on Robotics and Automation (ICRA), pp. 1397–1403. IEEE (2019)

18. Yu, S., Guo, Y., Meng, L., Qu, T., Chen, H.: MPC for path following problems of wheeled mobile robots**the work is supported by the national natural science foundation of china for financial support within the projects no. 61573165, no. 6171101085 and no. 61520106008. IFAC-PapersOnLine **51**(20), 247–252 (2018). https://doi.org/10.1016/j.ifacol.2018.11.021. https://www.sciencedirect.com/science/article/pii/S2405896318326752, 6th IFAC Conference on Nonlinear Model Predictive Control NMPC 2018

19. Zhao, W., Queralta, J.P., Westerlund, T.: Sim-to-real transfer in deep reinforcement learning for robotics: a survey. In: 2020 IEEE Symposium Series on Computational Intelligence (SSCI), pp. 737–744. IEEE (2020)

20. Zhu, Y., et al.: Target-driven visual navigation in indoor scenes using deep reinforcement learning. In: 2017 IEEE International Conference on Robotics and Automation (ICRA), pp. 3357–3364. IEEE (2017)

21. Zhu, Z., et al.: Nice-SLAM: neural implicit scalable encoding for SLAM. In: Proceedings of the IEEE/CVF Conference on Computer Vision and Pattern Recognition, pp. 12786–12796 (2022)

BiGSiD: Bionic Grasping with Edge-AI Slip Detection

Youssef Nassar[1]([✉])(ID), Mario Radke[1](ID), Atmaraaj Gopal[1], Tobias Knöller[1],
Thomas Weber[1], ZhaoHua Liu[2](ID), and Matthias Rätsch[1]

[1] ViSiR Group, Reutlingen University, Reutlingen, Germany
youssef.nassar@reutlingen-university.de
[2] Hunan University of Science and Technology, Xiangtan, Hunan, China

Abstract. Object grasping is a crucial task for robots, inspired by nature, where humans can flexibly grasp any object and detect whether it is slipping from grasp or not, more by the sense of touch than vision. In this work we present a bionic gripper with an Edge-AI device that is able to dexterously grasp the handled objects, sense and predict their slippage. In this paper, a bionic gripper with tactile sensors and a time-of-flight sensor is developed. We propose a LSTM model which is used to detect (incipient) slip/slippage, where a 6 degree-of-freedom robot manipulator is used for data collection and testing. The aim of this paper is to develop an efficient slip detection system which we can deploy on the edge device on our gripper, so it can be a stand-alone product that can be attached to almost any robotic manipulator. We have collected a dataset, trained the model and achieved a slip detection accuracy of 95.34%. Due to the efficiency of our model we were able to implement the slip detection on an edge device. We use the Nvidia Jetson AGX Orin development board to show the inference/prediction in a real-time scenario. We demonstrate in the our experiments how the on-gripper slip detection capability allows more robust grasping as the grip force is adjusted in response to a slippage.

Keywords: Slip detection · LSTM · Tactile sensor · AI-Edge-Device

1 Introduction

Slip detection was and is a critical research topic. Knowing the contact state of the grasped object by the robot manipulator is important for most robotic tasks. Slipping can occur due to insufficient gripping force or grasping slippery objects that need more grasping force or it can be by a wrong grasping position. Therefore, many sensors were developed to detect slip/slippage [6,10,20].

Humans can detect easily if the object in their hand is slipping, by either touch or vision, therefore, tactile sensors were used in our work alongside a proximity sensor. In this work, we prove that slip detection could improve grasping possibilities of general purpose robots in-the-wild i.e. home, supermarket, where the variety of objects to grasp is wide. In an attempt to mimic nature, we prototype a bionic gripper based on the fin-ray effect [7] to meet this challenge. Our developed bionic gripper is designed to

---

Y. Nassar and M. Radke—Equal contribution.

© The Author(s), under exclusive license to Springer Nature Switzerland AG 2024
J. Filipe and J. Röning (Eds.): ROBOVIS 2024, CCIS 2077, pp. 152–163, 2024.
https://doi.org/10.1007/978-3-031-59057-3_10

be modular on different robots, for that we bring everything from control to inference of our AImodel on an edge device. In our tests we use the Jetson Orin AGXboard [3]. Experiments were performed to collect data, which we then used to train our LSTMmodel. We attached the gripper to a 6 degree-of-freedom (6-DoF) UR3 robot arm. For the tactile sensing, we used Force Sensing Linear Potentiometers (FSLP) [2] due to their flexibility. They measure the pressure exerted by the object being grasped and its position. We also used a time-of-flight (ToF) sensor to measure the distance of the grasped object from the gripper. Different types of slipping events were needed to train the AImodel for better generalization, therefore we set up experiments with different types of slippages to create our dataset. This dataset was augmented with different procedures. The LSTMmodel trained on the dataset was able to detect slip in the test set with an accuracy of 95.34%. In the grasping experiments, we demonstrate that incipient slip in detected in near real-time, and the gripper is able to react by increasing the grip force applied reducing failed grasp attempts. This allows the gripper to increase the grasping force if needed, based on the model's predictions.

The main contribution of this paper is: (1) a slip detection LSTMmodel able to run interference on an edge device and adjusting the grasping force accordingly to prevent slipping, (2) a new dataset with tactile and ToFsensor data, (3) and training the AImodel with these data to achieve a test accuracy of 95.34%.

2   Related Work

Johansson et al. in [14], conducted experiments with volunteers. They highlighted the critical role of human tactile feedback in the act of grasping. Maintaining a stable grip proves to be challenging in the absence of tactile feedback. Furthermore, the information pertaining to force and tactile feedback is equally significant in the context of robotic grasping and the detection of slipping.

In [17,23], datasets were collected by moving the object to the sensor or making the later slide on the object, these datasets were limited in the types of slipping compared to ours. Yuan et al. [22] introduced a new a method of sensing the normal, shear and torsional load on the contact surface with a "GelSight" tactile sensor; they demonstrate the detection of incipient slip.

Dong et al. [8,9] used an improved "GelSight" sensor which is called "GelSlim" tactile sensor to monitor the sensor displacement field during grasping, with the aim of identifying initial slips. This approach demonstrates effective slip detection capabilities when applied to rigid objects; however, its performance decreases when dealing with deformed objects. Li et al. [15] used a "GelSight" tactile sensor along with an RGBcamera to detect slipping. They trained an LSTMmodel with data collected from these sensors by grasping and lifting 94 objects. Their model achieved an accuracy of 88.03%. While in [13] used a SVMto detect slip occurrence and controlled the robot in real-time to react to it.

Furthermore, slipping is naturally time dependent and many deep learning models were used to solve this issue. Yan et al. [18] directed their studies towards the temporal characteristics of tactile data. They employed a Convolution Neural Network (CNN) integrated with both spatial-channel and temporal attention mechanisms to predict the stability of grasps. This represents a pioneering application of an attention mechanism solely reliant on tactile data for predicting grasp stability. Temporal Convolution Neural Network (TCN) was proposed by [19], where they used the two modalities of vision and tactile sensors to detect slipping. While it was said that adding vision modality with the tactile sensor can improve slip detection, in this later research, the camera was fixed in front of the robot which makes this system less modular.

A new method for slip detection was proposed by Gao et al. in [11]. They used the multi-scale temporal convolution network (MS-TCN) to extract the temporal features of visual and tactile data, they collected data by using a RGBcamera and tactile sensor on 50 daily objects.

3   Data Collection

3.1   Hardware Setting

In order to collect the data required for training the slip detection model, we used three different modalities: (1) a Force Sensing Linear Potentiometer (FSLP) [2], (2) a Time-of-flight (ToF) sensor, (3) and double-hall encoder.

The fingers of the gripper are developed based on the Fin Ray effect [7] which give them the flexibility to adjust its grasping shape according to the grasped object. We needed our force sensor flexible as well, therefore we used a flexible FSLPon each finger, Fig. 1. In order to run our data collection process, we mounted our gripper on an UR3 robot which we controlled using ROS2 [5].

Fig. 1. Prototype of our Bionic gripper.

There exist different types of slipping: rotational, transitional, rotary, etc. We need to have training data that tackles all of these slipping types. This can be done by tying the object with an elastic band from the bottom and from the top as shown in Fig. 3. Then the robot moves its arm, which will create a gradual tension on the band and the object will be gradually slipping. For another transitional slip, we fix the objects to the table and move the robot arm upwards, see Fig. 4. This will result in getting slippage right from the beginning.

The sensors are connected to an "ESP32-DEV" [1], which transmits the read data via a serial connection to the edge device. The baud rate is 115200.

All data is saved in a matrix that has six features; ToF, Encoder position, two FSLPpressure values for each sensor and two FSLPposition values, alongside the label for each measurement as slip or no-slip. We manually labeled the data by pressing "Ctrl" key: the user sets the label of the specific measurement as slip, if nothing is pressed, it will be labeled automatically as no-slip.

3.2   Dataset

The selection of test objects is influenced by the geometry, the surface roughness and the weight. Since the weight of the object is already changing due to the attached rubber band as described in Fig. 3, the selection of the objects was not explicitly considered based on weight. The selected objects can be seen in Fig. 2.

An empty plastic bottle (Fig. 2a) that is on one hand transparent which could cause the ToFsensor to have difficulty measuring distance. On the other hand, the bottle is elastic, so it can be squeezed when grasped, giving the FSLPsensor a variety of position and pressure measurements. This is relevant for the model to detect slipping, even if the ToFsensor does not provide any meaningful data.

Another object is a chips can, that can be seen in Fig. 2b, which is a cylindrical, non-elastic object with a cardboard surface, giving different surface roughness and different behaviors of the ToFand the FSLPsensors. To vary the friction and reflection properties, it is also wrapped in aluminum foil. To obtain a non-cylindrical object geometry, a tetra pack, seen in Fig. 2c, is chosen.

After all samples were carried out, ~300 k measurements were recorded. Around 250 k measurements labeled as no-slip and only ~50 k as slip. The higher proportion of no-slip data is due to the fact, that there is a delay between the start of collecting the data and final slipping occurring.

This includes measurements while the gripper is still open, when closing and in the closed, stable state. Due to the five times higher number of no-slip data compared to slip data, this can lead to a biased prediction from the trained model; therefore some measurements are balanced slightly. To ensure the accuracy of our dataset, it was combed through after the initial recording, to eliminate any human error due to response time.

(a) Empty plastic bottle   (b) Chips can   (c) Tetra carton

Fig. 2. Different types of objects were used to train the LSTM model.

(a) Rubber band attached to the plas-
tic bottle. (b) Rubber band attached to the chips can. (c) Rubber band attached to the Tetra carton.

Fig. 3. A sample of the experiments carried out to simulate the changing of weight using rubber bands. The band was attached from different positions to initiate different types of slipping.

An example can be seen in Fig. 5 where slipping was recorded late and then it was adjusted to fit with the start of the sudden change of sensor readings. After balancing and re-labeling, we achieve ~180 k of no-slip measurements and ~50 k of slip.

Fig. 4. Experimental setup for transitional sliding with a fixed object.

This results in reduction of data, but for training the AImodel, more data is better in most cases, data augmentation is still carried out. This means the measurements are artificially changed and are saved as additional measurements. This results in a higher number of measured values, which leads to better generalization of the trained model.

A data augmentation by adding an offset to the original measurement was carried out. To apply this to all measurements, random offsets of 20% and −80% are applied. Furthermore, additional training data is also added by adding noise to the measured values, this is shown in Fig. 6, a normally distributed random number is added to, or subtracted from the measured value. This ensures that the model detects slips even when the measured values of the sensors are noisy which lead to not easily detectable slipping using conventional methods.

In addition, data augmentation is also achieved by zeroing random measured values in one measurement seen in Fig. 7. Between 60 and 120 measurements are chosen randomly to be set to 0. This simulates that the sensor does not receive any value that might be due to some faulty hardware or signal delivery.

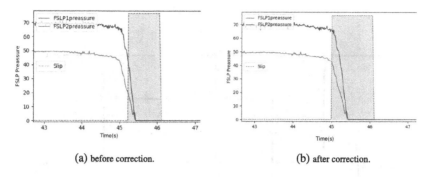

(a) before correction.   (b) after correction.

Fig. 5. Graphs showing the readings of the two FSLPsensors, where Fig. a shows the initial readings, where we can see the drop in the values indicating the slip while the label (green area) was indicated late. Figure b indicates the correction of the label which was done manually. (Color figure online)

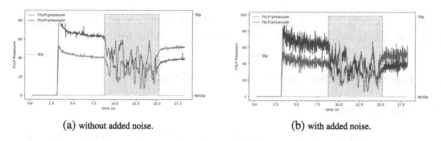

(a) without added noise.   (b) with added noise.

Fig. 6. Graphs showing the data augmentation procedure by adding normally distributed noise to the readings of the sensors.

New series of measurements are created by deleting individual measurements in a series of measurements. This simulates that the sampling rate is lower than in the original collected data.

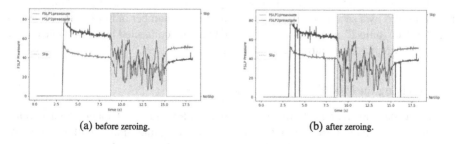

(a) before zeroing.   (b) after zeroing.

Fig. 7. Graphs showing the data augmentation procedure by zeroing.

After all the augmentation are carried out it leaves us with a dataset of ~350 k measurements, with ~250 k labeled as no-slip and ~100 k as slip. This indicates that

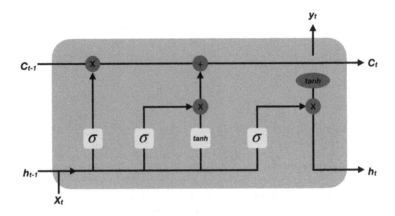

Fig. 8. LSTM architecture.

due to our augmentation processes we achieved a ratio between no-slip and slip of 2.5:1 rather than 3.6:1, which will help our AImodel to generalize better.

4   Proposed Method and Training the Model

4.1   Proposed Method

Slip detection is a time-dependent problem, so we needed to choose a method that could predict the output based on time series data. This could have been a vanilla recurrent neural network (Vanilla RNN) [16], but this can suffer later from the vanishing or exploding gradients. We then propose to use a LSTMnetwork [12,21] as seen in Fig. 8, not only to solve this problem, but LSTMcan be computationally cheap, which is needed to get this model to work on an edge device with far less capability than a normal computer.

The model proposed is built as the following, an LSTMlayer with a number of hidden units called "hidden_units1", followed by a dropout layer with a specified dropout rate, followed by a second LSTMlayer with a different number of hidden units referred to as "hidden_units2", at the end this is passed to a fully connected layer with one output which will predict the occurrence of slipping.

4.2   Training the Model

As already described, an LSTMnetwork is used. Before this can happen, the data must be put into a suitable form; the dataset is listed as two-dimensional, with one dimension describing the features, i.e. the different sensor readings, and the second describing the individual series of measurements. In order to find a suitable shape for the LSTM network, a three-dimensional matrix is required. Also the feature and the series of measurements are used, plus the number of series of measurements that the network should take into account. This is referred to below as timesteps. Figure 9 shows how this matrix looks like where we use the ToFsensor as an example for all features and where n indicates the number of timesteps. In measurement series 1, for example, timesteps = 50, then we fill the first row by the measured values 1–50 of the ToFsensor. In this example the values are 0, 10, 20, etc. The second row shows the measurements 2-51 (10, 20, 30, etc.). This creates a three-dimensional matrix with which the network can be trained on.

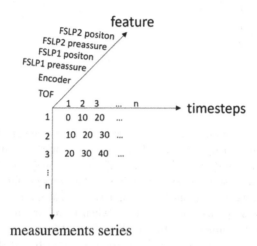

Fig. 9. Creating three-dimensional matrix for training the model.

Furthermore, prior to training, the data is normalised to [0, 1], that is done by using the "MinMaxScaler" function from the sklearn library [4], this means that each sensor has the same influence. To check how well the network is trained, test data is needed. This is done using the "train_test_split" function from sklearn splitting off 20% of the data to be used as test data. The remaining 80% of the data is saved as training data, of these another 20% is split off and used as validation data. What is important here is to set the "Shuffle" parameter to "False", so that not all measurement series get randomly mixed and prevent the loss of the temporal connection.

4.3   Experiments and Results

To have an overview on the influence of the number of hidden units in the LSTMlayer, the number of timesteps chosen for training and the choice of sensors, we train different models with different sets of parameters. Firstly, we fix the loss function to binary cross-entropy through all our training, this is due that we have a binary classification problem, we use the Adam optimizer with learning rate of 0.001. We set the batch size to 75 and the number of epochs to 120, we fix the dropout rate to 0.3. In order to test the influence of the timesteps chosen, we compare our trained models with three different timesteps; 1, 60, and 200.

As can be seen in Table 1, we compare the three different timesteps based on the test accuracy, while fixing the number of hidden units in each layer and using all of the

Table 1. Overall test results.

Sensors	Timesteps	hidden_units1	hidden_units2	#Layers	Accuracy [%]
all	1	64	128	2	86.29
all	60	64	128	2	93.46
all	60	128	256	2	93.44
all	60	64	0	1	94.32
all	60	128	0	1	94.54
all	200	64	128	2	**95.34**
Pressure	60	64	128	2	89.54
Pressure+ToF	60	64	128	2	91.10

sensor data. This shows an increase of accuracy of 7.17% when choosing 60 timesteps instead of 1. There is also an increase of 1.88% when changing the timesteps from 60 to 200. It is worth mentioning that this increase of timesteps will increase computational time and might result in some delays depending on the computational power.

We compare between different hidden unit values and fixing the timesteps to 60. This shows a decrease in accuracy by 0.02% when increasing the number of hidden units. Also, we test the influence of the number of LSTMlayers on the performance of the model. In Table 1 we can observe an increase in accuracy by y 0.86% when reducing the number of layers to 1 with 60 hidden units. When increasing the hidden units of this one layer to 128 there is an increase of 0.02% with respect to the later.

Lastly, we test the influence of every sensor on the performance of the model. We perform the test once with all the sensor data as features to the model. Once with only FSLPpressure values and once with FSLPpressure and ToFsensor values. During these three tests the number of hidden units and layers of the model were fixed. It is common for more features to result in better performance.

However more feature require more computational power, so it is always best to see how much each feature can influence the final accuracy. In this case we see that choosing only the pressure values decreases the accuracy to 89.54%. Choosing the later, combined with the ToFsensor values, the accuracy increases to 91.10%. Although, when choosing all the sensors, it gives the best performance as expected by the accuracy of 93.46%. To calculate accuracy, we count true positives if the prediction value is less than within 5% of the true label.

An experiment was conducted to adjust the torque of the gripper motor based on the detection of slipping, which was referred to as "slip reaction". The gripper was used to grasp a can of chips, and weights were gradually added to initiate slipping. Frames of a captured video of this experiment are shown in Fig. 10a to Fig. 10c, without applying "slip reaction". Figure 10d to Fig. 10f show the same experiment with the application of "slip reaction". In the second experiment, it is evident that the gripper exerted more force to prevent the can from falling and touching the below table. This demonstrates that our slip detection is sufficiently fast to allow the gripper to react and prevent the object from falling.

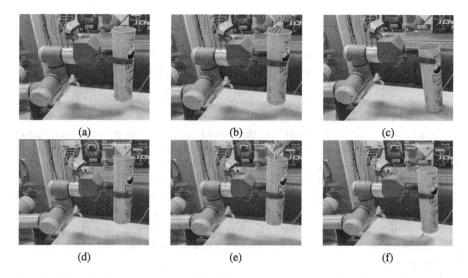

Fig. 10. Figure showing the difference of adding weights to can of chips without slip reaction (a to c) or with slip reaction (d to f).

5   AI Edge-Device

The goal is to port slip detection to edge devices to integrate each system component into the actuator. As a representative of this device category we use an Nvidia Jetson Orin Developer Kit. The Nvidia Orin is one of the most powerful devices in its class and includes a range of embedded system-on-modules (SoMs) equipped with a powerful GPU, multiple CPUcores and 64 GBLPDDR5memory and 64 GBeMMC5.1 storage. It delivers up to 275 TOPS(Tera Operations Per Second).

Obviously, it would be difficult to mount the development kit on the gripper itself, but there is a small form factor system-on-module variant with comparable character-istics, the Jetson Orin NX, which still has 21 TOPS, more than enough to run the slip detection model. Future research will focus on further downsizing of the hardware used.

5.1   Bringing AI to the Edge-Device

Porting the slip detection to the Nvidia Jeston Orin allows us to reduce the overall complexity. The aforementioned ESP32-DEVboard could be removed and instead the sensors could be connected directly to the GPIOpins of the Nvida Edge device. By making this transition, we are able to move away from relying on the serial connection from the ESP32-DEVto the computer.

As the Nvidia Jetson is only a representative of its class of devices, further down-scaling of the hardware may be possible. It is capable of running TensorFlow models directly, eliminating the need to convert and tune the model, thus avoiding any loss of accuracy. This development is an important step for our research, as we will now begin to face the challenges of hardware limitations.

6   Conclusion

We trained an LSTMmodel on data collected from three different objects, by running different experiments that included different types of slipping. The data was annotated manually. To achieve that, two FSLPsensors were attached to the bionic gripper to measure the pressure exerted from the force on the grasped object and its position, alongside a ToFsensor that can measure its distance from the gripper.

We performed data augmentation to the dataset collected to improve generalization of the model. In total, we have ∼350 k measurements for training and testing. Then, we analyzed the influences of different architectures of the LSTMwith different number of layers. We found the optimal choice of timesteps and the sensors for training to be training with all features from sensors, alongside having timesteps set to 200 with a two layer LSTMarchitecture. This gives the best test accuracy of 95.34%.

It is worth mentioning that, due to the non-existence of similar datasets, to the best of our knowledge, benchmarking was not feasible and would have not yielded a comparative analysis.

We wanted to have a compact AImodel that can run on any edge device. We tested our model on the Nvidia Jetson, that gave real-time predictions of the slipping occurrence by plotting its probability on an external monitor.

In future work, we can automate the data collection process to collect more data from different objects, test how the model perform related to different object parameters and also test the model on more edge devices to prove that it works efficiently and can be a modular gripper.

Acknowledgements. This work is partially supported by a grant of the EFRE and MWK ProFö-R&D program, no. FEIH_ProT_2517820 and MWK32-7535-30/10/2.

References

1. ESP32-DevKitC. https://www.espressif.com/en/products/devkits/esp32-devkitc. Accessed 20 Oct 2023
2. Force-sensing linear potentiometer. https://www.pololu.com/product/2730. Accessed 25 Oct 2023
3. Jetson Orin board. https://www.nvidia.com/en-us/autonomous-machines/embedded-systems/jetson-orin. Accessed 25 Oct 2023
4. Scikit-learn. https://scikit-learn.org. Accessed 01 Sept 2023
5. Why ROS2. https://design.ros2.org/articles/why_ros2.html. Accessed 24 Oct 2023
6. Chen, W., Khamis, H., Birznieks, I., Lepora, N.F., Redmond, S.J.: Tactile sensors for friction estimation and incipient slip detection-toward dexterous robotic manipulation: a review. IEEE Sens. J. **18**(22), 9049–9064 (2018)
7. Crooks, W., Vukasin, G., O'Sullivan, M., Messner, W., Rogers, C.: Fin ray® effect inspired soft robotic gripper: from the robosoft grand challenge toward optimization. Front. Robot. AI **3**, 70 (2016)
8. Dong, S., Ma, D., Donlon, E., Rodriguez, A.: Maintaining grasps within slipping bounds by monitoring incipient slip. In: 2019 International Conference on Robotics and Automation (ICRA), pp. 3818–3824. IEEE (2019)

9. Dong, S., Yuan, W., Adelson, E.H.: Improved gelsight tactile sensor for measuring geometry and slip. In: 2017 IEEE/RSJ International Conference on Intelligent Robots and Systems (IROS), pp. 137–144. IEEE (2017)
10. Francomano, M.T., Accoto, D., Guglielmelli, E.: Artificial sense of slip-a review. IEEE Sens. J. **13**(7), 2489–2498 (2013)
11. Gao, J., Huang, Z., Tang, Z., Song, H., Liang, W.: Visuo-tactile-based slip detection using a multi-scale temporal convolution network. arXiv preprint arXiv:2302.13564 (2023)
12. Graves, A., Graves, A.: Long short-term memory. In: Supervised Sequence Labelling with Recurrent Neural Networks, pp. 37–45 (2012)
13. James, J.W., Lepora, N.F.: Slip detection for grasp stabilization with a multifingered tactile robot hand. IEEE Trans. Rob. **37**(2), 506–519 (2020)
14. Johansson, R.S., Vallbo, A.B.: Tactile sensibility in the human hand: relative and absolute densities of four types of mechanoreceptive units in glabrous skin. J. Physiol. **286**(1), 283–300 (1979)
15. Li, J., Dong, S., Adelson, E.: Slip detection with combined tactile and visual information. In: 2018 IEEE International Conference on Robotics and Automation (ICRA), pp. 7772–7777. IEEE (2018)
16. Medsker, L., Jain, L.C.: Recurrent Neural Networks: Design and Applications. CRC Press (1999)
17. Meier, M., Patzelt, F., Haschke, R., Ritter, H.J.: Tactile convolutional networks for online slip and rotation detection. In: Villa, A.E.P., Masulli, P., Pons Rivero, A.J. (eds.) ICANN 2016. LNCS, vol. 9887, pp. 12–19. Springer, Cham (2016). https://doi.org/10.1007/978-3-319-44781-0_2
18. Yan, G., Schmitz, A., Funabashi, S., Somlor, S., Tomo, T.P., Sugano, S.: SCT-CNN: a spatio-channel-temporal attention CNN for grasp stability prediction. In: 2021 IEEE International Conference on Robotics and Automation (ICRA), pp. 2627–2634. IEEE (2021)
19. Yan, G., Schmitz, A., Tomo, T.P., Somlor, S., Funabashi, S., Sugano, S.: Detection of slip from vision and touch. In: 2022 International Conference on Robotics and Automation (ICRA), pp. 3537–3543. IEEE (2022)
20. Yousef, H., Boukallel, M., Althoefer, K.: Tactile sensing for dexterous in-hand manipulation in robotics—a review. Sens. Actuators A: Phys. **167**(2), 171–187 (2011)
21. Yu, Y., Si, X., Hu, C., Zhang, J.: A review of recurrent neural networks: LSTM cells and network architectures. Neural Comput. **31**(7), 1235–1270 (2019)
22. Yuan, W., Li, R., Srinivasan, M.A., Adelson, E.H.: Measurement of shear and slip with a gelsight tactile sensor. In: 2015 IEEE International Conference on Robotics and Automation (ICRA), pp. 304–311. IEEE (2015)
23. Zapata-Impata, B.S., Gil, P., Torres, F.: Learning spatio temporal tactile features with a ConvLSTM for the direction of slip detection. Sensors **19**(3), 523 (2019)

GAT-POSE: Graph Autoencoder-Transformer Fusion for Future Pose Prediction

Armin Danesh Pazho, Gabriel Maldonado, and Hamed Tabkhi[✉]

Department of Electrical and Computer Engineering, University of North Carolina at Charlotte, Charlotte, NC, USA
{adaneshp,gmaldon2,htabkhiv}@charlotte.edu

Abstract. Human pose prediction, interchangeably known as human pose forecasting, is a daunting endeavor within computer vision. Owing to its pivotal role in many advanced applications and research avenues like smart surveillance, autonomous vehicles, and healthcare, human pose prediction models must exhibit high precision and efficacy to curb error dissemination, especially in real-world settings. In this paper, we unveil GAT-POSE, an innovative fusion framework marrying the strengths of graph autoencoders and transformers crafted for deterministic future pose prediction. Our methodology encapsulates a singular compression and tokenization of pose sequences through graph autoencoders. By harnessing a transformer architecture for pose prediction and capitalizing on the tokenized pose sequences, we construct a new paradigm for precise pose prediction. The robustness of GAT-POSE is ascertained through its deployment in three diverse training and testing ecosystems, coupled with the utilization of multiple datasets for a thorough appraisal. The stringency of our experimental setup underscores that GAT-POSE outperforms contemporary methodologies in human pose prediction, bearing significant promise to influence a variety of real-world applications favorably and lay a robust foundation for subsequent explorations in computer vision research.

Keywords: Human pose prediction · Transformer neural networks · Autoencoders

1 Introduction

The exploration of human behavior has surfaced as a cornerstone topic within the sphere of computer vision, with human pose prediction—also termed human pose forecasting—standing as a primary objective to propel the field forward. The significance of human pose lies at the heart of numerous advanced computer vision applications such as autonomous vehicles [1,28,29], robotics [4,27,49], smart surveillance [36,37,46], fitness [13,41,50], and healthcare [10,21,44].

Delving into 3D pose prediction, a subset of human pose analysis entails forecasting ensuing pose sequences based on previous pose observations. Given the intricate nature of human motion and the unpredictability of future human behavior, 3D pose prediction poses a formidable challenge. Numerous studies adopt stochastic or probabilistic approaches, focusing on envisioning a range of possible motions and their likelihoods. Conversely, deterministic methodologies strive for a singular, decisive prediction of

J. Filipe and J. Röning (Eds.): ROBOVIS 2024, CCIS 2077, pp. 164–178, 2024.
https://doi.org/10.1007/978-3-031-59057-3_11

human body pose. The stochastic paradigm is often favored in scenarios mandating the consideration of uncertainty and multiple possible outcomes, finding its utility in realms such as robotics or human-computer interaction. However, deterministic approaches take precedence when a precise, singular prediction is necessitated without the contemplation of uncertainty, particularly in real-time systems like motion capture. Notably, deterministic methodologies, generally less computationally intensive than stochastic ones, are preferable in real-world real-time setups. On another note, the adoption of pose-based methods presents a notable advantage over pixel-based techniques concerning privacy conservation and bias minimization, attributed to the lesser incorporation of Personally Identifiable Information (PII) in pose data. Additionally, pose-based strategies demand lower computational resources thanks to their dependency on a limited set of joints instead of an extensive pixel count. However, it's paramount to recognize that the efficacy of pose-based applications is mainly contingent on the quality of the predicted pose, which often falls short when juxtaposed with pixel-based alternatives. This highlights the imperative of securing high-caliber predicted joints.

This paper presents GAT-POSE framework, a pioneering blueprint for future pose prediction, amalgamating the virtues of graph autoencoder (GA) and transformer architectures. The proposed framework employs the GA to skillfully discern the intrinsic interrelations and impacts among individual joint positions, facilitating the integration of vital temporal and spatial cues within pose sequences. The GA chiefly aims to craft a low-dimensional token representation of each pose sequence, optimizing computational efficiency while preserving indispensable information. In contrast, a decoder-only transformer model is harnessed to adeptly scrutinize these tokens, enabling precise forecasts of upcoming pose sequences. The attention mechanism inherent to the transformer setup permits focused analysis of relevant segments of the tokenized data, capturing long-range dependencies. Furthermore, the transformer's parallel processing prowess accelerates the training phase, simplifying scalability to larger datasets.

The contributions encompass introducing an innovative approach for pose sequence tokenization through the graph autoencoder architecture, unveiling a novel framework for pose prediction by fusing graph autoencoder and transformer architectures and proposing three unique environments alongside diverse datasets. This study effectively showcases the capabilities of GAT-POSE, highlighting its superior performance in contrast to state-of-the-art algorithms.

2 Related Works

Human future pose prediction can be bifurcated into two primary categories: deterministic human pose prediction and probabilistic human pose prediction [24].

2.1 Probabilistic Prediction

Probabilistic human pose prediction acknowledges the uncertainty inherent in forecasting future poses by delineating distributions over potential poses. A plethora of methodologies are encompassed within this categorization [2,3,12,14,25,42,47]. The most prevalently employed techniques within this domain are Generative Adversarial Networks (GANs) and Variational Autoencoders (VAEs) [24].

In the scope of Generative Adversarial Networks (GANs), a frequently employed strategy for motion prediction pivots on generating probabilistic future motions by melding random noise with the observed pose sequence. Through this tactic, GANs are capable of engendering diverse and stochastic motion predictions, thus propelling advancements in generative techniques bespoke for motion modeling applications. [3] pioneered the adoption of a GAN framework, with subsequent works [12, 14] elaborating on this foundation to unveil more dynamic and robust strategies. [25] advocates the employment of stochastic differential equations for future pose prediction, modeling each joint motion profile as a fundamental stochastic variable and leveraging a path integral-based approach for predicting forthcoming motion.

Conversely, methodologies utilizing Conditional Variational Autoencoders (CVAEs) bear similarities with Generative Adversarial Networks (GANs) in noise injection to modulate the output. However, a salient divergence arises in treating random noise, which transitions into an intermediate variable before propagating through the decoder. CVAEs can adeptly generate many stochastic motion predictions by capitalizing on this intermediary representation. [2] proposes a stochastic conditioning scheme amalgamating a random noise vector with anterior pose data to yield a diverse array of future motions. DLow [47] puts forth a sampling methodology, creating a diverse set of samples from a pre-trained deep generative model, demonstrating its efficacy in enhancing the performance of human motion prediction models.

PVRED [42] incorporates pose velocities and temporal positional data, employing a recurrent encoder-decoder architecture to decipher long-term dependencies among human poses. [25] and [2] provide alternative approaches for future pose prediction by harnessing stochastic differential equations and a stochastic conditioning scheme, respectively, thus broadening the spectrum of probabilistic human pose prediction methodologies and their potential for generating a diverse range of future motion predictions.

2.2 Deterministic Prediction

Deterministic human pose prediction aims to directly predict the exact pose of a human body with a high level of certainty. This approach represents the predominant method for human motion prediction employed in various applications. Human motion prediction is widely recognized as a regression task within predictive modeling. Recurrent Neural Networks (RNNs) [34] have granted heavy acknowledgment for their proficiency in addressing such tasks. Consequently, numerous researchers have endeavored to leverage the capabilities of RNNs for human motion prediction [6, 9, 43]. Many other approaches use Convolutional methods [15, 19, 22] benefiting from the kinematics for prediction. Recently, Graph Neural Networks (GNNs) have also been the center of attention for pose prediction tasks [5, 7, 17, 18].

With the growing prominence of attention networks in computer vision, numerous robust methodologies have been proposed to advance the state-of-the-art in future human pose estimation. Especially the use of transformers has been prominent in numerous endeavors [20, 27, 33, 35, 39, 45]. POTR [33] proposes a non-autoregressive transformer architecture for human motion prediction. This approach decodes elements parallel from a query sequence, which is less computationally intensive than autoregressive approaches. STPOTR [27] is a novel approach to predict the human trajectory and pose for robot follow-ahead simultaneously. It uses a non-autoregressive transformer to model the long-range dependencies in human motion. Overall, Transformers have exhibited considerable promise in forecasting future human pose by concurrently capturing contextual information, dependencies, and interdependencies.

3 Methodology

The primary objective of our research is to present a novel framework for forecasting the future pose of a human. Our approach capitalizes on the inherent characteristics of transformers in combination with autoencoders to accomplish this aim effectively. We introduce GAT-POSE as a non-autoregressive decoder-only Transformer-Autoencoder framework for future pose prediction.

3.1 Problem Formulation

In the context of a provided sequence of poses, our model undergoes training to forecast the subsequent sequence of pose vectors with the highest probabilistic likelihood.

In an abstract formulation, the model $\mathcal{M}$ is represented as a function that takes an input sequence of N-dimensional pose vectors $\mathcal{I} = X_{1:m} \in \mathcal{R}^N$ and produces an output sequence of N-dimensional pose vectors $\mathcal{O} = Y_{1:n} \in \mathcal{R}^N$. In simpler terms, the model $\mathcal{M}$ is designed to process a sequence of poses and predict the immediate following sequence of poses. It can be thought of as a predictive model that takes input poses and generates the subsequent poses.

The conventional approach to pose prediction has often relied on autoregressive methods, which incorporate temporal dependencies by utilizing the previously predicted output sequence as contextual input to the model [33]. This concept forms a feedback loop, emphasizing the interdependence between future pose predictions and past predicted pose sequences. However, autoregressive strategies are known to be computationally intensive [27], rendering them less suitable for real-world applications. Moreover, these methods tend to propagate errors, impacting the accuracy of all subsequent predictions [27]. To overcome these challenges, we propose a non-autoregressive approach in this paper. This alternative technique eliminates the need for sequential predictions, providing computational efficiency and reducing error propagation, thus making it a promising solution for practical applications.

3.2 Tokenization

We employ an autoencoder architecture to ensure the preparation of a suitable input token for the transformer model. The autoencoder consists of an encoder and a decoder network that work in tandem to compress the input data into a lower-dimensional latent space $\mathcal{L}$ representation and then reconstruct it back to its original form.

The encoder module operates on an input sequence (window) comprising m skeletons denoted as $X_{1:m}$. It leverages this input data to produce a compact latent space representation, represented by $\mathcal{L}_{1:L}$, where L corresponds to the number of latent values generated.

We initially deal with a substantial pose space input characterized by (m, K, D), with m denoting the number of skeletons per window, K representing the number of keypoints per pose, and D indicating the dimensionality of each keypoint, which can vary between 2D and 3D coordinates. The primary objective of the encoder is to effectively reduce the input dimensionality from $m \times K \times D$ to a more compact representation consisting of L latent values. Doing so significantly reduces the computational complexity and memory requirements while retaining the essential information that characterizes the original pose space.

The primary objective of the tokenizer decoder is to take as input the latent values $\mathcal{L}$ and accurately reconstruct the central $m/2$ skeletons of the given input window, called "Core Skeletons". We denote the decoder output as $Z_{1:m/2}$. The training process involves using the Mean Squared Error (MSE) loss function, modified to prioritize the 10 central core skeletons. The formulation of the autoencoder loss can be observed in Eq. 1.

$$\text{LOSS}_E = \frac{1}{m/2} \sum_{i=1}^{m/2} (X_{m/4+1:3m/4} - Z_{1:m/2})^2 \tag{1}$$

Utilizing a larger input size m compared to the smaller output size $m/2$ enhances the autoencoder's capability to comprehend the temporal and contextual information inherent in future and past skeletons, called "Context Skeletons", facilitating more accurate reconstructions. To ensure thorough training, a stride of $m/2$ is employed, which implies a $m/2$ overlap between each input window and its immediate successor and predecessor. This stride aids in covering the entire dataset and prevents information loss during training.

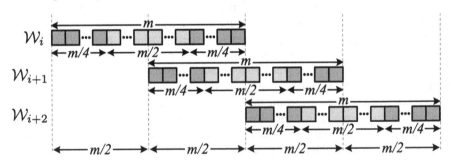

Fig. 1. Stride and core skeletons depiction. m represents the number of skeletons per each window $\mathcal{W}_j$. The stride is $m/2$, and an $m/2$ overlap between the windows. Green blocks represent the core skeletons, and red blocks represent context skeletons. (Color figure online)

The encoder accepts an input sequence (window) of m frames $X_{1:m}$, generating a latent space of L values $\mathcal{L}_{1:L}$. As we are moving from the large pose space of (W, K, D) where W is the number of skeletons per window, K is the number of key points per pose, and D is the dimension of each keypoint (varying between 2D and 3D), we are effectively reducing the input size from $W \times K \times C$ to L.

Figure 1 presents stride and core skeletons depiction. m represents the number of skeletons per each window $\mathcal{W}_j$. The stride is $m/2$, with an $m/2$ overlap between the windows. Green blocks represent the core skeletons, and red blocks represent context skeletons.

3.3   Transformer Autoencoder with Future Masking

Transitioning to the Transformer autoencoder, the GAT-POSE framework employs a decoder-only Transformer model, specifically the BERT (Bidirectional Encoder Representations from Transformers) Transformer, to judiciously analyze the tokens generated by the Graph Autoencoder. This innovative adaptation replaces the standard BERT methodology of random masking with a more strategic future masking approach. This nuanced modification aligns with the inherent goal of pose prediction—accurately forecasting future pose sequences. The future masking technique ensures that the model remains oblivious to the 'future' tokens during training, mirroring a real-world scenario where future poses are inherently unknown.

In the training, the loss function is another pivotal aspect where the GAT-POSE framework deviates from conventional practices. Rather than employing the typical cross-entropy loss, the Mean Square Error (MSE) is adopted as the loss function. This choice is symbolic of the continuous nature of the pose data, where MSE provides a more fitting measure of the deviations between the predicted and actual pose sequences.

The Transformer's architecture in GAT-POSE is not merely a passive recipient of the tokens; the built-in attention mechanism can identify the relevant segments of the tokenized data. It translates to a more nuanced understanding of pose evolution over time. Moreover, the parallel processing capability inherent to the Transformer architecture significantly accelerates the training phase, rendering the GAT-POSE framework amenable to scaling across larger datasets. This scalability feature is indispensable in exploring the vast and diverse datasets presented in three unique environments, as proposed in this study.

The novelty of GAT-POSE does not just reside in its unique architecture but extends to its proposition as a more generic domain-invariant approach for pose predictions. The usage of large pre-trained Transformers manifests as a versatile strategy, capable of traversing domain boundaries, thereby broadening the horizon for pose prediction applications. This generic approach, spurred by the GAT-POSE framework, embarks on a path less trodden, offering a fresh perspective and a robust methodology for tackling the challenges of future pose prediction.

How pose sequences are tokenized can significantly impact the performance and the insights garnered from the transformer model. In light of this, three distinct tokenization strategies are delineated: Normal, Relative, and Context tokenizations. Each approach encapsulates a unique perspective on how the pose data is represented and fed into the Transformer for subsequent analysis and prediction.

Normal: In the Normal tokenization strategy, each pose is treated as a standalone token. This straightforward approach encapsulates the inherent structure and information contained within individual poses. The tokens, representing distinct poses, are fed directly into the transformer model. This approach provides a direct and unaltered view of the pose data, allowing the Transformer to discern patterns and make predictions based on the original pose sequences.

Relative: The Relative tokenization strategy adopts a more nuanced approach by amalgamating both the absolute pose and the relative pose into a single token. This strategy aims to augment the pose data with additional spatial insights. By including the relative pose—which encapsulates the spatial relationships among different parts of the pose—the tokens carry a richer set of information compared to the Normal tokenization. This enriched token representation, comprising both absolute and relative pose data, provides a more comprehensive view of the pose dynamics, potentially enhancing the Transformer's ability to make more accurate predictions.

Context: Context tokenization dives deeper by introducing an additional layer of contextual information to the tokenization process. In this strategy, an 'action' token is prepended at the beginning of the pose sequence. This action token serves as a contextual cue, providing a broader understanding of the underlying activity. By integrating this contextual information, the Transformer is equipped with a more holistic understanding of the pose sequences it analyzes. This additional context may facilitate a more nuanced interpretation of the pose data, aiding in more accurate forecasting of future pose sequences.

Each of these tokenization strategies embodies a unique approach to representing pose data, and their efficacy may vary depending on the specific requirements of the pose prediction task at hand.

4 Experiment and Evaluation

4.1 Human3.6M

Human3.6M [11] is a widely used benchmark dataset for human motion analysis and pose prediction. It contains 3.6 million annotated 3D human poses captured by professional actors performing 15 daily activities such as walking, sitting, and eating. The dataset offers multi-view RGB videos and corresponding 3D ground-truth joint locations, recorded at 50 Frames Per Second (FPS). The dataset's original 3D pose skeleton, encompassing 32 joints, serves as the primary foundation; however, researchers have explored variations of this skeleton in their works.

Various experimental configurations have been employed across diverse studies. To ensure a rigorous and equitable comparison between our model and existing approaches, we define three distinct environments (Env), each characterized by specific parameters, including Observation Horizon (O_h), Prediction Horizon (P_h), and a subset of keypoints (K_s) out of the total 32 available joints. Notably, all environments share an expected downsampling rate of 25 frames per second (FPS). Table 1 presents comprehensive information about each environment. Following previous studies, training has been done on 5 subjects, while 2 subjects are left for validation and testing.

Table 1. Complete detail of each training and testing environment. All were chosen based on previous studies for fair comparison. O_h, P_h, and K_s are the Observation Horizon in frames, the Prediction Horizon in frames, and the number of joints available in the subset of keypoints.

Environment	O_h	P_h	K_s	Metric
Env-1	50	25	22	FDE (mm)
Env-2	10	25	22	ADE (mm)
Env-3	10	25	17	FDE (mm)

The dataset is resampled to a frame rate of 25 frames per second (FPS). The observation horizon spans 2 s, equivalent to 50 frames, while the prediction horizon extends to 1 s, encompassing 25 frames. Within this dataset, a subset of 22 keypoints, selected from the original 32, represents the human pose.

Table 2. Description of Environments.

Environment	Main Metric	Observation Frames	Predicted Frames	Downsampling	Keypoints	Train	Validation
Env-1	FDE mm	50 (2 s)	25 (1 s)	50 FPS to 25 FPS	22	5	2
Env-2	ADE mm	10	25	50 FPS to 25 FPS	22	5	2
Env-3	FDE mm	10	25	50 FPS to 25 FPS	17	5	2

Table 3. Configurations for three distinct experimental setups denoted as Env-1, Env-2, and Env-3. Different token variants—Normal, Normal+Relative, and Normal+Context—are assessed for each environment, showcasing a systematic exploration of configurations.

Environment	Token	# Heads	# Layers	FFL	Dropout	LR
Env-1	Normal	11	8	512	0.2	0.0001
	Normal+Relative	22	10	512	0.2	0.0001
	Normal+Context	11	8	512	0.2	0.0005
Env-2	Normal	11	8	512	0.2	0.0001
	Normal+Relative	22	10	512	0.2	0.0001
	Normal+Context	11	8	512	0.2	0.0005
Env-3	Normal	17	8	512	0.2	0.0005
	Normal+Relative	17	8	512	0.2	0.0005
	Normal+Context	17	8	512	0.2	0.0005

4.2   Evaluation Metrics

FDE stands for Final Displacement Error. It quantifies the disparity between the predicted positions of joints at their final time step per each predicted horizon and their actual ground truth positions. This discrepancy is measured using the L2 distance, which calculates the Euclidean distance between the predicted and ground truth joint positions in millimeters. FDE comprehensively evaluates the model's performance in predicting joint positions. Let N, K, G_i, and P_i be the number of last predicted poses in each horizon through the entire dataset, the number of keypoints per skeleton, the ground truth position of i-th joint, and the predicted position of i-th joint. FDE is calculated based on Eq. 2.

$$\text{FDE} = \frac{1}{N \times K} \sum_{n=1}^{N} \sum_{k=1}^{K} ||G_k^n - P_k^n|| \tag{2}$$

ADE stands for Average Displacement Error. It is very similar to FDE except that instead of averaging over the last predicted frame per each predicted horizon, the average is taken over all the joints in all the predicted skeletons up to the last predicted one in each prediction horizon. Let N, H, K, G_i, and P_i be the number of predicted horizons (equivalent to the total number of predicted windows) through the entire dataset, number of predicted skeletons per horizon, number of keypoints per skeleton, the ground truth position of i-th joint, and the predicted position of i-th joint. ADE is calculated based on Eq. 3.

$$\text{ADE} = \frac{1}{N \times K \times H} \sum_{n=1}^{N} \sum_{h=1}^{H} \sum_{k=1}^{K} ||G_{n,h,k} - P_{n,h,k}|| \tag{3}$$

4.3   Results and Comparative Analysis

Table 4. Comparative data across different models under two metrics—Average Displacement Error (ADE) and Final Displacement Error (FDE), across various timestamps (320, 560, 720, 880, 1000 ms). The models include established approaches like Res.Sup. [32], ConvSeq2Seq [16], LTD-50-25 [26,30,31], and [38], along with some modified versions like HRI+TCD and PGBIG+TCD.

Model	ADE					FDE				
Milliseconds	320	560	720	880	1000	320	560	720	880	1000
Res. Sup.	77	106.3	119.4	130	136.6	–	–	–	–	–
ConvSeq2Seq	61.4	90.7	104.7	116.7	124.2	–	–	–	–	–
LTD-50-25	50.7	79.6	93.6	105.2	112.4	–	–	–	–	–
HRI	47.1	77.3	91.8	104.1	112.1	–	–	–	–	–
PGBIG	46.6	76.3	90.9	102.6	110	–	–	–	–	–
TCD	48.8	73.7	84	94.3	103.3	–	–	–	–	–
HRI+TCD	47.3	72.9	83.8	94	102.9	–	–	–	–	–
PGBIG+TCD	46.1	72.4	83.6	93.9	102.8	–	–	–	–	–
Ours - Normal	119.4	184.6	224.63	261.1	287.19	80.08	113.34	134.81	155.34	170.11
Ours - Relative	366.11	432.72	416.88	409.26	409.5	178.18	283.23	314.26	331.9	341.17
Ours - Context	96.91	134.69	157.26	179.59	197.05	69.87	91.12	103.97	116.18	125.19

Table 2 describes the specifications of three distinct experimental environments, namely Env-1, Env-2, and Env-3, employed in a study pertaining to human pose prediction. The tabulated data encapsulates essential parameters for each environment, including the main metric used for evaluation—Final Displacement Error (FDE) in millimeters for Env-1 and Env-3 and Average Displacement Error (ADE) in millimeters for Env-2. Additionally, the table provides information on the number of observation frames and predicted frames, along with the downsampling rate used to convert the frame rate from 50 FPS to 25 FPS. The number of keypoints considered in each environment is also specified, with 22 keypoints for Env-1 and Env-2 and 17 keypoints for Env-3. Lastly, the table documents data division into training and validation sets, showcasing a uniform split across all three environments, with 5 units allocated for training and 2 for validation. Through such a detailed tabulation, the table offers a brief overview of the varying conditions under which the human pose prediction models were evaluated and compared.

Table 3 presents the configurations for three distinct experimental setups denoted as Env-1, Env-2, and Env-3. Different token variants—Normal, Normal+Relative, and Normal+Context—are assessed for each environment, showcasing a systematic exploration of configurations. The table delineates the parameters of the Transformer architecture used in each setup, specifying the number of attention heads (# of Heads), the number of layers (# of Layers), the size of the feed-forward layer (FFL), the dropout rate (Dropout), and the learning rate (LR) for every token variant across the three environments. These settings are crucial as they significantly impact the pose prediction models' learning process and performance. In particular, it reflects how variations in the Transformer architecture and learning configurations are applied to evaluate their efficacy in different scenarios, aiding in identifying an optimal setup for human pose prediction tasks.

Table 5. Performance of various models regarding ADE and FDE at different timestamps (320, 560, 720, 880, 1000 ms). Models include STSGCN [40], GAGCN [48], TCD [38], and three configurations of a new approach labeled as "Ours" - Normal, Relative, and Context.

Model	ADE					FDE				
Milliseconds	320	560	720	880	1000	320	560	720	880	1000
STSGCN	17.3	33.5	38.9	51.7	77.3	–	–	–	–	–
GAGCN	16.9	32.5	38.5	50	72.9	–	–	–	–	–
TCD	14	27.7	33.9	44.7	66.5	–	–	–	–	–
Ours - Normal	80.9	92.4	98.5	103.4	106.7	96.6	114.4	122.4	127.9	131.8
Ours - Relative	71.6	86	94	101	105.7	89	115	126.3	135.7	141.9
Ours - Context	85.7	103.8	115.1	126	134.2	107.8	141.5	162.3	183.2	200

Table 4 presents comparative data across different models under two metrics—Average Displacement Error (ADE) and Final Displacement Error (FDE), across various timestamps (320, 560, 720, 880, 1000 ms). The models include established approaches like

Res.Sup. [32], ConvSeq2Seq [16], LTD-50-25 [26,30,31], and [38], along with some modified versions like HRI+TCD and PGBIG+TCD. Additionally, the table showcases three configurations of a new approach labeled "Ours" - Normal, Relative, and Context. A noticeable trend is the increasing error values in ADE as the milliseconds increase, particularly pronounced in the "Ours - Relative" model. The FDE values are not provided for most models, except the "Ours" configurations, where the error values also tend to increase with milliseconds but at a less dramatic rate than in ADE.

Table 5 presents the performance of various models in terms of ADE and FDE at different timestamps (320, 560, 720, 880, 1000 ms). Models include STSGCN [40], GAGCN [48], TCD [38], and three configurations of a new approach labeled as "Ours" - Normal, Relative, and Context. In general, the error values in ADE increase as the timestamps progress, with "Ours - Context" model exhibiting the highest errors, especially as time progresses. The models STSGCN, GAGCN, and TCD show relatively lower error values compared to the "Ours" configurations, with TCD having the lowest ADE across all timestamps among all models. On the FDE metric, data is only available for the "Ours" configurations. Among these, the "Ours - Context" model again registers the highest error values across all timestamps, while "Ours - Normal" shows the lowest. The "Ours - Relative" configuration stands in between the other two "Ours" configurations concerning error values. This comparative data underscores the variance in performance among different models and configurations in predicting human pose over time under two other error metrics.

Table 6. The performance of various models under two metrics—ADE and FDE across different timestamps (320, 560, 720, 880, 1000 ms). The models include LDRGCN [8], MPT [23], TCD [38], and three configurations of a new approach labeled as "Ours" - Normal, Relative, and Context.

Model	ADE					FDE				
Milliseconds	320	560	720	880	1000	320	560	720	880	1000
LDRGCN	22.5	45.1	55.8	–	97.8	–	–	–	–	–
MPT	18.8	39	47.9	65.3	96.4	–	–	–	–	–
TCD	18.8	37.8	44.9	55.9	76.9	–	–	–	–	–
Ours - Normal	55.1	60.9	63.8	66.1	67.7	63.3	71.6	75	77.8	80.1
Ours - Relative	54.3	63.2	68.2	72.6	75.5	64.7	81.2	88.5	94.4	98.4
Ours - Context	58.08	69.53	76.89	84.22	89.8	71.96	93.71	107.95	122.83	134.79

Table 6 outlines the performance of various models under two metrics—ADE and FDE across different timestamps (320, 560, 720, 880, 1000 ms). The models include LDRGCN [8], MPT [23], TCD [38], and three configurations of a new approach labeled as "Ours" - Normal, Relative, and Context. In general, ADE increases with the progression of time for all models. Among the models, LDRGCN [8] and MPT [23] show a substantial increase in ADE from 320 to 1000 ms, while TCD maintains a relatively lower and steadier increase. The "Ours" configurations exhibit a moderate rise in ADE, with "Ours - Context" showing the highest ADE at 1000 ms among the three. For the FDE metric, data is provided only for the "Ours" configurations. All three "Ours" configurations show an increase in FDE as time progresses, with "Ours - Context" registering the highest error values across all timestamps and "Ours - Normal" showing the lowest. This table compares different models' performance in human pose prediction across various time intervals under two distinct error metrics.

5   Conclusions and Future Work

The GAT-POSE framework introduces a novel approach to pose prediction by harnessing the capabilities of the Transformer autoencoder. The framework's inherent scalability is a testament to its ability to manage larger datasets, making it apt for diverse data explorations. Furthermore, the domain-invariant nature of the GAT-POSE positions it as a versatile tool designed for an extensive range of pose prediction applications. The research presents three unique tokenization strategies, Normal, Relative, and Contex, that underscore the critical role of token representation in influencing model outcomes. Each tokenization method offers a distinct perspective on pose data interpretation, with findings suggesting that the richness of Context tokenization may not always translate to minimized error rates. In contrast, the straightforwardness of the Normal strategy seems to provide more consistent results in terms of the evaluated error metrics.

Building upon the insights derived from this study, there are multiple promising trajectories for future research. The exploration of enhanced tokenization techniques emerges as a potential area of study. Researchers could uncover methods leading to even more precise pose predictions by fusing the strengths of the discussed tokenization strategies. A deeper dive into this area could pave the way for performance enhancements. The framework's scalability invites exploration across diverse datasets from diverse environments. We will also look into practical implementations of the GAT-POSE framework in real-world scenarios, spanning sports analytics, healthcare, and entertainment.

References

1. Ahmed, S., Huda, M.N., Rajbhandari, S., Saha, C., Elshaw, M., Kanarachos, S.: Pedestrian and cyclist detection and intent estimation for autonomous vehicles: a survey. Appl. Sci. **9**(11), 2335 (2019)
2. Aliakbarian, S., Saleh, F.S., Salzmann, M., Petersson, L., Gould, S.: A stochastic conditioning scheme for diverse human motion prediction. In: Proceedings of the IEEE/CVF Conference on Computer Vision and Pattern Recognition, pp. 5223–5232 (2020)
3. Barsoum, E., Kender, J., Liu, Z.: HP-GAN: probabilistic 3D human motion prediction via GAN. In: Proceedings of the IEEE Conference on Computer Vision and Pattern Recognition Workshops, pp. 1418–1427 (2018)
4. Bütepage, J., Kjellström, H., Kragic, D.: Anticipating many futures: online human motion prediction and generation for human-robot interaction. In: 2018 IEEE International Conference on Robotics and Automation (ICRA), pp. 4563–4570. IEEE (2018)
5. Chao, X., et al.: Adversarial refinement network for human motion prediction. In: Proceedings of the Asian Conference on Computer Vision (2020)

6. Corona, E., Pumarola, A., Alenya, G., Moreno-Noguer, F.: Context-aware human motion prediction. In: Proceedings of the IEEE/CVF Conference on Computer Vision and Pattern Recognition, pp. 6992–7001 (2020)
7. Cui, Q., Sun, H., Yang, F.: Learning dynamic relationships for 3D human motion prediction. In: Proceedings of the IEEE/CVF Conference on Computer Vision and Pattern Recognition, pp. 6519–6527 (2020)
8. Cui, Q., Sun, H., Yang, F.: Learning dynamic relationships for 3D human motion prediction. In: IEEE/CVF Conference on Computer Vision and Pattern Recognition (CVPR), pp. 6519–6527 (2020)
9. Guo, X., Choi, J.: Human motion prediction via learning local structure representations and temporal dependencies. In: Proceedings of the AAAI Conference on Artificial Intelligence, vol. 33, pp. 2580–2587 (2019)
10. Huang, Z., Liu, Y., Fang, Y., Horn, B.K.: Video-based fall detection for seniors with human pose estimation. In: 2018 4th International Conference on Universal Village (UV), pp. 1–4. IEEE (2018)
11. Ionescu, C., Papava, D., Olaru, V., Sminchisescu, C.: Human3.6m: large scale datasets and predictive methods for 3D human sensing in natural environments. IEEE Trans. Pattern Anal. Mach. Intell. **36**(7), 1325–1339 (2013)
12. Jain, D.K., Zareapoor, M., Jain, R., Kathuria, A., Bachhety, S.: GAN-poser: an improvised bidirectional GAN model for human motion prediction. Neural Comput. Appl. **32**(18), 14579–14591 (2020)
13. Jeon, H., Yoon, Y., Kim, D.: Lightweight 2D human pose estimation for fitness coaching system. In: 2021 36th International Technical Conference on Circuits/Systems, Computers and Communications (ITC-CSCC), pp. 1–4. IEEE (2021)
14. Kundu, J.N., Gor, M., Babu, R.V.: BiHMP-GAN: bidirectional 3D human motion prediction GAN. In: Proceedings of the AAAI Conference on Artificial Intelligence, vol. 33, pp. 8553–8560 (2019)
15. Li, C., Zhang, Z., Lee, W.S., Lee, G.H.: Convolutional sequence to sequence model for human dynamics. In: Proceedings of the IEEE Conference on Computer Vision and Pattern Recognition, pp. 5226–5234 (2018)
16. Li, C., Zhang, Z., Lee, W.S., Lee, G.H.: Convolutional sequence to sequence model for human dynamics. In: IEEE/CVF Conference on Computer Vision and Pattern Recognition (CVPR), pp. 5226–5234 (2018)
17. Li, M., Chen, S., Zhao, Y., Zhang, Y., Wang, Y., Tian, Q.: Dynamic multiscale graph neural networks for 3D skeleton based human motion prediction. In: Proceedings of the IEEE/CVF Conference on Computer Vision and Pattern Recognition, pp. 214–223 (2020)
18. Li, M., Chen, S., Zhao, Y., Zhang, Y., Wang, Y., Tian, Q.: Multiscale spatio-temporal graph neural networks for 3D skeleton-based motion prediction. IEEE Trans. Image Process. **30**, 7760–7775 (2021)
19. Li, Y., et al.: Efficient convolutional hierarchical autoencoder for human motion prediction. Vis. Comput. **35**, 1143–1156 (2019)
20. Liu, D., Li, Q., Li, S., Kong, J., Qi, M.: Non-autoregressive sparse transformer networks for pedestrian trajectory prediction. Appl. Sci. **13**(5), 3296 (2023)
21. Liu, S., Huang, X., Fu, N., Li, C., Su, Z., Ostadabbas, S.: Simultaneously-collected multimodal lying pose dataset: enabling in-bed human pose monitoring. IEEE Trans. Pattern Anal. Mach. Intell. **45**(1), 1106–1118 (2022)
22. Liu, X., Yin, J., Liu, J., Ding, P., Liu, J., Liu, H.: TrajectoryCNN: a new spatio-temporal feature learning network for human motion prediction. IEEE Trans. Circuits Syst. Video Technol. **31**(6), 2133–2146 (2020)
23. Liu, Z., et al.: Motion prediction using trajectory cues. In: IEEE/CVF International Conference on Computer Vision (ICCV), pp. 13299–13308 (2021)

24. Lyu, K., Chen, H., Liu, Z., Zhang, B., Wang, R.: 3D human motion prediction: a survey. Neurocomputing **489**, 345–365 (2022)
25. Lyu, K., Liu, Z., Wu, S., Chen, H., Zhang, X., Yin, Y.: Learning human motion prediction via stochastic differential equations. In: Proceedings of the 29th ACM International Conference on Multimedia, pp. 4976–4984 (2021)
26. Ma, T., Nie, Y., Long, C., Zhang, Q., Li, G.: Progressively generating better initial guesses towards next stages for high-quality human motion prediction. In: IEEE/CVF Conference on Computer Vision and Pattern Recognition (CVPR), pp. 6437–6446 (2022)
27. Mahdavian, M., Nikdel, P., TaherAhmadi, M., Chen, M.: STPOTR: simultaneous human trajectory and pose prediction using a non-autoregressive transformer for robot follow-ahead. In: 2023 IEEE International Conference on Robotics and Automation (ICRA), pp. 9959–9965. IEEE (2023)
28. Mandal, S., Biswas, S., Balas, V.E., Shaw, R.N., Ghosh, A.: Motion prediction for autonomous vehicles from Lyft dataset using deep learning. In: 2020 IEEE 5th International Conference on Computing Communication and Automation (ICCCA), pp. 768–773. IEEE (2020)
29. Mangalam, K., Adeli, E., Lee, K.H., Gaidon, A., Niebles, J.C.: Disentangling human dynamics for pedestrian locomotion forecasting with noisy supervision. In: Proceedings of the IEEE/CVF Winter Conference on Applications of Computer Vision, pp. 2784–2793 (2020)
30. Mao, W., Liu, M., Salzmann, M.: History repeats itself: human motion prediction via motion attention. In: Vedaldi, A., Bischof, H., Brox, T., Frahm, J.-M. (eds.) ECCV 2020. LNCS, vol. 12359, pp. 474–489. Springer, Cham (2020). https://doi.org/10.1007/978-3-030-58568-6_28
31. Mao, W., Liu, M., Salzmann, M., Li, H.: Learning trajectory dependencies for human motion prediction. In: IEEE/CVF International Conference on Computer Vision (ICCV) (2019)
32. Martinez, J., Black, M.J., Romero, J.: On human motion prediction using recurrent neural networks. In: IEEE/CVF Conference on Computer Vision and Pattern Recognition (CVPR), pp. 2891–2900 (2017)
33. Martínez-González, A., Villamizar, M., Odobez, J.M.: Pose transformers (POTR): human motion prediction with non-autoregressive transformers. In: Proceedings of the IEEE/CVF International Conference on Computer Vision, pp. 2276–2284 (2021)
34. Medsker, L.R., Jain, L.: Recurrent neural networks. Des. Appl. **5**(64–67), 2 (2001)
35. Nikdel, P., Mahdavian, M., Chen, M.: DMMGAN: diverse multi motion prediction of 3D human joints using attention-based generative adversarial network. In: 2023 IEEE International Conference on Robotics and Automation (ICRA), pp. 9938–9944. IEEE (2023)
36. Noghre, G.A., Pazho, A.D., Katariya, V., Tabkhi, H.: Understanding the challenges and opportunities of pose-based anomaly detection. arXiv preprint arXiv:2303.05463 (2023)
37. Pazho, A.D., et al.: Ancilia: scalable intelligent video surveillance for the artificial intelligence of things. IEEE Internet Things J. (2023)
38. Saadatnejad, S., et al.: A generic diffusion-based approach for 3D human pose prediction in the wild. In: 2023 IEEE International Conference on Robotics and Automation (ICRA), pp. 8246–8253 (2023). https://doi.org/10.1109/ICRA48891.2023.10160399
39. Saadatnejad, S., et al.: A generic diffusion-based approach for 3D human pose prediction in the wild. In: 2023 IEEE International Conference on Robotics and Automation (ICRA), pp. 8246–8253. IEEE (2023)
40. Sofianos, T., Sampieri, A., Franco, L., Galasso, F.: Space-time-separable graph convolutional network for pose forecasting. In: IEEE/CVF International Conference on Computer Vision (ICCV), pp. 11209–11218 (2021)
41. Tang, Y., et al.: Flag3D: a 3D fitness activity dataset with language instruction. In: Proceedings of the IEEE/CVF Conference on Computer Vision and Pattern Recognition, pp. 22106–22117 (2023)

42. Wang, H., Dong, J., Cheng, B., Feng, J.: PVRED: a position-velocity recurrent encoder-decoder for human motion prediction. IEEE Trans. Image Process. **30**, 6096–6106 (2021)

43. Wang, Y., Wang, X., Jiang, P., Wang, F.: RNN-based human motion prediction via differential sequence representation. In: 2019 IEEE 6th International Conference on Cloud Computing and Intelligence Systems (CCIS), pp. 138–143. IEEE (2019)

44. Yang, X., Ren, X., Chen, M., Wang, L., Ding, Y.: Human posture recognition in intelligent healthcare. In: Journal of Physics: Conference Series, vol. 1437, p. 012014. IOP Publishing (2020)

45. Yu, H., et al.: Towards realistic 3D human motion prediction with a spatio-temporal cross-transformer approach. IEEE Trans. Circuits Syst. Video Technol. (2023)

46. Yu, S., et al.: Regularity learning via explicit distribution modeling for skeletal video anomaly detection. IEEE Trans. Circuits Syst. Video Technol. (2023)

47. Yuan, Y., Kitani, K.: DLow: diversifying latent flows for diverse human motion prediction. In: Vedaldi, A., Bischof, H., Brox, T., Frahm, J.-M. (eds.) ECCV 2020. LNCS, vol. 12354, pp. 346–364. Springer, Cham (2020). https://doi.org/10.1007/978-3-030-58545-7_20

48. Zhong, C., Hu, L., Zhang, Z., Ye, Y., Xia, S.: Spatio-temporal gating-adjacency GCN for human motion prediction. In: IEEE/CVF Conference on Computer Vision and Pattern Recognition (CVPR), pp. 6447–6456 (2022)

49. Zimmermann, C., Welschehold, T., Dornhege, C., Burgard, W., Brox, T.: 3D human pose estimation in RGBD images for robotic task learning. In: 2018 IEEE International Conference on Robotics and Automation (ICRA), pp. 1986–1992. IEEE (2018)

50. Zou, J., et al.: Intelligent fitness trainer system based on human pose estimation. In: Sun, S., Fu, M., Xu, L. (eds.) ICSINC 2018. LNEE, vol. 550, pp. 593–599. Springer, Singapore (2019). https://doi.org/10.1007/978-981-13-7123-3_69

UCorr: Wire Detection and Depth Estimation for Autonomous Drones

Benedikt Kolbeinsson$^{(\boxtimes)}$ and Krystian Mikolajczyk

Imperial College London, London, UK
{bk915,k.mikolajczyk}@imperial.ac.uk

Abstract. In the realm of fully autonomous drones, the accurate detection of obstacles is paramount to ensure safe navigation and prevent collisions. Among these challenges, the detection of wires stands out due to their slender profile, which poses a unique and intricate problem. To address this issue, we present an innovative solution in the form of a monocular end-to-end model for wire segmentation and depth estimation. Our approach leverages a temporal correlation layer trained on synthetic data, providing the model with the ability to effectively tackle the complex joint task of wire detection and depth estimation. We demonstrate the superiority of our proposed method over existing competitive approaches in the joint task of wire detection and depth estimation. Our results underscore the potential of our model to enhance the safety and precision of autonomous drones, shedding light on its promising applications in real-world scenarios.

Keywords: Wire detection · Depth estimation · Wire segmentation · Monocular vision · Drones · UAV

1 Introduction

In the era of autonomous systems and unmanned aerial vehicles (UAVs), the ability to navigate through complex environments with precision and safety is of paramount importance. One critical aspect of this challenge is the accurate detection of obstacles, a task that holds the key to preventing collisions and ensuring successful mission execution. Among these potential obstacles, wires, with their slim and inconspicuous profiles, represent a particularly formidable challenge. In this research, we delve into the intricate world of wire detection and depth estimation, unveiling a novel and effective approach that holds promise for enhancing the capabilities of autonomous drones in real-world scenarios.

UAVs have evolved to encompass a wide spectrum of capabilities, from those under remote human control to fully autonomous systems. UAVs have found extensive applications, including forestry research [40], autonomous inspections of electrical distribution networks [29] and package delivery [2]. Notably, the utilization of UAVs in disaster response operations has garnered significant attention due to their potential critical roles [1,8,13,14,32,33]. These versatile aerial platforms offer promising solutions for various real-world challenges, setting the stage for innovations that can enhance safety, efficiency, and effectiveness in diverse domains.

© The Author(s), under exclusive license to Springer Nature Switzerland AG 2024
J. Filipe and J. Röning (Eds.): ROBOVIS 2024, CCIS 2077, pp. 179–192, 2024.
https://doi.org/10.1007/978-3-031-59057-3_12

In the pursuit of safe and collision-free flight, UAVs have traditionally relied on obstacle detection systems, often employing proximity sensors based on ultrasound or computer vision. However, these existing systems face a notable limitation: their inability to consistently and reliably detect thin obstacles, such as power lines, telephone wires, and structural cables.

The weight of a UAV is a critical factor that directly influences its efficiency and maneuverability. Integrating additional sensors, such as LiDAR, for improved object detection can yield significant benefits but often comes at the cost of undesirable trade-offs. These compromises include adverse effects on flight characteristics and heightened expenditure. In this context, it is worth noting that nearly all UAVs are equipped with cameras for a multitude of purposes. Leveraging these onboard cameras to detect wires and obstacles not only eliminates the need for additional weight but also circumvents the burden of extra hardware costs.

Detecting wires in images presents a formidable challenge stemming from multiple factors. Wires possess inherent thinness, often manifesting as single-pixel or sub-pixel entities. Their subtle presence can seamlessly blend into complex and cluttered backgrounds, rendering them elusive even to human observers. With limited distinctive features, wires at the pixel level can bear a striking resemblance to other commonplace structures. However, merely identifying wires within an image is insufficient. Crucially, gauging the distance to these obstacles is paramount, as closer objects pose a heightened risk compared to distant ones. Moreover, to enable intelligent navigation through its environment, a drone must establish a comprehensive understanding of its surroundings

To tackle these challenges, we introduce UCorr, a monocular wire segmentation and depth estimation model. Utilizing a temporal correlation layer within an encoder-decoder architecture, as illustrated in Fig. 1, our approach surpasses the performance of existing methods in the domain of wire detection and depth estimation.

In summary, our contributions are as follows:

- We present UCorr, an innovative model tailored for monocular wire segmentation and depth estimation.
- We demonstrate that UCorr outperforms current methods, showcasing its potential to advance wire detection and depth estimation in autonomous systems.
- We introduce a novel wire depth evaluation metric designed to accurately assess wire depth estimation. This metric accounts for the unique characteristics of wires, providing a tailored and comprehensive evaluation.

2   Related Work

In this section, we provide an overview of related work on wire detection and depth estimation, discussing them separately due to limited research on their joint task.

2.1   Wire Detection

Academic research has predominantly concentrated on wire detection in images, with comparatively less emphasis placed on addressing the challenge of accurately determining the distance to the wires.

Traditional Computer Vision Techniques. Early work [19], proposed using the Steger algorithm [39] to detect edges on real images with synthetic wires, followed by a thresholded Hough transform [10]. This quickly became the standard approach for wire detection and following work used variations of these three stages: (1) An edge detector, (2) the Hough transform and finally (3) a filter.

For example, [23] first use a Pulse-Coupled Neural Network (PCNN) to filter the background of the images before using the Hough transform to detect straight lines. Then, using k-means clustering, power lines are detected and other line-like objects discarded. Similarly, [35] begin by removing large clutter using a Ring Median Filter and a SUSAN filter. To find wire like segments they use a gradient phase operator and vector path integration. Then merge small line segments together using morphological filters. Lastly, temporal information is used to remove non persistent line segments to reduce the false alarm rate. [43] start by using a gradient filter followed by the Hough transform to find line segments. Then k-means is used to select power lines and to discard other line-like objects. Lastly, using temporal information, the power lines are tracked using a Kalman filter. [5] combine temporal information to estimate pixel motion and a Canny edge detector [6] to form a feature map. This is followed by a windowed Hough transformation. The motion model is used to predict the next location of detected lines. [37] create an edge map using a matched filter and the first-order derivative of Gaussian. Morphological filtering is used to detect line segments before a graph-cut model groups line segments into whole lines. A final morphological filter is applied again to remove false lines. A slightly different approach was taken by [44] where they developed two methods. The first one, for a monocular camera which requires an inertial measurement unit and a second one, a stereo camera solution. Both start with a DoG edge detector [27] to detect edge points before reconstructing them in 3D space using temporal information.

Deep Learning Techniques. More recently, deep learning techniques have become more popular. [22] propose a weakly supervised CNN where the training images only have class labels. Multiple feature maps are generated at different depths of the network and are scaled and merged together to produce a final mask. [26] propose multiple variations of dilated convolutional networks trained on both synthetic data and real data. [38] use a CNN for feature generation then using two separate CNN networks, one of which classifies whether a wire is located near an anchor point while the other produces a Hesse norm line from the anchor to the detected wire. A Kalman filter helps tack the wires between frames and the wire's relative location is calculated. [42] use an edge detector proposed by [25] which is a modified version of VGG16 [36]. To remove the noise, only the longest edges with high confidence are kept. [30] use a CNN based on VGG16 to generate feature maps on different grids on the image. A classifier determines whether a wire appears on a grid and then a separate regressor network outputs the location of the longest line segment in each grid.

More recently, [7] propose a two-stage wire segmentation model where a coarse module focuses on capturing global contextual information and identifying regions potentially containing wires. Then a local module analyzes local wire-containing patches.

In contrast to these approaches, our model tackles wire detection and depth estimation simultaneously, trained end-to-end, and augmented with a correlation layer.

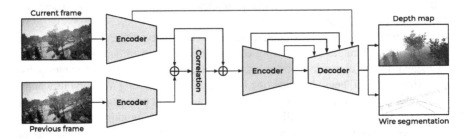

Fig. 1. Schematic of UCorr. Two sequential frames are used as input (both RGB). The leftmost encoders share weights. The output consist of a binary wire semantic segmentation map for the target image along with a full depth map. See Sect. 3 for more details.

2.2 Depth Estimation

Monocular depth estimation is an ongoing research problem that has seen continuous improvements over time. The problem of monocular depth estimation is comprised of a single image of a scene with the goal of producing the depth values for that scene. Here we present a brief overview over methods developed specifically for depth estimation.

Convolutional neural networks are a common method used to tackle this problem. For example, [12] propose a two stack approach. First a global network predicts a coarse depth map. The second local fine-scale network is applied to both the original image as well as the output of the global network, to produce the final output. Later [11] improve the network by making it deeper and add a third stage for higher resolution. Whereas, [21] propose a fully convolutional network in an encoder-decoder setup. The network uses ResNet-50 [18] as its backbone followed by unpooling and convolutional layers. They found that the reverse Huber loss, termed berHu [31], a mix between the standard L_1 and L_2 losses, performed well.

[16] present an unsupervised approach which uses image reconstruction loss as the training signal. In other words, instead of using the ground truth depth, which is difficult to acquire, they use a pair of binocular cameras (two cameras side-by-side) and learn to generate each image given its pair. Importantly, they compute both the left-to-right and right-to-left disparities using only the left input image. This allows them to achieve better depth prediction as both predictions should be consistent. Following this, [17] introduce an updated approach, Monodepth2, which uses a standard UNet [34] for depth prediction and a simple encoder to estimate the pose between images. By ignoring occluded pixels and pixels which violate motion assumption, they achieve greater performance.

More recently, methods [3,4,24] utilize a binning technique where the model estimates continuous depth by combining predicted probability distributions and discrete bins through a linear process.

3 Method

In this section, we present our method for wire detection and depth estimation. To begin, we will discuss the motivation and underlying principles that guided the development of our approach.

3.1 Motivation

From a visual perspective, wires have few unique visual features. The most obvious of which is their shape and color. One important feature common to most wires is their uniform construction. Note that significant differences still exist between wires, but individual wires will have consistent features, such as their width. However, an individual wire can be exposed to multiple different environmental factors across a scene resulting in perceived global differences.

To exploit some of this inherent local consistency, and occasional global consistency, we propose a self correlation layer. A correlation layer, much like a convolutional layer, applies a kernel to an input image. Unlike a convolutional layer, the kernel in the correlation layer does not include any learned weights but instead consists of data. This data can be a second image and thus the output represents the correlation between the input image and the second image. The output tensor consists of the correlation between each pixel or patch from both images. Given two patches of size $K = 2k + 1$, centered at $\mathbf{p}_1$ and $\mathbf{p}_2$, a single comparison between them can be defined as:

$$c(\mathbf{p}_1, \mathbf{p}_2) = \sum_{\mathbf{o} \in [-k,k] \times [-k,k]} \langle \mathbf{f}_1(\mathbf{p}_1 + \mathbf{o}), \mathbf{f}_2(\mathbf{p}_2 + \mathbf{o}) \rangle \tag{1}$$

where $\mathbf{f}_1$ and $\mathbf{f}_2$ and are multi-channel feature maps. Our implementation is inspired on FlowNet [9] which also introduces a maximum displacement parameter. This prevents calculating the correlation of pixels in completely different parts of the images. Instead, our proposed method only calculates the local correlation around each patch.

This correlation layer does not only benefit the wire segmentation capabilities of the model but also helps with depth estimation. Monocular depth estimation is inherently difficult due to the lack of three dimensional perspective. However, as a drone flies, multiple frames from the drone's camera can be recorded, which in turn provide rich temporal information. We hypothesize that the correlation layer helps extract this information as it allows the model to match objects between frames. Thus the flow of the scene can be understood as objects closer will have a larger displacement between frames compared to objects further away.

To fully utilize the correlation layer we propose UCorr, an end-to-end wire segmentation and depth estimation model. UCorr is the result of strategically adding a temporal correlation layer to the UNet [34] architecture. UNet, first developed for biomedical image segmentation, has now has become the *de facto* baseline for all segmentation tasks.

3.2 UCorr Network Architecture

UCorr comprises two independent input paths, illustrated in Fig. 1. The first path handles the current image frame from the drone's RGB camera, while the second path

Table 1. Wire segmentation on our simulated flights. Best results shown in bold. Due to the large class imbalance (very few pixels of wires), metrics such as AUC can be misleading. However, UCorr outperforms all the other methods in every metric.

Model	Depth	IoU (↑)	AUC (↑)	AP (↑)	Precision (↑)	Recall (↑)	F1 (↑)
Canny	No	0.011	–	–	0.012	0.220	0.022
DCNN	No	0.030	0.866	0.077	0.058	0.217	0.083
UNet	Yes	0.123	0.986	0.419	0.219	0.589	0.307
UCorr (ours)	Yes	**0.138**	**0.989**	**0.451**	**0.247**	**0.605**	**0.339**

processes the previous image frame. These initial encoders have common architecture and weights. The encoder pair use a set of convolutional layers and max pooling to compose an encoding of the input frames. This design enables the correlation layer to correlated between learned features from each image frame rather than raw pixel values. The remainder of the network features a convolutional auto-encoder with skip connections to alleviate information bottlenecks, similar to UNet. Importantly, there is a skip-connection from the first encoder (the one with the current frame) to the decoder.

In addition, we explore variations of this architecture in our ablation studies in Sect. 4.5.

3.3 Loss Function

We propose to use a loss function that incorporates both a wire segmentation component and a depth estimation component. The total loss function is defined as:

$$\mathcal{L}_{total} = \mathcal{L}_{wire} + \mathcal{L}_{depth} \tag{2}$$

where $\mathcal{L}_{wire}$ is the cross-entropy loss for pixel-wise binary classification of wires, thus:

$$\mathcal{L}_{wire} = -w(y\log(p) + (1-y)\log(1-p)) \tag{3}$$

where y is the binary label, p is the predicted label and w is an optional weight. Due to the class imbalance, the positive class is weighted 20 times the negative class in the loss. The depth loss has two components:

$$\mathcal{L}_{depth} = \mathcal{L}_{MAE} + \lambda\mathcal{L}_{MS-SSIM} \tag{4}$$

where $\mathcal{L}_{MAE}$ is the pixel-wise mean absolute error and $\mathcal{L}_{MS-SSIM}$ is the multi-scale structural similarity [41]. λ is set to 0.8.

4   Experiments

In this section, we provide an overview of the data and metrics used for our evaluation in the joint task of wire segmentation and depth estimation. Subsequently, we present both quantitative and qualitative results of our approach in this task. Additionally, we include an ablation study to analyze the individual components of our method and their contributions to the overall performance.

Table 2. Depth estimation on our simulated flights. Best results shown in bold. The Absolute Relative Error for Wire Depth (Abs. Rel. WD) is an especially challenging metric, which UCorr performs relatively well in.

Model	Segmentation	abs. rel. ($\downarrow$)	MAE ($\downarrow$)	abs. rel. WD ($\downarrow$)
UNet	Yes	0.129	**3.414**	0.606
UCorr (ours)	Yes	**0.128**	3.701	**0.564**

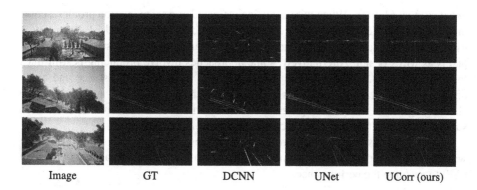

Image   GT   DCNN   UNet   UCorr (ours)

Fig. 2. Qualitative results for wire segmentation on our simulated flights. Each row showcases the output of various methods when applied to the input image as well as the ground truth (GT) segmentation. The visual representations are best observed in a digital format and can be examined more closely by zooming in. Our method tends to produce thinner segmentation masks, closely resembling the ground truth.

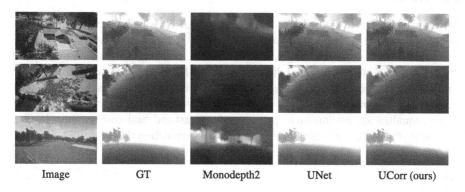

Image   GT   Monodepth2   UNet   UCorr (ours)

Fig. 3. Qualitative results for depth estimation on our simulated flights. Each row showcases the output of various methods when applied to the input image, as well as the ground truth (GT). Monodepth2 is trained on KITTI and fails to generalize to the less restrictive pose and more challenging data from the simulated drone flights. In the top row, the wires are clearly visible in the depth maps for both UNet and our method.

4.1 Data

No real-world annotated data exists for both wire segmentation and precise depth estimation from aerial views. Instead, we leverage the Drone Depth and Obstacle Segmentation (DDOS) dataset [20]. In total, DDOS contains 380 unique drone flights capturing 38 000 frames. 300 flights, are used for training while the remaining 80 flights are split evenly between validation and testing.

4.2 Metrics

Segmentation Metrics. When wire detection is treated as a segmentation problem, common metrics like IoU (Intersection over Union), precision, recall, and F1 score can be used. The advantage of this approach lies in its clear objective: classifying individual pixels as wires or not. Alternatively, some approaches involve producing best-fit lines to represent wires. These methods assess accuracy based on the distance and angle differences between proposed lines and ground truth. However, this approach can be challenging due to the non-straight nature of many wires. While various solutions exist, subtle metric variations can hinder comparisons among researchers.

Given the class imbalance (there are far fewer pixels of wires compared to not of wires), we also report the AUC (Area Under the Curve) score and average precision (AP) to evaluate the performance.

Depth Metrics. For depth estimation, we report the Absolute Relative Error (Abs. Rel.) and Mean Absolute Error (MAE). In addition, we introduce the Absolute Relative Error for Wire Depth (Abs. Rel. WD), a challenging metric designed for assessing models in drone-related tasks, where wires can be thin and appear free-floating.

4.3 Training

We train UCorr for 15 epochs on the training split of our synthetic dataset. We use a stochastic gradient descent (SGD) optimizer with momentum of 0.9 and weight decay equal to 0.01. An initial learning rate of 5×10^{-3}, decaying each epoch by a factor of 0.9. The maximum correlation disparity is set to 10. To increase generalization, we apply augmentation to the training data comprised of: motion blur, random flips, RGB shift, color jitter, randomize hue and saturation, invert, contrast limited adaptive histogram equalization, randomize brightness and contrast and randomize gamma. Images are rescaled to 853×480 using nearest neighbor interpolation (NNI).

4.4 Results

Quantitative Results. The quantitative results for wire segmentation and depth estimation can be found in Tables 1 and 2, respectively. In the wire segmentation task, our method demonstrates superior performance across all metrics, highlighting its effectiveness in accurately identifying wires. For depth estimation, our method particularly excels in the challenging absolute relative wire depth metric. This metric, which accounts for the thin nature of wires and their free-floating appearance, underscores our method's ability to accurately estimate the depth of wires in complex scenarios.

Overall, our model excels in this joint task, demonstrating superior performance across all but one evaluated metric. This highlights the effectiveness of our approach in simultaneously addressing wire segmentation and depth estimation.

Qualitative Results. Qualitative wire segmentation results, including comparisons with other methods, are displayed in Fig. 2. In these visual examples, we can observe the effectiveness of our method in accurately segmenting wires within the images, while also assessing how it performs in comparison to other approaches. Notably, our method tends to produce thinner segmentation masks that closely resemble the ground truth, as evident in the images. Qualitative depth estimation results from our simulated flights are presented in Fig. 3. Notably, Monodepth2 struggles to generalize to drone views, given its training on KITTI [15]. Meanwhile, the visible differences between our method and UNet are minimal.

4.5 Ablation Studies

Architecture Variants. First, the influence of architectural variants on UCorr's performance is explored. As detailed in Table 3, different locations for the correlation layer within the architecture are investigated. Specifically, UCorr variants based on pixel correlation, shallow features, and deep features are compared. The results are presented in terms of relative performance compared to UCorr with deep features. The superior performance of UCorr with deep features underscores the significance of this architectural choice.

Input Frames. Next, we examine the impact of the number of input frames on the model's performance. As shown in Table 4, UNet's performance is assessed with varying numbers of input frames, including 1, 2, and 3 frames. The relative performance is reported concerning UNet with a single input frame, which serves as the baseline for comparison. These findings emphasize that simply concatenating input frames is not sufficient. The correlation layer's role in integrating information across frames is a key factor in the model's success.

Skip-Connections. Finally, the role of skip-connections within the UCorr architecture is evaluated. Skip-connections are known for their ability to mitigate the information bottleneck and enhance feature propagation. In Table 5, the relative performance of UCorr without skip-connections is reported. The results highlight the critical role of skip-connections in enhancing the model's performance. The absence of skip connections leads to performance degradation, which can be attributed to the reduced capacity for information exchange between network layers.

5   Discussion

One limitation of our approach is its dependency on exactly two sequential input frames for temporal fusion. While this method is effective in many scenarios, it presents a

Table 3. Comparing UCorr architectural variants based on correlation layer location. UCorr (Pixel correlation) directly correlates input frame pixels. UCorr (Shallow features) employs small encoders for each input frame and correlates their shallow features. UCorr (Deep features) uses larger encoders and achieves the best performance, referred to as UCorr. Relative performance is reported compared to UCorr (Deep features).

Model	Δ Precision	Δ Recall	Δ F1
UCorr (Pixel correlation)	−15.7%	3.4%	−9.2%
UCorr (Shallow features)	−31.0%	4.5%	−20.6%
UCorr (Deep features)	−	−	−

Table 4. Comparing UNet performance with different numbers of input frames. UNet (1 frame) is the default version, while (2 frames) and (3 frames) involve simple frame concatenation. Relative performance is reported with respect to UNet (1 frame), which achieves the best overall performance.

Model	Δ Precision	Δ Recall	Δ F1
UNet (1 frame)	−	−	−
UNet (2 frames)	−6.2%	−5.1%	−6.0%
UNet (3 frames)	−1.6%	−9.1%	−2.8%

Table 5. Evaluating the influence of skip-connections in UCorr on performance. Skip-connections play a crucial role in the UCorr architecture, affecting its overall performance. We report relative performance in comparison to UCorr.

Model	Δ Precision	Δ Recall	Δ F1
UCorr	−	−	−
w/o skip-connections	−92.6%	15.6%	−88.5%

challenge when the drone is stationary or moving slowly, as there may be minimal discernible differences between consecutive frames. It would be advantageous if our method could adapt to varying frame numbers or capture and store scene flow during drone movement, addressing these situations more effectively.

A significant limitation is the absence of real-world data tailored for wire detection and depth estimation. Real-data testing is currently unfeasible as no such datasets exist, limiting the assessment of our method's real-world applicability. While testing against a broader range of benchmarks, especially those outside of methods tailored for wire detection, would have been beneficial, our work is constrained by computational resources.

This research also raises potential security and dual-use concerns, as the technology could be applied both for legitimate purposes and, in some cases, malicious applications. Researchers must remain vigilant in addressing these concerns and promoting the responsible and secure use of their findings.

The natural next step is implementing our method on a real drone, in collaboration with a dedicated hardware team. This practical deployment will validate the efficacy of our approach in real-world scenarios and pave the way for further enhancements based on empirical results. Additionally, exploring novel knowledge distillation techniques [28] offers opportunities to develop smaller, more efficient models.

6 Conclusion

Our contributions represent three significant advancements in the field. Firstly, we illuminate the underexplored domain of wire detection and depth estimation, recognizing its growing importance in applications like autonomous navigation and infrastructure maintenance. Secondly, our introduction of UCorr, an innovative model tailored for monocular wire segmentation and depth estimation, not only outperforms existing methods but also sets a valuable benchmark for the field. Finally, our novel wire depth evaluation metric enhances evaluation precision and comprehensiveness. Collectively, our work serves as a pivotal point for future research in this domain, opening doors for innovation and improved solutions.

References

1. Adams, S.M., Friedland, C.J.: A survey of unmanned aerial vehicle (UAV) usage for imagery collection in disaster research and management. In: 9th International Workshop on Remote Sensing for Disaster Response, vol. 8, pp. 1–8 (2011)
2. Benarbia, T., Kyamakya, K.: A literature review of drone-based package delivery logistics systems and their implementation feasibility. Sustainability **14**(1), 360 (2021)
3. Bhat, S.F., Alhashim, I., Wonka, P.: AdaBins: depth estimation using adaptive bins. In: IEEE Conference on Computer Vision and Pattern Recognition, CVPR 2021, Virtual, 19–25 June 2021, pp. 4009–4018. Computer Vision Foundation/IEEE (2021). https://doi.org/10.1109/CVPR46437.2021.00400, https://openaccess.thecvf.com/content/CVPR2021/html/Bhat_AdaBins_Depth_Estimation_Using_Adaptive_Bins_CVPR_2021_paper.html
4. Bhat, S.F., Birkl, R., Wofk, D., Wonka, P., Müller, M.: ZoeDepth: zero-shot transfer by combining relative and metric depth. ArXiv preprint abs/2302.12288 (2023). https://arxiv.org/abs/2302.12288
5. Candamo, J., Kasturi, R., Goldgof, D., Sarkar, S.: Detection of thin lines using low-quality video from low-altitude aircraft in urban settings. IEEE Trans. Aerosp. Electron. Syst. **45**(3), 937–949 (2009). https://doi.org/10.1109/TAES.2009.5259175
6. Canny, J.: A computational approach to edge detection. IEEE Trans. Pattern Anal. Mach. Intell. **6**, 679–698 (1986)
7. Chiu, M.T., et al.: Automatic high resolution wire segmentation and removal. In: Proceedings of the IEEE/CVF Conference on Computer Vision and Pattern Recognition, pp. 2183–2192 (2023)
8. Daud, S.M.S.M., et al.: Applications of drone in disaster management: a scoping review. Sci. Justice **62**(1), 30–42 (2022)
9. Dosovitskiy, A., et al.: FlowNet: learning optical flow with convolutional networks. In: 2015 IEEE International Conference on Computer Vision, ICCV 2015, Santiago, Chile, 7–13 December 2015, pp. 2758–2766. IEEE Computer Society (2015). https://doi.org/10.1109/ICCV.2015.316

10. Duda, R.O., Hart, P.E.: Use of the Hough transformation to detect lines and curves in pictures. Commun. ACM **15**(1), 11–15 (1972) https://doi.org/10.1145/361237.361242, http://portal.acm.org/citation.cfm?doid=361237.361242

11. Eigen, D., Fergus, R.: Predicting depth, surface normals and semantic labels with a common multi-scale convolutional architecture. In: 2015 IEEE International Conference on Computer Vision, ICCV 2015, Santiago, Chile, 7–13 December 2015, pp. 2650–2658. IEEE Computer Society (2015). https://doi.org/10.1109/ICCV.2015.304

12. Eigen, D., Puhrsch, C., Fergus, R.: Depth map prediction from a single image using a multi-scale deep network. In: Ghahramani, Z., Welling, M., Cortes, C., Lawrence, N.D., Weinberger, K.Q. (eds.) Advances in Neural Information Processing Systems 27: Annual Conference on Neural Information Processing Systems 2014, 8–13 December 2014, Montreal, Quebec, Canada, pp. 2366–2374 (2014). https://proceedings.neurips.cc/paper/2014/hash/7bccfde7714a1ebadf06c5f4cea752c1-Abstract.html

13. Erdelj, M., Natalizio, E., Chowdhury, K.R., Akyildiz, I.F.: Help from the sky: leveraging UAVs for disaster management. IEEE Pervasive Comput. **16**(1), 24–32 (2017). https://doi.org/10.1109/MPRV.2017.11

14. Estrada, M.A.R., Ndoma, A.: The uses of unmanned aerial vehicles-UAV's-(or drones) in social logistic: natural disasters response and humanitarian relief aid. Procedia Comput. Sci. **149**, 375–383 (2019)

15. Geiger, A., Lenz, P., Stiller, C., Urtasun, R.: Vision meets robotics: the KITTI dataset. Int. J. Robot. Res. (IJRR) **32**, 1231–1237 (2013)

16. Godard, C., Aodha, O.M., Brostow, G.J.: Unsupervised monocular depth estimation with left-right consistency. In: 2017 IEEE Conference on Computer Vision and Pattern Recognition, CVPR 2017, Honolulu, HI, USA, 21–26 July 2017, pp. 6602–6611. IEEE Computer Society (2017). https://doi.org/10.1109/CVPR.2017.699

17. Godard, C., Mac Aodha, O., Firman, M., Brostow, G.J.: Digging into self-supervised monocular depth prediction. In: Proceedings of the IEEE/CVF International Conference on Computer Vision, pp. 3828–3838 (2019)

18. He, K., Zhang, X., Ren, S., Sun, J.: Deep residual learning for image recognition. In: 2016 IEEE Conference on Computer Vision and Pattern Recognition, CVPR 2016, Las Vegas, NV, USA, 27–30 June 2016, pp. 770–778. IEEE Computer Society (2016). https://doi.org/10.1109/CVPR.2016.90

19. Kasturi, R., Camps, O., Huang, Y., Narasimhamurthy, A., Pande, N.: Wire detection algorithms for navigation. NASA Technical report (2002)

20. Kolbeinsson, B., Mikolajczyk, K.: DDOS: the drone depth and obstacle segmentation dataset. arXiv preprint arXiv:2312.12494 (2023)

21. Laina, I., Rupprecht, C., Belagiannis, V., Tombari, F., Navab, N.: Deeper depth prediction with fully convolutional residual networks. In: 2016 Fourth International Conference on 3D Vision (3DV), pp. 239–248. IEEE (2016)

22. Lee, S.J., Yun, J.P., Choi, H., Kwon, W., Koo, G., Kim, S.W.: Weakly supervised learning with convolutional neural networks for power line localization. In: 2017 IEEE Symposium Series on Computational Intelligence (SSCI), pp. 1–8 (2017). https://doi.org/10.1109/SSCI.2017.8285410

23. Li, Z., Liu, Y., Hayward, R., Zhang, J., Cai, J.: Knowledge-based power line detection for UAV surveillance and inspection systems. In: 2008 23rd International Conference Image and Vision Computing New Zealand, pp. 1–6 (2008). https://doi.org/10.1109/IVCNZ.2008.4762118, iSSN: 2151-2205

24. Li, Z., Wang, X., Liu, X., Jiang, J.: BinsFormer: revisiting adaptive bins for monocular depth estimation. ArXiv preprint abs/2204.00987 (2022). https://arxiv.org/abs/2204.00987

25. Liu, Y., Cheng, M., Hu, X., Wang, K., Bai, X.: Richer convolutional features for edge detection. In: 2017 IEEE Conference on Computer Vision and Pattern Recognition, CVPR 2017, Honolulu, HI, USA, 21–26 July 2017, pp. 5872–5881. IEEE Computer Society (2017). https://doi.org/10.1109/CVPR.2017.622, https://doi.org/10.1109/CVPR.2017.622

26. Madaan, R., Maturana, D., Scherer, S.: Wire detection using synthetic data and dilated convolutional networks for unmanned aerial vehicles. In: 2017 IEEE/RSJ International Conference on Intelligent Robots and Systems (IROS), pp. 3487–3494 (2017). https://doi.org/10.1109/IROS.2017.8206190. iSSN 2153-0866

27. Marr, D., Hildreth, E.: Theory of edge detection. Proc. Roy. Soc. London Ser. B Biol. Sci. **207**(1167), 187–217 (1980)

28. Miles, R., Mikolajczyk, K.: Understanding the role of the projector in knowledge distillation. ArXiv preprint abs/2303.11098 (2023). https://arxiv.org/abs/2303.11098

29. Nguyen, V.N., Jenssen, R., Roverso, D.: Automatic autonomous vision-based power line inspection: a review of current status and the potential role of deep learning. Int. J. Electr. Power Energy Syst. **99**, 107–120 (2018) https://doi.org/10.1016/j.ijepes.2017.12.016, http://www.sciencedirect.com/science/article/pii/S0142061517324444

30. Nguyen, V.N., Jenssen, R., Roverso, D.: LS-net: fast single-shot line-segment detector. ArXiv preprint abs/1912.09532 (2019). https://arxiv.org/abs/1912.09532

31. Owen, A.B.: A robust hybrid of lasso and ridge regression. Contemp. Math. **443**(7), 59–72 (2007)

32. Pi, Y., Nath, N.D., Behzadan, A.H.: Convolutional neural networks for object detection in aerial imagery for disaster response and recovery. Adv. Eng. Inform. **43**, 101009 (2020)

33. Qu, C., Sorbelli, F.B., Singh, R., Calyam, P., Das, S.K.: Environmentally-aware and energy-efficient multi-drone coordination and networking for disaster response. IEEE Trans. Netw. Serv. Manage. (2023)

34. Ronneberger, O., Fischer, P., Brox, T.: U-net: convolutional networks for biomedical image segmentation. In: Navab, N., Hornegger, J., Wells, W.M., Frangi, A.F. (eds.) MICCAI 2015. LNCS, vol. 9351, pp. 234–241. Springer, Cham (2015). https://doi.org/10.1007/978-3-319-24574-4_28

35. Sanders-Reed, J.N., Yelton, D.J., Witt, C.C., Galetti, R.R.: Passive obstacle detection system (PODS) for wire detection. In: Enhanced and Synthetic Vision 2009, vol. 7328, p. 732804. International Society for Optics and Photonics (2009)

36. Simonyan, K., Zisserman, A.: Very deep convolutional networks for large-scale image recognition. In: Bengio, Y., LeCun, Y. (eds.) 3rd International Conference on Learning Representations, ICLR 2015, San Diego, CA, USA, 7–9 May 2015, Conference Track Proceedings (2015). http://arxiv.org/abs/1409.1556

37. Song, B., Li, X.: Power line detection from optical images. Neurocomputing **129**, 350–361 (2014) https://doi.org/10.1016/j.neucom.2013.09.023, http://www.sciencedirect.com/science/article/pii/S0925231213009429

38. Stambler, A., Sherwin, G., Rowe, P.: Detection and reconstruction of wires using cameras for aircraft safety systems. In: 2019 International Conference on Robotics and Automation (ICRA), pp. 697–703 (2019). https://doi.org/10.1109/ICRA.2019.8793526, iSSN: 1050-4729

39. Steger, C.: An unbiased detector of curvilinear structures. IEEE Trans. Pattern Anal. Mach. Intell. **20**(2), 113–125 (1998)

40. Tang, L., Shao, G.: Drone remote sensing for forestry research and practices. J. For. Res. **26**(4), 791–797 (2015) https://doi.org/10.1007/s11676-015-0088-y

41. Wang, Z., Simoncelli, E.P., Bovik, A.C.: Multiscale structural similarity for image quality assessment. In: 2003 the Thrity-Seventh Asilomar Conference on Signals, Systems & Computers, vol. 2, pp. 1398–1402. IEEE (2003)

42. Zhang, H., Yang, W., Yu, H., Xu, F., Zhang, H.: Combined convolutional and structured features for power line detection in UAV images. In: IGARSS 2019–2019 IEEE International Geoscience and Remote Sensing Symposium, pp. 1306–1309 (2019). https://doi.org/10.1109/IGARSS.2019.8898033, iSSN: 2153-6996

43. Zhang, J., Liu, L., Wang, B., Chen, X., Wang, Q., Zheng, T.: High speed automatic power line detection and tracking for a UAV-based inspection. In: 2012 International Conference on Industrial Control and Electronics Engineering, pp. 266–269 (2012). https://doi.org/10.1109/ICICEE.2012.77. iSSN null

44. Zhou, C., Yang, J., Zhao, C., Hua, G.: Fast, accurate thin-structure obstacle detection for autonomous mobile robots. In: Proceedings of the IEEE Conference on Computer Vision and Pattern Recognition Workshops (2017)

A Quality-Based Criteria for Efficient View Selection

Rémy Alcouffe(✉), Sylvie Chambon⬛, Géraldine Morin⬛, and Simone Gasparini⬛

University of Toulouse, IRIT – Toulouse INP, Toulouse, France
{remy.alcouffe,sylvie.chambon,geraldine.morin,
simone.gasparini}@irit.fr

Abstract. The generation of complete 3D models of real-world objects is a well-known problem. The accuracy of a reconstruction can be defined as the fidelity to the original model, but in the context of the 3D reconstruction, the ground truth model is usually unavailable. In this paper, we propose to evaluate the quality of the model through local *intrinsic* metrics, that reflect the quality of the current reconstruction based on geometric measures of the reconstructed model. We then show how those metrics can be embedded in a Next Best View (NBV) framework as additional criteria for selecting optimal views that improve the quality of the reconstruction. Tests performed on simulated data and synthetic images show that using quality metrics helps the NBV algorithm to focus the view selection on the poor-quality parts of the reconstructed model, thus improving the overall quality.

Keywords: Iterative 3D reconstruction · View Selection · Accuracy

1 Introduction

The 3D reconstruction of real-world objects has become a key tool in revolutionising industries by converting the real world into digital shapes. 3D reconstruction can be performed using algorithms based on images [9,26,30] or depth sensors like LiDAR (Light Detection and Ranging) [12,25,29]. Although 3D reconstruction is reliable and efficient, it is not immune to imperfections: it may generate incomplete models, or models with noise, non-uniform, or inaccurate geometry [27], as illustrated in Fig. 1. Usually, they are caused by insufficient data collected by the sensor, whether because some parts of the scene are missed during the acquisition (*e.g.* because of occlusions), or because the complex shape and properties of the object prevent a complete reconstruction.

To palliate these issues, an iterative process integrating data acquisition and reconstruction can be used to strategically determine the *Next-Best-View* (NBV) [5] to enhance the 3D reconstruction of an object. NBV finds relevance in a multitude of applications spanning robotics, autonomous navigation, and exploration [28], virtual reality [21], and industrial inspection [8]. In this iterative paradigm, the next view is determined by maximising the contribution of an additional view to the quality of the reconstructed model. The contribution of a view to the reconstruction quality can be defined according to different metrics. Some methods focus on the completeness of the model, thus base their metrics on the visibility of the 3D model [5]: Massios et

ⓒ The Author(s), under exclusive license to Springer Nature Switzerland AG 2024
J. Filipe and J. Röning (Eds.): ROBOVIS 2024, CCIS 2077, pp. 193–209, 2024.
https://doi.org/10.1007/978-3-031-59057-3_13

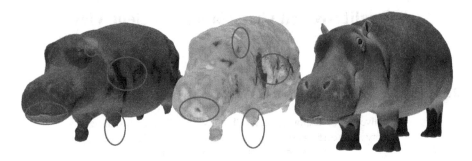

Fig. 1. Example of the assessment of a 3D reconstruction quality: the red circles highlight the poorly reconstructed parts (left model) of the original model (right model). The heat map (middle model) shows the response of the extrinsic metric MSDM2 [13], with the poorly reconstructed parts having a higher score (hot colors). (Color figure online)

al. [17] control the geometry of the model via the computation of the patch normals, Li et al. [16] minimize the Mass Vector Chain and Maver et al. [18] explicitly detect possible occlusions in the partial model. Other methods compute the uncertainty of the reconstructed model and select the next view by minimizing the entropy [32] or covariance matrix of the observations [7,10]. In the optimisation step, multiple metrics may be considered simultaneously. Mendez *et al.* [19] combine uncertainty and coverage to improve the current reconstruction and the baseline vergence angle to explore new parts of the scene. The APORA algorithm [6] considers the uncertainty, the visibility, and the proximity to frontier voxels. At the same time, in [2] a utility function maximizes the information gain (*i.e.* the entropy of voxels in a given viewpoint), and the density of the final model while penalizing viewpoints that are too far away.

The accuracy of the final 3D model is usually evaluated w.r.t. a reference model (*i.e.* the ground truth) with different metrics that rely on the geometric distance (*e.g.* Hausdorff [11], chamfer [3], *accuracy* and *completeness* [27]) between the points of the reconstructed model and the ground truth model, or perceptual measures [13,14, 31]. However, in general, the reference model is not available, thus making the task of assessing the accuracy a more challenging task.

In this paper, we propose to use local intrinsic quality metrics to assess the quality of a 3D model without a reference model. We show that these quality metrics can provide helpful insight to detect the regions of the model that are poorly reconstructed and thus require more acquisitions. We then show how the proposed metrics can be plugged into an existing NBV framework to guide the acquisition process to select the views that improve and ensure the quality of the final reconstructed model.

After presenting the NBV problem in Sect. 2, we present a full NBV pipeline that we adapted to account for quality functions in Sect. 3. We review the existing metrics for the assessment of the quality of 3D models that we propose to use for the determination of the NBV as well as validation metrics in Sect. 4. We conduct experiments on simulated data (Sect. 5) and synthetic images (Sect. 6) data to show the advantage of using intrinsic metrics in an NBV Selection context.

2   Next-Best-View Selection

In some applications, the image acquisitions involved in reconstructing a 3D model are conducted in a series of successive steps. This means that a first set of acquisitions is made, then, the 3D model is estimated and it is decided to acquire new images to improve the 3D model. Other applications involve sensor-equipped platforms with constrained mobility [15]. As a consequence, the choice of subsequent viewpoints is crucial in efficiently improving the reconstruction by minimizing occlusions, enhancing feature visibility, and mitigating the uncertainty of the reconstruction.

As explained in the introduction, the NBV selection consists of the optimal choice of the novel viewpoint in a sequence of viewpoints from which an object or scene should be observed to optimize quality improvement of the 3D reconstruction.

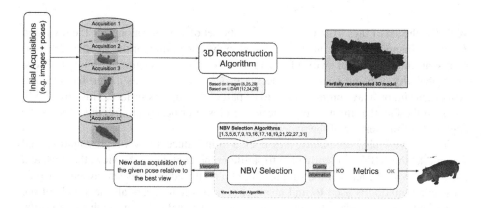

Fig. 2. NBV pipeline used in this paper.

Figure 2 presents a common NBV pipeline for an iterative reconstruction process. At each step, new data is acquired to generate the current reconstructed model. If the model achieves a sufficient level of reconstruction, the algorithm terminates; otherwise, the metrics are then used to evaluate the contributions of novel views. Once an optimal view is selected, the corresponding data is acquired and provided to the reconstruction algorithm to generate a novel reconstruction. The NBV problem is an optimisation problem involving the greedy selection of the next viewpoint for a given metric. The core concept of this algorithm concerns the choice of the metric for selecting the best view, as discussed in the next section.

3   Selected NBV Algorithm

3.1   A Global Max-Flow Based Method

Pan *et al.* [23] proposed a new approach based on the APORA [6] algorithm. Starting from the observation that a local iterative selection may lead to poor performance in view evaluation and that the fixed resolution of the 3D volumetric occupancy map may cause sampling problems for small objects, a max-flow-based approach is proposed that tackles the problem of small object reconstruction by adding a multi-resolution dimension.

Even though this method was designed for reconstruction using a LiDAR sensor, it can be suitable for any kind of 3D reconstruction algorithm, as the max-flow term ensures a certain overlap between the acquisitions. Like in APORA [6] algorithm, Pan et al. [23] choose the NBV from a selected set of views around the object. Then, for each view, they compute two terms: I_{local} and I_{flow}, which will further be combined to compute the information gain.

The local view quality function is defined as:

$$I_{local}(v) = \sum_{\forall r \in R_v} \sum_{\forall x \in X_r} H(x) \times P(vis_x) \times P(obj_x) \tag{1}$$

With R_v, the set of rays from the view v, X_r the set of voxels x alongside the ray r and $H(x)$ the Shannon entropy function, applied to the uncertainty of the voxel x. $P(vis_x)$ represents the visibility of a voxel from a given view: if it is seen through a lot of voxels, the probability of being visible will decrease. $P(obj_x)$ represents the probability of a voxel being hit by a ray coming from v to be part of the object's surface. This probability relies on the fact that most of the objects are closed or nearly closed, this models the continuity of the surface of the underlying model.

To achieve global optimality, they decide to introduce a novel representation, and they model the NBV problem with a tripartite graph containing the view, the rays, and the voxels, with the term of the sum in (Eq. (1)) on the edges between rays and voxels. This representation is used to find a subset of views that covers all the voxels of the model and that maximizes the information gain. It is solved as a graph optimisation problem, using network flow modeling.

From this solution, they define the flow-network information gain I_{flow} for each view, based on their history of appearance in the solution of the max flow problem.

This measure will then be mixed up with the local information gain I_{local}, using a weighted sum:

$$I_{global}(v) = (1 - \gamma) \times \frac{I_{local}(v)}{\sum_v I_{local}(v)} + \gamma \times \frac{I_{flow}(v)}{\sum_v I_{flow}(v)} \tag{2}$$

Finally, the NBV at a given iteration is defined as the view that maximizes the I_{global} function:

$$v^* = \underset{v \in V}{\operatorname{argmax}} \, I_{global}(v) \tag{3}$$

3.2   Problem Adaptation for Accuracy Improvement

These criteria mostly focus on the improvement of the completeness of the model. As for the accuracy of the final model, this is usually solved by reducing the entropy or uncertainty of the points, which is mostly based on the number of times a point has been seen by a camera, and it is not correlated to the geometric quality of the reconstructed model. During the process of acquiring data to create a 3D model, different parts of the object usually require varying levels of detail or complexity, which in turn, requires more data to accurately capture their geometry. To overcome this challenge, we propose to integrate new metrics into the NBV process that consider the geometric quality of the reconstructed parts of the model. This approach ensures that the acquisition process is guided by two opposing objectives: completing the model and ensuring sufficient accuracy. To test our approach, we used the NBV pipeline proposed by Pan *et al.* [23] and their available code. Moreover, we wanted to show that the proposed metrics may be integrated into an existing View Selection pipeline.

We replaced their local information metric I_{local} with a quality function containing, for each voxel of the model, the value of the quality ranging between 0 (low quality) and 1 (high quality), multiplied by the visibility criterion previously used in the proposed pipeline:

$$I_{local}(v) = \sum_{\forall r \in R_v} \sum_{\forall x \in X_r} P(vis_x) \times (1 - quality) \tag{4}$$

With that novel local information function, the selected views will tend to have a greater score if they are looking to poor quality voxels.

The next section presents the metrics that can be used to take the accuracy into account and how they can be easily integrated.

4   Estimation of 3D Model Quality

4.1   From Existing 3D Quality Metrics...

To assess the local quality of a 3D mesh, we perform a comparison to a reference mesh. We will refer to those metrics as *extrinsic* metrics because they rely on an external reference model. As shown in our previous work [1], the most common extrinsic metrics [11,13,14,31] are based on the computation of the Euclidean distance between two meshes to assess their differences.

Other more complex metrics use the intrinsic parameters of both the reference mesh and the reconstructed one. DAME [31] uses the difference in dihedral angle to assess the quality of a reconstructed mesh. MSDM [14] uses several parameters such as contrast, structure, and curvature, computed on both meshes. It can produce local quality maps that are then used to generate a global quality score on the model. A second version of that metric, called MSDM2 [13], takes into account the multi-scale dimension of the problem. These two last metrics have been proven to be correlated with subjective scores.

These metrics are interesting because they provide a quantitative and qualitative map of local quality by highlighting the differences between the original and reconstructed meshes. The provided different local maps can be used as a ground truth map to estimate the quality of a reconstructed mesh and as validation metrics in our context of experiments on 3D reconstruction.

However, as the reference model is rarely available, the use of that kind of metric is not suitable to assess the quality of the reconstruction. A metric that depends only on the intrinsic geometric properties of the 3D model is therefore more appropriate. This type of metric is called *intrinsic* and will be introduced in the next section.

4.2   ...to a Quality Metric for NBV

In our previous work [1], we proposed different intrinsic metrics (*i.e.* metrics that rely only on the geometry and the intrinsic parameters of the underlying 3D model). These metrics detect the different defects and issues of a 3D model, as well as respond to sharp and salient features of the 3D object. They are suitable in the context of 3D reconstruction as they do not need a reference mesh to be computed and can be iteratively computed on the go.

Different geometric properties of a 3D model can be computed such as curvature, dihedral angles, saliency, or local roughness. They are usually used and combined to give a global quality score for the mesh. In our context, we use them to express a quality factor for each point of the 3D model. In our precedent work, we presented three intrinsic metrics suitable for the problem of quality assessment. The Plane Local Roughness (PLR) as proposed by Rodríguez-Cuenca *et al.* [24], estimates the roughness of the 3D model by evaluating the reprojection error on the least square fitting plane of the neighboring patch for every vertex. This metric examines whether the existing vertex neighborhood can be characterized as planar. This gives us information on the underlying surface of the reconstructed model. For instance, when reconstructing a 3D object, if a surface is mostly planar, the need to have a high density of points is reduced. The Quadric Local Roughness [1] metric is similar to PLR, as it estimates the roughness of the model by computing the reprojection error on the least square-fitting quadric of the neighboring patch. Those two first metrics allow us to evaluate locally the regularity of the surface that should respect a plane or a quadric. The Mean Curvature introduced by Meynet *et al.* [20], assesses the mean curvature of a vertex by computing the derivative of the estimated least square fitting quadric of its neighborhood. As this metric is unbounded, it can not be used directly as a quality metric. However, it can give us information on high curvature areas that are either sharp features or defects of the object. These two kinds of surfaces are of interest for improving the reconstruction as they can correspond to parts of the model poorly reconstructed.

All these metrics are integrated in the NBV pipeline but we show in the first synthetic quality experiment that the metric needs to be monotonic as it will allow the camera to change positions. If a metric is not monotonic between every iteration and does not change, the NBV proposed by the algorithm will stay relatively close to the previous one as it was the best one according to the quality criterion. In that case, we need a quality function that is locally strictly monotonic. A way to achieve that is to multiply the quality factor by a new term that is correlated with the occupancy of each voxel in the Pan *et al.* [23] pipeline:

$$I_{local}(v) = \sum_{\forall r \in R_v} \sum_{\forall x \in X_r} P(vis_x) \times (1 - quality) \times H(x), \tag{5}$$

where the Shannon entropy function is

$$H(x) = -occ(x) \ln(occ(x)) - (1 - occ(x)) \ln(1 - occ(x)), \tag{6}$$

and $occ(x)$ is the occupancy of the voxel x. The occupancy of the occupied voxels is a function that tends to one as the number of iterations increases.

5 Experiments on Simulated Data

5.1 Experimental Setup

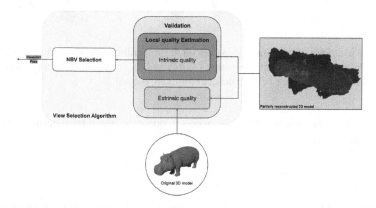

Fig. 3. A detailed view of the metric block of the global NBV pipeline. Note that the original 3D model is only used to render the images according to the selected viewpoints.

To add a quality criterion to the pipeline described in Fig. 2, we need to modify the metrics used for the view selection algorithm. We introduce two new stages in the metrics estimation scheme (*cf*. Fig. 3): the first one computes the intrinsic quality of the model used to determine the NBV. The second one computes the extrinsic quality of the model to validate the choice of the view and to verify the increase of the reconstructed model quality at each iteration. To that end, it needs a reference model for the comparison and the computation of extrinsic quality metrics.

First, we need to assess whether the addition of a local quality metric to the NBV pipeline has an impact and guides the views to explore the poor quality areas of the model. To that end, we performed synthetic experiments on a chosen 3D model, with an arbitrary given quality score for each vertex.

To perform this experiment, we adapted the NBV pipeline provided by Pan *et al.* [23] as described in the Sect. 3. The pipeline also comes with a LiDAR emulator, that can acquire the 3D points seen by a camera from a ground truth model. For our first synthetic experiments, we used this emulator.

We created a small dataset composed of a single 3D geometric object (*cf*. the armadillo in Fig. 4). To simulate the quality, we defined an arbitrary metric: for each vertex of the model, we associate a quality value that is either 0.5 for vertices considered with "poor quality" and 1.0 for those of "good quality". We defined 20 different, randomly generated quality versions for that same 3D object. In each version, the positions of the quality patches are randomly chosen as well as their sizes, as can be seen in Fig. 4.

Fig. 4. Some examples of poor quality patches on the armadillo model (in red). The patches are placed on the model by randomly selecting a vertex and its N-ring neighbours, where N is a parameter that defines the size of the patch. (Color figure online)

At each iteration, when performing a new acquisition, the quality term of the voxel is updated as follows:

$$qlt(v_i) = \begin{cases} qlt(v_i)^{0.9} & \text{if } v_i \in V_{seen} \\ 0.5 & \text{elsewhere.} \end{cases} \tag{7}$$

With v_i the voxel to update, $qlt(v_i)$ representing its quality in the working octomap, and V_{seen} the set of voxels that has already been seen during previous iterations. The quality of a voxel is defined to be updated only once during an iteration and not every time an acquired point falls into a voxel because it will help us in the validation process to compute the number of voxels of poor quality that have been modified at each iteration. We use the function $pow(x, 0.9)$ to ensure that the algorithm will not propose the same view at each iteration as the quality metric is not evolving on the ground truth model. We employ this function due to its asymptotic behavior approaching one as the number of iterations tends towards infinity. This update function allows us to see if the algorithm, is well suited for a quality metric that will improve itself and whether it can explore the poorly reconstructed parts of the model.

To validate the data we computed the completeness of the model at each iteration in two different ways. The first one corresponds to the number of voxels marked as *Seen* in the partially reconstructed model. The second one uses the completeness defined by Seitz *et al.* [27] and is computed by comparing the partial point cloud and the original model. Then we introduced another metric that corresponds to the number of times the quality of voxels has been updated using the Eq. (7). This metric will show us if the NBV is focusing more on poor quality areas compared to standard methods.

5.2 Results and Analysis

For this study, we compare the default reconstruction method proposed by Pan *et al.* [23], the APORA method proposed by Daudelin *et al.* [6], and our metric described in Sect. 3. We performed 20 iterations of the NBV algorithm.

As our method does not have any term that encourages the exploration of unknown areas of the object we needed to have an already complete 3D model. So if the first selected views do not see any "poor quality" voxels, our metric will show no results. To that end, for our method, the first 10 iterations will be computed using the APORA method. We chose the number of 10 iterations as the model will have sufficient completeness. We use APORA instead of the Pan *et al.* method, as it is deterministic so that different runs can be compared. Moreover, for every patch size and patch position, we will work on the same initial reconstructed model.

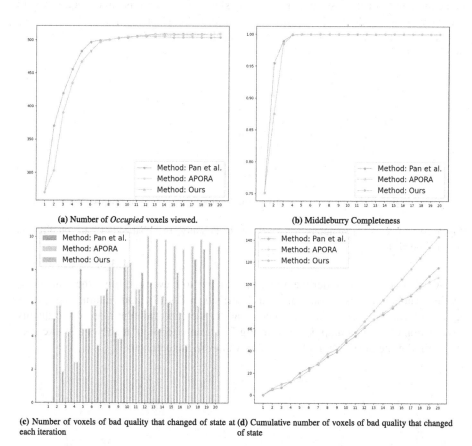

(a) Number of *Occupied* voxels viewed.

(b) Middleburry Completeness

(c) Number of voxels of bad quality that changed of state at each iteration

(d) Cumulative number of voxels of bad quality that changed of state

Fig. 5. Average values on different patch positions for a given patch size (here 10-ring neighborhood).

Figure 5 presents the average results on 5 different patch positions, for a given patch size. We used 10 iterations for the reconstruction of a complete model as the completeness metric and the number of *Occupied* voxels viewed at that stage seems constant. The maximum number of voxels viewed is achieved around the tenth iteration and changes very little afterward. Note that the blue and green curves (resp. APORA and Ours) are merged on the 10 first iterations as the APORA algorithm is used to perform the complete reconstruction on the first ten iterations of our method. Finally, the fourth graph,

presenting the cumulative number of voxels whose quality changed during the reconstruction, shows a huge improvement in the number of "poor quality" voxels seen at
each iteration. On average, for this size of the patch, the Pan *et al.* and the APORA
method view only 115 poor-quality voxels while our method can view more than 140
voxels.

The same kind of results are achieved for even smaller patch sizes, see Fig. 6. We
can denote that for the last ten iterations, the slope of the curve is almost equivalent to
the number of voxels that are considered to have a "poor quality". This demonstrates
that the algorithm selects views that show a patch of poor quality.

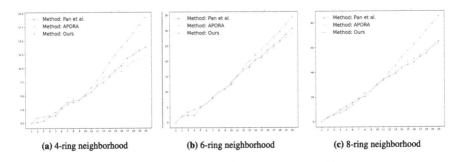

(a) 4-ring neighborhood   (b) 6-ring neighborhood   (c) 8-ring neighborhood

Fig. 6. Average cumulative number of voxels of "bad quality" that changed of state, on different
neighborhood sizes.

Another advantage of our method is that it tends to view more times the same poor-
quality patches. By using our function described in Eq. (7), and limiting the quality
update of voxels to only one time per iteration, we can draw the map of the quality
distribution of the octomap depicted in Fig. 7: at each iteration, it shows a stacked bar
histogram of the distribution of the quality values in the octomap.

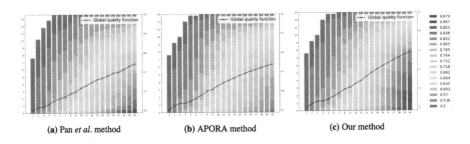

(a) Pan *et al.* method   (b) APORA method   (c) Our method

Fig. 7. Average map representing the distribution of the quality values in the octomap: at each
iteration (x-axis) the stacked bar histogram shows the evolution of the quality values. The colors
range from red (poor quality) to purple (better quality). (Color figure online)

On average, our method allows us to have a wider range of quality states, as it is
more likely to propose views that acquire the pre-defined poor-quality patches. We also
defined a global quality function score:

$$\gamma = \sum_{v_i \in V_{qlt}^i} qlt(v_i), \tag{8}$$

where V_{qlt}^i represents the set of voxels known to have a "poor quality" at the iteration i. This function, plotted in black in Fig. 6, shows how our method, designed to encourage the views containing poor quality voxels, contributes to the enhanced overall model quality compared to the other two methods.

The comparison of those 3 methods shows that there is a real interest in adding a quality criterion to an NBV pipeline to propose a novel view that will be focused on the poor-quality regions of the objects. The challenge is to apply this transformation to a real object using a real-life 3D reconstruction algorithm, with bigger uncertainty on the reconstruction and with the use of real quality metrics like the ones described in Sect. 4.2.

6 Experiments on Synthetic Images

6.1 Experimental Setup

We tested the proposed quality metrics in the context of a 3D reconstruction based on images. We relied on Meshroom [9], a 3D reconstruction framework for unordered sets of images. We considered textured 3D models and used Blender [4] to generate synthetic images from a given set of viewpoints. The NBV pipeline proposed by Pan *et al.* [23] was used as a reference and baseline for our comparisons. Since our goal is to show where the model quality can be improved, we used the reconstructed model obtained by Pan *et al.* after 20 iterations (that is, using 20 images) as a starting point. We call this reconstruction the *base model*; note so that the base model was mostly complete. Then, for each subsequent iteration, we ran the APORA algorithm [6] and its modified version that includes a term to take quality into account in the minimization process. The reconstruction (with Meshroom) provides the poses of the selected views. Pan *et al.* [23] focus on LiDAR for acquiring 3D but in photogrammetry more views are necessary since overlap is needed for the reconstruction. Thus, at each step, we consider the 4 best candidate views to render the relevant images and we add them to the set of input images for the reconstruction.

For this study, we changed the metric used in the NBV selection step. We used two different quality metrics presented earlier, the *Quadric Local Roughness* and the *Plane Local Roughness*. We used the mean version of them and they will be computed using their 50-nearest neighbors. Those metrics have a strong response on the areas of the objects that are considered as a default, but they also can have a high response regarding the geometry of the object as they are also sensitive to sharp and salient structures. While the response of the metrics in areas of poor quality vanishes if they are corrected, that is not the case for the areas with interesting geometry. To tackle this problem we propose to add the Shannon entropy term to the Local Information for the NBV Selection in Eq. (5). This term helps reduce the importance of the voxels marked as "poor quality" because they are just responding to the geometry of the model. The Shannon entropy $H(x)$ defined in Eq. (5) goes to 0 if the point has been seen many times (by many different views). Thus it will help to differentiate the metrics response corresponding to the sharp and salient features from the response corresponding to its defaults.

Finally, extrinsic metrics that we described in Sect. 4.1 are used for validation, to evaluate the quality of the reconstruction relative to ground truth. During our whole process, we will be able to follow the evolution of the quality metrics we use for the reconstruction, as well as other global and/or local *extrinsic* quality metrics such as Seitz *et al.* completeness and accuracy [27], Hausdorff distance [11], MSDM [14] and MSDM2 [13]. An example of local maps is given in Fig. 8. The Seitz *et al.* [27] metrics are defined using a certain threshold. For our study, we used an accuracy ratio of 99% and a completeness distance corresponding to 1% of the diagonal of the object. Those thresholds are restrictive, but allow us to better identify improvement in accuracy.

6.2 Results and Analysis

For our experiments, we have used a 3D model representing an Elephant from the Texture Quality Assessment Dataset [22]. This model has complex shapes but also has a good texture which is essential for the photogrammetry reconstruction pipeline.

From the base model, generated by 20 iterations of Pan *et al.* [23], we computed at each iteration the quality of the mesh, using either the *PLR* or *QLR*. For each iteration, the quality of the mesh is mapped to the octomap using a min function:

$$qlt_v(v) = min(qlt_p(x), \forall x \in v \subset X), \tag{9}$$

with $qlt_v(v)$ designing the quality of the voxel v in the octomap, $qlt_p(x)$ the quality of the point x in the reconstructed mesh, and X is the set of points of the reconstructed mesh. This function takes into account the fact that each voxel of the octomap can contain multiple points of the mesh. Since the points falling into one voxel might come from different parts of the mesh, the min function is to be preferred to *e.g. mean* and *median* to propagate the poor quality region in the octomap. An example of the octomap is shown in Fig. 9, with the poor-quality voxel highlighted in red. Figure 9b shows the PLR metric has high responses on the back, on the trunk, and the back feet of the elephant. The views selected by the algorithm (*cf*. Fig. 9.c–f) maximise the number of poor-quality voxels viewed, as they can be seen in the different selected views (trunk, feet, and back).

The choice of the views selected by the modified algorithm taking into account the quality shows an improvement of the accuracy of the model. For validation, Fig. 10 presents the results of extrinsic metrics on the Elephant model, for the three considered methods, a basic method using the APORA algorithm, our method using the *Plane Local Roughness* and using the *Quadric Local Roughness*.

The methods embedding the quality term achieve a similar reconstruction completeness after 15 iterations, where 87% of points are at a distance less than 1% of the object diagonal. It is also worth noting that the methods with quality reach better completeness for the first 5 iterations, thus showing that the quality metrics also help for the completeness of the model.

For the accuracy of the reconstructed model (second graph from the left of Fig. 10), the values have a similar evolution as the APORA method and are slightly lower (better accuracy). This is corroborated by the Hausdorff distance metric (middle graph of

(a) Original model   **(b)** Reconstructed model   **(c)** Geometry

(d) Hausdorff distance   **(e)** MSDM2 local map

(f) Mean PLR   **(g)** Mean QLR

Fig. 8. Example of local maps for extrinsic and intrinsic metrics for the reconstructed model.

Fig. 10), where the methods with the quality term converge more quickly to a threshold value. This value is mainly due to the poor reconstruction of the little elephant on the back of the big one, where the space between his legs is not well reconstructed.

Finally, the *Mesh Structural Distortion Measures* (last two graphs of Fig. 10) confirm that the methods with the quality term have in general better results.

This shows that integrating the proposed quality metrics in an NBV pipeline provides a better selection of views. In the case of photogrammetry, both the accuracy and the completeness of the reconstructed model are improved.

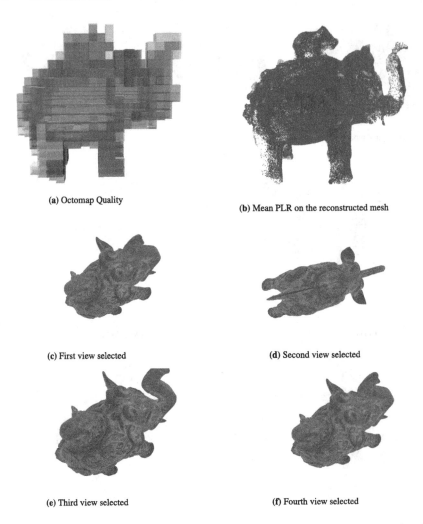

(a) Octomap Quality

(b) Mean PLR on the reconstructed mesh

(c) First view selected

(d) Second view selected

(e) Third view selected

(f) Fourth view selected

Fig. 9. Local map of the mean PLR metric and its corresponding octomap representation, followed by the associated selected views. (Color figure online)

The proposed quality metrics have, in general, a lower response on zones with high-density reconstructed points as they are computed on a 50-nearest-neighbor of each point. Hence they guide the view selection to focus on low-density areas of the object, which often correspond to poorly reconstructed zones of the object.

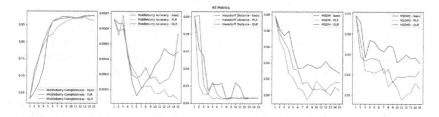

Fig. 10. The extrinsic metric response on 15 iterations for the 3 methods tested.

7 Conclusion

In this paper, we proposed the use and addition of local *intrinsic* metrics in the NBV Selection pipelines. In the first simulated experiment, we showed that using those metrics tends to encourage the views around the poor-quality regions of a 3D object. Then, we decided to test this method on real data, with an external photogrammetry reconstruction algorithm, using generated views from a reference 3D model. When using the local *intrinsic* metrics *PLR* and *QLR*, we show that it helps improve the accuracy of the model alongside its completeness and MSDM measures.

The metrics we proposed can detect the defaults of the 3D model, as well as the sharp and salient features of the object; The response of those metrics is defined according to a certain neighborhood, we can imagine developing a multiscale version of those metrics (like in MSDM2 [13]) to take into account the different sizes of features of the objects.

In the future, we would like to combine different metrics to be able to differentiate between salient features of the objects and actual defaults. This paper opens the way to the definition of new intrinsic quality metrics for NBV Selection algorithm, as it shows the interest of those metrics in a reconstruction process.

References

1. Alcouffe, R., Gasparini, S., Morin, G., Chambon, S.: Blind quality of a 3D reconstructed mesh. In: 29th IEEE International Conference on Image Processing (ICIP 2022), pp. 3406–3410. IEEE, Bordeaux (2022). https://doi.org/10.1109/ICIP46576.2022.9897783
2. Almadhoun, R., Abduldayem, A., Taha, T., Seneviratne, L., Zweiri, Y.: Guided next best view for 3D reconstruction of large complex structures. Remote Sens. **11**(20), 2440 (2019) https://doi.org/10.3390/rs11202440, https://www.mdpi.com/2072-4292/11/20/2440
3. Borgefors, G.: Distance transformations in arbitrary dimensions. Comput. Vision Graph. Image Process. **27**(3), 321–345 (1984). https://doi.org/10.1016/0734-189x(84)90035-5
4. Community, B.O.: Blender - a 3D modelling and rendering package (2018). http://www.blender.org
5. Connolly, C.: The determination of next best views. In: IEEE International Conference on Robotics and Automation, ICRA, vol. 2, pp. 432–435 (1985)
6. Daudelin, J., Campbell, M.: An adaptable, probabilistic, next-best view algorithm for reconstruction of unknown 3-D objects. IEEE Robot. Autom. Lett. (2017). https://doi.org/10.1109/LRA.2017.2660769

7. Dunn, E., Frahm, J.M.: Next best view planning for active model improvement. In: British Machine Vision Conference, BMVC (2009). https://doi.org/10.5244/C.23.53

8. Faria, M., Maza, I., Viguria, A.: Applying frontier cells based exploration and lazy Theta* path planning over single grid-based world representation for autonomous inspection of large 3D structures with an UAS. J. Intell. Robot. Syst. (2019). https://doi.org/10.1007/s10846-018-0798-4

9. Griwodz, C., et al.: AliceVision meshroom: an open-source 3D reconstruction pipeline. In: ACM Multimedia Systems Conference, pp. 241-247 (2021). https://doi.org/10.1145/3458305.3478443

10. Haner, S., Heyden, A.: Covariance propagation and next best view planning for 3D reconstruction. In: Fitzgibbon, A., Lazebnik, S., Perona, P., Sato, Y., Schmid, C. (eds.) ECCV 2012. LNCS, vol. 7573, pp. 545–556. Springer, Heidelberg (2012). https://doi.org/10.1007/978-3-642-33709-3_39

11. Hausdorff, F.: Set Theory, 2nd edn. Chelsea Publishing Company (1962)

12. Jun, C., Shiguang, Z., Xinyu, W.: Structured light-based shape measurement system. Signal Process. 93(6), 1435–1444 (2013)

13. Lavoué, G.: A multiscale metric for 3D mesh visual quality assessment. Comput. Graph. Forum 30, 1427–1437 (2011). https://doi.org/10.1111/j.1467-8659.2011.02017.x

14. Lavoué, G., Drelie Gelasca, E., Dupont, F., Baskurt, A., Ebrahimi, T.: Perceptually driven 3D distance metrics with application to watermarking. In: SPIE Optics + Photonics, p. 63120L (2006). https://doi.org/10.1117/12.686964

15. Lee, I., Seo, J., Kim, Y., Choi, J., Han, S., Yoo, B.: Automatic pose generation for robotic 3-D scanning of mechanical parts. IEEE Trans. Rob. (2020). https://doi.org/10.1109/TRO.2020.2980161

16. Li, Y., He, B., Bao, P.: Automatic view planning with self-termination in 3D object reconstructions. Sens. Actuat. A: Phys. 122(2) (2005). https://doi.org/10.1016/j.sna.2005.06.003

17. Massios, N.A., Fisher, R.B.: A best next view selection algorithm incorporating a quality criterion. In: British Machine Vision Conference, BMVC (1998). https://doi.org/10.5244/C.12.78

18. Maver, J., Bajcsy, R.: Occlusions as a guide for planning the next view. IEEE Trans. Pattern Anal. Mach. Intell. PAMI (1993). https://doi.org/10.1109/34.211463

19. Mendez, O., Hadfield, S., Pugeault, N., Bowden, R.: Next-best stereo: extending next-best view optimisation for collaborative sensors. In: British Machine Vision Conference, BMVC (2016). https://doi.org/10.5244/C.30.65

20. Meynet, G., Digne, J., Lavoué, G.: PC-MSDM: a quality metric for 3D point clouds. In: International Conference on Quality of Multimedia Experience, QoMEX (2019). https://doi.org/10.1109/QoMEX.2019.8743313

21. Mortezapoor, S., Schönauer, C., Rüggeberg, J., Kaufmann, H.: Photogrammabot: an autonomous ROS-based mobile photography robot for precise 3D reconstruction and mapping of large indoor spaces for mixed reality. In: IEEE Conference on Virtual Reality and 3D User Interfaces Abstracts and Workshops, VRW (2022). https://doi.org/10.1109/VRW55335.2022.00033

22. Nehmé, Y., Dupont, F., Farrugia, J., Le Callet, P., Lavoué, G.: Textured mesh quality assessment: large-scale dataset and deep learning-based quality metric. ACM Trans. Graph. (2023). https://doi.org/10.1145/3592786

23. Pan, S., Wei, H.: A global max-flow-based multi-resolution next-best-view method for reconstruction of 3D unknown objects. IEEE Robot. Autom. Lett. (2022). https://doi.org/10.1109/LRA.2021.3132430

24. Rodríguez-Cuenca, B., García-Cortés, S., Ordóñez, C., Alonso, M.C.: A study of the roughness and curvature in 3D point clouds to extract vertical and horizontal surfaces. In: IEEE

International Geoscience and Remote Sensing Symposium, IGARSS, pp. 4602–4605 (2015). https://doi.org/10.1109/IGARSS.2015.7326853

25. Roldao, L., de Charette, R., Verroust-Blondet, A.: 3D surface reconstruction from voxel-based lidar data. In: IEEE Intelligent Transportation Systems Conference, ITSC, pp. 2681–2686 (2019). https://doi.org/10.1109/ITSC.2019.8916881

26. Schonberger, J.L., Frahm, J.M.: Structure-from-motion revisited. In: IEEE Conference on Computer Vision and Pattern Recognition, CVPR (2016)

27. Seitz, S.M., Curless, B., Diebel, J., Scharstein, D., Szeliski, R.: A comparison and evaluation of multi-view stereo reconstruction algorithms. In: IEEE Conference on Computer Vision and Pattern Recognition, CVPR, pp. 519–528 (2006)

28. Selin, M., Tiger, M., Duberg, D., Heintz, F., Jensfelt, P.: Efficient autonomous exploration planning of large-scale 3-D environments. IEEE Robot. Autom. Lett. (2019). https://doi.org/10.1109/LRA.2019.2897343

29. Tachella, J., et al.: Real-time 3D reconstruction from single-photon lidar data using plug-and-play point cloud denoisers. Nat. Commun. **10**(1), 4984 (2019). https://doi.org/10.1038/s41467-019-12943-7

30. Tingdahl, D., Van Gool, L.: A public system for image based 3D model generation. In: International Conference on Computer Vision/Computer Graphics Collaboration Techniques and Applications, MIRAGE, vol. 6930/2011, pp. 262–273 (2011)

31. Váša, L., Rus, J.: Dihedral angle mesh error: a fast perception correlated distortion measure for fixed connectivity triangle meshes. Comput. Graph. Forum **31**(5), 1715–1724 (2012)

32. Wenhardt, S., Deutsch, B., Angelopoulou, E., Niemann, H.: Active visual object reconstruction using d-, e-, and t-optimal next best views. In: IEEE Conference on Computer Vision and Pattern Recognition, CVPR (2007). https://doi.org/10.1109/CVPR.2007.383363

Multi-UAV Weed Spraying

Ali Moltajaei Farid[1], Malek Mouhoub[1(✉)], Tony Arkles[2], and Greg Hutch[2]

[1] Department of Computer Science, University of Regina, Regina, Canada
{afarid,mouhoubm}@uregina.ca
[2] Engineering Team, Precision.ai, Regina, Canada
{tony,greg}@precision.ai

Abstract. In agriculture, weeds reduce soil productivity and harvest quality. A common practice for weed control is via weed spraying. Ground spray of weeds is a common approach that may be harmful, destructive, and too slow, while aerial UAV spraying can be safe, non-destructive, and quick. Spraying efficiency and accuracy can be enhanced when adopting multiple UAVs. In this context, we propose a new multiple UAV spraying system that autonomously and accurately sprays weeds within the field. In our proposed system, a weed pressure map is first clustered. Then, the voronoi approach generates the appropriate number of waypoints. Finally, a variant of the Traveling Salesman Problem (TSP) is solved to find the best UAV tour for each cluster. The latter task is performed using two nature-inspired techniques, namely, NSGA2 and MOEA/D. To assess the performance of each method, we conducted a set of simulation tests. The results reported in this paper demonstrate the superiority of NSGA2 over MOEA/D. In addition, the heterogeneity of UAVs is studied, where we have a mix of fixed-wing and multi-rotor drones for spraying.

Keywords: Precision farming · Path planning · Unmanned aerial vehicles (UAVs) · Evolutionary computation

1 Introduction

Agriculture has a significant impact on people's lives. Weeds use soil nutrients that the cultivated plants should use and can therefore reduce the harvest by a considerable amount. In addition, with the constant population growth, the world will need more food. Therefore, many technologies have been designed for weed control to improve the productivity of the agriculture sector [3, 16, 22]. These approaches include mechanical removal [4], laser removal [26], and spray removal [21]. These three techniques have advantages and disadvantages. Spraying can be challenging. In some cases, not enough sprayed areas may reduce the efficiency of the harvest, and the quality of spray is related to many parameters such as weather conditions, the speed of the UAV, the altitude of the UAV, the nozzle design, the droplet size, and dynamic design of UAVs. For instance, mechanical and laser weed removal will prevent pesticide spread. On the other hand, spraying liquid can be used more intelligently by solely spraying those parts of the field that contain weeds.

Supported by Mitacs Application IT23321.

We have three significant steps for weed control: detecting the weeds, access to the exact location of the weeds, and weed removal. For the first step, there are many reported research works to detect weeds with significant results. The most challenging parts of such systems are:

1. The various types of weeds,
2. the different views of the camera,
3. and the diverse climate conditions including windy, cloudy, or sunny weather

In addition, most of the mentioned solutions require massive images for each type of weed to train the system for proper detection [20]. Moreover, if there is a limitation in payload, then the processing power is another crucial factor that can play a role in real-time detection of weeds. After detecting weeds, many approaches can be applied to finding the precise locations of weeds if required [23]. We review the weed removal step in the following.

There are two general strategies for weed removal: online and offline systems [8]. Online systems are more time and cost efficient as they correspond to real-time actions as a see and spray. The latter, however, requires proper processing power and adequate sensors. On the other hand, offline systems are more costly as they require two separate phases: a mapping phase followed by a spraying phase.

In both strategies, we will need to cluster the detected weeds to spray the aerosol properly [25]. There are many approaches dedicated to this task in the literature. In [24], the authors applied the voronoi diagram to cluster the area containing weeds. In [14], the DBSCAN algorithm [6] was applied for clustering the weeds. Machine learning-based clustering attracted much attention [27], including neural networks [20], and K-means [29].

Spraying can be either blind or with prior data. Blind spraying means the sprayer does not have any information about the weed's location. Blind spraying can be time-consuming and inefficient in terms of aerosol consumption if it is performed on all fields regardless of their crop or weeds. Another type of spraying can include both weed mapping and weed spraying stages. This type of mission has challenges, such as the need to derive an exact location of weeds to send to the sprayer. Also, the sprayer should be able to determine its precise location during the spraying process.

Spraying can be done with different technologies. A comparison between fixed-wing and multi-rotor showed that fixed-wings have better performance in spraying [2]. In addition, multi-rotor UAVs are less complicated to control compared to fixed-wing drones. Several indoor and outdoor experiments have been conducted to check the effectiveness of spraying UAVs [15]. Hybrid fixed-wing/VTOL spraying UAVs is a new emerging approach in AgTech, such as Forward Robotics[1]. Otherwise, fixed-wing sprayers have attracted much attention, such as the case of Pelican[2].

In most developed systems, only one UAV is used, and consequently, the latter cannot fly for a long time and cannot cover a large area in one flight. For this reason, using multiple UAVs can improve time and mission efficiency. However, in such systems, we will have the additive costs of UAV collaboration, which benefits will outweigh its cost

---

[1] https://www.forwardrobotics.com.

[2] https://flypyka.com/agriculture.html.

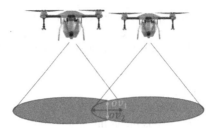

Fig. 1. The overlaps between two spraying drones.

in most agriculture applications. Using multiple UAVs will increase the system's complexity and requires proper communication among UAVs if needed. On the other hand, multiple UAVs can be more flexible and robust in various situations, especially when using swarm UAVs.

Many possible objectives are associated with multiple UAV missions, including the mission's duration, the number of recharging cycles, and the assessment of risks. When we have multiple objectives, we need to rely on a multiple-objective optimizer to handle such situations, as done in [8]. These optimizers are capable of finding a set of Pareto optimal solutions. Given this Pareto set, the decision maker can select the most appropriate ones for the mission.

In short, by identifying and spraying only the weeds in a field, we are forecasting a significant reduction in the amount of chemical entering the food supply without reducing yields.

In this paper, we propose a new system for spraying missions. The system can handle any number of UAVs. Unlike most of the work reported in the literature, our developed system works with both voronoi and DBSCAN. The designed system can deal with many objectives depending on the main goals of the spraying mission. These objectives include mission time, energy consumption, and risks. In addition, our system can estimate the number of aerosols for each cluster and the whole mission. Furthermore, the designed system can estimate the efficient number of UAVs to meet the mission's constraints. Finally, the proposed system is flexible with any shape and features of the farmland, such as non-flying zones. To the authors' knowledge, the proposed system is the first in this field to improve spray quality by comparing the number of spray zones using Voronoi cells, the intersection of sprayed zones. This feature can have applications under various conditions. For instance, if we have a large amount of drift due to wind, we can increase the amount of intersection by increasing the number of Voronoi cells to have a better spray quality.

2   Problem Definition

Assume we have a set of n spraying UAVs $U = \{s_1, s_2, \ldots, s_i, \ldots, s_n\}$. The three-dimensional position of each s_i at time t is denoted as $p_i(t)$. Each s_i has bottom spray nozzles with limited coverage. At time t, UAV s_i can cover the area $A(p_i(t))$. The total covered area by the set U is $A(t) = \cup_{1 \leq i \leq n} A(s_i(t))$. $A(t)$ is smaller than the area of interest (AoI) denoted by A_S. To ensure adequate spraying with no uncovered spraying area, we set side and front overlaps in the spraying zone taken by the drone, denoted by ov_1 and ov_2, respectively, as depicted in Fig. 1. We assume that each s_i moves in a 3D space with a fixed preset height.

For simplicity, we consider UAVs with a single nozzle that has a circular shape with radius of R_n. Details about spraying coverage will be covered later in this paper. Finally, each s_i has a limited communication range (R_c) to communicate with a set of m peers (neighbours) denoted by $N_i = \{s_{i1},..,s_{im}\}$.

The spraying process relies on both offline and online planners, as described in the previous section. The offline planner finds the number of clusters and outliers using the derived exact positions of weeds during the mapping. Suppose we have an AoI with n clusters, each denoted with Z_i and assigned to s_i. Z_i is decomposed into a number of voronoi cells. The proper number of cells is derived based on the proper intersection between spraying points which is set based on the spraying model. For simplicity, we assume that the spraying nozzle performs in real-time in a binary way (spray and not spray). Each center of the voronoi cell is assumed as a waypoint. A feasible path for a given UAV s_i consists of a sequence of H_{ij} cells covering the whole subarea Z_i. The main goal of the offline planner is to find a path covering the entire clustered areas $A_S = \cup_{1 \leq i \leq n} Z_i$ and optimizing the total time, energy consumption, and risk. The main goal of the online planner is to add adjustments when there are prospective collisions among UAVs. More formally, we define the MOO we are tackling as follows.

$$min(E_{total}, T_{total}, Risks) \quad subject\ to\ \eta_i \in B_i \tag{1}$$

where:

$$E_{total} = E_{turns} + E_{straight-lines} \tag{2}$$

$$T_{total} = T_{turns} + T_{straight-lines} \tag{3}$$

$$T_{straight-lines} = d_{ij}/v_{ij} \tag{4}$$

$$E_{straight-lines} = d_{ij} * \alpha_{v_{ij}} \tag{5}$$

$$Risks = w_{Energy} R_{Energy} + w_{Aerosol} R_{Aerosol} + w_{oc} R_{OC} \tag{6}$$

d_{ij} and v_{ij} are respectively the travelled distance and the velocity between cells i and j. Also, $\alpha_{v_{ij}}$ is a constant for velocity v_{ij}. Additionally, in multi-rotors, we have:

$$T_{turns} = \{ \begin{matrix} f_d(x) = \sum_{i,j \in x} d_{ij} \\ f_e(x) = \sum_{i,j \in x} e_{ij} \end{matrix} \tag{7}$$

$$E_{turns} = \{ \begin{matrix} f_d(x) = \sum_{i,j \in x} d_{ij} \\ f_e(x) = \sum_{i,j \in x} e_{ij} \end{matrix} \tag{8}$$

The time of turns in fixed-wing is based on the Dubin path, which is defined as follows:

$$T_{turns} = d_{Dubin}/v_{Dubin} \qquad (9)$$

where d_{Dubin} and v_{Dubin} are the distance and velocity that UAV passes during Dubin paths.

Equation 6 defines the risk factor as the sum of the Percentage of Fuel Usage (R_{Energy}), the required spraying liquid ($R_{Aerosol}$), and the total time when a given UAV leaves the ground station coverage (R_{OC}).

$$R_{Energy} = N_{Energy} \frac{f_c}{f_t} \qquad (10)$$

$$R_{Aerosol} = N_{Aerosol} \frac{a_c}{a_t} \qquad (11)$$

$$R_{OC} = N_{OC} \qquad (12)$$

N_{Energy}, $N_{Aerosol}$, N_{OC} are the total number of cells that are likely to be out of fuel, out of spraying liquid, and out of coverage, in the mission. f_c and f_t represent the current used fuel/energy and total fuel/energy of a given UAV. Similarly, a_c and a_t represent the UAV's current amount and total aerosol, respectively.

$\eta_i = (\eta_{i_1}, \eta_{i_2}, \ldots, \eta_{i_{n_i}})$ is the decision variable vector (representing a sequence of cells) for a given subarea Z_i and B_i is the set of feasible sequences according to the TSP definition (every cell should be visited exactly once) and the following constraints.

1. Time constraints: Each UAV s_i cannot fly more than a specific time τ_i. In addition, the completion time of the mission should not exceed a tolerable deadline.
2. Turning constraints: Fixed-wing UAVs cannot exceed the maximum turn angle each time due to aerodynamic limitations.

To solve the MOO we defined above, we use two evolutionary techniques: Non-dominated Sorting Genetic Algorithm version 2 (NSGA2) [5] and Multi-Objective Evolutionary algorithm based on Decomposition (MOEA/D) [28].

For simplicity, we assume that a UAV is a simple rigid body and the only constraint that we consider is the turning radius of fixed wings.

3 Proposed System

We assume that we have access to the mapping data of the area of interest; this includes the dimension, shapes, and weed locations. This information can be fed to our proposed system to find the optimal spraying method, maximizing the covered area, reducing time, aerosol waste, energy consumption, non sprayed areas, and risks. As shown in Fig. 2, the system contains five significant steps: clustering, finding the proper waypoints and path-planning, task allocation, take off location finding, and online collision avoidance. In the following, we will discuss these steps in detail.

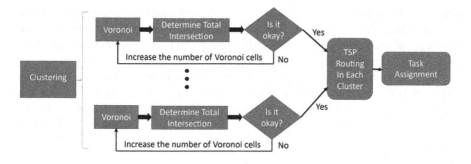

Fig. 2. The proposed system.

3.1 Clustering

We assume that we have access to the mapping details, including the precise location of weeds using current technologies [18] such as Trimble RTK GPS[3] Based on weed pressure, we can cluster through DBSCAN weeds to be sprayed with multiple UAVs.

Density-based clustering has the capability to uncover clusters of arbitrary shapes. The general idea behind these methods is to expand a particular group as long as the density in a predefined "neighborhood" exceeds a specific threshold value. Note that DBSCAN can cluster weeds without any number of predefined clusters, which can be very helpful.

3.2 Finding the Proper Way-Points

When we have several clusters, we need to find the best waypoints that can cover the area effectively. In this way, we assume that we have access to the configuration of the sprayer, including the number and the shape of spraying for nozzles based on the spraying liquid. With this information, the optimizer will check for the best number of waypoints and their locations. For this purpose, we used an iterative voronoi diagram which can cover the field with any number of voronoi centers.

The proposed system checks the different numbers of centers to find the best number of waypoints. In each of the voronoi centers, we put the shapes of the spraying model which can be used to determine the proper intersection between waypoints while minimizing these intersections. The intersection of these shapes should be minimized while preserving the minimum intersections. In addition, each spray model showing the details of spraying information of the UAVs can include the percentage of spraying coverage. For example, the intersection can be increased in windy situations to improve spraying efficiency.

3.3 Path-Planning

We must determine how to travel from a given waypoint to maximize our goal when we have a set of waypoints. The goal here is defined by a number of objectives. The

---
[3] www.trimble.com/en/solutions/technologies.

latter include energy consumption, mission time, and risk management. To optimize these (conflicting) objectives, we use a Multiple Objective Optimizer. The Optimizer finds a set of non-dominated solutions. Here, our path planning problem is viewed as a Traveling Salesman Problem (TSP) [10, 17].

The TSP consists of visiting all waypoints only once and returning to the starting waypoint. UAVs are clustered according to different factors including UAV's time span and energy consumption. Using path planning, the optimizer can determine the best location for UAVs to take off in order to optimize energy consumption and time as done in [8].

3.4 Online Collision Avoidance

Following on the recent algorithms we proposed in [7, 8], we add a collision avoidance system that will be activated only when there is a possibility of collision. Based on the algorithm, the UAV will slightly adjust its path until the collision risk is avoided.

4 Mapping

The mapping quality can affect the spraying performance and significantly affect precision farming. In [8], we developed a mapping system for weed control capable of working on farms with different shapes. The designed system's primary objective is to minimize time and energy. In addition to these two objectives, we consider the risk factor as well. We use both offline and online planning methods. Area decomposition, take-off location determination, and path planning are part of offline planning. Multi-drone optimization will consider the size of the area and the number of drones involved to develop the best plan that meets the requirements and optimizes time, energy, risks, and user preferences. We address this optimization problem through evolutionary techniques. Several unexpected events, such as sudden weather changes, communication failures, and nearby flying obstacles, can affect drone navigation during the execution of the optimal plan.

Online planning, implemented using a dynamic variant of the adopted evolutionary techniques, will be used to monitor and react to these unforeseen events. We assumed that we knew the camera capture frame at a specific altitude. Since we typically perform mapping at a certain altitude, our system determines the number of cells covering the area of interest. Next, we use a clustering technique to identify the set of sub-areas to cover by the UAVs. The assignment of each UAV to its specific sub-area depends on the maximum safe endurance and other technical details.

5 Spraying Technical Information

A model of nozzles plays a significant role in the quality of spraying missions. We adopted a single nozzle sprayer for each UAV. In practice, several experiments, such as wind tunnels or using sensitive papers in the field, are needed to model the behavior of a sprayer. In addition, the spraying quality varies from multi-rotor to fixed-wing UAVs [15], and many issues, such as the down-wash effect, affect the spraying quality.

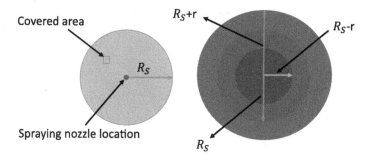

Fig. 3. The simplified spraying model.

According to Fig. 3, each spraying system has a specific model to help predict the spraying quality. As seen from the Figure, each radius has its specific spray quality. As we go far from the spraying nozzle location, spray quality will decrease. In addition, many factors, such as wind, can affect the spraying quality. We can take into account these factors when developing our system. For instance, in windy weather, the optimizer can increase the intersection of the spraying areas so that each of the regions without intersection is only within the radius that the spraying quality is the highest. Further considerations of wind and weather effects are left as future work.

Also, in case of the presence of wind, based on the wind strongness, our system can modify the intersections among voronoi cells and deal with wind. In addition, the density map of weeds is computed, and areas with more weed density will have more voronoi cells. In other words, more intersection of spray can increase the performance quality of the spraying. DBSCAN can be used for clustering; however, the operator must set some parameters for accurate results in DBSCAN.

6 Experimentation

We constructed our simulator using MathWorks Online Matlab with one virtual CPU and 16 GB of RAM. The details of the tuned parameters of MOEA/D and NSGA2 are listed in Table 1 [8]. Since the system is stochastic, all results are an average over five runs. Weeds are randomly scattered throughout the whole farmland. Figure 4 Shows a sample performance of the DBSCAN clustering algorithm. In addition, Fig. 5 shows how the number of voronoi cells can lead to different waypoints for UAVs. As we have a higher amount of cells, the spray intersection and the quality of spray will increase, as depicted in Fig. 3.

Figure 6 depicts the performance of MOEA/D vs NSGA2 for three scenarios involving different proportions of multi-rotor and fixed-wing UAVs. In all three cases NSGA2 is the most performing. We have to note however that these tests come with a layer of randomness related to the number of voronoi cells, the weed locations, and the TSP tours. We also notice that a multi-rotor leads to a faster mission if both types have equal recharging cycles. The fixed-wing has higher energy consumption and is slower in fulfilling the mission compared with multi-rotor sprayers. In the second set of experiments, we tested different groups of UAVs to see how their number might affect the mission

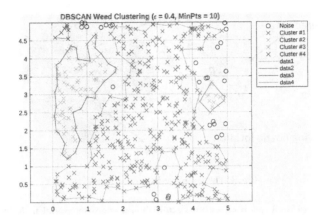

Fig. 4. The sample clustered weeds using the proposed system.

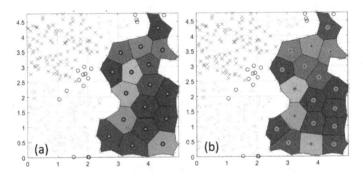

Fig. 5. The different number of voronoi cells in a sample field (a) 17, (b) 18.

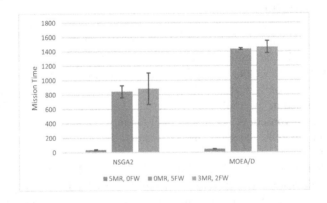

Fig. 6. The difference between MOEA/D and NSGA2 in the three different missions including fixed-wing and multi-rotor UAVs: blue (5 Multi-rotor only), orange (5 fixed-wing only), and grey (3 multi-rotor and 2 fixed-wing). (Color figure online)

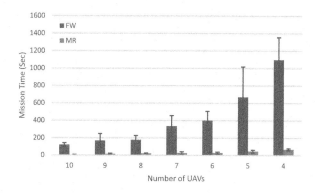

Fig. 7. The relation between mission time and the number of UAVs.

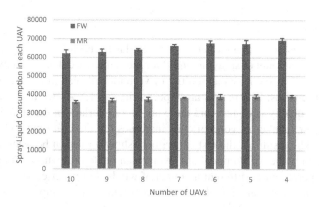

Fig. 8. The relation between spraying liquid and the number of UAVs.

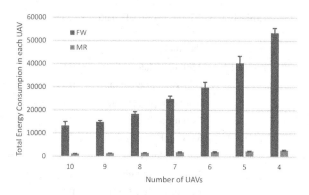

Fig. 9. The relation between the total energy consumption and the number of UAVs.

time, spraying liquid consumption, energy consumption, and the total mission time. As expected, the results listed in Figs. 7, 8, 9, 10 and 11 show that the mission time, energy, and liquid consumption decrease for each UAV, while the number of drones increases.

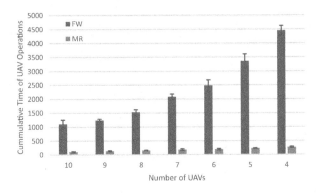

Fig. 10. The relation between the cumulative time of UAV operations during the mission and the number of UAVs.

In Fig. 8, the liquid consumption per UAV is similar for each UAV category given that UAVs use similar amount of spraying liquid for the same weed density. In the last experiments, the goal is to see how the number of voronoi cells can affect the total mission for different scenarios. The results are reported in Fig. 12. As we have more voronoi cells, the spray quality is higher, and there are more overlaps in the spraying. We also see that a higher number of voronoi cells increases the mission time and spray liquid consumption. The results of the last experiment show a relation between the spraying quality and the number of Voronoi cells, which can be helpful when trying to keep the spray quality persistent in different amounts of winds. In this case, we can increase or decrease the amount of cells based on the current wind, which impacts time and liquid consumption.

Table 1. NSGA2 and MOEA/D parameters [8].

Algorithm	Parameter	Value
$NSGA2$	Mutation Rate	0.02
	Cross-over percentage	0.7
	Mutation percentage	0.4
	Mutation Step Size	0.3
$MOEA/D$	Max archive size	20
	Subproblems	3
	Number of neighbors (T)	3
	Mutation rate (CR)	0.5

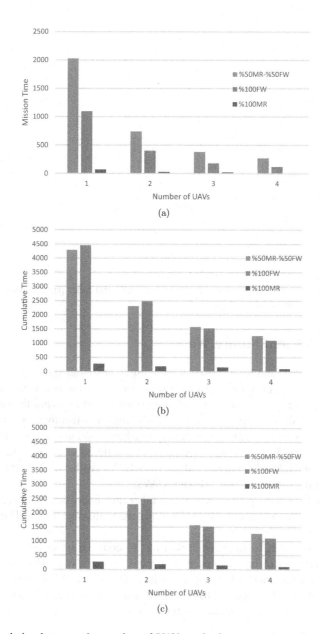

Fig. 11. The relation between the number of UAVs and other parameters when we have only multi-rotor, fixed-wing, and a combination of fixed-wing and multi-rotor.

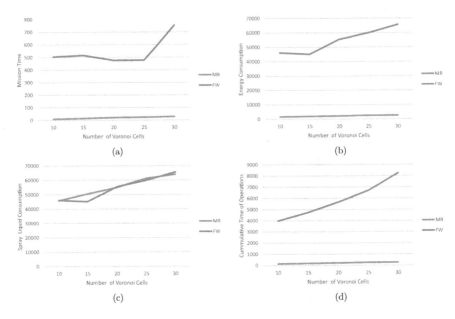

Fig. 12. The relation between the number of voronoi cells and other parameters when we have either multi-rotor or fixed-wing.

7   Conclusion and Future Work

We propose a new system for multi-UAV spraying in precision agriculture. To generate proper waypoints, the proposed algorithm relies on clustering and voronoi cells. Path planning is then developed for each cluster by viewing and solving the problem as a multi-objective TSP. We may have to use fixed-wings, multi-rotors, or a mix of both, depending on the situation. A multi-rotor may be a better option in areas with tight paths or a non-flying zone. We experimentally studied the differences between heterogeneous and homogeneous UAVs in spraying. Multi-rotor UAVs can have a longer mission time if recharged at the same rate as fixed-wing UAVs.

In the near future, we plan to investigate other metaheuristics [9, 11–13] as well as reinforcement learning methods [19] for solving the multi-objective TSP, especially in a reactive mode.

Moreover, we plan to improve clustering by considering other approaches [1]. DBSCAN can cluster without any excessive details of the system. However, the operator must set some parameters for proper results in DBSCAN. While some research has been conducted for self-adaptive DBSCAN, we manually tune parameters to their best and leave the self-adaptive clustering as future work.

References

1. Anowar, F., Sadaoui, S., Mouhoub, M.: Auction fraud classification based on clustering and sampling techniques. In: 2018 17th IEEE International Conference on Machine Learning and Applications (ICMLA), pp. 366–371. IEEE (2018)

2. Chen, P., Ouyang, F., Zhang, Y., Lan, Y.: Preliminary evaluation of spraying quality of multi-unmanned aerial vehicle (UAV) close formation spraying. Agriculture **12**(8), 1149 (2022)

3. Chen, Y., Qi, H., Li, G., Lan, Y.: Weed control effect of unmanned aerial vehicle (UAV) application in wheat field. Int. J. Precis. Agric. Aviat. **2**(2) (2019)

4. Cioni, F., Maines, G.: Weed control in SUGARBEET. Sugar Tech **12**(3), 243–255 (2010)

5. Deb, K., Agrawal, S., Pratap, A., Meyarivan, T.: A fast elitist non-dominated sorting genetic algorithm for multi-objective optimization: NSGA-II. In: Schoenauer, M., et al. (eds.) PPSN 2000. LNCS, vol. 1917, pp. 849–858. Springer, Heidelberg (2000). https://doi.org/10.1007/3-540-45356-3_83

6. Ester, M., Kriegel, H.P., Sander, J., Xu, X., et al.: A density-based algorithm for discovering clusters in large spatial databases with noise. In: KDD, vol. 96, pp. 226–231 (1996)

7. Farid, A.M., Egerton, S., Barca, J.C., Kamal, M.A.S.: Adaptive multi-objective search in a swarm vs swarm context. In: 2018 IEEE International Conference on Systems, Man, and Cybernetics (SMC), pp. 3641–3646. IEEE (2018)

8. Farid, A.M., Mouhoub, M.: Evolutionary mapping with multiple unmanned aerial vehicles. In: 2022 IEEE International Conference on Systems, Man and Cybernetics (SMC), pp. 1–7. IEEE (2022)

9. Hmer, A., Mouhoub, M.: A multi-phase hybrid metaheuristics approach for the exam timetabling. Int. J. Comput. Intell. Appl. **15**(04), 1650023 (2016)

10. Hoffman, K.L., Padberg, M., Rinaldi, G., et al.: Traveling salesman problem. Encycl. Oper. Res. Manage. Sci. **1**, 1573–1578 (2013)

11. Korani, W., Mouhoub, M.: Discrete mother tree optimization for the traveling salesman problem. In: Yang, H., Pasupa, K., Leung, A.C.-S., Kwok, J.T., Chan, J.H., King, I. (eds.) ICONIP 2020. LNCS, vol. 12533, pp. 25–37. Springer, Cham (2020). https://doi.org/10.1007/978-3-030-63833-7_3

12. Korani, W., Mouhoub, M.: Discrete mother tree optimization for the traveling salesman problem. In: Yang, H., Pasupa, K., Leung, A.C.-S., Kwok, J.T., Chan, J.H., King, I. (eds.) ICONIP 2020. LNCS, vol. 12533, pp. 25–37. Springer, Cham (2020). https://doi.org/10.1007/978-3-030-63833-7_3

13. Korani, W., Mouhoub, M.: Review on nature-inspired algorithms. Oper. Res. Forum **2**, 1–26 (2021). https://doi.org/10.1007/s43069-021-00068-x

14. Li, M., Shi, Y., Wang, X., Yuan, H.: Target recognition for the automatically targeting variable rate sprayer. In: Li, D., Liu, Y., Chen, Y. (eds.) CCTA 2010. IAICT, vol. 346, pp. 20–28. Springer, Heidelberg (2011). https://doi.org/10.1007/978-3-642-18354-6_4

15. Li, X., et al.: Comparison of UAV and fixed-wing aerial application for alfalfa insect pest control: evaluating efficacy, residues, and spray quality. Pest Manag. Sci. **77**(11), 4980–4992 (2021)

16. Lottes, P., Khanna, R., Pfeifer, J., Siegwart, R., Stachniss, C.: UAV-based crop and weed classification for smart farming. In: 2017 IEEE International Conference on Robotics and Automation (ICRA), pp. 3024–3031. IEEE (2017)

17. Matai, R., Singh, S.P., Mittal, M.L.: Traveling salesman problem: an overview of applications, formulations, and solution approaches. Travel. Salesman Probl. Theory Appl. **1**(1), 1–25 (2010)

18. Nørremark, M., Griepentrog, H., Nielsen, J., Søgaard, H.: Evaluation of an autonomous GPS-based system for intra-row weed control by assessing the tilled area. Precision Agric. **13**(2), 149–162 (2012)

19. Parasteh, S., Khorram, A., Mouhoub, M., Sadaoui, S.: A deep averaged reinforcement learning approach for the traveling salesman problem. In: IEEE International Conference on Systems, Man, and Cybernetics, SMC 2022, Prague, Czech Republic, 9–12 October 2022, pp. 2514–2519. IEEE (2022).https://doi.org/10.1109/SMC53654.2022.9945274

20. Partel, V., Kakarla, S.C., Ampatzidis, Y.: Development and evaluation of a low-cost and smart technology for precision weed management utilizing artificial intelligence. Comput. Electron. Agric. **157**, 339–350 (2019)

21. Pedersen, S.M., Fountas, S., Sørensen, C.G., Van Evert, F.K., Blackmore, B.S.: Robotic seeding: economic perspectives. In: Pedersen, S.M., Lind, K.M. (eds.) Precision Agriculture: Technology and Economic Perspectives. PPA, pp. 167–179. Springer, Cham (2017). https://doi.org/10.1007/978-3-319-68715-5_8

22. Rasmussen, J., Nielsen, J., Garcia-Ruiz, F., Christensen, S., Streibig, J.: Potential uses of small unmanned aircraft systems (UAS) in weed research. Weed Res. **53**(4), 242–248 (2013)

23. Shorewala, S., Ashfaque, A., Sidharth, R., Verma, U.: Weed density and distribution estimation for precision agriculture using semi-supervised learning. IEEE Access **9**, 27971–27986 (2021)

24. Srivastava, K., Pandey, P.C., Sharma, J.K.: An approach for route optimization in applications of precision agriculture using UAVs. Drones **4**(3), 58 (2020)

25. Wu, X., Aravecchia, S., Lottes, P., Stachniss, C., Pradalier, C.: Robotic weed control using automated weed and crop classification. J. Field Robot. **37**(2), 322–340 (2020)

26. Xiong, Y., Ge, Y., Liang, Y., Blackmore, S.: Development of a prototype robot and fast path-planning algorithm for static laser weeding. Comput. Electron. Agric. **142**, 494–503 (2017)

27. Yamamoto, K., Guo, W., Yoshioka, Y., Ninomiya, S.: On plant detection of intact tomato fruits using image analysis and machine learning methods. Sensors **14**(7), 12191–12206 (2014)

28. Zhang, Q., Li, H.: MOEA/D: a multiobjective evolutionary algorithm based on decomposition. IEEE Trans. Evol. Comput. **11**(6), 712–731 (2007)

29. Zhang, S., Guo, J., Wang, Z.: Combing k-means clustering and local weighted maximum discriminant projections for weed species recognition. Front. Comput. Sci. **1**, 4 (2019)

Human Comfort Factors in People Navigation: Literature Review, Taxonomy and Framework

Matthias Kalenberg$^{(\boxtimes)}$, Christian Hofmann , Sina Martin , and Jörg Franke

Institute for Factory Automation and Production Systems, Friedrich-Alexander Universität Erlangen-Nürnberg (FAU), Egerlandstraße 7, 91058 Erlangen, Germany
{matthias.kalenberg,christian.hofmann,sina.martin,
joerg.franke}@faps.fau.de

Abstract. Due to demographic shifts and improvements in medical care, person navigation systems (PNS) for people with disabilities are becoming increasingly important. So far, PNS have received less attention than mobile robots. However, the work on mobile robots cannot always be transferred to PNS because there are important differences in navigating people. In this paper, we address these differences by providing a comprehensive literature review on human comfort factors in people navigation, presenting a unified taxonomy for PNS and proposing a framework for integrating these factors into a navigation stack.

Based on the results, we extract the key differences and human comfort factors that have been addressed in current literature. Furthermore, the literature review shows that there is no unified taxonomy in this field. To address this, we introduce the term people navigation and a taxonomy to categorize existing systems. Finally, we summarize the human comfort factors that have been considered so far and provide an outlook on their implementation. Our survey serves as a foundation for a comprehensive research in people navigation and identifies open challenges.

Keywords: People navigation · Person navigation system · Human comfort factors

1 Introduction

PNS are becoming increasingly important for the transport of both healthy and disabled people. According to the survey of Singh et al. (2023), 56% of the participants believe that robots are appropriate for the transport sector, including self-driving cars, buses or trains. In addition, mobile robotics technology can provide invaluable assistance to people with disabilities, particularly through devices such as intelligent wheelchairs or travel assistance for the visually impaired. Simpson (2008) points out that 61% to 91% of wheelchair users could benefit from an intelligent wheelchair. Due to demographic changes, there will be a greater need for PNS to enable people with disabilities to maintain their independence.

The well-being of passengers using a PNS as well as the perception of the passenger by others are crucial. The comfort and safety of passengers are highly influenced by

© The Author(s), under exclusive license to Springer Nature Switzerland AG 2024
J. Filipe and J. Röning (Eds.): ROBOVIS 2024, CCIS 2077, pp. 225–243, 2024.
https://doi.org/10.1007/978-3-031-59057-3_15

parameters defining the driving behavior of a mobile system, such as speed, acceleration and jerk. In comparison, these factors are not relevant for mobile robots in terms of comfort. Furthermore, it is necessary to consider the comfort of pedestrians in the environment of a PNS. For instance, an intelligent wheelchair should navigate in a socially acceptable manner to avoid annoying other traffic participants.

Human-aware or social navigation is a well studied-problem of mobile robotics, but there is no review for PNS that includes human comfort factors of passengers. Therefore, we aim to bundle the research in the field of people navigation with a standardized taxonomy.

In this paper, we evaluate existing literature investigating both the comfort of the passenger and other traffic participants. The contributions of this paper are

- a comprehensive literature review on human comfort factors,
- a taxonomy for navigation systems that includes human comfort factors,
- a proposal for an implementation framework for human comfort factors.

We show that there is less research on the comfort factors for passengers of assistive mobile robots compared to social navigation of mobile robots. Furthermore, there is no taxonomy for such navigation systems available. Therefore, we introduce people navigation and a taxonomy to define PNS. In addition, we present a framework towards human comfortable navigation based on a common framework of human-aware navigation and explain which yet existing elements need to be extended.

This paper is structured as follows: First, we provide definitions of a passenger, people navigation and PNS. We then begin our review with a comprehensive search using the search string described in Sect. 2.2, to identify navigation systems that integrate human comfort factors. We classify the navigation systems following our novel taxonomy in Sect. 3.1. To discover additional navigation systems that meet our defined criteria of a PNS, a focused backward and forward search is performed. The references identified by the search string that match the definition of a PNS serve as a starting point. Finally, we present eight human comfort factors identified in the survey in Sect. 3. In Sect. 4, we introduce a navigation framework for incorporating human comfort factors, based on the findings presented before.

2   People Navigation: Definition, Review and Classification

To the best of our knowledge, there is no review paper that provides an overview of existing robotic navigation systems that navigate passengers and consider their comfort factors. There are surveys for human-aware navigation for mobile robots that point out some open challenges (Kruse et al., 2013, Mavrogiannis et al., 2021, Singh et al., 2022). Further, there are some reviews on specific assistance systems such as an intelligent wheelchair (Leaman et al., 2017, Simpson, 2005, Sivakanthan et al., 2022) or tools for visually impaired people (Kuriakose et al., 2022).

However, there is no standardized definition of systems that navigate people. Nor is there an overview of the factors that need to be considered for user comfort in navigation systems. To address this gap, we introduce definitions for the passenger, people navigation and PNS in Sect. 2.1. Based on these definitions, our systematic literature

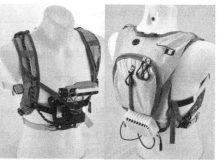

(a) Intelligent wheelchair (Kalenberg et al., 2023)   (b) Visual impaired assistance system (Sessner et al., 2022)

Fig. 1. Two assistance systems considered in our lab, (a) an intelligent wheelchair and (b) an assistance system for guiding visual impaired people.

review approach is described in Sect. 2.2. Finally, Sect. 2.3 describes our classification of the relevant literature.

2.1 Definitions

Passenger. In this paper, we define a passenger as a person who uses a navigation system to move towards a specific goal. The user can either operate independently with the aid of a guidance system or rely on an robotic system such as an intelligent wheelchair (Fig. 1a) or a visually impaired assistance system (Fig. 1b).

People Navigation. We introduce the term people navigation as an extension of human-aware navigation for frameworks that consider pedestrian comfort as well as passenger comfort. Human-aware or social navigation addresses the behavior of mobile robots, taking into account the well-being of people in the environment (Kruse et al. 2013, Mavrogiannis et al. 2021). When navigating a passenger, their comfort must also be taken into account. Therefore, it differs from the navigation of mobile robots or guidance systems that do not take passenger comfort into account. However, there is work in these related fields that has taken human comfort factors into account and can be applied to PNS.

Person Navigation System (PNS). A PNS has a passenger, controls the motion execution and is not a traffic vehicle. It navigates a passenger at human speed and ensures safe and socially accepted interaction with people in the environment. Depending on the system, it either executes the instructions autonomously or gives commands to the passenger. Existing systems that meet the definition of a PNS have different names in the literature, such as personal mobility vehicle, passenger vehicle, assistive mobile robot, micro-mobility transport vehicles or personal mobility devices. Examples are an intelligent wheelchair or a navigation system for visually impaired people (Fig. 1). Therefore, we propose PNS as a unified term for the research in people navigation.

2.2 Related Systematic Review

The following three research questions arise from the up-to-date insufficient overview of PNS, which are addressed in this publication:

– What are the differences between passenger and robot navigation?
– Are there specific navigation approaches for passengers?
– What factors contribute to passenger comfort?

Based on these questions, we derive a search string for the Web of Science database. We consider all publications that contain the words navigation and comfort. We restrict the search to systems that include passenger or pedestrian comfort. In this context, there is no consistent word for the human, that's why we consider passenger, pedestrian, people, human or person within our search string. The resulting syntax of the search string is: ALL = (navigation comfort) AND ALL = (passenger OR pedestrian OR people OR human OR person)[1]. We choose the Web of Science Core Collection to cover all fully indexed papers from different research areas that consider human comfort factors for navigation. This results in 137 publications.

To focus our search, we first examine the titles and the abstracts found for relevant sources. We are searching for navigation systems that in particular take human comfort factors into account. As outlined in Sect. 1, we consider both the passenger's and the pedestrian's point of view. Therefore, human factors of mobile robot navigation as well as passenger comfort factors must be included in this survey. By excluding papers without human comfort factors for navigation, such as comfortable interfaces, surgery navigation, virtual reality effects, teleportation, comfortable app navigation, thermal comfort or comfortable smart glasses, we reduce the number of papers to 46.

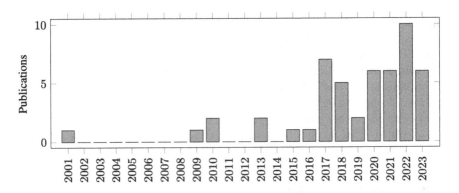

Fig. 2. Number of papers identified by publication year. The number of publications regarding human comfort factors has increased over the last decade.

The results show that people navigation is of current importance. As depicted in Fig 2 the number of publications on this topic has increased in the last decade. It is

---

[1] https://www.webofscience.com/wos/woscc/summary/688693e0-4ea9-41b9-be20-fc59ce8acd5a-b0f37689/relevance/1.

a more recent development than the research on human-aware navigation for mobile robots, which gained increased attention for about two decades (Kruse et al., 2013). Accordingly, the number of publications and different authors is limited (Fig. 3).

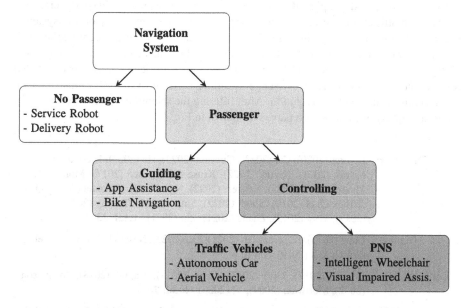

Fig. 3. Classification and examples of our proposed taxonomy. We distinguish whether the system has a passenger or not, is guiding or controlling the passenger and between traffic vehicles and PNS.

2.3   Taxonomy

To categorize the navigation systems identified by our search, we have developed a taxonomy. The aim of this search is to identify all relevant research areas related to human comfort factors in navigation, including mobile robots, apps, and autonomous vehicles. This leads to a range of different systems. We have created this taxonomy to structure the results for further researchers and to highlight relevant systems. The purpose of the taxonomy is twofold: first, to classify related navigation systems that have already taken into account human comfort factors. And second, to identify existing PNSs in the literature. The taxonomy is based on the following distinctions:

− no passenger or passenger,
− guiding or controlling,
− traffic vehicle or PNS.

The initial category differentiates between entirely robotic systems and systems that have a passenger. The second criterion differentiates between systems that propose a navigation command or information (guiding) and those that execute navigation commands (controlling). Controlling can be either the autonomous execution of navigation commands, as in the case of an intelligent wheelchair, or the transmission of navigation commands via a machine-human interface, as in the case of an assistance system for visually impaired people (cf. Fig. 1b). In the case of an assistance system, passengers can still check the navigation instructions, but they may rely on the system's decision. The final category distinguishes between navigation systems for traffic, such as autonomous cars, drones or boats and a PNS. A PNS has a passenger, controls the motion execution and is not a traffic vehicle as defined in Sect. 2.1. However, related research areas classified as no passenger, guiding or traffic vehicles do also include human comfort factors for navigation. After filtering the scientific papers resulting from our search query, we classify 46 papers as shown in Fig. 4.

No Passenger:	Boldrer (2020), Cai (2023), Guevara (2023), Hu (2022), Kidokoro (2015), Kivrak (2021), Kivrak (2022), Kruse (2013), Lee (2017), Mora (2022), Mavrogiannis (2023), Neggers (2022), Ngo (2020), Pimentel (2021), Qian (2010), Qian (2010), Singh (2022), Singh (2023), Truong (2018), Truong (2017), Vega (2019), Zhang (2021), Zhi (2021) - **total: 23**
Guiding:	Dang (2013), Kazemzadeh (2021), Liu (2022), Neset (2022), Vasconcellos (2001), Yan (2019) - **total: 6**
Traffic Vehicles:	Dousse (2017), Gim (2017), Guan (2017), Hamid (2018), Johannson (2022), Moriwaki (2009), Yi (2020) - **total: 7**
PNS:	Chen (2023), Jimenez (2020), Kim (2016), Moon (2022), Morales (2017), Morales (2018), Nguyen (2018), Sawabe (2018), Vanhaeren (2020), Wang (2020) - **total: 10**
Additional PNS:	Gulati (2008), Gulati (2009), Jimenez (2021), Jung (2020), Morales (2013), Morales (2014), Morales (2015), Morales (2018), Park (2011), Pineau (2007), Sawabe (2015), Zhang (2022) - **total: 12**

Fig. 4. The papers found by our search query were classified into four categories based on our taxonomy: No Passenger, Guiding, Traffic Vehicles, and PNS. The distribution of papers shows that PNS has received less attention than human-aware navigation of mobile robots. Additional PNS were identified by searching backward and forward on PNS found by our search query.

Our review shows that human comfort factors for passengers have received less attention than mobile robots (cf. Fig. 4). However, the number of publications has increased since the findings of Morales et al. (2013) and Sawabe et al. (2015) drew attention to this topic. To find other systems that match our definition of a PNS, we carry out a targeted backward-forward search. For this purpose, we use only those papers from the search string that were classified as PNS, resulting in additional 12 references (cf. Fig. 4).

3 Human Comfort Factors in People Navigation

Various aspects of passenger comfort have been analyzed in the relevant literature. To evaluate these aspects, we first examine in Sect. 3.1 which human comfort factors have previously been considered in their respective categories. We classify all discussed points into eight human comfort factors in Sect. 3.2.

3.1 Human Comfort Factors in Navigation Systems

No Passenger. This category does not meet the definition of a PNS, but remains relevant as a socially acceptable navigation is critical to passenger comfort. Irritated traffic participants do not contribute to the comfort of the passenger. This problem is well-known for mobile robots. Therefore, all papers in this category deal with the acceptance of the navigation behavior of mobile robots.

As human-aware navigation has received more and more attention in the last two decades, several reviews as presented by Kruse et al. (2013) or Singh et al. (2022) and approaches for frameworks as presented by Kivrak et al. (2021) or Qian et al. (2010) can be found in the literature. Kruse et al. (2013) define three main challenges for human-aware navigation: First, the robot must not cause stress or discomfort to people who interact with it. Second, the robot should behave as human-like as possible. Third, the robot should respect social norms. All of these challenges apply also to people navigation.

The social distances introduced by Hall (1966) that are shown in Table 1 are used by many approaches (Boldrer et al., 2020, Kivrak et al., 2022, Kruse et al. 2013, Mora et al., 2022, Neggers et al., 2022, Ngo et al., 2020, Qian et al., 2010, Truong et al., 2018). Most authors have extended the model proposed by Hall by adopting an elliptical shape to represent the movements of individuals. More recently, Neggers et al. (2022) have experimentally investigated the exact shape and size of personal spaces.

Table 1. Interpersonal distances introduced by Hall (1966).

Designation	Specification	Reserved for ...
Intimate distance	0 m–0.45 m	Embracing, touching, whispering
Personal distance	0.45 m–1.20 m	Friends
Social distance	1.20 m–3.60 m	Acquaintances and strangers
Public distance	>3.60 m	Public speaking

Smooth motion at a human-comfortable speed is also part of a human-aware robot, as pointed out by Kruse et al. (2013). They mention the work of Butler et al. (2001), who evaluated that a speed of 1 m/s feels uncomfortable for approaching humans, while 0.5 m/s is acceptable. Furthermore, Shi et al. (2008) point out that the velocity needs to be limited depending on the distance to the human to prevent emergency braking. Singh et al. (2023) demonstrate in their experiments that participants prefer robots, that move with a slower speed than humans. Kidokoro et al. (2015) consider speed in order to avoid their robot causing crowds. Zhang et al. (2021) restrict the velocity of their assistive robot based on virtual regions in the surrounding environment.

Humans generally tend to feel more comfortable when a robot is moving within their field of view (FOV) (Sisbot et al., 2007). If a mobile robot unexpectedly emerges from a blind spot, it may cause fear and discomfort. In addition, a robot passing behind a person also feels uncomfortable (Neggers et al., 2022). Therefore, Sisbot et al. (2007) introduce a visibility criterion which was later adopted by Qian et al. (2010). They propose a framework for human-compliant navigation and a socially acceptable navigation based on human prediction through human motion patterns (Qian et al., 2010).

When humans and robots interact, the robot should follow social conventions and avoid contact. This typically requires the robot to remain on the same side of a path like other traffic participants. To meet this requirement, Qian et al. (2010) propose the side-tendency criterion in addition to visibility and proxemics. This implementation of behavior can also be found in further literature (Kruse et al., 2013).

Another challenge is the understanding of groups in crowded environments, which is important in order not to disturb group formations (Kruse et al. 2013). Approaches including social spaces of groups typically use the position, orientation, movement and FOV of the people to classify groups (Kidokoro et al., 2015, Truong et al., 2017, Vega et al., 2019). After classification, a social space for the group can be mapped and included for behavior and path planning. Additionally, Kidokoro et al. (2015) point out that the robot's interaction with pedestrians may lead to crowding. Hence, this factor should be considered.

The comfort factors for human-aware navigation outlined in this study need to be considered but do not address the passenger. This is particularly evident through the introduction of the human-priority criterion by Qian et al. (2010). They utilize the prediction of human movements to always prioritize pedestrian right of way in encounters to ensure their comfort. This is not a drawback, but a method to guarantee pedestrians' comfort in any environment. However, it is inadequate for a PNS, it can support pedestrian comfort but needs to be extended for people navigation.

Guiding System. Systems that have a passenger but only guide, i.e. help the person driving the vehicle to navigate, are not defined as PNS. The main difference is that these systems propose a navigation instruction but do not execute it. Nevertheless, they take into account some human comfort factors that can be applied to PNS.

Yan et al. (2019) suggest evaluating sheltered environments to optimize pedestrian comfort on rainy days for navigation apps. They call these areas top-bounded spaces. Neset et al. (2022) propose to integrate thermal heat maps into pedestrian routing tools to address rising temperatures in cities due to climate change. To optimize pedestrian routing tools, Dang et al. (2013) present a framework for fusing multiple environmental sensors.

Further literature is considering navigation comfort of electric bicycle users (Kazemzadeh et al., 2021). Furthermore, Liu et al. (2022) present an approach to electric scooter interaction in pedestrian crowds. Incorporating these new types of road users into people navigation is important in traffic scenarios. Guidance systems show different human comfort factors.

Traffic Vehicle. As introduced with our taxonomy in Sect. 2.3, a PNS differs from traffic vehicles such as cars, air taxis or boats. A PNS is restricted to human speeds while ensuring safe and social interaction with the passenger and other humans in the environment. The environment of a PNS also differs from that of a traffic vehicle. A PNS will not be required to travel at the speed of cars or navigate on a motorway. However, it must be able to navigate in indoor environments, shopping malls or pedestrian areas. Consequently, our definition of PNS excludes traffic vehicles. Though, research in this area considers human comfort factors for navigation.

Research on autonomous transport vehicles addresses passenger comfort factors. There are papers, for instance, on aerial vehicles, buses or cars (Dousse et al., 2017, Johannson et al., 2022, Yi et al. 2020). Not all factors are transferable to a PNS, but in particular the lowest possible jerk while driving is often mentioned and also relevant (Dousse et al., 2017, Hamid et al., 2018, Yi et al., 2020). Though, most of these works focus on a car-like steering, for example by Moriwaki et al. (2009), which needs to be extended for each specific PNS.

Person Navigation System. A PNS has a passenger, controls the execution of the movement and is not a traffic vehicle. This includes, for example, intelligent wheelchairs, electronic travel aids (ETAs) for visually impaired people or smart walker assistance systems as presented in (Jimenez et al., 2020, Kim et al., 2016, Moon et al., 2022, Morales et al. 2018). Existing PNS comprise of a range of innovative solutions for different mobility needs. Further information on such systems can be found in specific reviews, like those on intelligent wheelchairs and ETAs (Kuriakose et al., 2022, Leaman et al., 2017, Simpson et al., 2005, Sivakanthan et al., 2022). However, none of the reviews cover passenger comfort factors.

When a PNS plans a path, it must consider both the proxemics of pedestrians and the comfort feeling experienced by the passenger. Approaches for human-aware navigation can be used but need to be extended in such a way that they take the passenger's proxemic into account. Jiménez et al. (2021) introduce an interpersonal-social zone (IPSz) and an interpersonal-public zone (IPPz) for interacting with their walking assistance system. IPSz is meant to allow relatively close interaction with people nearby. IPPz is used to prevent collisions with oncoming persons. Morales et al. (2017) propose a balanced navigation model which considers passenger and pedestrian comfort factors. Additionally, Morales et al. (2018) have conducted research on the comfort of passengers when taking certain positions in corridors. Furthermore, Morales et al. (2013) evaluate the comfort feeling of passengers taking the distance to obstacles and velocity into account. They found that people tend to walk slightly to the left or right of the centre of a corridor, depending on the direction of traffic. They implement their findings using social maps. In addition, Sawabe et al. (2018) have investigated preferred trajectories at intersections. Another approach by Kim et al. (2016) is to use reinforcement learning to train a cost function based on features evaluating the density and velocity of obstacles. The resulting function is used to create a local path planner based on their extracted features.

Visibility for a PNS is not only about moving in the FOV of pedestrians but also about the largest FOV for the passenger. Especially in areas around curves or intersections, this is important. People tend to choose trajectories that allow them to see as much as possible after a corner to avoid collisions or uncomfortable situations with other pedestrians. Therefore, Morales et al. (2014) introduce the visibility index, which depends on the ratio between visible and non-visible areas. Furthermore, Morales et al. (2015) implement this index into a multi-layered costmap to include human comfort factors in path planning. Their resulting path planner is perceived as more comfortable than the shortest path planner in experiments with 30 participants. Sawabe et al. (2015) conducted additional research on predicting collisions at intersections.

The graceful motion of a PNS, as introduced by Gulati et al. (2008), needs to be visibly safe, comfortable, fast and intuitive. Safe means not only free from collisions but also with minimal acceleration, as high acceleration can result in discomfort and even injury. For the comfort feeling, the movement should be smooth with minimal jerk. For comfortable navigation, a PNS should be as fast as possible, because an increased amount of time for transportation isn't comfortable in everyday life. Consequently, these constraints cannot be fulfilled solely by driving slowly. Furthermore, the movements should be intuitive for the passenger. Gulati et al. (2009) suggest a framework for planning comfortable and customizable motion by optimizing the human comfort factors based on a weighted sum. For that purpose, Morales et al. (2013) experimentally evaluated which forward velocities x and angular velocities Θ and corresponding accelerations feel comfortable for the passenger. Their results are shown in Table 2. Learning approaches are an alternative which are able to learn comfortable execution by demonstration trajectories (Kim et al., 2016).

Table 2. Human passenger comfort values by Morales et al. (2013).

Parameter	Numerical values
$\dot{x}_{\text{comfortable}}$	$0.80 \, \text{m/s}$
$\dot{\Theta}_{\text{comfortable}}$	$0.60 \, \text{rad/s}^2$
$\ddot{x}_{\text{comfortable}}$	$0.10 \, \text{m/s}^2$
$\ddot{\Theta}_{\text{comfortable}}$	$0.17 \, \text{rad/s}^2$

An essential issue for a PNS, which is irrelevant to mobile robotics, is the stress factor for the passenger. Swabe et al. (2018) consider three types of stress for PNS: stress factors from vehicle behavior, stress factors from a static environment and stress factors from a dynamic environment. Their main contribution is that they conduct experiments to provide an objective measurement of stress by using the heart rate and galvanic skin response (GSR). They argue that static stress factors, such as distances to walls or objects, have a robust strength and short interval characteristics which can be measured by the GSR. In contrast, dynamic stress factors, such as predicting collisions, have a weak strength but long stress interval features, which can be seen in the heart rate. In their experiments they show that these factors are measurable while driving in sections or approaching a wall or obstacles. Furthermore, these results show that the feeling of comfort and stress depends on each individual passenger. Vanhaeren et al. (2020) also demonstrate the individuality in video experiments in an online survey. In addition, Gulati et al. (2009) point out that customization for each passenger is important and suggest using the weights of a comfort function for this purpose.

The safety of the passenger should be the first priority. This factor is comparatively rarely mentioned as the development of both human-aware mobile robots and PNS are based on a collision avoidance and human comfort factors are seen as an extension of this. Several papers refer to the definition of safety proposed by Gulati et al. (2008). They state that safety requires a collision-free path but also that it must not cause excessive acceleration for the passenger. For example Sawabe et al. (2015), J. Park et al. (2011) and Y. Morales et al. (2015) refer to this. Furthermore, Wang et al. (2020) focus on the stable navigation of an autonomous wheelchair driving on a slope way. They use a sampling-based approach to indicate unsafe regions. Based on this, they optimize the chosen trajectory using a cost function. In summary, the examples show that it is essential for a PNS to ensure the safety and comfort of the passenger and other traffic participants.

3.2 Summary of Human Comfort Factors in People Navigation

We identified the following eight human comfort factors in people navigation:

- **Proxemics**, as introduced by Hall (1966), describes the observance of social distances and zones.
- **Graceful Motion** is defined by Gulati et al. (2008) as safe, comfortable, fast and intuitive motion. Additionally, we have incorporated literature that explores the speeds that offer the most comfort to passengers.
- **Visibility** includes the PNS being within the field of view of others and avoiding areas that are occluded.
- **Side-Tendency** refers to an individual's tendency to choose a specific side of a path, usually in compliance with traffic regulations.
- **Safety** means for PNS that the passenger and other humans are safe from collisions as well as from the effects of acceleration or the ground.
- **Crowd Density** is frequently mentioned for mobile robots, but it is also important for PNS to be able to navigate among people.
- **Stress** caused by the behavior of the PNS or by obstacles in the environment should be avoided for comfortable navigation.
- **Weather** conditions such as heat, rain or snow represent external factors that should be taken into account.

Finally, we summarize the relevant literature for each human comfort factor in order to guide researchers to the relevant literature to be considered for the development of a PNS (cf. Table 3).

Table 3. Relevant literature for the identified human comfort factors sorted by categories of our taxonomy.

Human Comfort Factor	Category			
	No Passenger	Guiding	Traffic vehicle	PNS
Proxemics	Boldrer (2020), Cai (2023) Guevara (2023), Hu (2022), Kidokoro (2015), Kivrak (2022), Kruse (2013), Lee (2017), Mora (2022), Neggers (2022), Ngo (2020), Pimentel (2021), Qian (2010), Singh (2022), Truong (2018)	–	–	Gulati (2008), Jimenez (2021), Kim 2016, Morales (2013), Morales (2017), Morales (2018), Nguyen (2018), Sawabe (2018)
Graceful Motion	Kidokoro (2015), Kruse (2013), Singh (2023), Zhang (2021)	Kazemzadeh (2021), Liu (2022)	Gim (2017), Dousse (2017), Yi (2020)	Gulati (2008), Gulati (2009), Kim (2016), Moon (2022), Morales (2013), Morales (2015), Morales (2017), Nguyen (2018), Park (2011), Sawabe (2015)
Visibility	Mavrogiannis (2021), Neggers (2022), Qian (2010), Qian (2010), Sisbot (2007)	–	–	Morales (2014), Morales (2015), Morales (2018), Nguyen (2018), Park (2011), Sawabe (2015)
Side-Tendency	Mavrogiannis (2021), Neggers (2022), Qian (2010), Qian (2010)	–	–	Morales (2017), Morales (2018)
Safety	Guevara (2023), Pimentel (2021), Qian (2010)	–	Hamid (2018)	Gulati (2008), Morales (2014), Park (2011), Pineau (2007), Sawabe (2015), Wang (2020)
Crowd Density	Boldrer (2020), Cai (2023), Hu (2022), Kidokoro (2015), Kruse (2013), Liu (2022), Mavrogiannis (2023), Truong (2017)	–	–	Kim (2016)
Stress	–	–	–	Gulati (2009), Sawabe (2018), Vanhaeren (2020)
Weather	–	Dang (2013), Neset (2022), Yan (2019)	–	–

4   Towards a People Navigation Framework

As introduced, a PNS should take the comfort of both pedestrians and passengers into account. Numerous publications in the field of mobile robotics are available in the literature, which concentrate on compliance with social distancing norms, and can be found in Table 3. Therefore, a PNS should be developed fulfilling these guidelines. Additionally, it is necessary to integrate the human comfort factors for the passenger.

4.1   Human-Aware Navigation

A framework for human-aware navigation typically includes four functional units that differ from those of a standard mobile robot, as illustrated in Fig. 5 (Kruse et al., 2013, Singh et al., 2022, Truong et al., 2017). These units are person detection, a social prediction model, social mapping and social behavior planning. Person detection can be done using data from cameras and laser scanners followed by a sensor fusion for different sensors and detectors as shown by Hofmann et al. (2022). Based on a social prediction model, the movement of the pedestrians can be predicted. The trajectories of pedestrians are integrated into a social layer in the map.

A common approach to social mapping is to build a multi-layered cost map as proposed by Lu et al. (2014). They present different layers for different obstacles, pedestrians or preferences. This map is the basis for the robot's behavior planning. Finally, a local path planning unit ensures responsive collision avoidance. If possible in real-time, it also takes social distances into account. Further approaches for implementing a human-aware navigation system are described by Kruse et al. (2013) and Singh et al. (2022).

4.2   Implementing Passenger Comfort Factors

Previous extensions to consider comfort factors in a human-aware navigation framework are based on static approaches with prior knowledge. One approach is to model pre-recorded maps in such a way that they take human comfort factors into account. Morales et al. (2013) implement comfortable positions in a corridor using a map. They extend it by a discomfort map based on a visibility index (Morales et al., 2017). Such approaches can be added to the mapping unit.

Another approach is to react to current sensor data. Kim et al. (2016) use a feature extraction module and a reinforcement learning approach to respond to these features. They learn a cost function which evaluates the cells of their local coastmap based on the features crowd density, speed, velocity and distance to the goal. This allows their path planning algorithm to adapt to different situations.

Graceful motion requires an intuitive path planner as well as comfortable speed limits. Gultati et al. (2008) propose B-splines for graceful path planning, which can be implemented in the path planner, taking social zones into account. Speed limits for passenger comfort can be set as constraints for the local path planner (Morales et al., 2017). However, constraints are not sufficient in all situations. Slow execution of the movement may increase the feeling of safety, but traveling too slowly will increase passenger stress due to inefficient travel.

As introduced in Sect. 3.1, each passenger's comfort level is different, so navigation should be adaptable to the individual passenger. General constraints or maps don't take personal preferences into account. For example, there are passengers who enjoy a faster or slower execution. Sawabe et al. (2018) show promising results in objectively measuring the passenger characteristic. This could be used in the future to adapt the navigation behavior of a PNS for each user by creating individual user profiles.

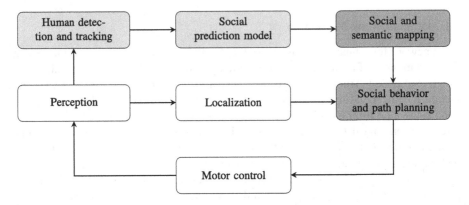

Fig. 5. A framework towards people navigation. White units are common for mobile robot navigation. Grey and green units are extensions for human-aware navigation. Green units need to be extended in terms of human comfort factors. (Color figure online)

5   Conclusion

This survey provides an overview of the existing literature on passenger comfort factors for a PNS. It aims to show researchers which comfort factors should be considered when developing such a system and where to find the corresponding literature. Furthermore, we introduce a taxonomy for people navigation and categorize the publications into eight comfort factors: proxemics, graceful motion, visibility, side-tendency, safety, crowd density, stress and weather. The aim of our work is to bundle the research in the field of people navigation with a standardized taxonomy and to point out open challenges.

Our review of recent publications, published in the last seven years, shows that the research field of people navigation is of current interest (cf. Fig. 2). However, there is only a small number of different authors in this field compared to social navigation of mobile robots. Therefore, there are still open challenges that need to be addressed in future work. It remains to be seen whether all the approaches used for mobile robots can be applied to PNS. Another open research field is how to adapt the navigation to each individual passenger.

References

Boldrer, M., Andreetto, M., Divan, S., Palopoli, L., Fontanelli, D.: Socially- aware reactive obstacle avoidance strategy based on limit cycle. IEEE Robot. Autom. Lett. **5**(2), 3251–3258 (2020). https://doi.org/10.1109/LRA.2020.2976302

Butler, J.T., Agah, A.: Psychological effects of behavior patterns of a mobile personal robot. Auton. Robot. **10**(2), 185–202 (2001). https://doi.org/10.1023/A:1008986004181

Cai, K.Q., Chen, W.N., Wang, C.Q., Song, S., Meng, M.Q.H.: Human-aware path planning with improved virtual doppler method in highly dynamic environments. IEEE Trans. Autom. Sci. Eng. **20**(2), 1304–1321 (2023). https://doi.org/10.1109/TASE.2022.3175039

Chen, W.J., Xie, Z.M., Yuan, P.X., Wang, R.L., Chen, H.W., Xiao, B.: A mobile intelligent guide system for visually impaired pedestrian. J. Syst. Softw. **195** (2023). https://doi.org/10.1016/j.jss.2022.111546

Dang, C.W., Iwai, M., Tobe, Y., Umeda, K., Sezaki, K.: A framework for pedestrian comfort navigation using multi-modal environmental sensors. Pervasive Mob. Comput. **9**(3), 421–436 (2013). https://doi.org/10.1016/j.pmcj.2013.01.002

Shi, D., Collins Jr, E.G., Goldiez, B., Donate, A., Liu, X., Dunlap, D.: Human-aware robot motion planning with velocity constraints. In: 2008 International Symposium on Collaborative Technologies and Systems, pp. 490–497. IEEE, Irvine (2008). https://doi.org/10.1109/CTS.2008.4543969

Dousse, N., Heitz, G., Schill, F., Floreano, D.: Human-comfortable collision-free navigation for personal aerial vehicles. IEEE Robot. Autom. Lett. **2**(1), 358–365 (2017). https://doi.org/10.1109/LRA.2016.2626520

Gim, S., Adouane, L., Lee, S., Derutin, J.P.: Clothoids composition method for smooth path generation of car-like vehicle navigation. J. Intell. Robot. Syst. **88**(1), 129–146 (2017). https://doi.org/10.1007/s10846-017-0531-8

Guan, Q.Z., Bao, H., Xuan, Z.X.: The research of prediction model on intelligent vehicle based on driver's perception. Clust. Comput. - J. Netw. Softw. Tools Appl. **20**(4), 2967–2979 (2017). https://doi.org/10.1007/s10586-017-0946-9

Guevara, L., Hanheide, M., Parsons, S.: Implementation of a human-aware robot navigation module for cooperative soft-fruit harvesting operations. J. Field Robot. (2023). https://doi.org/10.1002/rob.22227

Gulati, S., Jhurani, C., Kuipers, B., Longoria, R.: A framework for planning comfortable and customizable motion of an assistive mobile robot. In: 2009 IEEE/RSJ International Conference on Intelligent Robots and Systems, pp. 4253–4260. IEEE, St. Louis (2009). https://doi.org/10.1109/IROS.2009.5354172

Gulati, S., Kuipers, B.: High performance control for graceful motion of an intelligent wheelchair. In: 2008 IEEE International Conference on Robotics and Automation, pp. 3932–3938. IEEE, Pasadena (2008). https://doi.org/10.1109/ROBOT.2008.4543815

Hall, E.T.: The Hidden Dimension, 1st edn. Doubleday, Garden City (1966)

Hamid, U.Z.A., Zamzuri, H., Yamada, T., Rahman, M.A.A., Saito, Y., Raksincharoensak, P.: Modular design of artificial potential field and nonlinear model predictive control for a vehicle collision avoidance system with move blocking strategy. Proc. Inst. Mech. Eng. Part D J. Automob. Eng. **232**(10), 1353–1373 (2018). https://doi.org/10.1177/0954407017729057

Hofmann, C., Fichtner, M., Lieret, M., Franke, J.: Efficient semantic mapping in dynamic environments. In: Proceedings of the 17th International Joint Conference on Computer Vision, Imaging and Computer Graphics Theory and Applications, pp. 803–810. SCITEPRESS - Science and Technology Publications, Online Streaming, Select a Country (2022). https://doi.org/10.5220/0010770200003124

Hu, Z.X., Zhao, Y.L., Zhang, S., Zhou, L., Liu, J.T.: Crowd-comfort robot navigation among dynamic environment based on social-stressed deep reinforcement learning. Int. J. Soc. Robot. **14**(4), 913–929 (2022). https://doi.org/10.1007/s12369-021-00838-x

Jimenez, M.F., Mello, R.C., Bastos, T., Frizera, A.: Assistive locomotion device with haptic feedback for guiding visually impaired people. Med. Eng. Phys. **80**, 18–25 (2020). https://doi.org/10.1016/j.medengphy.2020.04.002

Johansson, M., Ekman, F., Karlsson, M., Stromberg, H., Jonsson, J.: ADAS at work: assessing professional bus drivers' experience and acceptance of a narrow navigation system. Cogn. Technol. Work **24**(4), 625–639 (2022). https://doi.org/10.1007/s10111-022-00704-4

Kalenberg, M., Lieret, M., Hofmann, C., Franke, J.: A multimodal A* algorithm to solve the two-dimensional optimization problem of accompanying a person for an intelligent wheelchair. In: 2023 IEEE Engineering in Medicine and Biology Society. IEEE (2023)

Kazemzadeh, K., Bansal, P.: Electric bike navigation comfort in pedestrian crowds. Sustain. Cities Soc. **69** (2021). https://doi.org/10.1016/j.scs.2021.102841

Kidokoro, H., Kanda, T., Brscic, D., Shiomi, M.: Simulation-based behavior planning to prevent congestion of pedestrians around a robot. IEEE Trans. Rob. **31**(6), 1419–1431 (2015). https://doi.org/10.1109/TRO.2015.2492862

Kim, B., Pineau, J.: Socially adaptive path planning in human environments using inverse reinforcement learning. Int. J. Soc. Robot. **8**(1), 51–66 (2016). https://doi.org/10.1007/s12369-015-0310-2

Kivrak, H., Cakmak, F., Kose, H., Yavuz, S.: Social navigation framework for assistive robots in human inhabited unknown environments. Eng. Sci. Technol.-Int. J.-JESTECH **24**(2), 284–298 (2021). https://doi.org/10.1016/j.jestch.2020.08.008

Kivrak, H., Cakmak, F., Kose, H., Yavuz, S.: Waypoint based path planner for socially aware robot navigation. Clust. Comput. - J. Netw. Softw. Tools Appl. **25**(3), 1665–1675 (2022). https://doi.org/10.1007/s10586-021-03479-x

Kruse, T., Pandey, A.K., Alami, R., Kirsch, A.: Human-aware robot navigation: a survey. Robot. Auton. Syst. **61**(12), 1726–1743 (2013). https://doi.org/10.1016/j.robot.2013.05.007

Kuriakose, B., Shrestha, R., Sandnes, F.E.: Tools and technologies for blind and visually impaired navigation support: a review. IETE Tech. Rev. **39**(1), 3–18 (2022). https://doi.org/10.1080/02564602.2020.1819893

Leaman, J., La, H.M.: A comprehensive review of smart wheelchairs: past, present, and future. IEEE Trans. Hum.-Mach. Syst. **47**(4), 486–499 (2017). https://doi.org/10.1109/THMS.2017.2706727

Lee, D., Liu, C., Liao, Y.W., Hedrick, J.K.: Parallel interacting multiple model-based human motion prediction for motion planning of companion robots. IEEE Trans. Autom. Sci. Eng. **14**(1), 52–61 (2017). https://doi.org/10.1109/TASE.2016.2623599

Liu, Y.C., Jafari, A., Shim, J.K., Paley, D.A.: Dynamic modeling and simulation of electric scooter interactions with a pedestrian crowd using a social force model. IEEE Trans. Intell. Transp. Syst. **23**(9), 16448–16461 (2022). https://doi.org/10.1109/TITS.2022.3150282

Lu, D.V., Hershberger, D., Smart, W.D.: Layered costmaps for context-sensitive navigation. In: 2014 IEEE/RSJ International Conference on Intelligent Robots and Systems, pp. 709–715. IEEE (2014). https://doi.org/10.1109/IROS.2014.6942636

Jimenez, M.F., Scheidegger, W.M., de Mello, R.C., Bastos-Filho, T., Bastos, T., Frizera, A.: Bringing proxemics to walker-assisted gait: using admittance control with spatial modulation to navigate in confined spaces. Pers. Ubiquit. Comput. **1**, 1–19 (2021). https://doi.org/10.1007/s00779-021-01521-8

Mavrogiannis, C., Balasubramanian, K., Poddar, S., Gandra, A., Srinivasa, S.S.: Winding through: crowd navigation via topological invariance. IEEE Robot. Autom. Lett. **8**(1), 121–128 (2023). https://doi.org/10.1109/LRA.2022.3223024

Mavrogiannis, C., et al.: Core challenges of social robot navigation: a survey. Technical report, arXiv (2021). https://doi.org/10.48550/arXiv.2103.05668

Moon, H.S., Seo, J.: Sample-efficient training of robotic guide using human path prediction network. IEEE Access **10**, 104996–105007 (2022). https://doi.org/10.1109/ACCESS.2022.3210932

Mora, A., Prados, A., Mendez, A., Barber, R., Garrido, S.: Sensor fusion for social navigation on a mobile robot based on fast marching square and gaussian mixture model. Sensors **22**(22) (2022). https://doi.org/10.3390/s22228728

Morales, Y., Miyashita, T., Hagita, N.: Social robotic wheelchair centered on passenger and pedestrian comfort. Robot. Auton. Syst. **87**, 355–362 (2017). https://doi.org/10.1016/j.robot.2016.09.010

Morales, Y., Watanabe, A., Ferreri, F., Even, J., Shinozawa, K., Hagita, N.: Passenger discomfort map for autonomous navigation in a robotic wheelchair. Robot. Auton. Syst. **103**, 13–26 (2018). https://doi.org/10.1016/j.robot.2018.02.002

Morales, Y., Akai, N., Murase H.: Personal mobility vehicle autonomous navigation through pedestrian flow: a data driven approach for parameter extraction. In: 2018 IEEE/RSJ International Conference on Intelligent Robots and Systems (IROS), Madrid, Spain, pp. 3438–3444 (2018). https://doi.org/10.1109/IROS.2018.8593902

Zhang, B., Barbareschi, G., Herrera, R., Carlson, T., Holloway, C.: Understanding Interactions for Smart Wheelchair Navigation in Crowds. In: Conference on Human Factors in Computing Systems (2022). https://doi.org/10.1145/3491102.3502085

Jung, Y., Kim, Y., Lee, W.H., Bang, M.S., Kim, Y., Kim, S.: Path planning algorithm for an autonomous electric wheelchair in hospitals. IEEE Access **8**, 208199–208213 (2020). https://doi.org/10.1109/ACCESS.2020.3038452

Morales, Y., et al.: Visibility analysis for autonomous vehicle comfortable navigation. In: IEEE International Conference on Robotics and Automation (ICRA), pp. 2197–2202 (2014). https://doi.org/10.1109/icra.2014.6907162

Morales, Y., Kallakuri, N., Shinozawa, K., Miyashita, T., Hagita, N.: Human comfortable navigation for an autonomous robotic wheelchair. In: 2013 IEEE/RSJ International Conference on Intelligent Robots and Systems, pp. 2737–2743. IEEE, Tokyo (2013). https://doi.org/10.1109/IROS.2013.6696743

Morales, Y., et al.: Including human factors for planning comfortable paths. In: 2015 IEEE International Conference on Robotics and Automation (ICRA), pp. 6153–6159. IEEE, Seattle (2015). https://doi.org/10.1109/ICRA.2015.7140063

Moriwaki, K., Tanaka, K.: Navigation control for electric vehicles using nonlinear state feedback H(infinity) control. Nonlinear Analy. Theory Methods Appl. **71**(12), E2920–E2933 (2009). https://doi.org/10.1016/j.na.2009.07.053

Neggers, M.M.E., Cuijpers, R.H., Ruijten, P.A.M., IJsselsteijn, W.A.: Determining shape and size of personal space of a human when passed by a robot. Int. J. Soc. Robot. **14**(2), 561–572 (2022). https://doi.org/10.1007/s12369-021-00805-6

Neset, T.S., et al.: Navigating urban heat-Assessing the potential of a pedestrian routing tool. Urban Clim. **46** (2022). https://doi.org/10.1016/j.uclim.2022.101333

Ngo, H.Q.T., Le, V.N., Thien, V.D.N., Nguyen, T.P., Nguyen, H.: Develop the socially human-aware navigation system using dynamic window approach and optimize cost function for autonomous medical robot. Adv. Mech. Eng. **12**(12) (2020). https://doi.org/10.1177/1687814020979430

Nguyen, V.T., Jayawardena, C., Ardekani, I.: A navigation model for sideby- side robotic wheelchairs for optimizing social comfort in crossing situations. Robot. Auton. Syst. **100**, 27–40 (2018). https://doi.org/10.1016/j.robot.2017.10.008

Park, J.J., Kuipers, B.: A smooth control law for graceful motion of differential wheeled mobile robots in 2D environment. In: 2011 IEEE International Conference on Robotics and Automation, pp. 4896–4902. IEEE, Shanghai (2011). https://doi.org/10.1109/ICRA.2011.5980167

Pimentel, F.D.M., Aquino, P.T.: Evaluation of ROS navigation stack for social navigation in simulated environments. J. Intell. Robot. Syst. **102**(4) (2021). https://doi.org/10.1007/s10846-021-01424-z

Pineau, J., Atrash, A.: SmartWheeler: a robotic wheelchair test-bed for investigating new models of human-robot interaction. In: AAAI Spring Symposium: Multidisciplinary Collaboration for Socially Assistive Robotics (2007)

Qian, K., Ma, X.D., Dai, X.Z., Fang, F.: Robotic etiquette: socially acceptable navigation of service robots with human motion pattern learning and prediction. J. Bionic Eng. **7**(2), 150–160 (2010). https://doi.org/10.1016/S1672-6529(09)60199-2

Qian, K., Ma, X.D., Dai, X.Z., Fang, F.: Socially acceptable pre-collision safety strategies for human-compliant navigation of service robots. Adv. Robot. **24**(13), 1813–1840 (2010). https://doi.org/10.1163/016918610X527176

Sawabe, T., Kanbara, M., Hagita, N.: Comfortable intelligence for evaluating passenger characteristics in autonomous wheelchairs. IEICE Trans. Fundam. Electron. Commun. Comput. Sci. **E101A**(9), 1308–1316 (2018). https://doi.org/10.1587/transfun.E101.A.1308

Sawabe, T., et al.: Comfortable autonomous navigation based on collision prediction in blind occluded regions. In: 2015 IEEE International Conference on Vehicular Electronics and Safety (ICVES), pp. 75–80. IEEE, Yokohama (2015). https://doi.org/10.1109/ICVES.2015.7396897

Sessner, J., Dellert, F., Franke, J.: Multimodal feedback to support the navigation of visually impaired people. In: 2022 IEEE/SICE International Symposium on System Integration (SII), pp. 196–201. IEEE, Narvik (2022). https://doi.org/10.1109/SII52469.2022.9708751

Simpson, R.C.: Smart wheelchairs: a literature review. J. Rehabil. Res. Dev. **42**(4), 423–36 (2005). https://doi.org/10.1682/jrrd.2004.08.0101

Simpson, R.C.: How many people would benefit from a smart wheelchair? J. Rehabil. Res. Dev. **45**(1), 53–72 (2008). https://doi.org/10.1682/JRRD.2007.01.0015

Singh, K.J., Kapoor, D.S., Abouhawwash, M., Al-Amri, J.F., Mahajan, S., Pandit, A.K.: Behavior of delivery robot in human-robot collaborative spaces during navigation. Intell. Autom. Soft Comput. **35**(1), 795-810 (2023). https://doi.org/10.32604/iasc.2023.025177

Singh, K.J., Kapoor, D.S., Sohi, B.S.: Understanding socially aware robot navigation. J. Eng. Res. **10**(1A), 131–149 (2022). https://doi.org/10.36909/jer.11123

Sisbot, E., Marin-Urias, L., Alami, R., Simeon, T.: A human aware mobile robot motion planner. IEEE Trans. Rob. **23**(5), 874–883 (2007). https://doi.org/10.1109/TRO.2007.904911

Sivakanthan, S., et al.: Mini-review: robotic wheelchair taxonomy and readiness. Neurosci. Lett. **772** (2022). https://doi.org/10.1016/j.neulet.2022.136482

Truong, X.T., Ngo, T.D.: Toward socially aware robot navigation in dynamic and crowded environments: a proactive social motion model. IEEE Trans. Autom. Sci. Eng. **14**(4), 1743–1760 (2017). https://doi.org/10.1109/TASE.2017.2731371

Truong, X.T., Ngo, T.D.: "To approach humans?": a unified framework for approaching pose prediction and socially aware robot navigation. IEEE Trans. Cogn. Dev. Syst. **10**(3), 557–572 (2018). https://doi.org/10.1109/TCDS.2017.2751963

Truong, X.T., Yoong, V.N., Ngo, T.D.: Socially aware robot navigation system in human interactive environments. Intel. Serv. Robot. **10**(4), 287–295 (2017). https://doi.org/10.1007/s11370-017-0232-y

Vanhaeren, N., De Cock, L., Lapon, L., Van de Weghe, N., Ooms, K., De Maeyer, P.: On the right track: comfort and confusion in indoor environments. ISPRS Int. J. Geo-Inf. **9**(2) (2020). https://doi.org/10.3390/ijgi9020132

Vasconcellos, J.M., Latorre, R.G.: Recreational boat noise level evaluation. Ocean Eng. **28**(9), 1309–1324 (2001). https://doi.org/10.1016/S0029-8018(00)00052-4

Vega, A., Manso, L.J., Macharet, D.G., Bustos, P., Nunez, P.: Socially aware robot navigation system in human-populated and interactive environments based on an adaptive spatial density function and space affordances. Pattern Recogn. Lett. **118**, 72–84 (2019). https://doi.org/10.1016/j.patrec.2018.07.015

Wang, C.Q., Xia, M., Meng, M.Q.H.: Stable autonomous robotic wheelchair navigation in the environment with slope way. IEEE Trans. Veh. Technol. **69**(10), 10759–10771 (2020). https://doi.org/10.1109/TVT.2020.3009979

Yan, J.J., Diakite, A.A., Zlatanova, S., Aleksandrov, M.: Top-bounded spaces formed by the built environment for navigation systems. ISPRS Int. J. Geo-Inf. **8**(5) (2019). https://doi.org/10.3390/ijgi8050224

Yi, Z.W., Li, L.H., Qu, X., Hong, Y., Mao, P.P., Ran, B.: Using artificial potential field theory for a cooperative control model in a connected and automated vehicles environment. Transp. Res. Rec. **2674**(9), 1005–1018 (2020). https://doi.org/10.1177/0361198120933271

Zhang, Y., Zhang, C.H., Shao, X.Y.: User preference-aware navigation for mobile robot in domestic via defined virtual area. J. Netw. Comput. Appl. **173** (2021). https://doi.org/10.1016/j.jnca.2020.102885

Zhi, J.X., Yu, L.F., Lien, J.M.: Designing human-robot coexistence space. IEEE Robot. Autom. Lett. **6**(4), 7161–7168 (2021). https://doi.org/10.1109/LRA.2021.3097061

Region Prediction for Efficient Robot Localization on Large Maps

Matteo Scucchia$^{(\boxtimes)}$ and Davide Maltoni

Dipartimento di Informatica—Scienza e Ingegneria (DISI), Universitá di Bologna,
47521 Cesena, Italy
matteo.scucchia2@unibo.it

Abstract. Recognizing already explored places (a.k.a. place recognition) is a fundamental task in Simultaneous Localization and Mapping (SLAM) to enable robot relocalization and loop closure detection. In topological SLAM the recognition takes place by comparing a signature (or feature vector) associated to the current node with the signatures of the nodes in the known map. However, as the number of nodes increases, matching the current node signature against all the existing ones becomes inefficient and thwarts real-time navigation. In this paper we propose a novel approach to pre-select a subset of map nodes for place recognition. The map nodes are clustered during exploration and each cluster is associated with a region. The region labels become the prediction targets of a deep neural network and, during navigation, only the nodes associated with the regions predicted with high probability are considered for matching. While the proposed technique can be integrated in different SLAM approaches, in this work we describe an effective integration with RTAB-Map (a popular framework for real-time topological SLAM) which allowed us to design and run several experiments to demonstrate its effectiveness.

Keywords: SLAM · Loop closure detection · Localization · Deep learning · Robotic vision

1 Introduction

The detection of loop closure, or the determination of whether an agent has returned to a previously visited location through the analysis of sensor data, is a crucial aspect of the Simultaneous Localization And Mapping (SLAM) problem because it significantly improves the accuracy of the map [1]. Due to intrinsic noise and unmodeled dynamics in its sensors and actuators, as a mobile robot explores its environment, it accumulates a localization error known as drift. By returning to a previously visited location this error can be corrected, resulting in an increase in the overall consistency of the map. From a philosophical point of view, place recognition provides robots with topological knowledge of the world, which is not a never-ending corridor but rather a space in which the same place can be reached through different paths. Therefore, loop closure detection through effective place recognition techniques is essential for mobile robotic systems capable of long-term autonomous navigation. Unfortunately, this problem is inherently complex and presents significant challenges [2]; in particular:

© The Author(s), under exclusive license to Springer Nature Switzerland AG 2024
J. Filipe and J. Röning (Eds.): ROBOVIS 2024, CCIS 2077, pp. 244–259, 2024.
https://doi.org/10.1007/978-3-031-59057-3_16

- variations in environmental conditions, such as differences in lighting between day and night or between different seasons, as well as changes/occlusions resulting from human interactions, can make place recognition difficult;
- to recognize previously visited locations, a robot must maintain a memory of prior observations and compare them with current observations. For large maps, the memory space and processing time required for this process may exceed available resources. For example, the authors of [3] indicate that a maximum of about 500 nodes can be maintained in memory for real-time loop closure detection during navigation.

The proposed method aims to solve this second problem. To this purpose, clustering of the map graph is performed during exploration, associating the map nodes to clusters (or regions); each region then becomes the target of a prediction process performed online during navigation. A deep neural network is trained to predict the probability that the current node belongs to the known regions, allowing the loop closure detector to focus only on the observations belonging to the most likely regions; this ensures real-time performance even when dealing with very large maps. The proposed technique can work with different SLAM approaches, independently of the algorithms used for pose estimation and map optimization. In this paper, we integrated it into RTAB-Map [4], a well-known approach that implements a graph-based SLAM with an appearance-based loop closure detector, to demonstrate its ability to improve loop closure detection and relocalization in large environments, while still adhering to real-time constraints.

After a discussion of the backgrounds and related literature in Sect. 2, the rest of the paper explains our method in detail. In Sect. 3, we present our methodology, which includes a comprehensive explanation of the dynamic clustering algorithm employed to partition the graph nodes into regions, the region prediction mechanism, and its integration into RTAB-Map. In Sect. 4 we present the experimental results and, finally, in Sect. 5 we provide some concluding remarks and future work.

2 Background and Related Works

To detect a loop closure or relocalize on a map, the common practice is to match the current observation against a database of known observations. To describe an image in a compact and robust way, the classic Bag-of-Words (BoW) [5] technique can be used, where visual words are extracted from each image and quantized into a visual vocabulary, making the comparison effective and efficient. Although modern deep learning techniques proved to be more effective than BoW in many tasks, BoW is still largely used in state-of-the-art SLAM systems [6]. The BoW vocabulary can be generated in different ways:

- offline, before starting navigation (and remains constant during navigation). This is a very practical and efficient choice, as it allows the use of an inverted index for fast computation of similarity scores between different keyframes; however, it does not adapt to the attributes of the operational environment, limiting the overall performance of loop closure detection [6]. ORB-SLAM2 [7], a well-known visual SLAM framework, implements this approach;

– online, during the exploration of the environment. Such a vocabulary is better for loop closure detection, as it better fits the current environment, but online modification of the vocabulary can hurt efficiency;
– in a mixed way, starting with an initial pre-trained vocabulary that incrementally updates during navigation.

Because long-term SLAM requires managing very large maps with places that change appearance over time, it is unlikely that an offline visual vocabulary would be sufficiently robust for this scenario. Moreover, in recent times deep learning and neural networks have been introduced to the SLAM problem, where features are learned and they are not fixed a priori. For these two reasons, research on long-term SLAM is focusing on online approaches and how to improve their performance, and the proposed method follows this philosophy. To this end, effective memory management is fundamental for the successful implementation of long-term loop closure detection. A few methods have been proposed in the literature for intelligently managing memory when exploring large environments. One approach, as outlined in [8], suggests dividing the exploration of the map into smaller submaps, with the creation of a new submap automatically triggered upon the passage through a door. This modular structure allows for independent maintenance of the map for each individual room or outdoor area, facilitating optimization and loop closure detection by considering only a selected portion of the entire map. However, switching between submaps can be complex in non-structured environments.

A more elegant approach is implemented in RTAB-Map, whose memory management system limits the number of comparisons performed for loop closure detection. To ensure real-time performance, RTAB-Map uses three types of memory:

1. Short Term Memory (STM): a buffer which contains the newest nodes of the graph;
2. Working Memory (WM): a working area for graph optimization and loop closure detection;
3. Long Term Memory (LTM): a local database storing all the knowledge about the map.

Thus, only the WM nodes are used for place recognition and loop closure detection. A continuous transfer takes place between WM and LTM in order to: i) retrieve from LTM nodes that are neighbors in time and space with respect to the recent highest loop closure hypothesis in WM; ii) transfer back to LTM the nodes that are the less likely to be involved in loop closures, allowing to keep the size of WM within a predefined capacity. Such memory management guarantees a constant time for loop closure detection, regardless of the size of the map (see Fig. 1). However, if the correct nodes are not present in WM because neither spatial nor temporal continuity is met, detection is unavoidably missed. This is the typical case of a large loop, where the robot returns to an already visited place after navigating for a long time elsewhere (see Fig. 2).

With the booming of deep learning, deep neural networks have been used to improve place recognition [9, 10] and continual learning techniques have also been used to help a robot learn how the appearance of places may change over time [11]. Novel bio-inspired approaches integrate deep neural networks, continual learning techniques and generative models to improve place recognition [12]. However, most of these methods

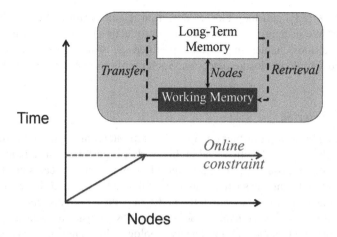

Fig. 1. The RTAB-Map computational cost of loop closure detection. The time grows linearly with the number of nodes in the map graph, until the WM is full. Then, the computational cost becomes constant, because always the same number of nodes are kept in the WM.

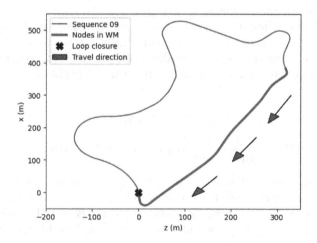

Fig. 2. In this example extracted from the sequence 09 of the KITTI odometry dataset, the robot is navigating the path denoted by the green arrows, and WM is populated with the nodes marked by the red trace according to spatio-temporal continuity criteria. Here, the loop closure cannot be detected when the robot crosses the previously explored location, denoted by the symbol x. (Color figure online)

still match the current node with the entire map and, for this reason, cannot scale to large maps. Therefore, the proposed approach is not an alternative, but can work in conjunction with them to improve efficiency on large maps.

3 Methodology

In the proposed approach, the overall SLAM process remains unchanged, as it continues to rely on traditional graph-based SLAM algorithms (such as pose estimation by PnP Ransac [13]) and loop closure detection is still performed using the conventional Bag-of-Words approach. However, the introduction of map clustering and neural network predictions enables an "effective prefiltering" of map nodes that are likely to be associated with loop closure detection. Such prefiltering ensures scalability to very large maps.

3.1   Map Clustering

Map clustering aims at partitioning map nodes into interconnected groups (or regions) according to their spatial location, and in this work it is performed using the scattering-based algorithm proposed in [14]. This algorithm dynamically creates clusters during exploration, by reducing the spatial scattering of the nodes within a cluster. The scattering metric reflects the extent to which the nodes of a cluster are dispersed compared to the equivalent radius. The equivalent radius describes a cluster regardless of its actual shape, comparing it to an ideal high-density topology. How a new node is assigned to a region depends on the desired cardinality of the clusters, a shape factor, and the radius upper bound of the equivalent circle. Depending on the environment explored and the speed at which the robot moves, these parameters can be tuned to obtain the desired clustering (avoiding too small or too large regions).

Equation 1 shows how the scattering for a cluster C_i is computed. For a cluster with cardinality $n_i > 1$, s'' is the sum of the squared Euclidean distances of all nodes v in the cluster from the centroid $\mathbf{pos}(C_i)$ divided by the equivalent radius $\mathrm{req}(C_i)$ (2). The threshold s' can be adjusted to regulate the cluster size. See [14] for more details and examples.

$$s(C_i) = s' + s''(C_i) \tag{1}$$

$$s''(C_i) = \frac{1}{\mathrm{req}(C_i)} \sum_{v \in C_i} \Delta(\mathbf{pos}(v), \mathbf{pos}(C_i))^2 \text{ if } n_i > 1 \tag{2}$$

Since this clustering is dynamic, a node can be reassigned to a different cluster; this is fundamental for the creation of compact and coherent clusters when the robot moves around in the same region or when it returns to previously visited locations; without such reassignment cluster shapes would be mostly linear and the different regions might overlap considerably. (see Fig. 3).

The concept of node clustering is crucial in our approach because signatures (i.e., images in our case) associated to single nodes are too specific and not stable with respect to the variations that may occur when the robot revisits the same location, while the set of images associated to a region (e.g., a room in a building or a square in a city) can collectively describe that place in a much more robust way. An example is shown in Fig. 4.

3.2   Region Prediction

While in the general case the neural network used for our region prediction method should be trained online and in continual learning fashion (i.e., without a clear distinction between training and inference), in this first work, aimed at demonstrating the underlying idea, we adopt some simplifications and identify three phases:

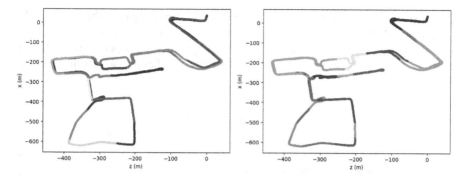

Fig. 3. The above images show the graph created by RTAB-Map runs on the sequence Week1 of the USyd [15] dataset. On the left, a static version of the clustering algorithm (i.e., without node reassignment); on the right the graph is clustered with the dynamic algorithm. In the static version, as the robot revisits the same locations, the nodes that were previously assigned cannot change their belonging region, resulting in linear clusters with high spatial overlapping. On the other hand, in the dynamic clustering, node reassignment moves nodes from a region to another when the robot returns to previously visited regions, leading to the formation of more compact clusters.

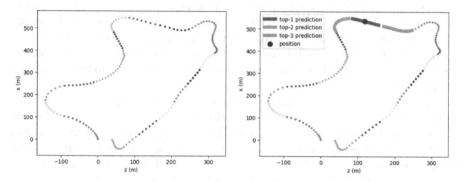

Fig. 4. The left image shows how the algorithm clusters the graph created by RTAB-Map [3] run on sequence 09 of the KITTI odometry dataset [16] (without loop closure detection). Each point in the image corresponds to a node in the graph and different colors correspond to different clusters. The image on the right highlights the regions predicted by the trained model in a subsequent navigation of the same sequence.

1. the exploration phase in which the robot explores its environment and clusters the map created by RTAB-Map into regions; at the end of this phase, a training dataset consisting of node images and their region labels is available;
2. the training phase, in which a neural network is trained offline as a classifier;
3. the inference phase, in which the neural network is utilized to predict the probabilities of the regions during successive robot's navigation including new visits of known places.

During the exploration phase, images acquired by the robot and regions assigned through map clustering are saved as a training set, so that in the training phase they can be used to train the neural network in a supervised manner. A lightweight MobileNetV2 [17] pretrained on ImageNet and with frozen weights is used as a convolutional backbone to extract features from images, while a simple multilayer perceptron (MLP) is trained on the top of the backbone as a classifier to predict region probabilities (see Fig. 5).

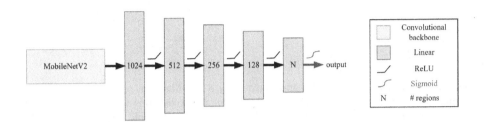

Fig. 5. The architecture of the neural network used for region prediction.

The model used in this work is very simple and allows to perform real-time inference even on embedded computing board. However, according to the desired accuracy/efficiency trade-off, it can be easily replaced with more complex models tailored to place recognition, such as NetVLAD [18] and RegionVLAD [19] or ResNet models pretrained on Places365 [20]. It is important to understand that these solutions are not competitors to our method, but can be used in place of MobileNetV2 to further improve classification performance.

The MLP is trained with supervision by assigning a probability of 1 to the correct region and 0 to all other regions. A focal loss is used as loss function, since the cardinality of the clusters may vary significantly, and focal loss better deals with class imbalances. Furthermore, in the last layer of the classifier, we replaced the classical softmax (leading to class probabilities to sum up to 1) with a logistic function to allow the network to predict with high confidence more regions; this is the case of places with scarce textures such as corridors, where the prediction should correctly return more regions (see Fig. 6). At inference time, to mitigate the possibility of retrieving wrong regions (because of high inter-region similarity), an exponential moving average (EMA) was used. The probability p_t^i for the region i at time t depends on the probability of the current observation o_t^i and the probability in the previous step p_{t-1}^i weighted by a parameter α. Through this method, the robot may encounter similar environments, but the confidence fusion tends to downweigh the probability of wrong selections.

$$p_t^i = \alpha o_t^i + (1 - \alpha)p_{t-1}^i \qquad (3)$$

3.3 Integration in RTAB-Map

The RTAB-Map transfer-retrieval process has been modified to incorporate the retrieval of nodes belonging to the most likely regions during navigation. As in the original solution, WM cannot exceed a maximum size of N nodes. The update procedure (WM_update in Algorithm 1) is called every time a new node v is created.

Fig. 6. Two distinct corridors (from our Campus dataset) whose visual appearance is very similar. In such a case, our model should predict both regions with high confidence.

Algorithm 1. Modified RTAB-Map Transfer-Retrieval.

1: **procedure** WM_UPDATE(v)
2:     $h \leftarrow$ highest loop closure hypothesis of v in WM
3:     $U_1 \leftarrow k_1$ neighboring nodes (in time and space) of h in LTM
4:     Retrieve U_1
5:     $U_2 \leftarrow k_2$ neighboring nodes of v in WM
6:     $O_t \leftarrow$ region predictions of the neural network
7:     $P_{t-1} \leftarrow$ regions probabilities at previous iteration
8:     $P_t \leftarrow \alpha O_t + (1 - \alpha)P_{t-1}$ // Equation 3
9:     $U_3 \leftarrow k_3$ node from LTM belonging to the most likely regions according to P_t
10:    Retrieve U_3
11:    **while** size(WM) $> N$ **do**
12:        $n \leftarrow$ node in WM belonging to the region with lowest probability according to P_t

13:        **if** n not in $U_1 \cup U_2$ **then**   // Nodes in U1 and U2 are immunized
14:            Transfer n
15:        **end if**
16:    **end while**
17: **end procedure**

At each step, a set of k_1 nodes is retrieved from the LTM, which are the neighbors in time and space to the node that turns out to be the highest loop closure hypothesis in WM. Our method adds to this the retrieval of other k_3 nodes belonging to the most likely regions. At this point, the nodes belonging to the less likely regions are transferred back to the LTM, excluding the k_1 neighbors retrieved in the current cycle and the k_2 neighbors of v already in WM (which are immunized), until WM size is equal to N.

4   Experiments and Results

Two types of experiments have been designed to assess the validity of the proposed approach. The former is aimed at estimating the ability of the neural network to predict the correct region when the robot revisits known places. The latter investigates the accuracy of loop closure detection by comparing the original version of RTAB-Map with the modified one. To this purpose, we report both the number of loop closures detected and the corresponding increase in overall pose accuracy. All the data (including manual and automatic labeling) and code necessary to set up our experiments will be made available for reproducibility and future comparisons.

For the experiments, we used three datasets. The first two are well known and widely used in SLAM:

- **OpenLoris:** the OpenLoris-Scene dataset [21], specifically created for lifelong SLAM, with different indoor sequences with variations in environmental conditions and with the presence of moving people introducing further variability and occlusions;
- **KITTI:** the KITTI odometry dataset [16], an outdoor dataset including 22 sequences (11 with ground truth to tune/train the algorithms and 11 without ground truth to test them) acquired with stereo cameras and a 3D velodyne laser in urban and rural settings.

A third dataset (denoted as **Campus**) was set up using sequences captured with the Xaxxon autocrawler robot [22] equipped with a 2D rotating lidar and an Intel D435 depth camera (see Fig. 7), navigating in three corridors of our university campus. Other datasets are available for visual place recognition (e.g. St Lucia Multiple Times of Day [23] and Nordland Dataset [24]). However, we cannot use them because of the lack of stereo or RGB-D data, which are necessary to perform visual-odometry estimation in a complete SLAM system. Furthermore, other interesting datasets, such as Oxford Robotcar Dataset [25], are not available for download.

In principle, other well-known place recognition/SLAM systems could be compared with the proposed approach, but in this work, we restricted comparison with the RTABMap baseline for the following reasons:

- NetVLAD [18] and other derived methods [19,26] are not competing techniques but modules that can be easily plugged in the proposed framework to improve place recognition. In particular, the MobileNetV2 backbone + MLP (Sect. 3.2) can be easily replaced with NetVLAD (preferably the mobile version), which demonstrated excellent robustness. All the rest of our systems (dynamic clustering + node retrieval) would remain identical.
- As discusses in Sect. 2, ORB-SLAM2, which is one of the most popular SLAM system, uses a fixed vocabulary with inverted index retrieval, so it does not suffer efficiency problems on large maps (except on very large ones). On the other side, the fixed vocabulary can be a limitation for adaptability and robustness. A meaningful comparison between our approach and ORB-SLAM2 would require to perform accuracy/efficiency evaluations over large maps characterized by relevant variations of the acquisition conditions during successive revisiting of the same places. This is beyond the scope of this work and left for future research.

For the experiments performed in this paper, we only used RGB data for region prediction.

Fig. 7. The Xaxxon autocrawler robot employed to acquire the Campus dataset.

4.1 Prediction Accuracy

For the first type of experiments, we used Campus and two OpenLoris packages, where the robot navigates the same locations in different sequences:

- the **Market** package, comprising three sequences captured inside a large market-place, with relatively consistent lighting conditions across sequences;
- the **Corridor** package, comprising five sequences captured along a single corridor with large windows, with strongly varying lighting conditions (including artificial illumination turned off).

KITTI was not used here because of the lack of sequences revisiting the same locations. For OpenLoris and Campus, the first sequence is used to train the neural network and the others for testing. The pairing of the regions between the training and test sequences was manually identified, by visually matching the images and assigning consistent region labels.

The top-1 and the top-3 accuracy metrics are used for these experiments because they highlight the network's ability to predict the correct region and to capture similarities between the different regions.

Table 1 shows the results. In the OpenLoris Market and Campus Corridors sequences, the top-3 accuracy is good, indicating that the correct region is almost always among the three most likely predictions and therefore its nodes have a high chance of being retrieved in WM. Sometimes incorrect regions may be predicted as top-1, however, this behavior is even desirable in some cases, to deal with region similarities.

The prediction accuracy is not as good on the Corridor sequences of OpenLoris, due to the strong variation in the lighting conditions (see the example in Fig. 8). To deal with such variation a continual learning of region prediction would be necessary as discussed in Sect. 5.

Table 1. Top-1 and top-3 region prediction accuracy. The numbering x-y at the end of each sequence name means that the predictor was trained on sequence x and tested on y.

Sequences	Top-1 accuracy	Top-3 accuracy
OpenLoris/Market 1–2	0.81	0.92
OpenLoris/Market 1–3	0.79	0.93
OpenLoris/Corridor 1–2	0.27	0.45
OpenLoris/Corridor 1–3	0.06	0.14
OpenLoris/Corridor 1–4	0.17	0.44
OpenLoris/Corridor 1–5	0.65	0.90
Campus/Corridor-Biolab 1–2	0.53	0.79
Campus/Corridor-DEI 1–2	0.47	0.77
Campus/Corridor-Arc 1–2	0.33	0.76

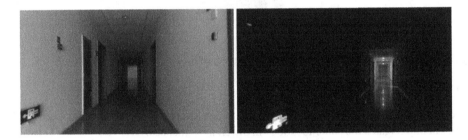

Fig. 8. The left image depicts an acquisition from the first Corridor sequence of OpenLoris, captured under good lighting conditions. On the right, the same corridor is shown in the fourth sequence, with artificial illumination turned off.

4.2   Loop Closure Detection

In the experiments of loop closure detection, in addition to the OpenLoris Market package and Campus sequences, we also used KITTI sequences which contain loop closures, namely sequences 00, 02, 05, 06, 07 and 09, (loop closures are not present in the other sequences). Since the ground truth robot pose is known for KITTI and OpenLoris, we implemented a simple algorithm to match poses across the sequences, in order to identify correspondences (and then loop closure candidates) in an automatic way. In particular, if the distance between the (x,y) location in the 2D plane and the angle (also in the 2D plane) between the two poses are less than two given thresholds, then the two poses are considered as a match.

In these experiments we made a fundamental assumption: in explorations of very large environments (potentially the whole world) only a subset of map nodes can be considered for loop closure detection and map optimization to avoid violating the real-time constraint. To demonstrate the effectiveness of the proposed method under this assumption, we limited the WM size of RTAB-Map to a fixed number of nodes, simulating in this way the exploration of large maps, where not the entire map can be hosted in WM. Referring to the Algorithm 1, the WM size was limited to $N = 50$ nodes (approximately 15% of the average size of the sequences considered). The parameters k_1 and k_2 were set to default RTAB-Map values of 2 and 0.25 (that is, 25% $\times$ $N = 12$ neighboring nodes in WM cannot be transferred to LTM, avoiding the transfer of too recent nodes), respectively. According to the constraints, $k_3 = N - k_1 - k_2$.

As shown in Table 2, our approach was able to recognize all the loop closure in all the sequences considered (except one) totaling 95% of loop closure detection, even with a very limited WM. On the contrary, the default RTAB-Map memory management was able to detect loop closure only 15% of times because the spatial and temporal closeness criteria can be unsatisfactory when navigating large maps.

Table 2. Loop closure detection results. For Campus and OpenLoris, the numbering x-y at the end of each sequence name means that the predictor was trained on sequence x and tested on y.

Sequences	N° Loop closures	Loops detected	
		RTAB-Map baseline	Our
KITTI/00	4	1	**4**
KITTI/02	2	0	**2**
KITTI/05	3	0	**3**
KITTI/06	1	0	**1**
KITTI/07	1	1	1
KITTI/09	1	0	**1**
Campus/Corridor-Biolab 1–2	2	0	**2**
Campus/Corridor-DEI 1–2	2	0	**2**
Campus/Corridor-Arc 1–2	3	1	**2**
OpenLoris/Market 1–3	1	0	**1**
Total	20	3 (15%)	**19 (95%)**

OpenLoris sequences often have no loop closures within the single sequence, but in different sequences the robot returns to the same places and relocalization can be performed (see Table 3). To deal with these cases, RTAB-Map allows reloading all memory in the WM when a new sequence is started or reloading only the WM as it was at the end of the previous exploration. To keep the WM limited to 50 nodes, the latter option was chosen.

Table 3. Relocalization results. The numbering x-y at the end of each sequence name means that the predictor was trained on sequence x and tested on y.

Sequences	N° Relocalization	Relocalizations performed	
		RTAB-Map baseline	Our
OpenLoris/Market 1–2	3	1	**3**
OpenLoris/Market 1–3	3	1	**3**
Total	6	2 (33%)	**6 (100%)**

The common metric used to evaluate loop closure detection is the Precision-Recall metric [27]. Tables 4 and 5 report Precision-Recall for loop closure detection and relocalization, respectively. The proposed method, compared to the RTAB-Map baseline, greatly increases the recall in the large maps scenario. Furthermore, the precision does not worsen, as the loop closure detection process is not modified. On the contrary, precision could increase because only nodes belonging to regions predicted with high probability are considered, discarding other observations that could lead to false positives.

Table 4. Precision-Recall on loop closure detection. For Campus and OpenLoris, the numbering x-y at the end of each sequence name means that the predictor was trained on sequence x and tested on y.

Sequences	RTAB-Map baseline		Our	
	Precision	Recall	Precision	Recall
KITTI/00	1	0.25	1	1
KITTI/02	–	0	1	1
KITTI/05	–	0	1	1
KITTI/06	–	0	1	1
KITTI/07	1	1	1	1
KITTI/09	–	0	1	1
Campus/Corridor-Biolab 1–2	–	0	1	1
Campus/Corridor-DEI 1–2	–	0	1	1
Campus/Corridor-Arc 1–2	1	0.33	1	**0.66**
OpenLoris/Market 1–3	–	0	1	1

Table 5. Precision-Recall on relocalization. The numbering x-y at the end of each sequence name means that the predictor was trained on sequence x and tested on y.

Sequences	RTAB-Map baseline		Our	
	Precision	Recall	Precision	Recall
OpenLoris/Market 1–2	1	0.33	1	**1**
OpenLoris/Market 1–3	1	0.33	1	**1**

Finally, it is worth noting that even if our node preselection was perfect (i.e., ensuring that the right nodes are always in WM), the native loop closure algorithm of the SLAM used could miss some closures because of insufficient similarity of the corresponding signatures. A posterior analysis of the results showed that the only loop missed by our approach in Table 2 falls into this category.

4.3 Pose Estimation Accuracy

Since loop closure detection is critical for optimizing the map and reducing localization error, we also report the accuracy of pose estimation on different sequences of the

KITTI odometry dataset. The absolute trajectory error (ATE) [28] reported in Table 6 highlights that even on small maps (such as the KITTI sequences) where the drift is not so large, the error correction achieved through loop closure detection has a strong impact on pose accuracy, especially in presence of large loops (e.g., sequence 09, see Fig. 9).

Table 6. Absolute trajectory errors results. Both the baseline and our method have to be considered with the WM size limited to 50 nodes. For the baseline, the ATE is higher because fewer loop closures are detected, while for our method it decreases because all loop closures are detected. Since the entire map cannot be corrected due to the limited WM size, results are different from those reported in the original RTAB-Map paper [3].

Sequences	ATE(m)	
	RTAB-Map baseline	Our
KITTI/00	4.754	**3.107**
KITTI/02	6.891	**6.080**
KITTI/05	2.188	**1.946**
KITTI/06	3.791	**1.811**
KITTI/07	1.116	**1.079**
KITTI/09	13.222	**5.623**

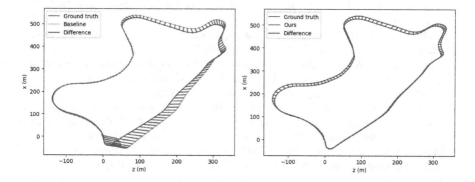

Fig. 9. Both images display the absolute trajectory error (ATE) on sequence 09 of the KITTI odometry dataset. In the left image, the ATE for the RTAB-Map baseline is depicted, where no loop closure is detected. On the right, the ATE for our method is shown, where a loop closure has been successfully detected.

5 Conclusions and Future Works

In this work we introduced a region prediction technique, where map clustering is used to partition nodes into regions and a deep model is trained to predict the region that the robot is currently navigating. This approach enables an efficient implementation of place recognition for real-time loop closure detection. Our experiments validate the effectiveness of the idea but leave some issues open. In fact, in this preliminary work, the proposed technique cannot be entirely performed in real-time, because the predictor is trained offline on the whole accumulated map knowledge. Its natural evolution is toward an online continual learning implementation as required in lifelong SLAM. To this end, the model needs to incrementally learn new regions and new instances (e.g., day/night variations) of already known regions without forgetting old knowledge (a scenario known as NIC in the terminology of continual learning [29]). Our previous experiences on continual learning make us confident that this target is feasible: in particular, latent replay techniques [30] seem to be very appropriate in this context because they allow to update the model by storing only a small subset of latent representation of past data. Finally, we re-emphasize that our method can be implemented in every graph-based SLAM framework as long as a memory management system is introduced to select only a subset of graph nodes for loop closure detection.

References

1. Cadena, C., et al.: Simultaneous localization and mapping: present, future, and the robust-perception age. IEEE Trans. Rob. **32** (2016). https://doi.org/10.1109/TRO.2016.2624754
2. Nashed, S.B.: A brief survey of loop closure detection: a case for rethinking evaluation of intelligent systems. In: NeurIPS 2020 Workshop: ML Retrospectives, Surveys Meta-Analyses (ML-RSA) (2020)
3. Labbé, M.: RTAB-Map as an open-source lidar and visual simultaneous localization and mapping library for large-scale and long-term online operation. J. Field Robot. **36**(2), 416–446 (2019)
4. Labbé, M., Michaud, F.: Appearance-based loop closure detection in real-time for large-scale and long-term operation. IEEE Trans. Robot. **29**(3), 734–745 (2013)
5. Fraundorferh, F., Wu, C., Frahm, J.M., Pollefeys, M.: Visual word based location recognition in 3d models using distance augmented weighting. In: 4th International Symposium on 3D Data Processing, Visualization, andTransmission, pp. 1–8 (2008)
6. Konstantinos, T.A., Bampis, L., Gasteratos, A.: The revisiting problem in simultaneous localization and mapping: a survey on visual loop closure detection. IEEE Trans. Intell. Transp. Syst. **23**(11), 19929–19953 (2022). https://doi.org/10.1109/tits.2022.3175656
7. Mur-Artal, R., Tardos, J.D.: ORB-SLAM2: an open-source SLAM system for monocular, stereo, and RGB-D cameras. IEEE Trans. Rob. **33**(5), 1255–1262 (2017). https://doi.org/10.1109/tro.2017.2705103
8. Ehlers, S.F.G., Stuede, M., Nuelle, K., Ortmaier, T.: Map Management approach for SLAM in large-scale indoor and outdoor areas. In: 2020 IEEE International Conference on Robotics and Automation (ICRA), pp. 9652–9658 (2020)
9. Arshad, S., Kim, G.W.: Role of deep learning in loop closure detection for visual and lidar SLAM: a survey. Sensors **21**(4) (2021)
10. Masone, C., Caputo, B.: A survey on deep visual place recognition, vol. 9. IEEE (2021)
11. Gao, D., Wang, C., Scherer, S.: AirLoop: lifelong loop closure detection. In: 2022 International Conference on Robotics and Automation (ICRA) (2022)
12. Yin, P., Abuduweili, A., Zhao, S., Liu, C., Scherer, S.: BioSLAM: a bio-inspired lifelong memory system for general place recognition (2022)
13. Scaramuzza, D., Fraundorfer, F.: Visual odometry [tutorial]. IEEE Robot. Autom. Mag. **18**(4), 80–92 (2011). https://doi.org/10.1109/MRA.2011.943233

14. Maio, D., Maltoni, D., Rizzi, S.: Dynamic clustering of maps in autonomous agents. IEEE Trans. Pattern Anal. Mach. Intell. **18**(11), 1080–1091 (1996)
15. Zhou, W., et al.: The USyd campus dataset (2019). https://doi.org/10.21227/sk74-7419
16. Geiger, A., Lenz, P., Urtasun, R.: Are we ready for autonomous driving? The KITTI vision benchmark suite. In: Conference on Computer Vision and Pattern Recognition (CVPR) (2012)
17. Sandler, M., Howard, A., Zhu, M., Zhmoginov, A., Chen, L.C.: MobileNetV2: inverted residuals and linear bottlenecks (2018)
18. Arandjelović, R., Gronát, P., Torii, A., Pajdla, T., Sivic, J.: NetVLAD: CNN architecture for weakly supervised place recognition (CoRR) (2015)
19. Khaliq, A., Ehsan, S., Chen, Z., Milford, M., McDonald-Maier, K.: A holistic visual place recognition approach using lightweight CNNs for significant viewpoint and appearance changes. IEEE Trans. Rob. **36**(2), 561–569 (2020). https://doi.org/10.1109/TRO.2019.2956352
20. Zhou, B., Lapedriza, A., Khosla, A., Oliva, A., Torralba, A.: Places: a 10 million image database for scene recognition. IEEE Trans. Pattern Anal. Mach. Intell. (2017)
21. Shi, X., et al.: Are we ready for service robots? The OpenLORIS-Scene Datasets for Lifelong SLAM, pp. 3139–3145 (2020)
22. Xaxxon, Xaxxon AutoCRAWLER Autonomous Robot. http://www.xaxxon.com/xaxxon/autocrawler
23. Glover, A., Maddern, W., Milford, M., Wyeth, G.: FAB-MAP + RatSLAM: appearance-based SLAM for multiple times of day. In: The International Conference on Robotics and Automation (2010)
24. Olid, D., Fácil, J.M., Civera, J.: Single-view place recognition under seasonal changes. In: PPNIV Workshop at IROS (2018)
25. Maddern, W., Pascoe, G., Linegar, C., Newman, P.: 1 year, 1000km: the Oxford RobotCar dataset. Int. J. Robot. Res. (IJRR) (2016)
26. Sarlin, P.E., Debraine, F., Dymczyk, M., Siegwart, R., Cadena, C.: Leveraging deep visual descriptors for hierarchical efficient localization (2018)
27. Precision and recall. https://en.wikipedia.org/wiki/Precision_and_recall
28. Sturm, J., Felix, E., Felix, N., Felix, E., Burgard, W., Cremers, D.: A benchmark for the evaluation of RGB-D SLAM systems. In: IEEE/RSJ International Conference on Intelligent Robots and Systems, pp. 573–580 (2012). https://doi.org/10.1109/IROS.2012.6385773.
29. Lesort, T., Lomonaco, V., Stoian, A., Maltoni, D., Filliat, D., Díaz-Rodríguez, N.: Continual learning for robotics: definition, framework, learning strategies, opportunities and challenges. Inf. Fusion **58**, 52–68 (2020). https://doi.org/10.1016/j.inffus.2019.12.004
30. Pellegrini, L., Graffieti, G., Lomonaco, V., Maltoni, D.: Latent replay for real-time continual learning. In: 2020 IEEE/RSJ International Conference on Intelligent Robots and Systems (IROS), Las Vegas, NV, USA, pp. 10203–10209 (2020). https://doi.org/10.1109/IROS45743.2020.9341460

Utilizing Dataset Affinity Prediction in Object Detection to Assess Training Data

Stefan Becker[1,2(✉)] [iD], Jens Bayer[1,2] [iD], Ronny Hug[1,2] [iD], Wolfgang Huebner[1,2] [iD], and Michael Arens[1,2] [iD]

[1] Fraunhofer IOSB, Ettlingen, Germany
Stefan.Becker@iosb.fraunhofer.de
https://www.iosb.fraunhofer.de
[2] Fraunhofer Center for Machine Learning, Munich, Germany

Abstract. Data pooling offers various advantages, such as increasing the sample size, improving generalization, reducing sampling bias, and addressing data sparsity and quality, but it is not straightforward and may even be counterproductive. Assessing the effectiveness of pooling datasets in a principled manner is challenging due to the difficulty in estimating the overall information content of individual datasets. Towards this end, we propose incorporating a data source prediction module into standard object detection pipelines. The module runs with minimal overhead during inference time, providing additional information about the data source assigned to individual detections. We show the benefits of the so-called dataset affinity score by automatically selecting samples from a heterogeneous pool of vehicle datasets. The results show that object detectors can be trained on a significantly sparser set of training samples without losing detection accuracy.

Keywords: Training data analysis · Ante-hoc explanation · Object detection · Sample selection · Dataset label prediction · Dataset origin prediction · Selection bias

1 Introduction and Related Work

Despite their growing scale, single datasets capture only limited visual aspects of a target domain, and obtaining more label data takes time and effort. One way to overcome these limitations is data pooling, the combination of datasets. Combining datasets results in a larger sample size, providing more instances for model training, which can lead to more robust and generalizable models, especially in situations where the original datasets are relatively small. Data pooling also aims to increase diversity in the data to avoid overfitting to specific patterns present in one dataset but not in another, but also increase intra-class variations and scene variation. It can also be useful when dealing with imbalanced datasets by combining datasets with different class distributions. However, an arbitrary combination of datasets capturing a specific object category does not guarantee an improved detection performance and can be counterproductive. For example, extending with samples too far away from the target domain can lead to a decline in the detector's performance. Combining strongly correlated datasets can be redundant and provides no new information.

© The Author(s), under exclusive license to Springer Nature Switzerland AG 2024
J. Filipe and J. Röning (Eds.): ROBOVIS 2024, CCIS 2077, pp. 260–277, 2024.
https://doi.org/10.1007/978-3-031-59057-3_17

One central problem is that the effectiveness of pooling datasets can not be assessed in a principled way because the overall information content of individual datasets is hard to estimate. Towards this end, we propose extending standard object detection pipelines with an additional inference head to predict a dataset affinity score. The affinity prediction assigns every detection to the set of pooled datasets realized as a multinomial logistic regression task. Thus scoring the affinity between detections and training datasets. This enables direct model-depend feedback to the training data during inference. Thereby, we gain information on which dataset contributed to individual detections. This can be seen as a kind of ante-hoc detection explanation. We use the affinity scores to identify datasets that support the overall detection performance and datasets where the scores suggest a higher domain gap between the training and target sets. Based on the assigned dataset affinity distribution, we prune the training set and show that detectors trained on a significantly sparser set achieve similar detection accuracy. By providing the dataset affinity score during inference, our approach stands in contrast to post-hoc explanation methods, producing visual explanations.

These methods specify saliency maps to interpret the object predictions. There are gradient-based methods such as Grad-CAM [55] or GradCAM++ [8] where the saliency maps are based on the gradient of the model's output with respect to the input features and perturbation-based methods where generating these maps involve perturbing or altering input features and observing the impact on the model's prediction (e.g., RISE [48], D-RISE [49], LIME [53]). For a more detailed view of explainable artificial intelligence (XAI), including post-hoc explanation methods, we refer to the survey of Burkart et al. [7] and for a comparison of several saliency maps generation methods for object detection to Bayer et al. [3].

The dataset affinity score provides information on whether an object in the target domain can be explained with samples from particular datasets. So, assessing the model performance during processing with estimating the detector's uncertainty can be seen as an alternative concept of getting direct feedback on the target domain. Several techniques have been proposed to integrate uncertainty estimation into a detector. There are approaches using *variational inference* by relying on *Bayesian neural networks* (BNNs) [41] or using *Monte-Carlo dropout* [18] as more a practical way to perform approximate inference, such as the work of Azevedo et al. [2]. Then there are approaches using *direct modeling* by assuming a certain probability distribution over the detector outputs (e.g., [11]). Further, there are approaches estimating predictive probability using an ensemble of models where the outputs from each detector are treated as independent samples from a mixture model [34]. For a more detailed view of uncertainty estimation in the context of object detection, we refer to the surveys of Feng et al. [16] and Hall et al. [25].

Other concepts to assess the efficiency of data pooling are not part of the model itself. These concepts use statistical measures like the *Kullback-Leibler* divergence or *Wasserstein* distance to quantify the difference between probability distributions of domains [27] or make a feature space analysis by examining the distribution of features in different domains with histograms, scatter plots, or kernel density estimation [22]. Thus, these concepts use external post-processing steps to compare learned representation. This comparing and assessing dataset domain gaps, and therefor data pooling, is closely related to or rather part of the broader problem of dataset shift.

Dataset shift is a concept that encompasses various distribution changes that can occur within or between domains, leading to the failure of even high-capacity models. Reasons for domain shift include seasonal or weather change. For a detailed overview of dataset shift and related sub-problems, we refer to the work of [50]. Domain adaptation is a specific technique to address dataset shifts in cases where the change in data distribution is due to a shift between domains.

In the context of domain adaptation for object detection, corresponding methods try to align the source domain distribution to a particular target domain. Some approaches [9, 10] try to learn invariant features by feature alignment via adversarial training [19]. Other methods try to align object instances across domains utilizing category-level centroids [71] or attention maps [59]. Domain generalization aims to generalize to domains unseen in training. For example, the approach form Vidit et al. [58] leverages a pre-trained vision model to develop a semantic augmentation strategy for altering image embeddings.

Besides the problems of data pooling, training from multiple datasets also faces the problem of varying label sets. To align multiple datasets, we unify the label sets by mapping sub-categories to a subsuming super-category or, rather, a more general category. In our case, we subsume different land-vehicle types such as 'car, 'van', 'truck' under the super-category 'vehicle'. In the context of unifying label sets, Redmon et al. [51] introduced a hierarchical model of visual concepts (WordTree) to combine the labels of ImageNet [54] and MS COCO [37]. ImageNet labels are pulled from WordNet [43], a language database that structures concepts and their relation. Redmon et al. [51] utilizes several classification scores over co-hyponyms of the WordTree to realize a more fine-grained object classification along the hierarchical label tree. Nevertheless, considering a hierarchical tree with different levels of information and intra-class differences, we follow the concept of mapping all intra-class variations of vehicle classes to one comprehensive super-category. Merging datasets this way for an object category has already been proven to learn more general and robust models. For example, Hasan et al. [26] combined multiple pedestrian datasets, showing improved cross-dataset performance. For segmentation, Lampert et al. [35] merged and split different classes from datasets to realize a unified flat taxonomy to be still compatible with the standard training method.

Although approaches that learn a label space from visual data go beyond this paper's scope, we also mention a few to cover this aspect. The task is considered universal representational or universal detectors. Another approach toward a universal detector is the work of Wang et al. [61] They proposed to train a detector from multiple datasets in a multi-task setting. Zhao et al. [67] train a universal detector on multiple datasets by manually merging the taxonomies and train with cross-datasets pseudo-labels generated by dataset-specific models. In the work of Zhou et al. [69] they fuse multiple annotated datasets without manually merging by formulating an optimization problem on which dataset-specific output should be merged.

Since the proposed additional affinity prediction relies on an object detector, we refer to the following works [30, 38, 63, 64, 68, 72] for an overview on current trends and state-of-the-art models for object detection.

The main contribution of this paper is to present a new idea to assess the effectiveness of data pooling. We propose to extend detection pipelines with an additional inference head to predict the affinity to pooled training data sets. With minimal overhead, the affinity scores allow direct feedback to training samples during run-time. The score provides information on which dataset is responsible for explaining individual detections and the selection of a sparser training set without performance decrease.

The paper is structured as follows. The next section provides a description of the proposed additional dataset affinity prediction (Sect. 2). In Sect. 3, the selected datasets for training and their alignment are described. The evaluation and achieved results are discussed in Sect. 4. Finally, a conclusion is given in Sect. 5.

2   Dataset Affinity Prediction

To better assess the efficiency of data pooling, we propose to use an additional inference head to estimate the affinity to datasets in the data pool for every detection. Since current object detectors are designed in a way that they internally use separate heads for different inference tasks, this concept is applicable to almost all current detection pipelines. Given an image $\mathbf{I}_k$ with index k applying a modified detector with the additional dataset affinity score results in the following output:

$$detector_\Theta(\mathbf{I}_k) \rightarrow \{\vec{d}_{i,k} = (o, \vec{b}, \vec{c}, \vec{a})\}_i^{N_{d,k}} \tag{1}$$

Θ are the model parameters. The output is a set of $N_{d,k}$ detected objects $\vec{d}$ with object index i, where o is the objectness or confidence score, $\vec{b}$ the object location description in the image (i.e., the bounding box with central point, width and height of the object $\vec{b} = \{b_x, b_y, b_w, b_h\}$), $\vec{c}$ the class labels, and $\vec{a}$ the dataset affinity scores where the dimension corresponds to number of datasets in the training pool. Adding the affinity score is stated as a multinomial logistic regression task to distinguish between the individual datasets of the combined training pool.

Here, we exemplarily build on a recent variant of the *You Only Look Once* (YOLO) object detection family, in particular on the YOLOv7-X [60] detector. YOLO is a so-called *single shot detector*. This means that objects are detected in a single forward pass without additional steps such as *region proposal networks* [21,52]. Thus, YOLO variants are particularly suitable for real-time applications. YOLO variants use separate inference heads for localization and classification and thus fulfill the requirements to apply the proposed extension. During training, this is considered with multiple loss terms. In particular, YOLOv7-X uses an objectness loss $\mathcal{L}_{obj}$, a classification loss $\mathcal{L}_{cls}$, and a localization loss $\mathcal{L}_{loc}$ to form the complete loss function that guides the training process of the model. The objectness loss assists in accurate object localization and classification by distinguishing between cells that contain objects and those that do not. $\mathcal{L}_{loc}$ corresponds to the bounding box regression head that is responsible for refining the precise location and size of detected objects. The classification head and hence $\mathcal{L}_{cls}$ focuses on classifying detected objects into predefined categories. It typically involves using *softmax* functions to assign each object to a specific class label. Relying on the same information as the classification head that distinguishes between object classes, a

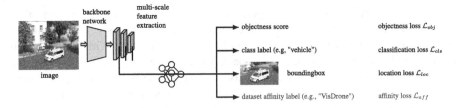

Fig. 1. Schematic visualization of an object detection pipeline with an additional inference head to predict the dataset affinity. The dataset affinity is inferred on object level or rather for every detected object and not on image level.

similar head is added that distinguishes between every dataset added in the training set. With this adaptation, the overall loss term, including the affinity loss $\mathcal{L}_{aff}$, is given by:

$$\mathcal{L} = \lambda_{obj}\mathcal{L}_{obj} + \lambda_{cls}\mathcal{L}_{cls} + \lambda_{loc}\mathcal{L}_{loc} + \lambda_{aff}\mathcal{L}_{aff} \tag{2}$$

Similar to Wang et al. [60], the weighting factors of the loss terms are set to $\lambda_{obj} = 0.7$, $\lambda_{cls} = 0.3$, $\lambda_{loc} = 0.05$, and we set $\lambda_{aff} = 0.3$ after a grid search. $\mathcal{L}_{objectness}$ uses *binary cross entropy*. To calculate $\mathcal{L}_{loc}$ the *complete intersection over union* (CIoU) is utilized. The classification loss and the affinity loss are realized using *focal loss* [36]. However, in the case of a single class detector such as for 'vehicle', also *binary cross entropy* is used as classification loss. A schematic illustration of the proposed object detection pipeline is depicted in Fig. 1.

The model is implemented using *Pytorch* [47] building on the YOLOv7-X detector implementation of [60][1]. For training, an *ADAM* optimizer variant [32,40] with a starting learning rate of 0.001 is used.

3   Dataset Alignment

Besides getting insights into the training data pool, we follow the concept of combining datasets for an object category to learn more general and robust models. A problem that arises from this is differing label sets. Concepts of unifying label sets have already been discussed in Sect. 1. To build a general 'vehicle' detector, we map different sub-categories of vehicles to the more general parent class or rather super-category for aligning the datasets in terms of object labels. In addition to the class labels used, we categorize vehicle datasets according to two criteria: dataset types and sensor positions (viewing angle) during data recording. For other dataset characteristics, we refer to the following reviews and surveys [4,5,13,29,39,46,56,65,66].

For dataset types, we distinguish between *general* datasets and *domain-specific* datasets. *General* datasets, also called *foundation data*, are designed to capture a diverse range of objects or scenes. Examples of such datasets include ImageNet [54], MS COCO [37], and OpenImages [33]. *General* datasets typically contain a large number of diverse images with a broad range of object categories, allowing researchers to test

---

[1] https://github.com/WongKinYiu/yolov7 (accessed 14.11.2023).

the performance of their models on a wide variety of objects and backgrounds. *Domain-specific* or *task-specific* datasets, on the other hand, are designed to capture a specific type of object or scene that is relevant to a particular domain or application. Examples of such datasets for the application domain of autonomous driving include FLIR [17], Cityscapes [12], and KITTI [20]. These datasets are often smaller in size compared to general datasets, but they are curated to capture the specific challenges and characteristics of the domain or task, and have only a small set of class labels. The advantage of using *domain-specific* datasets is that they are tailored to the specific requirements and constraints of the application or domain. However, this restriction may hinder an object detector trained on these datasets from generalizing to other domains.

An additional difference between *general* and *domain-specific* datasets is that *general* datasets consist of randomly pooled image collections instead of data recorded with a specific sensor. For example, the image sensors for autonomous driving. Despite the extremely large variation these datasets have to capture, the sensor position is always close to ground-level with a specific viewing angle of the scene. Thus, our next criterion to categorize datasets is the sensor position corresponding to the sensor platform or the altitude of the sensor platform. These are ground-level datasets captured from car sensors or body cams. Then, there are low, mid, and high-altitude datasets. Low-altitude datasets are commonly captured with fixed surveillance cams and are widespread in the application domain of traffic monitoring. Mid-altitude datasets often come from the same application domain but are captured with small UAVs. Lastly, high-altitude datasets or aerial datasets where the data is recorded with a sensor on a satellite or high-flying drones, etc.

Table 1. Key characteristic of the aligned datasets used for training a general 'vehicle' detector.

dataset	dataset type	resolution / pixel	# images	# aligned images	# categories	# vehicle categories	# instances
MS COCO [37]	general	640 × 640	328.0k	118.3k	80	4 ('car', 'motorcycle', 'truck', 'bus')	68634
DETRAC [62]	domain-specific	960 × 540	84.0k	8.1k	4	4 ('car', 'van', 'bus', 'others')	46814
UAVDT [14]	domain-specific	1024 × 540	80.0k	4.1k	3	3 ('car', 'truck', 'bus')	33942
VisDrone [70]	domain-specific	960 × 540	10.2k	1.0k	10	8 (car', 'van', 'truck', 'tricycle', 'awning-tricycle', 'bus', 'motor', 'other')	124977
FLIR VIS [17]	domain-specific	1800 × 1600	10.3k	9.3k	15	6 ('car', 'motor', 'bus', 'truck', 'scooter', 'other vehicle')	76946
FLIR IR [17]	domain-specific	640 × 512	10.3k	9.3k	15	6 ('car', 'motor', 'bus', 'truck', 'scooter', 'other vehicle')	76946

For the combination of datasets in our experiments, we choose the following datasets to be included in the training set. From the category of *general* datasets, the MS COCO dataset is included. The basic object detector YOLOv7-X is also trained on MS COCO. From the category of *domain-specific* datasets, we use one dataset from autonomous driving, recorded from ground-level, the FLIR dataset. We split this dataset into sub-sets along the spectral range (infrared (IR) and visual-optical (VIS)). Thus the sub-set of the FLIR dataset gets separate labels for the affinity prediction. From the category of low-level altitude dataset, recorded from a surveillance cam, the DETRAC dataset [62] is included. The boundary between different altitudes to categorize datasets is not sharp. So, from the category of mid to high-level altitude datasets, we include the

Fig. 2. Example images from selected datasets included in the overall training set. The top images show samples from MS COCO (left), DETRAC (middle), and FLIR IR. The bottom images depict samples from VisDrone, UAVDT, and FLIR VIS. The gray areas are masked out regions that are not annotated but labeled as 'ignore regions'. From the original categories only vehicle categories are considered and mapped to the super-category 'vehicle'. (Color figure online)

VisDrone [70] and UAVDT dataset [14]. The key characteristics of the selected datasets are summarized in Table 1. This includes the considered vehicle child classes that are mapped to the super-category 'vehicle'.

In addition to aligning the labels, datasets, where the ratio of average object height to image resolution differs strongly from the ratio present in *general* object datasets, are further adapted. These datasets are the *domain-specific* dataset from the categories above ground-level (DETRAC, VisDrone, UAVDT). For these datasets, the original images are sliced into overlapping patches in the range of 600 to 800 pixels (see for example Akyon et al. [1]). The patches also fit better the image resolution of the basic detector of 640×640 pixel. The actual patch size is randomly sampled. We set an overlap ratio of 0.1. For datasets containing video data, such as DETRAC, we only add every 20th frame in the training set to prevent including extremely correlated frames. Further, image regions that are not annotated but masking information is provided are colored gray, preventing negative effects during training. Example images from the selected aligned datasets are shown in Fig. 2. It should be noted that the number of instances is not completely balanced, but every dataset contains at least over $30k$ instances. Due to the fact that the number of instances per image varies, perfect balancing is also difficult to achieve.

4 Evaluation

The evaluation is done on unseen datasets to assess the generalization and robustness of the object detector. In the experiments, we use our own dataset captured with the *Fraunhofer* measuring vehicle MODISSA [6] and the publically available Multi-Spectral Object Detection dataset (MSOD) [31].

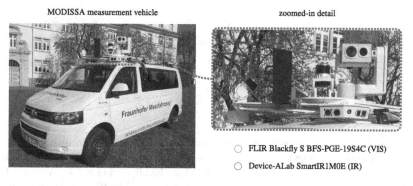

| MODISSA measurement vehicle | zoomed-in detail |

○ FLIR Blackfly S BFS-PGE-19S4C (VIS)
○ Device-ALab SmartIR1M0E (IR)

Fig. 3. The MODISSA measurement vehicle with the used sensors for the recording of the test datasets.

The MODISSA measuring vehicle is equipped with a range of sensors as well as a visible and infrared panoramic camera setup. For the recording of the test datasets, only the front cameras are used. The visible cameras (VIS) are FLIR Blackfly S BFS-PGE-19S4C with a resolution of 1616×1240 pixel, and the infrared cameras (IR) are Device-ALab SmartIR1M0E with a of 1024×768 pixel. Figure 3 shows the MODISSA measurement vehicle with a detailed view of the sensor suite at the front of the vehicle.

Table 2. Key characteristic of the MODISSA [6] test datasets used for evaluation.

dataset	dataset type	resolution / pixel	# images	# categories	# vehicle categories	# instances
MODISSA *Vogelsang* (VIS)	domain-specific	1616×1240	10k	6	4 ('car', 'motorcycle', 'bus', 'truck')	18214
MODISSA *Vogelsang* (IR)	domain-specific	1024×768	8k	6	4 ('car', 'motorcycle', 'bus', 'truck')	10250
MODISSA *Realfahrt* (VIS)	domain-specific	1616×1240	5.3k	6	4 ('car', 'motorcycle', 'bus', 'truck')	6530
MODISSA *Realfahrt* (IR)	domain-specific	1024×768	5.3k	6	4 ('car', 'motorcycle', 'bus', 'truck')	6530

The test datasets consist of two different recordings called *Vogelsang* and *Realfahrt*, where we distinguish between the spectral ranges. Thus, four test datasets are separately evaluated. *Vogelsang* captures mainly a residential area with parked vehicles and road traffic. For the *Realfahrt*, only one IR and VIS camera pair is used. The dataset shows further scenes with road traffic and a parking lot. There are more dynamic

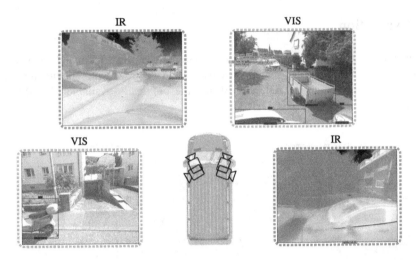

Fig. 4. Exemplary detection results of the universal 'vehicle' detector trained with the aligned dataset on the unseen MODISSA *Vogelsang* dataset. The color of the bounding boxes encode the assigned dataset. Detections assigned to MS COCO are highlighted in red ■. Assigned FLIR IR detections are shown in aqua ■ and detections assigned to FLIR VIS are shown in lime ■. (Color figure online)

Table 3. Key characteristic of the MSOD [31] test datasets used for evaluation.

dataset	dataset type	resolution / pixel	# images	# categories	# vehicle categories	# instances
MSOD (VIS) [31]	domain-specific	640 × 480	7.5k	9	1 ('car')	7426
MSOD (NIR) [31]	domain-specific	320 × 256	7.5k	9	1 ('car')	5209
MSOD (MIR) [31]	domain-specific	320 × 256	7.5k	9	1 ('car')	4472
MSOD (FIR) [31]	domain-specific	640 × 480	7.5k	9	4 ('car')	5042

objects than in the *Vogelsang* dataset. To ensure privacy-preserving (e.g., image recordings of license plates) and complying with corresponding guidelines, we follow the data protection concept of Münch et al. [23,44]. The annotations contain six classes with four vehicle classes ('car', 'motorcycle', 'bus', 'truck'). Similar to the training data, these sub-categories are mapped to one 'vehicle' class. All key characteristics of the MODISSA test datasets are summarized in Table 2.

The selected public MSOD dataset [31] is a *domain-specific* dataset for autonomous driving that consists of multi-spectral (VIS, NIR, MIR, and FIR) images. Similarity to the MODISSA dataset, the different spectral ranges are separately evaluated. The nine original ground truth class labels include only one class ('car') mapped to 'vehicle'. The images show traffic scene in an university environment at daytime and nighttime. All key characteristics of the MSOD test datasets are summarized in Table 3.

Table 4. Comparison of reference detectors trained on different combinations of aligned datasets for the MODISSA datasets. In addition, the percentage of assigned datasets for true positive detection based on the dataset affinity score is depicted.

test dataset	spectral range		training datasets + percentage of assigned true positive detection						mAP ↑	
	VIS	IR	MS COCO	DETRAC	UAVDT	VisDrone	FLIR VIS	FLIR IR	mAP@.5	mAP@.5-.95
MODISSA *Vogelsang*	✓	✗	✓(45.6%)	✓(0.1%)	✓(≈0%)	✓(≈0%)	✓(54.3%)	✓(≈0%)	0.921	0.802
MODISSA *Vogelsang*	✓	✗	✓(44.7%)	✗(-%)	✗(-%)	✗(-%)	✓(55.3%)	✗(-%)	0.913	0.785
MODISSA *Vogelsang*	✓	✗	✗(-%)	✓(99.7%)	✓(0.1%)	✓(0.1%)	✗(-%)	✓(0.1%)	0.662	0.482
MODISSA *Vogelsang*	✗	✓	✓(1.2%)	✓(0.1%)	✓(0.1%)	✓(0.1%)	✓(0.1%)	✓(98.4%)	0.914	0.780
MODISSA *Vogelsang*	✗	✓	✓(0.6%)	✗(-%)	✗(-%)	✗(-%)	✗(-%)	✓(99.4%)	0.911	0.781
MODISSA *Vogelsang*	✗	✓	✗(-%)	✓(99.1%)	✓(0.3%)	✓(0.3%)	✓(0.1%)	✗(-%)	0.528	0.396
MODISSA *Realfahrt*	✓	✗	✓(29.5%)	✓(≈0%)	✓(≈0%)	✓(≈0%)	✓(70.5%)	✓(≈0%)	0.822	0.617
MODISSA *Realfahrt*	✓	✗	✓(30.8%)	✗(-%)	✗(-%)	✗(-%)	✓(69.2%)	✗(-%)	0.780	0.561
MODISSA *Realfahrt*	✓	✗	✗(-%)	✓(99.4%)	✓(0.4%)	✓(0.2%)	✗(-%)	✓(≈0%)	0.716	0.416
MODISSA *Realfahrt*	✗	✓	✓(1.2%)	✓(0.1%)	✓(0.1%)	✓(0.1%)	✓(3.9%)	✓(94.6%)	0.674	0.400
MODISSA *Realfahrt*	✗	✓	✓(1.9%)	✗(-%)	✗(-%)	✗(-%)	✗(-%)	✓(98.1%)	0.673	0.400
MODISSA *Realfahrt*	✗	✓	✗(-%)	✓(99.2%)	✓(0.3%)	✓(0.3%)	✓(0.2%)	✗(-%)	0.449	0.238

To quantify the results, we use the *mean average precision* (mAP) object detector metrics. In particular, mAP@.5 [15] and mAP@.5:.95 [37] are used. While mAP@.5 is the mAP for an IoU threshold of at least fifty percent, the mAP@.5:.95 is the average across ten IoU thresholds, hence more strict.

After aligning the label sets as described in Sect. 3, we first train a 'vehicle' detector with the selected six datasets (MS COCO, DETRAC, VisDrone, UAVDT, FLIR VIS, FLIR IR) for the experiments. Besides calculating the mAP values, the maximum score of the affinity prediction is used to estimate the contributing dataset of a true positive (TP) detection. The distribution of assigned training datasets of truly detected vehicles is calculated over the evaluation dataset. It is used to split the training into the sets of the two highest assigned datasets and the remaining datasets. After training on the split sets, the performance between detectors is compared. The quantitative results of these experiments for the MODISSA datasets are shown in Table 4, and some exemplary qualitative results are visualized in Fig. 4. Detections assigned to MS COCO are highlighted in red ■. The assigned FLIR IR detections are shown in aqua ▬ and detections assigned to FLIR VIS are shown in lime ▬.

The results show that the best performance could be achieved by using all the complete aligned training data. This applies to all MODISSA test datasets. Thus, increasing the variation and number of training samples helped to generalize to these datasets. Hence, the concept of merging datasets has also here proven to learn more robust and general models. When looking at the distribution of the assigned dataset by the affinity scores, one can see that for the VIS *Vogelsang* and *Realfahrt* mainly the MS COCO and FLIR VIS datasets are classified as origin dataset. For the IR *Vogelsang* and *Realfahrt*, almost all true positive detections are classified as originating from the FLIR IR dataset. Since the test dataset is in the application of autonomous driving captured from ground-level, this might not be surprising. Mainly because only one IR dataset is in the training set. However, this can be seen as some sanity check that the proposed idea of adding the dataset affinity prediction as additional inference enables useful feedback over the training set.

Table 5. Comparison of reference detectors trained on different combinations of aligned datasets for the MSOD datasets. In addition, the percentage of assigned datasets for true positive detection based on the dataset affinity score is depicted.

test dataset	spectral range				training datasets + percentage of assigned true positive detection						mAP ↑	
	VIS	NIR	MIR	FIR	MS COCO	DETRAC	UAVDT	VisDrone	FLIR VIS	FLIR IR	mAP@.5	mAP@.5-.95
MSOD	✓	✗	✗	✗	✓(86.3%)	✓(0.1%)	✓(≈0%)	✓(4.0%)	✓(9.6%)	✓(≈0%)	0.490	0.293
MSOD	✓	✗	✗	✗	✓(88.2%)	✗(-%)	✗(-%)	✗(-%)	✓(11.8%)	✗(-%)	0.487	0.280
MSOD	✓	✗	✗	✗	✗(-%)	✓(99.3%)	✓(0.1%)	✓(0.5%)	✗(-%)	✓(0.1%)	0.314	0.177
MSOD	✗	✓	✗	✗	✓(49.1%)	✓(0.8%)	✓(0.1%)	✓(0.1%)	✓(43.4%)	✓(6.5%)	0.458	0.260
MSOD	✗	✓	✗	✗	✓(38.8%)	✗(-%)	✗(-%)	✗(-%)	✓(61.2%)	✗(-%)	0.429	0.238
MSOD	✗	✓	✗	✗	✗(-%)	✓(99.6%)	✓(0.2%)	✓(0.1%)	✗(-%)	✓(0.1%)	0.284	0.154
MSOD	✗	✗	✓	✗	✓(1.8%)	✓(≈0%)	✓(≈0%)	✓(0.8%)	✓(≈0%)	✓(97.4%)	0.496	0.316
MSOD	✗	✗	✓	✗	✓(7.2%)	✗(-%)	✗(-%)	✗(-%)	✗(-%)	✓(92.8%)	0.489	0.306
MSOD	✗	✗	✓	✗	✗(-%)	✓(98.8%)	✓(0.4%)	✓(0.8%)	✓(≈0%)	✗(-%)	0.239	0.141
MSOD	✗	✗	✗	✓	✓(0.3%)	✓(≈0%)	✓(≈0%)	✓(≈0%)	✓(≈0%)	✓(99.7%)	0.505	0.293
MSOD	✗	✗	✗	✓	✓(0.2%)	✗(-%)	✗(-%)	✗(-%)	✗(-%)	✓(99.8%)	0.520	0.302
MSOD	✗	✗	✗	✓	✗(-%)	✓(93.2%)	✓(3.8%)	✓(2.5%)	✓(0.5%)	✗(-%)	0.153	0.0825

Moreover, when we look at the results achieved using only the data from the datasets with the highest percentage of assigned dataset affinity, it becomes visible that the drop in performance is relatively low compared to the full set. In contrast, using the remaining datasets led to a drastic performance drop despite the total number of training images and instances being higher (see Table 1). The fact that from the remaining datasets, DETRAC is then the most assigned dataset also corresponds to the intuition that the low-level altitude dataset is closest to the test domain.

This also applies to the results of the experiments for the MSOD datasets, shown in Table 5, and some quantitative results are shown in Fig. 5. The colors of the bounding boxes encode the assigned dataset. Red ■ corresponds to MS COCO, lime ■ to FLIR VIS, and aqua ■ to FLIR IR. The overall tendency complies with the result of the MODISSA datasets, although there are minor differences. The full training pool achieves the best performance for almost all MSOD test datasets. The only exception is the FIR data, where using only the main supporting datasets achieved even better results. What can be seen from these results is the shift along the spectral range what datasets are responsible for the detections. Whereas for the VIS data, the detector mainly assigns MS COCO and FLIR VIS. The lower mAP values for the MSOD datasets can be explained with the lower image resolution and correspondingly lower object sizes in the image. The shift towards FLIR IR can be seen when considering images corresponding to higher wavelength spectra. Interestingly, the detector still relies on MS COCO and FLIR VIS in the NIR data. A minor difference is that MS COCO is the dataset with the estimated strongest support for the VIS data. Nonetheless, also these results show the proposed dataset affinity score can be used to automatically select samples from a heterogeneous pool of vehicle datasets. Besides, the model is trained on a significantly sparser set of training samples, there is almost no performance decrease and even a counterproductive training data combination could be identified. Since the selected dataset pool spans across different categories, adding a dataset from often assigned categories is a way to optimize an object detector on a specific application.

MSOD (VIS)

MSOD (NIR)

MSOD (MIR)

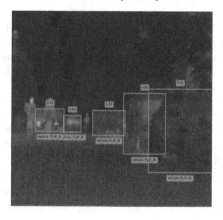

MSOD (FIR)

Fig. 5. Sample detection results of the universal 'vehicle' detector trained with the aligned dataset on the unseen MSOD dataset [31]. The color of the bounding boxes encode the assigned origin dataset. Detections assigned to MS COCO are highlighted in red ▬. Assigned FLIR IR detections are shown in aqua ▬ and detections assigned to FLIR VIS are shown in lime ▬. (Color figure online)

The benefit of the ante-hoc detection explanation provided by the affinity prediction can be seen without a quantitative evaluation. By applying the adapted detector to desired target domain data, it is possible to directly get insights how to possible extend the training set and if samples from the target domain can already be explained by included datasets. Figure 6 shows some exemplary detections on datasets outside the training domain to depict this effect. Images are taken from the DroneVehicle dataset [57], the KAIST Multispectral Pedestrian Dataset (KAIST MPD) [28], the Dense Depth for Automated Driving dataset (DDAD) [24], the REalistic and Diverse Scenes dataset

Fig. 6. Sample detection results of the universal 'vehicle' detector on different unseen datsets (DroneVehicle [57], AMVD [42], KAIST MPD [28], DDAD [24], REDS [45]). The color of the bounding boxes encode the assigned origin dataset. Detections assigned to VisDrone are highlighted in blue ▬ and to MS COCO in red ▬. Assigned FLIR IR detections are shown in aqua ▬ and detections assigned to FLIR VIS are shown in lime ▬. (Color figure online)

(REDS) [45], and Aerial Multi-Vehicle Detection Dataset (AMVD). The colors of the bounding boxes encode the assigned dataset. Red ▬, blue ▬, lime ▬, and aqua ▬ correspond to respectively MS COCO, VisDrone, FLIR VIS, FLIR IR. For the examples from datasets captured from a high altitude, the VisDrone dataset is assigned. Although the results, together with the chosen set of aligned datasets and the test dataset, follow an intuition of what dataset combination should work, the proposed affinity score can help to find dataset bias and outliers in the data and offers an additional tool to assess the training data.

5   Conclusion

In this paper, we proposed to add an additional inference head to an object detection pipeline for predicting the training data affinity. Since current detectors have inherent different heads for separated inference tasks, this extension can be applied to most current detectors. By merging existing datasets to learn a more robust model, we first aligned several datasets toward this end. Then, we evaluated an exemplary detector and used the affinity score to assess the contribution of specific datasets on individual detections. We demonstrated the efficacy of the dataset affinity prediction by achieving comparable results with significantly fewer training samples by focusing on datasets with more substantial support, as indicated by the affinity scores. Moreover, the proposed dataset affinity prediction offers some kind of ante-hoc detection explanation during inference and helps to assess the effectiveness of pooling datasets.

References

1. Akyon, F.C., Altinuc, S.O., Temizel, A.: Slicing aided hyper inference and fine-tuning for small object detection. In: 2022 IEEE International Conference on Image Processing (ICIP), pp. 966–970 (2022). https://doi.org/10.1109/ICIP46576.2022.9897990
2. Azevedo, T., de Jong, R., Maji, P.: Stochastic-yolo: efficient probabilistic object detection under dataset shifts. In: NeurIPS Workshop on Machine Learning for Autonomous Driving (ML4AD) (2020)
3. Bayer, J., Münch, D., Arens, M.: APMD: adversarial pixel masking derivative for multispectral object detectors. In: Counterterrorism, Crime Fighting, Forensics, and Surveillance Technologies VI, vol. 12275, p. 122750F. International Society for Optics and Photonics, SPIE (2022). https://doi.org/10.1117/12.2637977
4. Bogdoll., D., Schreyer., F., Zöllner., J.M.: Ad-datasets: a meta-collection of data sets for autonomous driving. In: Proceedings of the 8th International Conference on Vehicle Technology and Intelligent Transport Systems - VEHITS, pp. 46–56. INSTICC, SciTePress (2022). https://doi.org/10.5220/0011001900003191
5. Bogdoll, D., Uhlemeyer, S., Kowol, K., Zöllner, J.M.: Perception datasets for anomaly detection in autonomous driving: a survey (2023). https://doi.org/10.48550/ARXIV.2302.02790, https://arxiv.org/abs/2302.02790
6. Borgmann, B., Schatz, V., Hammer, M., Hebel, M., Arens, M., Stilla, U.: Modissa: a multi-purpose platform for the prototypical realization of vehicle-related applications using optical sensors. Appl. Opt. **60**(22), F50–F65 (2021). https://doi.org/10.1364/AO.423599, https://opg.optica.org/ao/abstract.cfm?URI=ao-60-22-F50
7. Burkart, N., Huber, M.F.: A survey on the explainability of supervised machine learning. J. Artif. Intell. Res. **70**, 245–317 (2021)
8. Chattopadhay, A., Sarkar, A., Howlader, P., Balasubramanian, V.N.: Grad-CAM++: generalized gradient-based visual explanations for deep convolutional networks. In: 2018 IEEE Winter Conference on Applications of Computer Vision (WACV), pp. 839–847 (2018). https://doi.org/10.1109/WACV.2018.00097
9. Chen, C., Zheng, Z., Ding, X., Huang, Y., Dou, Q.: Harmonizing transferability and discriminability for adapting object detectors. In: 2020 IEEE/CVF Conference on Computer Vision and Pattern Recognition (CVPR), pp. 8866–8875 (2020). https://doi.org/10.1109/CVPR42600.2020.00889
10. Chen, Y., Li, W., Sakaridis, C., Dai, D., Van Gool, L.: Domain adaptive faster R-CNN for object detection in the wild. In: 2018 IEEE/CVF Conference on Computer Vision and Pattern Recognition, pp. 3339–3348 (2018). https://doi.org/10.1109/CVPR.2018.00352
11. Choi, J., Chun, D., Kim, H., Lee, H.J.: Gaussian yolov3: an accurate and fast object detector using localization uncertainty for autonomous driving. In: The IEEE International Conference on Computer Vision (ICCV), October 2019
12. Cordts, M., et al.: The cityscapes dataset for semantic urban scene understanding. In: Proceedings of the IEEE Conference on Computer Vision and Pattern Recognition (CVPR), pp. 3213–3223 (2016)
13. Danaci, K.I., Akagunduz, E.: A survey on infrared image and video sets (2023)
14. Du, D., et al.: The unmanned aerial vehicle benchmark: object detection and tracking. In: Ferrari, V., Hebert, M., Sminchisescu, C., Weiss, Y. (eds.) ECCV 2018. LNCS, vol. 11214, pp. 375–391. Springer, Cham (2018). https://doi.org/10.1007/978-3-030-01249-6_23
15. Everingham, M., Van Gool, L., Williams, C.K., Winn, J., Zisserman, A.: The pascal visual object classes (VOC) challenge. Int. J. Comput. Vis. **88**, 303–338 (2010)
16. Feng, D., Harakeh, A., Waslander, S.L., Dietmayer, K.C.J.: A review and comparative study on probabilistic object detection in autonomous driving. IEEE Trans. Intell. Transp. Syst. **23**, 9961–9980 (2020)

17. FLIR (V2): Free flir thermal dataset for algorithm training (2022). https://www.flir.com/oem/adas/dataset/european-regional-thermal-dataset/

18. Gal, Y., Ghahramani, Z.: Dropout as a bayesian approximation: representing model uncertainty in deep learning. In: Proceedings of the 33rd International Conference on International Conference on Machine Learning, vol. 48, pp. 1050–1059. ICML'16, JMLR.org (2016)

19. Ganin, Y., et al.: Domain-adversarial training of neural networks. J. Mach. Learn. Res. **17**(59), 1–35 (2016). http://jmlr.org/papers/v17/15-239.html

20. Geiger, A., Lenz, P., Urtasun, R.: Are we ready for autonomous driving? The kitti vision benchmark suite. In: Conference on Computer Vision and Pattern Recognition (CVPR) (2012)

21. Girshick, R.: Fast R-CNN. In: 2015 IEEE International Conference on Computer Vision (ICCV), pp. 1440–1448 (2015). https://doi.org/10.1109/ICCV.2015.169

22. Goodfellow, I., Bengio, Y., Courville, A.: Deep Learning. MIT Press, Cambridge, MA, USA (2016). http://www.deeplearningbook.org

23. Grosselfinger, A.K., Münch, D., Arens, M.: An architecture for automatic multimodal video data anonymization to ensure data protection. In: Bouma, H., Prabhu, R., Stokes, R.J., Yitzhaky, Y. (eds.) Counterterrorism, Crime Fighting, Forensics, and Surveillance Technologies III, vol. 11166, pp. 206 – 217. International Society for Optics and Photonics, SPIE (2019).https://doi.org/10.1117/12.2533031

24. Guizilini, V., Ambruş, R., Pillai, S., Raventos, A., Gaidon, A.: 3D packing for self-supervised monocular depth estimation. In: 2020 IEEE/CVF Conference on Computer Vision and Pattern Recognition (CVPR), pp. 2482–2491 (2020). https://doi.org/10.1109/CVPR42600.2020.00256

25. Hall, D., et al.: Probabilistic object detection: Definition and evaluation. In: The IEEE Winter Conference on Applications of Computer Vision, pp. 1031–1040 (2020)

26. Hasan, I., Liao, S., Li, J., Akram, S.U., Shao, L.: Generalizable pedestrian detection: the elephant in the room. In: IEEE Conference on Computer Vision and Pattern Recognition, CVPR 2021, virtual, 19–25 June 2021, pp. 11328–11337. Computer Vision Foundation/IEEE (2021). https://doi.org/10.1109/CVPR46437.2021.01117

27. Hinton, G., Roweis, S.: Stochastic neighbor embedding. Adv. Neural Inf. Process. Syst. **15**, 833–840 (2003). https://www.bibsonomy.org/bibtex/2a0d72c90aa3348858a647e7603ad7323/gromgull

28. Hwang, S., Park, J., Kim, N., Choi, Y., Kweon, I.S.: Multispectral pedestrian detection: benchmark dataset and baselines. In: Proceedings of IEEE Conference on Computer Vision and Pattern Recognition CVPR (2015)

29. Janai, J., Güney, F., Behl, A., Geiger, A.: Computer Vision for Autonomous Vehicles: Problems, Datasets and State-of-the-Art. Foundations and Trends in Computer Graphics and Vision (2020)

30. Jiao, L., et al.: A survey of deep learning-based object detection. IEEE Access **7**, 128837–128868 (2019). https://doi.org/10.1109/ACCESS.2019.2939201

31. Karasawa, T., Kohei, W., Qishen, H., Antonio, T.D.P., Yoshitaka, U., Tatsuya, H.: Multispectral object detection for autonomous vehicles. In: Proceedings of the on Thematic Workshops of ACM Multimedia 2017, pp. 35–43. Thematic Workshops '17, Association for Computing Machinery, New York, NY, USA (2017). https://doi.org/10.1145/3126686.3126727

32. Kingma, D., Ba, J.: Adam: a method for stochastic optimization. In: International Conference on Learning Representations (ICLR) (2015)

33. Kuznetsova, A., et al.: The open images dataset v4: unified image classification, object detection, and visual relationship detection at scale. IJCV (2020)

34. Lakshminarayanan, B., Pritzel, A., Blundell, C.: Simple and scalable predictive uncertainty estimation using deep ensembles. In: Guyon, I., Luxburg, U.V., Bengio, S., Wallach, H.,

Fergus, R., Vishwanathan, S., Garnett, R. (eds.) Advances in Neural Information Processing Systems, vol. 30. Curran Associates, Inc. (2017). https://proceedings.neurips.cc/paper_files/paper/2017/file/9ef2ed4b7fd2c810847ffa5fa85bce38-Paper.pdf

35. Lambert, J., Liu, Z., Sener, O., Hays, J., Koltun, V.: MSeg: a composite dataset for multi-domain semantic segmentation. In: Computer Vision and Pattern Recognition (CVPR) (2020)

36. Lin, T.Y., Goyal, P., Girshick, R., He, K., Dollár, P.: Focal loss for dense object detection. In: 2017 IEEE International Conference on Computer Vision (ICCV), pp. 2999–3007 (2017). https://doi.org/10.1109/ICCV.2017.324

37. Lin, T.-Y., et al.: Microsoft COCO: common objects in context. In: Fleet, D., Pajdla, T., Schiele, B., Tuytelaars, T. (eds.) ECCV 2014. LNCS, vol. 8693, pp. 740–755. Springer, Cham (2014). https://doi.org/10.1007/978-3-319-10602-1_48

38. Liu, L., et al.: deep learning for generic object detection: a survey. Int. J. Comput. Vis. **128**(2), 261–318 (2020). https://doi.org/10.1007/s11263-019-01247-4

39. Long, Y., et al.: On creating benchmark dataset for aerial image interpretation: reviews, guidances and million-aid. IEEE J. Sel. Top. Appl. Earth Obs. Remote Sens. **14**, 4205–4230 (2021). https://doi.org/10.1109/JSTARS.2021.3070368

40. Loshchilov, I., Hutter, F.: Decoupled weight decay regularization. In: International Conference on Learning Representations (ICLR) (2019)

41. MacKay, D.J.C.: A practical bayesian framework for backpropagation networks. Neural Comput. **4**(3), 448–472 (1992). https://doi.org/10.1162/neco.1992.4.3.448

42. Makrigiorgis, R., Kolios, P., Kyrkou, C.: Aerial multi-vehicle detection dataset, September 2022. https://doi.org/10.5281/zenodo.7053442

43. Miller, G.A.: Wordnet: a lexical database for English. Commun. ACM **38**(11), 39–41 (1995). https://doi.org/10.1145/219717.219748

44. Münch, D., Grosselfinger, A.-K., Krempel, E., Hebel, M., Arens, M.: Data anonymization for data protection on publicly recorded data. In: Tzovaras, D., Giakoumis, D., Vincze, M., Argyros, A. (eds.) ICVS 2019. LNCS, vol. 11754, pp. 245–258. Springer, Cham (2019). https://doi.org/10.1007/978-3-030-34995-0_23

45. Nah, S., et al.: NTIRE 2019 challenge on video deblurring and super-resolution: Dataset and study. In: 2019 IEEE/CVF Conference on Computer Vision and Pattern Recognition Workshops (CVPRW), pp. 1996–2005 (2019). https://doi.org/10.1109/CVPRW.2019.00251

46. Éric Noël Laflamme, C., Pomerleau, F., Giguère, P.: Driving datasets literature review. ArXiv **abs/1910.11968** (2019). https://api.semanticscholar.org/CorpusID:204904177

47. Paszke, A., et al.: PyTorch: an imperative style, high-performance deep learning library. In: Advances in Neural Information Processing Systems (NeurIPS), pp. 8024–8035. Curran Associates, Inc. (2019)

48. Petsiuk, V., Das, A., Saenko, K.: Rise: randomized input sampling for explanation of black-box models. In: British Machine Vision Conference (BMVC) (2018). http://bmvc2018.org/contents/papers/1064.pdf

49. Petsiuk, V., et al.: Black-box explanation of object detectors via saliency maps. 2021 IEEE/CVF Conference on Computer Vision and Pattern Recognition (CVPR), pp. 11438–11447 (2020). https://api.semanticscholar.org/CorpusID:219401828

50. Quionero-Candela, J., Sugiyama, M., Schwaighofer, A., Lawrence, N.D.: Dataset Shift in Machine Learning. The MIT Press, Cambridge (2009)

51. Redmon, J., Farhadi, A.: Yolo9000: better, faster, stronger. In: Proceedings of the IEEE Conference on Computer Vision and Pattern Recognition (CVPR), July 2017

52. Ren, S., He, K., Girshick, R., Sun, J.: Faster R-CNN: towards real-time object detection with region proposal networks. IEEE Trans. Pattern Anal. Mach. Intell. **39**(6), 1137–1149 (2017). https://doi.org/10.1109/TPAMI.2016.2577031

53. Ribeiro, M.T., Singh, S., Guestrin, C.: Why should i trust you?: Explaining the predictions of any classifier. In: Proceedings of the 22nd ACM SIGKDD International Conference on Knowledge Discovery and Data Mining, pp. 1135–1144. KDD '16, Association for Computing Machinery, New York, NY, USA (2016). https://doi.org/10.1145/2939672.2939778

54. Russakovsky, O., et al.: ImageNet large scale visual recognition challenge. Int. J. Comput. Vis. (IJCV) **115**(3), 211–252 (2015). https://doi.org/10.1007/s11263-015-0816-y

55. Selvaraju, R.R., Cogswell, M., Das, A., Vedantam, R., Parikh, D., Batra, D.: Grad-CAM: visual explanations from deep networks via gradient-based localization. In: 2017 IEEE International Conference on Computer Vision (ICCV), pp. 618–626 (2017). https://doi.org/10.1109/ICCV.2017.74

56. Song, Z., et al.: Synthetic datasets for autonomous driving: a survey (2023)

57. Sun, Y., Cao, B., Zhu, P., Hu, Q.: Drone-based RGB-infrared cross-modality vehicle detection via uncertainty-aware learning. IEEE Trans. Circuits Syst. Video Technol. 1 (2022). https://doi.org/10.1109/TCSVT.2022.3168279

58. Vidit, V., Engilberge, M., Salzmann, M.: Clip the gap: a single domain generalization approach for object detection. In: Proceedings of the IEEE/CVF Conference on Computer Vision and Pattern Recognition (CVPR), pp. 3219–3229, June 2023

59. Vs, V., Gupta, V., Oza, P., Sindagi, V.A., Patel, V.M.: Mega-CDA: memory guided attention for category-aware unsupervised domain adaptive object detection. In: Proceedings of the IEEE/CVF Conference on Computer Vision and Pattern Recognition, pp. 4516–4526 (2021)

60. Wang, C.Y., Bochkovskiy, A., Mark Liao, H.Y.: Yolov7: trainable bag-of-freebies sets new state-of-the-art for real-time object detectors. In: Proceedings of the IEEE Conference on Computer Vision and Pattern Recognition (CVPR) (2023)

61. Wang, X., Cai, Z., Gao, D., Vasconcelos, N.: Towards universal object detection by domain attention. In: Proceedings of the IEEE Conference on Computer Vision and Pattern Recognition, pp. 7289–7298 (2019)

62. Wen, L., et al.: UA-DETRAC: a new benchmark and protocol for multi-object detection and tracking. Comput. Vis. Image Underst. (2020)

63. Wu, X., Sahoo, D., Hoi, S.C.: Recent advances in deep learning for object detection. Neurocomputing **396**, 39–64 (2020). https://doi.org/10.1016/j.neucom.2020.01.085, http://www.sciencedirect.com/science/article/pii/S0925231220301430

64. Xiao, Y., et al.: A review of object detection based on deep learning. Multimed. Tools Appl. **79**(33), 23729–23791 (2020). https://doi.org/10.1007/s11042-020-08976-6

65. Yin, H., Berger, C.: When to use what data set for your self-driving car algorithm: an overview of publicly available driving datasets. In: 2017 IEEE 20th International Conference on Intelligent Transportation Systems (ITSC), pp. 1–8 (2017). https://doi.org/10.1109/ITSC.2017.8317828

66. Yurtsever, E., Lambert, J., Carballo, A., Takeda, K.: A survey of autonomous driving: common practices and emerging technologies. IEEE Access **8**, 58443–58469 (2020). https://doi.org/10.1109/ACCESS.2020.2983149

67. Zhao, X., Schulter, S., Sharma, G., Tsai, Y.-H., Chandraker, M., Wu, Y.: Object detection with a unified label space from multiple datasets. In: Vedaldi, A., Bischof, H., Brox, T., Frahm, J.-M. (eds.) ECCV 2020. LNCS, vol. 12359, pp. 178–193. Springer, Cham (2020). https://doi.org/10.1007/978-3-030-58568-6_11

68. Zhao, Z., Zheng, P., Xu, S., Wu, X.: Object detection with deep learning: a review. IEEE Trans. Neural Netw. Learn. Syst. **30**(11), 3212–3232 (2019). https://doi.org/10.1109/TNNLS.2018.2876865

69. Zhou, X., Koltun, V., Krähenbühl, P.: Simple multi-dataset detection. In: Proceedings of the IEEE/CVF Conference on Computer Vision and Pattern Recognition (CVPR), pp. 7571–7580, June 2022

70. Zhu, P., et al.: Detection and tracking meet drones challenge. IEEE Trans. Pattern Anal. Mach. Intell. 1 (2021). https://doi.org/10.1109/TPAMI.2021.3119563
71. Zhu, X., Pang, J., Yang, C., Shi, J., Lin, D.: Adapting object detectors via selective cross-domain alignment. In: 2019 IEEE/CVF Conference on Computer Vision and Pattern Recognition (CVPR), pp. 687–696 (2019). https://doi.org/10.1109/CVPR.2019.00078
72. Zou, Z., Shi, Z., Guo, Y., Ye, J.: Object detection in 20 years: a survey (2019)

Optimizing Mobile Robot Navigation Through Neuro-Symbolic Fusion of Deep Deterministic Policy Gradient (DDPG) and Fuzzy Logic

Muhammad Faqiihuddin Nasary⬤, Azhar Mohd Ibrahim⬤, Suaib Al Mahmud⬤,
Amir Akramin Shafie$^{(\boxtimes)}$ ⬤, and Muhammad Imran Mardzuki⬤

Advanced Multi-Agent System Lab, Department of Mechatronics Engineering, International
Islamic University Malaysia, Kuala Lumpur, Malaysia
aashafie@iium.edu.my

Abstract. Mobile robot navigation has been a sector of great importance in the autonomous systems research arena for a while. For ensuring successful navigation in complex environments several rule-based traditional approaches have been employed previously which possess several drawbacks in terms of ensuring navigation and obstacle avoidance efficiency. Compared to them, reinforcement learning is a novel technique being assessed for this purpose lately. However, the constant reward values in reinforcement learning algorithms limits their performance capabilities. This study enhances the Deep Deterministic Policy Gradient (DDPG) algorithm by integrating fuzzy logic, creating a neuro-symbolic approach that imparts advanced reasoning capabilities to the mobile agents. The outcomes observed in the environment resembling real-world scenarios, highlighted remarkable performance improvements of the neuro-symbolic approach, displaying a success rate of 0.71% compared to 0.39%, an average path length of 35 m compared to 25 m, and an average execution time of 120 s compared to 97 s. The results suggest that the employed approach enhances the navigation performance in terms of obstacle avoidance success rate and path length, hence could be reliable for navigation purpose of mobile agents.

Keywords: DDPG · Fuzzy logic · Mobile robot navigation · Obstacle avoidance · Simulation

1 Introduction

Mobile robotics has advanced significantly, with a growing focus on incorporating AI and machine learning techniques to improve navigation capabilities [1–6]. Deep reinforcement learning, a subset of reinforcement learning that employs deep neural networks, has been highly effective in various tasks, including mobile robot navigation.

In this regard, the DDPG algorithm, a variant of deep reinforcement learning [7] is used in this study to enhance the navigation capabilities of a mobile robot. The DDPG algorithm is implemented using MATLAB and Simulink software, which are widely used in the field of control systems and robotics. DDPG algorithm is a classic deep

© The Author(s), under exclusive license to Springer Nature Switzerland AG 2024
J. Filipe and J. Röning (Eds.): ROBOVIS 2024, CCIS 2077, pp. 278–292, 2024.
https://doi.org/10.1007/978-3-031-59057-3_18

reinforcement learning technique [8–10], which has a significant advantage in continuous control issues. The DDPG algorithm is built around the actor critical method, the DQN algorithm, and the deterministic strategy gradient (DPG). DQN algorithm uses deep neural network's powerful function fitting ability to map environmental state into action strategy and state action pair to value function, avoiding the problem of Q table's large storage space. The integration of the Deep Q- Network (DQN) algorithm within the Deep Deterministic Policy Gradient (DDPG) algorithm is significant as it leverages the powerful function fitting ability of deep neural networks to map environmental states to action strategies and state-action pairs to value functions [3, 11, 12], effectively addressing the issue of large storage space required by Q tables. This integration enhances the overall performance and scalability of the DDPG algorithm, enabling it to tackle complex decision-making problems in reinforcement learning with greater efficiency and effectiveness.

The current limitations of mobile robot navigation in dynamic and unstructured environments pose significant challenges in the field of robotics. So many traditional methods have been employed before for navigation, obstacle avoidances and path planning purposes [13–22]. Traditional navigation methods, such as pre- programmed paths or sensor-based localization, may prove inadequate in such scenarios [23]. Therefore, more sophisticated navigation approaches are required to enable mobile robots to learn and adapt to dynamic environments [11]. Self-learning approaches have been employed in a few studies before to tackle this issue [23–36]. Still the problems persist to several degrees because of the existence of non-reasoning capabilities in self-learning algorithms.

This research aims to examine the efficacy of the DDPG algorithm, particularly in conjunction with a neuro-symbolic approach, in enhancing the navigation capabilities of a mobile robot within dynamic and unstructured environments and to assess the navigational accuracy, adaptability, and robustness exhibited by the DDPG algorithm across a diverse array of simulated environments, thus quantitatively evaluating its performance in a comprehensive manner. Specifically, the ability of the algorithm to guide a mobile robot through complex and dynamic environments while avoiding obstacles and reaching a desired target will be assessed [37]. The outcomes of this study will not only demonstrate the potential of the DDPG algorithm but also highlight areas for improvement, paving the way for future research in this exciting field.

1.1 Deep Deterministic Policy Gradient Algorithm

This study investigates the use of the DDPG algorithm for reinforcement learning in a scenario where a mobile robot equipped with range sensors navigates an environment to avoid obstacles. The DDPG algorithm is well-suited for continuous action spaces and utilizes an actor-critic architecture where the actor network represents the policy, and the critic network represents the value function. To simulate range sensor readings, an occupancy map of a known environment was employed, and collision avoidance was achieved by determining optimal controls for the robot in terms of linear and angular velocity. The DDPG agent utilized sensor readings as input and generated velocity controls as output. By iteratively exploring the environment and receiving rewards as feedback, the agent learned to make better decisions and effectively avoid obstacles.

1.2 Neuro-Symbolic Approach Through Fuzzy Logic in Reward Function

This research work introduces a novel neuro-symbolic approach that enhances AI with reasoning capabilities for mobile robot navigation.

By integrating evaluative Fuzzy logic functions, the proposed system harmonizes deep reinforcement learning (DRL) with symbolic reasoning, enabling the robot to reason and optimize DRL computations during navigation. The key emphasis lies in the construction of the reward function, where fuzzy logic plays a pivotal role. This integration empowers the system with the ability to learn, adapt, and operate effectively in unknown environments, facilitating seamless real-world deployment and interaction. The incorporation of fuzzy logic in the reward function enables the system to achieve robust and interpretable decision-making capabilities, thus significantly enhancing the overall efficiency and reliability of the navigation process. This research highlights the crucial significance of incorporating fuzzy logic to enhance reasoning and optimize DRL computations in mobile robot navigation systems.

The paper is organized into the following sections: Sect. 2 details the methodological framework, Sect. 3 presents experiment results, Sect. 4 engages in discussion, and Sect. 5 concludes by summarizing key insights and suggesting future research directions.

2 Methods

2.1 Overview of the Hybrid System Architecture of DDPG and Fuzzy Logic

In the hybrid system architecture as shown in Fig. 1, fuzzy logic is integrated into the DDPG algorithm by incorporating it into the reward function. The reward function serves as a critical component in reinforcement learning algorithms, providing feedback to the agent based on its actions in the environment. In this case, the fuzzy logic system is used to define the reward values based on the inputs obtained from the environment. These inputs can include various factors such as proximity to obstacles, speed, and other relevant information. The fuzzy logic system processes these inputs and generates a reward value that captures the desirability or undesirability of the agent's actions.

2.2 Constructing DDPG Agent

Similar to Actor–Critic, the DDPG algorithm comprises two primary networks known as the Actor-networks and Critic-networks [38]. The Actor network produces a determined action defined by $a = \mu (s, a |\theta^u)$. The network responsible for generating real-time actions is represented as $\mu\theta(s)$. Through updates to the parameter denoted by θ^μ, it generates action A based on the current state described by st and engages with the environment to produce the next state, s_{t+1} and next reward, r_{t+1}. The Actor target network updates parameters within the Critic network and determines the subsequent best action, at + 1 based on the next state, s_{t+1} sampled from the experience replay [38].

HYBRID SYSTEM ARCHITECTURE OF DDPG AND FUZZY LOGIC

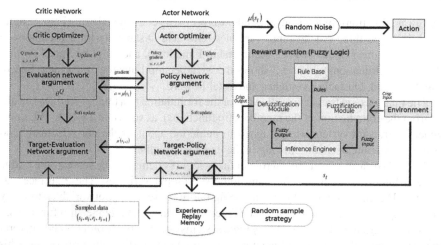

Fig. 1. Environment Interface which responsible to take the action, give the observation and reward signals.

The primary objective of the critic network in the DDPG algorithm is to approximate the $Q(s, a |\theta^Q)$. To achieve this, the Critic network modifies its parameters, θ^Q and computes two crucial values which are the Q value, $Q(s_t, a_t, \theta^Q)$ and the target Q value defined as $y_i = r + \gamma^{Q'} (st + 1, a^{t+1}, \theta^{Q'})$ [38]. The target Q value involves the Q' component, which is computed by the Critic target network. In this context, the discount factor, γ plays a crucial role, as it determines the weightage given to future rewards. Its value ranges between 0 and 1. In this research, the value used for γ is 0.995. The critic network undergoes a training process to optimize the loss function, L, as depicted in Eq. (1).

$$L = \frac{1}{N} \sum_i (y_i - Q(s_i, a_i | \theta^Q))^2 \tag{1}$$

where y_i is given by Eq. (2).

$$y_i = r(s_i a_i) + \gamma Q'(s_{i+1}, \mu'(s_{i+1} | \theta^{\mu'}) | \theta^{Q'}) \tag{2}$$

The Actor network undergoes an update process via a policy gradient show in Eq. (3).

$$\nabla_{\theta^\mu} J \approx \frac{1}{N} \sum_i \nabla_a Q(s, a | \theta^Q) \Big|_{s=s_i, a=\mu(s_i)} \nabla_{\theta^\mu} \mu(s | \theta^\mu) \Big|_{s_i} \tag{3}$$

whereas, the Target networks are optimized through Eq. (4) and Eq. (5), with $\tau \ll 1$.

$$\theta^{Q'} \leftarrow \tau \theta^Q + (1 - \tau)\theta^{Q'} \tag{4}$$

$$\theta^{\mu'} \leftarrow \tau \theta^\mu + (1 - \tau)\theta^{\mu'} \tag{5}$$

2.3 Constructing Reward Function Using Fuzzy Logic

The reward function employed in this study was primarily constructed using Fuzzy Logic, which involved three crucial input variables: Obstacle Distance (with 5 Membership Functions), Linear Speed (with 5 Membership Functions), and Angular Speed (with 3 Membership Functions). Figure 2 shows the Membership Functions for Linear Speed, Angular Speed, Obstacle Avoidance and Total Reward.

The Fuzzy Logic framework allowed for the formulation of a total of 75 rules (resulting from the combination of the membership functions), as shown in Table 1. This comprehensive reward system was designed to guide the agent's behavior effectively and ensure appropriate decision- making in the given environment.

Control surfaces play a crucial role in fuzzy logic systems as they serve as the bridge between linguistic input variables and linguistic output variables. These surfaces, as shown in Fig. 3, are responsible for mapping the fuzzy sets of input variables to fuzzy sets of output variables, based on a set of predefined rules and membership functions.

By utilizing control surfaces, fuzzy logic systems can effectively process and interpret linguistic input information and generate appropriate linguistic output responses. This enables the system to handle imprecise, uncertain, or qualitative data and make intelligent decisions based on human-like reasoning. Thus, control surfaces in fuzzy logic form a fundamental component that facilitates the transformation of linguistic information into actionable control actions, making them essential for a wide range of applications in decision-making, control systems, and artificial intelligence domains.

Table 1. Rules table for reward function using three main input variables.

OD	AS	LS VL	LS L	LS M	LS H	LS VH
VNR	L	P	P	P	G	G
	M	P	P	P	P	G
	H	VP	VP	VP	VP	G
NR	L	G	G	G	G	G
	M	P	P	P	P	E
	H	VG	VG	VG	VG	E
M	L	VG	VG	VG	VG	E
	M	G	G	G	VG	E
	H	P	G	G	G	VG
F	L	E	VE	VE	VE	VE
	M	VG	E	E	E	E
	H	VG	E	E	E	VE
VF	L	A	A	A	A	A
	M	VE	VE	A	A	A
	H	VE	VE	VE	VE	VE

OD: Obstacle Avoidance
MF: Very Near (VNR), Near (NR), Medium (M), Far (F), Very Far (VF)

AS: Angular Speed
MF: Low (L), Medium (M), High (H)

LS: Linear Speed
MF: Very Low (VL), Low (L), Medium (M), High (H), Very High (VH)

Total Rewards (Grey Box)
MF: Very Poor (VP), Poor (P), Good (G), Very Good (VG), Excellent (E), Very Excellent (VE), Amazing (A)

INPUT 1: LINEAR SPEED		
Range [0 0.3] m/s		
Name	Type	Parameters (m/s)
Very Low	Triangular	[0 0 0.075]
Low	Triangular	[0 0.075 0.15]
Medium	Triangular	[0.075 0.15 0.225]
High	Triangular	[0.15 0.225 0.3]
Very High	Triangular	[0.225 0.3 0.3]

(a)

INPUT 2: ANGULAR SPEED		
Range [-0.3 0.3] rad/s		
Name	Type	Parameters (rad/s)
Low	Triangular	[-0.3 -0.3 0]
Medium	Triangular	[-0.3 0 0.3]
High	Triangular	[0 0.3 0.3]

(b)

INPUT 3: OBSTACLE AVOIDANCE		
Range [0 15] m		
Name	Type	Parameters (m)
Very Near	Triangular	[0 0 4]
Near	Triangular	[0 4 8]
Moderate	Triangular	[4 8 12]
Far	Triangular	[8 12 15]
Very Far	Triangular	[12 15 15]

(c)

OUTPUT: TOTAL REWARD		
Range [0 0.6]		
Name	Type	Parameters
Very Poor	Triangular	[0 0 0.1]
Poor	Triangular	[0 0.1 0.2]
Good	Triangular	[0.1 0.2 0.3]
Very Good	Triangular	[0.2 0.3 0.4]
Excellent	Triangular	[0.3 0.4 0.5]
Very Excellent	Triangular	[0.4 0.5 0.6]
Amazing	Triangular	[0.5 0.6 0.6]

(d)

Fig. 2. The membership Functions for (a) Linear Speed. (b) Angular Speed. (c) Obstacle Avoidance. (d) Total Reward.

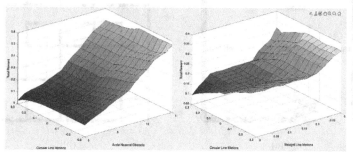

Fig. 3. Control Surface between two input variables. Obstacle Distance & Angular Speed (Left), Obstacle Distance & Linear Speed.

2.4 Agents' Training

To effectively train agents, it is crucial to determine the appropriate training options. In this study, the agent undergoes training for a maximum of 6000 episodes, with each episode limited to a certain number of time steps. The Episode Manager dialog box in breakdown of the agent's performance at each step. Adjustable hyperparameters such as the maximum number of episodes, maxSteps, and stopping criteria are dependent on the specific task and available resources. The Reinforcement Learning Episode Manager dialog box facilitates the visual assessment of the agent's performance, while the command line display provides a comprehensive analysis that aids in understanding the agent's behavior and interpreting the results. The environment of the whole training can be seen in Fig. 4. The significance of training and testing an agent in different environments lies in evaluating the robustness and adaptability of the trained model.

The initial simulation employed the DDPG algorithm, focusing on training and testing an agent in a simple environment named "simplemap." This environment was basic, with few obstacles. In contrast, the current simulation pushed the agent into a more intricate setting, such as "complexMap" and "officeMap" replicating a real office environment via lidar scans. The goal was to evaluate the agent's adaptability to novel environments.

Understanding DDPG's traits in this experiment is crucial. This algorithm aims to optimize return by approximating the Q-function and policy using neural networks: critic and actor networks. The capacity of these networks significantly impacts the agent's adaptability. Notably, DDPG excels in scenarios with continuous action spaces.

The latest simulation showcased the agent's proficiency in navigating a new environment using the same trained model, emphasizing DDPG's adaptability, as evident in Fig. 4. This hints that DDPG has learned a policy effective not only in the simplemap but also in more complex settings. It's noteworthy that the DDPG algorithm, designed for continuous action spaces, hinges on the capabilities of its neural networks: the critic and actor networks, pivotal for its generalization ability.

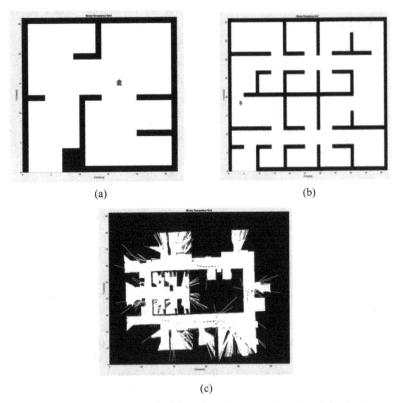

(a)   (b)

(c)

Fig. 4. Snapshots of collision-free trajectories of mobile robots based on the trained agents using (a) simple map. (b) complex map. (c) office map.

3   Experiments and Results

3.1   DDPG Agent Training Results

As shown in Fig. 5, the observed rise in average reward per episode demonstrates the successful learning of the agent using the DDPG algorithm. This improvement in reward, both on a per-episode basis and when considering the average across all episodes, indicates the agent's enhanced decision- making capabilities as it accumulates more experience. This progress aligns with the fundamental objective of reinforcement learning, emphasizing the effectiveness of the DDPG algorithm in maximizing cumulative rewards over time by enabling the agent to refine its decision-making through experiential learning.

3.2   Mobile Robot Simulation Results

In the obstacle avoidance simulation for a mobile robot, the rewards and penalties were carefully designed to guide the robot's navigation. Rewards were assigned for achieving objectives, such as avoiding the nearest obstacle or moving in a straight line, while penalties were imposed for undesirable actions like circular movements. The DDPG algorithm aims to maximize the expected return, which is the cumulative sum of rewards while minimizing penalties. The agent's behavior is encouraged to avoid obstacles, maintain linear velocity, and avoid circular motions.

It is important to consider that the reward and penalty scheme was tailored to the specific task and environment of the simulation and may require adjustments for different scenarios. Nonetheless, the simulation demonstrates the effectiveness of the DDPG algorithm in learning an effective obstacle avoidance policy within the given environment for both maps.

Evaluating the performance of an agent navigating an environment involves key characteristics such as the success rate, representing the agent's proficiency in obstacle avoidance. A higher success rate indicates superior performance. Additionally, the average path length, reflecting the mean distance covered in successful navigation, and the average execution time, indicating the mean duration for completion, are crucial metrics. Higher values for average path length and execution time are desirable, signaling the agent's ability to cover more distance and sustain collision-free movement over extended periods. These characteristics collectively provide a concise yet comprehensive evaluation of the agent's efficiency and effectiveness in navigation and obstacle avoidance.

4   Discussions

4.1   Overall Reward for DDPG Training

The increase in average reward per episode as shown in Fig. 5 can be attributed to two key factors in the DDPG algorithm. Firstly, the actor network learns an improved policy by adjusting its parameters to select actions that lead to higher rewards. This process, known as policy gradient, enables the agent to make better decisions over time. Secondly, the critic network learns a more accurate value function by adjusting its parameters to estimate the expected cumulative reward of state-action pairs. This process, known as Q-learning, enhances the agent's ability to assess the value of actions. The successful learning of both the actor and critic networks contributes to the observed rise in average reward per episode, showcasing the effectiveness of the DDPG algorithm in optimizing decision-making and overall performance.

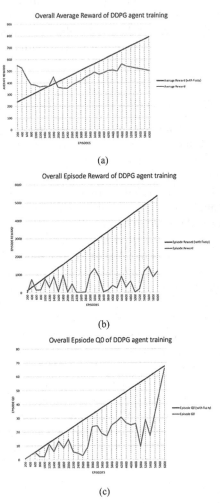

(a)

(b)

(c)

Fig. 5. 6000 navigation tasks are generated in each testing environment (**a**) Average reward represents the average reward over multiple episodes. (**b**) Episode Reward reflects the reward obtained during a single episode (**c**) Episode Q0 represents the estimate of the discounted long-term reward at the beginning of each episode, based on the initial observation of the environment.

4.2 Mobile Robot Simulation Performance

In the initial mobile robot simulation, the DDPG algorithm was employed to train and test an agent in a simplified environment called Simple Map and Complex Map. This environment had minimal obstacles and flat terrain. In contrast, the current simulation introduced the agent to a more realistic and complex environment called Office Map (Fig. 6), generated from lidar scans of a real-world office setting. This extension aimed to assess the algorithm's ability to generalize to unfamiliar environments. The results, depicted in Fig. 6 using the same trained model, demonstrate the DDPG algorithm's capacity for generalization as the agent successfully navigated the new environment. This suggests that the algorithm has learned a policy that is effective in both simplified and realistic environments.

The use of fuzzy logic within the neuro-symbolic approach has notably surpassed the initial method (non-fuzzy) reliant on fixed values. Quantitative analysis showcases a substantial enhancement in obstacle avoidance efficiency. The incorporation of multiple input variables—such as obstacle distance, linear, and angular speeds—within the fuzzy logic system enables a more intricate decision-making process. This approach capitalizes on fuzzy logic's capacity to manage imprecise data, effectively capturing complex interrelationships between variables to generate refined and adaptable actions.

When navigating narrow passages, the neuro-symbolic approach employing fuzzy logic outperforms the fixed values approach. The system's sensitivity to obstacle proximity allows the mobile robot to detect and respond more effectively to tight spaces. Leveraging membership functions and fuzzy inference, this approach finely adjusts the robot's actions, adeptly maneuvering obstacles in confined areas while maintaining safety. Such precision results in smoother and more dependable navigation within constrained environments.

Additionally, the neuro-symbolic approach utilizing fuzzy logic showcases heightened caution in handling obstacles. Employing membership functions and rule-based reasoning enables the system to assess potential risks associated with varying levels of obstacle proximity. With a broader range of input values and membership functions, the system offers a detailed evaluation of the environment, ensuring the robot maintains a safe distance, reducing collision risks, and enhancing overall safety during navigation.

4.3 Implementation of Fuzzy Logic in Reward Function

The integration of fuzzy logic into the reward and penalty system of the Deep Deterministic Policy Gradient (DDPG) algorithm as shown in Fig. 1 bestows an excessive of advantageous traits to mobile robot navigation. This ingenious process endows the system with remarkable adaptability, allowing it to adeptly handle imprecise or uncertain environments. By seamlessly incorporating fuzzy logic into the reward and penalty system, the system becomes resilient, capable of acclimating to diverse environmental conditions, and deftly responding to situations that lack precise numerical values. Consequently, this heightened adaptability amplifies the learning and training process by enabling the robot to glean insights from a wider array of scenarios, making astute decisions based on fuzzy inputs.

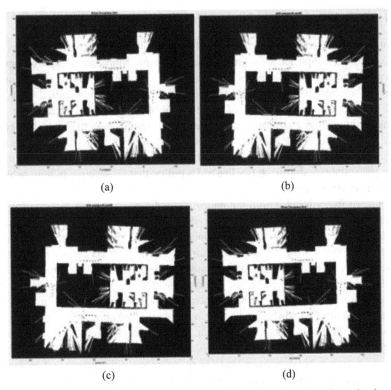

(a)   (b)

(c)   (d)

Fig. 6. Snapshots of collision-free trajectories of mobile robots based on the trained agents in office map at time (a) 15 s. (b) 30 s. (c) 45 s. (d) 60 s.

Another notable advantage of integrating fuzzy logic compared to using constant values approach as shown in Fig. 7, lies in its ability to bestow robustness upon the system, mitigating the deleterious effects of noise, uncertainties, and variations commonly encountered in real- world settings. The inclusion of fuzzy inputs in the reward and penalty system imparts a formidable shield against external disturbances, bolstering the system's fortitude in less controlled and unpredictable environments. Such fortitude enhances the system's ability to learn and navigate with utmost efficacy, regardless of the surrounding uncertainties.

Based on Fig. 7, it shows that by employing Fuzzy Logic in the reward function, yields superior navigation performance, even if it comes at the cost of increased execution time. The incremental time required for processing the Fuzzy Logic-based reward function as our second approach is justified by the substantial improvements achieved in terms of success rates, average path lengths, and the robot's overall ability to navigate through dynamic and unstructured environments.

This approach outperforms the first approach that relies on constant values in terms of quantitative performance metrics and qualitative aspects of adaptability and robustness. The flexibility of the neuro-symbolic approach allows for iterative refinement and optimization of the reward function, resulting in improved navigation capabilities and learning outcomes. The findings emphasize the trade-off between execution time and performance and highlight the value of integrating neuro- symbolic approaches, such as Fuzzy Logic, to enhance the navigation capabilities of mobile robots.

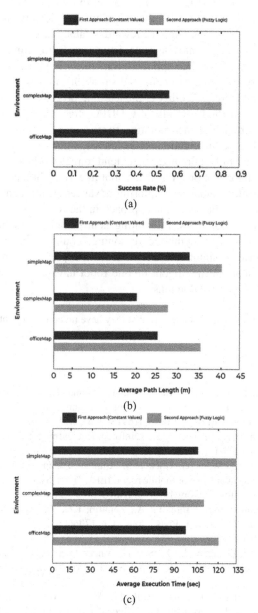

Fig. 7. 6000 navigation tasks are generated in each testing environments. (a) Success rate demonstrates the successful probability to avoid obstacle. (b) Average path demonstrates the mean path lengths for all successful navigation. (c) Average execution time demonstrates the average value of execution time for all successful navigation

5 Conclusion

The successful implementation of the DDPG algorithm in MATLAB and Simulink enabled the simulation of mobile robot navigation in dynamic and unstructured environments. The results demonstrate that the algorithm significantly enhanced the robot's navigation capabilities by maximizing the reward obtained in the simulation. Moreover, the integration of fuzzy logic into the reward function further improved the system's performance and adaptability. The application of fuzzy logic successfully introduced enhanced adaptability, robustness to noise and variability, human-like decision making, smooth transitions, and interpretability to the learning process. This research highlights the potential of DRL methods, specifically DDPG, for mobile robot navigation, and underscores the importance of incorporating fuzzy logic to optimize and validate the performance of DRL-based navigation algorithms in simulation-based studies.

In future work, the study's findings can extend to real-world applications by implementing the DDPG algorithm on a physical robot like TurtleBot, enabling autonomous navigation and obstacle avoidance. Exploring advanced reinforcement learning algorithms and optimizing the Fuzzy Logic approach in the reward system are avenues for improving navigation capabilities. Integrating neuro-symbolic techniques, like combining neural networks with symbolic reasoning, could enhance decision-making. Bridging the gap between simulation and real-world deployment, these advancements aim to develop efficient and intelligent mobile robot navigation systems for practical implementation across diverse domains.

Disclosure Statement. The authors declare that they have no competing interests.

References

1. Lu, X., Woo, H., Faragasso, A., Yamashita, A., Asama, H.: Robot navigation in crowds via deep reinforcement learning with modeling of obstacle uni-action. Adv. Robot. **37**(4), 257–269 (2023). https://doi.org/10.1080/01691864.2022.2142068
2. Shyalika, C., Silva, T., Karunananda, A.: Reinforcement learning in dynamic task scheduling: a review. SN Comput. Sci. **1**(6) (2020). https://doi.org/10.1007/s42979-020-00326-5
3. Gao, X., Yan, L., Li, Z., Wang, G., Chen, I.-M.: Improved deep deterministic policy gradient for dynamic obstacle avoidance of mobile robot. IEEE Trans. Syst. Man, Cybern. Syst. **53**(6), 3675–3682 (2023). https://doi.org/10.1109/TSMC.2022.3230666
4. Bahamid, A., Ibrahim, A.M., Ibrahim, A., Zahurin, I.Z., Wahid, A.N.: Intelligent robot-assisted evacuation: a review. J. Phys. Conf. Ser. **1706**(1) (2020). https://doi.org/10.1088/1742-6596/1706/1/012159
5. Chen, Y., Cheng, C., Zhang, Y., Li, X., Sun, L.: A neural network-based navigation approach for autonomous mobile robot systems. Appl. Sci. **12**(15) (2022). https://doi.org/10.3390/app12157796
6. Romlay, M.R.M., Azhar, M.I., Toha, S.F., Rashid, M.M.: Two-wheel balancing robot; review on control methods and experiments. Int. J. Recent Technol. Eng. **7**(6), 106–112 (2019)
7. Lillicrap, T.P., et al.: Continuous control with deep reinforcement learning. In: 4th International Conference on Learning Representations, ICLR 2016 - Conference Track Proceedings (2016)

8. Lashin, M.M.A., Saleh, W.S.E.S.: Road safety policies for Saudi females: a fuzzy logic analysis. Sustainability **14**(7) (2022). https://doi.org/10.3390/su14074154
9. Çimen, M.E., Garip, Z., Emekli, M., Boz, A.F.: Fuzzy logic PID design using genetic algorithm under overshoot constrained conditions for heat exchanger control. Iğdır Üniversitesi Fen Bilim. Enstitüsü Derg. **12**(1), 164–181 (2022). https://doi.org/10.21597/jist.980726
10. Nguyen, L.A.: Fuzzy simulations and bisimulations between fuzzy automata. Int. J. Approx. Reason. **155**, 113–131 (2023). https://doi.org/10.1016/j.ijar.2023.02.002
11. Wang, Y., Fang, Y., Lou, P., Yan, J., Liu, N.: Deep reinforcement learning based path planning for mobile robot in unknown environment. J. Phys. Conf. Ser. **1576**(1) (2020). https://doi.org/10.1088/1742-6596/1576/1/012009
12. Li, Y., et al.: Prediction model for geologically complicated fault structure based on artificial neural network and fuzzy logic. Sci. Program. **2022** (2022). https://doi.org/10.1155/2022/2630953
13. Ni, J., Wu, L., Fan, X., Yang, S.X.: Bioinspired intelligent algorithm and its applications for mobile robot control: a survey. Comput. Intell. Neurosci. **2016** (2016). https://doi.org/10.1155/2016/3810903
14. Takahashi, O., Schilling, R.J.: Motion planning in a plane using generalized voronoi diagrams. IEEE Trans. Robot. Autom. **5**(2), 143–150 (1989). https://doi.org/10.1109/70.88035
15. Bhattacharya, P., Gavrilova, M.L.: Roadmap-based path planning - using the voronoi diagram for a clearance-based shortest path. IEEE Robot. Autom. Mag. **15**(2), 58–66 (2008). https://doi.org/10.1109/MRA.2008.921540
16. Gómez, E.J., Santa, F.M.M., Sarmiento, F.H.M.: A comparative study of geometric path planning methods for a mobile robot: potential field and voronoi diagrams. In: 2013 II International Congress of Engineering Mechatronics and Automation (CIIMA), pp. 1–6 (2013). https://doi.org/10.1109/CIIMA.2013.6682776
17. Abiyev, R., Ibrahim, D., Erin, B.: Navigation of mobile robots in the presence of obstacles. Adv. Eng. Softw. **41**(10), 1179–1186 (2010). https://doi.org/10.1016/j.advengsoft.2010.08.001
18. Soltani, A.R., Tawfik, H., Goulermas, J.Y., Fernando, T.: Path planning in construction sites: performance evaluation of the Dijkstra, A*, and GA search algorithms. Adv. Eng. Inform. **16**(4), 291–303 (2002). https://doi.org/10.1016/S1474-0346(03)00018-1
19. Masehian, E., Amin-Naseri, M.R.: A voronoi diagram-visibility graph-potencial field compound algorith for robot path planning. J. Robot. Syst. **21**(6), 275–300 (2004). https://doi.org/10.1002/rob.20014
20. Weigl, M., Siemiáatkowska, B., Sikorski, K.A., Borkowski, A.: Grid-based mapping for autonomous mobile robot. Rob. Auton. Syst. **11**(1), 13–21 (1993). https://doi.org/10.1016/0921-8890(93)90004-V
21. Ghorbani, A., Shiry, S., Nodehi, A.: Using genetic algorithm for a mobile robot path planning. In: 2009 International Conference on Future Computer and Communication, pp. 164–166 (2009). https://doi.org/10.1109/ICFCC.2009.28
22. Ahmadzadeh, S., Ghanavati, M.: Navigation of mobile robot using the PSO particle swarm optimization. J. Acad. Appl. Stud. **2** (2012). https://api.semanticscholar.org/CorpusID:18077178
23. Zhu, K., Zhang, T.: Deep reinforcement learning based mobile robot navigation: a review. Tsinghua Sci. Technol. **26**(5), 674–691 (2021). https://doi.org/10.26599/TST.2021.9010012
24. Hu, H., Zhang, K., Tan, A.H., Ruan, M., Agia, C., Nejat, G.: A sim-to-real pipeline for deep reinforcement learning for autonomous robot navigation in cluttered rough terrain. IEEE Robot. Autom. Lett. **6**(4), 6569–6576 (2021). https://doi.org/10.1109/LRA.2021.3093551
25. Liu, B., Wang, L., Liu, M.: Lifelong federated reinforcement learning: a learning architecture for navigation in cloud robotic systems. IEEE Robot. Autom. Lett. **4**(4), 4555–4562 (2019). https://doi.org/10.1109/LRA.2019.2931179

26. Algabri, M.: Self-learning Mobile Robot Navigation in Unknown Environment Using Evolutionary Learning, vol. 20, no. 10, pp. 1459–1468 (2014)

27. Yusuf, S.H.: Mobile Robot Navigation Using Deep Reinforcement Learning (2022)

28. Fathinezhad, F., Derhami, V., Rezaeian, M.: Supervised fuzzy reinforcement learning for robot navigation. Appl. Soft Comput. **40**, 33–41 (2016). https://doi.org/10.1016/j.asoc.2015.11.030

29. Ciou, P.-H., Hsiao, Y.-T., Wu, Z.-Z., Tseng, S.-H., Fu, L.-C.: Composite reinforcement learning for social robot navigation. In: 2018 IEEE/RSJ International Conference on Intelligent Robots and Systems (IROS), pp. 2553–2558 (2018). https://doi.org/10.1109/IROS.2018.8593410

30. Bernstein, A.V., Burnaev, E.V., Kachan, O.N.: Reinforcement learning for computer vision and robot navigation. In: Perner, P. (eds.) Machine Learning and Data Mining in Pattern Recognition. MLDM 2018. LNCS, vol. 10935, pp. 258–272. Springer, Cham (2018). https://doi.org/10.1007/978-3-319-96133-0_20

31. Hase, H., et al.: Ultrasound-guided robotic navigation with deep reinforcement learning. In: 2020 IEEE/RSJ International Conference on Intelligent Robots and Systems (IROS), pp. 5534–5541 (2020). https://doi.org/10.1109/IROS45743.2020.9340913

32. Liu, L., Dugas, D., Cesari, G., Siegwart, R., Dubé, R.: Robot navigation in crowded environments using deep reinforcement learning. In: 2020 IEEE/RSJ International Conference on Intelligent Robots and Systems (IROS), pp. 5671–5677 (2020). https://doi.org/10.1109/IROS45743.2020.9341540

33. Chen, G., et al.: Robot Navigation with Map-Based Deep Reinforcement Learning, February 2020. http://arxiv.org/abs/2002.04349

34. Sun, S., Zhao, X., Li, Q., Tan, M.: Inverse reinforcement learning-based time-dependent A* planner for human-aware robot navigation with local vision. Adv. Robot. **34**(13), 888–901 (2020). https://doi.org/10.1080/01691864.2020.1753569

35. Bruce, J., Sünderhauf, N., Mirowski, P.: One-Shot Reinforcement Learning for Robot Navigation with Interactive Replay, no. Nips, 2017

36. Su, M.-C., Huang, D.-Y., Chou, C.-H., Hsieh, C.-C.: A reinforcement-learning approach to robot navigation. In: IEEE International Conference on Networking, Sensing and Control, 2004, vol. 1, pp. 665–669 (2004). https://doi.org/10.1109/ICNSC.2004.1297519

37. Dong, Y., Zou, X.: Mobile robot path planning based on improved DDPG reinforcement learning algorithm. In: 2020 IEEE 11th International Conference on Software Engineering and Service Science (ICSESS), pp. 52–56 (2020). https://doi.org/10.1109/ICSESS49938.2020.9237641

38. Chen, Y., Liang, L.: SLP-improved DDPG path-planning algorithm for mobile robot in large-scale dynamic environment. Sensors **23**(7), 3521 (2023)

DAFDeTr: Deformable Attention Fusion Based 3D Detection Transformer

Gopi Krishna Erabati[(✉)] and Helder Araujo

Institute of Systems and Robotics, University of Coimbra, 3030-290 Coimbra, Portugal
{gopi.erabati,helder}@isr.uc.pt

Abstract. Existing approaches fuse the LiDAR points and image pixels by hard association relying on highly accurate calibration matrices. We propose Deformable Attention Fusion based 3D Detection Transformer (DAFDeTr) to attentively and adaptively fuse the image features to the LiDAR features with soft association using deformable attention mechanism. Specifically, our detection head consists of two decoders for sequential fusion: LiDAR and image decoder powered by deformable cross-attention to link the multi-modal features to the 3D object predictions leveraging a sparse set of object queries. The refined object queries from the LiDAR decoder attentively fuse with the corresponding and required image features establishing a soft association, thereby making our model robust for any camera malfunction. We conduct extensive experiments and analysis on nuScenes and Waymo datasets. Our DAFDeTr-L achieves 63.4 mAP and outperforms well established networks on the nuScenes dataset and obtains competitive performance on the Waymo dataset. Our fusion model DAFDeTr achieves 64.6 mAP on the nuScenes dataset. We also extend our model to the 3D tracking task and our model outperforms state-of-the-art methods on 3D tracking.

Keywords: 3D Object detection · Transformer · Attention · LiDAR · Fusion

1 Introduction

Perception tasks play a significant role in an autonomous system, specifically in autonomous driving scenarios. 3D object detection is one of the most crucial perception task in autonomous driving as it provides location, size, orientation and category of objects. LiDAR and camera are two crucial sensors in autonomous driving. LiDAR provides accurate depth information but it is difficult to detect distant objects due to sparse nature of point clouds. On the other hand, camera provides dense information of the scene to detect small/distant objects but it does not provide the depth information and it is very sensitive to illumination effects. We can fuse the LiDAR and camera data to develop a multi-modal 3D object detector leveraging the complementary nature of both the sensor modalities.

Earlier approaches [38,39] find the hard association between LiDAR points and image pixels to augment LiDAR points with the associated image features by concatenation. The main problem with fusion approaches using hard association is that they rely on the accuracy of the calibration matrices of two sensors and many of the dense

© The Author(s), under exclusive license to Springer Nature Switzerland AG 2024
J. Filipe and J. Röning (Eds.): ROBOVIS 2024, CCIS 2077, pp. 293–315, 2024.
https://doi.org/10.1007/978-3-031-59057-3_19

image features are wasted due to hard association of sparse LiDAR points. Motivated by [1], we design a multi-modal sequential fusion approach with soft association of LiDAR and image data.

Our Deformable Attention Fusion based 3D Detection Transformer (DAFDeTr) is an end-to-end, single-stage and NMS-free 3D object detector which inputs LiDAR point cloud and multi-view images to predict 3D bounding boxes. The sequential fusion detection head in our approach consists of two decoders: LiDAR and image decoder. Similar to [1], we employ input-dependent and category-aware object queries so that the object queries better represent potential object candidates not only during training but also during inference. The LiDAR decoder employs multi-scale deformable cross-attention [50] to link the LiDAR features to the 3D object predictions leveraging the object queries. The deformable image cross-attention in image decoder attentively fuses LiDAR and image data by adaptively and efficiently linking the useful multi-view image features to the 3D object predictions leveraging the refined object queries from the LiDAR decoder. The refined object queries are finally transformed into 3D object parameters for LiDAR-only and LiDAR-camera fusion model. The network is trained end-to-end using set-to-set loss [3] to formulate 3D object detection as a direct set pre-diction problem to avoid post-processing steps like non-maximum suppression (NMS).

The vanilla cross-attention [37] in [1] attends all possible spatial locations of the multi-modal input features which increases the computational complexity. To reduce the computational complexity we can think of a sparse attention mechanism where each object query only attends certain learnt useful spatial locations which are relevant to the corresponding query. To achieve this, we employ deformable attention mechanism [50] that attends only a small set of key sampling points around a reference point (for each object query) on the multi-modal input features.

We conduct extensive experiments on publicly available autonomous driving datasets: nuScenes [2] and Waymo [34]. Our DAFDeTr-L (LiDAR-only) achieves 63.4 mAP and 69.1 NDS on the nuScenes dataset surpassing the established networks like CenterPoint [45] by 5.4 mAP, Object-DGCNN [42] by 4.7 mAP, Li3DeTr [11] by 2.1 mAP and VISTA-OHS [10] by 0.4 mAP. Our network DAFDeTr-L surpasses SEC-OND [43], PointPillars [18], VoTr-SSD [23] and achieves competitive performance on Waymo dataset. Compared to TransFusion [1], our DAFDeTr-L model achieves around 23% increase in inference speed at a cost of 3% (2.1 mAP) drop in performance. Our LiDAR-camera fusion model DAFDeTr achieves 64.6 mAP and 69.3 NDS on the nuScenes dataset. Our DAFDeTr network achieves 69.0 AMOTA on the nuScenes dataset for 3D tracking task and surpasses the existing approaches.

We summarize our main contributions as follows:

- We fuse the multi-modal features using a soft-association leveraging the image cross-attention (ICA) mechanism. In order to reduce the computational cost of the attention mechanism, we employ deformable attention [50] in LiDAR and image decoders.
- The soft-association and sequential method of fusion is robust to different weather scenarios (Table 9) and camera malfunction (Table 10).
- We conduct comprehensive experiments and analysis on the nuScenes [2] and Waymo [34] datasets. We also extend our approach to 3D tracking-by-detection and surpasses well established methods in 3D tracking task.

2 Related Work

2.1 LiDAR-Only Approaches

Due to the sparse and unordered nature of point clouds the 2D CNN-based object detectors [21,30,36] can not be directly applied to LiDAR point clouds. The LiDAR-only approaches can be classified into three types depending on the representation of data: point-type, grid-type and point-voxel hybrid approaches. Earlier approaches [27,32,44] directly operate on point clouds using multi-scale set abstraction [28,29]. The methods which directly operate on point clouds are generally computationally expensive due to large number of points. Many approaches project the point cloud into a grid-like structure such as voxels [11,42,45,48], pillars [18,40] or range images [12,35]. VoxelNet [48] discretizes the point cloud into 3D voxels and employ 3D convolutions to extract voxel features. SECOND [43] extracts voxel features by employing 3D sparse convolutions [13] as vanilla 3D convolutions are computationally expensive. In [45] the height feature of the 3D voxels is flattened to transform 3D voxels into a 2D grid-like LiDAR BEV features. In our work, we employ a voxel-based 3D sparse convolutional backbone and transform the voxel features to grid-like LiDAR BEV features and sent them to the decoder.

2.2 Multi-modal Approaches

Due to the complementary nature of LiDAR and camera data, many approaches are built upon the fusion of multi-modal LiDAR and camera input data. Depending on the level at which the multi-modal features are fused, the fusion methods are classified into three types: early-level, proposal-level and output-level fusion. Early-level fusion methods [38,39] involve the fusion of points and image features by a hard association of both the modalities leveraging the calibration matrices. PointPainitng [38] augments the points with the corresponding image semantic features extracted by the 2D segmentation network. In [39], instead of the semantic features deep image features extracted by 2D object detection network are used to augment the points. However, the main problems of these approaches are: 1) The hard association heavily relies on the accuracy of calibration matrices, 2) As the LiDAR points are sparse, many dense image features are left unused, 3) The point-wise concatenation of image features does not represent accurate contextual relationships between both the modalities, and 4) The accuracy of such models depends on the accuracy of pretrained 2D segmentation and detection approaches which are used to extract features to decorate the points. MV3D [7] and AVOD [16] are proposal-level (mid-level) fusion approaches where the corresponding LiDAR and camera features are fused for different shared proposals using RoIAlign [31] for each modality. In output-level fusion approaches [27,33], 2D object detection/segmentation network is used to locate the potential objects in the image space and then lift the proposals to a 3D frustum and employ [28] for 3D object detection. The main drawback of such approaches is that they heavily rely on off-the-shelf 2D detection/segmentation approaches for initial potential proposals. In our approach we formulate a soft association between multi-modal features leveraging the deformable cross-attention mechanism making the model robust to different weather scenarios and camera malfunction.

3   Methodology

Our DAFDeTr network inputs LiDAR point cloud and multi-view RGB images to output 3D bounding box predictions for different object categories in an autonomous driving scenario, as shown in Fig. 1. It mainly consists of backbone modules for multi-modal feature extraction, LiDAR encoder, query initialization, LiDAR decoder and image decoder modules as detailed below.

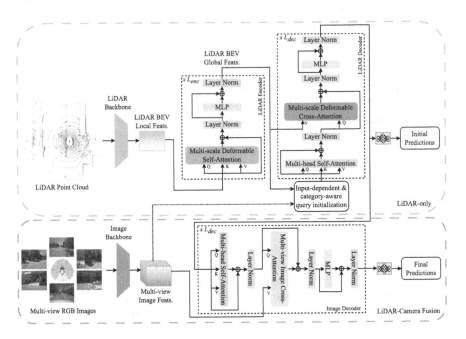

Fig. 1. An overview of DAFDeTr architecture. It consists of backbones (Sect. 3.1) for multi-modal feature extraction, LiDAR encoder (Sect. 3.2), query initialization (Sect. 3.3) and detection head with two decoders for sequential fusion: LiDAR decoder (Sect. 3.4) and image decoder (Sect. 3.5). The sequential fusion of LiDAR and image data by the deformable cross-attention mechanism provides a soft association of both the modalities making it robust for camera malfunction.

3.1   Backbones

LiDAR Backbone. We employ VoxelNet [48] to obtain LiDAR BEV local features. Specifically, we voxelize the point cloud with [0.075, 0.075, 0.2] m voxel size and employ 3D sparse convolutions [13] to obtain voxel features. The sparse voxel features are projected to BEV grid and SECOND [43] feature extraction network is employed to extract BEV features. Finally, a FPN [20] is employed to obtain multi-scale LiDAR BEV local features.

Image Backbone. We employ a shared VoVNetV2-99 [19] to extract multi-view multi-scale image features. The image features are further enhanced by a FPN [20] to obtain semantically strong multi-view image features.

3.2   LiDAR Encoder

The 3D sparse convolutions in the LiDAR backbone are capable of obtaining local voxel features. In order to obtain the LiDAR BEV global features we employ attention mechanism to capture the long range dependencies between BEV features. As the vanilla attention [37] mechanism leads to very high computational complexities to capture long range dependencies in high resolution feature maps, we employ multi-scale deformable attention [50] to encode the LiDAR BEV local features. The LiDAR encoder inputs multi-scale local BEV feature maps and outputs encoded global BEV feature maps with the same resolution. The computational complexity of deformable attention is lower than vanilla attention because the former only attends a small set of key sampling points around a reference point. The LiDAR encoder consists of multi-scale deformable self-attention and MLP blocks with skip connections and is repeated L_{enc} times. The LiDAR BEV global features are passed to cross-attention module in the LiDAR decoder.

3.3   Query Initialization

In earlier approaches [11,41,42] the object queries are learnt during the training and are static for different inputs during inference. Following [1], we obtain input-dependent and category-aware object queries which provides potential object candidates not only during training but also during inference. Given the LiDAR BEV global feature map $\mathcal{F}_{bev} \in \mathbb{R}^{X \times Y \times C}$, we predict category-specific heatmap $\mathcal{H}_{bev} \in \mathbb{R}^{X \times Y \times k}$, where $X \times Y$ is the dimension of the BEV feature map and k is the number of classes. We select the top-N_q (number of queries) candidates as the initial object queries. The positions and features of the selected queries are used to initialize the object query positions and object query features. In order to make the object queries category-aware, we add the query feature with a category embedding vector obtained by transforming one-hot category vector into a $\mathbb{R}^C$ vector.

In the LiDAR-camera fusion model, we also use the multi-view image features along with LiDAR features for query initialization. Specifically, the LiDAR-camera BEV feature map $\mathcal{F}_{bev}^{img}$ is generated by projecting the multi-view image features $\{\mathcal{F}_i^{img}\}_{i=1}^{6}$ onto the BEV plane through the cross-attention with LiDAR BEV features $\mathcal{F}_{bev}$. The multi-view image features are collapsed along the height axis and used as key-value pair for attention mechanism similar to [1]. The LiDAR-camera BEV feature map $\mathcal{F}_{bev}^{img}$ is used to predict category-specific heatmap $\mathcal{H}^{img}$ similar to $\mathcal{H}_{bev}$. The final heat map $\mathcal{H}_{bev}^{img}$ is obtained by mean of the two heatmaps and is used to obtain the final object query features and query positions.

3.4   LiDAR Decoder

The LiDAR decoder transforms the LiDAR BEV global features into initial predictions leveraging the initialized object queries. The LiDAR decoder inputs a set of object queries $\{q_i^l\}_{i=1}^{N_q} \in \mathbb{R}^C$ (where $l \in \{1, 2, \ldots, L_{dec}\}$, N_q is number of queries) and LiDAR BEV global features $\mathcal{F}_{bev}$ and it consists of L_{dec} number of decoder layers to refine the object queries.

Each decoder layer consists of multi-head self-attention block, multi-scale deformable cross-attention block and MLP block with the skip connections as shown in Fig. 1. The multi-head self-attention block reasons the interaction of different objects candidates with each other. The query positions are transformed into a latent vector using an MLP layer and added element-wise to the query features to reason jointly about context and position. The multi-scale deformable cross-attention block links the LiDAR BEV global features to the box predictions leveraging the object queries.

Instead of employing vanilla attention as in [1], we employ deformable attention to formulate the cross-attention mechanism to reduce the computational complexity of the network. The vanilla attention mechanism attends all possible spatial locations on the LiDAR BEV feature map for each object query which increases the computational complexity. It is reasonable if each object query attends only the regions of feature map that are relevant to the respective object query to reduce the computational complexity. In order to achieve this, we employ deformable cross-attention mechanism [50] which attends only a small set of key sampling points on LiDAR BEV feature map for each object query rather than all possible spatial locations.

Let the object query feature be q_f, it's respective query position be q_p and LiDAR BEV global multi-scale feature maps $\mathcal{F}_{bev} = \{\mathcal{F}_{bev}^j\}_{j=1}^4$, where $\mathcal{F}_{bev}^j \in \mathbb{R}^{H \times W \times C}$. The query position q_p is treated as reference point for it's respective query feature and $\hat{q}_p \in [0,1]^2$ be the normalized coordinates of the reference point. The multi-scale deformable cross-attention is applied as

$$\text{MSDeformCrossAttn}(q_f, \hat{q}_p, \{\mathcal{F}_{bev}^j\}_{j=1}^4)$$
$$= \sum_{m=1}^M W_m [\sum_{j=1}^4 \sum_{k=1}^K A_{mjk} W_m' \mathcal{F}_{bev}^j (\phi(\hat{q}_p) + \Delta p_{mjk})] \quad (1)$$

where, m indexes the attention head, j indexes the LiDAR BEV feature level, k indexes the sampling point and K is the total number of key sampling points. Δp_{mjk} and A_{mjk} are sampling offset and attention weights respectively for m-th head, j-th feature level and k-th sampling point. Both Δp_{mjk} and A_{mjk} are obtained by linear transformation of the query feature q_f. W_m and W_m' are learnable weights. The function $\phi(\hat{q}_p)$ re-scales the normalized coordinates of reference point $\hat{q}_p$ to the input feature map of the j-th level. We compute the loss from the predictions of each decoder layer but we only use the predictions of last decoder layer during inference.

The object queries are decoded into box parameters and class labels using an MLP layer. The MLP layer for each decoder layer l predicts the center offset from object query position as $\delta q_p^l = (\delta x^l, \delta y^l)$, box height z^l, box size (l^l, w^l, h^l), box orientation $(\sin \alpha^l, \cos \alpha^l)$, box velocity (v_x^l, v_y^l) and class label $\hat{y}^l$ for each object query q^l.

We refine the query position for each query of each decoder layer by using the center offset predictions of the previous decoder layer as,

$$q_p^{l+1} = q_p^l + \delta q_p^l \quad (2)$$

The refined object queries along with the initial predictions from the LiDAR decoder are leveraged for the LiDAR-camera fusion in the image decoder, as explained in next section.

3.5 Image Decoder

The image decoder is designed similar to the LiDAR decoder except for the cross-attention block, where the object queries need to attend multi-view image features to aggregate relevant context information. The image decoder transforms the multi-view image features into the final predictions leveraging the refined object queries and initial predictions from the LiDAR decoder. The image decoder inputs the refined object queries from the LiDAR decoder, multi-view image feature maps $\{\mathcal{F}_{img}^v\}_{v=1}^6$ and it consists of L_{dec} number of decoder layers to refine the object queries. Similar to LiDAR decoder it consists of multi-head self-attention block, multi-view image cross-attention block and MLP block with the skip connections as shown in Fig. 1.

The computational complexity of vanilla multi-head cross-attention [37] is extremely high due to large dimensions of multi-scale multi-view image feature maps. To tackle this issue, we adapt the 2D deformable attention [50] to perform the resource-efficient multi-view image cross-attention (ICA) between object queries and multi-view image features, where each object query only attends its corresponding useful regions across camera views. The image cross-attention in the image decoder performs the LiDAR-camera feature fusion in a sparse-to-sparse manner by building a soft association between LiDAR and camera images. The soft association by image cross-attention enables the network to adaptively focus on where the information should be taken from the multi-view images.

We can apply the image cross-attention using Eq. (1) by specifically making two changes to adapt for multi-view image features. 1) The query positions (q_p) which are treated as reference points for deformable attention are in LiDAR BEV space, so we need to project the query positions to image space using camera matrices. 2) As the image features are from different camera views, we need to know which camera views are valid for each object query.

Let the object query position in LiDAR BEV space be $q_p = (x, y)$. The real world coordinates (X, Y) of q_p are given as:

$$(X, Y) = (x, y) \times \text{stride} \times \text{voxel size} \qquad (3)$$

where stride is the feature map stride of LiDAR BEV feature map and voxel size is the size of resolution of BEV grid. The 3D reference point of each object query in world coordinate system is (X, Y, Z), where Z is the height of the respective object query as predicted by initial prediction using LiDAR-only model. We project the 3D point of each object query onto multi-view image feature maps using the camera projection matrices of different cameras as:

$$f(q_p, v) = (x_v, y_v, 1) \simeq R_v \left[X\ Y\ Z\ 1 \right]^T \qquad (4)$$

where $f(q_p, v)$ is the projection function of object query (q_p) onto the v-th view which results in a 2D point (x_v, y_v), $R_v \in \mathbb{R}^{3 \times 4}$ is the camera projection matrix for v-th view.

Here, for each object query, the projected 2D points on multi-view images fall only in some views and does not fall in other views. We term the views onto which the projected 2D points fall as *valid* views $(\mathcal{V}_{val})$. The valid 2D projected points on the valid views are treated as reference points and corresponding image features are sampled around these reference points using Eq. (1). Finally, we average the sampled features across all *valid* views to get the final image cross-attention (ICA) result, as:

$$
\begin{aligned}
&\mathrm{ICA}(q_f, q_p, \{\mathcal{F}_{img}^v\}_{v=1}^6) \\
&\qquad = \frac{1}{|\mathcal{V}_{val}|} \sum_{v \in \mathcal{V}_{val}} \mathrm{MSDeformCrossAttn}(q_f, f(q_p, v), \mathcal{F}_{img}^v) \quad (5)
\end{aligned}
$$

3.6 Loss

We follow set-to-set loss [3] by finding the bipartite matching between the ground truth objects and 3D object predictions through the Hungarian algorithm [17]. The matching cost is the weighted sum of classification cost (Focal loss), regression cost (L1 loss) and 3D IoU cost. After obtaining one-to-one matching between predictions and ground truth, we compute the total loss between the matched pairs. The total loss is the sum of classification loss (Focal loss), regression loss (L1 loss) and heatmap loss (Gaussian Focal loss [45]).

4 Experiments

We evaluate our network DAFDeTr on autonomous driving datasets: nuScenes [2] and Waymo Open Dataset [34]. In this section, we provide the implementation details, present the results, analysis and ablation studies.

4.1 Implementation Details

nuScenes Dataset. There are 28K, 6K and 6K samples for training, validation and testing respectively. Each sample consists of LiDAR point cloud and RGB camera images from 6 different views [front, back, front_left, back_left, front_right, back_right]. The detection metrics are computed for 10 different object categories. We follow the official evaluation protocol to compute two main metrics, mean average precision (mAP) and nuScenes Detection Score (NDS), in addition to true positive metrics such as, average translation error (ATE), average scale error (ASE), average orientation error (AOE), average velocity error (AVE), average attribute error (AAE).

Waymo Dataset. There are 798 and 202 scenes each of 20 s duration for training and validation respectively. Each sample in the dataset consists of LiDAR point cloud and RGB camera images from 5 different views [front, front_right, `front_left, side_right, side_left`. *vehicle*, *pedestrian* and *cyclist* are the object classes to compute evaluation metrics. mAPH (mean average precision weighted by heading) is the main evaluation metric. The IoU threshold for *vehicle* class is 0.7 and *pedestrian* and *cyclist* class is 0.5. LEVEL_1 difficulty is for boxes with more than 5 LiDAR points and LEVEL_2 difficulty is for boxes with at least 1 LiDAR point.

Model Details. The point cloud range is set to [−55.2 m, 55.2 m] × [−55.2 m, 55.2 m] × [−5.0 m, 3.0 m] and [−76.8 m, 76.8 m] × [−76.8 m, 76.8 m] × [−2.0 m, 4.0 m] for nuScenes and Waymo dataset respectively. The voxel resolution is set to [0.075 m, 0.075 m, 0.2 m] and [0.1 m, 0.1 m, 0.15 m] for nuScenes and Waymo dataset respectively. 3D SparseConv [13], SECOND [43] and FPN [20] are employed for LiDAR BEV local feature extraction. The multi-scale deformable self-attention in the LiDAR encoder is set with 8 attention heads, 4 key sampling points and hidden dimension of 128. The number of LiDAR encoder layers (L_{enc}) is set to 3. The number of attention heads in multi-head self-attention in LiDAR decoder is set to 8 with hidden dimension of 128. The number of object queries (N_q) is set to 300. The multi-scale deformable cross-attention in LiDAR decoder is set with hidden dimension 128, 8 attention heads and 8 key sampling points. The number of LiDAR decoder layers (L_{dec}) is set to 4.

A shared VoVNetV2-99 [19] backbone along with FPN is employed to extract the multi-view image features. The multi-head self-attention in image decoder is set with a hidden dimension of 128 and 8 attention heads. The image cross-attention (ICA) is set with 8 attention heads, 8 key sampling points and hidden dimension of 128. The number of image decoder layers (L_{dec}) is set to 4. The image size is set to 448 × 768.

Training Details. Our DAFDeTr is implemented in PyTorch [26] using the MMDetection3D [9]. Following [45], we adopt the same data augmentation along with CBGS [49]. We follow two stage training pipeline similar to [1]: 1) We train the LiDAR-only model for 20 epochs to predict initial predictions. We disable the copy-and-paste augmentation [43] to apply the fade strategy for the last 5 epochs. 2) We train the LiDAR-camera fusion model for another 5 epochs by freezing the LiDAR-only model during this stage. The two-stage training policy helps than joint training since we can apply better augmentations for LiDAR-only model. The network is trained with AdamW [22] optimizer with initial learning rate of 1×10^{-4} and weight decay of 10^{-2}. The models are trained on two RTX 4090 GPUs.

During inference, the final score is computed as geometric average of heatmap score and classification score. As the network is trained with one-to-one matching, we can avoid post-processing step like Non-maximum Suppression (NMS).

4.2 Results and Discussion

nuScenes Dataset. The comparison of our DAFDeTr approach with the state-of-the-art approaches on the nuScenes [2] *test* set is as shown in Table 1. Our LiDAR-only model DAFDeTr-L achieves 63.4 mAP and 69.1 NDS surpassing the state-of-the-art models such as PolarStream [6] by 9.6 mAP, CenterPoint [45] by 5.4 mAP, Object-DGCNN [42] by 4.7 mAP and Li3DeTr [11] by 2.1 mAP and VISTA-OHS [10] by 0.4 mAP. Our LiDAR-Camera fusion model DAFDeTr achieves 64.6 mAP and 69.3 NDS surpassing the well established networks such as PointPainting [38] and 3D-CVF

[47]. MVP [46] and PointAugmenting [39] employ virtual points/objects into the point clouds and images and MVP is a two-stage method whose first stage depends on 2D segmentation results and it predicts objects for individual multi-view images instead of processing multi-view images all at once.

Table 1. Comparison of recent works on nuScenes [2] *test* set.

Method	mAP ↑	NDS ↑	mATE ↓	mASE ↓	mAOE ↓	mAVE ↓	mAAE ↓
LiDAR-only							
CBGS [49]	52.8	63.3	30.0	24.7	37.9	24.5	14.0
PolarStream [6]	53.8	61.3	33.9	26.4	49.1	33.9	12.3
CenterPoint [45]	58.0	65.5	–	–	–	–	–
CVCNet-ens [4]	58.2	66.6	28.4	24.1	37.2	22.4	12.6
Object-DGCNN [42]	58.7	66.0	33.3	26.3	28.8	25.1	19.0
HotSpotNet [5]	59.3	66.0	27.4	23.9	38.4	33.3	13.3
Li3DeTr [11]	61.3	67.6	30.5	25.4	35.2	26.7	12.5
VISTA-OHS [10]	63.0	**69.8**	25.6	23.3	32.1	21.6	12.2
DAFDeTr-L (Ours)	**63.4**	69.1	26.6	24.4	33.9	27.5	13.1
LiDAR+Camera							
PointPainting [38]	46.4	58.1	–	–	–	–	–
3D-CVF [47]	57.8	66.3	28.0	24.6	36.7	23.8	13.0
MVP [46]	66.4	70.5	26.3	23.8	32.1	31.3	13.4
PointAugmenting [39]	**66.8**	**71.1**	25.3	23.5	35.4	26.6	12.3
DAFDeTr (Ours)	64.6	69.3	26.4	24.9	35.9	28.9	13.2

We also compare our approach with a similar method [1] on the nuScenes *test* set in terms of mAP and inference speed (FPS-Frames Per Second) for a fair comparison as shown in Table 2. TransFusion [1] employs cross-attention using vanilla attention [37] in its decoder layers to decode object queries into box predictions using the LiDAR and image feature maps. The computational complexity of cross-attention using vanilla attention is of $\mathcal{O}(HWC^2 + N_qHWC)$, where N_q is the number of queries, $H \times W$ is the size of feature map and C is the feature dimension. The computational complexity of vanilla attention is directly related to the spatial size of feature maps. As a trade-off between accuracy and speed, we employ deformable attention [50] instead of a vanilla attention for the cross-attention in the decoder to increase the inference speed of our approach. The computational complexity of deformable cross-attention is $\mathcal{O}(N_qKC^2)$, where K is the total number of key sampling points, which is independent of the spatial size of feature maps. We can observe from Table 2 that our approach achieves around 23% higher inference speed than TransFusion for LiDAR-only model at the cost of 2 mAP. The complexity in our approach depends on K number of sampling key points in the decoder cross-attention, which can be adjusted according to accuracy-speed trade-off requirements.

Tracking. We adopt tracking-by-detection algorithm from CenterPoint [45] to evaluate 3D multi object tracking (MOT) on our model on the nuScenes dataset [2] as shown in Table 3. The probabilistic MOT [8] adapts Kalman filter-based Mahalanobis distance matching and CenterPoint uses velocity-based closest point matching. As the tracking is by detection, our model outperforms CenterPoint and achieves competitive performance to EagerMOT [15].

Table 2. Comparison in terms of mAP and inference speed (FPS) on nuScenes [2] dataset. FPS is measured on an Intel Core i9 CPU and a RTX 3090 GPU. L - LiDAR and LC - LiDAR+Camera.

Method	Modality	mAP	FPS
TransFusion	L	**65.5**	3.2
DAFDeTr (Ours)	L	63.4	**4.2**
TransFusion	LC	**68.9**	2.7
DAFDeTr (Ours)	LC	64.6	**3.0**

Table 3. Performance of tracking results on nuScenes dataset. (AMOTA: Average Multi Object Tracking Accuracy, FP: False Positives, FN: False Negatives, IDS: ID Switches).

Method	AMOTA ↑	FP ↓	FN ↓	IDS ↓
Prob-MOT [8]	55.0	17533	33216	950
CenterPoint [45]	63.8	18612	22928	760
EagerMOT [15]	67.7	17705	24925	1156
DAFDeTr-L (Ours)	67.8	12416	**21409**	**861**
DAFDeTr (Ours)	**69.0**	**11877**	21430	873

Waymo Open Dataset. The comparison of our DAFDeTr-L approach with the state-of-the-art approaches on the Waymo [34] *val* set in terms of mAPH is as shown in Table 4. Our method achieves 71.8 mAPH and 63.5 mAPH for LEVEL_1 and LEVEL_2 *vehicle* category respectively. It surpasses the well established approaches such as SECOND [43], PointPillars [18] and VoTr-SSD [23] by good margin for *vehicle*, *pedestrian* and *cyclist* categories. Our method achieves a competitive performance with TransFusion [1] on *vehicle* and *cyclist* categories but fails to match the performance for smaller objects like *pedestrian*. The dense nature of vanilla attention [37] in TransFusion [1] could better represent small objects than the sparse deformable attention [50] in our approach. However, the inference speed of our approach on Waymo dataset is 10 FPS which is 25% higher than that of TransFusion [1], thanks to sparse nature of deformable attention.

Table 4. Comparison of recent works in terms of mAPH on Waymo [34] *val* set. Scores in second position of respective metric are shown in underline.

Method	Vehicle		Pedestrian		Cyclist	
	L1 mAPH	L2 mAPH	L1 mAPH	L2 mAPH	L1 mAPH	L2 mAPH
SECOND [43]	57.9	51.1	54.9	48.0	47.6	45.8
PointPillars [18]	71.0	62.5	56.7	50.2	62.3	59.9
VoTr-SSD [23]	68.3	59.6	–	–	–	–
TransFusion-L [1]	–	**65.1**	–	**63.7**	–	**65.9**
DAFDeTr-L (Ours)	71.8	<u>63.5</u>	61.7	<u>54.2</u>	66.0	<u>63.5</u>

Analysis. The performance analysis of our method by object category, object distance, object size, different weather scenarios and robustness for camera malfunction is detailed below.

Object Category. We compare the performance of our approach DAFDeTr by object category on the nuScenes [2] *val* set in terms of Average Precision (AP) as shown in

Table 5. The input-dependent and category-aware object queries provide potential 3D object locations for not only larger objects like *bus* and *construction vehicle* but also for smaller objects like *motorcycle*. The deformable cross-attention in the decoder links the multi-modal feature maps to the 3D object predictions leveraging object queries not only for larger objects but also for smaller object categories. The LiDAR-Camera fusion model DAFDeTr achieves huge improvement in the performance of objects such as *bicycle*, *motorcycle* and *traffic cone*, which proves the significance of soft-fusion of multi-view image features with the queries generated from LiDAR-only model.

Table 5. Performance of our model by object category on the nuScenes *val* set in terms of Average Precision (AP). Motor - Motorcycle, Ped - Pedestrian, CV - Construction Vehicle, TC - Traffic Cone, Barr - Barrier. The scores in green indicate the increase in performance with respect to scores in underline and scores in blue indicate the increase in performance with respect to LiDAR-only model.

Method	Car	Truck	Trailer	Bus	CV	Bicycle	Motor	Ped	TC	Barr	mAP
Obj-DGCNN [42]	84.0	54.0	40.4	66.8	20.2	44.7	66.2	81.6	64.7	62.6	58.5
VISTA [10]	85.0	57.4	39.9	66.4	21.2	51.7	66.6	84.5	68.5	66.8	60.9
Li3DeTr [11]	85.8	56.5	43.0	70.9	22.9	51.6	66.9	83.9	66.8	65.7	61.4
DAFDeTr-L (Ours)	87.2	52.1	46.7	75.1 ↑ 4.2	28.6 ↑ 5.7	45.6	71.9 ↑ 5.0	85.1	72.7	65.8	**63.1**
DAFDeTr (Ours)	87.5	52.2	47.3	75.7	28.6	52.8 ↑ 7.2	74.6 ↑ 2.7	85.6	75.0 ↑ 2.3	66.1	**64.6**

Object Distance. We compare the performance of our DAFDeTr network by object distance on the nuScenes [2] *val* set in terms of mAP as shown in Table 6. The 3D objects are split into three categories basing on the distance between object center and ego vehicle: [0m,20m], [20m,30m] and [30m,+∞]. Our DAFDeTr-L model improves the performance of objects which far from ego vehicle because of the deformable cross-attention in the decoder which captures long range dependencies. The LiDAR point clouds at large distance become sparse and the fusion of LiDAR and camera modalities improve the performance of objects at far distance by leveraging dense image features as shown in Table 6.

Table 6. Performance of our model by object distance on the nuScenes *val* set in terms of mAP. The scores in green indicate the increase in performance with respect to scores in underline and scores in blue indicate the increase in performance with respect to LiDAR-only model.

Method	[0m,20m]	[20m,30m]	[30m,+∞]
Obj-DGCNN [42]	73.2	55.5	30.3
VISTA [10]	75.2	56.3	21.4
Li3DeTr [11]	75.6	56.9	32.7
DAFDeTr-L (Ours)	75.7	59.2 ↑ 2.3	34.7 ↑ 2.0
DAFDeTr (Ours)	76.9	60.6 ↑ 1.4	36.8 ↑ 2.1

We compare the performance of DAFDeTr-L network by object distance on the Waymo [34] *val* set in terms of LEVEL_1 mAPH for *vehicle* category. Our network achieves improvement not only for near objects but also for far objects as shown in Table 7, thanks to the effective deformable cross-attention in the decoder.

Table 7. Performance of our DAFDeTr-L by object distance on the Waymo *val* set in terms of LEVEL_1 mAPH for *vehicle* category. The scores in green indicate the increase in performance with respect to scores in underline.

Method	[0m, 30m]	[30m, 50m]	[50m, +∞]
StarNet [25]	82.4	53.2	25.7
PointPillars [18]	84.4	58.6	35.2
VoTr-SSD [23]	87.6	66.0	41.3
DAFDeTr-L (Ours)	89.9	69.3 ↑ 3.3	46.3 ↑ 5.0

Object Size. We compare the performance of our approach DAFDeTr by object size on the nuScenes [2] *val* set in terms of mAP as shown in Table 8. The 3D objects are divided into two categories basing on the longer edge of the object: [0m, 4m] and [4m, +∞]. The performance of smaller objects (<4 m) is significantly improved by 2.0 mAP compared to Li3DeTr [11]. The LiDAR-Camera model DAFDeTr shows slight improvement for smaller objects leveraging the dense image features.

Table 8. Performance of our model by object size on the nuScenes *val* set in terms of mAP. The scores in green indicate the increase in performance with respect to scores in underline.

Method	[0m, 4m]	[4m, +∞]
Obj-DGCNN [42]	36.0	25.4
Li3DeTr [11]	37.9	27.8
DAFDeTr-L (Ours)	39.9 ↑ 2.0	27.9
DAFDeTr (Ours)	40.3	28.0

Weather Scenarios. We compare the performance of our approach DAFDeTr on the nuScenes *val* set in terms of mAP for different weather scenarios such as *sunny*, *rainy* and *night* as shown in Table 9. During sunny scenarios the performance of our model is leveraged by the bright image data available on sunny days whereas during rainy and night weather scenarios the LiDAR data complements the image data for accurate detection of objects. The soft association between LiDAR and camera image features using the object queries achieves the high performance gain during night driving scenarios as shown in Table 9.

Table 9. Performance of our model on the nuScenes *val* set in terms of mAP for different weather scenarios. The scores in blue indicate the increase in performance with respect to LiDAR-only model.

Method	Sunny	Rainy	Night
DAFDeTr-L	62.9	61.7	58.0
DAFDeTr	64.2	64.1 ↑ 2.4	64.3 ↑ 6.3

Camera Malfunction. We test the performance of our fusion approach against the multi-view camera malfunction on nuScenes *val* set as shown in Table 10. To simulate camera malfunction we randomly drop the several multi-view images for each sample by setting the image features to zero during inference. We randomly drop 2, 4 and 6 images from each sample and our DAFDeTr network is able to maintain the mAP in case of a camera malfunction which shows the robustness of our fusion approach. This advantage is leveraged by initially predicting with LiDAR-only model and then attending only useful multi-view image features using deformable image cross-attention module.

Table 10. Performance of our model in terms of mAP for different number of multi-view camera malfunction on nuScenes *val* set. The scores in red indicate the decrease in performance with respect to scores in underline.

# cameras malfunction	DAFDeTr
0	<u>64.6</u>
2	63.9 ↓ 0.7
4	63.6 ↓ 1.0
6	63.0 ↓ 1.6

4.3   Ablation Studies

Number of Queries. We compare the performance of our approach in terms of mAP and NDS on nuScenes *val* set for different number of queries in the decoder as shown in Table 11. As the object queries are input-dependent and category-aware, unlike previous approaches [11,24,42], we can dynamically change the number of queries during inference time to adapt for performance-latency trade-off. The performance of our model increases with the increase in number of queries because input-dependent category-aware object queries represent potential object candidates. However, the performance of the model has slight impact above 300 queries. Therefore, we fix number of object queries (N_q) to 300.

Table 11. Performance of our model on the nuScenes *val* set in terms of mAP and NDS for different number of object queries.

No. of queries	DAFDeTr-L		DAFDeTr	
	mAP	NDS	mAP	NDS
100	61.4	66.3	62.9	67.1
200	62.2	67.5	63.8	68.4
300	**63.1**	**68.9**	**64.6**	**69.7**
500	63.1	68.7	64.4	69.3

Number of Key Sampling Points. We compare the performance of our network in terms of mAP and NDS on the nuScenes *val* set for different number of key sampling points (K) in deformable cross-attention in the decoder as shown in Table 12. The key sampling points are the learnable points on the feature maps around a given reference point, wherein each query attends in the deformable cross-attention. As the number of key sampling points increases the computational complexity of the model increases, therefore we have to find an optimum number of key sampling points for the optimized performance of the network. In our model the number of key sampling points is set to 8.

Table 12. Performance of our model on the nuScenes *val* set in terms of mAP and NDS for different number of key sampling points.

K	DAFDeTr-L		DAFDeTr	
	mAP	NDS	mAP	NDS
1	60.8	66.1	61.9	67.1
4	61.9	67.4	63.1	68.1
8	**63.1**	**68.9**	**64.6**	**69.7**

Backbones. We compare the performance of our network in terms of mAP and NDS on nuScenes *val* set with different type of backbone networks for LiDAR and camera inputs as shown in Table 13. For the LiDAR input modality we test with VoxelNet [48] and PointPillars [18] and for the camera input modality we test with ResNet-50 [14] and ResNet-101 networks. The deep and complex image backbone ResNet-101 with a powerful LiDAR backbone VoxelNet achieves the best performance. Our model is flexible enough to plug and play any type of LiDAR BEV and image backbone depending upon the performance-latency requirements of the application.

Table 13. Performance of our model on the nuScenes *val* set in terms of mAP and NDS for different backbone architectures.

Camera	LiDAR	mAP	NDS
LiDAR-Only			
–	PointPillars	52.5	61.1
–	Voxelnet	**63.1**	**68.9**
LiDAR+Camera			
ResNet-50	PointPillar	51.8	60.1
ResNet-50	VoxelNet	62.4	67.5
ResNet-101	PointPillar	53.9	61.2
ResNet-101	VoxelNet	**64.6**	**69.7**

Decoder Layers. We compare the performance of our DAFDeTr-L model on the nuScenes *val* set for different number of decoder layers as shown in Table 14. Each decoder layer iteratively refines the object queries conditioned on the multi-modal input features with the help of cross-attention mechanism. Therefore, the performance of our model improves as we increase the number of decoder layers. There is a slight improvement in the performance of network until 4 decoder layers. Therefore, we set the number of decoder layers (L_{dec}) to 4.

4.4 Qualitative Results

The qualitative results of our DAFDeTr model on the nuScenes dataset [2] predicting the objects projected onto the LiDAR BEV space and image space are illustrated for three scenarios: *sunny day* in Fig. 2, *rainy day* in Fig. 3 and *night time* in Fig. 4. Although the LiDAR point cloud far away from ego vehicle is sparse, our network is able to detect the objects. This is possible by effective fusion of LiDAR-camera data in our approach as image features provide the dense information to detect objects far away from ego vehicle complementing the LiDAR features. A short video demonstrating the predictions of our DAFDeTr network on the nuScenes dataset [2] for three weather scenarios: sunny, rainy and night is presented at https://youtu.be/MVAg9ydZuBg.

Table 14. Performance of our model on the nuScenes *val* set in terms of mAP and NDS for different number of decoder layers.

Layer	DAFDeTr-L		DAFDeTr	
	mAP	NDS	mAP	NDS
1	62.7	67.9	64.1	69.4
2	62.8	68.6	64.3	69.5
3	63.0	68.8	64.4	69.5
4	**63.1**	**68.9**	**64.6**	**69.7**
5	63.1	68.8	64.3	69.5

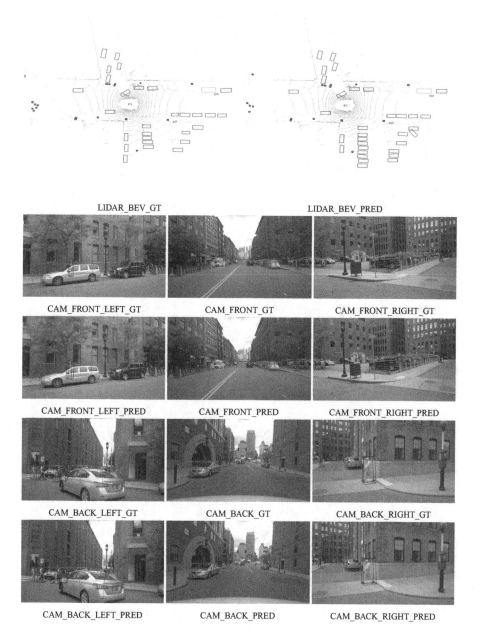

Fig. 2. Qualitative results of our DAFDeTr network on nuScenes dataset (weather: sunny) [2] both in LiDAR BEV plane and 3D bounding boxes projected onto multi-view image planes. Different object categories are shown in different colors. Image best viewed in zoom and color.

Fig. 3. Qualitative results of our DAFDeTr network on nuScenes dataset (weather: rainy) [2] both in LiDAR BEV plane and 3D bounding boxes projected onto multi-view image planes. Different object categories are shown in different colors. Image best viewed in zoom and color.

Fig. 4. Qualitative results of our DAFDeTr network on nuScenes dataset (night time) [2] both in LiDAR BEV plane and 3D bounding boxes projected onto multi-view image planes. Different object categories are shown in different colors. Image best viewed in zoom and color.

5 Conclusion

Existing approaches [38, 39] fuse LiDAR and image data by hard association heavily relying on the accuracy of calibration matrices. In our approach, we propose a sequential fusion of LiDAR and image data by soft association leveraged by deformable cross-attention [50] mechanism. Our DAFDeTr is a single-stage and NMS-free network which inputs LiDAR point cloud and multi-view images to predict 3D bounding boxes in an autonomous driving scenario. DAFDeTr consists of a backbone network for multi-modal feature extraction and a detection head which consists of two decoders for sequential fusion: LiDAR and image decoder. The deformable cross-attention in LiDAR decoder transforms the LiDAR global BEV features to 3D box predictions leveraging the input-dependent object queries. The image cross-attention in the image decoder adaptively and attentively fuse the LiDAR and image features establishing a soft association and making the model robust to different weather scenarios and camera malfunction. We present extensive experiments and analysis on nuScenes [2] and Waymo [34] datasets. Our DAFDeTr outperform well established models on nuScenes dataset and obtains competitive performance on Waymo dataset. To reduce the computational complexity and increase the inference speed, we employ deformable cross-attention mechanism where each query only attends learnt key sampling spatial locations of multi-modal feature maps that are useful and relevant to the corresponding object query. Compared to TransFusion [1], our DAFDeTr-L model achieves around 23% increase in inference speed at a cost of 3% (2.1 mAP) drop in performance. We also extend our model for 3D tracking task and achieve state-of-the-art performance compared to existing approaches.

Acknowledgments. This work has been supported by European Union's H2020 MSCA-ITN-ACHIEVE [Grant No. 765866], Fundação para a Ciência e a Tecnologia (FCT) for ISR - Coimbra [Ref. No. UIDB/00048/2020 https://doi.org/10.54499/UIDB/00048/2020] and FCT Portugal PhD research grant [Ref. No. 2021.06219.BD].

References

1. Bai, X., et al.: Transfusion: robust lidar-camera fusion for 3D object detection with transformers. In: Proceedings of the IEEE/CVF Conference on Computer Vision and Pattern Recognition, pp. 1090–1099 (2022)
2. Caesar, H., et al.: nuScenes: a multimodal dataset for autonomous driving. In: Proceedings of the IEEE/CVF Conference on Computer Vision and Pattern Recognition, pp. 11621–11631 (2020)
3. Carion, N., Massa, F., Synnaeve, G., Usunier, N., Kirillov, A., Zagoruyko, S.: End-to-end object detection with transformers. In: Vedaldi, A., Bischof, H., Brox, T., Frahm, J.-M. (eds.) ECCV 2020. LNCS, vol. 12346, pp. 213–229. Springer, Cham (2020). https://doi.org/10.1007/978-3-030-58452-8_13
4. Chen, Q., Sun, L., Cheung, E., Yuille, A.L.: Every view counts: cross-view consistency in 3d object detection with hybrid-cylindrical-spherical voxelization. Adv. Neural. Inf. Process. Syst. **33**, 21224–21235 (2020)
5. Chen, Q., Sun, L., Wang, Z., Jia, K., Yuille, A.: Object as hotspots: an anchor-free 3D Object detection approach via firing of hotspots. In: Vedaldi, A., Bischof, H., Brox, T., Frahm, J.-M.

(eds.) ECCV 2020. LNCS, vol. 12366, pp. 68–84. Springer, Cham (2020). https://doi.org/10.1007/978-3-030-58589-1_5

6. Chen, Q., Vora, S., Beijbom, O.: Polarstream: streaming object detection and segmentation with polar pillars. Adv. Neural. Inf. Process. Syst. **34**, 26871–26883 (2021)

7. Chen, X., Ma, H., Wan, J., Li, B., Xia, T.: Multi-view 3D object detection network for autonomous driving. In: Proceedings of the IEEE Conference on Computer Vision and Pattern Recognition, pp. 1907–1915 (2017)

8. Chiu, H.k., Prioletti, A., Li, J., Bohg, J.: Probabilistic 3d multi-object tracking for autonomous driving. arXiv preprint arXiv:2001.05673 (2020)

9. Contributors, M.: MMDetection3D: OpenMMLab next-generation platform for general 3D object detection (2020). https://github.com/open-mmlab/mmdetection3d

10. Deng, S., Liang, Z., Sun, L., Jia, K.: Vista: boosting 3d object detection via dual cross-view spatial attention. In: Proceedings of the IEEE/CVF Conference on Computer Vision and Pattern Recognition, pp. 8448–8457 (2022)

11. Erabati, G.K., Araujo, H.: Li3detr: a lidar based 3d detection transformer. In: Proceedings of the IEEE/CVF Winter Conference on Applications of Computer Vision, pp. 4250–4259 (2023)

12. Fan, L., Xiong, X., Wang, F., Wang, N., Zhang, Z.: RangeDet: in defense of range view for lidar-based 3d object detection. In: Proceedings of the IEEE/CVF International Conference on Computer Vision, pp. 2918–2927 (2021)

13. Graham, B., Engelcke, M., Van Der Maaten, L.: 3D semantic segmentation with submanifold sparse convolutional networks. In: Proceedings of the IEEE Conference on Computer Vision and Pattern Recognition, pp. 9224–9232 (2018)

14. He, K., Zhang, X., Ren, S., Sun, J.: Deep residual learning for image recognition. In: Proceedings of the IEEE Conference on Computer Vision and Pattern Recognition, pp. 770–778 (2016)

15. Kim, A., Ošep, A., Leal-Taixé, L.: Eagermot: 3d multi-object tracking via sensor fusion. In: 2021 IEEE International conference on Robotics and Automation (ICRA), pp. 11315–11321. IEEE (2021)

16. Ku, J., Mozifian, M., Lee, J., Harakeh, A., Waslander, S.L.: Joint 3d proposal generation and object detection from view aggregation. In: 2018 IEEE/RSJ International Conference on Intelligent Robots and Systems (IROS), pp. 1–8. IEEE (2018)

17. Kuhn, H.W.: The hungarian method for the assignment problem. Nav. Res. Logist. q. **2**(1–2), 83–97 (1955)

18. Lang, A.H., Vora, S., Caesar, H., Zhou, L., Yang, J., Beijbom, O.: Pointpillars: fast encoders for object detection from point clouds. In: Proceedings of the IEEE/CVF Conference on Computer Vision and Pattern Recognition, pp. 12697–12705 (2019)

19. Lee, Y., Park, J.: Centermask: real-time anchor-free instance segmentation. In: Proceedings of the IEEE/CVF Conference on Computer Vision and Pattern Recognition, pp. 13906–13915 (2020)

20. Lin, T.Y., Dollár, P., Girshick, R., He, K., Hariharan, B., Belongie, S.: Feature pyramid networks for object detection. In: Proceedings of the IEEE Conference on Computer Vision and Pattern Recognition, pp. 2117–2125 (2017)

21. Liu, W., et al.: SSD: single shot multibox detector. In: Leibe, B., Matas, J., Sebe, N., Welling, M. (eds.) ECCV 2016. LNCS, vol. 9905, pp. 21–37. Springer, Cham (2016). https://doi.org/10.1007/978-3-319-46448-0_2

22. Loshchilov, I., Hutter, F.: Decoupled weight decay regularization. arXiv preprint arXiv:1711.05101 (2017)

23. Mao, J., et al.: Voxel transformer for 3d object detection. In: Proceedings of the IEEE/CVF International Conference on Computer Vision, pp. 3164–3173 (2021)

24. Misra, I., Girdhar, R., Joulin, A.: An end-to-end transformer model for 3d object detection. In: Proceedings of the IEEE/CVF International Conference on Computer Vision, pp. 2906–2917 (2021)
25. Ngiam, J., et al.: Starnet: targeted computation for object detection in point clouds. arXiv preprint arXiv:1908.11069 (2019)
26. Paszke, A., et al.: Pytorch: an imperative style, high-performance deep learning library. In: Wallach, H., Larochelle, H., Beygelzimer, A., d'Alché-Buc, F., Fox, E., Garnett, R. (eds.) Advances in Neural Information Processing Systems, vol. 32, pp. 8024–8035. Curran Associates, Inc. (2019). http://papers.neurips.cc/paper/9015-pytorch-an-imperative-style-high-performance-deep-learning-library.pdf
27. Qi, C.R., Liu, W., Wu, C., Su, H., Guibas, L.J.: Frustum pointnets for 3d object detection from RGB-D data. In: Proceedings of the IEEE Conference on Computer Vision and Pattern Recognition, pp. 918–927 (2018)
28. Qi, C.R., Su, H., Mo, K., Guibas, L.J.: Pointnet: deep learning on point sets for 3d classification and segmentation. In: Proceedings of the IEEE Conference on Computer Vision and Pattern Recognition, pp. 652–660 (2017)
29. Qi, C.R., Yi, L., Su, H., Guibas, L.J.: Pointnet++: deep hierarchical feature learning on point sets in a metric space. Adv. Neural Inf. Process. Syst. **30** (2017)
30. Redmon, J., Farhadi, A.: Yolov3: an incremental improvement. arXiv preprint arXiv:1804.02767 (2018)
31. Ren, S., He, K., Girshick, R., Sun, J.: Faster r-cnn: towards real-time object detection with region proposal networks. Adv. Neural Inf. Process. Syst. **28** (2015)
32. Shi, S., Wang, X., Li, H.: Pointrcnn: 3d object proposal generation and detection from point cloud. In: Proceedings of the IEEE/CVF Conference on Computer Vision and Pattern Recognition, pp. 770–779 (2019)
33. Shin, K., Kwon, Y.P., Tomizuka, M.: Roarnet: a robust 3d object detection based on region approximation refinement. In: 2019 IEEE Intelligent Vehicles Symposium (IV), pp. 2510–2515. IEEE (2019)
34. Sun, P., et al.: Scalability in perception for autonomous driving: waymo open dataset. In: Proceedings of the IEEE/CVF Conference on Computer Vision and Pattern Recognition, pp. 2446–2454 (2020)
35. Sun, P., et al.: RSN: range sparse net for efficient, accurate lidar 3D object detection. In: Proceedings of the IEEE/CVF Conference on Computer Vision and Pattern Recognition, pp. 5725–5734 (2021)
36. Tian, Z., Shen, C., Chen, H., He, T.: FCOS: fully convolutional one-stage object detection. In: Proceedings of the IEEE/CVF International Conference on Computer Vision, pp. 9627–9636 (2019)
37. Vaswani, A., et al.: Attention is all you need. Adv. Neural Inf. Process. Syst. **30** (2017)
38. Vora, S., Lang, A.H., Helou, B., Beijbom, O.: Pointpainting: sequential fusion for 3d object detection. In: Proceedings of the IEEE/CVF Conference on Computer Vision and Pattern Recognition, pp. 4604–4612 (2020)
39. Wang, C., Ma, C., Zhu, M., Yang, X.: Pointaugmenting: cross-modal augmentation for 3d object detection. In: Proceedings of the IEEE/CVF Conference on Computer Vision and Pattern Recognition, pp. 11794–11803 (2021)
40. Wang, Y., et al.: Pillar-based object detection for autonomous driving. In: Vedaldi, A., Bischof, H., Brox, T., Frahm, J.-M. (eds.) ECCV 2020. LNCS, vol. 12367, pp. 18–34. Springer, Cham (2020). https://doi.org/10.1007/978-3-030-58542-6_2
41. Wang, Y., Guizilini, V.C., Zhang, T., Wang, Y., Zhao, H., Solomon, J.: Detr3d: 3d object detection from multi-view images via 3d-to-2d queries. In: Conference on Robot Learning, pp. 180–191. PMLR (2022)

42. Wang, Y., Solomon, J.M.: Object DGCNN: 3d object detection using dynamic graphs. Adv. Neural Inf. Process. Syst. **34** (2021)
43. Yan, Y., Mao, Y., Li, B.: Second: sparsely embedded convolutional detection. Sensors **18**(10), 3337 (2018)
44. Yang, Z., Sun, Y., Liu, S., Jia, J.: 3DSSD: point-based 3D single stage object detector. In: Proceedings of the IEEE/CVF Conference on Computer Vision and Pattern Recognition, pp. 11040–11048 (2020)
45. Yin, T., Zhou, X., Krahenbuhl, P.: Center-based 3d object detection and tracking. In: Proceedings of the IEEE/CVF Conference on Computer Vision and Pattern Recognition, pp. 11784–11793 (2021)
46. Yin, T., Zhou, X., Krähenbühl, P.: Multimodal virtual point 3d detection. Adv. Neural Inf. Process. Syst. **34** (2021)
47. Yoo, J.H., Kim, Y., Kim, J., Choi, J.W.: 3D-CVF: generating joint camera and LiDAR features using cross-view spatial feature fusion for 3D object detection. In: Vedaldi, A., Bischof, H., Brox, T., Frahm, J.-M. (eds.) ECCV 2020. LNCS, vol. 12372, pp. 720–736. Springer, Cham (2020). https://doi.org/10.1007/978-3-030-58583-9_43
48. Zhou, Y., Tuzel, O.: VoxelNet: end-to-end learning for point cloud based 3d object detection. In: Proceedings of the IEEE Conference on Computer Vision and Pattern Recognition, pp. 4490–4499 (2018)
49. Zhu, B., Jiang, Z., Zhou, X., Li, Z., Yu, G.: Class-balanced grouping and sampling for point cloud 3d object detection. arXiv preprint arXiv:1908.09492 (2019)
50. Zhu, X., Su, W., Lu, L., Li, B., Wang, X., Dai, J.: Deformable detr: deformable transformers for end-to-end object detection. arXiv preprint arXiv:2010.04159 (2020)

MDC-Net: Multimodal Detection and Captioning Network for Steel Surface Defects

Anthony Ashwin Peter Chazhoor[1] , Shanfeng Hu[1] , Bin Gao[2] ,
and Wai Lok Woo[1(✉)]

[1] Department of Computer and Information Sciences, Northumbria University,
Newcastle upon Tyne NE1 8ST, U.K.
{anthony.chazhoor,shanfeng2.hu,wailok.woo}@northumbria.ac.uk
[2] School of Automation Engineering, University of Electronic Science and Technology
of China, Chengdu, China
bin_gao@uestc.edu.cn

Abstract. In the highly competitive steel sector, product quality, particularly in terms of surface integrity, is critical. Surface defect detection (SDD) is essential in maintaining high production standards, as it directly impacts product quality and manufacturing efficiency. Traditional SDD approaches, which rely primarily on manual inspection or traditional computer vision techniques, are plagued with difficulties, including reduced accuracy and potential health concerns to inspectors. This research describes an innovative solution that uses a sequence generation model with transformers to improve the defect detection process while manufacturing hot-rolled steel sheets and generating captions about the defect and its spatial location. This method, which views object detection as a sequence generation problem, allows for a more sophisticated understanding of image content and a complete and contextually rich investigation of surface defects whilst providing captions. While this method can potentially improve detection accuracy, its actual power rests in its scalability and flexibility to various industrial applications. Furthermore, this technique has the potential to be further enhanced for visual question-answering applications, opening up opportunities for interactive and intelligent image analysis.

Keywords: Steel defect detection · Image captioning · Pixel to sequence

1 Introduction

A customer's decision to purchase a product is frequently influenced by its visual appeal. When even minor defects are apparent, it can impede purchases. This scenario is crucial for producers who want to maintain their products constantly to avoid financial disasters. The steel industry is a prime example of this, as it provides critical materials for diverse industries such as construction, automobile, and appliance manufacturing while also playing an essential part in economic

J. Filipe and J. Röning (Eds.): ROBOVIS 2024, CCIS 2077, pp. 316–333, 2024.
https://doi.org/10.1007/978-3-031-59057-3_20

development. As a result, strict quality control is required in this industry. Any defect in steel manufacturing results in financial losses and poses significant threats to safety and operational performance.

Surface defect detection (SDD) is integral to the manufacturing process. It impacts not just the ultimate product's quality but also the efficiency of the following procedures. Traditional methods of detecting defects in steel, such as manual examinations and older computer vision approaches, have significant limitations varying from potential inaccuracy to health dangers for the inspectors.

A significant gap can be seen in the current state of Steel Surface Defect Detection (SDD). Conventional object detectors such as YOLO and Faster R-CNN have inadequate contextual awareness when it comes to defect detection [1, 2]. Although these models are in the forefront of defect detection, they frequently fall short of offering a more in-depth, contextualised analysis that is essential for a thorough defect analysis [3]. This discrepancy emphasises the need for novel methods that can both precisely identify defects and meaningfully understand them. We close this gap by using the captioning-capable Pix2Seq framework in our research [4]. By providing comprehensive, contextual insights into every defect found, this method improves defect detection and greatly increases its interpretability and usefulness in industrial environments, especially for quality assurance and inspection procedures.

This contribution puts our work ahead in this field by integrating improved descriptive capabilities for defect detection with deep learning. Our study's theoretical framework is based on the use of transformer models in image processing. We will talk about the relevance of this paradigm to our findings. We'll also briefly explain our process, emphasising how Pix2Seq is used and how it may be extended to image captioning. This will offer an insight into our research approach.

Our contribution are as follows:

Application of Pix2Seq in Steel Defect Detection: Existing literature confirms that, to our knowledge, this study is the first to use the Pix2Seq framework in steel defect detection and its captioning. This innovative method represents an essential advancement in the practical implementation of deep learning methods in the industrial world, especially in improving quality assurance and inspection processes.

Extending Pix2Seq with Captioning Capabilities: Our work integrates captioning features into the Pix2Seq framework, improving it. This advancement allows the model to produce comprehensive and perceptive analyses for every observed defect. This capability enhances the interpretability and industrial applicability of the model's results.

The structure of this paper is as follows: following this introduction, we will provide a thorough assessment of the literature, outline our methodology, go over the results of our experiments, and then explain the implications of our conclusions and future development possibilities.

2   Literature Review

In the steel industry, ensuring the quality of products is crucial for maintaining the structural integrity and safety essential to their end-use. One key aspect of quality assurance is the detection of surface defects, which is vital for upholding the standards of the final steel products. This challenge has been approached through various historical techniques, evolving through three primary categories: manual inspection, traditional vision-based, and deep learning-based methods. Manual inspections are known for their laborious and time-consuming nature, with a significant risk of random error due to the subjective nature of the inspection process. Such variability in judgment among inspectors can lead to inconsistent quality, which may result in delivering substandard products to the market [5].

Technological advancements have brought forward methods employing eddy currents [6,7], infrared technology [8,9], and X-ray imaging [10]. Despite their benefits in specific contexts, the high cost of operation and infrastructure requirements limit their widespread adoption. Meanwhile, the digital revolution has introduced automated SSDD (Steel Surface Defect Detection) techniques that promise non-destructive testing and improved accuracy through pattern recognition and image processing advancements [11]. These modern techniques have provided substantial technical backing to the field, including using Local Binary Patterns, thresholding, morphological operations, Fourier and wavelet transforms [12]. However, there remains to be a gap in these methods' ability to generalise across different defect types, with current techniques sometimes failing under various conditions such as changes in lighting, camera angles, and backgrounds [11].

Maintaining high accuracy and throughput is the primary requirement of an effective SSDD system. For this system to be robust, it must understand various types of defects on steel surfaces with varying backgrounds and high noise. The ulterior objective is to elevate the detection process while integrating it with the existing manufacturing flow, simultaneously minimising false detections and ensuring the high quality of the steel product. Advancements in deep learning have mitigated many challenges inherent to industrial defect detection that relied on traditional techniques. The synergy of high-performance computing hardware and the proliferation of big data has propelled deep learning to the forefront of image analysis [13]. Convolutional Neural Networks (CNN) have been pivotal in recent research developments, demonstrating exceptional efficacy in image-processing tasks. Their application in SSDD has yielded significant research breakthroughs, leveraging deep learning's robust feature extraction capabilities. CNNs have shown excellent efficacy in image-processing tasks, and their applications extend beyond industrial defect detection [14]. For example, Chazhoor et al. (2022) showed how transfer learning with CNNs can effectively classify plastic waste, demonstrating the models' versatility across different domains [15,16].

Recent advancements in the field of steel defect detection have seen a variety of innovative contributions from several researchers in this field. Fityanul Akhyar et al. enhanced the Cascade R-CNN model with deformable convolutions and Region of Interest (ROI) pooling to better adapt to the geometric shapes of defects [12]. This model also utilises guided anchoring for more accurate bounding box generation and employs random scaling of images to maintain the aspect ratio. Similarly, Yu et al. developed a multilevel feature fusion network that builds on the feature map of CNNs, merging them at each stage to create a single hierarchical feature that enhances the detailing of defect characteristics. This is then used with a region proposal network to generate regions of interest ROIs [17]. Further contributions by Yongfang Xie et al. include the proposal of a loss function and a feature-enhanced YOLO algorithm that streamlines the YOLO model for improved efficiency while also increasing its accuracy through an upgraded feature pyramid network [3]. Another significant contribution is made in a recent study that benchmarks five state-of-the-art object detection models, including Faster R-CNN, Deformable DETR, Double Head R-CNN, Retinanet, and Deformable Convolutional Network, on steel surfaces. This research, providing detailed analyses of each model, aids in understanding the complexity of steel defect patterns and highlights the distinct performance of different models against contrasting and homogeneous defects [18]. Zhao et al. systematically approached the defect detection problem by advancing the Faster R-CNN model, optimising its algorithm, and reconfiguring its network structure. This adaptation allows multiscale fusion training aimed at smaller targets and employs a Deformable Convolutional Network (DCN) to delineate more complex features [19]. Zhang et al. recently introduced a cross-scale weighted feature fusion network that integrates Laplace sharpening with YOLOv5 for robust feature scale extraction. This innovative network utilises bidirectional and residual models for precise defect representation and applies K-means clustering for enhanced bounding box prediction [11].

These scholarly endeavours have collectively contributed to the progressive enhancement of defect detection accuracy and efficiency, showcasing the dynamic nature of research in this domain. Like object detection, image captioning plays a crucial role in translating the complex visual cues of surface defects into comprehensive textual descriptions. This technology bridges the gap between vision and language, allowing for a multimodal interpretation of defects. Image captioning goes beyond the confines of bounding box detections by offering detailed narratives that encapsulate the defect's nature, seriousness, and potential corrective measures. Such rich descriptions provide contextual clarity, allowing operators to gain a deeper understanding of the issues at hand and make informed decisions leading to explainiablity [20].

Wang et al. argues the importance of explicit object detections in end-to-end image captioning systems and highlight the importance of object characteristics and categories playing a crucial role in the captioning process [21]. With image captioning, each identified defect is accompanied by an automatically generated report, which not only aids in immediate decision-making but also serves as an archived record for future reference, quality assurance, and regulatory compliance. The granularity of the descriptions ensures that everything is noticed, and the maintenance can be appropriately prioritised based on the severity and implications of the defects described. They also prove to be an exceptional educational tool for new operators, who can learn to recognise and understand defects through detailed, annotated examples [22]. This aspect of image captioning is in line with the evolving nature of training, where experiential learning is enhanced by technology. Applying image captioning to steel defect detection creates a notable leap in data inspection. It lays the foundation for a workflow that's not just smarter but swifter, meeting the complex demands of the workforce. This facilitates greater involvement across different departmental teams; image captioning is critical in pushing forward the industry's standards, guaranteeing that the quality checks are thorough, streamlined, and universally understandable across the board in the steel sector.

Iwamura et al. proposed a novel end-to-end trainable method to generate captions with object detection using CNN, (Long Short Term Memory) LSTM, and attention. The authors suggest motion features around object regions to improve the accuracy of the caption generation [23]. Shao et al. proposed the Variational Joint Self-Attention model (VJSA) to overcome the limitations made by the attention models. This model innovatively employs self-attention mechanisms to capture both the relationships within and between sequences. Additionally, it incorporates a variational neural inference component that learns the distributional characteristics of image features in relation to their corresponding textual descriptions [24]. Wei et al. developed RTLCap and Faster RTLCap, two deep-learning models for automated railway track inspection. Using ResNet-50-FPN and YOLOv3, these models efficiently generate inspection reports from images, tackling challenges like object occlusion and category imbalance [25]. Yong et al. developed the FMSeq2Seq model by combining Seq2Seq along with Factorization Machines for efficient defect image captioning for dam inspections. By leveraging LSTM and attention mechanisms, the model enhances keyword interpretation and text semantics, showing high improvements in recall and precision for real-world captioning tasks [26].

From the literature, we can see image captioning for defect detection majorly involves LSTM's and attention-based models. After Vasvani et al. proposed transformer-based models the literature slowly shifted to transformers due to their strong attention capabilities [27]. Following Vaswani et al.'s introduction of transformer-based models, there has been a noticeable shift in the literature on image captioning for defect detection. LSTM and attention-based architectures were first popular because they were critical in image captioning. However, these had limitations regarding training efficiency and expression capabilities. The introduction of transformer-based models, with their strong attention capabilities, has resulted in considerable advances in the field. Researchers have begun to investigate CNN-Transformer-based models with remarkable success. These transformer models have proved valuable in overcoming restrictions associated with long-sequence data processing and managing data complexity, which were the issues with previous CNN and RNN procedures. The state-of-the-art in image captioning now broadly integrates transformer-based techniques, indicating a substantial shift in image captioning system methodology and efficiency, notably in defect detection applications [28–30].

Chen et al. introduced a transformative approach to object detection by reconceptualising it as a language modelling task through their Pix2Seq framework [4]. By harnessing the capabilities of transformers, this innovative framework transitions from traditional methods, which involved numerous processing steps such as anchor box generation and non-maximum suppression, to a more streamlined, end-to-end process. Pix2seq could also be used for tasks such as keypoint detection, image captioning, visual questions, and answering. Nevertheless, Pix2Seq's autoregressive modeling framework has limitations. For instance, its reliance on sequence termination upon encountering an end token can limit the detection of objects, particularly in densely populated images. This necessitates further refinement to ensure robustness across different detection scenarios [4].

To overcome conventional techniques' drawbacks, object detection and image captioning are combined in the steel defect detection process using the Pix2Seq framework. Beyond only bounding box detections, this integrated method offers comprehensive narratives about defects. It provides a more comprehensive, contextual knowledge of defects and their severity. This system uses transformer models, which address data complexity and other difficulties, to process long-sequence and complicated data more efficiently than earlier CNN and RNN models. However, there are also issues, such as possible data overload, model complexity, and the requirement for real-time processing in industrial settings. Notwithstanding these difficulties, some advantages exist, such as increased precision in identifying defects, more outstanding predictive maintenance, superior quality control, and the capacity to tailor the system to particular industrial requirements.

3 Methodology

This research methodology is explained in the following section: Dataset used for training and inference, preprocessing done to the data, vocabulary management, model architecture, initialisation and training Strategy and Inference, followed by discussion and conclusion.

3.1 Dataset Description

This study employs the NEU steel defect dataset, annotated explicitly for identifying steel manufacturing surface defects as shown in Fig. 1. The dataset was originally annotated in XML format, detailing defects with bounding box coordinates and class names. For this research, these annotations have been converted into a text format to streamline the process, with each record now containing an image name, path, bounding box coordinates, and defect class.

The 1,800 grayscale images in the (NEU) surface defect database record are split into six classes, each with 300 samples. Crazing (Cr), inclusion (In), patches (Pa), pitted surface (PS), rolled-in scale (RS), and scratches (Sc) are the six classes of surface defects as seen in hot-rolled steel strips. The resolution of every image in the dataset is 200 by 200 pixels. Due to their interclass similarities, the defect's crazing, pitted surface, and rolled-in scale are difficult to detect. Defects like scratches are hard to find because of the intraclass similarities in diagonal, vertical, and horizontal patterns. Because the dataset is grayscale, lighting circumstances may lead to inaccurate intraclass defect identification [31].

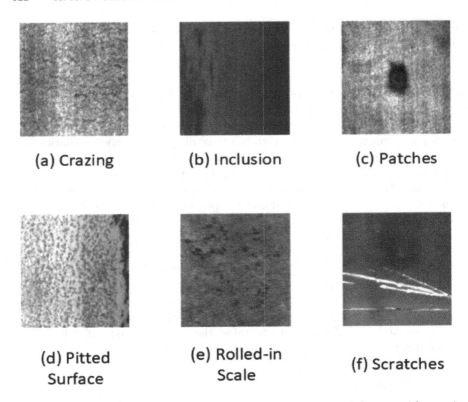

(a) Crazing   (b) Inclusion   (c) Patches

(d) Pitted   (e) Rolled-in   (f) Scratches
Surface   Scale

Fig. 1. Sample images from across all classes from the NEU steel dataset with associated defect descriptions: (a) Crazing - The defect is located at the top of the image. (b) Inclusion - The defect is located at the left of the image. (c) Patches - The defect is located at the center of the image. (d) Rolled-in Scale - The defect is located at the top left of the image. (e) Pitted Surface - [Description of the Pitted Surface defect location]. (f) Scratches - The defect is located at the bottom of the image.

Caption Generation and Validation. We generated descriptive captions for each defect using a Python script to support multimodal learning. This script produced textual descriptions that complement the visual data, focusing on the defects' attributes and locations. We created a sample for all the captions, which provides a solid foundation for initial model training. Even though many of the images had multiple bounding boxes, we concentrated on considering only one bounding box per image throughout the research phase. While each image contains multiple defects, our approach annotates only one defect per image with its bounding box coordinates and corresponding caption.

Dataset Suitability for Deep Learning. Combining images with textual descriptions, a dataset well-suited for deep learning applications in automated defect detection and captioning was prepared. For this research, images are standardised at 200 × 200 pixels, with only one defect type annotated per image to maintain clarity and focus on the learning task. This specificity ensures that the model can learn from a clear, unambiguous set of examples, which is critical for achieving high accuracy in practical quality control scenarios.

Only one defect was annotated for each image to simplify the model and improve its learning efficiency. This decision is in line with our objective of developing a training regime that is both thorough and manageable, ensuring the creation of a robust model that can accurately detect and describe defects. Its focus, which improves the model's performance and the methodology's scalability, justifies the simplification.

3.2 Dataset Preprocessing

Preprocessing data is crucial when preparing it for a specific neural network architecture. In this study, we adjusted the size of all images in our dataset from 200×200 pixels to 224×224 pixels. This change was necessary to fit the requirements of the Data-Efficient Image Transformers (DeiT3) small model, designed for processing images at this size using small patches of 16×16 pixelsData [32]. After adjusting image dimensions to meet the input requirements of the selected DeiT3 small architecture, we proceeded to delineate the dataset into subsets for training and validation. This segregation is crucial to furnish the model with ample learning material while reserving a share for evaluating model accuracy and its application to unseen data. We adopted a conventional partition ratio, dedicating 80% of the dataset to develop the model and earmarking 20% for subsequent performance validation. Stratified sampling was utilised during the split to maintain a balanced representation of defect categories across both subsets, thereby preventing potential learning biases and ensuring the validation set mirrors the composite class variety in the entire dataset.

Image and Augmentation Transformations. To prepare the images for training, we apply a range of augmentations. These include flipping the images horizontally or vertically, rotating them, changing brightness and contrast, and adding blur effects. These steps introduce variation to the data, which helps make our model more capable of dealing with different visual scenarios. For the validation dataset, we keep things simpler by just resizing and normalising the images, ensuring they are in a uniform format for the model to evaluate. By training our model with these diverse conditions, we're teaching it to recognise defects in less-than-ideal circumstances, making it more effective for real-world applications. We balance our use of augmentations to avoid confusing the model with too much variation, which could otherwise reduce its accuracy.

Data Preparation: Bounding Boxes, Captions, and Labels. Three principal components are meticulously structured in preparing data for the proposed model: quantised bounding box coordinates, tokenised image captions, and class labels. Bounding box values are scaled and quantised to discrete integers, facilitating uniformity in input data dimensions and mitigating overfitting due to minute positional variances. These quantised values offer a compact numerical representation of spatial information, encapsulating the location and dimension of objects within images.

Consider a normalised value x to be quantised. The quantisation process can be represented as:

$$Q(x) = \text{int}\left(x \times (N-1)\right) \tag{1}$$

where $Q(x)$ represents the quantised value of x, N is the number of quantisation levels, and int($\cdot$) is the function that converts the product into an integer. This quantisation formula scales the input x to a discrete level within the range of 0 to $N-1$, where N denotes the total number of available quantisation levels.

Captions undergo tokenisation to convert textual descriptions into a format valid for computational processing. This process involves deconstructing sentences into constituent tokens and mapping each token to a corresponding integer identifier based on a pre-established vocabulary. The vocabulary is constructed by cataloguing token occurrences throughout the corpus and assigning indices to those surpassing a defined frequency threshold. This methodical assignment yields a sequence of integers that effectively replaces raw textual data, making it suitable for subsequent learning tasks.

Class labels convert categorical object identifications into a numerical schema, assigning an unequivocal integer to each unique object class. The synthesised input feature vector for the learning model amalgamates these three data facets, presenting a cohesive framework that aligns visual descriptors with linguistic elements.

3.3   Model Architecture

Our research used an EncoderDecoder network structure inspired by the Pix2Seq technique for transforming visual data into descriptive language. The synergy of two unique aspects underpins our method: the encoder, which refines images into feature-rich vectors, and the decoder, which reconstructs these vectors into narrative text. The encoder can extract detailed visual features using the Data-Efficient Image Transformers (DeiT3) compact architecture [32]. The decoder takes in tokenised captions, quantised bounding box coordinates, and image features. It uses these rich traits to output a sequence which contains the textual descriptions togethed with the bounding box coordinates that accurately reflect the visual data. Pix2Seq's approach and our refined additions enable a more accurate depiction of defects, increasing the model's utility in industrial quality control.

Encoder Module. The encoder module is the first part of our image-processing journey. Constructed on the DeiT3 small model framework, it transforms images into a compact feature vector format, rendering them suitable for interpretation [32]. An adaptive average pooling layer is strategically employed to refine the output feature set to a fixed dimensionality, streamlining subsequent computational steps.

Decoder Module. Complementing the encoder, the decoder module's role is to reconstruct the feature vectors into textual descriptions. It comprises an embedding layer to transform vocabulary indices into vector representations, enhanced by positional embeddings to preserve the sequential character of natural language. Including a dropout mechanism safeguards against overfitting, promoting a generalisable model across diverse data inputs. The decoder utilises a series of transformer layers renowned for their self-attention capabilities, enabling the model to discern and emphasise pertinent information throughout the decoding process.

End-to-End Model Workflow. The EncoderDecoder class encapsulates the workflow, making a seamless transition from image input to textual output. This synergy ensures the integrity of the model's end-to-end learning capability, underpinned by a coherent forward propagation strategy from raw image to final caption. The predict function within this class serves a dual purpose: refining the generation of descriptions and validating the model's predictive prowess

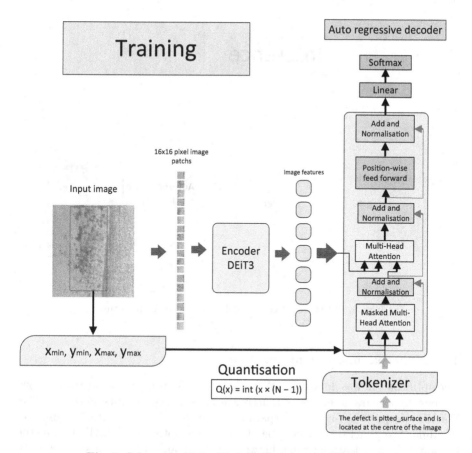

Fig. 2. Schematic of the Model's Training Architecture.

on partial text inputs. The model can break down and understand the text that describes industrial defects. Complementing this, we've also implemented a vectorisation technique for bounding box coordinates, ensuring a seamless integration of spatial data with textual information. This dual strategy enhances the model's ability to correlate visual data with descriptive text and improves defect detection and characterisation accuracy. Hence, the model stands out as a specialised solution, finely tuned for the intricacies and challenges of industrial quality control and defect analysis (Figs. 2 and 3).

4   Implementation and Training

Our training process employs a standard epoch-based approach, iterating over the dataset for a predefined number of epochs, which in our case is 50. At each epoch, the model is trained on the entire training dataset and evaluated on the validation dataset. An initial learning rate of 0.00001 and a weight decay of 0.0001 were selected to balance the model's learning speed and regularisation needs.

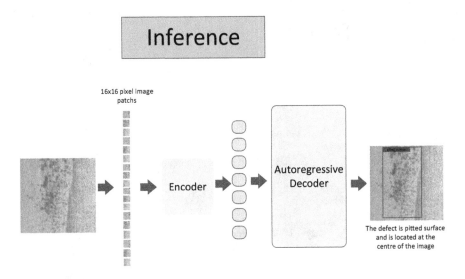

Fig. 3. Overview of the Model's Inference Architecture.

4.1   Hyperparameter Optimization

The optimisation was done using WandB Sweeps. This helped in narrowing down the best hyperparameters by conducting a series of experiments. Setup: Utilized WandB sweeps to optimise hyperparameters such as learning rate, learning rate schedule, loss function, epochs, batch size, and optimiser [33,34]. Parameters Explored: Tested learning rates between 0.00001 and 0.1, batch sizes of 8, 16,

32, weight decay of 1e-5 and 1e-4, and optimisers including 'AdamW' and Adam. Dynamic Configuration: Each sweep iteration dynamically adjusted the model's loss function, optimiser, and learning rate scheduler based on the sweep's current configuration.

4.2   Reproducibility and Model Consistency

We emphasise reproducibility and model consistency by using a fixed seed for all elements of stochasticity in our computational environment. This ensures that other researchers can consistently regenerate our results. The dataset underwent a precise split of 80% for training and 20% for validation to maintain our experimental design's integrity.

4.3   Loss Function and Optimization

Focal loss was selected as the loss function parameterised by $\alpha = 1$ and $\gamma = 2$, significantly improving model performance compared to cross-entropy loss [35]. This improvement was notable even though our dataset had a balanced set of classes. The critical advantage of focal loss lies in its ability to prioritise learning from challenging examples. In our context, despite class balance, there were notable interclass and intraclass similarities, with some examples being complicated to detect and classify. Focal loss focuses more on these complex examples, dynamically scaling the loss to emphasise learning from these challenging cases. The γ parameter, set at 2, was instrumental in reducing the influence of easily classified examples, thereby compelling the model to learn more discriminative features [36]. The model's capacity to distinguish and correctly classify instances—even those belonging to identical classes—was significantly enhanced by concentrating on the more intricate cases. This proved the usefulness of focal loss when subtle feature differentiation is essential.

Code Accessibility. The complete implementation code and datasets are available upon request to ensure controlled distribution and usage.

5   Results and Discussion

The encouraging trend in our experimental results can be attributed to the model's learning efficacy. From the graph in Fig. 4, We see a steady drop in loss during training, with the training loss impressively decreasing to 0.2. At the same time, the validation loss demonstrated a positive convergence, falling to 0.15 by the eighth epoch as seen in Fig. 5. This convergence pattern is a reliable sign of the model's capacity for efficient learning. Notable in particular is the relatively small difference between training and validation losses, which suggests a well-balanced model fit that effectively avoids overfitting while preserving strong generalisation.

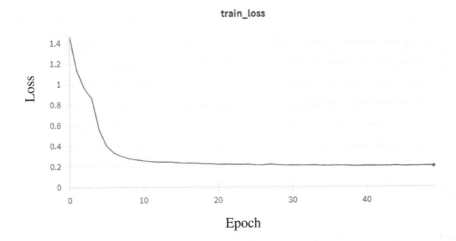

Fig. 4. Graph depicting the training loss across epochs for the model.

The model exhibits an adequate learning curve, as evidenced by the convergence of training and validation losses, indicating its capability to learn efficiently from the dataset. This is particularly noteworthy given the limited data available for training and validation. When benchmarked against baseline LSTM Attention models, our framework demonstrates comparable performance, reinforcing the model's effectiveness even within the constraints of a limited dataset. Additionally, the framework's design presents opportunities for extension, particularly in incorporating more detailed captions and adapting to visual question-answering tasks, which are increasingly relevant in advanced AI (Artificial Intelligence) applications. Figure 6 shows the correct bounding box prediction with the underlying captions.

Despite these limitations, the model's performance with a limited dataset is encouraging, particularly for potential applications in industrial settings where precise visual inspection and automated captioning are valuable. The observed gap in bounding box and caption accuracy underscores the need for a model that can achieve a more complex and human-like understanding of visual data. Comparatively, the extension of the Pix2Seq model to captioning exhibits potential advantages over traditional LSTM-CNN approaches, especially in generating more detailed and contextually relevant captions.

When it comes to defect detection, our suggested method has two advantages over traditional acoustic emission techniques. Our method tackles both detection and contextual understanding using a single pipeline, in contrast to vanilla object detectors that only detect defects. By combining global contextual perspective with parallel processing power of the transformers, it gives detailed analysis in addition to defect detection. This adaptability makes our method more comprehensive and suitable for a wide range of industrial purposes. It also opens up potential applications in segmentation and other sequence-based tasks. This dual-capability, coupled with its flexible application range, significantly outper-

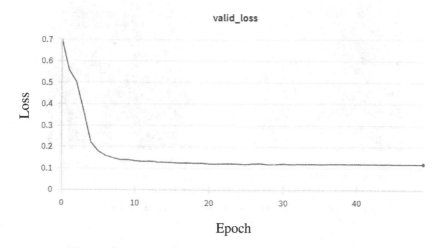

Fig. 5. Graph depicting the validation loss across epochs for the model.

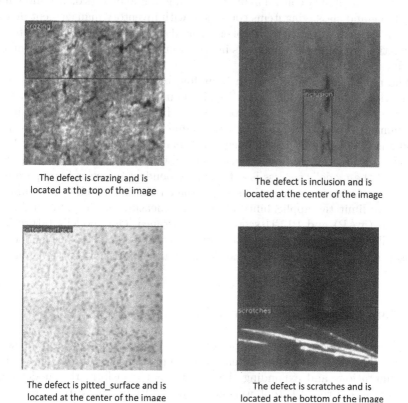

The defect is crazing and is
located at the top of the image

The defect is inclusion and is
located at the center of the image

The defect is pitted_surface and is
located at the center of the image

The defect is scratches and is
located at the bottom of the image

Fig. 6. Correct output results of defects and captions.

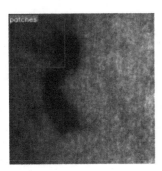 

The defect is patches and is located at the top left of the image

The defect is pitted_surface and is located at the top left of the image

Fig. 7. Incorrect output predictions of defects and captions.

forms traditional single-focus methods in both scope and efficacy. This model is practically adaptable to a variety of industrial applications. It could be applied, for example, to quality control in manufacturing to find defects on assembly lines. Identifying and classifying items could help with inventory management in logistics. The model's capacity to decipher visual data and deliver important textual information would be advantageous in each scenario, improving decision-making processes' accuracy and efficiency.

The model faces limitations in bounding box accuracy and caption generation, with notable discrepancies (Fig. 7). Our present technique uses a single bounding box per image, which we see as a limitations, especially for images with numerous or overlaid defects. This is due in part to the size and nature of our dataset, which may impede generalisation in complicated settings. At the moment, automated captioning lacks the subtle context that a person would offer, and the model's success is extremely dependent on exact hyperparameter tuning. Furthermore, training biases and the emphasis on technical accuracy in captioning limit the applicability of common measures such as Mean Average Precision (mAP) and BLEU score in our instance. Our model's future iterations will strive to integrate multi-object detection capabilities and increase the dataset, improving applicability and accuracy in a variety of industrial environments.

6 Conclusion and Future Direction

The current model demonstrates promising results within its constraints showing that there is considerable potential for improvement. Addressing the identified limitations and expanding the dataset can transform the model into a more robust and versatile tool, well-suited for industrial applications and potentially pioneering new standards in automated visual inspection and captioning. The findings from this research could pave the way for future studies in automated visual inspection and caption generation, particularly in industrial settings. Demonstrating the effectiveness of transformer models in this domain could inspire further research into more complex and refined applications, pushing the boundaries of what these models can achieve.

Several avenues exist to enhance the model's performance and utility. Integrating human-created captions into the training process could substantially improve the quality and relevance of the generated captions, bringing a level of sophistication and accuracy that automated methods alone cannot achieve. Expanding the dataset in size and diversity and including multiple bounding boxes per image with corresponding captions will provide a more realistic and challenging training environment for the model. Implementing advanced quantitative metrics like mean average precision for multiple bounding boxes will enable a more concrete evaluation of the model's performance.

Disclosure of Interests. The authors declare that there are no competing interests to disclose that are relevant to the content of this article. No funding has been allocated for this project.

References

1. Redmon, J., Divvala, S., Girshick, R., Farhadi, A.: You only look once: unified, real-time object detection. In: Proceedings of the IEEE Conference on Computer Vision and Pattern Recognition, pp. 779–788 (2016)
2. Girshick, R.: Fast r-cnn. In: Proceedings of the IEEE International Conference on Computer Vision, pp. 1440–1448 (2015)
3. Xie, Y., Hu, W., Xie, S., He, L.: Surface defect detection algorithm based on feature-enhanced yolo. Cogn. Comput. **15**(2), 565–579 (2023)
4. Chen, T., Saxena, S., Li, L., Fleet, D.J., Hinton, G.: Pix2seq: a language modeling framework for object detection. arXiv preprint arXiv:2109.10852 (2021)
5. Luo, Q., He, Y.: A cost-effective and automatic surface defect inspection system for hot-rolled flat steel. Robot. Comput.-Integr. Manuf. **38**, 16–30 (2016)
6. Helifa, B., Oulhadj, A., Benbelghit, A., Lefkaier, I., Boubenider, F., Boutassouna, D.: Detection and measurement of surface cracks in ferromagnetic materials using eddy current testing. Ndt & E Int. **39**(5), 384–390 (2006)
7. Li, X., Gao, B., Woo, W.L., Tian, G.Y., Qiu, X., Gu, L.: Quantitative surface crack evaluation based on eddy current pulsed thermography. IEEE Sens. J. **17**(2), 412–421 (2016)
8. Shrestha, R., Park, J., Kim, W.: Application of thermal wave imaging and phase shifting method for defect detection in stainless steel. Infrared Phys. Technol. **76**, 676–683 (2016)
9. Gao, B., Li, X., Woo, W.L., Yun Tian, G.: Physics-based image segmentation using first order statistical properties and genetic algorithm for inductive thermography imaging. IEEE Trans. Image Process. **27**(5) (2017) 2160–2175
10. Li, X.G., Miao, C.Y., Wang, J., Zhang, Y.: Automatic defect detection method for the steel cord conveyor belt based on its x-ray images. In: 2011 International Conference on Control, Automation and Systems Engineering (CASE), pp. 1–4. IEEE (2011)
11. Zhang, Y., et al.: Development of a cross-scale weighted feature fusion network for hot-rolled steel surface defect detection. Eng. Appl. Artif. Intell. **117**, 105628 (2023)

12. Demir, K., Ay, M., Cavas, M., Demir, F.: Automated steel surface defect detection and classification using a new deep learning-based approach. Neural Comput. Appl. **35**(11), 8389–8406 (2023)

13. Yang, L., Xu, S., Fan, J., Li, E., Liu, Y.: A pixel-level deep segmentation network for automatic defect detection. Expert Syst. Appl. **215**, 119388 (2023)

14. Ji, A., Thee, Q.Y., Woo, W.L., Wong, E.: Experimental investigations of a convolutional neural network model for detecting railway track anomalies. In: IECON 2023-49th Annual Conference of the IEEE Industrial Electronics Society, pp. 1–7. IEEE (2023)

15. Chazhoor, A.A.P., Zhu, M., Ho, E.S.L., Gao, B., Woo, W.L.: Classification of different types of plastics using deep transfer learning. In: ROBOVIS, SciTePress, Science and Technology Publications, pp. 190–195 (2021)

16. Chazhoor, A.A.P., Ho, E.S., Gao, B., Woo, W.L.: Deep transfer learning benchmark for plastic waste classification. Intell. Robot. **2**, 1–19 (2022)

17. He, Y., Song, K., Meng, Q., Yan, Y.: An end-to-end steel surface defect detection approach via fusing multiple hierarchical features. IEEE Trans. Instrum. Meas. **69**(4), 1493–1504 (2019)

18. Chazhoor, A.A.P., Ho, E.S., Gao, B., Woo, W.L.: A review and benchmark on state-of-the-art steel defects detection. SN Comput. Sci. **5**(1), 114 (2023)

19. Zhao, W., Chen, F., Huang, H., Li, D., Cheng, W.: A new steel defect detection algorithm based on deep learning. Comput. Intell. Neurosci. **2021**, 1–13 (2021)

20. Mirzaei, S., Mao, H., Al-Nima, R.R.O., Woo, W.L.: Explainable AI evaluation: a top-down approach for selecting optimal explanations for black box models. Information **15**(1), 4 (2023)

21. Wang, J., Madhyastha, P., Specia, L.: Object counts! bringing explicit detections back into image captioning. arXiv preprint arXiv:1805.00314 (2018)

22. Chun, P.J., Yamane, T., Maemura, Y.: A deep learning-based image captioning method to automatically generate comprehensive explanations of bridge damage. Comput.-Aided Civ. Infrastruct. Eng. **37**(11), 1387–1401 (2022)

23. Iwamura, K., Louhi Kasahara, J.Y., Moro, A., Yamashita, A., Asama, H.: Image captioning using motion-CNN with object detection. Sensors **21**(4), 1270 (2021)

24. Shao, X., Xiang, Z., Li, Y., Zhang, M.: Variational joint self-attention for image captioning. IET Image Process. **16**(8), 2075–2086 (2022)

25. Wei, D., Wei, X., Jia, L.: Automatic defect description of railway track line image based on dense captioning. Sensors **22**(17), 6419 (2022)

26. Yong, C., Yingchi, M., Yi, W., Ping, P., Longbao, W.: Keywords-based dam defect image caption generation. In: 2021 IEEE Seventh International Conference on Big Data Computing Service and Applications (BigDataService), pp. 214–221. IEEE (2021)

27. Vaswani, A., et al.: Attention is all you need. Adv. Neural Inf. Process. Syst. **30** (2017)

28. Tsaniya, H., Fatichah, C., Suciati, N.: Transformer approaches in image captioning: a literature review. In: 2022 14th International Conference on Information Technology and Electrical Engineering (ICITEE), pp. 1–6. IEEE (2022)

29. Wang, Y., Xu, J., Sun, Y.: End-to-end transformer based model for image captioning. In: Proceedings of the AAAI Conference on Artificial Intelligence, vol. 36, pp. 2585–2594 (2022)

30. Dittakan, K., Prompitak, K., Thungklang, P., Wongwattanakit, C.: Image caption generation using transformer learning methods: a case study on instagram image. Multimed. Tools Appl. 1–21 (2023)

31. Song, K., Yan, Y.: A noise robust method based on completed local binary patterns for hot-rolled steel strip surface defects. Appl. Surf. Sci. **285**, 858–864 (2013)
32. Touvron, H., Cord, M., Jégou, H.: DeiT III: revenge of the ViT. In: Avidan, S., Brostow, G., Cisse, M., Farinella, G.M., Hassner, T. (eds.) Computer Vision – ECCV 2022. ECCV 2022. LNCS, vol. 13684, pp. 516–533. Springer, Cham (2022). https://doi.org/10.1007/978-3-031-20053-3_30
33. Zhang, Z.: Improved adam optimizer for deep neural networks. In: IEEE/ACM 26th International Symposium on Quality of Service (IWQoS). IEEE 2018, pp. 1–2 (2018)
34. Yao, Z., Gholami, A., Shen, S., Mustafa, M., Keutzer, K., Mahoney, M.: Adahessian: an adaptive second order optimizer for machine learning. In: Proceedings of the AAAI Conference on Artificial Intelligence, vol. 35, pp. 10665–10673 (2021)
35. Zhang, Z., Sabuncu, M.: Generalized cross entropy loss for training deep neural networks with noisy labels. Adv. Neural Inf. Process. Syst. **31** (2018)
36. Lin, T.Y., Goyal, P., Girshick, R., He, K., Dollár, P.: Focal loss for dense object detection. In: Proceedings of the IEEE International Conference on Computer Vision, pp. 2980–2988 (2017)

Operational Modeling of Temporal Intervals for Intelligent Systems

J. I. Olszewska$^{(\boxtimes)}$ iD

School of Computing and Engineering, University of the West of Scotland, Paisley, UK
joanna.olszewska@ieee.org

Abstract. Time is a crucial notion for intelligent systems, such as robotic systems, cognitive systems, multi-agent systems, cyber-physical systems, or autonomous systems, since it is inherent to any real-world process and/or environment. Hence, in this paper, we present operational temporal logic notations for modeling the time aspect of intelligent systems in terms of temporal interval concepts. Their application to intelligent systems' application scenarios have demonstrated the usefulness and effectiveness of our developed approach.

Keywords: Intelligent systems · Robotic systems · Knowledge-based systems · Cognitive systems · Multi-agent systems · System of systems · Cyber-physical systems · Autonomous systems · Intelligent control · Temporal intervals · Allen's temporal relations · Description logic · Unified modeling language · Knowledge representation and reasoning · Verification and validation · Explainable Artificial intelligence

1 Introduction

With the current development of smart manufacturing and Industry 4.0 [63] as well as related technologies such as cloud robotics [25], or Internet of Things (IoT) [67], intelligent and autonomous systems intrinsically involve temporal processes [58], and thus their study requires the conceptualisation of temporal notions [45].

Hence, Logic and in particular Temporal Logic (TL) [39] have been used for the design [28] and planning – task planning [38], motion planning [32] – as well as the testing [46] and verification [23] of intelligent and autonomous systems. Temporal logic has also been applied for checking safety [61] and privacy [66] of systems such as autonomous driving systems or autonomous flying systems.

Moreover, the design [52], the requirement specification [30] and the verification [4] of of complex software [17], real-time systems [37], distributed systems [36], cognitive and knowledge-based systems (KBS) [10], artificial intelligence-based systems [21], multi-agent systems (MAS) [48], or cyber-physical systems (CPS) [26], robotic systems [42], or system of systems (SoS) [13] also require the use of temporal logic [27].

For this purpose, Signal Temporal Logic (STL) [5] and Metric Temporal Logic (MTL) [34], which extends the expressiveness of the Linear Temporal Logic (LTL) [60], are commonly used as well as their further enhancements such as Chance Constrained Temporal Logic (C2TL) extending STL to capture perception uncertainty [35],

© The Author(s), under exclusive license to Springer Nature Switzerland AG 2024
J. Filipe and J. Röning (Eds.): ROBOVIS 2024, CCIS 2077, pp. 334–344, 2024.
https://doi.org/10.1007/978-3-031-59057-3_21

or Spatio-Temporal Specification Language (STSL), i.e. STL with spatial logic [41], to name a few. On the other hand, some works present high-level definitions of time concepts [18] using e.g., the Semantic Web Rule Language (SWRL) [9].

In this study, we model our temporal relations in Description Logic (DL) for both operational-ability and interoperability. Furthermore, while DL notations could be directly integrated in the building of potential OWL-DL ontologies requiring temporal aspect [7], DL knowledge specifications are also closely connected to the Unified Modeling Language (UML) [11], which is useful to model intelligent, robotic and autonomous systems [52].

Indeed, our operational modeling uses DL rather than other logics such as MTL [62] or STL [31], in order to provide intelligent systems with the possibility of further integration with ontologies [53,55] and ontological standards [54,56] for robotics and automation such as IEEE 1872-2015, IEEE P1872.1, IEEE 1872.2-2021, IEEE 1872.3 [22,49] as well as IEEE 7007-2021 [33,59].

Another advantage of using temporal DL over other temporal logic languages is that UML can be embedded in the DL modeling [44]. Since UML is useful for designing intelligent systems, e.g. robotic systems [65], this constitutes an important benefit for the developed operational modeling.

UML is a well-established notational language to describe the structure and behaviour of complex systems [24]. It is useful for building softwares and ontologies [57], maintaining information in databases [29], as well as modeling and describing processes [8]. However, UML is a non-temporal modeling language [15]. Some attempts to introduce temporal aspect into UML have been done by [1,11,15,16], but there were mostly limited to class diagrams.

Therefore, in this work, we aim also to fully integrate temporal notions such as temporal interval relations [2] with UML activity diagrams [14].

It is worth noting that we focus in this study on activity diagrams only, because they have been demonstrated to be very powerful to capture dynamic processes of an intelligent system [50,51] and also to represent time concurrent systems [3].

Thence, the main contributions of this work are the study of the conceptualization of dynamic behaviours of intelligent systems and their operational modeling in an ontologically appropriate form through the use of Temporal Description Logic (TDL) notations and enhanced by Unified Modeling Language (UML) activity diagrams, in context of dependable software systems [12] and verifiable autonomous systems [20].

The paper is structured as follows. In Sect. 2, we introduce the operational modeling of the temporal interval relations. Then, we present our approach for both formal and semantic time concept's representation using DL and UML on real-world intelligent systems, as reported and discussed in Sect. 3. Conclusions are drawn up in Sect. 4.

2   Proposed Approach

Time notion could be conceptualised in terms of time points or in terms of time intervals [19]. In particular, [2] considered the temporal axis as indefinitely dense and defined a time interval as an ordered set of points $T = \{t\}$ defined by end-points t^- and t^+, leading to the formal logic definition as follows:

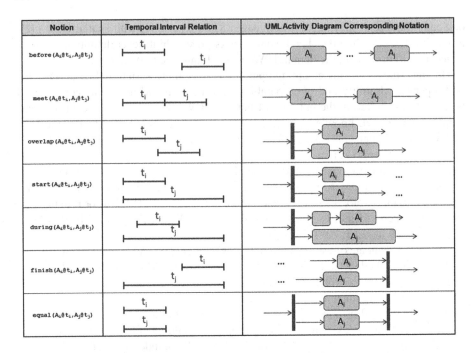

Fig. 1. Mapping temporal interval relations with UML activity diagram notations.

$$(t^-, t^+) : (\forall t \in T)(t > t^-) \wedge (t < t^+). \tag{1}$$

Then, for the intervals t_i and t_j, [2] sets seven temporal relations, i.e. before: $t_i < t_j$, meets: $t_i \, m \, t_j$, overlap: $t_i \, o \, t_j$, starts: $t_i \, s \, t_j$, during: $t_i \, d \, t_j$, finishes: $t_i \, f \, t_j$, and equal: $t_i = t_j$. These temporal relations mentioned in Fig. 1 (column 1) are further illustrated in Fig. 1 (column 2), assuming an abstract time axis from left to right.

In this work, we formalize thus time concepts based on Allen's temporal intervals, because time intervals appear to be a well-suited knowledge representation of the time of activities/states of intelligent systems [36, 40, 64].

The formalization of our operational model involves DL and leads to the axioms as follows:

$$before(A_i@t_i, A_j@t_j) \sqsubseteq Temporal\_Relation$$
$$\sqcap (\Diamond t_i)(\Diamond t_j)$$
$$(t_{i+} < t_{j-})$$
$$\cdot (A_i@t_i \sqcap A_j@t_j), \tag{2}$$

$$meet(A_i@t_i, A_j@t_j) \sqsubseteq Temporal\_Relation$$
$$\sqcap (\Diamond t_i)(\Diamond t_j)$$
$$(t_{i+} = t_{j-})$$
$$\cdot (A_i@t_i \sqcap A_j@t_j), \tag{3}$$

$$overlap(A_i@t_i, A_j@t_j) \sqsubseteq Temporal\_Relation$$
$$\sqcap (\diamond t_i)(\diamond t_j)$$
$$(t_{i-} < t_{j-})$$
$$\sqcap (t_{i+} > t_{j-})$$
$$\sqcap (t_{i+} < t_{j+})$$
$$\cdot (A_i@t_i \sqcap A_j@t_j), \tag{4}$$

$$start(A_i@t_i, A_j@t_j) \sqsubseteq Temporal\_Relation$$
$$\sqcap (\diamond t_i)(\diamond t_j)$$
$$(t_{i-} = t_{j-})$$
$$\cdot (A_i@t_i \sqcap A_j@t_j), \tag{5}$$

$$during(A_i@t_i, A_j@t_j) \sqsubseteq Temporal\_Relation$$
$$\sqcap (\diamond t_i)(\diamond t_j)$$
$$(t_{i-} > t_{j-}) \sqcap (t_{i+} < t_{j+})$$
$$\cdot (A_i@t_i \sqcap A_j@t_j), \tag{6}$$

$$finish(A_i@t_i, A_j@t_j) \sqsubseteq Temporal\_Relation$$
$$\sqcap (\diamond t_i)(\diamond t_j)$$
$$(t_{i+} = t_{j+})$$
$$\cdot (A_i@t_i \sqcap A_j@t_j), \tag{7}$$

$$equal(A_i@t_i, A_j@t_j) \sqsubseteq Temporal\_Relation$$
$$\sqcap (\diamond t_i)(\diamond t_j)$$
$$(t_{i-} = t_{j-}) \sqcap (t_{i+} = t_{j+})$$
$$\cdot (A_i@t_i \sqcap A_j@t_j), \tag{8}$$

where the temporal DL symbol $\diamond$ introduced by [6] represents the temporal existential qualifier.

The temporal model as specified by Eqs. 2–8 relates activities two by two. For example, temporal relations like $before(A_i@t_i, A_j@t_j)$ or its counterpart $after(A_i@t_i, A_j@t_j)$ help to order the pairs of activities, while temporal relations like $start(A_i@t_i, A_j@t_j)$, $finish(A_i@t_i, A_j@t_j)$, $equal(A_i@t_i, A_j@t_j)$ as well as $meet(A_i@t_i, A_j@t_j)$ contribute to the synchronization of the overall process.

3   Application and Discussion

In order to validate our presented operational approach, we studied a real-world scenario of an intelligent system which performs activities we captured using UML activity diagram notations. Indeed, UML activity diagrams [47] are state-transition diagrams that consist of activities/states and transitions between them, such as displayed in Fig. 1 (column 3).

Activities are where the tasks of a process are performed, and they could be short or long. They are represented by rounded rectangles labeled inside with the name of the related activity [43]. Activities could also be simultaneous. Thus, they could start simultaneously as graphically notated by a fork or finish simultaneously as visually symbolized by a join [50].

Moreover, activities could be performed by different actors, organized into swimlanes which are represented by columns with a heading containing the corresponding actor's name (see Fig. 2). On the other hand, states are activities where nothing happen [43]. In particular, the initial state, which is depicted as a black circle, is the initialization of the process, while the final state denotes the end of the process and is drawn as a black bullseye [43]. Transitions capture the work flow of the system from one activity to another and are symbolized by an arrow [43]. Other most common activity patterns consist of decisions which lead to different flow paths of the process, and which are determined by some conditions constraining then the work flow [43]. Decisions are illustrated by a diamond shape as in Fig. 2.

In the scenario as presented in Fig. 2, activities are assumed to be represented chronologically from top to bottom, and the height of each rectangle corresponding to an activity is proportional to its duration in time. These notations as well as their relative positions within the activity diagram can be used to set the appropriate temporal relations between any pair of these activities.

It is worth to note we abstracted the names of these activities to A_1, etc. for the sake of confidentiality as well as anonymity of the carried-out study.

While our proposed model in the previous section can map the temporal interval relations to UML activity diagram notations as displayed in Fig. 1, it can also deal with the various actors and the related swimlanes such as those present in this case study. For example, in the swimlane 1, the activity A_1 performed by the actor 1 meets the activity A_2 performed by the actor 2. Hence, this could be formalized by:

$$meet(A_1@t_1, A_2@t_2) \sqsubseteq Temporal\_Relation$$
$$\sqcap (\Diamond t_1)(\Diamond t_2)$$
$$(t_{1+} = t_{2-}) \tag{9}$$
$$\cdot (A_1@t_1 \sqcap A_2@t_2).$$

In particular, concurrent actions such as A_6 and A_{12} could be conceptualized by:

$$equal(A_6@t_6, A_{12}@t_{12}) \sqsubseteq Temporal\_Relation$$
$$\sqcap (\Diamond t_6)(\Diamond t_{12})$$
$$(t_{6-} = t_{12-}) \tag{10}$$
$$\sqcap (t_{6+} = t_{12+})$$
$$\cdot (A_6@t_6 \sqcap A_{12}@t_{12}).$$

On the other hand, activities such as A_{15} and A_{16} could occur within a loop if the c_2 condition is met. For example, if there is one loop ($l = [0, 1]$, $l \in \mathbb{N}$), this could lead to the following relations:

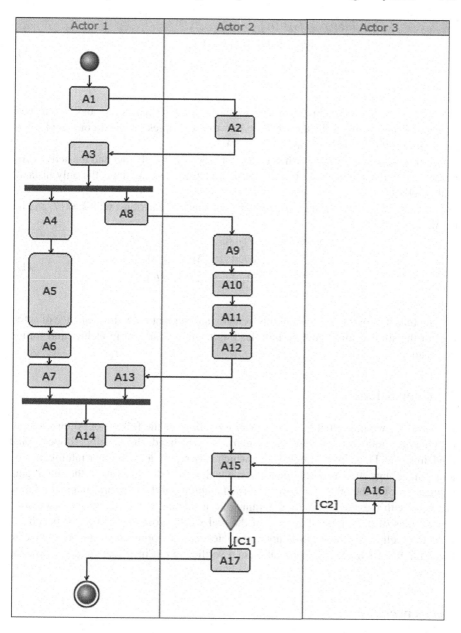

Fig. 2. UML activity diagram of a scenario example.

$$loop \doteq \diamond(t_0)\diamond(t_1)$$
$$(A_{15_0} < A_{16_1})(A_{16_1}mA_{15_1})$$
$$\cdot (A_{15_0}@t_{15_0} \sqcap A_{16_1}@t_{16_1} \sqcap A_{15_1}@t_{15_1}). \tag{11}$$

A_{15_l} and A_{16_l} are the chronological instances of the activities A_{15} and A_{16}, respectively, and they result from the lth loop due to the l-times satisfied constraint c_2. In particular for the single loop case, $A_{16_{l=1}} = A_{16}$.

In the case when $l = 0$, i.e. when the c_1 condition is directly met and the activity A_{16} never occurs, the activity A_{15_0} is then considered as A_{15}, since this is the only instance of this activity.

Our notation for the entire scenario which consists of k actions, with $k = 17$, and for $l = 0$, is as follows:

$$scenario \doteq \diamond(t_1...t_k)$$
$$(A_1mA_2)...(A_{15} < A_{17})$$
$$\cdot (A_1@t_1 \sqcap ... \sqcap A_k@t_k), \tag{12}$$

and thus it allows to represent both formally and semantically the sequence of activities of the studied intelligent system, leading to its operational modeling and formal verification.

4   Conclusions

In this work, we presented the operational modelling of the full set of Allen's temporal interval relations for intelligent systems. On one hand, the developed operational modeling uses Description Logic (DL), which is compatible with other intelligent system's modelings such as ontological ones, opening thus the doors to further intelligent applications. On the other hand, the proposed mapping of the temporal-interval relation concepts with the UML activity diagram patterns enhances both formal and semantic descriptions of the temporal aspects of the real-world processes while still benefiting from the well-established UML notations. Hence, our approach could be applied to temporal process modeling, automation and verification of intelligent and autonomous systems.

References

1. Al-Lail, M., Abdunabi, R., France, R.B., Ray, I.: An approach to analyzing temporal properties in UML class models. In: Proceedings of the ACM/IEEE International Conference on Model Driven Engineering Languages and Systems Workshop (MODELS), pp. 77–86 (2013)
2. Allen, J.F.: Maintaining knowledge about temporal intervals. Commun. ACM **26**(11), 832–843 (1983)

3. André, É., Choppy, C., Noulamo, T.: Modelling timed concurrent systems using activity diagram patterns. In: Nguyen, V.-H., Le, A.-C., Huynh, V.-N. (eds.) Knowledge and Systems Engineering. AISC, vol. 326, pp. 339–351. Springer, Cham (2015). https://doi.org/10.1007/978-3-319-11680-8_27

4. Araiza-Illan, D., Fisher, M., Leahy, K., Olszewska, J.I., Redfield, S.: Verification of autonomous systems. IEEE Robot. Autom. Mag. **29**(1), 2–3 (2022)

5. Arechiga, N.: Specifying safety of autonomous vehicles in signal temporal logic. In: Proceedings of the IEEE Intelligent Vehicles Symposium (IV), pp. 58–63 (2019)

6. Artale, A., Franconi, E.: Temporal description logics. Handb. Time Temporal Reason. Artif. Intell. **1**, 375–388 (2005)

7. Artale, A., Kontchakov, R., Ryzhikov, V., Zakharyaschev, M.: Tractable interval temporal propositional and description logics. In: Proceedings of the AAAI Conference on Artificial Intelligence (AAAI) (2015)

8. Bastos, R., Ruiz, D.: Extending UML activity diagram for workflow modeling in production systems. In: Proceedings of the IEEE Annual Hawaii International Conference on System Sciences, pp. 3786–3795 (2002)

9. Batsakis, S., Petrakis, E., Tachmazidis, I., Antoniou, G.: Temporal representation and reasoning in OWL 2. Semant. Web J. **8**(6), 1–20 (2016)

10. Bayat, B., et al.: Requirements for building an ontology for autonomous robots. Ind. Robot. **43**(5), 469–480 (2016)

11. Berardi, D., Calvanese, D., Giacomo, G.D.: Reasoning on UML class diagrams using description logic based systems. In: Proceedings of the KI Workshop on Applications of Description Logics, vol. 44 (2001)

12. Binder, R.: Software dependability measurement at the age of 36. IEEE Comput. **57**(4), 1–18 (2024). https://arxiv.org/abs/2311.10039

13. Black, R., Davenport, J.H., Olszewska, J.I., Roessler, J., Smith, A.L., Wright, J.: Artificial Intelligence and Software Testing: Building Systems You Can Trust. BCS Press, London (2022)

14. Booch, G., Rumbaugh, J., Jacobson, I.: The Unified Modeling Language User Guide. Pearson, London (2005)

15. Cabot, J., Olivé, A., Teniente, E.: Representing temporal information in UML. In: Stevens, P., Whittle, J., Booch, G. (eds.) UML 2003. LNCS, vol. 2863, pp. 44–59. Springer, Heidelberg (2003). https://doi.org/10.1007/978-3-540-45221-8_5

16. Cali, A., Calvanese, D., Giacomo, G.D., Lenzerini, M.: Reasoning on UML class diagrams in description logics. In: Proceedings of IJCAR Workshop on Precise Modelling and Deduction for Object-Oriented Software Development, pp. 77–86 (2001)

17. Clarke, E.M., Wing, J.M.: Formal methods: state of the art and future directions. ACM Comput. Surv. **28**(4), 626–643 (1996)

18. Cox, S., Little, C.: Time ontology in owl. A w3c candidate recommendation draft for a time ontology. W3C recommendation (2022). https://www.w3.org/TR/2022/CRD-owl-time-20221115/

19. Della Monica, D., Goranko, V., Montanari, A., Sciavicco, G.: Interval temporal logics: a journey. Bull. EATCS **3**(105), 73–99 (2013)

20. Dennis, L., Fisher, M.: Verifiable Autonomous Systems. Cambridge University Press, Cambridge (2023)

21. Dreossi, T., et al.: Verifai: a toolkit for the formal design and analysis of artificial intelligence-based systems. In: Proceedings of the International Conference on Computer Aided Verification (CAV), pp. 432–442 (2019)

22. Fiorini, S.R., et al.: A suite of ontologies for robotics and automation. IEEE Robot. Autom. Mag. **24**(1), 8–11 (2017)

23. Fisher, M.: An Introduction to Practical Formal Methods Using Temporal Logic. Wiley, Hoboken (2011)
24. Fowler, M.: UML Distilled, 3rd edn. Addison-Wesley, USA (2004)
25. Pignaton de Freitas, E., et al.: Ontological concepts for information sharing in cloud robotics. J. Ambient Intell. Humaniz. Comput. **14**(5), 4921–4932 (2023)
26. Ghosh, S., et al.: Diagnosis and repair for synthesis from signal temporal logic specifications. In: Proceedings of the ACM International Conference on Hybrid Systems: Computation and Control (HSCC), pp. 31–40 (2016)
27. Goranko, V.: Temporal Logics. Cambridge University Press, Cambridge (2023)
28. Goranko, V., Montanari, A., Sciavicco, G.: Propositional interval neighborhood temporal logics. J. Univ. Comput. Sci. **9**(9), 1137–1167 (2003)
29. Hariri, B.B., Calvanese, D., Montali, M., Giacomo, G.D., Masellis, R.D., Felli, P.: Description logic knowledge and action bases. J. Artif. Intell. Res. **46**, 651–686 (2013)
30. He, J., Bartocci, E., Nickovic, D., Isakovic, H., Grosu, R.: Deepstl - from English requirements to signal temporal logic. In: Proceedings of the IEEE/ACM International Conference on Software Engineering (ICSE), pp. 610–622 (2022)
31. Hekmatnejad, M., et al.: Encoding and monitoring responsibility sensitive safety rules for automated vehicles in signal temporal logic. In: Proceedings of the ACM International Conference on Formal Methods and Models for System Design, pp. 1–11 (2019)
32. Ho, Q.H., Ilyes, R.B., Sunberg, Z.N., Lahijanian, M.: Automaton-guided control synthesis for signal temporal logic specifications. In: Proceedings of the IEEE International Conference on Decision and Control (CDC), pp. 1–8 (2022)
33. Houghtaling, M.A., et al.: Standardizing an ontology for ethically aligned robotic and autonomous systems. IEEE Trans. Syst. Man Cybern. Syst. 1–14 (2023)
34. Hoxha, B., Fainekos, G.: Planning in dynamic environments through temporal logic monitoring. In: Proceedings of the AAAI International Conference on Artificial Intelligence Workshops (AAAI), pp. 601–607 (2016)
35. Jha, S., Raman, V., Sadigh, D., Seshia, S.A.: Safe autonomy under perception uncertainty using chance-constrained temporal logic. J. Autom. Reason. **60**(1), 43–62 (2018)
36. Kortenkamp, D., Simmons, R., Milam, T., Fernandez, J.L.: A suite of tools for debugging distributed autonomous systems. Form. Methods Syst. Des. **24**(2), 157–188 (2004)
37. Koymans, R.: Specifying real-time properties with metric temporal logic. Real-Time Syst. **2**(4), 255–299 (1990)
38. Kvarnstrom, J., Heintz, F., Doherty, P.: A temporal logic-based planning and execution monitoring system. In: Proceedings of the AAAI International Conference on Automated Planning and Scheduling (ICAPS), pp. 198–205 (2008)
39. de Leng, D., Heintz, F.: Approximate stream reasoning with metric temporal logic under uncertainty. In: Proceedings of the AAAI International Conference on Artificial Intelligence (AAAI), pp. 2760–2767 (2019)
40. Lewandowski, R., Olszewska, J.I.: Automated task scheduling for automotive industry. In: Proceedings of the IEEE International Conference on Intelligent Engineering Systems, pp. 159–164 (2020)
41. Li, T., et al.: STSL: a novel spatio-temporal specification language for cyber-physical systems. In: Proceedings of the IEEE International Conference on Software Quality, Reliability and Security (QRS), pp. 309–319 (2020)
42. Liu, J., Prabhakar, P.: Switching control of dynamical systems from metric temporal logic specifications. In: Proceedings of the IEEE International Conference on Robotics and Automation (ICRA), pp. 5333–5338 (2014)
43. Lunn, K.: Software Development with UML. Palgrave MacMillan, New York, USA (2003)

44. Lutz, C., Wolter, F., Zakharyashev, M.: Temporal description logics: a survey. In: Proceedings of the IEEE International Symposium on Temporal Representation and Reasoning, pp. 3–14 (2008)
45. Maierhofer, S., Rettinger, A.K., Mayer, E.C., Althoff, M.: Formalization of interstate traffic rules in temporal logic. In: Proceedings of the IEEE Intelligent Vehicles Symposium (IV), pp. 752–759 (2020)
46. Menghi, C., Nejati, S., Briand, L., Parache, Y.I.: Approximation-refinement testing of compute-intensive cyber-physical models: an approach based on system identification. In: Proceedings of the IEEE/ACM International Conference on Software Engineering (ICSE), pp. 372–384 (2020)
47. Mijatov, S., Langer, P., Mayerhofer, T., Kappel, G.: A framework for testing UML activities based on fUML. In: Proceedings of the ACM/IEEE International Conference on Model Driven Engineering Languages and Systems, pp. 1–10 (2013)
48. Muniraj, D., Vamvoudakis, K.G., Farhood, M.: Enforcing signal temporal logic specifications in multi-agent adversarial environments: a deep q-learning approach. In: Proceedings of the IEEE International Conference on Decision and Control (CDC), pp. 4141–4146 (2018)
49. Olivares-Alarcos, A., et al.: A review and comparison of ontology-based approaches to robot autonomy. Knowl. Eng. Rev. **34**, 1–38 (2019)
50. Olszewska, J.I.: UML activity diagrams for OWL ontology building. In: Proceedings of the International Conference on Knowledge Engineering and Ontology Development (KEOD), pp. 370–374 (2015)
51. Olszewska, J.I.: Temporal interval modeling for UML activity diagrams. In: Proceedings of International Conference on Knowledge Engineering and Ontology Development (KEOD), pp. 566–569 (2016)
52. Olszewska, J.I.: Designing transparent and autonomous intelligent vision systems. In: Proceedings of the International Conference on Agents and Artificial Intelligence (ICAART), pp. 850–856 (2019)
53. Olszewska, J.I.: AI-T: Software testing ontology for AI-based systems. In: Proceedings of the International Joint Conference on Knowledge Discovery, Knowledge Engineering and Knowledge Management (KEOD), pp. 291–298 (2020)
54. Olszewska, J.I.: Formal approaches, ontologies, and standards for the verification of autonomous systems. In: IEEE International Conference on Robotics and Automation (ICRA) (2022)
55. Olszewska, J.I.: Trustworthy intelligent systems: an ontological model. In: Proceedings of the International Joint Conference on Knowledge Discovery, Knowledge Engineering and Knowledge Management (KEOD), pp. 207–214 (2022)
56. Olszewska, J.I., Bermejo-Alonso, J., Sanz, R.: Special issue on ontologies and standards for intelligent systems. Knowl. Eng. Rev. **37**, 1–4 (2022)
57. Olszewska, J.I., Simpson, R.M., McCluskey, T.L.: Dynamic OWL ontology design using UML and BPMN. In: Proceedings of the International Conference on Knowledge Engineering and Ontology Development (KEOD), pp. 436–444 (2014)
58. Pant, Y.V., Quaye, R.A., Abbas, H., Varre, A., Mangharam, R.: Fly-by-logic: a tool for unmanned aircraft system fleet planning using temporal logic. In: Proceedings of the NASA Formal Methods Symposium, pp. 355–362 (2019)
59. Prestes, E., et al.: IEEE P7007: the first global ontological standard for ethically driven robotics and automation systems. IEEE Robot. Autom. Mag. **28**(4), 120–124 (2021)
60. Rajabli, N., Flammini, F., Nardone, R., Vittorini, V.: Software verification and validation of safe autonomous cars: a systematic literature review. IEEE Access **9**, 4797–4819 (2021)
61. Riedmaier, S., Ponn, T., Ludwig, D., Schick, B., Diermeyer, F.: Survey on scenario-based safety assessment of automated vehicles. IEEE Access **8**, 87456–87477 (2020)

62. Rodionova, A., Alvarez, I., Elli, M.S., Oboril, F., Quast, J., Mangharam, R.: How safe is safe enough? Automatic safety constraints boundary estimation for decision-making in automated vehicles. In: Proceedings of the IEEE Intelligent Vehicles Symposium (IV), pp. 1457–1464 (2020)

63. Sampath Kumar, V.R., et al.: Ontologies for industry 4.0. Knowl. Eng. Rev. **34**, 1–14 (2019)

64. Slee, D., Cain, S., Vichare, P., Olszewska, J.I.: Smart lifts: an ontological perspective. In: Proceedings of the International Joint Conference on Knowledge Discovery, Knowledge Engineering and Knowledge Management (KEOD), pp. 210–219 (2021)

65. Thomas, U., Hirzinger, G., Rumpe, B., Schulze, C., Wortmann, A.: A new skill based robot programming language using UML/P statecharts. In: Proceedings of the IEEE International Conference on Robotics and Automation (ICRA), pp. 461–466 (2013)

66. Xu, Z., Yazdani, K., Hale, M.T., Topcu, U.: Differentially private controller synthesis with metric temporal logic specifications. In: Proceedings of the IEEE American Control Conference (ACC), pp. 4745–4750 (2020)

67. Zhu, Y., Al-Ahmed, S.A., Shakir, M.Z., Olszewska, J.I.: LSTM-based IoT enabled co2 steady state forecasting for indoor air quality monitoring. Electronics **12**(1), 1–12 (2023)

A Meta-MDP Approach for Information Gathering Heterogeneous Multi-agent Systems

Alvin Gandois[1,2]([✉]) [ID], Abdel-Illah Mouaddib[1] [ID], Simon Le Gloannec[2],
and Ayman Alfalou[2]

[1] University of Caen Normandy, GREYC-CNRS UMR6072, Caen, France
{alvin.gandois,abdel-illah.mouaddib}@unicaen.fr
[2] L@bISEN - YNCREA OUEST, Brest, France
{simon.le-gloannec,ayman.al-falou}@isen-ouest.yncrea.fr

Abstract. In this paper, we address the problem of heterogeneous multi-robot cooperation for information gathering and situation evaluation in a stochastic and partially observable environment. The goal is to optimally gather information about targets in the environment with several robots having different capabilities. The classical Dec-POMDP framework is a good tool to compute an optimal joint policy for such problems. However, its scalability is weak. To overcome this limitation, we developed a Meta-MDP model with actions being individual policies of information gathering based on POMDPs. We compute an optimal exploration policy for each couple of robot and target, and the Meta-MDP model acts as a long-term optimal task allocation algorithm. We experiment our model on a simulation environment and compare to an optimal MPOMDP approach and show promising results on solution quality and scalability.

Keywords: Heterogeneous robots · Information gathering · Markov decision process

1 Introduction

We are considering a situation evaluation problem with heterogeneous robots (robots having different observation abilities, navigation abilities, embedding abilities) in a stochastic and partially observable environment (for example evaluating a situation after a disaster). The robots need to cooperate in order to efficiently evaluate the situation without any human intervention. The objective will be to gather information about a set of targets in the environment in the least amount of time. The stochasticity of the environment appears in several forms: (1) the actions of the robots can be nondeterministic, for example a robot can slip and slightly deviate from its expected position; (2) the plan of the environment can be different than the expected plan, for example when evaluating the situation after a disaster, some ways could be not reachable anymore or too dangerous; (3) the precision of robots' sensors which are not accurate.

The Markov Decision Process (MDP) framework allows us to deal with the two first kind of stochasticity by providing an action policy for every state of the environment while maximizing a desired performance criterion. However, due to the inaccuracy of

J. Filipe and J. Röning (Eds.): ROBOVIS 2024, CCIS 2077, pp. 345–360, 2024.
https://doi.org/10.1007/978-3-031-59057-3_22

the robots' sensors, we cannot know for sure in which state we are at every time step, so the MDP framework is not appropriate.

The Partially Observable Markov Decision Process (POMDP) framework extends the MDP framework to the case where there is uncertainty on the state of the model. POMDPs are used in many applications [5], and especially in target detection and information gathering [4, 26]

For the multi-agent setting, MDP and POMDP frameworks have been extended to DEC-MDP and DEC-POMDP (decentralized POMDP). However, due to the complexity of the DEC-POMDP being NEXP-complete [2], solving a DEC-POMDP is often intractable, although algorithms have been developed to solve them [27].

In this paper, we propose a Meta-MDP approach to solve the situation evaluation problem. The goal is to break down the complexity of the DEC-POMDP framework by computing exploration policies for each robot and each target, and then optimally allocating targets to robots. The Meta-MDP will act as a task allocation algorithm, considering long term rewards, where tasks are POMDP policies that needs to be executed by the agent until it reaches the corresponding target.

The use of MDPs for task allocation is not novel but faces the curse of dimensionality [11] and hierarchical MDPs with macro actions [12] have been developed to overcome this difficulty. The actions of the Meta-MDP are individual policies, which would have different time steps leading to durative actions in MDPs [14]. In [3, 25], the authors used task allocation with auctioning to allocate tasks to robots, where the execution of a task is formulated as a POMDP policy, which allows them to use the policies' value function as the value the robot should bid for this task. The key difference is that in our model, tasks are allocated optimally according to global long-term rewards, because the task allocation process is repeated until the situation is fully evaluated, while in [3, 25], the authors propose a myopic method. Our method outputs a meta-policy for situation evaluation where actions are task execution policies.

For this work, we will focus on the uncertainty of the environment rather than the uncertainty of the robots' states. This kind of problem can be found in the literature as a Mixed Observability Markov Decision Process [16]. To deal with the uncertainty of the other robots, the Interactive POMDP [10] model has been developed and has been subject to multiple research [7, 8]. Another model, ρPOMDP [1], has been developed to give rewards to the agent depending on the belief state, and thus allowing us to optimize according to our knowledge of the environment. Our approach considers the multi-agent settings of this problem. Moreover, recent work on this model led to new interesting theoretical results [9] and solution algorithm [28].

An issue we could face is when different robots seek for the same target, for example when collecting information on their route to their allocated target. To prevent this kind of behavior, Distributed Value Functions [13] can be used to add penalties to robots for example when exploring a target that another robot is already exploring, or is closer to, or has better capacities to explore it.

An important inspiration for this work is [20], which focuses more on information theory and information pertinence to develop optimal exploration and communication policies, while our work is more focused on the heterogeneous aspect of the problem and the use of the Meta-MDP that reduces the complexity.

The paper is organized in the following way: first, we provide background on the MDP and POMDP formalism and their solution methods and algorithms. Then, we present our model which we break down in two parts: the exploration models using POMDPs, and the allocation model using a Meta-MDP where the actions are policies of the exploration models. We also go deeper in details on the transition function of the Meta-MDP and approximations techniques we implemented to improve computation times. Then, in Sect. 4, we evaluate our model in a simulation environment and compare results to two other approaches before concluding in Sect. 5. Finally, in Sect. 6, we present short term and long term perspectives for this work.

2 Background

2.1 Markov Decision Process

A Markov Decision Process (MDP) [19] is a framework for solving decision making problems in stochastic environments. It is defined by the tuple $\langle S, A, T, R \rangle$, where S is a finite set of states, A is a finite set of actions, $T : S \times A \times S \to [0, 1]$ is the state transition function, where $T(s, a, s')$ is the probability to reach state s' given that the robot is in state s and executes the action a, and $R : S \times A \times S \to \mathbb{R}$ is the immediate reward (or utility) function, where $R(s, a, s')$ is the reward given to the robot when it executes the action a in state s and lands on state s'. This function is also often defined as $R(s, a)$ (the reward for taking the action a in state s), or simply $R(s)$ (the reward for being in state s). A solution to a MDP is a policy $\pi : S \to A$, where $\pi(s)$ is the action the robot has to execute in state s. The value function of a policy $V : S \to \mathbb{R}$ gives the expected total reward the robot will receive by following this policy. It is defined as follows:

$$V^\pi(s) = R(s, \pi(s)) + \gamma \sum_{s' \in S} T(s, \pi(s), s')V^\pi(s') \quad \forall s \in S \tag{1}$$

where $0 < \gamma \leq 1$ is the discount factor, i.e. how much future rewards are decreased compared to direct rewards.

An optimal policy, denoted as π^*, is a policy such that, for all state $s \in S$ and for every other policy $\pi \neq \pi^*$, $V^{\pi^*}(s) \geq V^\pi(s)$. Computing a such policy can be done by solving the following Bellman optimality equation:

$$V^*(s) = \max_{a \in A} \left(R(s, a) + \gamma \sum_{s' \in S} T(s, a, s')V^*(s') \right) \forall s \in S \tag{2}$$

Most used algorithms to solve a Markov Decision Process are Value Iteration and Policy Iteration. Value Iteration algorithm consists of repeatedly iterating over the set of states to improve the value function until convergence. Policy Iteration algorithm consists of repeatedly evaluating the policy and iterating over the set of states to find improvements until convergence. Both algorithms share the same time complexity of $O(|S^2||A|)$ and the choice of the algorithm often depends of the kind of the problem.

2.2   Partially Observable Markov Decision Process

The Partially Observable Markov Decision Process (POMDP) [24] framework is an extension of the MDP framework to the case where the state is not completely observable. It is defined by the tuple $\langle S, A, T, R, \Omega, O \rangle$, where $\langle S, A, T, R \rangle$ is an MDP such as defined in the previous section, Ω is the finite set of observations the robot can receive, and $O : A \times S$ is the observation function which is probability distribution over Ω. We denote $O(a, s, o)$ the probability of receiving observation o in state s after taking action a. Due to partial observability, we cannot define a policy over the set of states as in a classical MDP. A common way to define a policy for a POMDP is to use the history of observations, by mapping every possible observation history to an action. However, the number of observation history grows exponentially and quickly becomes intractable. Instead, we will define a belief state b, which is, for each state of the environment, how much the robot believes that this is the real state. When the robot takes an action and receives an observation, the belief state is updated using the following Bayesian update formula: $b(s) = P(s|a, o, b)$. Now, we can define a policy over the set of belief states, denoted as $\mathcal{B}$. Since there is an infinite number of belief states, it is not possible to use resolution techniques used for classical MDPs. Solving a POMDP is not an easy task and many resolution techniques and algorithms have been developed throughout the years. Interested readers may refer to [6, 18, 21–23].

3   Model

We consider a set of targets, X (variable states of the environment to evaluate), which are independent probabilistic variables. Each target $x \in X$ takes a value in its domain $DOM(x)$.

The state of the environment, ϵ, is described as an affectation of values to targets. The set $\mathcal{E}$ is the set of all possibles states of the environment (i.e. all possible values affectations to targets).

Our goal is to find information about the real state of the environment (find the real value of each target) with agents having different abilities to sense them. As an illustrative example, we consider two kinds of autonomous agents: agents with a local but precise observation ability, and agents with a global but imprecise observation ability, evolving in a grid environment as depicted in Fig. 1. Each kind of robot can possibly be fully heterogeneous, which means not having the same action abilities or not the same observation abilities, but all evolve in the same environment, therefore they share the same set of joint states and the same set of environment states.

For now, our model considers the following assumptions:

1. Each robot knows the model of the other robots (action set, state set, observation set, observation function)
2. Each robot knows the current internal state (e.g. location, orientation, etc.) of the other robots
3. Information is instantly shared among all robots without cost (i.e. they all share the same belief state)

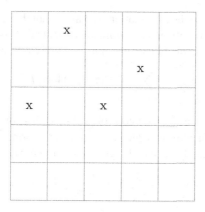

Fig. 1. A 5×5 grid with 4 targets (marked with a "x" letter).

3.1 The Exploration POMDPs

The macro actions of our Meta-MDP are POMDP policies of robots to accomplish targets. Thus, for each robot i and each target j, we define the following POMDP model:

$$POMDP_{i,j}\langle S, \mathcal{E}, A_i \cup \{OBSERVE, STAY\}, T_{i,j}, R_{i,j}, \Omega_i, O_i \rangle$$

The set S of states is common to all robots, and represents all the possible internal states of the robots, such that $S = S_1 \times S_2 \times \cdots \times S_k$, where k is the number of robots, and S_k the set of possible internal states for the robot k (e.g. its location, orientation, etc.). The state is completely observable.

The set $\mathcal{E}$ is the set of all possible states of the environment, such that $\mathcal{E} = DOM(X_1) \times DOM(X_2) \times \cdots \times DOM(X_n)$. The state of the environment is partially observable.

We have a model where the state is completely observable and the environment state is partially observable.

The set A_i represents the set of actions the robot i can perform, to which we add an action "STAY" which is a "do nothing" action, and an action "OBSERVE" which is an action to observe the current target the robot is close to.

The transition function $T_{i,j}$ is a classical transition function for a POMDP model, which gives a probability distribution $T_i(s, a)$ over the possible states when the robot i executes the action a in the state s.

To represent robots' knowledge of the environment, we also define a belief state b as in classical POMDP models. However, in our case, we want to measure the knowledge of each target individually, so, instead of defining a belief state over the full environment state, we define a set of belief states, $b = \{b(x_1), \ldots, b(x_n)\}$, where $b(x_i)$ is the belief state for the environment variable i, which represents the current knowledge about the target i (a probability distribution over the domain of its variable). Then, when the robot evolves in the environment and receives an observation, only the belief states for the corresponding targets are updated.

Our goal is to maximize the information we have about the environment. A common way to represent the uncertainty of a probabilistic variable is to use the Shannon entropy. The Shannon entropy of a probabilistic variable, denoted as $H(x)$, is defined as follows:

$$H(x) = - \sum_{v \in DOM(x)} P(x = v) \log_2 P(x = v)$$

However, in information-oriented control problems, it is often more appropriate to use the Negative Shannon entropy, which measures the information quantity rather than the uncertainty quantity, and thus can directly be used in reward functions:

$$H^-(x) = \log_2(|DOM(x)|) + \sum_{v \in DOM(x)} b(x = v) \log_2 b(x = v) \qquad (3)$$

The Negative Shannon Entropy is maximal in the corners of the simplex and minimal in the center [1], which means that the reward is maximal when there is no ambiguity about the variable.

Finally, to define the quantity of information contained in a belief state b (which is, for a reminder, the set of the belief states of every single environment variable), we will sum the negative entropy of each variable:

$$I(b) = \sum_{x \in X} H^-(x)$$

By including the entropy in the reward function of the robots, our goal will be to optimize to gather as much information as possible. The reward function $R_{i,j}((s, b), a, (s, b)')$ defines the reward the robot i with target j will receive when performing the action a in state (s, b) (with s its internal state and b the belief state) and transits into state $(s, b)'$. We define $R_{i,j}((s, b), a, (s, b)')$ as follows:

$$I(b') - H^-(x_j) + \begin{cases} \log_2 |DOM(x_j)| & \text{if } s \models j \wedge a = OBSERVE \\ 0 & \text{otherwise} \end{cases}$$

Here, $H^-(x_j)$ is the negative entropy of the current target of the robot, and $I(b')$ is the sum of the negative entropies of all targets in belief state b'. $\log_2 |DOM(x_j)|$ is the maximum of the negative entropy of the allocated target (when $P(x = v) = 1$ or $P(x = v) = 0$ for any $v \in DOM(x)$).

So, when the robot explores its environment, it receives a reward corresponding to the negative entropy of its new belief state, but ignores its allocated target. However, when the robot observes its allocated target (by performing the OBSERVE action), it also optimistically receives the maximum reward possible for this target, as if it had completely disambiguated this target.

Finally, the Ω_i set is the set of observations the robot i can receive. A robot can receive an observation about the state of a target, so the set of observation is the set of all possibles values for each target.

$O_i(s', a)$ is a classical POMDP observation function, which gives a probability distribution over the observation set of the robot, when the robot performs the action a and lands in state s'.

These models allows us to compute policies for each robot and each target, so that each robot has an optimal policy to reach and explore each target. We denote $\pi_{i,j}^*$ the optimal policy of the robot i for the target j, and $V_{i,j}^*$ the value function of the optimal policy of the robot i for the target j (see Eq. 2).

3.2 The Meta-MDP

In this section we will describe our main model to compute an optimal assignment for the current state while taking into account possible future rewards. We define an MDP $\langle S, \mathcal{E}, A, T, R \rangle$ where $S = \{S_1 \times \cdots \times S_k\}$ is the set of all possible internal states of the robots and $\mathcal{E}$ the set of all possible states of the environment, as already defined in Sect. 3.1. The originality of our approach is that the set of joint actions is the set of all possible assignments for each robot represented by the exploration policies introduced in Sect. 3.1. For example, if we have two robots and three targets, $A = \{(\pi_{1,1}^*, \pi_{2,2}^*), (\pi_{1,1}^*, \pi_{2,3}^*), (\pi_{1,2}^*, \pi_{2,1}^*), (\pi_{1,2}^*, \pi_{2,3}^*), (\pi_{1,3}^*, \pi_{2,1}^*), (\pi_{1,3}^*, \pi_{2,2}^*)\}$. The aim is to compute an optimal policy to assign individual policies (targets) to robots.

The reward function is defined as follows:

$$R(\epsilon, a, \epsilon') = I(\epsilon')$$

Again, we use the negative Shannon entropy defined in Eq. 3 to measure the quantity of information we have, and for this model the only thing we need is to gather as much information as possible, this is why the reward function is the negative entropy of the next state of the environment.

The transition function of the Meta-MDP is a bit complicated. Given that the actions are joint policies that are executed, we need to compute all possibles resulting states after executing theses policies, which can be a lot. We do this by computing the trajectories of the policies, bounded by an adjustable maximum depth parameter d. One other issue is that we don't know for sure, for a given time step, which robot will perform its action first. For example, if two robots are close to the same target, maybe the robot 1 will observe the target first, or maybe the robot 2 will observe the target first. This can affect the resulting states and we need to take this into account. As we don't need the whole trajectories but only the final states, we can compute trajectories step by step by using the dynamic programming algorithm described in Algorithm 1. For simplicity, the algorithm is described for two agents.

This algorithm starts by computing the possible states at depth t then uses states at depth t to compute states at depth $t + 1$. As said before, we need to take into account the order in which the actions are executed by the robots, this is why the lines 9 and 11–13 are duplicated. One is for the case where the robot 1 executes its action first, the other when the robot 2 executes its action first. As you can see, the algorithm is described only for the two robots case, but can easily be extended to the general case with n robots, knowing that for n robots we have $n!$ possible action orders to evaluate. Also, we are supposing that each robot has an even chance to execute its action first, but this can also be easily configured, for example by adding weights to the terms of the sums. And, if the order of the actions is already known and always the same, then only this order needs to be computed.

Algorithm 1. Meta-TransitionFunction.

Input: state s, joint action a, depth d
Output: T^d is the probability distribution of the possible states at depth d
1 T^0 : (empty) probability distribution over the states at step 0
2 $T^0(s) = 1$
3 **foreach** $t \in \{1, \ldots, d\}$ **do**
4 $\quad$ $T^t : S \to \mathbb{R}$
5 $\quad$ **foreach** $s^{t-1} \in T^{t-1}$ **do**
6 $\quad\quad$ **if** s^{t-1} *is final* **then**
7 $\quad\quad\quad$ | continue
8 $\quad\quad$ **end**
9 $\quad\quad$ $tr_1 = T_{2,a_2}(T_{1,a_1}(s^{t-1}, \pi_{1,a_1}), \pi_{2,a_2})$
10 $\quad\quad$ $tr_2 = T_{1,a_1}(T_{2,a_2}(s^{t-1}, \pi_{2,a_2}), \pi_{1,a_1})$
11 $\quad\quad$ **foreach** $s^t \in tr_1$ **do**
12 $\quad\quad\quad$ | $T^t(s^t) = T^{t-1}(s^{t-1}) * \frac{1}{2}(tr_1(s^t) + tr_2(s^t))$
13 $\quad\quad$ **end**
14 $\quad\quad$ **foreach** $s^t \in tr_2$ **do**
15 $\quad\quad\quad$ | $T^t(s^t) = T^{t-1}(s^{t-1}) * \frac{1}{2}(tr_1(s^t) + tr_2(s^t))$
16 $\quad\quad$ **end**
17 $\quad$ **end**
18 **end**
19 **return** T^d

This algorithm provides higher quality with higher depth but leads to higher computation time. However, this algorithm has an anytime behavior and can be able to provide a solution at any time and the quality of the solution improves according to the depth.

Solving the Meta-MDP consists of computing a joint policy $\pi(\epsilon) = (\pi_1, \ldots, \pi_k)$ where, for each state ϵ, we have the optimal joint action dictated by the joint policy, as described in the following reformulation of the Bellman equation:

$$V(\epsilon) = \max_{(\pi_1, \ldots, \pi_k) \in A} [R(\epsilon, (\pi_1, \ldots, \pi_k), \epsilon') + \gamma \sum_{\epsilon' \in \mathcal{E}} T^d(\epsilon, (\pi_1, \ldots, \pi_k), \epsilon') V(\epsilon')] \quad (4)$$

3.3 Approximating the Meta Transition Function

The algorithm of the transition function computation is very costly as shown in the previous section. That's why in this section we aim at reducing the cost of this algorithm. We will describe two probabilistic approximation techniques commonly used to reduce computation times.

Monte Carlo Sampling. Monte Carlo sampling [15] is an approximation method that uses random number generation to find a probability distribution. For example, for a sample of size $k = 10$, we will pick randomly 10 possible outcomes of the transition function for the current state and action chosen. Then, the resulting sample is considered to be the true probability distribution of the transition function. For example, if after 10 random picks, we have the following sample: 3x s_1, 5x s_2, 2x s_3, we will consider that the transitions probabilities are $\{s_1 : 0.3, s_2 : 0.5, s_3 : 0.2\}$. Unfortunately, this method gives poor results on our problem, since that the higher the depth, the more states we have in our transition function, each one with a possibly very small probability, and it would need a very large sample size to be representative, which would be worse than our original algorithm in computation time.

Pruning of Least Probable States. This method consists of taking only the most probable states and pruning the other ones. This way, we reduce the branching factor of our search tree. To do so, we define a parameter, γ, which will represent the precision of our approximation. For example, with $\gamma = 0.75$, we will prune the 25% least probable states. This method is applied after computing the transition function at depth t (between lines 17 and 18 in Algorithm 1). This approximation method is described in Algorithm 2.

Algorithm 2. TransitionFunctionPruning.

Input: Transition function at step t T^t, precision factor γ
Output: The pruned transition function at step t

1   $S : \{\}$
2   $sum = 0$
3   Sort T^t by probability in descending order
4   **foreach** $(s, p) \in T^t$ **do**
5      $S = S \cup \{s\}$
6      $sum = sum + p$
7   **if** $sum > \gamma$ **then**
8   **break**
9   **end**
10 **end**
11 T'^t: new probability distribution
     // Normalization of the new distribution
12 **foreach** $s \in S$ **do**
13      $T'^t[s] = T^t[s]/sum$
14 **end**
15 **return** T'^t

3.4   Complexity Analysis

For simplicity, we implemented our models on a discrete belief space, so that we can represent the Meta-MDP as an MDP over the belief space. Therefore, the complexity of computing a policy for our model is the same as for computing a policy in a classical MDP, which is $O(|S^2||A|)$. Our state space includes all internal states of the robots and all possible environment instances. In the example of Fig. 1, a $n \times m$ grid with k robots, the internal state of the robots is their location, thus we have $(n \times m)^k$ internal states. Then, for $|X|$ targets which are Boolean variables (so that their belief state can be represented as an unique value), and d discrete belief points, we have $d^{|X|}$ belief states. Therefore, the total number of states is $|S| = (n \times m)^k \times d^{|X|}$. For the experimental example we used, with 10 belief points, generating a total of 6,250,000 states. However, our approximation method reduces drastically the number of states as we will present in the experimental section.

4   Experimentation

4.1   Experimental Setup

To evaluate our model, we will use a grid domain where we have some targets placed on a grid, which are Boolean variables, that can represent for example the presence of a threat in this area. The goal will be to evaluate all the targets in the least amount of time. Figure 1 shows an example of environment. For this experiment, we will have two agents: an autonomous agent (e.g. UGV) with a local but high precision observation capability (which will almost always receive true information), denoted later as AAL, and an autonomous agent (e.g. UAV) with a global but low precision observation capability (which will often receive false information), denoted later as AAG.

The AAL has 4 possible actions: UP, RIGHT, DOWN, LEFT. As presented in the model, we add 2 more actions: STAY and OBSERVE. The STAY action does nothing and the robot stays in the same cell without receiving any information. The 4 moving actions moves the robot 1 cell in the chosen direction, and if the new cell contains a target, it receives an information corresponding to Table 1.

Table 1. AAL observation function for the moving actions.

Real value	Observation	
	True	False
True	0.55	0.45
False	0.45	0.55

When using the OBSERVE action on a cell containing a target, the robot receives an information corresponding to Table 2.

Table 2. AAL observation function for the OBSERVE action.

Real value	Observation	
	True	False
True	0.80	0.20
False	0.20	0.80

The AAG has the same set of actions, but the observations are less precise. It has only 60% chance to observe the real state of the target for the OBSERVE action, and 55% for the moving actions.

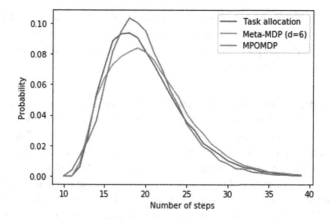

Fig. 2. Number of steps required to completely evaluate the situation, 100,000 runs.

4.2 Comparative Models and Measures

We will compare our model against two other approaches which we will not describe in details here. The first approach is a MPOMDP-based approach (Multi-agent POMDP) which is the optimal solution considering our specific assumptions (complete information sharing). The other approach is using an optimal task allocation algorithm to directly allocate targets to robots using value function of the individual exploration policies as rewards. The difference between the Meta-MDP and the simple task allocation is that the Meta-MDP considers long-term rewards while the task allocation algorithm considers only direct and myopic rewards (relating to the macro-level, because the exploration policies are always optimally calculated for long-term exploration). The task allocation approach can be seen as a Meta-MDP where the horizon is 1 and the depth of the Meta-transition function is equivalent to the horizon of the exploration policies. Expected results are that the MPOMDP provides a better solution than the Meta-MDP, which is supposed to be better than the task allocation approach. However, the Meta-MDP scales better than MPOMDP.

We will evaluate the three approaches for the following criterion: the average number of time steps (actions performed by the robots) required to completely evaluate the situation (i.e. fully determine the value of each target). For simplicity, all models have been implemented with discrete belief state spaces as described in Sect. 3.4. Each target belief space has 10 discrete beliefs points distributed as follows: $\{0.0, 0.11, 0.22, \ldots, 1.0\}$ (which is probably a bit too much for this kind of problem). We also evaluated the Meta-MDP for different depth settings, with and without approximation, to show how much performance increases with depth, and eventually the loss that the approximation occurs.

4.3 Experimental and Theoretical Results

In this section, we will present the experimental results obtained on the example we previously described. We will start by evaluating the solution quality and compare it to other approaches and how it evolves with different depth settings and by adding approximations. Then we will measure how the computation time scales when increasing the depth, with and without approximation. Lastly, we will state about the time complexity of the comparative models we used.

Solution Quality. Figure 2 shows the result for the three approaches. The depth parameter used for the Meta-Transition function is 6 without any approximation (which is the maximum depth we could compute in a reasonable amount of time). The x-axis is the number of steps required to completely evaluate the situation, and the y-axis is the probability that the model will completely evaluate the situation in the given number of steps. First, we can notice that all three models are close to each other, the curves have the same shape, and the standard deviation seems relatively close. As expected, the MPOMDP model is the most efficient, with an average step number of 19.85. The baseline approach (task allocation algorithm) is very close to the optimal approach with an average step number of 20.01. Our Meta-MDP shows a good performance (20.49 average step number) representing 96.73% of the optimal solution. Average number of steps required for each models are summed up in Table 3.

Table 3. Average number of steps required to fully evaluate the situation for the three models.

Model	Average steps required
MPOMDP	19.85
Meta-MDP (d = 6)	20.49
Task allocation algorithm	20.01

We will now measure how the Meta-MDP performance evolves when increasing the depth parameter and how the approximation method impacts its performance. For all experiments, we used the approximation method presented in Sect. 2 (pruning of least probable states) with a γ value of 0.75.

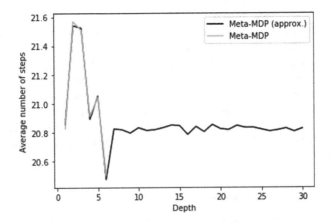

Fig. 3. Average number of steps required to completely evaluate the situation using the Meta-MDP for different depth settings, with and without approximation.

Figure 3 shows the result for increasing depth parameter for the Meta-Transition Function with and without approximation. As we can see, the performance of the approach is not degraded by the approximation, while we can achieve higher depths. Also, we can see that the solution does not seem to improve when increasing the depth (and at some points it loses quality), which is not the result we expected. To understand what is happening, we also compared in Fig. 4 the number of allocation (meta-time steps, i.e. the number of time a new target is allocated to each robot) required to evaluate the situation. We can see that the higher the depth, the less reallocation are done, and again there is no visible difference when adding approximation. The reason is that our Meta-MDP model aims at minimizing the number of meta-time steps. More precisely, since the reward function only takes into account the entropy of the next state, it will optimize to gather as much information as possible in a single meta-time step, which leads to more actions per meta-time step, and overall reduces the number of meta-time steps. This point will be discussed in Sect. 6.

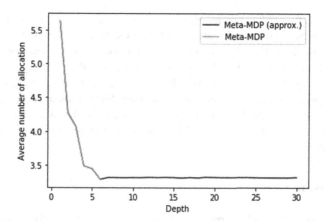

Fig. 4. Average number of target allocation used to completely evaluate the situation using the Meta-MDP for different depth settings, with and without approximation.

Computation Time. In Fig. 5, we measured the computation time of the policy of the Meta-MDP when increasing the depth parameter and adding approximation. We can see that the computation time without approximation grows exponentially while the approximation method is almost linear, supporting thus our claim in Sect. 3.4. An interesting point is that around depth 13, the computation time with the approximation method decreases and then grows much slowly. The decreasing is due to the policy computation algorithm that has converged earlier than with the previous depths values, and we suppose that the γ value is such that increasing the depth doesn't lead to much more new probable states.

Time Complexity. For the task allocation approach, we used the well-known Hungarian Algorithm which has a time complexity of $O(n^3)$ (with n being the number

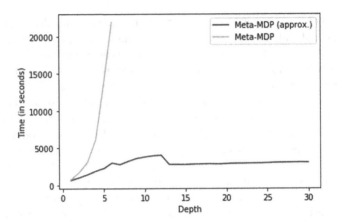

Fig. 5. Policy computation time for the Meta-MDP for different depth settings with and without approximations.

of tasks). As we do not have so many tasks in our example, the computation time for this approach is negligible, and scales better than the two other approaches. The classical POMDP model is PSPACE-hard for finite horizon problems, and undecidable for infinite time horizons [17]. The MPOMDP model being the multi-agent case of the POMDP, its complexity is also PSPACE-hard. For the model we presented, the Meta-MDP with approximation scales better than the Meta-MDP without approximation, and in the worst case, the Meta-MDP without approximation scales at least as much as the MPOMDP, but further work is needed to state about the comparison between Meta-MDP and MPOMDP.

5   Conclusion

In this paper, we addressed the problem of heterogeneous multi-robot cooperation for information gathering and situation evaluation in a stochastic and partially observable environment. We presented Meta-MDP which takes as actions individual policies from exploration POMDPs. We developed algorithms to compute the transition function of the Meta-MDP and proposed approximation techniques to reduce computation time. We evaluated our model on simulations and compared it to a MPOMDP and a baseline approach in a simple grid environment and shown that the model gives promising results that could be improved by a well defined reward function. We also shown that the approximation techniques we developed allows us to substantially reduce the complexity of our transition function algorithm with comparative quality results according to the optimal solution.

6   Future Work

A first perspective for this work would be to find better reward functions for the explorations models and the allocation model to avoid the issue we faced in Sect. 4. An idea would be to take as reward the sum of the rewards of the sequence of actions of the meta-time step with a discount factor for every consecutive action, similar to what is done in the hierarchical MDPs [12].

Currently, our model works only for evaluating one target at a time per robot. However, in real world, we can have robots (typically UAVs) with sensors with a large field of view that are able to observe multiple targets at a time, or for example if two targets are close to each other, it could be interesting to aggregate them so that one robot observe both targets. So a next step for this work would be to consider actions that consist of exploring multiple targets at a time. To do so, it is needed to redefine the set of actions of the explorations POMDPs or the Meta-MDP to explore multiple targets. Our model relies on three assumptions, with two being relatively strong (free communication and full observability of the other robots). It would be interesting in the future work to relax these assumptions. In this case, instead of comparing our work to MPOMDP, we could compare to DEC-POMDP, which is known to be intractable [2]. Finally, our model relies on a previous knowledge about the targets to be effective (the number of target and their positions, their domains, etc.). In real situation evaluation problems, possibly all areas of the environment are targets, but considering all areas as targets would conduct to combinatorial explosion, as our state space is exponential in the number of targets.

Acknowledgements. We would like to thank the AID (french Agence de l'Innovation de Défense - Defense Innovation Agency) for their support to this work.

References

1. Araya, M., Buffet, O., Thomas, V., Charpillet, F.: A POMDP extension with belief-dependent rewards. In: Advances in Neural Information Processing Systems, vol. 23 (2010)
2. Bernstein, D.S., Givan, R., Immerman, N., Zilberstein, S.: The complexity of decentralized control of Markov decision processes. Math. Oper. Res. **27**(4), 819–840 (2002)
3. Capitan, J., Spaan, M.T., Merino, L., Ollero, A.: Decentralized multi-robot cooperation with auctioned POMDPs. Int. J. Robot. Res. **32**(6), 650–671 (2013)
4. Carvalho Chanel, C.P., Teichteil-Königsbuch, F., Lesire, C.: POMDP-based online target detection and recognition for autonomous UAVs. In: ECAI 2012, pp. 955–960. IOS Press (2012)
5. Cassandra, A.R.: A survey of POMDP applications. In: Working Notes of AAAI 1998 Fall Symposium on Planning with Partially Observable Markov Decision Processes, vol. 1724 (1998)
6. Cassandra, A.R., Kaelbling, L.P., Littman, M.L.: Acting optimally in partially observable stochastic domains. In: AAAI, vol. 94, pp. 1023–1028 (1994)
7. Doshi, P., Gmytrasiewicz, P.J.: Monte Carlo sampling methods for approximating interactive POMDPs. J. Artif. Intell. Res. **34**, 297–337 (2009)
8. Doshi, P., Zeng, Y., Chen, Q.: Graphical models for interactive POMDPs: representations and solutions. Auton. Agent. Multi-Agent Syst. **18**(3), 376–416 (2009)
9. Fehr, M., Buffet, O., Thomas, V., Dibangoye, J.: rho-POMDPs have Lipschitz-continuous epsilon-optimal value functions. In: Advances in Neural Information Processing Systems, vol. 31 (2018)
10. Gmytrasiewicz, P.J., Doshi, P.: A framework for sequential planning in multi-agent settings. J. Artif. Intell. Res. **24**, 49–79 (2005)

11. Hanna, H., Mouaddib, A.I.: Task selection problem under uncertainty as decision-making. In: Proceedings of the First International Joint Conference on Autonomous Agents and Multiagent Systems: Part 3, pp. 1303–1308 (2002)

12. Hauskrecht, M., Meuleau, N., Kaelbling, L.P., Dean, T.L., Boutilier, C.: Hierarchical solution of Markov decision processes using macro-actions. arXiv preprint arXiv:1301.7381 (2013)

13. Matignon, L., Jeanpierre, L., Mouaddib, A.I.: Distributed value functions for multi-robot exploration. In: 2012 IEEE International Conference on Robotics and Automation, pp. 1544–1550. IEEE (2012)

14. Mausam, M., Weld, D.: Planning with durative actions in stochastic domains. J. Artif. Intell. Res. (JAIR) **31**, 33–82 (2008). https://doi.org/10.1613/jair.2269

15. Metropolis, N., Ulam, S.: The Monte Carlo method. J. Am. Stat. Assoc. **44**(247), 335–341 (1949)

16. Ong, S.C., Png, S.W., Hsu, D., Lee, W.S.: Planning under uncertainty for robotic tasks with mixed observability. Int. J. Robot. Res. **29**(8), 1053–1068 (2010)

17. Papadimitriou, C.H., Tsitsiklis, J.N.: The complexity of Markov decision processes. Math. Oper. Res. **12**(3), 441–450 (1987)

18. Pineau, J., Gordon, G., Thrun, S., et al.: Point-based value iteration: an anytime algorithm for pomdps. In: IJCAI, vol. 3, pp. 1025–1032 (2003)

19. Puterman, M.L.: Markov Decision Processes: Discrete Stochastic Dynamic Programming. Wiley Series in Probability and Statistics, Wiley, Hoboken (1994). https://doi.org/10.1002/9780470316887

20. Renoux, J.: Contribution to multiagent planning for active information gathering. Ph.D. thesis, Normandie Université (2015)

21. Shani, G., Pineau, J., Kaplow, R.: A survey of point-based POMDP solvers. Auton. Agent. Multi-Agent Syst. **27**, 1–51 (2013)

22. Silver, D., Veness, J.: Monte-Carlo planning in large POMDPs. Advances in neural information processing systems **23** (2010)

23. Smith, T., Simmons, R.: Heuristic search value iteration for POMDPs. arXiv preprint arXiv:1207.4166 (2012)

24. Sondik, E.J.: The optimal control of partially observable Markov processes over the infinite horizon: Discounted costs. Oper. Res. **26**(2), 282–304 (1978)

25. Spaan, M.T., Gonçalves, N., Sequeira, J.: Multirobot coordination by auctioning POMDPs. In: 2010 IEEE International Conference on Robotics and Automation, pp. 1446–1451. IEEE (2010)

26. Spaan, M.T., Veiga, T.S., Lima, P.U.: Active cooperative perception in network robot systems using pomdps. In: 2010 IEEE/RSJ International Conference on Intelligent Robots and Systems, pp. 4800–4805. IEEE (2010)

27. Szer, D., Charpillet, F., Zilberstein, S.: Maa*: a heuristic search algorithm for solving decentralized pomdps. arXiv preprint arXiv:1207.1359 (2012)

28. Thomas, V., Hutin, G., Buffet, O.: Monte Carlo information-oriented planning. arXiv preprint arXiv:2103.11345 (2021)

Interacting with a Visuotactile Countertop

Michael Jenkin[1,2]($\boxtimes$)(iD), Francois R. Hogan[1], Kaleem Siddiqi[1,3](iD),
Jean-François Tremblay[1,3](iD), Bobak Baghi[1](iD), and Gregory Dudek[1,3](iD)

[1] Samsung AI Center, Montreal, Canada
jenkin@cse.yorku.ca
[2] Lassonde School of Engineering, York University, Toronto, Canada
[3] School of Computer Science, McGill University, Montreal, Canada

Abstract. We present the See-Through-your-Skin Display (STS-d), a device that integrates visual and tactile sensing with a surface display to provide an interactive user experience. The STS-d expands the application of visuo-tactile optical sensors to Human-Robot Interaction (HRI) tasks and Human-Computer Interaction (HCI) tasks more generally. A key finding of this paper is that it is possible to display graphics on the reflective membrane of semi-transparent optical tactile sensors without interfering with their sensing capabilities, thus permitting simultaneous sensing and visual display. A proof of concept demonstration of the technology is presented where the STS Visual Display (STS-d) is used to provide an animated countertop that responds to visual and tactile events. We show that the integrated sensor can monitor interactions with the countertop, such as predicting the timing and location of contact with an object, or the amount of liquid in a container being placed on it, while displaying visual cues to the user.

Keywords: Visuo-tactile optical sensor · Interactive visual display

1 Introduction

Tactile sensors can provide considerable information about the nature of interactions with the device. Although commercial tactile technologies typically concentrate on capturing finger-touch interactions with the interaction surface, technologies exist that can capture more complex two-dimensional interactions. For modern high-resolution sensors this can include information about mass, texture, friction, and other dynamic properties related to the interaction of the sensor with an external object [1].

The last few years have seen the development of a number of optical tactile sensing technologies that can obtain complex information related to physical interaction with the tactile surface, but to date there have been few efforts to integrate dense tactile sensing with an interactive visual display. Recognizing the potential synergy between the domains of optical tactile sensing and interactive displays, here we integrate properties of both technologies to develop a high-resolution display and tactile interaction surface, capable of monitoring and visually responding to, interactions with objects in touch with, or near the surface of, the device. Our STS Visual Display (STS-d), shown in Fig. 1, integrates high-resolution tactile sensing with an interactive display. We also

© The Author(s), under exclusive license to Springer Nature Switzerland AG 2024
J. Filipe and J. Röning (Eds.): ROBOVIS 2024, CCIS 2077, pp. 361–374, 2024.
https://doi.org/10.1007/978-3-031-59057-3_23

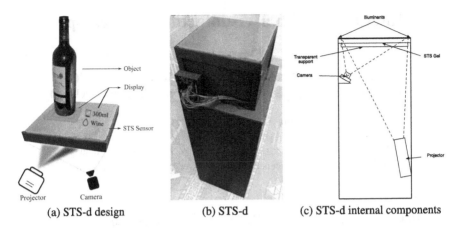

(a) STS-d design   (b) STS-d   (c) STS-d internal components

Fig. 1. The STS-d and a sketch of its internal components. An interior wide field of view camera, a display projector and a controllable illumination array are mounted within the STS-d. Note that the entire STS-d is enclosed so as to enable the internal illumination conditions to be fully controlled. Illumination within the STS-d is provided by a ring of individually controllable LEDs.

present a "smart interactive countertop" proof of concept that highlights the potential of this display as a smart-home technology. This prototype countertop can both "see" through the surface of the sensor to track objects as they are moved above it, and also "feel" the portion of the objects in contact with the surface, enabling precise judgement of both object identity as well as its physical properties such as weight and surface texture. For example, by recognizing the associated container the STS-d can track which of a set of possible liquids is currently being added to a container, and can inform the user, in real-time, about how to adjust the ratio of materials for a perfect mix. To our knowledge, this is the first effort to integrate display technology within a high-resolution tactile sensor.

The contributions of this paper are threefold. First, we introduce a new sensor prototype, the STS-d, an interactive display technology that leverages the high-tactile resolution of optical tactile sensors to provide an interactive user experience with a heightened degree of precision. Second, we show that it is possible to display graphics on the surface of a family of optical tactile sensors without interfering with the sensor's internal illumination model, thus simultaneously capturing the deformation of the membrane's surface while projecting information on it. Finally, we present a proof of concept demonstration of the technology as a smart kitchen countertop that responds to visual and tactile events with interactive animations.

This article is organized as follows. Section 2 summarizes previous work on high-resolution tactile sensors, including multi-modal devices such as the STS. Section 3 introduces the STS Visual Display (STS-d) showing how display and sensing technology can be integrated within a single sensor/display surface. Section 4 describes the "Countertop Application" highlighting its tactile, visual and interaction components.

Finally, Sect. 5 summarizes the manuscript and describes our ongoing work with the sensor.

2 Previous Work

2.1 Dense Tactile Sensors

High resolution optical tactile sensors such as Gelsight [2], GelSlim [3], Soft-bubble [4], OmniTact [5], GelTip [6], STS [7], a system based on a compound eye model [8], TouchRoller [9] and a number of others, have been successfully applied to a range of tasks, from monitoring the nature of contact to characterizing the object in contact with the sensor. Although there exist a number of different aspects of the various technologies, one common underlying approach – see [10] for an example – is to provide an interaction membrane, which is typically opaque, and then to light and view this membrane from within the sensor. Through an appropriate choice of illumination the image of the opaque interaction surface transduces tactile interaction which is then captured by the camera within the sensor. A range of different illumination and image processing algorithms can then be used to capture interactions with the surface.

A common approach to developing this type of sensor is to fabricate the interaction surface as a supported transparent inner support surface, and then to bind a deformable gel above this followed by an opaque membrane. The support surface prevents wide-scale deformation of the interaction surface and thus localizes interactions with the outer membrane. The deformable gel actually captures interactions with the device, while the outer surface serves two purposes. It blocks the view of the external environment and any external illuminants while also providing a surface that can be imaged to capture distortions of the deformable gel as it interacts with physical items in the world. This may optimize the sensor's performance when viewing interactions with the tactile sensor but it prevents the option of using the sensor to also capture images of the environment not in contact with the sensor. In contrast to fully opaque optical-tactile sensors the STS sensor [7] utilizes a semi-transparent interaction surface which enables the sensor to operate in both a tactile and visual mode. When operating in the opaque mode, the sensor operates in a manner similar to traditional gel-based tactile sensors, capturing tactile interactions. When operating in the transparent mode, visual sensors within the sensor view the visual world outside of the sensor, enabling the sensor to capture the appearance of objects in close proximity to the surface. Full details of the STS sensor can be found in [7] and [11]. Application of the STS sensor to a robot manipulation task can be found in [1].

2.2 Visual Tactile Displays

Touch screens are ubiquitous, with early technology based on identifying the timing of the cathode ray tube refresh [12]. Modern display technology relies on a range of different technologies including resistive, capacitive, audio, visual and other signals, to localize single or multiple interactions with the display surface. Indeed, the technology is so common that some non-interactive displays are equipped with signage to inform viewers that the particular device is not an interactive one.

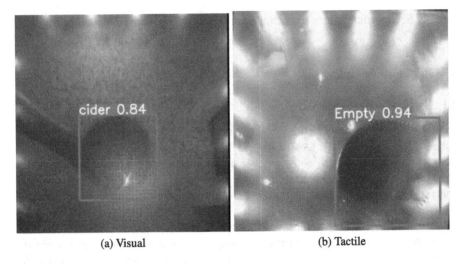

(a) Visual   (b) Tactile

Fig. 2. View obtained by the STS-d in tactile and visual modes. Shown overlaid over the views is the STS identification and localization of the object in view. In the visual view the object is identified as a 'cider' bottle, while in the tactile view a different bottle is identified as being 'empty'. The white bands around the periphery of the image correspond to regions of strong illumination from the LED illumination ring mounted around the edge of the sensor.

One problem common with monitoring interaction with a display surface is that the technology being used must not occlude the display itself. For small scale displays, e.g., cellphones and tablets, it is possible to embed the transparent interaction technology within the device itself. For larger displays, including rear-projection display and interaction surfaces, the scale of the surface introduces its own complications. Here again, a number of different display and interaction technologies exist (e.g., [13]). It is also possible to assemble larger displays by tessellating smaller ones, integrating both the display and interaction components (e.g., [14]).

Interestingly, most tactile displays are designed to deal with users who are interacting directly (e.g., touching) the display and not dealing with interactions in close proximity to the display, although there are exceptions. For example, devices such as the Leap Motion (see [15]) can provide proximal interaction with the display.

3   The STS Display

The STS Display (STS-d) integrates the key components of an optical tactile sensor, namely a deformable gel, a transparent rigid support, illuminants, and a camera, with a rear projection display. A prototype of the device is shown in Fig. 1. This combination enables the STS-d to capture visually the slight deformation of the gel membrane when an external object is placed or pressed on the surface, and to display information on the surface. The STS includes an external membrane that is coated with a thin layer of semi-transparent paint. By regulating the internal illumination of the sensor and the camera parameters it is possible to obtain streams of visual and tactile information from a co-located perspective. An example of these two modalities is shown in Fig. 2. Figure 2(a) shows the visual modality while Fig. 2(b) shows the tactile modality, where a bottle is placed at rest on the sensor, allowing it to visualize its texture and contact area. Figure 2 shows sample imagery captured by the STS-d with the output of the recognition step (described below) overlaid. In the original STS described in [7], the camera was mounted in the centre of the sensor. In the STS-d, the sensor is offset to provide a clear projection path for the visual display presented on the sensor. This is illustrated in the sketch of the internal components shown in Fig. 1(c).

The STS-d includes an internal projector that displays graphics onto the interaction surface. In this paper, we study the potential interaction between displayed material and the process of recovering tactile and visual information from the sensor. We examine if the display projected on the tactile sensor's surface interferes with the lighting from the internal illuminants that are essential to highlight the tactile deformations or if it interferes with the process of visual tracking when the sensor is operating in visual mode. We explore and discuss this question further in Sect. 4, where we demonstrate that it is possible to simultaneously capture the deformation of the membrane's surface and tracking information while projecting on the surface of the sensor.

In the original STS, the camera placement allowed for a straightforward mapping from camera image to position on the external interaction surface of the STS. Given the oblique mounting position for the camera within the STS-d to provide a clear line of sight for display projection, standard image processing techniques were used to correct for the barrel distortion caused by the wide field of view of the camera and to rectify the off axis viewing of the interaction surface. These image manipulations provide a straightforward mapping from the display and interaction surface to pixel locations in the rectifed camera view, but slightly distorts objects at some distance from the surface of the STS-d. This also accounts for the distorted view of the LEDs shown in Fig. 2. For the interactive countertop application considered here, specific tasks and their algorithmic solutions are described in the subsections below.

3.1 Identifying Interaction Objects

We leverage advances in deep learning and computer vision for object detection to recognize objects in both the visual and tactile modalities of the sensor [16]. As the operational mode of the sensor (tactile vs. visual) is known during inference, separate YoloV5 object detection networks are trained for each modality. For each modality training data was collected while visual displays associated with the tabletop were presented. Default YoloV5 hyperparameter settings were used for both the tactile and visual training sets.

This recognition process not only identifies the object but also computes its bounding box, a property that we utilize below. The sensor views shown in Fig. 2 show the output of the YoloV5 recognition process for each of the two views. Beyond object recognition, there are two aspects of the use of an object recognizer that are of particular interest in the application considered here. First, in tactile mode, the force acting on the gel is proportional to the mass of the object. Thus by training the YoloV5 network with containers containing different amounts of liquid we can identify not only the object being interacted with but also the current amount of material present in it.

Table 1. Tactile mode confusion matrix. In the tactile mode confusion matrix, the labels empty, full and half refer to the state of the cider bottle. Vertical axis is predicted, horizontal axis is the true label. FP (false positive) corresponds to images within which no bottle was present in contact with the sensor. FN (false negative) corresponds to the null label result.

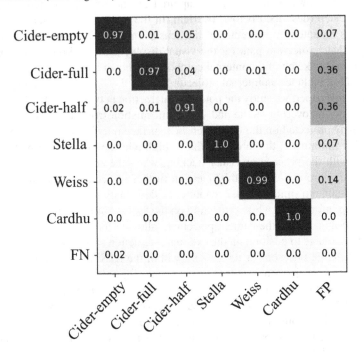

	Cider-empty	Cider-full	Cider-half	Stella	Weiss	Cardhu	FP
Cider-empty	0.97	0.01	0.05	0.0	0.0	0.0	0.07
Cider-full	0.0	0.97	0.04	0.0	0.01	0.0	0.36
Cider-half	0.02	0.01	0.91	0.0	0.0	0.0	0.36
Stella	0.0	0.0	0.0	1.0	0.0	0.0	0.07
Weiss	0.0	0.0	0.0	0.0	0.99	0.0	0.14
Cardhu	0.0	0.0	0.0	0.0	0.0	1.0	0.0
FN	0.02	0.0	0.0	0.0	0.0	0.0	0.0

Second, in visual mode, the apparent visual size of the object provides a strong cue of the distance of the target to the sensor.

3.2 Tactile/Visual Duty Cycle

The STS-d sensor relies on changing the internal illuminant to swap between the visual and tactile modes of the sensor. This introduces an interesting question related to the visual/tactile duty cycle. When an STS device is being used as part of a robot-controlled interaction, it may be possible to determine the appropriate mode of operation *a priori*. For example, if an STS sensor is mounted on the end effector of a robot arm, the commanded nature of the interaction provides a strong prior as to the appropriate mode of the STS. In the application considered here, we choose a duty cycle based on proximity. Prior to contact the STS-d operates in vision-only mode. Once the visual channel indicates that contact is imminent, the sensor swaps to a tactile mode, until either a tactile contact is detected or the interaction times out and the sensor returns to visual mode.

Table 2. Visual mode confusion matrix. The Cider bottle only appears once in the visual confusion matrix, as the bottle appears the same regardless of the volume of its liquid contents. Vertical axis is predicted, horizontal axis is the true label. FP (false positive) corresponds to images within which no bottle was present in contact with the sensor. FN (false negative) corresponds to the null label result.

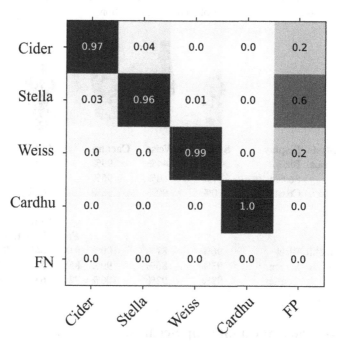

3.3   The STS-D Display

The display that is rendered on the STS is provided by a rear-projection Digital Light Processing (DLP) projector mounted below the sensor surface. The projector is an ultra short-throw projector that overscans the projection surface. The projector is aligned so as to reduce the projector hotspot. In general, the display aspect of the STS-d operates independently. However, imagery displayed on the STS-d display will be captured by the camera that images the sensor. This motivates either time multi-plexing the image capture and display processes, or adapting algorithms that process the visual and tactile image streams to cope with the effect of projected display imagery on the image processing pipeline. Here we choose the later approach and train the image processing mechanism with a range of likely rendered imagery in order to accommodate potential interactions.

When the STS-d is operating in tactile mode the DLP projector must compete with the LEDs in terms of illuminating the surface. The current implementation of the STS-d relies on visible light LEDs. In practice this means that rendering in tactile mode is less clear than rendering when the STS-d is operating in visual mode.

Table 3. Machine label fractional accuracy per condition. For each of the mode/display conditions, the fraction of labels for the 28,085 labelled frames that corresponds to the correct label are shown. Even with a distracting display being rendered on the STS-d, object recognition can be very good. Note that the poorest performance is seen in the visual mode, likely due to the more complex nature of the visual mode including the potential for small target size and the presence of visual distractors and less well controlled lighting conditions.

Mode	Display	Stella	Weiss	Cardhu	Cider		
Visual	Black	81%	44%	99%	62%		
	Screen	87%	80%	96%	41%		
	Coaster	70%	90%	98%	82%		
					Cider		
					Full	**Half**	**Empty**
Tactile	Black	96%	87%	100%	91%	66%	90%
	Screen	93%	86%	99%	85%	53%	98%
	Coaster	99%	92%	100%	72%	63%	98%

4   The Interactive Countertop Scenario

The modern home kitchen has changed dramatically over the years. [17] provides a thoughtful introduction into the role of the development of kitchen technology and its relationship to culture and societal expectations. Over the last 100 years kitchens have evolved from the "anonymous workspace of an individual" to the "social hub" of the home [18]. This evolution of the role of the kitchen (and the role of those who prepare meals within it) is reflected in advances in kitchen technology. Smart, interconnected kitchen devices are already available to the consumer. For example, devices like Samsung's Family Hub™ [19] perform both as a traditional appliance (here a refrigerator), but also house a standard touch-based computer with display, as well as acting as an interaction point for a range of other networked kitchen appliances.

The future of modern home kitchen technology appears very bright. Speculative articles including [20] and [21], highlight a range of different technologies that we can expect to be deployed in home kitchens over the next few years. Of particular interest here is the concept of providing integrated display, interaction and measurement functionality in the kitchen of the future. Such systems are already in production. For example Bosch's Projection and Interaction device [22] provides an under-counter projector that utilizes the kitchen countertop as a display and interaction surface. This front projection display is monitored by a camera within the projector to capture interactions with the display.

Although there are many advantages with projecting a display onto a countertop with a camera to capture interactions, the approach is not without its drawbacks. Projection onto the surface is complicated by the user interfering with the beam of the projected imagery. But perhaps most problematically, interactions are limited to capturing information from above the surface, so surface interactions must be inferred rather than observed directly.

Although the STS-d can be applied to a range of different tasks, here we consider the potential of deploying an STS-d device as part of an interactive countertop. As such, we concentrate on a single interaction task rather than a general application. We consider the task of having a countertop recognize that the user is interacting with it, signalling this interaction to the user, and then finally providing the user with information related to their interaction. More specifically, we envision an interaction in which a homeowner wishes to obtain information about an object (in this demonstration, a bottle), including its content and the amount of liquid within it. This might be a bottle containing material to be used in some recipe, or just a drink to be consumed. We break this process down into a sequence of steps and identify how the STS-d interacts with the object and the user, at each step.

1. **Prior to Interaction** Prior to interaction the STS-d idles, displaying a background image. For the purposes of the demonstration we provide an animated screensaver during this phase. The STS-d operates in visual sensing mode at this time.
2. **Human Communicating Intent** To indicate that the human wishes to interact with the countertop, the object of interest is brought in close proximity of the countertop. The STS-d detects visual objects and monitors their proximity.
3. **Countertop Response** The countertop responds by replacing the screen saver display with a drink coaster display. This display fades in as the object is brought closer to the countertop. The countertop tracks the detected object and moves the drink coaster to be displayed under the point at which the object is viewed. The intensity of the projected image is adjusted based on the object's proximity to the surface of the STS-d.
4. **Human Confirming Intent** If the human moves the object away from the countertop the drink coaster fades out and the display returns to the idle mode and the screen saver is displayed as described above.
5. **Countertop Response** Should the object be brought into very close proximity or contact with the STS-d the STS-d transits into tactile mode. If the object is brought into contact with the tabletop then the object is classified and the display is updated to reflect this.
6. **After Interaction** The countertop response remains in tactile mode until the object is moved off of the STS-d interaction surface, at which point the content display is removed and the display returns to the screen saver mode awaiting the next interaction.

4.1 Sample Interaction with the STS-d

Figure 3 provides a sequence of snapshots of a typical interaction with the STS-d in a smart countertop demonstration. Images (a) through (d) are from the camera mounted

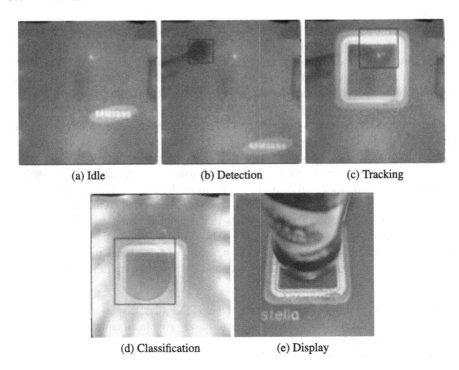

(a) Idle   (b) Detection   (c) Tracking

(d) Classification   (e) Display

Fig. 3. A summary of the interaction of the STS-d with an object, here a bottle. Images (a) through (d) left are from the camera mounted inside the STS-d. Image (e) right is an external view. The bottle in (e) was blurred for publication. Images (a) through (d) were flipped to present the view as it would appear if viewed externally of the STS-d. (a) Initially the STS-d displays a floating logo to indicate that the sensor is waiting for interaction. (b) When the object is brought in close proximity to the STS-d it is detected and tracked, and then as shown in (c) a coaster is displayed on the device. When the sensor predicts that the object is in contact with the surface, the sensor utilizes its tactile mode (d) to classify the object and this information is communicated to the user (e).

inside the STS-d. Image (e) is an external view. The bottle in (e) right was blurred for publication. (a) through (d) were flipped to present the view external to the STS-d. (a) Initially the STS-d displays a floating logo to indicate that the sensor is waiting for interaction. (b) When the object is brought in close proximity to the STS-d it is tracked, and then as shown in (c) a coaster is displayed on the device. When the sensor predicts that the object is in contact with the surface, the sensor utilizes its tactile mode (d) to classify the object and this information is communicated to the user (e). When the bottle is moved away from the sensor the countertop reverts to the idle mode shown in (a).

4.2   Interaction Object Dataset

Training was performed using 100 manually-labelled sample images of each of the interaction objects under each of the display conditions (black screen, screen saver, coaster) and for each of the tactile and visual data sets, for a total of 1200 labelled images for the visual data set and 1800 labelled images for the tactile data set. Data was collected with objects with their "bottom side down". For the tactile dataset, data was collected with the objects in normal contact with the STS-d surface such that the tactile imprint on the sensor is consistent with the natural weighting of the object. Sample imagery from the dataset is shown in Fig. 2 for both the visual and tactile modalities of the STS. Images of the actual containers used can be found in Table 3.

4.3 Training and Recognition

For each of the visual and tactile mode datasets separately, a YoloV5 network was trained from the pretrained yolo5s configuration using 50% of the data set conditions for each object with the remaining 50% of the data set retained for validation (25%) and testing (25%). Each of the networks were trained for 300 epochs using the default hyperparameters resulting in mAP@[.5:.95] scores of 0.82 for the visual recognizer and 0.92 for the tactile recognizer. The confusion matrices for the visual and tactile modes are shown in Tables 1 and 2.

Although only 3000 images were hand labelled, the nature of the training data enables other insights into the performance of the two recognizers. This is of particular interest in terms of assessing the potential impact of the display being rendered on their recognition performance. Each training dataset collection video captured many more images of a known interaction object than were actually labelled. It was therefore possible to run the trained networks on these much larger datasets and to count the fraction of times the label assigned to the object that was interacting with the tabletop corresponded to the object used in that video sequence. There were a total of 28085 frames with objects recognized by the networks, resulting in approximately 906 labels on average for each condition of (visual, tactile) × object × display. The fraction of these labels that correspond to the correct object labels are provided in Table 3. Note that the training data is included in this fraction.

This STS-d tabletop realization provides some interesting insights into the impact of the display on the recognition process in both modes. First, the recognition process can be quite accurate even in the presence of the projected graphical display. The recognition network was trained on an equal number of examples from each background, and although there was considerable variability in performance over the different classes, there is no obvious impairment of recognition performance when a non-black display is provided. One effect that can be observed is that performance of the visual mode recognizer is generally inferior to the performance of the tactile mode recognizer. This is to be expected as the visual mode recognizer is presented with samples over a much broader range of imaging conditions (e.g., they appear at different distances and the images are subject to the effects of perspective and external illumination conditions) while the tactile recognizer operates under much more controlled lighting conditions and is presented with what is primarily a two-dimensional recognition process.

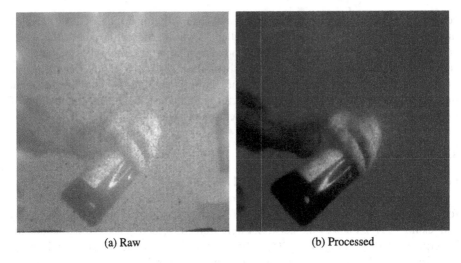

| | (a) Raw | (b) Processed |

Fig. 4. By estimating unchanging pixel locations in the STS visual channel it is possible to compute a "background" image that accounts for opacities and imperfections in the gel. This process can allow the images on the surface to be corrected, and can potentially even discount the effect of material (i.e. dirt) deposited on the surface externally.

4.4   Estimating Object Pose and Trajectory

Assuming the entirety of an object is placed on the surface, each object has a known maximum size (given by the size of the bounding box when the object is viewed in tactile mode). We can thus estimate both position when the object is in contact with the STS-d and displacement from the STS-d in visual mode, as well as for visual mode the approximate height of the object above the STS-d given the size of the bounding box returned by the recognizer.

5   Summary and Ongoing Work

In this paper, we introduced a new sensor realization that combines optically-based visuotactile sensing methods with interactive displays to enable novel applications. The STS Visual Display combines some of the advantages of tactile sensing, classical computer vision and modern machine learning to create a new display technology that can better characterize the nature of interaction with a heightened degree of precision. A key finding of this paper is that it is possible and practical to display graphics on the reflective membrane of the STS sensor. This is possible due to the semi-transparent nature of the membrane, that enables the projector to display graphics from the inside of the sensor. We show experimentally that displaying on the membrane does not interfere with the tactile sensing modalitiy, thus permitting simultaneous sensing and visual animation.

We have demonstrated the sensing and animation capabilities of the STS-d sensor on a smart kitchen countertop scenario, using the high resolution sensing to perform object detection and the projector to display key object properties, such as the contact area, object name, and fullness level when the objects are bottles filled with liquid. The STS-d is an exciting new technology that combines high resolution sensing with interactive display and presents a number of opportunities in applied and commercially relevant tasks, including interactive displays, haptic devices and human-machine interaction.

Ongoing work includes exploring the use of non-visible internal illuminants within the STS and STS-d devices so as to enable visual, tactile and display modes to operate even more independently, and the application of STS sensors in a range of manipulation and HRI tasks. We are also exploring mechanisms to process the visual STS channel to obtain clearer visual imagery. This process is akin to the correction process using in astronomical equipment and is based on both permanent and transient imperfections on the surface using "dark frames" [23]. In astrophotography, a dark frame refers to an image collected in the absence of any actual content (e.g., with a lens cover on) which can be used to calibrate an image system with respect to non-uniform sensitivity. In our case, a geometric mask is computed when no object is in view, and the irregularities in the mask are used to correct subsequent images for gel imperfections when objects are present. For example, Fig. 4 shows a raw visual channel image as well as a processed version in which the effect of the visual artifacts associated with the background and viewing through the STS gel have been removed.

References

1. Hogan, F.R., Tremblay, J.F., Baghi, B.H., Jenkin, M., Siddiqi, K., Dudek, G.: Finger-STS: combined proximity and tactile sensing for robotic manipulation. IEEE Robot. Autom. Lett. **7**, 10865–10872 (2022)
2. Yuan, W., Dong, S., Adelson, E.H.: GelSight: high-resolution robot tactile sensors for estimating geometry and force. Sensors **17**(12), 2762 (2017)
3. Donlon, E., Dong, S., Liu, M., Li, J., Adelson, E., Rodriguez, A.: GelSlim: a high-resolution, compact, robust, and calibrated tactile-sensing finger. In: IEEE/RSJ International Conference on Intelligent Robots and Systems (IROS), pp. 1927–1934 Madrid, Spain (2018)
4. Alspach, A., Hashimoto, K., Kuppuswarny, N., Tedrake, R.: Soft-bubble: a highly compliant dense geometry tactile sensor for robot manipulation. In: IEEE International Conference on Soft Robotics (RoboSoft), pp. 597–604 Seoul, Korea (2019)
5. Padmanabha, A., Ebert, F., Tian, S., Calandra, R., Finn, C., Levine, S.: OmniTact: a multi-directional high-resolution touch sensor. In: IEEE International Conference on Robotics and Automation (ICRA), pp. 618–624 Held Online (2020)
6. Gomes, D.F., Lin, Z., Luo, S.: GelTip: a finger-shaped optical tac- tile sensor for robotic manipulation. In: IEEE/RSJ International Conference on Intelligent Robots and Systems (IROS), pp. 9903–9909. Las Vegas, NV, (2020)
7. Hogan, F.R., Jenkin, M., Rezaei-Shoshtari, S. Girdhar, Y., Meger, D., Dudek, G.: Seeing through your skin: recognizing objects with a novel visuotactile sensor. In: WACV, Held Online (2021)
8. Zhang, Y., Chen, X., Wang, M.Y., Yu, H.: Multidimensional tactile sensor with a thin compound eye-inspired imaging system. Soft Robot. **9**(5), 861–870 (2022)
9. Cao, G., Jiang, J., Lu, C., Gomes, D.F., Luo, S.: TouchRoller: a rolling optical tactile sensor for rapid assessment of textures for large surface areas. Sensors **23**, 2661 (2023)

10. Abad, A., Ranasinghe, A.: Visuotactile sensors with emphasis on GelSight sensor: a review. IEEE Sens. **20**, 7628–7638 (2020)
11. Hogan, F., Jenkin, M., Dudek, G.L., Girdhar, Y., Rezaei-Shoshtari, S., Meger, D.: Semitransparent tactile surface sensor and a method of sensing an interaction with an object using the semitransparent tactile surface sensor (2023). US Patent 11656759
12. Denk, W.E.: Electronic pointer for television images (1946). US Patent 2,487,641
13. Brandl, P., et al.: An adapatable rear-projection screen using digital pens and hand gestures. In: 17th International Conference on Artificial Reality and Telexistence (ICAT), Esbjerg, Denmark (2007)
14. Jenkin, M., Tsotsos, J., Andreopoulos, A., Rotenstein, A., Robinson, M., Laurence, J.: A large-scale touch sensitive display. In: 6th International Conference on Informatics and Systems, Cairo, Egypt (2008)
15. Bachmann, D., Weichert, F., Rinkenauer, G.: Evaluation of the leap motion controller as a pointing device. Sensors (Basel) **15**, 214–233 (2015)
16. Redmon, J., Divvala, S., Girshick, R., Farhadi, A.: You only look once: Unified, real-time object detection. In: IEEE Conference on Computer Vision and Pattern Recognition (CVPR), pp. 779–788. Las Vegas, NV (2016)
17. Parr, J.: Modern kitchen, good home, strong nation. Technol. Cult. **43**, 657–667 (2002)
18. Surmann, A.: The evolution of kitchen design: a yearning for a modern stone age cave. In: van der Meulen, N., Wiesel, J. (eds.) Culinary Turn: Aesthetic Practice of Cookery, pp. 47–56. Transcript Verlag (2017)
19. Samsung connected hub for smart appliances (2022). https://www.samsung.com/us/explore/family-hub-refrigerator/connected-hub/. Accessed Feb 23 2022
20. The rise of kitchen technology and what to expect in future homes (2021). https://www.hippo.com/blog/future-of-kitchen-technology. Accessed 23 Feb 2022
21. Smriti, R.: A quick glimpse into the future of kitchen technology (2021). https://techversions.com/blogs/a-quick-glimpse-into-the-future-of-kitchen-technology/. Accessed 23 Feb 2022
22. Prospero, M.: Bosch's projector turns your countertop into a touchscreen (2019). https://www.tomsguide.com/us/bosch-pai-smart-kitchen-projector,news-29077.html. Accessed 23 Feb 2022
23. Gomez-Rodriguez, M., Kober, J., Schölkopf, B.: Denoising photographs using dark frames optimized by quadratic programming. In: 2009 IEEE International Conference on Computational Photography (ICCP), pp. 1–9. IEEE (2009)

A Color Event-Based Camera Emulator for Robot Vision

Ignacio Bugueno-Cordova[1], Miguel Campusano[2], Robert Guaman-Rivera[1],
and Rodrigo Verschae[1($\boxtimes$)]

[1] Institute of Engineering Sciences, Universidad de O'Higgins, Rancagua, Chile
{ignacio.bugueno,robert.guaman,rodrigo.verschae}@uoh.cl
[2] University of Southern Denmark, Odense, Denmark
mica@mmmi.sdu.dk

Abstract. Event-based cameras are becoming increasingly popular due to their asynchronous spatial-temporal information, high temporal resolution, power efficiency, and high dynamic range advantages. Despite these benefits, the adoption of these sensors has been hindered, mainly due to their high cost. While prices are decreasing and commercial options exist, researchers and developers face barriers to addressing the potential of event-based vision, especially with more specialized models. Although accurate event-based simulators and emulators exist, their primary limitation lies in their inability to operate in real-time and in that they are designed only for grey-scale video streams. This limitation creates a gap between theoretical exploration and practical application, hindering the seamless integration of event-based systems into real-world applications, especially in robotics. Moreover, the importance of color information is well recognized for many tasks, and most existing event-based cameras do not handle color information, except for a few exceptions. To address this challenge, we propose a ROS-based color event camera emulator to aid in reducing the gap between the real-world applicability of event-based color cameras by presenting its software design and implementation. Finally, we present a preliminary evaluation to demonstrate its performance.

Keywords: Event-Based camera · Color vision · Asynchronous sensors · Robot vision · Emulator · Robot Operating System (ROS)

1 Introduction

Event-based cameras, also known as neuromorphic vision sensors, are rapidly becoming popular in various research communities. These sensors –*designed to capture visual and temporal information asynchronously*– offer significant advantages in speed and efficiency [9]. However, their adoption has been limited by several challenges, most notably the cost of these specialized sensors. Although their price is decreasing and some commercial options exist, there are still significant barriers for researchers and developers seeking to exploit the potential of event-based vision, particularly in the case of more specialized models. While the alternative of accurate simulators and emulators has emerged –*such as ESIM* [24] *and V2E* [12]– their main limitation lies in their

© The Author(s), under exclusive license to Springer Nature Switzerland AG 2024
J. Filipe and J. Röning (Eds.): ROBOVIS 2024, CCIS 2077, pp. 375–390, 2024.
https://doi.org/10.1007/978-3-031-59057-3_24

inability to operate in real-time. This limitation introduces a gap between theoretical exploration and practical application, hindering the integration of event-based systems into real-world applications and some research areas, especially in robotics. Moreover, most event-based cameras do not handle color information, with a few exceptions, and it is well known that color information is essential for segmentation, tracking, classification, and many other tasks in computer vision, machine vision, and robot vision [7, 11].

In the present paper, we propose a ROS-based color event camera emulator, which addresses the critical need to bridge the gap between theoretical accuracy and real-world applicability of event-based color cameras, describing its design and implementation and giving a preliminary evaluation.

The present paper is structured as follows: Sect. 1 introduces the problem under study; Sect. 2 provides an overview of the state-of-the-art in event-based camera simulators and emulators; Sect. 3 describes the working principle of this sensor and proposes a color event camera emulator; Sect. 4 outlines the obtained results; Sect. 5 discuss software perspective considerations around the design and implementation of the emulator, and Sect. 6 concludes and projects this work.

2   Related Work

This section provides a comprehensive overview of event-based cameras. Specifically, we review the working principle of this kind of neuromorphic vision sensor, examine the current state-of-the-art in event-based simulators and emulators, and describe the fundamentals of color event-based camera hardware implementation as a reference framework for designing the proposed emulator.

2.1   Event-Based Cameras Working Principle

Biological Inspiration. The fundamental principle behind the design of an event-based pixel is to emulate how the mammalian retina works, a remarkable biological structure that consists of ten functional layers [26]. Consequently, the implementation of an event-based pixel necessarily requires a simplification of this biological complexity. Figure 1 shows a simplified event-based pixel representation consisting of three layers: the photoreceptor layer, the outer plexiform layer, and the inner plexiform layer. The complexity of these three layers refers to the cone (photoreceptor), ON/OFF bipolar cells, and ON/OFF ganglion cells [25]. Together, these cells are the optimal structure for a silicon retina that can be used for most imaging applications while mimicking the mammalian retina. The silicon equivalent reproduces this structure by introducing a photoreceptor, a differentiation circuit (bipolar cells), and a pair of comparators (ganglion cells).

From Silicon Circuit to Event Generation. In the pixel schematic, Fig. 2a shows the simplified event-based circuit that detects rapid changes and measures light simultaneously without interference. This process memorizes the logarithmic intensity each time an event occurs while constantly monitoring any change of sufficient magnitude from

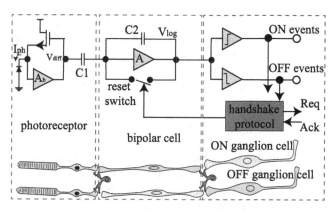

Fig. 1. Three-layer model of a human retina and its corresponding DVS pixel circuit. Based on [8].

the memorized value. In this context, Fig. 2b shows that the Dynamic Vision Sensor (DVS) responds asynchronously and independently to changes in brightness at each pixel (compared to standard cameras, which acquire complete frames at a rate specified by an external clock). Hence, the events camera generates a variable data rate sequence of digital "events" or "spikes", such as shown in Fig. 2d, triggering information about the pixel location(x, y), timestamp (t), and change polarity (p).

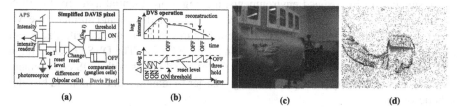

Fig. 2. Simplified working principle of asynchronous pixel generation in event-based cameras. (a) Simplified circuit diagram of the DAVIS pixel (event-based pixel in red, frame-based pixel in blue); (b) Schematic of the event-based data generation; (c) Frame of a DAVIS346 event camera; (d) Accumulated events of a DAVIS346 event camera (blue for positive polarity, red for negative). (a, b) based on [9] and (c, d) own elaboration. (Color figure online)

Event cameras are data-based sensors: their output depends on the motion or brightness change in the scene. The faster the motion, the more events per second are generated as each pixel adapts its delta modulator's sampling rate to the change rate of the logarithmic intensity signal. Events are marked with microsecond resolution and transmitted with sub-millisecond latency, enabling these sensors to react quickly to visual stimulation. The incident light on a pixel is a product of the scene's illumination and the surface's reflectance. If the lighting is approximately constant, a change in logarithmic intensity signals a change in reflectance. These changes in reflectance are mainly the result of the movement of objects in the field of view. For this reason, DVS brightness change events have a built-in invariance concerning scene illumination [17].

Event Data. As described above, event-based cameras asynchronously respond to changes in the received logarithmic brightness signal $L(\mathbf{u}_k, t_k) \doteq \log(I(\mathbf{u}_k, t_k))$, where $\mathbf{u}_k$ corresponds to the sensor pixel, t_k to the associated time, L to the luminosity, and I to the brightness signal [9]. Then, an event is triggered at pixel $\mathbf{u}_k = (x_k, y_k)^T$ and at time t_k as soon as the brightness change since the last event at the pixel reaches a threshold $\pm C$ (with $C > 0$):

$$L(\mathbf{u}_k, t_k) - L(\mathbf{u}_k, t_k - \Delta t_k) \geq p_k C, \tag{1}$$

where $p_k \in \{-1, +1\}$ is the sign of the brightness change and Δt_k is the time since the last event at $\mathbf{u}_k$. Then, in a given time interval, an event camera produces a sequence of events, $\mathcal{E}(t_N) = \{e_k\}_{k=1}^N = \{(x_k, y_k, t_k, p_k)\}_{k=1}^N$ with microsecond resolution, where t_N denotes the last timestamp in the event stream $\mathcal{E}$.

2.2 Simulators and Emulators

Due to the high prices of sensors and the early lack of event-based data to develop, train, and test algorithms for event-based cameras, several simulators and offline emulators have been proposed. Therefore, we describe the systems that simulate event-based data and emulate event sequences from video sequences under an offline approach.

DVS Gazebo Plugin. This plugin simulates a DVS in the 3D simulator Gazebo [13], being suitable for high-speed environments, making it an essential asset for the ROS community due to its adaptability to different robotic platforms and simulation environments. The plugin configures key camera features such as update rate and event detection threshold by defining parameters in the SDF format. The DVS Gazebo Plugin can publish events to specific topics within Gazebo and aligns with ROS communication and interoperability principles, making it easier to integrate into simulated broader robotic systems.

AirSim. This simulator is an advanced Unreal Engine-based simulator designed for testing and developing autonomous ground and aerial systems algorithms [27]. In recent years, AirSim has integrated a simulated implementation of event-based cameras, distinguished by comparing successive frames to detect significant changes in light intensity, generating events when noticeable variations are observed [1]. Despite its usefulness, the AirSim implementation does not fully replicate real event cameras' asynchronous nature and high temporal resolution. Therefore, the results obtained must be carefully validated in real scenarios.

ESIM: An Open Event Camera Simulator. This simulator provides a software environment that simulates the output of neuromorphic cameras [24]. ESIM uses lighting and motion models to simulate optical flow in a 3D environment, allowing the virtual camera to react to changes in light intensity similarly to a physical event-based camera. This tool stands out for its flexibility and accuracy in simulating several scenarios and lighting conditions, being highly relevant for validating vision-based algorithms from robotics to autonomous driving. In addition, it offers the possibility of injecting noise into the simulation, allowing to understand how methods designed for this type of sensor might behave in less ideal situations and closer to real-world conditions.

V2E from Video Frames to DVS Events. This offline emulator aims to replicate the working principle of event cameras to generate realistic DVS event streams [12], allowing the conversion of conventional videos to event sequences. This capability is essential for bridging the gap between computational and neuromorphic vision. V2E uses state-of-the-art methods to emulate the pixel response of an event-based camera. First, it converts the color frames to grayscale, then uses the SuperSloMo interpolation method [21] to increase the number of frames per second to guarantee a high temporal resolution. Therefore, the threshold of intensity change is calculated to represent the different sensitivity characteristics of real event cameras. Afterward, it measures per-pixel temporal differences in logarithmic intensity with a high dynamic range to generate the emulated events asynchronously. Finally, V2E incorporates sensory imperfections, providing a realistic approximation of event camera-based cameras.

Despite V2E's pioneering contribution to event emulation, it has significant challenges in terms of computational efficiency:

1. It uses large temporary memory buffers for frame processing and event generation. This implies a considerable use of memory and GPU, limiting its use in resource-constrained systems.
2. The lack of real-time capability restricts its application in dynamic environments that require instantaneous interaction, such as robotic systems in ROS, reducing its viability in practical applications.
3. The emulation of large datasets requires huge processing time that can only be reduced by simplifying the spatial-temporal features or using High-Performance Computing infrastructures.

These limitations highlight the need for a highly efficient emulator to expand the applicability of event-based cameras to robotics and bridge the existing gap.

2.3 Hardware Implementation of Color Event-Based Cameras

We can identify three general categories for capturing color information using event-based cameras. In the first one, sensors are derived from the DAVIS camera using Bayer filters; the second combines three monochrome event-based cameras and a light splitter; and the third uses a monochrome event-based sensor and structured lighting.

The DAVIS camera [5] is a monochrome camera that can capture frames and events, with a spatial resolution of 240×180 pixels for DAVIS240 and 346×240 pixels for DAVIS346. One of the first color event cameras, based on the DAVIS camera, is the C-DAVIS camera [16], which can capture RGBW frames and monochrome events at VGA (640×480) and QVGA resolution (320×240), respectively. Later, the SDAVIS192 [20] was proposed, exhibiting enhanced sensitivity compared to the DAVIS, capable of generating color (RGBW) events and frames with a resolution of 188×192 pixels.

Finally, the Color-DAVIS346 [29] stands as the most recent color event camera commercially available, which uses a 2×2 RGBG Bayer pattern on top of the CCD sensor, having a 346×260 resolution.

A different approach was proposed in [19], where a combination of three Asynchronous Time-based Image Sensors (ATIS) and dichroic filters to split a single light beam is used. Finally, a third approach was proposed in [4], where an Event-Based RGB Sensing system that uses a monochrome event-based camera aid by Structured Light to detect full RGB events, which can capture events event in static situations. These two last approaches do not need to trade-off for the sensor resolution, as the DAVIS-based sensors do, but are large, requiring three cameras or an active vision device.

3   Color Event Camera Emulator for Robotic Vision

One of the biggest problems with existing event camera emulators is their inability to work in real-time robotic vision applications. The main reason is that the frame interpolation methods used to emulate the high temporal resolution of events often have long inference and processing times. This is due to several factors, including: a) the complexity of the implemented architecture, b) sub-optimal design of the frame interpolation method and event generation algorithm, c) and the high-performance hardware requirements. Therefore, it is unfeasible to integrate this kind of emulator in frameworks such as ROS.

This section presents the proposed color event-based camera emulator for robotic vision integrated with ROS. Our proposal aims to be an efficient implementation using the state-of-the-art frame interpolation method FLAVR [14], the respective event-based data generation for each RGB channel, and a ROS-based software integration.

Event Color Data. As described above, event-based cameras asynchronously respond to changes in the received logarithmic brightness signal $L(\mathbf{u}_k, t_k) \doteq \log(I(\mathbf{u}_k, t_k))$, where $\mathbf{u}_k$ corresponds to the sensor pixel, t_k to the associated time, L to the luminosity, and I to the brightness signal [9]. Our emulator generates three sequences, each associated with each color channel c, $\mathcal{E}^c(t_N^c) = \{e_k^c\}_{k=1}^{N^c} = \{(x_k^c, y_k^c, t_k^c, p_k^c)\}_{k=1}^{N^c}$, each of these being managed concurrently.

Proposed Efficient Emulator. We propose an efficient color event-based camera emulator, as shown in Fig. 3. In this proposal, the first step is to use an RGB frames buffer, followed by a frame interpolation method (more details later), which generates a set of interpolated RGB frames according to the interpolation factor chosen to guarantee high temporal resolution. Then, by interspersing the original frames with the interpolated frames, the intensity change threshold that triggers an event for each channel is captured between frames. Subsequently, the temporal differences per pixel are measured in logarithmic intensity for each RGB channel with a high dynamic range, and the respective logarithmic curves are compared with the corresponding trigger thresholds to finally generate the emulated color events asynchronously.

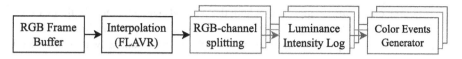

Fig. 3. Proposed color event-based camera emulator pipeline.

Efficient Emulator and High Temporal Resolution Using FLAVR. To ensure high temporal resolution of the events and accurate performance, we employ FLAVR [14], a state-of-the-art frame interpolation method that achieves high performance in multi-frame prediction with low inference times. FLAVR uses a customized encoder-decoder architecture with 3D spatio-temporal convolutions and channel gating to capture and interpolate complex motion trajectories between frames. The first layer of the encoder receives an input of $2 \cdot C \cdot H \cdot W \cdot 3$, where $2 \cdot C$ corresponds to a temporal window of only the immediate neighbors, H, W are the spatial dimensions of the input frames and 3 to the RGB channels. The final prediction layer projects the 3D feature maps into $(k - 1)$ frame predictions, where k is the interpolation factor used. This design allows FLAVR to predict multiple frames in one inference forward pass, as shown in Fig. 4.

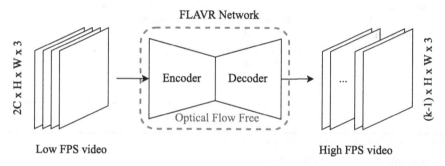

Fig. 4. Flow-Agnostic Video Representations (FLAVR) for fast video frame interpolation. Based on [14].

An essential feature of FLAVR is pre-trained weights, which reduces inference times compared to traditional methods, regardless of the interpolation factor used. Thus, the authors [14] provide three pre-trained weights ($k = 2, k = 4, k = 8$) for an architecture with four input frames. Thus, if we take as FLAVR input a buffer of 4 RGB frames and an interpolation factor of 4 (i.e., increase by four times the original FPS), we will have $C = 2$ and $k = 4$. If a different interpolation factor is required (e.g., $k = 16$), the network must be retrained, or a combination of the above interpolation factors must be used [14].

3.1 ROS Software Integration

As described in Sect. 2.2 and mentioned in Sect. 3, existing event camera emulators are designed to guarantee high temporal resolution, trading off the execution time. This design works on an offline approach, where the methods can be lenient with the execution time. However, these methods do not work adequately in a real-time case, where event generation/interpolation must keep up with the data source, which is an RGB camera.

We integrated our highly efficient emulator with the Robot Operation System (ROS) [23], which allows it to be used with any ROS-compatible robot. Then, we developed a ROS node to work in parallel using two threads. This parallel approach allows for an optimal use of resources where events are being published. In contrast, new events are generated, giving extra time to generate events before publishing them.

The first thread processes the frames of an RGB camera and generates an array of events between frames, which then is added to a queue shared between threads. The second thread publishes the generated events into the ROS system. If there are no events to be published due to the shared queue being empty or because the timestamp of the following array of events to be published is greater than the current timestamp (*i.e.,* the events should be published in the future), the thread sleeps for a moment. These threads can be implemented in Algorithm 1 and Algorithm 2.

Algorithm 1. Thread 1: Generate emulated events.

1: **procedure** GENERATEEVENT($queue, previousFrame, currentFrame$)
2:     $eventsArray \leftarrow eventsBetween(previousFrame, currentFrame)$
3:     **for each** $events \in eventsArray$ **do**
4:         $timestamp \leftarrow events.first().timestamp$
5:         $queue.push(< events, timestamp >)$
6:     **end for**
7: **end procedure**

Algorithm 2. Thread 2: Publish emulated events.

1: **procedure** PUBLISHEVENT($queue$)
2:     $events$ ▷ events to be published
3:     **while** $true$ **do**
4:         **if** $events \neq null$ &   **not** $queue.empty()$ **then**
5:             $events \leftarrow queue.pop()$ ▷ get next events
6:         **end if**
7:         **if** $events$ & $time.now() \geq events.timestamp$ **then**
8:             $publishEvents(events)$
9:         **else**
10:             $sleep(0.001)$ ▷ If no events to publish, then wait
11:         **end if**
12:     **end while**
13: **end procedure**

Figure 5 shows the interaction between the two threads. This algorithm allows the node to handle both the generation of events and the publication of the same events independently at the proper time.

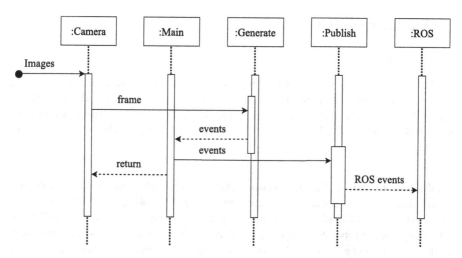

Fig. 5. Sequential Diagram of the color event-based camera emulator using two threads: Generate and Publish.

Due to the nature of the emulator, when events are generated, the timestamps associated with those events will always be in the past. For ROS to correctly publish the emulated events, the emulator incorporates a delay based on how much time is left until the next frame in the ROS node and from that frame to publish the generated events. Therefore, the emulated events are stored in a shared queue with the timestamp corresponding to when the event will be published. For this reason, the second thread only has to worry about publishing at the correct time. As a result, we implement an efficient ROS-based event camera emulator to which a node can subscribe and use such events (considering its delay), as shown in Fig. 6.

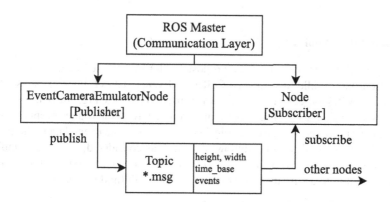

Fig. 6. ROS flowchart of the color event-based camera emulator proposal.

4   Qualitative Results

4.1   Datasets

Databases derived from event cameras represent a valuable resource that facilitates the evaluation of several computer vision algorithms, particularly those related to three-dimensional reconstruction, object recognition, and motion analysis (optical flow) [9]. In the following, we briefly describe the datasets used in the qualitative analysis presented below.

Middle Size League Collected Events Dataset. Released in August 2023, this pioneering database [2] of event-based records in environment robotic football (specifically the RoboCup 2023 Middle Size League) was captured using also a Color-DAVIS346 [29]. on one of the robot goalkeepers to analyze: a) the movement of the ball approaching the goal (air and ground level); b) the movement of the ball away from the goal (air and ground level); c) the dribbling of the ball by opponents; d) throwing the ball from the penalty spot; e) robots moving along the field of play.

MVSEC and DSEC Datasets. Stereo event capture in [30] mounts the cameras on a car, hexacopter, motorcycle, handheld device, and LIDAR, IMU, GPS, and standard stereo cameras. Data acquisition includes day and night recordings in both indoor and outdoor environments. DAVIS 346B cameras with stereo configuration, 346×260 resolution, 4 mm lens, and vertical field of view of approximately $70°$ were used, and synchronization was performed using a hardware trigger. In contrast to the previously reported MVSEC database, the DSEC database was created using two event cameras with VGA resolution. The authors in [10] have reported the first large-scale, high-resolution stereo event dataset in a driving environment. Data was captured using two Prophesee monochrome cameras with (640×480) resolution in various lighting conditions.

4.2   Qualitative Analysis

In Fig. 7, we illustrate the use of the proposed color event-based camera emulator of images from the Middle Size League Collected Events Dataset. For this dataset (captured by a DAVIS346C camera), color frames are available (see Fig. 7(a, d)); color event sequences are available (see Fig. 7(b, e)) and from the available frames events are emulated with our proposed systems (see Fig. 7(c, f)). To show the event data in the figures, for both (b, e) and (c, f), a time window of 33ms was considered, and an accumulated image was employed based on an RGBG pattern. It can be observed that the emulated results (left column) are pretty similar to the ground truth (middle column).

4.3   Example Application

Motion analysis is critical in various tasks, such as navigation, mapping, visual control, pose estimation, and optical flow estimation. We have implemented a surface distance algorithm (*DistSurf*) proposed by [3], which used event camera information to estimate

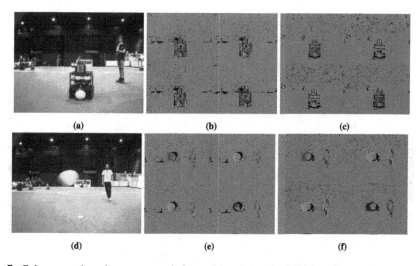

Fig. 7. Color event-based camera emulation achieved for the Middle Size League Collected Events Dataset, with a 346 × 260 spatial resolution, $5ms$ temporal resolution and $33ms$ time window: (a, d) the original color frames captured by a DAVIS346C camera; (b, e) the original events captured; (c, f) emulated color event sequences. The corresponding RGBG sequences are shown for each case.

the optical flow. The algorithm reports the use of distance transformations derived from DVS-generated events to estimate object texture, involving a distance surface concept to calculate pixel velocity from multiple edge pixels with different edge orientations (Fig. 8).

4.4 Processing Times

The average execution time performance analysis of the proposed color event-based camera emulator is evaluated on an NVIDIA®GeForce GTX 1650 (4 GB) and a NVIDIA®DGX-1^{TM} (32 GB), with the results for the different emulators listed in Table 1.

5 Software Implementation Discussion

GPU-CPU Memory Transfer. As shown in Table 1, a critical issue in deep learning-based real-time systems is the memory transfer bottleneck between the GPU and CPU [6]. Using asynchronous transfers and data prefetching techniques can speed up these transfers [18], reducing latency in real-time systems. On the hardware side, the GPU-CPU memory transfer takes place over the PCIe bus (Fig. 9), whose speed may not be on par with the ultra-fast processing capabilities of modern GPUs [22]. This may result in a bottleneck that negatively affects the responsiveness of the real-time inference system. Hardware optimization, such as parallelizing the use of multiple CPUs and GPUs [28] or selecting GPUs with higher memory bandwidths and faster PCIe buses, is critical to minimize these delays.

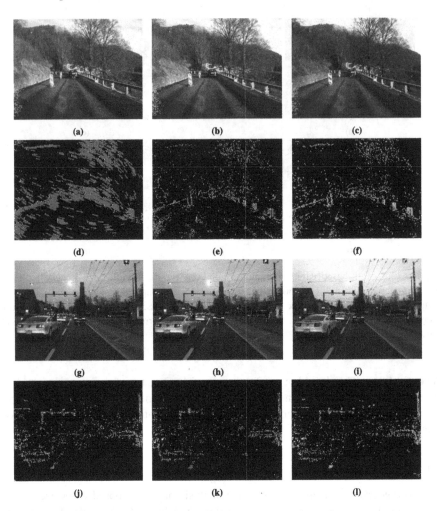

Fig. 8. DistSurf optical flow algorithm qualitative performance, using color event sequences generated by the proposed emulator applied to MVSEC and DSEC.

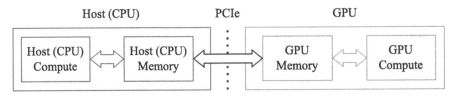

Fig. 9. Host-to-device data transfer in NVIDIA CUDA Memory. Based on [15].

Another challenge is handling *unfinished kernels* during GPU-CPU memory transfers. Therefore, ensuring proper CPU-GPU synchronization is essential, waiting for all

Table 1. Average execution time of the color event-based camera emulator modules, from frame interpolation to color event emulation. We analyze the proposal performance using different spatial resolutions (128 × 128 for DVS128, 240 × 180 for DAVIS240, 346 × 260 for DAVIS346), frame interpolation factors (k), frame interpolation methods (SuperSlomo [21] and FLAVR [14]), and specialized hardware.

Hardware	Emulated sensor	Frame interpolation method			GPU-CPU	Color events generation
		Factor	SuperSlomo	FLAVR		
	Dimension	k	t_{exec} [ms]	t_{exec} [ms]	t_{exec} [ms]	t_{exec} [ms]
GTX 1650	128 × 128	2	38,33	6,89	68,33	16,98
	240 × 180		74,88	5,97	69,91	22,24
	346 × 260		242,85	5,73	68,47	51,57
	128 × 128	4	38,12	8,32	70,31	32,19
	240 × 180		80,52	7,05	69,45	36,87
	346 × 260		253,30	7,98	70,18	97,35
	128 × 128	8	36,89	6,21	71,77	58,10
	240 × 180		89,77	6,58	70,78	92,00
	346 × 260		261,63	8,10	71,05	108,86
DGX-1	128 × 128	2	14,60	2,62	71,81	6,23
	240 × 180		28,39	2,33	68,68	8,78
	346 × 260		91,28	2,08	71,52	18,90
	128 × 128	4	14,37	2,83	69,71	11,79
	240 × 180		30,25	2,56	68,26	13,64
	346 × 260		95,10	3,06	69,11	36,67
	128 × 128	8	13,69	2,47	71,09	21,52
	240 × 180		33,70	2,21	71,64	34,58
	346 × 260		98,22	2,73	71,91	40,35

kernels to complete before initiating the data transfer. This synchronization must be carefully managed to avoid unsuitable delays.

Emulator Modularity. From a software engineering approach, modularity allows greater flexibility and adaptability to different contexts. The system's modular design allows a clear and logical separation of responsibilities. For example, the color event-based camera emulator works with a ROS Node that registers to an RGB camera and generates events that should be published with an unavoidable delay. This preserves the principle of single responsibility and provides the flexibility to modify or replace specific algorithms without affecting the rest of the system. This means the algorithm for generating events could be easily selected or modified through a configuration file, allowing adjustments based on external factors such as the camera's frame rate. This approach makes the initial setup easier and allows the system to be tuned to different hardware, which is especially valuable in environments where hardware may vary or where rapid reconfiguration is required.

Handling Large Volumes of Events in ROS. Efficient handling of large data volumes in ROS *–especially in an event emulator–* is critically important due to variability, asynchrony, and the potentially massive volume of data. In highly dynamic scenarios, such as those with rapid motion or lighting changes, the data flow can be vast and fluctuating, requiring a robust and scalable system capable of queuing, processing, and transmitting these data spikes without compromising performance. Data asynchrony in ROS adds complexity, as it was not originally conceived to handle data at irregular intervals consistently. This implies flexibility in data processing to ensure that the system responds in real-time without losing critical information. Therefore, it is essential for an efficient event camera emulator to implement modules that can adapt to variable demand, handle data efficiently, and maintain consistency in the generation and publication of real-time emulated events.

6   Conclusions and Future Work

This paper presents an efficient color event-based camera emulator implemented in ROS, focusing on robot vision. As a contribution, it includes: a) the software engineering considerations that every event emulator should take into account, b) the integration of the fastest state-of-the-art frame interpolation method, c) the qualitative evaluation of the proposal in different databases with a focus on robotics, d) a time performance analysis of the proposed emulator, e) a discussion of relevant issues detected that prevent a delay-free implementation, f) and the ROS code provided to the community (by prior request).

As future work, the goal is to: a) implement a real-time color event emulator (by predicting the subsequent frames for delay reduction), b) to be ROS distro agnostic, c) to be hardware agnostic (using a low-cost frame interpolation method that avoids GPU-CPU transfer times), d) and release the ROS code to the entire community as an open-source contribution.

Also, a modular implementation should be made from a software engineering approach, making the emulator adaptable to different factors and scenarios. It will also be interesting to analyze which event publishing approach is best for robotics applications: publishing events as they are emulated or grouping and publishing them with a constant time window. Another relevant aspect is the integration of the emulator to Gazebo and RViz to enable the visualization and analysis of color events in robotic vision applications. Finally, a quantitative evaluation and validation in other applications, such as classification, segmentation, etc., are required.

Acknowledgement. This work was partly supported by the Programa de Equipamiento Científico y Tecnológico, ANID, Chile (FONDEQUIP) Project under Grant EQM170041.

References

1. Event camera - airsim (2021). https://microsoft.github.io/AirSim/event_sim/
2. Mist lab collected events with event-based cameras (2023). https://github.com/MISTLab/event_based_data
3. Almatrafi, M., Baldwin, R., Aizawa, K., Hirakawa, K.: Distance surface for event-based optical flow. IEEE Trans. Pattern Anal. Mach. Intell. **42**(7), 1547–1556 (2020)
4. Bajestani, S.E.M., Beltrame, G.: Event-based RGB sensing with structured light. In: Proceedings of the IEEE/CVF Winter Conference on Applications of Computer Vision (WACV), pp. 5458–5467 (2023)
5. Brandli, C., Berner, R., Yang, M., Liu, S.C., Delbruck, T.: A 240× 180 130 db 3 μs latency global shutter spatiotemporal vision sensor. IEEE J. Solid-State Circ. **49**(10), 2333–2341 (2014)
6. Buber, E., Diri, B.: Performance analysis and CPU vs GPU comparison for deep learning. In: 2018 6th International Conference on Control Engineering & Information Technology (CEIT), pp. 1–6 (2018)
7. Finlayson, G.D.: Colour and illumination in computer vision. Interface focus **8**(4), 20180008 (2018)
8. Furmonas, J., Liobe, J., Barzdenas, V.: Analytical review of event-based camera depth estimation methods and systems. Sensors **22**(3), 1201 (2022)
9. Gallego, G., et al.: Event-based vision: a survey. IEEE Trans. Pattern Anal. Mach. Intell. **44**(1), 154–180 (2022)
10. Gehrig, M., Aarents, W., Gehrig, D., Scaramuzza, D.: Dsec: a stereo event camera dataset for driving scenarios. IEEE Robot. Autom. Lett. **6**(3), 4947–4954 (2021)
11. Gowda, S.N., Yuan, C.: ColorNet: investigating the importance of color spaces for image classification. In: Jawahar, C., Li, H., Mori, G., Schindler, K. (eds.) ACCV 2018. LNCS, pp. 581–596. Springer, Cham (2019). https://doi.org/10.1007/978-3-030-20870-7_36
12. Hu, Y., Liu, S.C., Delbruck, T.: v2e: From video frames to realistic DVS events. In: 2021 IEEE/CVF Conference on Computer Vision and Pattern Recognition Workshops (CVPRW), pp. 1312–1321 (2021)
13. Kaiser, J., et al.: Towards a framework for end-to-end control of a simulated vehicle with spiking neural networks. In: 2016 IEEE International Conference on Simulation, Modeling, and Programming for Autonomous Robots, pp. 127–134 (2016)
14. Kalluri, T., Pathak, D., Chandraker, M., Tran, D.: Flavr: flow-free architecture for fast video frame interpolation. Mach. Vis. Appl. **34**(5), 83 (2023)
15. Kessler, C., et al.: Programmability and performance portability aspects of heterogeneous multi-/manycore systems. In: 2012 Design, Automation & Test in Europe Conference & Exhibition (DATE), pp. 1403–1408 (2012)
16. Li, C., et al.: Design of an RGBW color VGA rolling and global shutter dynamic and active-pixel vision sensor. In: 2015 IEEE International Symposium on Circuits and Systems (ISCAS), pp. 718–721. IEEE (2015)
17. Lichtsteiner, P., Posch, C., Delbruck, T.: A 128×128 120 db 15 μs latency asynchronous temporal contrast vision sensor. IEEE J. Solid-State Circ. **43**, 566–576 (2008)
18. Long, X., Gong, X., Zhang, B., Zhou, H.: Deep learning based data prefetching in CPU-GPU unified virtual memory. J. Parallel Distrib. Comput. **174**, 19–31 (2023)
19. Marcireau, A., Ieng, S.H., Simon-Chane, C., Benosman, R.B.: Event-based color segmentation with a high dynamic range sensor. Front. Neurosci. **12**, 317614 (2018)
20. Moeys, D.P., et al.: A sensitive dynamic and active pixel vision sensor for color or neural imaging applications. IEEE Trans. Biomed. Circuits Syst. **12**(1), 123–136 (2017)

21. Niklaus, S., Mai, L., Liu, F.: Video frame interpolation via adaptive convolution. In: 2017 IEEE Conference on Computer Vision and Pattern Recognition (CVPR), pp. 2270–2279 (2017)
22. Nikolić, G.S., Dimitrijević, B.R., Nikolić, T.R., Stojcev, M.K.: A survey of three types of processing units: CPU, GPU and TPU. In: 2022 57th International Scientific Conference on Information, Communication and Energy Systems and Technologies (ICEST), pp. 1–6 (2022)
23. Quigley, M., et al.: ROS: an open-source robot operating system. In: Proceedings of the IEEE International Conference on Robotics and Automation (ICRA) Workshop on Open Source Robotics. Kobe, Japan (2009)
24. Rebecq, H., Gehrig, D., Scaramuzza, D.: ESIM: an open event camera simulator. In: Billard, A., Dragan, A., Peters, J., Morimoto, J. (eds.) Proceedings of The 2nd Conference on Robot Learning. Proceedings of Machine Learning Research, vol. 87, pp. 969–982. PMLR (2018)
25. Sawant, A., Saha, A., Khoussine, J., Sinha, R., Hoon, M.: New insights into retinal circuits through EM connectomics: what we have learnt and what remains to be learned. Front. Ophthalmol. **3**, 1168548 (2023)
26. Shah, P., Rathod, S.S.: Review of bio-inspired silicon retina: from cell to system level implementation. In: 2021 International Conference on Communication information and Computing Technology (ICCICT), pp. 1–13. IEEE (2021)
27. Shah, S., Dey, D., Lovett, C., Kapoor, A.: Airsim: high-fidelity visual and physical simulation for autonomous vehicles. In: Hutter, M., Siegwart, R. (eds.) Field and Service Robotics. Springer Proceedings in Advanced Robotics, vol. 5, pp. 621–635. Springer, Cham (2017). https://doi.org/10.1007/978-3-319-67361-5_40
28. Skorych, V., Dosta, M.: Parallel CPU-GPU computing technique for discrete element method. Concurrency Comput. Pract. Experience **34**(11), e6839 (2022)
29. Taverni, G., et al.: Front and back illuminated dynamic and active pixel vision sensors comparison. IEEE Trans. Circ. Syst. II Express Briefs **65**(5), 677–681 (2018)
30. Zhu, A.Z., Thakur, D., Özaslan, T., Pfrommer, B., Kumar, V., Daniilidis, K.: The multivehicle stereo event camera dataset: an event camera dataset for 3D perception. IEEE Robot. Autom. Lett. **3**(3), 2032–2039 (2018)

Fast Point Cloud to Mesh Reconstruction for Deformable Object Tracking

Elham Amin Mansour[1]([✉]) [iD], Hehui Zheng[1,2] [iD], and Robert K. Katzschmann[1] [iD]

[1] Soft Robotics Lab, ETH Zürich, Zürich, Switzerland
elham.aminmansour@inf.ethz.ch
[2] ETH AI Center, Zürich, Switzerland
https://srl.ethz.ch, https://ai.ethz.ch/

Abstract. The world around us is full of soft objects we perceive and deform with dexterous hand movements. For a robotic hand to control soft objects, it has to acquire online state feedback of the deforming object. While RGB-D cameras can collect occluded point clouds at a rate of 30 Hz, this does not represent a continuously trackable object surface. Hence, in this work, we developed a method that takes as input a template mesh which is the mesh of an object in its non-deformed state and a deformed point cloud of the same object, and then shapes the template mesh such that it matches the deformed point cloud. The reconstruction of meshes from point clouds has long been studied in the field of Computer graphics under 3D reconstruction and 4D reconstruction, however, both lack the speed and generalizability needed for robotics applications. Our model is designed using a point cloud auto-encoder and a Real-NVP architecture. Our trained model can perform mesh reconstruction and tracking at a rate of 58 Hz on a template mesh of 3000 vertices and a deformed point cloud of 5000 points and is generalizable to the deformations of six different object categories which are assumed to be made of soft material in our experiments (scissors, hammer, foam brick, cleanser bottle, orange, and dice). The object meshes are taken from the YCB benchmark dataset. An instance of a downstream application can be the control algorithm for a robotic hand that requires online feedback from the state of the manipulated object which would allow online grasp adaptation in a closed-loop manner. Furthermore, the tracking capacity of our method can help in the system identification of deforming objects in a marker-free approach. In future work, we will extend our trained model to generalize beyond six object categories and additionally to real-world deforming point clouds.

Keywords: Deformation · Manipulation · Reconstruction · Tracking

1 Introduction

The interaction between robots and soft objects is a milestone yet to be hit in the field of robotics. For instance, a robotic hand should be able to quickly learn how an unseen soft object changes shape while it is manipulated and should be able to continuously track the deformations of a soft object to adapt its grasping method accordingly.

© The Author(s), under exclusive license to Springer Nature Switzerland AG 2024
J. Filipe and J. Röning (Eds.): ROBOVIS 2024, CCIS 2077, pp. 391–409, 2024.
https://doi.org/10.1007/978-3-031-59057-3_25

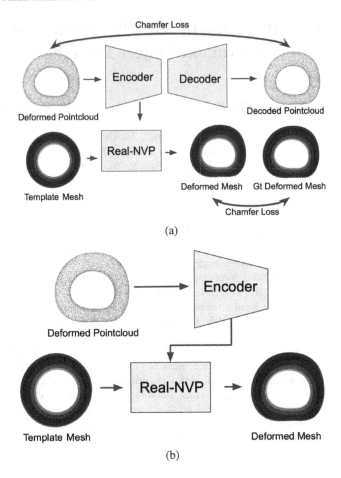

Fig. 1. Our pipeline for the two stages of training (a) and testing (b), respectively, both take as input a deformed point cloud of an object and a mesh of the same object in a non-deformed state (template mesh). It is designed to reconstruct the deformed point cloud into a deformed mesh by deforming the template mesh. (a) Training stage: The auto-encoder, comprised of an encoder and decoder, takes the deformed point cloud as input and learns an encoding through chamfer loss by comparing the decoded/reconstructed deformed point cloud with the groundtruth deformed point cloud. Then, the conditional Real-NVP model takes as input the auto-encoder's encoding and the template mesh and learns the coordinates of the deformed mesh using chamfer loss supervised by the ground truth deformed mesh. (b) Inference stage: The encoder encodes the deformed point cloud, and then the conditional Real-NVP model takes the template mesh and the encoding as input and predicts the new coordinate for every vertex in the template mesh. Therefore, in both stages of training and inference, the deformed mesh consists of the template mesh vertices moved around by the Real-NVP, and faces consistent with those of the template mesh.

The first step towards dexterous manipulation of complex objects is seeing the object. This can be achieved through a model that takes a live stream of point clouds of a deforming object as input and performs an online reconstruction to trackable deforming meshes. The stream of point clouds would be collected via RGB-D cameras positioned at different angles around the object.

The task of creating meshes from point clouds is a long-studied problem in the computer graphics field. Works in 3D reconstruction generate a mesh for one point cloud [8, 10, 17, 22], while 4D reconstruction works generate meshes for a sequence of deforming point clouds [3, 9, 12, 14, 19]. The main focus of both works is the accurate generation of refined meshes and hence time efficiency is compromised. Furthermore, most of the 4D reconstruction works are based on learning the canonical (or template) mesh, which limits them to training a separate model for each object category with the main focus on humans and animals. In 3D reconstruction, on one hand, implicit algorithms [17] which use marching cubes are accurate but time inefficient, and on the other hand, explicit models [8, 10, 22] that deform one or more initial template meshes are speed efficient with poor accuracy and topology. Overall, prior works in 3D reconstruction do not apply to the time dimension and hence do not allow for the tracking of the vertex positions of the deformed meshes. This proves to be limiting in robotics applications.

In our work, to find a balance between speed and accuracy, we assume a template mesh can be generated from the first point cloud of the deforming point cloud sequence using a SOTA method, e.g. [17] which operates in the implicit domain and generates meshes of the right topology with a speed of 25 Hz. The main focus of our work is generating deformed meshes for the remaining deformed point cloud frames by continuously deforming and tracking the template mesh. In this work, we assume that within a sequence of deforming point clouds of an object, the topology does not change and hence, the template mesh has the same topology as the deformed point cloud of any frame within the sequence. To predict the mesh coordinates of the deformed mesh, we use our model, as illustrated in Fig. 1, which consists of an encoder and decoder for extracting an encoding from the deformed point cloud and a Real-NVP [6] component which deforms the template mesh given the deformed encoding. The resulting pipeline has an inference speed of 0.017 s for a template mesh of 3000 vertices and a point cloud of 5000 points on an Omen Desktop (24-core, 3.2 GHz Intel Core i9-12900K CPU, 64 GB memory, NVIDIA GeForce 3090 GPU with 24 GB memory).

In summary, our main contributions are a trained model:

- With a capacity of generating deformable meshes in an online manner of 58 Hz given a template mesh of 3000 vertices and a deformed point cloud of 5000 points.
- Generalizable to the deformations of different object categories.
- With the capacity to track the vertices.

2 Related Work

Previous works in the computer graphics field demonstrate point cloud to mesh reconstruction approaches that either work for a single point cloud (3D mesh reconstruction) or a sequence of point clouds (4D mesh reconstruction). In the following, we briefly discuss the most related works and the gaps that need to be addressed.

2.1   3D Mesh Reconstruction of a Point Cloud

This category of work reconstructs a separate mesh for each frame of point cloud input, lacking consistent tracking of vertex positions, which can be crucial for robotic applications. These works fall into two categories. In the first category, the vertex positions of a template mesh are modified using a deformation network to best fit the input point cloud that needs to be reconstructed [7, 8, 10, 20, 22].

To move around vertices, three different methods are widely used: Neural ordinary differential equations(NODE) [5], Real-NVP [6], and MLP. MLP is not homeomorphic and hence does not guarantee manifoldness by the proof in the supplementary material of ShapeFlow [10]. While normalizing flows using NODE [5] are homeomorphic and guarantee manifoldness, they come at a cost of time inefficiency due to the integrals in their constructions. One pass through the construction takes 0.04 s on our hardware. In contrast, a normalizing flow using Real-NVP [6] guarantees manifoldness at a speed of 0.017 s.

Some papers such as 3DN [22], ShapeFlow [10], and Deformation-Aware 3D Model [20] use a retrieval network to find a template mesh similar to the input point cloud from a mesh template bank. The disadvantage of 3DN [22] is that the deforming is done using an MLP which does not guarantee the preservation of the manifoldness of the mesh. Furthermore, in contrast to our work, these works do not take into account the deformations of one single instance but rather go from one object instance to another object instance. Some other deforming papers such as NMF [7], Point2Mesh [8] and Neural Parts [16] start with one or multiple sphere meshes as a template. Point2Mesh [8] fits a sphere to one point cloud during inference(which is also its training stage) over three hours which is unfeasible for downstream robotic applications. NMF [7] makes use of flow networks consisting of neural ordinary differential equations to find the flow direction of the sphere template vertices. Therefore, their work, while preserving topology can not reconstruct meshes of a higher genus than zero. Neural Parts [16] deforms five template spheres using Real-NVP [6]. Starting with multiple template meshes gives the possibility of reconstructing meshes of more complex topology such as a chair with a backseat hole (genus of one). However, this method suffers from disconnectivity between the five resulting component meshes and needs prior knowledge of the number of initial spheres.

The second category of 3D mesh reconstruction papers, models implicit functions such as signed distance functions or an indicator function and then uses marching cubes to reconstruct them. For instance, Shape As Points [17] uses marching cubes and deep Poisson reconstruction [11] and works at a rate of 25 Hz which is the fastest 3D mesh reconstruction in the state of the arts to the best of our knowledge. Additionally, it can reconstruct meshes of arbitrary topology with thin structures.

Another category of papers combines both the implicit function learning and the flow of the vertices [18]. This medical paper [18] is used for the reconstruction of body organs and the point correspondence e.g. livers of different patients. However, due to the template learning of their pipeline, they have a separate pre-trained model for each organ of the human body. Additionally, their inference time is 180.10 s which is not feasible for a robotics case of use.

In summary, the fastest model for 3D mesh reconstruction to our knowledge is Shape As Points [17] with a rate of 25 Hz which can also generate the right mesh topology. However, this method still falls short in speed, particularly in the field of robotic manipulation, and lacks the essential capability of vertex tracking throughout the deformation sequence.

2.2 4D Mesh Reconstruction of Point Clouds

In the Computer graphics domain, a lot of work has been done in the 4D mesh reconstruction field [3, 9, 12, 14, 19, 21]. This consists of firstly, a sequence of point clouds of an object deforming (human or animal in motion, articulated object opening/closing, non-rigid object twisting) being fed to the network. Then, the network predicts a mesh for every point cloud. In some of these papers, the correspondence between meshes (vertex tracking) is also predicted, and in some not [9]. For time-efficiency purposes, some of the works in the 4D field reconstruct only one single mesh of either a canonical state or the first state. This single mesh is referred to as the template mesh. Sequentially like Occupancy Flow [14] or in parallel like CaDeX [12]), the template vertices are mapped to new point coordinates for the remaining point cloud frames. The mesh of each frame is reconstructed using the same faces as the template mesh along with the newly mapped vertex coordinates. For instance, the Occupancy Flow [14] paper and the LPDC [19] paper, use an occupancy field and the multi-resolution isosurface extraction algorithm to reconstruct the mesh of the first point cloud frame and use it as a template mesh. Subsequently, Occupancy Flow [14] uses normalizing flows consisting of neural ordinary differential equations(LPDC [19] uses MLP) to move around the vertices of the template mesh. In CaDeX [12], the canonical state which is an implicit field is predicted in parallel to vertex tracking. Then, the marching cubes algorithm is used to reconstruct the canonical implicit field as the template mesh. Subsequently, the meshes of other point cloud frames are reconstructed with vertex tracking. This method also uses normalizing flows to move around the vertex coordinates. Its normalizing flow uses Real-NVP [6] consisting of coupling blocks which is more time efficient than NODE [5]. Although CaDeX [12] achieves outstanding results, they have an individual pre-trained model for every specific object category because of their template-learning-based pipeline. For instance, there is a separate pre-trained model for animals, humans, laptops, doors, etc. Similarly, LPDC [19] is limited to a pre-trained model for the motion of only humans. Furthermore, these works are not fast enough for the field of robotics: CaDeX [12] takes 0.365 s for its rest frames on our machine and 0.68 s according to their own recordings. Occupancy Flow [14] takes 0.212 s for its rest frames on our machine. The rest frame speed does not take into account the template reconstruction that is done only in the beginning.

The mainstream datasets used in these works Occupancy Flow [14], CaDeX [12], LPDC [19] are deforming human identities from DFAUST [2], articulated objects from Shape2Motion [23], humans and animals from DeformingThings4D [13] and warped objects using the Occupancy flow [14] deformable data generation code.

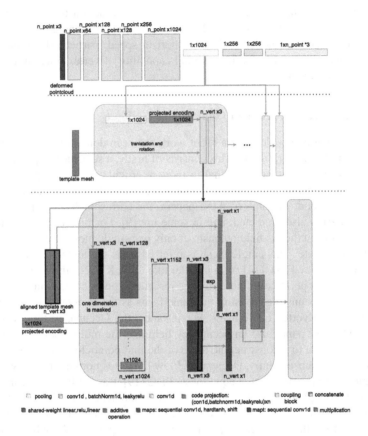

Fig. 2. The overall architecture of our method contains an auto-encoder (Top) and a conditional Real-NVP (Middle). The main goal of the model is to deform the mesh of a non-deformed object (template mesh) such that it fits the deformed point cloud of the same object. The auto-encoder takes the coordinates of a deformed point cloud and encodes it into an encoding with one-by-one convolutions and pooling. The Real-NVP which consists of coupling blocks takes the template mesh and the auto-encoder's encoding as input. The architecture within each coupling block (purple block) is shown on the bottom. Within the coupling block, one randomly chosen dimension of the coordinates is masked to zero (randomly chosen for each coupling block) and then the projections of all coordinates to 128 dimensions (brown block) are concatenated to the encoding from the auto-encoder (orange block). This concatenation is shown with a yellow accolade where the encoding is repeated for all coordinates. Subsequently, sequential Conv1d networks called map_s (pink block) and map_t (dark blue block), with and without an activation function, are applied to the results. The chosen dimension of the coordinates from the pink block is exponentiated and then multiplied by the corresponding dimension of the template mesh. The result which is the lemon green block is multiplied by the corresponding dimension of the map_t network (dark blue block). The result (bright blue block) replaces the chosen dimension of the template mesh while the two other dimensions are kept as they were before. This result is passed on to the next coupling block as the new template and hence the template mesh coordinates are gradually modified to fit the deformed point cloud. (Color figure online)

3   Methodology

The overall scheme of our method can be seen in Fig. 1. Our model takes as input a mesh of an object in a non-deformed state (template mesh) and a point cloud of the same object in a deformed state. The model learns to deform the template mesh to fit the deformed point cloud. The main components are an auto-encoder and a conditional Real-NVP. The auto-encoder is responsible for the encoding of the deformed point cloud, while the Real-NVP is responsible for the deformation of the template mesh coordinates conditioned on the auto-encoder encoding. Our model can be trained on objects of different categories which also means that during inference, our trained model can be applied to unseen deformations of different object categories as long as the object categories have been seen during training.

3.1   Auto-Encoder

During training, an encoder and decoder (auto-encoder model) are firstly pre-trained on the reconstruction of sampled point clouds from our training data using chamfer distance loss reconstruction as can be seen in Fig. 1(a). Henceforth, we refer to this loss as the chamfer distance reconstruction loss ($\mathcal{L}_{CDR}$). The encoder learns how to encode vital features of a deformed point cloud such that it can be decoded into a reconstructed point cloud. Subsequently, the Real-NVP is trained with the pre-trained encoder on the same training data. We do ablation studies in Sect. 4.2 to investigate whether the auto-encoder needs to be frozen while we train the Real-NVP. The pre-training is done in order to ensure that the encoding contains the important features of the point cloud. The final employed auto-encoder model is from [1]. In order to find a suitable architecture, the auto-pointcloud architecture [1] is compared with FoldingNet architecture [25] in Sect. 4.2.

3.2   Real-NVP

Similarly to prior works [12,16], we use Real-NVP in a conditional way. The conditional Real-NVP learns how to deform the template mesh vertices conditioned on the encoding of the deformed point cloud such that it fits the deformed point cloud. Real-NVP consists of several conditional coupling blocks. Each coupling block is a continuous bijective function which makes Real-NVP homeomorphic. Homeomorphisms are continuous bijective maps between two topological spaces that conserve topological properties. The homeomorphic property of the Real-NVP guarantees a stable deformation of the template mesh without causing any holes in the deformed mesh. The coupling block operation which is a conditional affine transformation is explained in Eq. 1. For each coupling block, one random dimension of the coordinates is chosen and is redefined based on all of the three dimensions of the coordinates and the auto-encoder encoding (which is marked as enc in Eq. 1) while the two unchosen dimensions of the coordinates remain unchanged. In Eq. 1, the randomly chosen coordinate dimension is z. map_s and map_t are sequential one-by-one convolutions with and without nonlinearity respectively. The coupling block is applied several times and gradually moves around the template mesh coordinates. The deforming mesh results from the deformed coordinates and shares the same face topology as the template mesh. The learning is done using the chamfer distance loss between the final deformed mesh output from the Real-NVP and the groundtruth deformed mesh as illustrated in Fig. 1(a). Henceforth, we refer to this loss as the chamfer distance deformation loss($\mathcal{L}_{CDD}$).

$$[x', y', z'] = [x, y, z \exp (map_s(x, y \mid enc)) + map_t(x, y \mid enc)] \tag{1}$$

3.3 Network Architecture

In Fig. 2, the in-depth architecture of our method is presented. In Fig. 2, the auto-encoder is found on the top and the Real-NVP in the middle. The architecture within the coupling block is shown in Fig. 2 bottom. The Real-NVP's main elements are coupling blocks which are homeomorphic (bijective and continuous). Homeomorphisms preserve properties linked to the topology which makes this mapping suitable for stable deformation. Furthermore, a run through the entire models takes about 0.017 s for a mesh of 3000 vertices making it all the more suitable for robotic applications. The auto-encoder's main components are one-by-one convolutional layers, batch normalization, rectification non-linearities (ReLU), and max pooling operations. The convolutions help in the extraction of the point cloud features and the pooling maintains the permutation in-variance property. The auto-encoder encodes the deformed point cloud into an encoding and then decodes it back into a point cloud which is compared to the deformed point cloud so that the encoding can be better learned during the pre-training of the auto-encoder. The Real-NVP takes as input the template mesh coordinates and the auto-encoder's encoding. Within each coupling block (purple blocks in Fig. 2), one random dimension of the coordinates is masked to zero. Then the changed coordinates are concatenated to the encoding from the auto-encoder. This concatenation is shown with a yellow accolade in Fig. 2right where the encoding is repeated for each coordinate. Subsequently, sequential one-by-one convolutional networks called map_s (pink block) and map_t (dark blue block), with and without an activation function, respectively, are applied to the results. The chosen dimension of the coordinates from the pink block are exponentiated and then multiplied by the corresponding dimension of the template mesh. The result which is the lemon green block is multiplied by the corresponding dimension of the map_t network (dark blue block). The result (bright blue block) replaces the chosen dimension of the template mesh while the two other dimensions are kept as they were before. This result is used as the new template for the next coupling block and hence the template mesh gradually deforms into the deformed mesh.

3.4 Inference

During test time, as illustrated in Fig. 1(b), the encoder extracts the encoding from the deformed point cloud and afterwards the Real-NVP deforms the given template mesh using the deformed encoding. The trained model can be applied to unseen deformations of objects it has seen during training. The model can be generalized to different object categories during training. Our final model is trained on the deformations of six different object categories as discussed in Sect. 4.2.

3.5 Dataset

For the training and testing datasets, the simulation of object deformation is automated using the code from [14]. The code applies random displacement fields to a $3\times3\times3$ grid using a gaussian random variable and then obtains a continuous displacement field by interpolating between the grid points using RBF [15]. The random warping field can then be applied as many times as possible. This consecutive application of the same warping field creates a deformation trajectory containing steps as can be seen in Fig. 3(a).

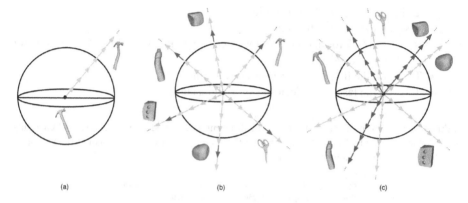

Fig. 3. The generation of our different datasets for training and evaluating the model: (a) An arrow in a unique direction represents a unique warping field generated by the deformation code of the Occflow [14] authors. If a warping field is repeatedly applied to a mesh, then a trajectory is created. (b) Dataset B: The red arrows correspond to unseen deformations and the green arrows correspond to seen deformations during training. One trajectory containing 51 deformations is simulated for each of the six instances from the YCB benchmark dataset [4] where steps divisible by five are unseen and the steps indivisible by five are seen. (c) Dataset D: The red arrows correspond to unseen deformations and the green arrows correspond to seen deformations during training. 1000 trajectories are simulated for each of the six YCB instances where 800 of the trajectories are seen and 200 trajectories are unseen. (Color figure online)

4   Experiments

4.1   Dataset Generation

For the preliminary experiments, we have a small dataset containing deformations of a car and a donut mesh. The donut has 576 vertices and the car contains 15018 vertices. For each mesh, 50 deformed meshes were generated. This is used in Sect. 4.2 to show our model's adaptive resolution capacity and to evaluate SOTA pre-trained auto-encoder models. Additionally, to be able to demonstrate the manipulation capacity, six mesh instances were taken from the YCB benchmark dataset [4]. These meshes were chosen such that they are all watertight meaning that there are no holes within the mesh surface. We generated four different datasets as explained below using the deformation code from [14]. The six meshes include a pair of scissors, a hammer, an orange, a dice, a foam brick, and a bleach-cleanser bottle. Datasets B and D are visualized in Fig. 3(b)(c).

- Dataset A: One deformation trajectory containing 50 deformation steps for scissors
  - Train set: all deformation steps not divisible by five
  - Test set: all deformation steps divisible by five
- Dataset B: One deformation trajectory containing 50 deformation steps for all six YCB instances
  - Train set: all deformation steps not divisible by five
  - Test set: all deformation steps divisible by five
- Dataset C: 1000 deformation trajectories each containing 21 deformation steps for scissors
  - Train set: the first 800 trajectories
  - Test set: the last 200 trajectories
- Dataset D: 1000 deformation trajectories each containing 21 deformation steps for all six YCB instances
  - Train set: the first 800 trajectories of each instance
  - Test set: the last 200 trajectories of each instance

Table 1. Comparison of the performance of different auto-encoders(architecture and encoding size are the main studied variants). The metric $\mathcal{L}_{CDD}$ indicates the final mesh quality in comparison to the groundtruth deformed mesh.

Exp.	Set	Arch.	Encoding Size	$\mathcal{L}_{CDR}$	$\mathcal{L}_{CDD}$	End2end*
Exp.1	B	Auto-pointcloud	256	0.0010	0.0011	no
Exp.2	B	Auto-pointcloud	1024	0.0010	0.0012	no
Exp.3	B	FoldingNet	256	0.0011	0.0016	no
Exp.4	B	FoldingNet	1024	0.0011	0.0017	no
Exp.5	B	Auto-pointcloud	1024	-	0.0012	yes
Exp.6	B	FoldingNet	1024	-	0.0013	yes

*The encoder is not frozen while the Real-NVP is trained.

Table 2. Generalizability capacity: assessing the generalizability of the model by comparing the performance of a model trained on the deformations of six instances(Datasets B and D) in contrast to one instance(Datasets A and C). The test set of Dataset B contains unseen step deformations and dataset C contains unseen deformation directions. The metric $\mathcal{L}_{CDD}$ indicates the final mesh quality in comparison to the groundtruth deformed mesh.

Exp.	Train set	Test set	Arch.	Encoding Size	$\mathcal{L}_{CDR}$	$\mathcal{L}_{CDD}$	End2end*
Exp.7	A	A	Auto-pointcloud	1024	0.0002	0.0002	yes
Exp.8	B	A	Auto-pointcloud	1024	0.0007	0.0003	yes
Exp.9	C	C	Auto-pointcloud	1024	0.0002	0.0004	yes
Exp.10	D	C	Auto-pointcloud	1024	0.0003	0.0005	yes

*The encoder is not frozen while the Real-NVP is trained.

Table 3. Exp.7 Individual object $\mathcal{L}_{CDD}$.

Object type	$\mathcal{L}_{CDD}$
Scissors	0.0004
Hammer	0.0003
Dice	0.0016
Bleach-cleanser	0.0006
Brick	0.0015

Table 4. Comparison of different methods for reconstructing meshes in terms of the essential robotic application properties of generalizability and speed on an Omen desktop computer (24-core, 3.2 GHz Intel Core i9-12900K CPU, 64 GB memory, NVIDIA GeForce 3090 GPU with 24 GB memory).

Work	Time	Method	(Sub)Problem	#Categories
Ours	0.017 s	Real-NVP	Template deformation	6
CaDeX	0.365 s	Real-NVP	Template deformation	1
Occflow	0.212 s	NODE	Template deformation	2
topology	185.27 s	NODE	Template deformation	1
NMF	0.14 s	NODE	Reconstruction	Shapenet
Point2Mesh	3h	MLP	Reconstruction	1

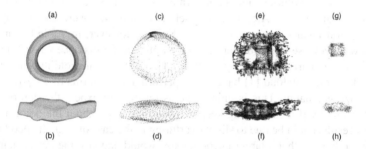

Fig. 4. Comparison of different pre-trained encoders trained on 8–10 Shapenet categories(containing no deformations) which contain a car category but not a donut category: (a) Groundtruth mesh of the deformed donut at step 50 (b) Groundtruth mesh of deformed car at step 27 (b) Decoded donut point cloud using FoldingNet [25] (d) Decoded car point cloud using FoldingNet [25] (e) Decoded donut point cloud using GRNET [24] (f) Decoded car point cloud using GRNET [24] (e) Decoded donut using PCN [26] (h) Decoded car point cloud using PCN [26].

4.2 Discussion

All of the experiments were done on an Omen desktop computer (24-core, 3.2 GHz Intel Core i9-12900K CPU, 64 GB memory, NVIDIA GeForce 3090 GPU with 24 GB memory).

Auto-Encoder. As the auto-encoder architecture is an important part of this model, several experiments were done in order to explore its capacity and suitable architecture.

In a first stage, the possibility of using pre-trained encoders from other works was considered. These pre-trained encoders are trained on some of the Shapenet categories

(8–10 different categories) where the training data does not contain any deformations. The purpose of this experiment was to see whether such pre-trained models are generalizable to deformations. The reuse of pre-trained encoders would save time and allow our work to focus solely on the training of the conditional Real-NVP. The works that were considered include PCN [26], GRNET [24], and FoldingNet [25] which are the SOTA of point cloud reconstruction on benchmarks. As can be seen in Fig. 4, qualitatively, none of the pre-trained encoders worked well on the deformed donut which was an unseen category during training. Additionally, PCN [26] and GRNET [24] did not do well on the deformed car which was a seen category. The trained FoldingNet also failed to capture the tires of the car. Thus, in the following experiments, the auto-encoder was retrained on datasets containing deformations. Furthermore, we tried different variations of these auto-encoders by changing the encoding size in order to preserve more features from the deformed point cloud.

During the training of the encoder, two different architectures were tested, the FoldingNet [25] and the Auto-pointcloud [1]. Additionally, the encoding size of these architectures was also studied. The results in terms of $\mathcal{L}_{CDR}$ and $\mathcal{L}_{CDD}$ are reported in Table 1. The most indicative metric of the final quality is $\mathcal{L}_{CDD}$ because it compares the final output mesh with the groundtruth mesh. Current literature states that independent one-by-one convolutions maintain permutation invariance of point clouds but do not capture local features. Architectures such as FoldingNet overcome this by applying poolings on local neighborhoods using KNNs. However, in Table 1, our experiments show a decrease in performance in terms of chamfer distance when using FoldingNet [25] in comparison to Auto-pointcloud [1]. Moreover, the FoldingNet [25] architecture and Auto-pointcloud [1] have better performance in terms of $\mathcal{L}_{CDD}$ when the encoding size is smaller. This is unintuitive as one would expect the deformation to be of better quality if the encoding keeps more information about the deformed point cloud. Our results could be due to slight overfitting in the case of a small encoding size. However, we believe that a larger encoding size would enhance the performance considerably if the model were to be trained on many more object categories. When trained on a very diverse training set, the encoding would have to keep a lot of information in order to be generalizable to many object categories.

In Exp. 5 and 6, reported in Table 1, we consider whether unfreezing the auto-encoder while training it with the Real-NVP worsens the performance (End2End). It appears that when changing only this End2End factor, the FoldingNet method improves as seen in Table 1 by comparing Exp. 4 and Exp. 6, however, the Auto-pointcloud performance does not change as can be deduced by comparing Exp. 2 and Exp. 5. We continue our experiments with the Auto-pointcloud architecture and encoding size 1024 given that Auto-pointcloud performs better than FoldingNet and the 1024 encoding size allows for more information encoding.

Generalizibility. The generalizability capacity of our method was evaluated on different levels in Table 2. Overall, the performance decreases when more generalizability is demanded of the model. The final mesh quality is assessed with the $\mathcal{L}_{CDD}$ metric and therefore is the most indicative when comparing our experiments. In particular, when comparing the $\mathcal{L}_{CDD}$ of Exp. 7(8) with Exp. 9(10), one can see that evaluat-

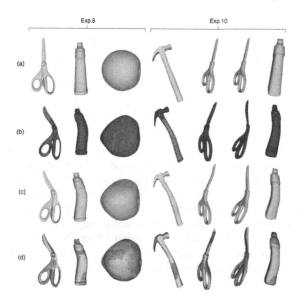

Fig. 5. Some visual results where each column corresponds to one deformation. The first three columns are generated using the trained model from Exp. 8 on test set A samples and the last four columns are generated by applying the trained model from Exp. 10 on some samples from test set C (a) Template mesh (b) Groundtruth deformed mesh (c) Predicted deformed mesh (d) Overlay of predicted and groundtruth deformed mesh.

ing on unseen deformations of seen deformation directions (red arrows in Fig. 3(b)) has a better performance than unseen deformations of unseen directions (red arrows in Fig. 3(c)). Furthermore, when the model is trained on more object categories, the evaluation performance on one single category degrades. This can be observed by comparing the $\mathcal{L}_{CDD}$ of Exp. 7(9) with Exp. 8(10) where the training set of B(D) contains deformations of all six items while the training set of A(C) contains only the deformations of one item (scissors). The test set of all four experiments contains only the deformations of scissors. In Fig. 6, the visual quality of predicted scissors by models trained on different generalizability conditions is shown. Such generalizability conditions include the number of training object categories and having unseen deformation directions in the test set. Some visual results of Exp. 8 and 10 can be seen in Fig. 5.

As can be seen in Table 3, the numbers depict that the deformation works better for rod-like objects such as the bleach-cleanser, the scissors, and the hammer in contrast to the orange, the dice, and the brick.

Comparison of Different Works. In Table 4, the factors of generalizability and speed of the most relevant works to ours are compared. As discussed before, these two factors are essential for robotics applications. If a method works slower than 30 Hz then its application may not be considered in a robotics context. Furthermore, the generalizability of a method to different object categories is essential for robotics manipulation

Fig. 6. Generalizability of our model: Some visual results from the Exp. 7–10, see Table 2. All of the items visualize the overlay of the predicted and groundtruth deformed mesh. (a) Exp. 7 (b) Exp. 8 (c) Exp. 9 (d) Exp. 10, The overlay of (b) is less perfect than (a), and (d) is less perfect than (c) as pointed out in the encircled area. In Exp. 8 and Exp. 10 the model is trained on the deformations of all six YCB instances while in Exp. 7 and Exp. 9 the model is only trained on the deformations of one YCB instance and hence training the model on a larger set of objects worsens the performance on individual objects. (a) and (b) depict the meshes of unseen deformed point clouds from seen deformation trajectories while (c) and (d) depict the meshes of unseen deformed point clouds in unseen deformation trajectories.

tasks where any object of an unpredictable category could need manipulation. Therefore, methods that have been designed for one single object category are not suitable for the problem addressed in our work. Some of the works mentioned in Table 4, address our problem only in part. For instance, in the works, OccFlow [14], CaDeX [12] and Topology [18], the template mesh is learned in addition to the deformation and hence every trained model works on only one category of objects. For instance, they have individually trained models for each of the categories humans, animals, doors, etc. In contrast, we consider the template mesh learning as a separate problem resolved by SOTA methods such as Shape As Points [17] and therefore our model remains generalizable to different object categories. Furthermore, despite both our method and CaDeX using Real-NVP [6], separating template learning from deformation learning in our approach leads to an increased speed over CaDeX. Moreover, the work, Point2Mesh [8], does not do any vertex tracking in addition to being slow for robotic applications. The NMF [7] is also not time efficient as it works at around 5 Hz which makes it incompatible with robotics settings.

Nevertheless, in order to have a baseline to compare against in terms of quality, we retrained the Occupancy flow [14] model from scratch on our dataset D. In contrast to their training dataset, we have different object categories within the dataset D. The Occupancy flow [14] is the most recent work in the 4D reconstruction SOTA to the best of our knowledge. In Table 5, our work is quantitatively compared against Occupancy flow [14]. Our work has a lower chamfer loss. In Fig. 12 of the Appendix, our deformed meshes are qualitatively compared against the deformed meshes generated by Occupancy flow [14] for two YCB objects. As illustrated, the bleach cleanser and the scissors are, respectively, missing details and partially reconstructed. Furthermore, the model does not generalize to the 18th-frame deformation of the bleach cleanser. We speculate that because Occupancy flow [14] needs to learn the template mesh, its generalizability capacity to different YCB objects is limited.

(a)   (b)

Fig. 7. Adaptive resolution (a) During training: the template mesh of the car contains 15018 vertices and 30032 faces and hence the deformed mesh contains just as many faces and vertices. (b) During Inference: the template mesh given to the trained model has 27000 vertices and 55172 faces. This shows that the network has the ability to take in templates of different sizes.

Table 5. Comparison of $\mathcal{L}_{CDD}$ of our model and the Occupancy Flow model both having been trained on dataset D.

Method	$\mathcal{L}_{CDD}$
ours	0.0016
Occflow [14]	0.0173

Adaptive-Resolution. The Real-NVP uses operations that operate on each vertex independently and in a permutation-invariant way and hence, for every pass, a different number of template mesh vertices can be used as input. This allows for the template mesh during training to be of a smaller resolution than during test time, thereby facilitating a more time-efficient training process. As depicted in Fig. 7, this implies that our model is not constrained by template meshes of a predetermined resolution.

5   Conclusion and Future Work

In conclusion, with our method, it is possible to generate meshes from the deforming point clouds (5000 points) of an object and its template mesh (3000 vertices) at a rate of above 50 Hz with simulated data. Additionally, we demonstrate that our model can be generalized to the deformations of at least six objects of different categories and also allows for tracking the vertices of the object. This method has downstream applications such as deformable object manipulation and material learning. In future works, we will focus on firstly generalizing to more object categories which is achievable given higher computational power. In a second step, we will focus on generalizing to real-world point clouds and making the model robust to the occlusions and noises of real-world experiments.

Appendix

In this section, some visualizations are provided in order to give a clearer understanding of the SOTA qualitative quality. In deforming methods, the mesh is generated by moving around the vertices of the initial mesh in order to fit the target point cloud. For instance, for reconstructing a giraffe point cloud, the deformation network starts off with a convex block mesh as can be seen in Fig. 8. The method Point2Mesh [8] results in non-watertight meshes as can be seen in Fig. 8. The NMF [7] method, which deforms a sphere, can not reconstruct meshes of a higher genus than zero as can be seen in Fig. 9. The NMF [7] is incapable of fitting thin structures such as lamps as can be seen in Fig. 9(b). The Neural Parts [16] method deforms five template spheres as can be seen in Fig. 10(a). Starting with multiple template meshes gives the possibility of reconstructing meshes of more complex topology as can be seen in Fig. 10(b).

Works using implicit models for mesh reconstruction can reconstruct meshes of arbitrary topology with thin structures(lamp) as can be seen in Fig. 11.

Fig. 8. Rerun of the Point2Mesh code [8] code: From left to right: the input point cloud, the deformed output mesh, the overlay of the point cloud and the deformed mesh, the template bounding box from which the deformation is started from. The mesh reconstructed with this method is not water-tight as can be seen in the encircled hole.

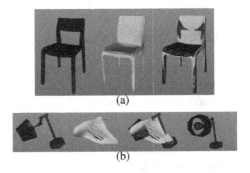

(a)

(b)

Fig. 9. The NMF code [7] rerun: from left to right: (a) The input point cloud, the deformed mesh, the overlay of the input point cloud, and the deformed mesh. (b) The input point cloud, the deformed mesh, the overlay of the input point cloud and the deformed mesh, the lamp point cloud input shown from a different angle. The NMF model can not reconstruct the thin structure of the lamp nor the topology of genus one(one hole) in the chair backseat and the lamp.

In Fig. 12 the results of our method and the results of the method Occupancy flow [14] both trained on our dataset D are visualized.

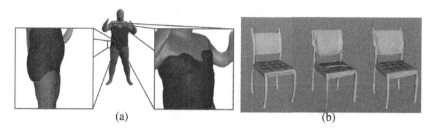

(a)   (b)

Fig. 10. (a) Image from the Neural Parts paper [16] where each color represents the deformation of a sphere: there are five spheres (b) The rerun of the Neural parts code [16]: from left to right: the groundtruth mesh, the deformed mesh using five spherical template meshes as a template and input images of a chair, the overlay of the groundtruth mesh and the output mesh. The final mesh captures the hole inside the chair back-rest however the final mesh is composed of multiple disconnected meshes.

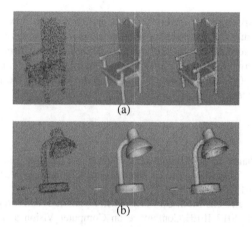

Fig. 11. The Shape As Points [17] rerun: from left to right: the input point cloud, the reconstructed mesh of the chair or lamp, the overlay of the output mesh, and the input point cloud. The topology of the chair point cloud which is of genus two is preserved in its reconstructed mesh.

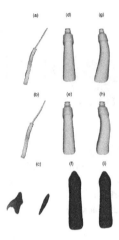

Fig. 12. Visual comparison of our method's results and Occupancy flow [14] retrained on our dataset D (a) Groundtruth deformed scissor mesh(side view) (b) Our deformed mesh(side view) (c) Occupancy flow deformed mesh(side/front view) d) Groundtruth 1st frame of bleach cleanser (e) Our 1st frame deformed mesh (f) Occupancy flow 1st frame deformed mesh (g) Groundtruth 17th deformed frame of bleach cleanser (h) Our 17th frame deformed mesh (i) Occupancy flow 17th frame deformed mesh.

References

1. Achlioptas, P., Diamanti, O., Mitliagkas, I., Guibas, L.: Learning representations and generative models for 3d point clouds. In: International Conference on Machine Learning, pp. 40–49. PMLR (2018)
2. Bogo, F., Romero, J., Pons-Moll, G., Black, M.J.: Dynamic FAUST: registering human bodies in motion. In: 2017 IEEE Conference on Computer Vision and Pattern Recognition (CVPR), pp. 5573–5582 (2017). https://doi.org/10.1109/CVPR.2017.591
3. Božič, A., Palafox, P., Zollhöfer, M., Thies, J., Dai, A., Nießner, M.: Neural deformation graphs for globally-consistent non-rigid reconstruction (2020). https://doi.org/10.48550/ARXIV.2012.01451, https://arxiv.org/abs/2012.01451
4. Calli, B., Walsman, A., Singh, A., Srinivasa, S., Abbeel, P., Dollar, A.M.: Benchmarking in manipulation research: the YCB object and model set and benchmarking protocols. arXiv preprint arXiv:1502.03143 (2015)
5. Chen, R.T.Q., Rubanova, Y., Bettencourt, J., Duvenaud, D.: Neural ordinary differential equations (2018). https://doi.org/10.48550/ARXIV.1806.07366, https://arxiv.org/abs/1806.07366
6. Dinh, L., Sohl-Dickstein, J., Bengio, S.: Density estimation using real NVP. arXiv preprint arXiv:1605.08803 (2016)
7. Gupta, K., Chandraker, M.: Neural mesh flow: 3d manifold mesh generation via diffeomorphic flows (2020). https://doi.org/10.48550/ARXIV.2007.10973, https://arxiv.org/abs/2007.10973
8. Hanocka, R., Metzer, G., Giryes, R., Cohen-Or, D.: Point2mesh: a self-prior for deformable meshes. arXiv preprint arXiv:2005.11084 (2020)
9. Jiang, B., Zhang, Y., Wei, X., Xue, X., Fu, Y.: Learning compositional representation for 4D captures with neural ode (2021). https://doi.org/10.48550/ARXIV.2103.08271, https://arxiv.org/abs/2103.08271

10. Jiang, C.M., Huang, J., Tagliasacchi, A., Guibas, L.: Shapeflow: learnable deformations among 3d shapes (2020). https://doi.org/10.48550/ARXIV.2006.07982, https://arxiv.org/abs/2006.07982

11. Kazhdan, M., Bolitho, M., Hoppe, H.: Poisson Surface Reconstruction. In: Sheffer, A., Polthier, K. (eds.) Symposium on Geometry Processing. The Eurographics Association (2006). https://doi.org/10.2312/SGP/SGP06/061-070

12. Lei, J., Daniilidis, K.: Cadex: learning canonical deformation coordinate space for dynamic surface representation via neural homeomorphism (2022). https://doi.org/10.48550/ARXIV.2203.16529, https://arxiv.org/abs/2203.16529

13. Li, Y., Takehara, H., Taketomi, T., Zheng, B., Nießner, M.: 4dcomplete: non-rigid motion estimation beyond the observable surface (2021). https://doi.org/10.48550/ARXIV.2105.01905, https://arxiv.org/abs/2105.01905

14. Niemeyer, M., Mescheder, L., Oechsle, M., Geiger, A.: Occupancy flow: 4d reconstruction by learning particle dynamics. In: Proceedings of the IEEE/CVF International Conference on Computer Vision, pp. 5379–5389 (2019)

15. Park, J., Sandberg, I.W.: Universal approximation using radial-basis-function networks. Neural Comput. 3(2), 246–257 (1991)

16. Paschalidou, D., Katharopoulos, A., Geiger, A., Fidler, S.: Neural parts: learning expressive 3d shape abstractions with invertible neural networks (2021). https://doi.org/10.48550/ARXIV.2103.10429, https://arxiv.org/abs/2103.10429

17. Peng, S., Jiang, C.M., Liao, Y., Niemeyer, M., Pollefeys, M., Geiger, A.: Shape as points: a differentiable Poisson solver (2021). https://doi.org/10.48550/ARXIV.2106.03452, https://arxiv.org/abs/2106.03452

18. Sun, S., Han, K., Kong, D., Tang, H., Yan, X., Xie, X.: Topology-preserving shape reconstruction and registration via neural diffeomorphic flow. In: Proceedings of the IEEE/CVF Conference on Computer Vision and Pattern Recognition, pp. 20845–20855 (2022)

19. Tang, J., Xu, D., Jia, K., Zhang, L.: Learning parallel dense correspondence from spatiotemporal descriptors for efficient and robust 4d reconstruction. In: Proceedings of the IEEE/CVF Conference on Computer Vision and Pattern Recognition, pp. 6022–6031 (2021)

20. Uy, M.A., Huang, J., Sung, M., Birdal, T., Guibas, L.: Deformation-aware 3d model embedding and retrieval (2020). https://doi.org/10.48550/ARXIV.2004.01228, https://arxiv.org/abs/2004.01228

21. Vu, T.A., Nguyen, D.T., Hua, B.S., Pham, Q.H., Yeung, S.K.: Rfnet-4D: joint object reconstruction and flow estimation from 4d point clouds (2022). https://doi.org/10.48550/ARXIV.2203.16482, https://arxiv.org/abs/2203.16482

22. Wang, W., Ceylan, D., Mech, R., Neumann, U.: 3dn: 3d deformation network (2019). https://doi.org/10.48550/ARXIV.1903.03322, https://arxiv.org/abs/1903.03322

23. Wang, X., Zhou, B., Shi, Y., Chen, X., Zhao, Q., Xu, K.: Shape2motion: joint analysis of motion parts and attributes from 3d shapes (2019). https://doi.org/10.48550/ARXIV.1903.03911, https://arxiv.org/abs/1903.03911

24. Xie, H., Yao, H., Zhou, S., Mao, J., Zhang, S., Sun, W.: GRNet: gridding residual network for dense point cloud completion. In: Vedaldi, A., Bischof, H., Brox, T., Frahm, J.M. (eds.) ECCV 2020, Part IX. LNCS, vol. 12354, pp. 365–381. Springer, Cham (2020). https://doi.org/10.1007/978-3-030-58545-7_21

25. Yang, Y., Feng, C., Shen, Y., Tian, D.: Foldingnet: point cloud auto-encoder via deep grid deformation. In: Proceedings of the IEEE Conference on Computer Vision and Pattern Recognition, pp. 206–215 (2018)

26. Yuan, W., Khot, T., Held, D., Mertz, C., Hebert, M.: PCN: point completion network. In: 2018 International Conference on 3D Vision (3DV), pp. 728–737. IEEE (2018)

Estimation of Optimal Gripper Configuration Through an Embedded Array of Proximity Sensors

Jonathas Henrique Mariano Pereira[1,2], Carlos Fernando Joventino[1,2],

João Alberto Fabro[2], and André Schneider de Oliveira[2(✉)]

[1] Federal Institute of São Paulo (IFSP), Registro, São Paulo, Brazil
{jonathashmp,jcarlosfernando}@ifsp.edu.br
[2] Federal University of Technology - Parana (UTFPR), Curitiba, Paraná, Brazil
{fabro,andreoliveira}@utfpr.edu.br

Abstract. The task of picking up and handling objects is a great robotic challenge. Estimating the best point where the gripper fingers should come into contact with the object before performing the pick-up task is essential to avoid failures. This study presents a new approach to estimating the grasping pose of objects using a database generated by a gripper through its proximity sensors. The grasping pose estimation simulates the points where the fingers should be positioned to obtain the best grasp of the object. In this study, we used a database generated by a reconfigurable gripper with three fingers that can scan different objects through distance sensors attached to the fingers and palm of the gripper. The grasping pose of 13 objects was estimated, which were classified according to their geometries. The analysis of the grasping pose estimates considered the versatility of the gripper used. These object grasping pose estimates were validated using the CoppeliaSim software, where it was possible to configure the gripper according to the estimates generated and pick up the objects using just two or three fingers of the reconfigurable gripper.

Keywords: Object estimation · Robotic grasping · Proximity sensor

1 Introduction

When picking up an object, human beings first observe its size, shape, estimate its weight and compare this information with its experience stored in the brain, all using our vision sensor. After this identification, the brain adjusts the hands in a configuration to successfully pick up the object. This situation is so natural to us that it seems like an easy task, but when we try to put it to work in a robot, we find that picking up an object is a very complex task.

Many robots use the camera system to identify the object [11, 16], as they can estimate the object's position and geometry and generate a cloud of points to compare with a previously registered database. Although the camera is widely used to identify objects due to its ease of implementation and many reading points, it cannot obtain data from

J. Filipe and J. Röning (Eds.): ROBOVIS 2024, CCIS 2077, pp. 410–425, 2024.
https://doi.org/10.1007/978-3-031-59057-3_26

all sides of the object, requiring extensive training until the robot fully recognizes it. The studies [4, 14] use proximity sensors attached to the gripper to identify objects. In the study [4], proximity sensors complement information not captured by a depth camera when identifying objects. In the study [14], the sensors are attached to the fingers and palm of a reconfigurable claw to identify objects without cameras. With this information captured by the sensors, a database was generated, and only the reconstruction of the geometry of different objects was analyzed.

Object identification is the first step in picking up an object, but it is necessary to estimate the grip position and finger configuration to pick up objects. The study [6] presents a broad analysis of different approaches to locating the object, estimating the object's pose, and finally estimating the claw configuration to pick up the objects. In this study, we can observe that all the analyzed approaches used cameras to read information from the objects, and most of the time, a database and neural networks were used to find the best configuration to get the objects. It is observed that for a robot to be able to pick up objects is a more complex task than for us human beings.

Another study [1] analyzes how the human hand picks up different types of objects. For this, ten cameras were used at different angles, and a thermographic camera was used to identify the points where human hands touched the objects. This analysis shows which fingers are most used to pick up objects. In all, twenty-five objects were used, and an extensive database was generated that can be used as a basis for estimating the pose of the claw when picking up objects.

When analyzing the studies presented, we identified that knowing where the gripper will be positioned to pick up the object is essential, as this information increases the chances of the task being successfully performed. Following this analogy, this study presents a new approach to estimating the grasping pose of objects using only the database generated by the study [14] with proximity sensors. This study presents a difference in that it does not use any camera resources to collect data to estimate the objects' grasping pose.

This study is organized into eight sections, as described below. In Sect. 2, related work is discussed. Section 3 presents the gripper model used. In Sect. 4, the sensors and database were used, and in Sect. 5, the grasping pose of the objects was estimated. In Sect. 6, the experiments are presented, and in Sect. 7, an analysis of the results obtained is carried out. Finally, conclusions and suggestions for future research are presented in Sect. 8.

2 Related Works

Finding the optimal pose for the gripper before it picks up the object is a vast topic. We can find several approaches that present different strategies for identifying the best points to pick up different types of objects. In the study [7], a simulator presents different poses of a parallel pincer claw for 8,872 types of objects. This study used a database where two existing learning-based grasping methods were retrained, resulting in a new grasping dataset called ACRONYM with 17.7 million pick-up poses. In the study [8], 97,280 RGB-D images were generated using a RealSense camera and a Kinect camera with different views. All these images enabled a database with more than 1 billion grasping poses for 38 objects from a YCB dataset using a gripper. This database of more than 1 billion grasping poses was used by the study [5] to be trained by another object grasping method, considering the restriction of grasping poses according to where the object was positioned. In this study, the Robotiq gripper with two fingers was used, and the restriction of the environment was based on its dimensions. We can observe in these three studies that the objects have numerous ways of being captured by the robots, increasing the possibilities of objects being successfully captured, as the grippers will have more than one option to be configured before the pick-up task.

In [2], a neuromorphic vision sensor was used to generate a database of robotic prehension called NeuroGrasp. In all, 8,753 images of 154 objects were captured. These data were processed, and the best seizure points for each object were identified. In the study [15], no database was used to define the object's grasping points. In this study, a camera is attached to the robotic arm, and when an object is identified, a contour is created, and the grasping points are defined. In [12], a camera was also attached to a robotic arm, but in a more dynamic way to capture images at different angles to define the grasping points of the objects. In this study, collision points where the gripper cannot act are identified in addition to grasping points. This multitasking dynamic defines the grasping points according to the obstacles the gripper encounters.

Some studies simulate grippers in the shape of human hands to estimate the grasping points of objects, as can be seen in [3, 9, 13]. In the study [3], 133,000 images of 21 YCB objects were generated, and numerous ways of picking up the objects were identified. We can observe that the same object has several ways of being captured, including when these objects are positioned in cluttered environments with several objects in close contact. In the study [9], the grip estimate was used for harvesting and placing fruits and vegetables in agricultural environments. Fruits and vegetables are very delicate objects, and their sizes and geometry can vary from one object to another. In this study, to estimate the pressure pose, the objects were first classified into well-known geometries such as spheres, cylinders, and cones, and later they were reconstructed in the shape of fruits. Finally, possible ways of apprehension were defined to pick up the objects more safely. In the study [13], a method was presented to resolve the ambiguity of the grasping poses for each object, as the same object can have numerous ways of being captured, generating difficulties in the neural network during decision-making.

The related works present different results and approaches to how grippers can grasp different objects. We can observe that in these studies, different camera models and types of neural networks were used to process a large amount of information to obtain the results. This study presents a new approach to estimating the object's grasping pose using a database generated by the study [14] using proximity sensors attached directly to the fingers and palm of the Hybrid-Active gripper.

3   The Hybrid-Active Gripper

The use of reconfigurable grippers is essential to increase the chances of performing the task of picking up objects. Reconfigurable grips allow fingers to vary their positions to find the best pick-up configuration.

In this study, the Hybrid-Active (H-A) gripper [14] with three fingers that can reconfigure its position according to the identified object was used to perform the pick-up task. In Fig. 1, we have the 3D design of the H-A gripper divided into three structures: the yellow outline, the red outline, and the purple outline. The structure with the yellow outline controls the angular displacement of the fingers. This structure is at the base of the claw, and each finger has a servomotor to perform its control, being able to vary up to 180° the position of the finger around the object. The structure with the red outline is responsible for the tilt of the finger. This inclination allows the finger to vary up to 10° to the right side and up to 10° to the left side, allowing one more option for reconfigurability of the gripper to increase the chances of the object being successfully caught. On the other hand, the purple structure is where the servomotor is located, which triggers the movement of opening and closing the fingers, or rather, picking up and releasing the object. This structure is coupled to the red structure's servomotor and controls the finger's closing, as seen in Fig. 1.

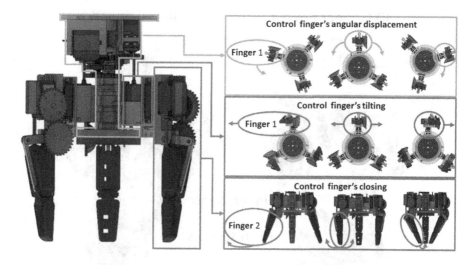

Fig. 1. Topology of Hybrid-Active Gripper.

In addition to these structures, the fingers of the H-A gripper are composed of two phalanges, the middle phalanx, and the distal phalanx. The servomotor drives the middle phalanx directly through two transmission gears, and the distal phalanx has indirect control. A link controls the distal phalanx and is only activated when the middle phalanx comes into contact with the finger.

The H-A gripper uses nine MG996R High Torque servomotors with up to 180° of variation, allowing each finger to have its control. The H-A gripper has twelve degrees of freedom, nine generated directly by the servomotors and three through the link that controls the distal phalanx. We can observe that the H-A gripper has a great reconfigurability that can be adjusted according to the characteristics of each object.

This 3D model of the H-A gripper was imported into the CoppeliaSim software and used to perform the object pick-up task using the grip pose estimates discussed in the next sections.

4   Embedded Array of Proximity Sensors

Sensors are essential for a robotic gripper to pick up an object. Usually, they are used to knowing if the object was captured. In the previously cited studies, we saw that cameras are widely used to identify objects and plan the grasping point of the gripper, as they collect numerous points of objects and generate broad databases. Usually, the cameras are attached to an external structure and sometimes to robotic arms.

The H-A gripper, the gripper used in this study, is a gripper that was designed to attach sensors to the structure of your palm and your fingers, as can be seen in Fig. 2. Note that the palm has five points, and the fingers have two sensor points on each phalanx. Proximity sensors were attached to each of these points to identify the presence of objects.

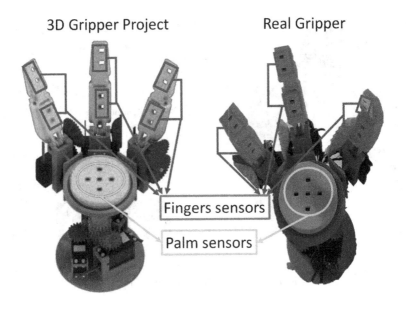

Fig. 2. Proximity Sensors Array.

In all, seventeen time-of-flight (ToF) proximity sensors of the VL53L0X model were coupled, five in the palm and, twelve in the fingers, four in each finger. The sensors attached to the palm identify the object, centering the claw according to the object and bringing the gripper closer or farther away, as seen in [14]. Finger sensors, however, identify the object and control whether or not the gripper caught the object. All sensors were adjusted to obtain high accuracy in object identification, with a minimum reading of 10 mm and a maximum reading of 2000 mm.

This set of sensors coupled to the H-A gripper was used in [14], and a database was generated with 84,060 reading points that allowed the analysis and reconstruction of 13 objects. This database did not use any camera image capture, and the object scanning process was performed directly by the claw through variations of the angles of its fingers. Another point to highlight is that this database was used to generate the grasping pose estimate discussed in the next section. The Delaunay triangulation function in Matlab was used to predict objects.

5   Estimation of Grasp Pose Configuration

The grasp pose estimation is an excellent help for carrying out the task of picking up objects, as it means that the object to be captured is already known and that the gripper already has the definition of the position of the fingers at the pick-up, even before if the gripper comes into contact with the object.

In this study, the estimation of grasping pose used data collected by the gripper itself through [14] proximity sensors. The data generated by the sensors has information from the top of the object, collected by the palm sensors, and 360° information around the object, collected by the finger sensors. During the object scanning process, the sensors identified several points, and later, these points were used to predict the object.

The grasping pose of the 13 objects scanned by the gripper was estimated. The objects were classified according to their geometries, forming six groups: cube, parallelepiped, sphere, cylinder (objects and can soda), cone (cups), and an irregular object (bottle), as can be seen in Fig. 3.

Fig. 3. Objects organized by shapes and sizes.

To improve the visualization of the prediction of objects, a voxelization was performed in 3D and later plotted the points in the estimated locations to carry out the pick-up, as seen in Fig. 4. To perform the voxelization, the polygon2voxel function of [10] was used, which converts the triangulated mesh by the Delaunay triangulation function to a discretized mesh.

We can see in Fig. 4 the entire process used to find the grasp pose estimation, firstly the selected object, in this case, a large cube, then its prediction using the Delaunay triangulation function and the voxelization of the object reconstruction using the polygon2voxel function. Note that in the voxelization stage, there are two red and two green dots. These points refer to estimating the grasping pose of objects and will be explained in more detail in a later section.

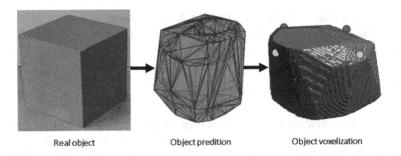

Real object   Object predition   Object voxelization

Fig. 4. Steps to generate object grip pose estimation.

6   Analysis of Gripper Configuration Estimation

The experimental grasping pose estimation used the [14] database to find object pick-up points for the H-A gripper. The H-A gripper has three fingers that can reconfigure their positions around the object, increasing the possibility of grasping the same object. All processes were carried out in Matlab, with the Delaunay triangulation function to redo the prediction of the objects, the voxel function of [10] to improve the contours of the objects, and a function called pick-up was created that plots the possible points in the estimated grasping position.

In Fig. 5, we have an example of the procedure performed to find the pick-up points of an object, in this case, the cube. In image A, we have the cube point cloud; in image B, we have the prediction of the object with the pick-up points. The point cloud contains the information read by the sensors and is used to predict the object. The prediction of the object was carried out using Matlab's Delaunay triangulation function, where the points were connected using triangles to reconstruct the object's geometry. These triangles form the face of the object prediction and were used to identify the pick-up points, as they have different sizes due to the dispersion of the points.

To find the pick-up points, first, the centers of the triangles were identified, which can be seen in image B of Fig. 5 in the shape of black circles. After identifying the center of the triangles, the centers of the most distant triangles were found in the positive part of the x, y, and z axes and the negative part of the x, y, and z axes. This distance had as a reference the central point of the object $(0,0,0)$. After finding the centers of the most distant triangles, four pick-up points were defined, with $Pmax_{x+}$, $Pmax_{y+}$, $Pmax_{x-}$, and $Pmax_{y-}$ being the midpoints of the centers of the most distant triangles on their respective axes. These four pick-up points can be observed in image B of Fig. 5, with the $Pmax_{x+}$ and $Pmax_{y+}$ points highlighted in green circles and the $Pmax_{x-}$ and $Pmax_{y-}$ points highlighted in red circles.

After finding the pick-up points, the respective angles at which each finger will be positioned to pick up the object were calculated. First, the distance that the pick-up point is in relation to the center point of the claw palm $(0,0)$ was calculated to find the angular displacement of the finger. For this, Eq. 1 was used, where $dp_{ab(j)}$ is the distance between the starting point and the endpoint, and $Pmax_{x(j)}$ and $Pmax_{y(j)}$ are the

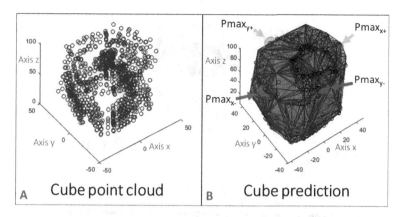

Fig. 5. Defining the pick-up points: A-) point cloud of the cube extracted from the database; B-) Reconstruction of the cube with the Delaunay triangulation function, black circles are the centers of the triangles and the red and green circles are the pick-up points. (Color figure online)

pick-up points, where j varies from one to four, with 1 being the $x+$ axis, 2 being the $y+$ axis, 3 being the $x-$ axis and 4 being the $y-$ axis.

$$dp_{ab(j)} = \sqrt{((Pmax_{x(j)})^2 + (Pmax_{y(j)})^2)} \tag{1}$$

After knowing the distances between the points, Eq. 2 was used to find the angle at which each finger was positioned, where θ is the angle position of the finger around the object, f_i is the identification of the finger, where i corresponds to finger number 1, 2 or 3.

$$\theta f_i = \cos^{-1} \frac{Pmax_{x(j)}}{dp_{ab(j)}} \tag{2}$$

In Fig. 6, we can observe the positioning of the fingers according to the θf_i calculated in Eq. 2. It can be seen that the fingers move to be positioned in the same direction as the estimated point to perform the pick-up. As the H-A gripper is a gripper in which the three fingers have individual control over their movements, the estimated pick-up point can have two configuration options. This can be observed at the pick-up point $Pmax_{y-j}$, which can be configured with finger 2 or finger 3 to perform the pick-up.

After finding the angle at which the fingers will be positioned around the object, the closing angle of each finger was found. The closing angles of the fingers can differ; it all depends on the estimated points. To find the closing angle, the analysis is more complex, as it was necessary to use the initial position of the finger at 90° as a reference, with the initial distance d_i from the center of the palm to the finger being 84 mm and the height initial finger h_i from base to tip is 110 mm.

Firstly, the distances dp_{af} and dp_{ao} were found, where dp_{af} is the distance from the central point of the palm to the tip of the finger, and dp_{ao} is the distance between the central point of the gripper and the pick-up points found in the prediction of objects. In Eq. 3, we consider that the fingertip is in the position $x = 0$, $y = d_i$, $z = h_i$, and at an angle of 90° to the palm of the gripper. Now, in Eq. 4, we have the calculations for

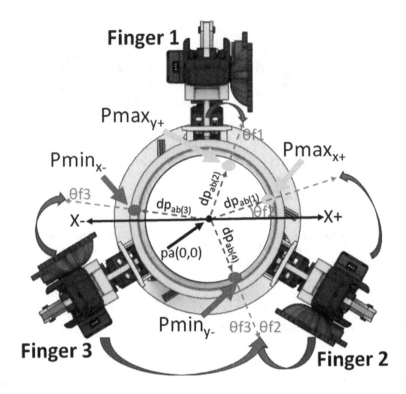

Fig. 6. New finger positioning according to estimated pick-up points.

the pick-up points $Pmax_{x(j)}$, $Pmax_{y(j)}$ and $Pmax_{z(j)}$, considering the central point of the gripper being $(0,0,0)$.

$$dp_{af} = \sqrt{(0^2 + (d_i)^2 + (h_i)^2)} \tag{3}$$

$$dp_{ao} = \sqrt{((Pmax_{x(j)})^2 + (Pmax_{y(j)})^2 + (Pmax_{z(j)})^2)} \tag{4}$$

The angle of inclination γ of dp_{af} considering the finger at $90°$ to the palm of the gripper is given by:

$$\gamma = sin^{-1} \frac{h_i}{dp_{af}} \tag{5}$$

The next step is to find the variation obtained between the distances dp_{af} and dp_{ao}, which shows how much the finger needs to move to contact the object. The variation is given by:

$$\Delta dp = dp_{af} - dp_{ao} \tag{6}$$

After finding how much the finger needs to move to touch the object, the new height of the fingertip h_f and its new distance d_f to the palm were found in Eqs. 7 and 8.

$$h_f = h_i - (\Delta dp.sin(\gamma)) \tag{7}$$

$$d_f = d_i - (\Delta dp.cos(\gamma)) \tag{8}$$

With the information of the new position of the finger, it was possible to find the angle α_f that the finger moved to touch the object, and later, it was found the angle $\Delta\alpha$ that was configured for the gripper to position the fingers to the estimated pick-up position. The following equations were used to find these angles, where α_i is the 90° angle referring to the initial position of the finger.

$$\alpha_f = tg^{-1}\left(\frac{d_f}{h_f}\right) \tag{9}$$

$$\Delta\alpha = \alpha_i - \alpha_f \tag{10}$$

This entire equation of the angle of closure of the fingers is represented in Fig. 7. We can observe that to obtain the final inclination angle is necessary to find the height h_f from the estimated point to the palm and the distance d_f at which the estimated point is on the finger. To complete this, it is necessary to consider the initial position of the finger at the 90° angle, α_i, and also know the height h_i and distance d_i of the finger in relation to the palm. Subsequently, we find the distance from the pick-up points and the distance from the fingertip, all in relation to the center of the palm (0,0,0). Finally, h_f and d_f are found to obtain the finger closing angle to perform the object pick-up task.

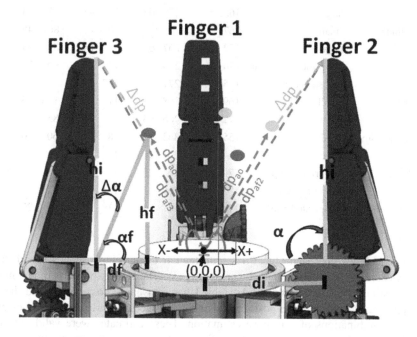

Fig. 7. Representation of the equation of the finger closure angle.

All these equations were used to find the angles used to define the estimated grasping pose of the objects. In the subsequent section, the angles identified for estimating the pick-up of objects can be observed.

7   Results Analysis of Grasp Pose Estimation

In this section, the angles obtained for the points $Pmax_{x+}$, $Pmax_{y+}$, $Pmax_{x-}$, and $Pmax_{y-}$ will be presented through the equations of the previous section. These angles were used to configure the angular displacement of each finger (θ) and the closing angle of the finger (α).

In Table 1, we can see that the objects were separated according to their format and their size or type. In the case of cylindrical objects, they were separated by size and type to compare the results of printed objects with real objects. This division of the object type also occurs in conical objects, where they are separated into 3D-printed and real objects. Another point to observe is the pick-up points in $Pmax_{x+}$, $Pmax_{y+}$, $Pmax_{x-}$, and $Pmax_{y-}$, each with their respective angles θ and α.

Table 1. The angular displacement θ and finger closure angles α can be used for grip pose estimation.

Shape	Size	$Pmax_{x-}(°)$		$Pmax_{y-}(°)$		$Pmax_{x+}(°)$		$Pmax_{y+}(°)$	
		θ	α	θ	α	θ	α	θ	α
Sphere	small	170	28	270	31	12	26	72	25
	large	165	54	270	63	16	41	87	43
Cylinder	small	167	50	271	49	10	49	86	45
	large	172	65	267	65	356	64	89	64
	3D-printed soda can	170	75	275	58	13	63	90	72
	real soda can	175	51	271	41	357	55	98	53
Cube	small	169	31	258	33	17	29	103	35
	large	172	63	266	63	25	36	85	51
Parallelepiped	small	155	30	262	35	18	31	60	30
	large	164	39	264	26	11	36	71	34
Conic	3D-printed cup	170	61	265	25	10	37	98	63
	real cup glass	171	27	260	35	1	26	92	27
Irregular	3D-printed bottle	170	36	267	25	11	27	59	27

Table 1 shows that each object has four angular displacement angles θ with four finger closure angles α to estimate the grasping pose. The H-A gripper has three fingers that can adjust to different angles. As Table 1 has four angle possibilities and the H-A gripper can reconfigure the positions of its three fingers, it was possible to perform different combinations of grip pose estimation. These estimates were valid with the H-A gripper, using only two or all three fingers. In this way, we carry out a greater number of pick-up experiments. All object pick-up experiments were carried out using CoppeliaSim software.

The following subsections present the results obtained with the H-A gripper using only two fingers and the H-A gripper using three fingers.

7.1   Pose Estimation Gripper with Two Fingers

In this analysis, the versatility of the H-A gripper was used to estimate the grasping pose using only two fingers of the gripper and the angles found in Table 1. In Table 2, we have the selection of some objects and some selected points to estimate the grasping pose of the objects: small cube, large parallelepiped, and irregular object.

Table 2. Selected points for estimating grasp pose using two fingers.

Objects	$Finger_1$	$Finger_2$	$Finger_3$
Cube large	None	$Pmax_{x+}$	$Pmax_{x-}$
Parallelepiped small	$Pmax_{y+}$	None	$Pmax_{y-}$
Irregular	None	$Pmax_{x+}$	$Pmax_{x-}$

The objects presented in Table 2 can also be analyzed in Fig. 8 with the 3D design configuration of the H-A gripper with the angles θ and α according to the estimation of the grasping pose presented in Table 2. Figure 6 shows that in the three selected grasp estimates, the fingers are practically 180° out of phase, placing the object as the central target. Another point to note in Fig. 6 is that in images 1-A, 1-B, and 1-C, we have the positioning of the fingers before performing the pick-up, where only the θ angles were adjusted. In images 2-A, 2-B, and 2-C, we have the pick-up of the objects from the experiments carried out in the CoppeliaSim software, where adjustments were made to the angles θ and α. In these 3 experiments presented, the object pick-up was carried out successfully.

In total, 78 experiments were carried out, with six variations of grasp pose estimates for each object. These six variations were carried out through different combinations between the pick-up points $Pmax_{x+}$, $Pmax_{y+}$, $Pmax_{x-}$, and $Pmax_{y-}$. Of the 78 experiments, only 33% of the estimated pose of grasping the object with two fingers were successfully performed. In these experiments, we were able to observe that when the finger adjustments were between $Pmax_{x+}$ and $Pmax_{x-}$ and between $Pmax_{y+}$ and $Pmax_{y-}$, the objects were captured successfully. In other configurations, for example, $Pmax_{x+}$ and $Pmax_{y-}$, the objects were not captured correctly by the fingers, as the objects were not centered between the fingers.

When analyzing the percentage of success in estimating the object's grasp, considering all combinations between the estimated pick-up points, we observed low accuracy. Let us analyze only the configurations where the H-A gripper had the two fingers in parallel or the gripper as a pincer. We can compare with the estimates presented in the studies [2, 5, 12, 15], which also used or considered parallel-jaw grippers to make the estimates.

When considering only the combinations between $Pmax_{x+}$ and $Pmax_{x-}$ and between $Pmax_{y+}$ and $Pmax_{y-}$, where the gripper had two fingers in the same configuration as the studies [2, 5, 12, 15], the pick-up accuracy was 100%. The highest pick-up accuracy found in the studies mentioned above was 88.16 % obtained by the study [15]. It is worth mentioning that in these studies, a large database with countless points was

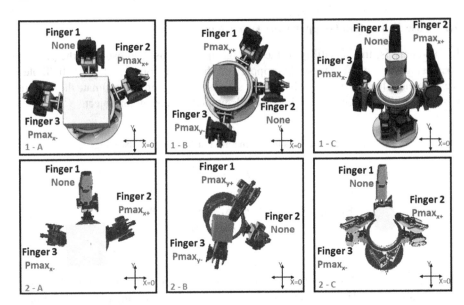

Fig. 8. 1-A, 1-B, 1-C: positioning of the fingers to pick up objects in the 3D software; 2-A, 2-B, 2-C: picking up objects in the CoppeliaSim simulator. Objects: A: large cube; B: small parallelepiped; C: irregular.

processed by different neural networks to find estimates of the grasping pose of different objects. Another relevant point is that the objects used in this study are different from the studies mentioned, but the geometries of the objects are similar.

7.2 Pose Estimation Gripper with Three Fingers

Another analysis carried out was to pick up the objects in CoppeliaSim according to the objects' estimated grasping pose using the H-A gripper's three fingers. In Table 3, we have the selection of just three objects: the small sphere, the large cylinder, and the 3D-printed cup, to demonstrate how the angles presented in Table 1 were used to estimating the grasping pose.

Table 3. Selected points for estimating grasp pose using three fingers.

Objects	$Finger_1$	$Finger_2$	$Finger_3$
Small Sphere	$Pmax_{y+}$	$Pmax_{y-}$	$Pmax_{x-}$
Small Cylinder	$Pmax_{y+}$	$Pmax_{y-}$	$Pmax_{x-}$
3D-printed Cup	$Pmax_{y+}$	$Pmax_{x+}$	$Pmax_{y-}$

To better understand Table 3 and visualize the estimated angles of the gripping pose, we can observe that Fig. 9 has images 1-A, 1-B, and 1-C that show the configuration of the θ angles in the three fingers. In these adjustments of the angles θ, we can observe that two fingers are almost 180° apart. This occurs because we are using three fingers to perform the pick-up. In images 2-A, 2-B, and 2-C, we have the object pick-up experiments carried out in the CoppeliaSim software, where we can observe that in addition to the adjustments to the θ angles, adjustments were made to the angles α to attach the objects.

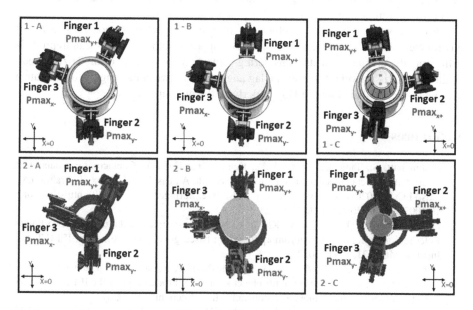

Fig. 9. 1-A, 1-B, 1-C: positioning of the fingers to pick up objects in the 3D software; 2-A, 2-B, 2-C: picking up objects in the CoppeliaSim simulator. Objects: A: small sphere; B: small cylinder; C: 3D-printed cup.

In total, 52 pick-up experiments were carried out with the three fingers configured according to the grip pose estimation in Table 1. In these experiments, we obtained an accuracy of 100%, as in all configurations, a balance of forces was applied to the object, ensuring that the pick-up was carried out successfully.

8   Conclusion

The new approach proposed to estimate the grasping pose of objects showed that a database generated directly by the gripper, through distance sensors embedded in its fingers and palm, can be used to define the points where the object will be captured. This new approach presented calculations for estimating the grasping pose of objects, considering only the four points furthest from the centers of the object prediction triangles. Another point to highlight is that no camera system was used to generate the estimates in this study. The database used can be considered small compared to those used in the studies mentioned.

This study also presented significant results in the experiments carried out in the CoppeliaSim software to validate the estimation of the grasping pose of objects through the pick-up task. The low accuracy of 33% obtained when using just two fingers of the H-A gripper was increased to an accuracy of 100% when comparing this study with other studies [2,5,12,15] using a parallel-jaw gripper. This significant increase in accuracy was due to the comparison considering only the pick-up points, configuring the H-A gripper in the parallel-jaw format. The results using the three fingers of the H-A gripper were all satisfactory, reaching an accuracy of 100%.

In future work, we have the challenge of validating all these concepts in a real environment using these objects and the H-A gripper. Another point we can improve is estimating the grasp of objects, considering using only two fingers of the H-A gripper. In this case, it is important to create a lag angle limit between the fingers to generate a grasping estimate that is more likely to perform the pick-up task.

References

1. Brahmbhatt, S., Tang, C., Twigg, C.D., Kemp, C.C., Hays, J.: Contactpose: a dataset of grasps with object contact and hand pose. In: Vedaldi, A., Bischof, H., Brox, T., Frahm, J.M. (eds.) ECCV 2020. LNCS, vol. 12358, pp. 361–378. Springer, Cham (2020). https://doi.org/10.1007/978-3-030-58601-0_22
2. Cao, H., Chen, G., Li, Z., Hu, Y., Knoll, A.: NeuroGrasp: multimodal neural network with Euler region regression for neuromorphic vision-based grasp pose estimation. IEEE Trans. Instrum. Meas. **71**, 1–11 (2022)
3. Corona, E., Pumarola, A., Alenyà, G., Moreno-Noguer, F., Rogez, G.: Ganhand: predicting human grasp affordances in multi-object scenes. In: Proceedings of the IEEE Computer Society Conference on Computer Vision and Pattern Recognition (2020)
4. Cox, R., Correll, N.: Merging local and global 3D perception using contact sensing. AAAI Spring Symposium - Technical report (2017)
5. Dong, Z., Tian, H., Bao, X., Yan, Y., Chen, F.: GraspVDN: scene-oriented grasp estimation by learning vector representations of grasps. Complex Intell. Syst. **8**, 2911–2922 (2022)
6. Du, G., Wang, K., Lian, S., Zhao, K.: Vision-based robotic grasping from object localization, object pose estimation to grasp estimation for parallel grippers: a review. Artif. Intell. Rev. **54**, 1677–1734 (2021)
7. Eppner, C., Mousavian, A., Fox, D.: Acronym: a large-scale grasp dataset based on simulation. In: Proceedings - IEEE International Conference on Robotics and Automation (2021)
8. Fang, H.S., Wang, C., Gou, M., Lu, C.: Graspnet-1billion: a large-scale benchmark for general object grasping. In: Proceedings of the IEEE Computer Society Conference on Computer Vision and Pattern Recognition (2020)
9. Guo, N., Zhang, B., Zhou, J., Zhan, K., Lai, S.: Pose estimation and adaptable grasp configuration with point cloud registration and geometry understanding for fruit grasp planning. Comput. Electron. Agric. **179**, 105818 (2020)
10. Kroon, D.J.: Polygon2voxel (2023). https://www.mathworks.com/matlabcentral/fileexchange/24086-polygon2voxel. Accessed 30 June 2023
11. Kulecki, B., Młodzikowski, K., Staszak, R., Belter, D.: Practical aspects of detection and grasping objects by a mobile manipulating robot. Ind. Robot **48**, 688–699 (2021)
12. Li, Y., Kong, T., Chu, R., Li, Y., Wang, P., Li, L.: Simultaneous semantic and collision learning for 6-DoF grasp pose estimation. In: IEEE International Conference on Intelligent Robots and Systems (2021)

13. Liu, M., Pan, Z., Xu, K., Ganguly, K., Manocha, D.: Generating grasp poses for a high-DoF gripper using neural networks. In: IEEE International Conference on Intelligent Robots and Systems (2019)
14. Pereira, J.H., Joventino, C.F., Fabro, J.A., Oliveira, A.S.: Non-contact tactile perception for hybrid-active gripper. IEEE Robot. Autom. Lett. **8**, 3047–3054 (2023)
15. Vohra, M., Prakash, R., Behera, L.: Real-time grasp pose estimation for novel objects in densely cluttered environment. 2019 28th IEEE International Conference on Robot and Human Interactive Communication, RO-MAN 2019 (2019)
16. Yu, Y., Cao, Z., Liang, S., Geng, W., Yu, J.: A novel vision-based grasping method under occlusion for manipulating robotic system. IEEE Sens. J. **20**, 10996–11006 (2020)

The Twinning Technique of the SyncLMKD Method

Fabiano Stingelin Cardoso[1] (ORCID), Ronnier Frates Rohrich[2] (ORCID), and André Schneider de Oliveira[2(✉)] (ORCID)

[1] Federal Institute of Paraná (IFPR), Ivaiporã, Paraná 86870-000, Brazil
fabiano.cardoso@ifpr.edu.br
[2] Federal University of Technology – Parana (UTFPR), Curitiba, Paraná 80230-901, Brazil
{rohrich,andreoliveira}@utfpr.edu.br

Abstract. This article introduces a novel technique for establishing a Digital Twin counterpart twinning methodology, aiming to attain elevated fidelity levels for mobile robots. The proposed technique, denominated as Synchronization Logarithmic Mean Kinematic Difference (SyncLMKD), is elucidated in detail within the confines of this study. Addressing the diverse fidelity requirements intrinsic to Industry 4.0's dynamic landscape necessitates a sophisticated numerical method. The SyncLMKD technique, being numerical, facilitates the dynamic and decoupled adjustment of compensations about trajectory planning. Consequently, this numerical methodology empowers the definition of various degrees of freedom when configuring environmental layouts. Moreover, this technique incorporates considerations such as the predictability of distances between counterparts and path planning. The article also comprehensively explores tuning control, insights, metrics, and control strategies associated with the SyncLMKD approach. Experimental validations of the proposed methodology were conducted on a virtual platform designed to support the SyncLMKD technique, affirming its efficacy in achieving the desired level of high fidelity for mobile robots across diverse operational scenarios.

Keywords: Digital twin · High fidelity · Path planning · Predictability · SyncLMKD method

1 Introduction

The Digital Twin is conceived as a tangible entity, constituting a virtual counterpart and the interconnected data relationships between them [14]. This conceptual framework has continually evolved to address numerous use cases to which it is tethered. Presently, novel applications for Digital Twins are incessantly emerging, encompassing applications for both fixed Digital Twins, as illustrated in [5]. It was presented as Stationary Digital Twins in [13], and mobile Digital Twins were developed in two works [4]. Consequently, a Digital Twin (DT) can comprise fixed and mobile components concurrently. Furthermore, depending on contextual insertion, a Digital Twin may be fixed or mobile. Closing the disparity between simulation and reality remains a fundamental challenge, as simulation does not invariably mirror the authentic model faithfully [4].

J. Filipe and J. Röning (Eds.): ROBOVIS 2024, CCIS 2077, pp. 426–440, 2024.
https://doi.org/10.1007/978-3-031-59057-3_27

The synchronization of virtual and physical states, characterized by virtual parameters mirroring the values of their physical counterparts in the Digital Twin, is acknowledged in the literature as "twinning". Therefore, it is apt to assert that entities are in a state of "twinning" or "synchronized" [12]. In practical terms, a mobile robot may deviate from its planned path due to environmental factors or errors in the joints of various robot components, compromising its movement [3]. Concurrently, the absence of feedback from crucial robot data during their movements impedes the detection and correction of errors, rendering them incapable of performing tasks requiring high operational precision [9, 15]. Consequently, to navigate a dynamic world, mobile robots necessitate input data, a technique to decipher inputs, and a method for execution (including their movement) [1]. In this context, various measuring instruments strive to collect data to formulate models representing the real world through mathematical equations [11]. Enhancing results in a virtual environment and amalgamating models, data, and mechanisms with the physical entity pose ongoing challenges for the Digital Twin.

This article advances a novel technique for twinning mobile robots in Digital Twin applications in the above context. It introduces the Kinematics Difference Mean Logarithmic of Synchronization - SyncLMKD, emphasizing the aspects of monitoring, efficiency measurement, and synchronization adjustment. The SyncLMKD method underwent evaluation within a simulated scenario tailored for the Digital Twin application, thereby enabling the validation of the proposed technique. The organizational framework of the article unfolds as follows: Sect. 2 provides an overview of related works, coupled with the proposed approach for the twinning technique inherent to the SyncLMKD method; Sect. 3 delineates the evaluation of results; and Sect. 4 encapsulates concluding remarks and outlines prospective avenues for further research.

2   The Challenges for Twinning and the Solutions

In the pursuit of the theme of this article, a phase of bibliographic research was conducted to substantiate the theoretical concepts, methods, and perceptions within the current state-of-the-art scenario. A comprehensive bibliographic review was undertaken, focusing on the following topics: suggested solutions in software for twinning counterparts, an exploration of applications of Digital Twins, and the techniques employed for twinning. Kuts, Cherezova, Sarkans, and Otto [6] investigated the precision of the digital environment by transferring a mathematical model to the virtual realm, thereby creating a precise and scaled virtual model of an industrial robot. Although employing a parametric virtual model with identical scales to the real model, the tests revealed a synchronization gap of approximately 4 mm. Notably, the Jacobian matrix was not utilized for adjusting linear and angular aspects; instead, the frames of velocities of the Unit3D motor were employed. Liang, Mcgee, Menassa, and Kamat [7] developed a PCA (pose checking algorithm) to verify robot pose Synchronization between robotic arms. The algorithm assesses the differences between the virtual and real arms' poses. If the discrepancy exceeds a predefined threshold, the following joint angle is assigned with the current joint angles to ensure the physical robot reaches the desired joint angles. The authors suggest that trajectory adjustments may be necessary to accommodate the updated joint angles. Müller, Jazdi, and Weyrich [10] identified three essential steps in both cyber and physical domains: data acquisition, pre-processing, and transference. They observed nonlinearity in the speed of the physical robot attributed to friction during displacement. A reinforcement learning was applied, allowing non-linear relations between requested and defined speeds, resulting in a deviation correction exceeding 2 cm. Liu et al. [8] employed genetic algorithms for trajectory planning, optimizing mobile robot trajectories and reducing errors in physical robot movements by integrating virtual and real data. This approach facilitates the mapping of virtual domain learning to the physical robot. The articles above in this section introduce four methods to enhance Synchronization in Digital Twins applications. The mathematical transfer model for the virtual model, aimed at precisely reflecting the real model, proves unfeasible in dynamic and complex physical environments. The PCA algorithm addresses differences in the following position or angle, potentially leading to unstable control or robotized movements. Reinforcement learning, applied for model validation through simulation repetition, demands time and additional processing. Even in a controlled and invariant environment, genetic algorithms require numerous repetitions to reduce twinning errors among counterparts in Digital Twin applications gradually. The approach presented in this article addresses the highlighted limitations. The Twinning Technique SyncLMKD method (Kinematics et al. of Synchronization) incorporates a spread considering global displacement in real-time, facilitating dynamic path planning adjustments. It generates kinematic rectilinear and uniform movement adjustments, offering flexible control by decoupling controls in both counterparts and path planning. Furthermore, the technique exhibits a degree of predictiveness by enabling the forecast of convergence behaviors for Digital Twins.

This work introduces the SyncLMKD twinning technique, specifying its insights, metrics, and control strategies. More details about the modeling method of SyncLMKD, the simulation environment, topics used by ROS, and the preliminary control of synchronization are described in [2].

2.1 Proposed Approach for Twinning Technique

As illustrated in Fig. 1, the presented approach furnishes information regarding the robotic environment and the relationships between the robots and the simulation environment. The world coordinates arrow conveys real-time pose tracking information in meters for both counterparts and path planning, encompassing the x and y axes. This information undergoes processing by the SyncLMKD method and its associated Effect function. The adjustment arrow signifies a bidirectional channel facilitating data exchange after transmitting respective speeds in centimeters per second by the Feedback arrows. These speeds are then added to the pre-set speeds, denoted by the Reference arrows. Once the environment and the robot's direction, destination, or purpose are understood, the path planning communicates the dynamic displacement direction for the counterparts to the SyncLMKD method, guiding them toward their objectives. Consequently, the World speeds arrow transmits the speeds that propel the counterparts and the path planning in real-time and dynamically throughout the entire operation.

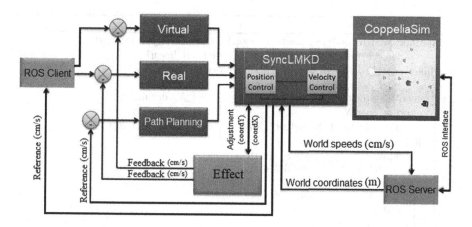

Fig. 1. Diagram of the Twinning Technique.

2.2 Control

Within the CoppeliaSim environment, it is feasible to manipulate inertial mass and various other nonlinearities for testing purposes. In cases with applied linearities, where counterparts and path planning assume different positions while maintaining uniform speeds, they present a unique challenge. This scenario poses a considerable challenge for synchronization, thus providing a platform to demonstrate the superior effectiveness of the SyncLMKD Method.

In Algorithm 1 of the SyncLMKD method, a loop is employed to ascertain whether the counterparts have reached the final destination, denoted by the fixed yellow cylinder while maintaining a preconfigured distance, as presented in Fig. 1. Within this loop, conditions for maximum tolerance are assessed between the counterparts and the path planned. Consequently, if the path planned-represented by the dynamic object in purple moving along the black line-encounters different configurations in environmental layouts, the tolerance allows a certain degree of freedom between the counterparts and the path planned.

The output values of the SyncLMKD are calculated in coordinates Y and X. It is crucial to underscore that, for the modeling to be meaningful, correct calculation of the position of terms and precedence in the calculation is imperative. The calculation is exemplified through values obtained in line 1 of Table 1. The expression is represented as follows:

$$\Delta V = Planned[y] - Virtual[y] \tag{1}$$

$$\Delta R = Planned[y] - Real[y] \tag{2}$$

$$coordY = (\Delta V - \Delta R/log(\Delta V/\Delta R)) \tag{3}$$

Algorithm 1. SyncLMKD.

---

input: position_robot1[x, y], position_robot2[x, y], position_planned[x, y],
    tolerance_max, tolerance_min, vel_linearR1, vel_linearR2
while *(robot1_euclidean_object_fixed > tolerance_min)* **and**
(robot2_euclidean_object_fixed > tolerance_min) **do**
| coordY ← (deltaR1_Y - deltaR2_Y / log(deltaR1_Y / deltaR2_Y))
| effect ← coordY
| coordX ← (deltaR1_X - deltaR2_X / log(deltaR1_X / deltaR2_X))
| **if** *flag_sincY* **then**
| | **if** *deltaR2_Y > tolerance_max* **then**
| | | robot2 ← vel_linearR2 + adjustment(effect)
| | **else**
| | | robot1 ← vel_linearR1
| | **end**
| **else**
| | **if** *deltaR1_Y > tolerance_max* **then**
| | | robot1 ← vel_linearR1 + adjustment(effect)
| | **else**
| | | robot2 ← vel_linearR2
| | **end**
| **end**
| **if** *flag_sincX* **then**
| | robot1 ← vel_angularErro, robot2 ← vel_angularErro
| **end**
| **if** *flag_nan_sincY* **then**
| | robot1 ← vel_linearR1 + adjustment(effect)
| | robot2 ← vel_linearR2 + adjustment(effect)
| **end**
| **if** *flag_nan_sincX* **then**
| | robot1 ← vel_angularErro, robot2 ← vel_angularErro
| **end**
end

If the resultant value of the expression is 57.36, the operation is deemed correct, affirming the viability of replicating the presented technique. Following the control signals, Flag_sincY and Flag_sincX indicate the precedence of one counterpart over another, be it along the y-axis or the x-axis. The control signals Flag_nan_sincY and Flag_nan_sincX signify the resynchronization of counterparts and the idealized path, once again, whether along the y-axis or the x-axis. The simulation's dataset is available in a repository of open access[1].

2.3   Timestamps

The retrieval of data during simulation is contingent upon the elapsed time between the initiation and termination of the simulation, a temporal interval specified by the user. Positions of robots to displacement, along with the corresponding elapsed time

---

[1] Simulation dataset - https://github.com/facardoso-sudo/2024.

values at which positions or odometry are recorded, are systematically stored in a matrix denoted as Matrix 1 to N. This meticulous organization ensures that each reading of x and y coordinates is associated with a specific moment, facilitating accurate plotting of position changes over time. Consequently, upon completion of the simulation, the position and time value's matrix yields meaningful timestamps.

For every elapsed simulation second, a duration of 20 µs is generated. Consequently, Table 1 presents noteworthy timestamps delineated from left to right: simulation time in seconds, virtual robot position, real robot position, path planned position (in meters), and the resultant value of CoordY calculation in percentage for each timestamp. Notably, this table pertains explicitly to the y-axis for linear displacement.

Table 1. Timestamps.

Time (seg.)	Virtual (m)	Real (m)	Planned (m)	CoordY (%)
1.30	2.5702	1.7192	8.5531	57.36
20.30	4.2845	3.8463	9.4087	72.90
39,35	5.8570	5.8019	10.2299	357.58
42.15	6.0828	6.0814	10.3508	12556.09
42.20	6.0868	6.0863	10.3530	35916.25
42.25	6.0909	6.0913	10.3551	−41171.13
42.35	6.0989	6.1012	10.3594	−7734.57
42.55	6.1150	6.1211	10.3680	−2938.00
61.10	7.5750	7.9152	11.1681	−29.11
92.60	9.8996	10.7124	11.9271	−0.34
95.60	10.1137	10.9680	11.9271	−0.30
107.00	11.9318	11.9306	11.9372	NaN

Table 1 illustrates three discernible stages in the synchronization process:

1. At time 1.30 s, variations between the positions of the counterparts and the idealized path are significant, indicating a lack of synchronization;
2. During the elapsed time from 42.15 s to 42.35 s, a notable increase in the observed output percentage is evident, accompanied by a change in the signal. This signifies the synchronization of the counterparts, both virtual and real;
3. Within the time interval from 92.60 s to 107.00 s, a minimal percentage is observed, approaching zero. This observation suggests that synchronization between the counterparts and the planned path is imminent.

2.4 Mirroring

The defining characteristic of the reflectivity of mobile robot counterparts during displacement lies primarily in the spatial separation among them. Dynamic flexibility in distances up to 1 m is perceptible to the human eye. Conversely, dynamic flexibility in centimeters is less discernible and even less so in millimeters or thousandths of a millimeter, rendering it practically imperceptible. In such cases, the level of fidelity is robust for the latter scenarios and more relaxed for the former. Figure 2 illustrates correlations identified in the output of CoordY, representing the aforementioned logical discussion.

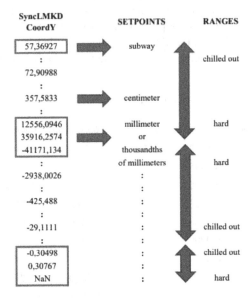

Fig. 2. Mirroring logic.

The simulations have established that logarithmic propagation can effectively manage the controllable degree of freedom. This control is further modifiable by establishing set points, allowing for customization along the trajectory within the displacement interface.

2.5 Predictability and Effect Function

The logarithmic propagation serves as a tool to illustrate fluctuations in the stock market trend, encompassing declines, increases, and stabilization. Likewise, the outputs of CoordY and CoordX can anticipate the proximity and displacement between the counterparts and the planned path. While the Euclidean distance measures the spatial separation in "meters" between two points, the SyncLMKD method calculates the distance in "percentages" among three points: the virtual entity, the actual entity, and the planned path. Consequently, establishing the relationship of proximity and synchronization is sufficient to derive the values of their respective positions.

The adjustment function, depicted in Fig. 1 as the Effect function, within the SyncLMKD method plays a pivotal role in coordinating the movement of counterparts to achieve proximity, stabilization, and mirrored movements. It is represented by the Algorithm 2.

Algorithm 2. Effect.

---

    procedure ADJUSTMENT($effect$)
    coordY ← effect
    k ← (1/coordY) + weight
    profile ← selectProfile(1,2,3,4,5,6,7,8)
    K ← k * profile
    return K
    end procedure

The output of percentage values generated by the SyncLMKD method represents the mean logarithmic propagation derived from positional differences. Logically, these outputs exhibit an inversely proportional relationship with the required velocities essential for achieving synchronized movement initially between the counterparts and subsequently among the counterparts and the planned path. In the initial simulations, the output values of CoordY were directly integrated into the subsequent Eq. 4:

$$adjustment = \frac{1}{coordY} \tag{4}$$

However, rather than observing a straightforward and uniform effect on the prearranged robot speeds, a slingshot effect was noted. Although this phenomenon facilitates proximity and synchronization, it led to the formulation of the following correlation.

$$adjustment = \left(\frac{1}{coordY} + weight \right) X\ effect \tag{5}$$

Equation 5 illustrates the inclusion of the weight term, a variable dependent on speed detection and initial displacements between the counterparts and the planned path. The term "effect", which multiplies the equation, is essential in controlling stabilization. Subsequently, eight distinct profiles were delineated based on the data presented in Table 2.

Table 2. Effects.

No	Profiles	PE, IE, DE	PE, DE, DE	PE, PE, PE
1	coordY > 2 and coordY < 200	0.02	0.02	0.02
2	coordY > 201 and coordY < 800	0.001	0.01	0.02
3	coordY > 801 and coordY < 200.000	0.01	0.01	0.02
4	coordY < −801 and coordY > −200.000	0.01	0.01	0.02
5	coordY < −201 and coordY > −800	0.001	0.01	0.02
6	coordY < −2 and coordY > −200	0.02	0.02	0.02
7	coordY < 2 and coordY > NaN	0.01	0.01	0.01
8	coordY > −2 and coordY < NaN	0.01	0.01	0.01

The profiles (PE, IE, DE) have been designed to facilitate gradual proximity. When the distance between counterparts is equivalent in meters, regardless of one being ahead of the other, the proportional effect (PE) of 0.02 is applied. If the relation is in centimeters, the integrative effect (IE) of 0.001 is employed. In the case of proximity relations approaching millimeters or thousandths of a millimeter, the derivative effect (DE) is applied, with a value of 0.01. Typically, Euclidean distance errors are incorporated to apply the gains. In this specific instance, the output value of CoordY was utilized for the effects (PE, IE, DE), (PE, DE, DE), and (PE, PE, PE). The profiles (PE, DE, DE) and (PE, PE, PE) will be further employed in Sect. 3 to validate the technique. Table 3 illustrates the profiles for the slingshot effect (SE). In each profile, instead of using the numerator 1 in Eq. 4, numerators are altered to 100, 10, and 1, respectively. This adjustment ensures valid values that are subsequently added to the prefixed speeds of the counterparts.

Table 3. Slingshot Effect.

No	Profiles	SE
1	coordY > 2 and coordY < 99	100
2	coordY > 100 and coordY < 999	10
3	coordY > 1000 and coordY < 200.000	1
4	coordY < −1000 and coordY > −200.000	1
5	coordY < −100 and coordY > −999	10
6	coordY < −2 and coordY > −99	100
7	coordY < 2 and coordY > NaN	1
8	coordY > −2 and coordY < NaN	1

3   Evaluation

The conducted simulation operates within a closed-loop control framework, fully implemented in the CoppeliaSim with ROS framework. The primary objective of this simulation was to validate the twinning technique employed by the SyncLMKD method. Figure 3 illustrates three distinct surfaces for displacement, all aligned to the z-axis at the origin. In this configuration, the red robot symbolizes the virtual counterpart, the black line depicting the displacement of the purple sphere represents the path planning, and the blue robot represents the real counterpart. Each element possesses a surface for displacement identical to the others. For enhanced visualization, the displacement surfaces for both the path planning and the real robot were configured as transparent. Sequential frames of the simulation (PE, IE, DE) were subsequently incorporated to assess proximity displacement visually.

Table 4. Main parameterized data.

Elements	Position (m) (x, y)	Speed (cm/s)	Weight
Virtual	2.75, 2.76	4	40
Real	1.86, 1.71	4	40
Planned	6.73, 8.55	2	-

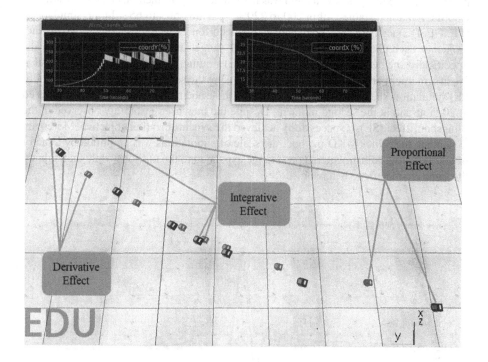

Fig. 3. Experiment PE, IE, DE in CoppeliaSim.

Table 4 presents the main parameterized data for the simulation, where speeds and weights were intentionally set to be equal for each counterpart category, both virtual and real. This intentional configuration facilitates adjustments based on the output variation of the SyncLMKD. Given that weight directly influences the speeds of the counterparts, a higher weight becomes imperative when the distance between elements is greater. In the conducted tests, it was observed that a delay in intersection was noticeable without the incorporation of weights. Conversely, with the inclusion of weights, a reduction in intersection time was achieved. Three simulations were executed with the effects outlined in Table 2.

In Fig. 4, a pronounced spike is observed in the graph when the intersection between the counterparts transpires, whether along the x-axis or y-axis. The simulations conducted to explore different effects contribute to a comprehensive understanding of this phenomenon. Furthermore, the simulations presented in this article not only facilitated the control of peaks, but also provided insights into the significance of peak saturation concerning the predictability of the SyncLMKD method. In the context of CoordY, as depicted in Fig. 4, limiting the peaks to facilitate comparisons across all four simulations became necessary. Upon execution of the (PE, IE, DE) simulation, it was evident that there were no instances of intersection between the counterparts along the y-axis throughout the simulation, resulting in peaks occurring exclusively at intersection points. The proximity between them was maintained in centimeters, and the variation of CoordY remained stable within 200 to 220%, spanning 50 s to 65 s. In the simulations (PE, DE, DE) and (PE, PE, PE), intersection occurrences were observed at two distinct moments, each characterized by different peak ranges and approximate time intervals. Specifically, the peak range in the (PE, DE, DE) simulation was around 100 thousand at the first moment and approximately 50 thousand at the second moment. In the (PE, PE, PE) simulation, the peak range was around 50 thousand at the first moment and reduced to 20 thousand at the second moment. Despite the increased instability observed in the Slingshot Effect (SE), it successfully achieved the synchronization objective. Moreover, to validate the SyncLMKD method, the scale of simulations was amplified by a factor of ten. With this adjustment, the peak range expanded to the millions while maintaining the same characteristic behavior.

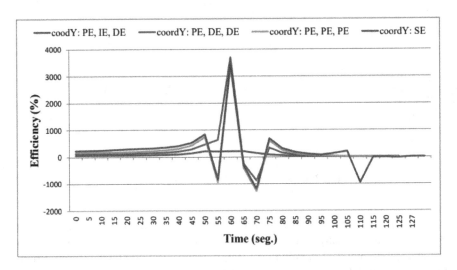

Fig. 4. Simulations of Y coordinates.

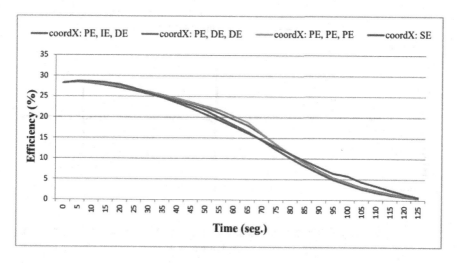

Fig. 5. Simulations of X coordinates.

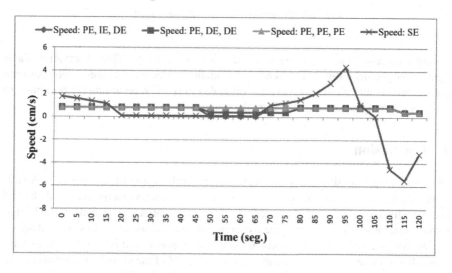

Fig. 6. Return speed of the activation function.

Figure 5 shows the confluence from the beginning to the end of the simulation for the x-axis. However, there was no intersection.

Figure 6 illustrates the return speeds of the activation function without an augmentation of the pre-fixed speed. Notably, the application of effects contributed to the stabilization of speeds, which contrasts the behavior observed in the Slingshot Effect.

In Fig. 7, specifically in the simulation (PE, DE, DE), the limitation applied was solely to the time duration of the simulation, spanning from 47.75 s to 75.75 s, without imposing any restriction on the peak range. During this interval, it became apparent that a saturation occurred, starting from the peak of the first moment and extending

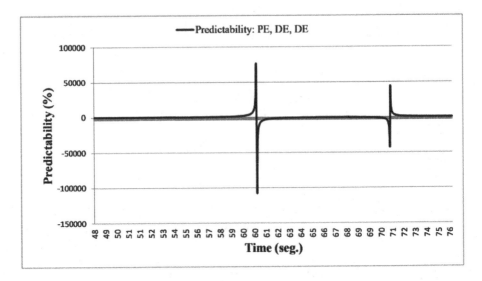

Fig. 7. Predictability of the SyncLMKD method.

toward the second one, resulting in a reduction of the range. This observation sheds light on the predictability of the SyncLMKD method. Whether the intersection between counterparts is intentionally generated, valuable information regarding the proximity to the path planning can be gleaned from the outputs.

4   Conclusion

Disregarding the nonlinearities inherent to mobile robots becomes imperative. A software solution that detects and corrects these nonconformities in a bidirectional channel is crucial for Digital Twin applications. This importance arises because the virtual counterpart simulator aims to mirror the dynamics of the real world, representing discrepancies from the simulator. The software solution proposed in this article demonstrates feasibility without considering the mathematical model of the virtual counterpart and its environment. The twinning technique employed by the SyncLMKD method produces global percentages of kinematic differences in real time, regardless of nonconformities and nonlinearities.

The decoupling of planning path and the counterparts by SyncLMKD control made it possible to carry out the adjustment through overshoot from the Adjust function (effect). The investigation on coordY percentage values instructed the establishment of set points and ranges for speed profiles. Thus, the proportional effect (PE) was applied when disparities between the counterparts' distances were superior, and when their distances were inferior, the integrative effect (IE) was used to maintain distances equal in centimeters of regularity. Derivative effect (DE) made it possible to reduce those differences to the point of reversing the synchronization signal, i.e., the counterparts exchange the front among themselves and then generate the peaks. The peaks, in turn, introduce the predictability of the counterpart's approximation to the planning path (dynamic target).

The proposed approach introduces a novel twining behavior; unlike standard approaches that generally used the Euclidean distance errors sum to apply the gains, the CoordY output value was managed with more reliable effects PE, IE, and DE. The slingshot effect (SE) is promising to be applied in robots or machines that use propulsion, like rockets, aircraft, and vessels, because the peak climb is fast and high, and it was just possible to use it in simulation when the decimal places were decreased according to the indicated profile. Therefore, as part of future research, the twinning technique of the SyncLMKD method will be evaluated with physical and virtual sensors within Digital Twin applications.

References

1. Brunete, A., Ranganath, A., Segovia, S., De Frutos, J.P., Hernando, M., Gambao, E.: Current trends in reconfigurable modular robots design. Int. J. Adv. Robot. Syst. **14**(3), 1729881417710457 (2017)
2. Cardoso, F.S., Cantieri, A.R., de Oliveira, A.S.: Controle Cinemático de Sincronização para as Contrapartes do Gêmeo Digital Através do Novo Método SyncLMKD. Simpósio Brasileiro de Automação Inteligente - SBAI (2023)
3. Chen, T., Yin, X., Peng, L., Rong, J., Yang, J., Cong, G.: Monitoring and recognizing enterprise public opinion from high-risk users based on user portrait and random forest algorithm. Axioms **10**(2), 106 (2021)
4. Emara, M.B., Youssef, A.W., Mashaly, M., Kiefer, J., Shihata, L.A., Azab, E.: Digital twinning for closed-loop control of a three-wheeled omnidirectional mobile robot. Procedia CIRP **107**, 1245–1250 (2022)
5. Gardner, L., Kyvelou, P., Herbert, G., Buchanan, C.: Testing and initial verification of the world's first metal 3D printed bridge. J. Constr. Steel Res. **172**, 106233 (2020)
6. Kuts, V., Cherezova, N., Sarkans, M., Otto, T.: Digital twin: industrial robot kinematic model integration to the virtual reality environment. J. Mach. Eng. **20**(2), 53–64 (2020)
7. Liang, C.J., McGee, W., Menassa, C., Kamat, V.: Bi-directional communication bridge for state synchronization between digital twin simulations and physical construction robots. In: Proceedings of the International Symposium on Automation and Robotics in Construction (IAARC) (2020)
8. Liu, X., et al.: Genetic algorithm-based trajectory optimization for digital twin robots. Front. Bioeng. Biotechnol. **9**, 793782 (2022)
9. Luo, R.C., Hsu, W.L.: Autonomous mobile robot localization based on multisensor fusion approach. In: 2012 IEEE International Symposium on Industrial Electronics, pp. 1262–1267. IEEE (2012)
10. Müller, M.S., Jazdi, N., Weyrich, M.: Self-improving models for the intelligent digital twin: towards closing the reality-to-simulation gap. IFAC-PapersOnLine **55**(2), 126–131 (2022)
11. Qi, Q., et al.: Enabling technologies and tools for digital twin. J. Manuf. Syst. **58**, 3–21 (2021)
12. Schleich, B., Anwer, N., Mathieu, L., Wartzack, S.: Shaping the digital twin for design and production engineering. CIRP Ann. **66**(1), 141–144 (2017)
13. Xuan, D.T., Huynh, T.V., Hung, N.T., Thang, V.T.: Applying digital twin and multi-adaptive genetic algorithms in human-robot cooperative assembly optimization. Appl. Sci. **13**(7), 4229 (2023)

14. Yildiz, E., Møller, C., Bilberg, A.: Demonstration and evaluation of a digital twin-based virtual factory. Int. J. Adv. Manuf. Technol. **114**(1), 185–203 (2021)

15. Yu, M., Li, G., Jiang, D., Jiang, G., Tao, B., Chen, D.: Hand medical monitoring system based on machine learning and optimal EMG feature set. Pers. Ubiquit. Comput. 1–17 (2019)

Intuitive Multi-modal Human-Robot Interaction via Posture and Voice

Yuzhi Lai[1] [ID], Mario Radke[1] [ID], Youssef Nassar[1(✉)] [ID], Atmaraaj Gopal[1(✉)],
Thomas Weber[1(✉)], ZhaoHua Liu[2(✉)], Yihong Zhang[3(✉)], and Matthias Rätsch[1(✉)]

[1] Reutlingen University, 72762 Reutlingen, Germany
{yuzhi.lai,youssef.nassar,atmaraaj.gopal,
thomas.weber,matthias.ratsch}@reutlingen-university.de,
mario.radke@student.reutlingen-university.de
[2] Hunan University of Science and Technology, Xiangtan 411199, China
zhaohualiu2009@hotmail.com
[3] Donghua University, Shanghai 201620, China
zhangyh@dhu.edu.cn

Abstract. Collaborative robots promise to greatly improve the quality-of-life for the aging population and also easing elder care. However existing systems often rely on hand gestures, which can be restrictive and less accessible for users with cognitive disability. This paper introduces a multi-modal command input, which combines voice and deictic postures, to create a natural humanrobot interaction. In addition, we combine our system with a chatbot to make the interaction responsive. The demonstrated deictic postures, voice and the perceived table-top scene are processed in real-time to extract the human's intention. The system is evaluated for increasingly complex tasks using a real Universal Robots UR3e 6-DoF robot arm. The preliminary results demonstrate a high success rate in task completion and a notable improvement compared to gesture-based systems. Controlling robots through multi-modal commands, as opposed to gesture control, can save up to 48.1% of the time taken to issue commands to the robot. Our system adeptly integrates the advantages of voice commands and deictic postures to facilitate intuitive human-robot interaction. Compared to conventional gesture control methods, our approach requires minimal training, eliminating the need to memorize complex gestures, and results in shorter interaction times.

Keywords: Human-Robot collaboration · Multi-Modal control · Intent recognition

1 Introduction

The increase in labor costs due to an aging population has led to the growing integration of collaborative robots into everyday life scenarios such as home service [7] and entertainment [16]. Most elderly individuals find it challenging to master complex human-robot interaction (HRI) methods. Consequently, there is an urgent need for a natural and

---

Y. Lai and M. Radke—These authors contributed equally to this work.

J. Filipe and J. Röning (Eds.): ROBOVIS 2024, CCIS 2077, pp. 441–456, 2024.
https://doi.org/10.1007/978-3-031-59057-3_28

intuitive HRI [24]. One of the most commonly used methods is gestures [6,22]. Conveying human intentions to robots through gestures has distinct advantages under certain conditions, such as underwater environments [5], quiet library environment [11], and for deaf-muted people [2]. However, this method is not intuitive as it requires individuals to learn and memorize numerous complex gestures to control robots. For example, for most elderly and cognitively disabled people, memorizing these gestures can be particularly challenging. Many other vocal-based commands also require memorizing tedious instruction sets, and it is prone to ambiguity in the environment [12]. Consequently, there is a need for an intuitive HRI method that is particularly suited to the elderly and cognitively disabled people.

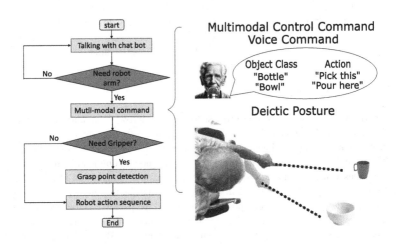

Fig. 1. We combine voice and deictic postures to realize multi-modal command.

Language is appropriate to assist robots in creating actions, while deictic postures are meant for indicating objects or locations [12]. Integrating the respective advantages of these approaches for multi-modal HRI proves highly effective in addressing the aforementioned issues. This method also aligns more closely with everyday communication practices, substantially reducing the need for prior learning.

In this paper, we propose a multi-modal command for HRI via voice and posture that enables users to communicate their intentions to robots intuitively (see Fig. 1). Compared to complex gestures, verbal communication is a more natural method of interaction, requiring no prior training. We resolved the issue of difficulty in distinguishing the target object, when two objects of different classes are too close together, by adding a class command. To further facilitate intelligent HRI, we have integrated multi-modal commands with our chatbot, enabling users to perform robotic grasping tasks more naturally. A modern robot should be able to perceive and interact with its environment based on embedded sensors. Grasping tasks are among the most fundamental of these tasks [4]. To better facilitate grasping tasks, we employed multi-view grasping detection based on point clouds [20] combined with GQ-CNN (Dex/Net3.0) [9].

The main contributions of the paper are:

1. A multi-modal command, composed of deictic posture and voice command. This allows for a more intuitive representation of human intent.
2. Evaluation of the tasks in a real world setup and comparison with other HRI method, that uses only hand gestures.
3. A combined system with multi-view grasp detection and GQ-CNN, to complete the grasping task more stably.
4. An additional chatbot in the multi-modal command for a more natural realization of robot grasping tasks.

2 Related Work

Current systems predominantly employ single-modality interactions. Some researchers focus on commanding robots either through pure hand gestures [22] or through a variety of body language, including hand gestures and body postures [10]. Often, commercial devices such as the Leap Motion sensor are utilized to detect hand movements for classifying dynamic and static gestures [22]. Due to the use of the narrow field of view sensors, the hand must remain continuously above the sensor, which makes it very unpractical. Some researchers [10] deployed open-source works such as OpenPose [3] framework to detect human skeleton points and then developed a hand gesture detection pipeline based on the Microsoft Kinect camera. It allows the camera to be placed far away for more observations. However, gesture-based methods are not intuitive. For most of the elderly and general population, memorizing standard hand gestures accurately can be difficult. Voice command is another popular approach [18] to address the HRI problem. Often, voice control can be integrated as a Bayesian-based behavior controller to allow humans to control robots via voice command. Yet this method has issues when dealing with identical objects and often can not resolve the actual location by a simple command.

There are several works focused on multi-modal HRI. In [17], they proposed a universal architecture for multi-modal HRI, where commands across multiple modalities complement and enhance each other. Moon et al. in [12] combined electromyography (EMG), facial gestures, and voice signals to control the direction of a wheelchair's movement. In their system, multi-modal information was used to distinguish intentional user actions, with sonar detectors employed for obstacle avoidance. However, in these works, the information conveyed by different modalities is redundant, and an alternate modality is utilized only when one fails to accurately express human intentions. For example, in noisy environments, auditory information is disregarded in favor of solely relying on gesture-based communication.

In other works, like [8], they compared two different multi-modal HRI techniques using mixed reality (MR) devices (head orientation or pointing, both in combination with speech) and applied them to robotic grasping and placing tasks. But MR devices are expensive and not able to apply to outdoor environment, more over, most people feel discomfort when wearing VR/AR glass.

Grasping, as a foundational task in robotics, is of paramount importance. In work [23], transformers were applied to grasping detection for the first time and achieved a success rate of 97.9% in Cornell grasping dataset. However, the accuracy of grasping for real objects is significantly lower and due to the use of transformers, the memory consumption is particularly high.

3   Multi-modal Human-Robot-Interaction

In this section we discuss the problem formulation of multi-modal HRI, implementation methods, and validation.

3.1   Problem Formulation

From the given multi-modal observed result o, the human intention i is derived through a simple combination of action intention (target action) and object intention (target object) and then converted into a sequence of robotic actions a.

The *multi-modal observed result* is defined as $o = [v, p, s]$. It consist of time-series voice features v and static deictic postures p. s represents the context of the scene, including the status of objects and the robot arm. This encompasses the recognized objects and the state of the robot arm.

The *Human intention* represents how humans desire to change the state of the scene s. To predict human intentions, we divide them into two parts: object intention and action intention. Object intention denotes the object that humans desire to manipulate. Action intention represents the action that humans want to apply to the object indicated by the object intention.

Individual vocal features can express a variety of information, including the desired action and the class of the desired object. Our system integrates three types of vocal features into our voice commands, including nouns (class), verbs (action), and demonstrative pronouns (pronouns). Among these, demonstrative pronouns work in conjunction with deictic postures. Mapping $\mathcal{M}$ transforms vocal features into text. The main types of vocal features and deictic postures are:

Class Command: vocal features are transcribed into text, with nouns predefining specific classes, such as bowls, bottles, cups, and plates. It is essential to determine the class of an object before proceeding with a deictic gesture. This stipulation is especially critical in instances where two objects of disparate classes are positioned in close proximity. Adhering to this prerequisite is pivotal for the detection system to accurately identify the object.

Action Command: In our system, verbs indicative of specific actions. Simple robotic actions need to specify only the type of the action and have no object dependency (e.g., *go to initial position* based on grid world step). However, for more complex actions like *Pick up a cup*, it becomes imperative to clearly define both the action and the object intention. Our system encompasses the set of robotic actions, as follows: 1. Without object intention: Home, Throw. 2. With object intention: Pick, Put, Pour.

Pronouns Command: In our system, the pronoun command is employed in conjunction with the deictic posture. When the demonstrative pronoun is recognized by the system, it records the location of the object that has been selected through the deictic posture.

Deictic Posture: This static posture facilitates users in selecting an object within a scene. The direction line, denoted as p_{line}, represents the direction in which the arm is pointing. The symbol o_{poses} denotes the poses of known objects in the scene. Furthermore, the vector to_{dists} represents the distance from each object in the scene to the vector p_{line}, as in Eq. (1). Function $\mathcal{P}$ involves finding the closest distance of an object $s_i \in o_{poses}$ to a directional line by counting individual distances to the directional line p_{line}, as in Eq. (2).

Where p_1 and p_2 are two random points from p_{line} and s_i is a position of the object i. All vectors are in 3D Cartesian space.

$$to_{dists} = \mathcal{P}(p_{line}, o_{poses}) \tag{1}$$

$$d_i^2 = \frac{|(p_2 - p_1) \times (p_1 - s_i)|^2}{|p_2 - p_1|^2} \tag{2}$$

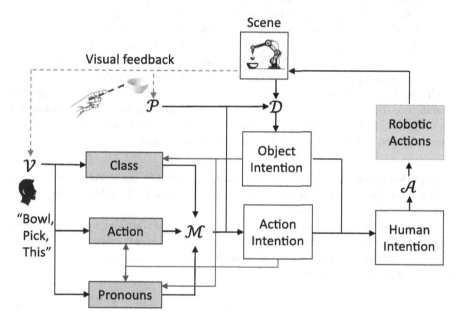

Fig. 2. System diagram. $\mathcal{V}$ represents voice command, $\mathcal{M}$ is mapping vocal features to text, $\mathcal{A}$ is robotic action generation, $\mathcal{P}$ is deictic posture execution. Blue blocks represent user inputs, and yellow blocks are robot output modes. (Color figure online)

Finally, the multi-modal command C can be defined as a tuple of vocal feature class, action, pronouns, and object specified by deictic posture, Eq. (3).

While the action command is always required. Object reference commands are only required for specific operations and must specify class and demonstrative pronouns.

Individual command corresponds to the user intention i, which included action intention a_i and object intention o_i, according to Eq. (4).

Where to_{dists} is the distance from the target object to the direction of the deictic posture. a_i denotes action intention and o_i denotes object intent.

The whole structure can be seen in Fig. 2.

$$C = (class, \ action, \ pronouns, \ object) \tag{3}$$

$$i = (\underbrace{action}_{a_i}, \underbrace{argmin(to_{dists}(p_{line}, o_{poses})))}_{o_i} \tag{4}$$

3.2 Materials and Methods

The problem described in Sect. 3.1 can be divided into the following parts: 1. speech-to-text conversion, 2. object detection, 3. user posture detection, 4. robot action generation, and 5. execution.

Visual signals are collected through the Intel Realsense D435i RGBD camera, while auditory signals are captured through a microphone.

Speech-to-Text Conversion. Speech recognition serves as the foundation of our system. In work [21], after comparing five of the most popular real-time speech-to-text tools, the VOSK API [1] and WhisperAI [14] are particularly well-suited for integration with robotic systems. For our application, we have chosen to employ the VOSK API, primarily due to its capability to recognize individual speakers, a feature that is advantageous for potential future enhancements of the system's functionality.

To increase the accuracy of recognition, we crafted three tailored vocabulary lists that include the class command, the action command, and the pronouns command. The model is designed to identify a word as an item from these vocabulary lists whenever it detects a word that closely resembles one of the listed words.

Object Detection. The primary aim of object detection in our system is to ascertain both the position and class of objects in the given scene S. To achieve this goal, we utilized the YOLOV5 [15] model.

In order to determine the position of objects in a 3D Cartesian space, our system utilizes a Intel Realsense D435i RGBD camera. This camera is employed to apply the YOLOV5 model on RGB images. Within these RGB images, the 2D position of an object, represented as Eq. (5).

$$(x, y) = (\frac{1}{2}(x_{max} - x_{min}), \frac{1}{2}(y_{max} - y_{min})) \tag{5}$$

where $x_{max}, x_{min}, y_{max}, y_{min}$ represents the coordinates of the bounding box of the detected object. In the aligned depth map, the depth information at the coordinates (x, y), denoted z, contributes to forming the 3D Cartesian coordinates (x_c, y_c, z_c) of the detected object. The coordinates of the 3D position of object o_{pose} obtained here are used to calculate the distance in Eq. (2).

In our system, we determine the detected object by the class command (see Sect. 3.2). Only objects defined by class command in multi-modal command (see Eq. (3)) are detected.

Deictic Posture Detection. The deictic posture is a special type of static gesture. In our system, deictic posture are defined by the direction of the user's right arm to detect potential object intentions (see Eq. (1) and Eq. (2) how the closest object to the direction line is found).

Human skeletal detection in our system is detected using the OpenPose [3] framework, in conjunction with an Intel Realsense D435i RGBD camera. OpenPose detects and extracts the 2D positions of human skeletal joints from RGB images, identifying key body joints such as the head, shoulders, arms, and legs. By mapping these 2D joints onto the depth image, the pixel coordinates of each 2D joint are transformed into 3D world coordinates. The extension of the right little arm of the human skeleton is expressed as the direction line, p_{line}, in 3D Cartesian coordinates for the deictic posture.

When two objects belonging to different classes are situated near each other, specifying class command in advance significantly aids in more accurately distinguishing the object intention. This concept is illustrated in Fig. 3. Despite the deictic posture being identical in both scenarios, the object intention can be distinctly identified either as a "bowl" (below) or a "cup" (above), depending on the class command.

a) Class "cup" as object intention   b) Class "bowl" as object intention

Fig. 3. Through the use of class command, it becomes easy to distinguish nearby object intentions even when the deictic posture remains unchanged.

Generalised Grasp Detection. In order to maximise the grasp detection options in GPD and Dex-Net and at the same time minimise the gaps that each method presents, we seek to have a qualifier that evaluates the grasp candidates from both modules. The two grasp pose detection methods, GPD 2.0 [20] and GQ-CNN (DexNet 3.0) [9], are combined. For example, GPD fails at detecting ideal grasps with hollow objects with thin sides, such as a porcelain cup, as the normal estimation of the thin sides in the point cloud are frequently inaccurate with the sensor used [13]. The DexNet grasp detection could compensate for this lacking as it generates better grasp candidates with the cup. DexNet, on the other hand, is trained to detect top-down grasps, and therefore fails at other approach directions. DexNet only works with a single viewpoint RGBD data, while GPD could detect grasps in a reconstructed point cloud.

Robot Action Sequence Generation and Execution. Figure 4 shows the flowchart for generating a sequence of robotic actions. Our system contains the following set of robotic actions with an increasing complexity:

– Without object dependency: go to initial position, throw,
– With object dependency: pick, put, pour

Additionally, the pronouns command include: here, there, this, and that. The class commands encompass terms: cup and bowl. We can readily expand the functionalities of our system by simply adding voice commands corresponding to new actions and incorporating these action sequences into the existing flowchart.

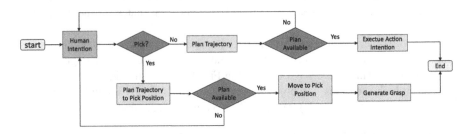

Fig. 4. Flowchart for generating robot action sequences.

Figure 5 shows the process of executing a multi-modal command to pour water from Cup 1 into Cup 2, as represented by a textured 3D point cloud. After issuing a class command (*cup*), objects are then detected (indicated by green boxes). The red

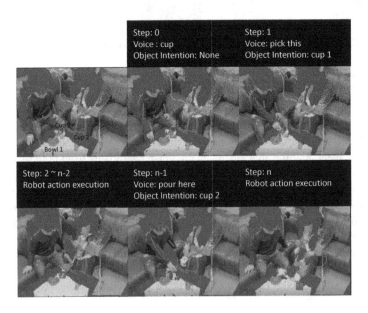

Fig. 5. The process of implementing multi-modal commands. Green boxes indicate detected objects, while red boxes signify potential object intentions. The human intention is to pour water from Cup 1 into Cup 2. (Color figure online)

box represents the object closest to the deictic posture, which is recorded as the object intention only after the user utters a pronoun command (*this*). In the case of executing a "pick" action, the initial step involves manipulating the robot to a predetermined pick position. This position is strategically designed within our system to be 10 cm above the object's position. This approach not only simplifies the subsequent trajectory planning process, but also minimizes the risk of the robot's collision with other objects during the grasping phase.

3.3 Experimental Setup

Robot Environment. Our system is tested only in real environments. The scene contains a Universal Robots UR3e 6-DoF robot arm and several manipulation objects. An Intel Realsense D435i RGBD camera opposing the robot is used for object detection and deictic posture detection.

Description of Experimental Scenarios. We designed a set of typical manipulation experiments of the increasing human intention complexity:

1. move the robot arm to initial position, $\mathcal{V} = (home)$, $\mathcal{P} = (None)$
2. pick up the cup1 the table, $\mathcal{V} = (cup, pick, this)$, $\mathcal{P} = (cup1)$
3. pick up the cup1 the table and pour the water in cup2, $\mathcal{V} = (cup, pick, this)$, $(cup, pour, this)$, $\mathcal{P} = (cup1)$, $(cup2)$
4. pick up the cup1 the table and put the water in bowl1, $\mathcal{V} = (cup, pick, this)$, $(bowl, put, this)$, $\mathcal{P} = (cup1)$, $(bowl1)$

The completion time of each scenario visualized in Table 2.

3.4 Experimental Results

We show results for the following experiments:

1. comparison with hand gestures based HRI,
2. deictic posture accuracy, and
3. scenario completion

All the scenes and tasks are set so that the robot is able to complete tasks using objects in the scene.

Comparison with Hand Gestures Based HRI. In work [22], a gesture-based human-robot interaction (HRI) method is proposed. In this approach, Leap Motion sensor [25] is used to obtain the hand bone structure. However, this method presents several issues.

1. Due to the use of the narrow field of view sensors, the hand must remain continuously above the sensor, which makes it very unpractical.
2. The efficiency of the system is somewhat hindered due to the requirement that hands must be moved out of the sensor's range following each gesture before initiating the next one.

3. In gesture-based HRI, it typically necessitates memorizing a complex table of gestures corresponding to commands. Moreover, as the number of commands increases, the complexity of the gestures also escalates (see Fig. 6, which illustrates some common gestures used in gesture-based HRI systems). This method is neither intuitive nor natural, which is particularly challenging for the elderly and those with cognition disabilities.

Fig. 6. Compared to other systems that solely rely on gesture control, our system facilitates more intuitive human-machine interaction without necessitating the use of complex gestures.

Table 1. Time used to enter the same commands as the gesture-based HRI.

Command	Ours	Vanc et al. [22]
pick	1.21 s	2.25 s
put	1.38 s	2.64 s
pour	1.43 s	2.86 s

For this experiment, we enlisted five participants. All participants were only verbally briefed on the interaction method, without undergoing any formal training. Table 1 shows the result of the experiment.

The results demonstrated that our system required 48.1% less time in comparison with [22]. Furthermore, our methodology offers a more intuitive interaction experience and significantly reduces, if not entirely eliminates, the need for users to learn new command mappings.

Deictic Posture Accuracy. In our tests, we placed six cups on a table, setting the distance between every two cups at 25 cm. Overall, the accuracy of the detected object intentions depends on the precision of human skeletal detection and the error in the point cloud generated by the Intel Realsense D435i RGBD camera. Initially, we used the index finger as the deictic posture, but due to instability, we opted for the right forearm.

Visual feedback (see Fig. 7) shows the user which object is in aim. Figure 8 shows the detailed accuracy rates for different categories of users. With little training, the accuracy improves significantly, especially when visual feedback is available for reference. The accuracy is relatively lower in the absence of visual feedback, as instances where the arm and multiple objects align linearly can lead to misidentification. Specifically, when the deictic posture is directed towards a distant object, a nearer object may be erroneously recognized as the intended target.

Scenarios Evaluation. A total of five users with an average age of 26 years were introduced to our multi-modal control command. Without previous knowledge, users were guided to do predefined tasks (see Table 2). Most of the errors occurred due to the misdetections of the object. Fluctuations in the 3D point cloud can lead to errors in coordinate calculation. Occlusion of the body may result in objects not being detected.

Fig. 7. Visual feedback for deictic posture evaluation.

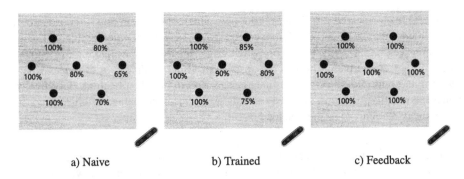

a) Naive   b) Trained   c) Feedback

Fig. 8. Deictic posture evaluation results. Intel Realsense D435i RGBD camera is at the right rear of the test table. Black circles are target objects. The percentage represents the accuracy of all tested users for each object.

Some voice commands might not be heard, might be recognized incorrectly, or the system might experience crashes. During the experimentation phase, some participants indicated that using individual words as commands was still not sufficiently intuitive. Consequently, we sought a method that could utilize complete sentences as voice commands. To this end, we developed a Chatbot based on a large language model, with detailed information presented in Sect. 4.

Table 2. Task completion by time per scenario.

Scenario	Time to complete [s]
move the robot arm to initial position	8
pick up the cup1 the table	18
pick up the cup1 the table and pour the water in cup2	35
pick up the cup1 the table and pour the water in bowl1	39

4   Chatbot

In addition to the basic Speech-to-Text (STT) implementation showed in Sect. 3.2, we have integrated it with a sophisticated chatbot originating from our ongoing research in mental health and depression detection. Our primary objective is to investigate the chatbot's capability to engage with the physical world through the robotic arm, while maintaining the smalltalk functionality.

Figure 9 shows that the chatbot is equipped with an avatar that has human-like characteristics. When integrated with STT and Text-to-Speech (TTS) capabilities, it achieves a higher level of conversational naturalness. The underlying technology uses OpenAI's GPT-4 Large Language Model (LLM), utilizing the Larynx speech model

Fig. 9. Visual chatbot avatar.

for TTS and the Whispers large model for the STT component. Simultaneously, the facial animation sequence is synchronized with the generated audio output, enhancing the immersive quality of the interaction. Following Zhou et al.'s insights [26], we recognize that machines capable of simulating empathy are more likely to be embraced by users. Therefore, we adopt this approach to increase the acceptance of the robot in everyday life.

In order to integrate multi-modal commands with the chatbot, we implement a robot control extension, as shown in Fig. 10. This extension analyses the content of each prompt for a control intention and initiates a sub-conversation with the chatbot. In our configuration, "Help me, please" serves as the reference control intention, requiring a semantic match between the prompt and the reference phrase, constrained by some simple conditions such as maximum prompt length to trigger the sub-conversation. This matching is also realised with the used LLM.

In this sub-conversation, the LLM receives the structure of the vocal command as described in Sect. 3.1. Together with a list of allowed command words, it matches the user's intention expressed in natural language with a valid vocal feature of the multi-modal command and forwards it to the Human Intention Module to initiate the robot's movement.

This method offers significant advantages over the basic TTS implementation showed in Sect. 3.2. One notable advantage is that users do not need to memorise specific keywords and their order to initiate actions; a natural, ordinary phrase is sufficient. The LLM is configured to attempt matching any sentence to a valid command whenever possible. Another significant advantage is that commands are language-independent. For example, if a user usually interacts with the chatbot in English, but issues a command in German, the action will still be executed. This feature results from the LLM's inherent ability to handle multiple languages and can be seen as a welcome by-product. The only limitations are the languages supported by the LLM and STT models. These advantages could significantly reduce the learning curve for new users. The only remaining user requirements are the ability to point to the desired object and to articulate commands with sufficient accuracy to ensure that essential information is included in the articulated text.

As Song et al. state, service robots require a wider range of capabilities beyond their primary function to improve the perceived usefulness of the robot [19]. With the addition of our chatbot, we provide the system with some of these required capabilities to improve the HRI.

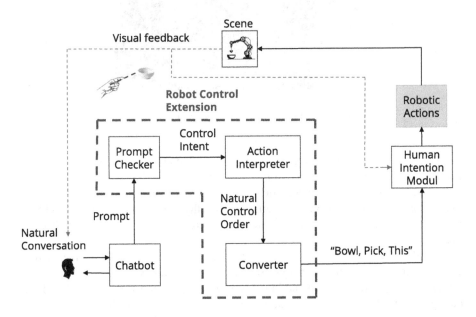

Fig. 10. System diagram. Chatbot with added robot control extension.

5 Conclusion

We proposed a system that can handle multi-modal command for HRI while handling different vocal feature types and deictic posture and combining its information to express and execute the user intent. Deictic posture test on users gave us information that visual feedback is a crucial component of such a system. Compared to other gesture-based HRI systems, our system is more intuitive, obviating the need to learn complex gestures. Furthermore, without narrow field of view sensors allows users freedom of movement. In addition, the time taken to input identical commands is reduced by 48%. From the scenario test, we can see that users will be able to fully grasp the use of the system with a simple explanation. In the future, we aim to expand the capabilities of multi-modal commands, allowing our system to perform more and more complex tasks, for example, pouring water into another cup through a single command.

Acknowledgments. This work is partially supported by a grant of the EFRE and MWK ProFö-R&D program, no. FEIH_ProT_2517820 and MWK32-7535-30/10/2.

References

1. Alpha Cephei: Vosk homepage. https://alphacephei.com/vosk/
2. Babour, A., et al.: Intelligent gloves: an IT intervention for deaf-mute people. J. Intell. Syst. **32**(1), 20220076 (2023)
3. Cao, Z., Simon, T., Wei, S.E., Sheikh, Y.: Realtime multi-person 2D pose estimation using part affinity fields. In: Proceedings of the IEEE Conference on Computer Vision and Pattern Recognition, pp. 7291–7299 (2017)
4. Cheng, H., Wang, Y., Meng, M.Q.H.: A vision-based robot grasping system. IEEE Sens. J. **22**(10), 9610–9620 (2022)
5. Enan, S.S., Fulton, M., Sattar, J.: Robotic detection of a human-comprehensible gestural language for underwater multi-human-robot collaboration. In: 2022 IEEE/RSJ International Conference on Intelligent Robots and Systems (IROS), pp. 3085–3092. IEEE (2022)
6. Ende, T., Haddadin, S., Parusel, S., Wüsthoff, T., Hassenzahl, M., Albu-Schäffer, A.: A human-centered approach to robot gesture based communication within collaborative working processes. In: 2011 IEEE/RSJ International Conference on Intelligent Robots and Systems, pp. 3367–3374. IEEE (2011)
7. Fujii, T., Lee, J.H., Okamoto, S.: Gesture recognition system for human-robot interaction and its application to robotic service task. In: Proceedings of the International Multi-Conference of Engineers and Computer Scientists (IMECS), vol. 1 (2014)
8. Krupke, D., Steinicke, F., Lubos, P., Jonetzko, Y., Görner, M., Zhang, J.: Comparison of multimodal heading and pointing gestures for co-located mixed reality human-robot interaction. In: 2018 IEEE/RSJ International Conference on Intelligent Robots and Systems (IROS), pp. 1–9. IEEE (2018)
9. Mahler, J., Matl, M., Liu, X., Li, A., Gealy, D., Goldberg, K.: Dex-Net 3.0: computing robust robot suction grasp targets in point clouds using a new analytic model and deep learning. arXiv preprint arXiv:1709.06670 (2017)
10. Mazhar, O., Ramdani, S., Navarro, B., Passama, R., Cherubini, A.: Towards real-time physical human-robot interaction using skeleton information and hand gestures. In: 2018 IEEE/RSJ International Conference on Intelligent Robots and Systems (IROS), pp. 1–6. IEEE (2018)
11. Mikawa, M., Morimoto, Y., Tanaka, K.: Guidance method using laser pointer and gestures for librarian robot. In: 19th International Symposium in Robot and Human Interactive Communication, pp. 373–378. IEEE (2010)
12. Moon, I., Lee, M., Ryu, J., Mun, M.: Intelligent robotic wheelchair with EMG-, gesture-, and voice-based interfaces. In: Proceedings 2003 IEEE/RSJ International Conference on Intelligent Robots and Systems (IROS 2003) (Cat. No. 03CH37453), vol. 4, pp. 3453–3458. IEEE (2003)
13. Mousavian, A., Eppner, C., Fox, D.: 6-DOF GraspNet: variational grasp generation for object manipulation. In: Proceedings of the IEEE/CVF International Conference on Computer Vision, pp. 2901–2910 (2019)
14. Radford, A., Kim, J.W., Xu, T., Brockman, G., McLeavey, C., Sutskever, I.: Robust speech recognition via large-scale weak supervision. In: International Conference on Machine Learning, pp. 28492–28518. PMLR (2023)
15. Redmon, J., Divvala, S., Girshick, R., Farhadi, A.: You only look once: unified, real-time object detection. In: Proceedings of the IEEE Conference on Computer Vision and Pattern Recognition, pp. 779–788 (2016)
16. Ren, Z., Meng, J., Yuan, J.: Depth camera based hand gesture recognition and its applications in human-computer-interaction. In: 2011 8th International Conference on Information, Communications & Signal Processing, pp. 1–5. IEEE (2011)

17. Rossi, S., Leone, E., Fiore, M., Finzi, A., Cutugno, F.: An extensible architecture for robust multimodal human-robot communication. In: 2013 IEEE/RSJ International Conference on Intelligent Robots and Systems, pp. 2208–2213. IEEE (2013)

18. Skrzypek, A., Panfil, W., Kosior, M., Przysta, P., et al.: Control system shell of mobile robot with voice recognition module. In: 2019 12th International Workshop on Robot Motion and Control (RoMoCo), pp. 191–196. IEEE (2019)

19. Song, C.S., Kim, Y.K.: The role of the human-robot interaction in consumers' acceptance of humanoid retail service robots. J. Bus. Res. **146**, 489–503 (2022). https://doi.org/10.1016/j.jbusres.2022.03.087. https://www.sciencedirect.com/science/article/pii/S014829632200323X

20. Ten Pas, A., Gualtieri, M., Saenko, K., Platt, R.: Grasp pose detection in point clouds. Int. J. Robot. Res. **36**(13–14), 1455–1473 (2017)

21. Trabelsi, A., Warichet, S., Aajaoun, Y., Soussilane, S.: Evaluation of the efficiency of state-of-the-art speech recognition engines. Procedia Comput. Sci. **207**, 2242–2252 (2022)

22. Vanc, P., Behrens, J.K., Stepanova, K., Hlavac, V.: Communicating human intent to a robotic companion by multi-type gesture sentences. arXiv preprint arXiv:2303.04451 (2023)

23. Wang, S., Zhou, Z., Kan, Z.: When transformer meets robotic grasping: exploits context for efficient grasp detection. IEEE Robot. Autom. Lett. **7**(3), 8170–8177 (2022)

24. Wang, X., Shen, H., Yu, H., Guo, J., Wei, X.: Hand and arm gesture-based human-robot interaction: a review. In: Proceedings of the 6th International Conference on Algorithms, Computing and Systems, pp. 1–7 (2022)

25. Weichert, F., Bachmann, D., Rudak, B., Fisseler, D.: Analysis of the accuracy and robustness of the leap motion controller. Sensors **13**(5), 6380–6393 (2013)

26. Zhou, L., Gao, J., Li, D., Shum, H.Y.: The design and implementation of xiaoice, an empathetic social chatbot. Comput. Linguist. **46**(1), 53–93 (2020). https://doi.org/10.1162/coli_a_00368

Virtual Model of a Robotic Arm Digital Twin with MuJoCo

Bernardo Perez Inturias⬤, João Pedro Garbelini Marques de Oliveira⬤, and Mauricio Becerra Vargas⁽✉⁾⬤

Institute of Science and Technology, São Paulo State University (Unesp), Sorocaba, São Paulo, Brazil
{bernardo.perez,joao.garbelini,mauricio.b.vargas}@unesp.br

Abstract. In this paper, a digital twin architecture for a *Robotis* manipulator's arm is constructed on the Mujoco physics engine SDK. The virtual model in the Mujoco OpenGL virtual environment runs synchronously with the real robot via a TTL-USB physical communication and a C++ script running in Linux. The robot servomotor *Dynamixel* SDK and the MuJoCo SDK are segregated through threads for parallel execution in the C++ script. From the data flow perspective, we have proposed three scenarios in real-time: Digital Shadow, Digital Driven, and a Digital Twin itself. A preliminary test is performed to confirm the system is functioning as expected. This test compares the motor's real and virtual torque in a static home position and a digital twin scenario. As this study is to be used as an exemplar for future research on Digital Twin frameworks, we propose future works to continue this research.

Keywords: Digital Twin · Mujoco · Robotic Arm

1 Introduction

For the sake of this paper, we consider the system framework of a digital twin robotic arm, as shown in Fig. 1.

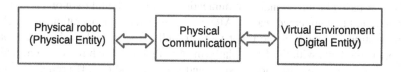

Fig. 1. Generic Framework of Digital Twin Robotic Arm.

Thus, according to Fig. 1, we adopt the following definition for a digital twin [1]: *A digital twin framework involves a "physical entity" consisting of a physical robot, digitally reproduced in a counterpart "digital entity". Bidirectional information flows between the physical and digital entity by physical communication, supporting synchronous or asynchronous behavioral influence on each other.*

J. Filipe and J. Röning (Eds.): ROBOVIS 2024, CCIS 2077, pp. 457–469, 2024.
https://doi.org/10.1007/978-3-031-59057-3_29

From the data flow perspective, we can characterize a generic framework (Fig. 1) as follow:

- Digital Shadow Framework: Information data flows unidirectionally from the physical robot to the virtual environment (virtual model). Information data can flow from the virtual environment to the physical robot but can not influence the physical robot.
- Digital Driven Framework: Information data flows unidirectionally from the virtual model to the physical robot. Information data can flow from the physical robot to the virtual model but can not influence the virtual robot.
- Digital Twin Framework: Bidirectional information flows between the physical robot and the virtual model and can influence each other.

1.1 Related Works

The digital twin approach has gained interest in academia and industry, being listed as a top strategic technology in the last few years [12]. Despite the many published works (by the end of 2021, 2934 papers were published [12]), only some are related to robotic arm applications, and some, in our understanding, are not considered digital twins. [14] proposed a digital shadow of a system with two robotic arms (Kuka and UR5) as a first step to developing a Digital Twin. The physical communication with the robots was implemented using a Java client - Python server and a Python *urinterface*. They used the *Unity* physics engine for virtual model simulation (kinematic simulation from desired joint angles). In [8], a 6-DOF robotic arm digital shadow is constructed on the *Unity* platform. The virtual model runs synchronously with the real robot, and the joint rotation angle of each axis is monitored in real-time. The digital shadow is used to observe the robotic arm in real-time, efficiently store data in the cloud, and consult the history to apply predictions or diagnoses in applications that require it. In [9], a 3D-printed physical 6DOF robot arm digital twin is constructed on the *Unity* platform. The digital twin trains an artificial intelligence model for robotic arms in specific tasks and applies it to Industry 4.0. [3] implemented a cyber-physical system-based digital twin of a robot and a human operator for human-robot collaboration (HRC). They implemented the proposed physical and virtual environment using the *Unity* platform and a UR3 robot. All the joint information is synchronized with the digital twin in the virtual environment via TCP/IP-based bi-directional communication. In [7], a digital twin of a 6 DoF UR5 robot is ported to augmented reality (AR) glasses to offer a teleoperation approach and an observation approach of the robot more friendly. The virtual model of the physical robot is modeled with the *Unity* platform. An ethernet switch router connected and communicated between the robot system and the AR module. [4] proposed a digital driven for a FANUC robot. The digital driven assists in the online/remote programming of the robot. The virtual model of the physical robot is modeled with the *Unity* platform. A virtual reality (VR) interface, programmed through the Unity platform, controls the robot movement of both digital and physical robots. When a VR controller moves in the digital environment, it generates a position value for the movement of a robot arm. In [5], a Digital Twin of a UR10 6 DoF cobotic arm is used in combination with virtual reality to create dynamic and immersive virtual environments that facilitate remote or collaborative interaction with these systems, as well as using it to design, simulate and optimize cyber-physical production systems. The visualization and interaction tool in virtual reality is based on the *Unity* platform. [6] developed a novel digital twin prototype to analyze communication requirements in a mission-critical application such as mobile networks supported by remote surgery. The system comprised a robotic arm (UR3) and HTC Vive Virtual Reality (VR) system connected over a 4G mobile network. They used the *Unity* platform and OpenVR to create a virtual reality scene for the prototype system that loosely resembles a medical setting. The network connection setup utilized the UDP Protocol. In [15], a digital driven is used to correct the position error of an industrial robot (J601 of Anno robot) using an attitude sensor and a digital model. The robot is driven by a stepper motor, which lacks a closed-loop control. This one uses *ThingJS*, which is a 3D visualization engine. [1] implemented a ROS-based digital twin with Franka-Emika robotic arm and Gazebo physics engine for the digital robot. The ROS runs with RT-kernel on a powerful computer, which runs the Gazebo simulation in almost real-time.

1.2 Contribution

Most of the related works use the *Unity* platform to model the virtual entity. Unity is a game physics engine that allows users to create games and experiences in both 2D and 3D. This game engine can be described as an excellent rendering engine but a reasonably accurate physics engine, especially in contact, collision, and deformation physics simulations. On the other hand, MuJoCo can be described as an excellent physics simulator with decent rendering. However, there needs to be more published work on Mujoco as a virtual model in digital twin robotics applications. In this context, the main contribution of this research is integrating the Mujoco physics simulator [13] as a virtual representation of a robot within the context of a digital twin for robotic manipulators. Additionally, according to the literature review, this is the first time a *Robotis* manipulator arm is used in this application.

2 Hardware and Software Architecture

The digital twin proposed in this paper is divided into three layers, as shown in Figs. 1 and 2: the physical, communication, and virtual layers.

2.1 Physical Robot

The OpenManipulator-X, an articulated robotic system developed by Robotis within the OpenManipulator series, stands as a well-designed robotic system for its adaptability and open-source nature. The manipulator's core functionality involves a group of five servo motors powered by a 12-v input voltage. The XM430-W350 servo motor incorporates the 12-bit rotary position sensor AS5045 from AMS, intricately integrated with the 32-bit ARM Cortex-M microcontroller unit, guarantees a 4096 pulses per revolution resolution, maintaining an acceptable accuracy over controlling operations. This integration empowers the servo motors with various controlling operations and operating modes, including current, velocity, position, extended position, current-based position,

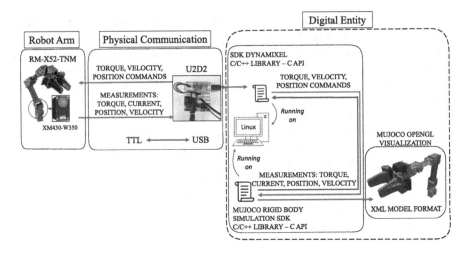

Fig. 2. Hardware and Software Architecture.

and PWM. As an open-hardware platform, the OpenManipulator-X allows for the integration of STL files. This unique feature enables the articulation of the physical system in various software applications, including Unity and MuJoCo, which promotes the creation of virtual systems that can be implemented as a digital twin feature.

2.2 Physical Communication

As shown in Fig. 3, the communication is facilitated by the U2D2 small USB converter, providing the means to regulate and operate the Dynamixels. This communication is instantiated through a USB cable, utilizing connectors designed for TTL communications. By utilizing this form of communication, the physical and digital entities can exchange sensor-measured information (such as position, velocity, current, etc.) and input data for the robot, including commands specifying position, velocity, and other relevant parameters.

2.3 Digital Entity

The digital entity utilizes two libraries: the Dynamixel SDK and MuJoCo SDK, both implemented in the C/C++ programming language. Information from the physical realm is managed through the Dynamixel SDK. The computational system employed operates on the Ubuntu Linux platform. These two SDKs work in parallel, sharing readings and command transmission if necessary.

SDK Dynamixel. The manipulator relies on a Software Development Kit (SDK) from Robotis as an open software. This SDK, developed for the Dynamixel XM430-W350 [11] servo motors, offers a range of tools, libraries, and documentation that facilitates the creation, customization, and seamless integration of software within the project's

Fig. 3. Physical Robotis Manipulator.

development environment and ensures precise control for the servo motors. It supports multiple programming languages, including C, C++, and Python.

For this practice, C++ is used and all the libraries can be downloaded for free in the Robotis' GitHub page. During the installation process, templates are provided that exemplify the control of a servo motor using a specific operating mode. These templates showcase essential functions, notably *Read* and *Write*. The execution of these commands on the robot depends on both the established operational mode and the length of information intended for *reading* or *writing*. Specifying the byte quantity for each instance of deploying these commands is imperative. This SDK needs a Packet Handler instance for controlling the servo motors.

Another consideration is the need to specify the physical ID for each servo motor, as the *read* or *write* commands are tailored for a singular servo motor per instance.

SDK Mujoco Virtual Model. Mujoco [13] is a multibody physics engine SDK based on a C/C++ library with a C API. In this work, the API is accessed through a C/C++ script. MuJoCo's primary modeling is an XML formatted file representing a robot model by defining the position of the links (rigid bodies) and the joints that connect the links. In XML format, the parent-child relationship is defined, where the base (body fixed) is a parent, and consecutive links are the child to it. The XML file allows defining meshes from STL files for 3D visualization and the mass and inertia for simulation purposes. 3D Model STL files were downloaded from the Robotis site. Mujoco includes interactive visualization with a native GUI, rendered in OpenGL as shown in Fig. 4.

3   Proposed Frameworks

As mentioned in Sect. 2.1, the physical robot arm used in this file has several modes
of operation. In the proposed frameworks, it is exemplified with the position operation mode. That is, the data of the servo motors are angular positions saved in a variable called Joint Angles. Another can replace this parameter if the operation mode is
changed.

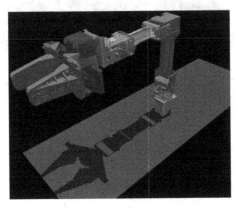

Fig. 4. Robot Rendering from Mujoco Open-GL.

3.1   Digital Shadow

Framework. Following Fig. 2, the framework of the Digital Shadow initiates with
measurements obtained from the RM-X52-TNM robot arm, transmitted through the
physical communication interface, utilizing a unidirectional data exchange with the
U2D2. Subsequently, this information is directed towards the Dynamixel SDK and
concurrently shared with the MuJoCo SDK, as both operate in parallel in the Linux
computer. This collaborative operation leads to a modification in the visualization of
MuJoCo's digital entity.

Flow Diagram. The proposed Digital Shadow replicates the ongoing actions of the
manipulator robot using position sensors embedded in the motors. As seen in Fig. 5, it
necessitates initializing of specific parameters, such as opening the communication port,
defining the baud rate, setting the operational mode of Dynamixel motors, configuring
their respective gains, limiting current, and specifying desired current and torque values.
Subsequently, the robot transitions to the Home Position by adjusting the values of a
variable named Joint Angles to zero.

The Dynamixel SDK and the MuJoCo SDK are segregated through threads for parallel execution. The Dynamixel SDK, the left side of Fig. 5, handles the communication
interface with the user and the physical motor control. The right side is for the MuJoCo
SDK for the Digital Entity.

Users input desired positions for each motor, and if these positions fall within per-
missible limits, the Joint Angles variable is updated. Concurrently, the motors adjust
to the values specified by the Joint Angles variable using specific writing commands,

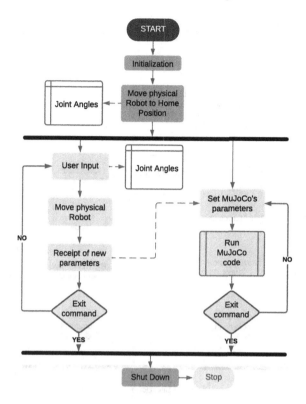

Fig. 5. Information Flow Diagram - Digital Shadow Framework.

as mentioned in Sect. 2.1. By using reading commands, position sensors relay this new parameters to the MuJoCo code governing the movement of the digital manipulator robot.

In the MuJoCo code block, as we set the real servomotor to position operation mode, we simulate the same effect by defining a direct-drive torque actuator for each joint in the MuJoCo XML model. Each actuator's PD position control loop computes the desired torque at each joint motor and is then sent to the direct-drive actuator (we can scale it up by a specific gear relation). Desired joint angles to the MuJoCo PD position control are obtained from the real servomotor position sensor.

In Fig. 5, the segmented lines delineate the directional flow of data, while the continuous line illustrates the sequential order of the code. Both loops continue their operations until an exit command is issued, terminating the program. All three frameworks have the same shutting down process.

3.2 Digital Driven

Framework. In line with Fig. 2, the architecture of the Digital Driven commences within the MuJoCo SDK, where the robot's parameters are modified using commands. Subsequently, this updated information is shared with the Dynamixel SDK, leveraging the parallel operation on the Linux computer. This information is transmitted through the physical communication interface, employing a unidirectional data

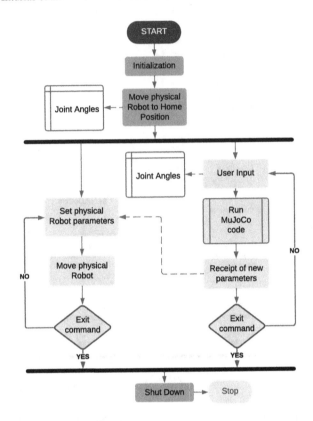

Fig. 6. Information Flow Diagram - Digital Driven Framework.

exchange facilitated by the U2D2 to the robot arm. These commands instigate modifications in the physical robot, impacting its position, torque, and other relevant parameters.

Flow Diagram. The proposed Digital Driven system empowers the user to manipulate a digital manipulator robot, with the physical robot replicating these movements, a digital-to-physical synchronized replication process.

The physical motor control is handled by the Dynamixel SDK, which is on the left side of Fig. 6. The right side is for the MuJoCo SDK, the communication interface for user input, and the Digital Entity.

Users input the desired position for each virtual motor (input to MuJoCo block). Then, each actuator's PD position control loop computes the desired torque at each joint motor and is sent to the direct-drive actuator (we can scale it up by a specific gear relation). Finally, joint angles measured from MuJoCo (receipt of new parameters block in Fig. 6) are transmitted to the physical motors, directing them to move to the corresponding angles using specific writing commands, as mentioned in Sect. 2.1.

In Fig. 6, the segmented lines delineate the directional flow of data, while the continuous line illustrates the sequential order of the code.

3.3 Digital Twin

Framework. Aligned with Fig. 2, the architecture of the Digital Twin incorporates all proposed features, distinguished by its bidirectional data exchange capabilities, unlike the other frameworks. Essential measurements traverse the U2D2 physical communication interface to reach the Dynamixel SDK, facilitating sharing this information with the MuJoCo SDK. Leveraging their parallel operation on the Linux computer, this bidirectional information flow can impact the digital entity's visualization. Moreover, this architecture enables data to flow in the opposite direction, allowing commands from the MuJoCo SDK to be transmitted to the Dynamixel SDK. By using the physical communication interface, these commands can then modify the parameters of the physical robot, thus completing the definition of Digital Twin exposed.

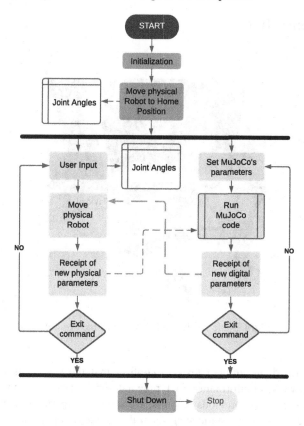

Fig. 7. Information Flow Diagram - Digital Twin Framework.

Flow Diagram. The proposed digital twin enables users to manipulate a digital manipulator robot and its physical counterpart concurrently. With the proposed definition, bidirectional communication becomes feasible within the application, rendering it applicable across diverse domains.

The Dynamixel SDK, on the left side of Fig. 7, handles the communication interface with the user and the physical motor control. The right side is for the MuJoCo SDK and the Digital Entity.

The user input works exactly the same as the Digital Shadow framework. The robot in the MuJoCo environment and the physical robot move synchronously to the values of the Joint Angles parameter.

The physical and the digital realms have bidirectional data exchange by sending and receiving new important physical and digital parameters depending on the application using specific reading and writing commands, as mentioned in Sect. 2.1.

In Fig. 7, the segmented lines delineate the directional flow of data, while the continuous line illustrates the sequential order of the code.

4   Preliminary Tests

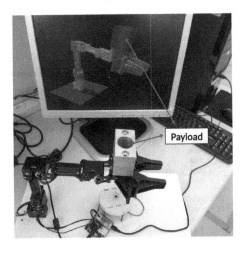

Fig. 8. Static Analysis of Torque - Home Position.

We have performed preliminary tests to confirm that the system is functioning as expected. First, we send information by typing a desired set of joint angles in the three scenarios discussed in the previous sections. We show an experiment demonstration in [2]. Second, we carried out a static analysis of the torque of a joint under a payload, as shown in Fig. 8.

We tried setting the same control scheme and parameters for the virtual and real systems in a digital twin configuration (see Fig. 7). Figure 9 shows the position controller in Position Control Mode. Setting to zero feedforward parameters and derivative and integrative gains, we obtain a simple proportional current controller.

We calculate an approximation of this gain at the proportional torque controller by multiplying this gain by the motor's constant torque. And that is the simplest way to

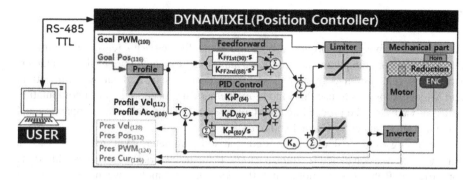

Fig. 9. Block diagram describing the position controller in Position Control Mode [11].

Table 1. Proportional Gain - Controller Parameters.

Control Table Value	Motor Controller Conversion	Mujoco Controller
$\mathbf{P}_{table}$	$\mathbf{P}_{table}/128$	$(\mathbf{P}_{table}/128)\mathbf{K}_t$
2000	2000/128	(2000/128) * 1.99

control a joint in a Mujoco environment. Table 1 shows the parameters configured in the virtual and real controllers for joint 3. Similar calculations can be done for the other joints.

Table 2. Current to Torque Conversion.

Control Table Value	Current Conversion	Torque Conversion
$\mathbf{I}_{table}$	$2.69\mathbf{I}_{table}$ (mA)	$2.69\mathbf{I}_{table}\mathbf{K}_t/1000$ (Nm)

Be aware that the Control Table is a data structure implemented in the servomotor. We can *read/write* a specific *Data* from the Control Table with *read/write* instruction packets [11]. In Mujoco, we configure the gain in the XML file and use the *ctrl*[*i*] command in the C++ file to define the desired joint position in the proportional torque controller.

To compare the joint torques (for joint 3), we *read* the current value from the Control Table Structure. Table 2 shows the conversion. We calculated the torque constant, K_t, from the performance graph (curve) in [11]. As we are recording in a static condition, the values from the current sensor are close to each other. Thus, the Table 3 shows the average value of the actual torque in the servomotor. The MuJuCo torque is constant.

Table 3. Torque Comparison.

Real Servomotor	Virtual Servomotor - Mujoco
= 0.42 Nm (Average)	−1.1 Nm

5 Discussion

As shown in Table 3, the torques in both situations differed. This reaffirms the importance of adjusting the parameters of the virtual model to match the physical characteristics of the real system. Adjusting these parameters can be carried out by optimization, and Mujoco allows us to use this kind of mathematical procedure in a fast computation platform via C++. The proceeding could also be carried out with joint comparison and using a desired trajectory (virtual and real).

Regarding torque calculation as a comparison parameter, some researchers use a parameter conversion called *torque_to_current_value_ratio*. We can access this value for different Robotis servomotor in [10]. For our servomotor, we have a value of 149.795386991; thus, from the Control Table current value, we can calculate the motor torque as:

$$Torque = \frac{1}{149.795386991} CurrentValue$$

Thus, by applying the former equation, we have an average torque of -0.524 Nm for joint 3. In fact, with the current values (from the control table) and MuJuCo Torques, we can approximate this parameter, which results in 71 (average).

6 Concluding Remarks and Futures Works

In this study, we attempt to demonstrate the feasibility of the MuJoCo integration in the context of the digital twin for a robotic arm as a virtual model tool. We choose a position, torque and currents variable as flow information between the physical and virtual layers, but it could be any other parameter, such as velocity. The Virtual and real servomotor handles these variables either as sensor or command variables, depending on the operation modes of the servomotor. The system was able to run the physics simulation, the rendering model via OpenGL, and the driving of the physical robot synchronously in all of the three frameworks proposed: digital shadow, digital-driven, and digital twin itself.

Finally, future works must focus on the following aspects:

- To adjust the virtual model parameters to match the physical characteristics of the real system via optimization.
- Performance evaluation: validation between the physical and virtual model.
- To implement other communications protocols between the physical and virtual entities.
- MuJoCo integration with virtual reality interface.
- MuJoCo Plugin and Unity Integration: the goal of the MuJoCo Plugin and Unity Integration package is to combine the best of both worlds: use MuJoCo physics and Unity rendering within the same project.
- To implement different case studies as shown in related works.

References

1. Baidya, S., Das, S.K., Uddin, M.H., Kosek, C., Summers, C.: Digital twin in safety-critical robotics applications: opportunities and challenges. In: 2022 IEEE International Performance, Computing, and Communications Conference (IPCCC), pp. 101–107. IEEE (2022)
2. Becerra-Vargas, M.: Full dynamic model with contacts of a quadruped robot. Comparison with MuJoCo (2023). https://www.youtube.com/watch?v=iYzmyULJ3Tk
3. Choi, S.H., et al.: An integrated mixed reality system for safety-aware human-robot collaboration using deep learning and digital twin generation. Robot. Comput.-Integr. Manuf. **73**, 102258 (2022)
4. Garg, G., Kuts, V., Anbarjafari, G.: Digital twin for fanuc robots: industrial robot programming and simulation using virtual reality. Sustainability **13**(18), 10336 (2021)
5. Havard, V., Jeanne, B., Lacomblez, M., Baudry, D.: Digital twin and virtual reality: a co-simulation environment for design and assessment of industrial workstations. Prod. Manuf. Res. **7**(1), 472–489 (2019)
6. Laaki, H., Miche, Y., Tammi, K.: Prototyping a digital twin for real time remote control over mobile networks: application of remote surgery. IEEE Access **7**, 20325–20336 (2019)
7. Li, C., Zheng, P., Li, S., Pang, Y., Lee, C.K.: AR-assisted digital twin-enabled robot collaborative manufacturing system with human-in-the-loop. Robot. Comput.-Integr. Manuf. **76**, 102321 (2022)
8. Lou, Y., Wang, Z., Du, S., Liu, W., Kong, S.: A hybrid data storage method for a robotic arm digital twin prototype. In: 2022 6th International Conference on Automation, Control and Robots (ICACR), pp. 83–87. IEEE (2022)
9. Matulis, M., Harvey, C.: A robot arm digital twin utilising reinforcement learning. Comput. Graph. **95**, 106–114 (2021)
10. Robotis: Robotis-framework (2023). https://github.com/ROBOTIS-GIT/ROBOTIS-Framework/blob/master/robotis_device/devices/dynamixel/XM430-W350.device
11. Robotis: xm430-w350 manual (2023). https://emanual.robotis.com/docs/en/dxl/x/xm430-w350/#specifications
12. Tao, F., Xiao, B., Qi, Q., Cheng, J., Ji, P.: Digital twin modeling. J. Manuf. Syst. **64**, 372–389 (2022)
13. Todorov, E., Erez, T., Tassa, Y.: MuJoCo: a physics engine for model-based control. In: 2012 IEEE/RSJ International Conference on Intelligent Robots and Systems, pp. 5026–5033. IEEE (2012). https://doi.org/10.1109/IROS.2012.6386109
14. Tola, D., Böttjer, T., Larsen, P.G., Esterle, L.: Towards modular digital twins of robot systems. In: 2022 IEEE International Conference on Autonomic Computing and Self-Organizing Systems Companion (ACSOS-C), pp. 95–100. IEEE (2022)
15. Wu, Z., Chen, S., Han, J., Zhang, S., Liang, J., Yang, X.: A low-cost digital twin-driven positioning error compensation method for industrial robotic arm. IEEE Sens. J. **22**(23), 22885–22893 (2022)

Author Index

A

Achour, Abdessalem 115
Aguilar, Iu 82
Al Assaad, Hiba 115
Al Mahmud, Suaib 278
Alcouffe, Rémy 193
Alfalou, Ayman 345
Alj, Youssef 134
Alonso, Pablo 31
Amin Mansour, Elham 391
Aranjuelo, Nerea 31
Araujo, Helder 293
Arens, Michael 260
Arkles, Tony 210

B

Baghi, Bobak 361
Bayer, Jens 260
Becerra Vargas, Mauricio 457
Becker, Stefan 260
Blohm, Ivar 47
Bouzid, Taha 134
Brodskiy, Yury 66
Bueno, Gloria 100
Bugueno-Cordova, Ignacio 375

C

Campusano, Miguel 375
Cardoso, Fabiano Stingelin 426
Chambon, Sylvie 193
Chazhoor, Anthony Ashwin Peter 316

D

de Gordoa, Jon Ander Íñiguez 82
de Oliveira, André Schneider 410, 426
Delgado, Guillem 31, 82
Deniz, Oscar 100
Dudek, Gregory 361
Dupuis, Yohan 115

E

El Zaher, Madeleine 115
Erabati, Gopi Krishna 293

F

Fabro, João Alberto 410
Farid, Ali Moltajaei 210
Franke, Jörg 225

G

Gandois, Alvin 345
Gao, Bin 316
Garcia, Mikel 82
Gasparini, Simone 193
Gopal, Atmaraaj 152, 441
Grasshof, Stella 66
Guaman-Rivera, Robert 375

H

Hast, Anders 47
Hofmann, Christian 225
Hogan, Francois R. 361
Hu, Shanfeng 316
Huebner, Wolfgang 260
Hug, Ronny 260
Hutch, Greg 210

I

Ibrahim, Azhar Mohd 278

J

Jenkin, Michael 361
Jevtić, Aleksandar 31, 82
Joventino, Carlos Fernando 410

K

Kalenberg, Matthias 225
Katzschmann, Robert K. 391
Knöller, Tobias 152

J. Filipe and J. Röning (Eds.): ROBOVIS 2024, CCIS 2077, pp. 471–472, 2024.
https://doi.org/10.1007/978-3-031-59057-3

Kolbeinsson, Benedikt   179
Kuzhippallil, Francis A.   21

L
Lai, Congting   47
Lai, Yuzhi   441
Latha, Abhishek V.   21
Le Gloannec, Simon   345
Liu, ZhaoHua   152, 441

M
Maldonado, Gabriel   164
Maltoni, Davide   244
Mardzuki, Muhammad Imran   278
Marques de Oliveira, João Pedro Garbelini   457
Martin, Sina   225
Merabet, Adel   21
Mikolajczyk, Krystian   179
Miranda, Alejandro   82
Morin, Géraldine   193
Mouaddib, Abdel-Illah   345
Mouhoub, Malek   210
Muñoz, Juan Daniel   100

N
Naranjo, Ruben   31
Nasary, Muhammad Faqiihuddin   278
Nassar, Youssef   152, 441
Nieto, Marcos   82

O
Olszewska, J. I.   334

P
Pazho, Armin Danesh   164
Pereira, Jonathas Henrique Mariano   410
Perez Inturias, Bernardo   457

Pérez-Benito, Cristina   31, 82
Pujol, David   82

R
Radke, Mario   152, 441
Rahimipour, Mohammad   21
Rätsch, Matthias   152, 441
Rhinelander, Jason   21
Ribeiro Marnet, Luiza   66
Rohrich, Ronnier Frates   426
Roth, Jörg   1
Ruiz-Santaquiteria, Jesus   100

S
Scucchia, Matteo   244
Shafie, Amir Akramin   278
Siddiqi, Kaleem   361
Sintes, Joan   31

T
Tabkhi, Hamed   164
Tremblay, Jean-François   361

V
Velez, Gorka   82
Venkat, Ramesh   21
Verschae, Rodrigo   375

W
Wąsowski, Andrzej   66
Weber, Thomas   152, 441
Woo, Wai Lok   316

Z
Zhang, Yihong   441
Zheng, Hehui   391
Zhou, Yijie   47

Printed in the United States
by Baker & Taylor Publisher Services